MACROECONOMICS

The Monetary Foundations of the Macroeconomy

Volume 1

First Edition

Edited by Thomas Rustici, James Caton,
Dima Shamoun, and Theo Shamoun

Bassim Hamadeh, CEO and Publisher
Michael Simpson, Vice President of Acquisitions
Jamie Giganti, Managing Editor
Jess Busch, Senior Graphic Designer
Amy Stone, Acquisitions Editor
Mirasol Enriquez, Project Editor
Luiz Ferreira, Senior Licensing Specialist
Mandy Licata, Interior Designer

First published in the United States of America in 2015 by Cognella, Inc.

Cover image copyright © 2012 Depositphotos Inc./digiart.

Printed in the United States of America

ISBN: 978-1-63487-013-9 (pbk)/ 978-1-63487-014-6 (br)

www.cognella.com   800-200-3908

"This compilation of key works from the classical tradition in macroeconomics fills a gap that I didn't know existed, until I saw the table of contents. The book contains an amazing range of classical pieces on macroeconomics as well as the microeconomics underpinnings of money and macro. It's a great idea to put all of these important articles together in one volume, especially for academics who don't have the time to waste searching through library catalogs, and who may not even recall where a classic paper first appeared."

Scott Sumner Ph.D., Bentley University
The Money Illusion blog

"In this two-volume collection, Rustici, Caton, Shamoun, and Shamoun have gathered many of the 'greatest hits' of macroeconomics, and smartly supplemented them with excellent but less-known pieces and their own helpful contributions. The result is a set of readings that will be extremely valuable for any macroeconomics student—and for any instructor who wants to expose students to the field's key insights and broad range of approaches."

Lawrence H. White, Ph.D., George Mason University
The Clash of Economic Ideas: The Great Policy Debates and Experiments of the Last Hundred Years

"The editors of these two volumes have created a truly ambitious and valuable resource. It is a wonderful compilation of important writings on an amazing variety of macroeconomic topics. The selections range from classics accessible to anyone untutored in economics all the way to sophisticated contributions that were path-breaking when they first appeared. Anyone who teaches or writes about economics will want to consult these volumes."

Jeffrey Rogers Hummel, Ph.D., San Jose State University
Emancipating Slaves, Enslaving Free Men: A History of the American Civil War

"This read is an excellent compilation of classical articles on macroeconomics and monetary theory as well as some new and original articles. Selections from the reader would be appropriate for a variety of courses from introductory macroeconomics to intermediate macroeconomics and money and banking. Advanced students of macroeconomics will find the reader an excellent companion in a course that emphasizes contemporary critique."

W. William Woolsey, Ph. D., The Citadel, Military College of South Carolina

Macroeconomics: The Monetary Foundation of the Macroeconomy, Volume 1 edited by Thomas Rustici, James Caton, Dima Shamoun, and Theo Shamoun

The essays featured in *Macroeconomics: The Monetary Foundations of the Macroeconomy, Volume I* come from a broad range of pre-Keynesian classical thinkers. They represent differing traditions, primarily the divide between a more monetarist approach and the Austrian school, which is reflected in diverging views on capital theory, interest rates, price level effects, and sometimes in the study of institutions and public policy.

The readings introduce economics as a form of unplanned order emerging from seeming chaos. Students will learn about microeconomics, the quantity theory of money, inflation and hyperinflation. This prepares them for a deeper exploration of macroeconomics. The section on the classical macroeconomic model introduces a variety of topics including real and nominal prices, real interest rates, Say's Law, and price flexibility.

Volume II builds on this foundation, including empirical and theoretical literature that is indispensable for adequate training as a technical macroeconomist. It is an ideal collection for advanced undergraduate and graduate students.

Dr. Thomas Rustici was the Freedom Professor of Economics at the Fund for American Studies, Georgetown University. He is currently an assistant professor of economics and the Associate Director of Undergraduate Studies in Economics at George Mason University.

James Caton is a graduate teaching assistant and Ph.D. candidate in the economics program at George Mason University. He blogs regularly at *Money, Markets, and Misperceptions.*

Dima Yazji Shamoun is a research fellow with the Regulatory Studies Program at the Mercatus Center. She earned her Ph.D. in economics from George Mason University.

Theo Shamoun earned both his B.A., summa cum laude, and M.A. degrees in economics from George Mason University.

Contents

PUBLIC CHOICE

ENTREPRENEURSHIP

CHAPTER 3: MONEY

CHAPTER 4: THE QUANTITY THEORY OF MONEY

CHAPTER 5: INFLATION AND EPISODES IN HYPERINFLATION

INFLATION

CHAPTER 6: CLASSICAL MACRO MODEL

REAL AND NOMINAL PRICES

REAL INTEREST RATE

SAY'S LAW

PRICE FLEXIBILITY

CHAPTER 7: CONCLUSION

APPENDICES

Editor's Note

While the various essays come from a broad range of pre-Keynesian classical thinkers, not each author is in agreement with each other on every point. There are different traditions within this set of classical thinkers, primarily between a more monetarist approach (Irving Fisher) and the Austrian school (F. A. Hayek). These conflicts show up in capital theory, interest rates, price level effects and occasionally in the study of institutions and public policy. Moreover, even among the editors of this anthology there is not agreement on, or endorsement of, every point made in every essay that we have collected for reprinting. We are not mind clones and don't expect others to be so. On the other hand, we are in agreement that Keynesian theory was a fundamental mistake—or, as Professor Leland Yeager might say, a "diversion"—from a basically sound classical model (with some important modifications and clarifications). It is up to each student to make up their own mind only after being exposed to the fullest breadth of this scientific literature.

CHAPTER 1

Introduction

Spontaneous Order and the Science of Economics

By Thomas Rustici

"[E]very individual ... generally, indeed, neither intends to promote the publick interest, nor knows how much he is promoting it ... and by directing [his capital] in such a manner as its produce may be of the greatest value, he intends only his own gain, and he is in this, as in many other cases, *led by an invisible hand to promote an end which was no part of his intention*."
– Adam Smith, 1776

Economics may be described as the study of purposeful human action and the consequences, both intended and unintended, of that action. Individuals make numerous choices every day of their life. These actions successfully interact with the decisions of millions of others, most often total strangers. The great Nobel Prize--winning economist Friedrich Von Hayek explained this phenomenon as "spontaneous or unplanned emergent order," the product of human action, but not of human design or intention. But even if benevolent intention is missing from the list of necessary ingredients for a well-- ordered society and economy, it should not be missed, as Smith reminds us at the end of his famous passage quoted above. "Nor is it always worse for the society that it was no part of it. By pursuing his own interest he frequently promotes that of the society more effectually than when he really intends to promote it. I have never known much good done by those who affected to trade for the publick good."

The essays in Section 1 develop this "big picture" of economics – the idea of unplanned order emerging from seeming chaos, and of the futility and counterproductive nature of man's attempts to centrally plan and manufacture that order. Leonard Reed's classic essay, "*I Pencil*", illustrates the process by which the intelligence, effort, and values of millions of strangers are involved in the production of a humble pencil, **yet no one knows how to make a pencil, and in fact this is the only reason people are able to acquire them**. Through the complex division of labor and the division of knowledge that make up a modern market economy, millions of strangers combine their disparate knowledge and skills to make seeming miracles occur with routine ease. An economy has no grand design or overall centralized plan, yet our activities coordinate in such a way that logical and coherent life is made possible. The study of Economics explains this hidden order, Smith's *Invisible Hand*, and teaches to look both for "what is seen, and what is not seen" in our grand designs and plans.

I, Pencil

My Family Tree as Told to Leonard E. Read

By Leonard E. Read

I am a lead pencil—the ordinary wooden pencil familiar to all boys and girls and adults who can read and write.[1]

Writing is both my vocation and my avocation; that's all I do.

You may wonder why I should write a genealogy. Well, to begin with, my story is interesting. And, next, I am a mystery—more so than a tree or a sunset or even a flash of lightning. But, sadly, I am taken for granted by those who use me, as if I were a mere incident and without background. This supercilious attitude relegates me to the level of the commonplace.

This is a species of the grievous error in which mankind cannot too long persist without peril. For, the wise G. K. Chesterton observed, "We are perishing for want of wonder, not for want of wonders."

I, Pencil, simple though I appear to be, merit your wonder and awe, a claim I shall attempt to prove. In fact, if you can understand me—no, that's too much to ask of anyone—if you can become aware of the miraculousness which I symbolize, you can help save the freedom mankind is so unhappily losing. I have a profound lesson to teach. And I can teach this lesson

better than can an automobile or an airplane or a mechanical dishwasher because—well, because I am seemingly so simple.

Simple? Yet, *not a single person on the face of this earth knows how to make me*. This sounds fantastic, doesn't it? Especially when it is realized that there are about one and one-half billion of my kind produced in the U.S.A. each year.

Pick me up and look me over. What do you see? Not much meets the eye—there's some wood, lacquer, the printed labeling, graphite lead, a bit of metal, and an eraser.

INNUMERABLE ANTECEDENTS

Just as you cannot trace your family tree back very far, so is it impossible for me to name and explain all my antecedents. But I would like to suggest enough of them to impress upon you the richness and complexity of my background.

My family tree begins with what in fact is a tree, a cedar of straight grain that grows in Northern California and Oregon. Now contemplate all the

---

1 My official name is "Mongol 482." My many ingredients are assembled, fabricated, and finished by Eberhard Faber Pencil Company.

saws and trucks and rope and the countless other gear used in harvesting and carting the cedar logs to the railroad siding. Think of all the persons and the numberless skills that went into their fabrication: the mining of ore, the making of steel and its refinement into saws, axes, motors; the growing of hemp and bringing it through all the stages to heavy and strong rope; the logging camps with their beds and mess halls, the cookery and the raising of all the foods. Why, untold thousands of persons had a hand in every cup of coffee the loggers drink!

The logs are shipped to a mill in San Leandro, California. Can you imagine the individuals who make flat cars and rails and railroad engines and who construct and install the communication systems incidental thereto? These legions are among my antecedents.

Consider the millwork in San Leandro. The cedar logs are cut into small, pencil-length slats less than one-fourth of an inch in thickness. These are kiln dried and then tinted for the same reason women put rouge on their faces. People prefer that I look pretty, not a pallid white. The slats are waxed and kiln dried again. How many skills went into the making of the tint and the kilns, into supplying the heat, the light and power, the belts, motors, and all the other things a mill requires? Sweepers in the mill among my ancestors? Yes, and included are the men who poured the concrete for the dam of a Pacific Gas & Electric Company hydroplant which supplies the mill's power!

Don't overlook the ancestors present and distant who have a hand in transporting sixty carloads of slats across the nation.

Once in the pencil factory—$4,000,000 in machinery and building, all capital accumulated by thrifty and saving parents of mine—each slat is given eight grooves by a complex machine, after which another machine lays leads in every other slat, applies glue, and places another slat atop—a lead sandwich, so to speak. Seven brothers and I are mechanically carved from this "wood-clinched" sandwich.

My "lead" itself—it contains no lead at all—is complex. The graphite is mined in Ceylon. Consider these miners and those who make their many tools and the makers of the paper sacks in which the graphite is shipped and those who make the string that ties the sacks and those who put them aboard ships and those who make the ships. Even the lighthouse keepers along the way assisted in my birth—and the harbor pilots.

The graphite is mixed with clay from Mississippi in which ammonium hydroxide is used in the refining process. Then wetting agents are added such as sulfonated tallow—animal fats chemically reacted with sulfuric acid. After passing through numerous machines, the mixture finally appears as endless extrusions—as from a sausage grinder-cut to size, dried, and baked for several hours at 1,850 degrees Fahrenheit. To increase their strength and smoothness the leads are then treated with a hot mixture which includes candelilla wax from Mexico, paraffin wax, and hydrogenated natural fats.

My cedar receives six coats of lacquer. Do you know all the ingredients of lacquer? Who would think that the growers of castor beans and the refiners of castor oil are a part of it? They are. Why, even the processes by which the lacquer is made a beautiful yellow involve the skills of more persons than one can enumerate!

Observe the labeling. That's a film formed by applying heat to carbon black mixed with resins. How do you make resins and what, pray, is carbon black?

My bit of metal—the ferrule—is brass. Think of all the persons who mine zinc and copper and those who have the skills to make shiny sheet brass from these products of nature. Those black rings on my ferrule are black nickel. What is black nickel and how is it applied? The complete story of why the center of my ferrule has no black nickel on it would take pages to explain.

Then there's my crowning glory, inelegantly referred to in the trade as "the plug," the part man uses to erase the errors he makes with me. An ingredient called "factice" is what does the erasing. It is a rubber-like product made by reacting rape-seed oil from the Dutch East Indies with sulfur chloride. Rubber, contrary to the common notion, is only for binding purposes. Then, too, there are numerous vulcanizing and accelerating agents. The pumice comes from Italy; and the pigment which gives "the plug" its color is cadmium sulfide.

NO ONE KNOWS

Does anyone wish to challenge my earlier assertion that no single person on the face of this earth knows how to make me?

Actually, millions of human beings have had a hand in my creation, no one of whom even knows more than a very few of the others. Now, you may say that I go too far in relating the picker of a coffee berry in far off Brazil and food growers elsewhere to my creation; that this is an extreme position. I shall stand by my claim. There isn't a single person in all these millions, including the president of the pencil company, who contributes more than a tiny, infinitesimal bit of know-how. From the standpoint of know-how the only difference between the miner of graphite in Ceylon and the logger in Oregon is in the *type* of know-how. Neither the miner nor the logger can be dispensed with, any more than can the chemist at the factory or the worker in the oil field—paraffin being a by-product of petroleum.

Here is an astounding fact: Neither the worker in the oil field nor the chemist nor the digger of graphite or clay nor any who mans or makes the ships or trains or trucks nor the one who runs the machine that does the knurling on my bit of metal nor the president of the company performs his singular task because he wants me. Each one wants me less, perhaps, than does a child in the first grade. Indeed, there are some among this vast multitude who never saw a pencil nor would they know how to use one. Their motivation is other than me. Perhaps it is something like this: Each of these millions sees that he can thus exchange his tiny know-how for the goods and services he needs or wants. I may or may not be among these items.

NO MASTER MIND

There is a fact still more astounding: the absence of a master mind, of anyone dictating or forcibly directing these countless actions which bring me into being. No trace of such a person can be found. Instead, we find the Invisible Hand at work. This is the mystery to which I earlier referred.

It has been said that "only God can make a tree." Why do we agree with this? Isn't it because we realize that we ourselves could not make one? Indeed, can we even describe a tree? We cannot, except in superficial terms. We can say, for instance, that a certain molecular configuration manifests itself as a tree. But what mind is there among men that could even record, let alone direct, the constant changes in molecules that transpire in the life span of a tree? Such a feat is utterly unthinkable!

I, Pencil, am a complex combination of miracles: a tree, zinc, copper, graphite, and so on. But to these miracles which manifest themselves in Nature an even more extraordinary miracle has been added: the configuration of creative human energies—millions of tiny know-hows configurating naturally and spontaneously in response to human necessity and desire and *in the absence of any human masterminding!* Since only God can make a tree, I insist that only God could make me. Man can no more direct these millions of know-hows to bring me into being than he can put molecules together to create a tree.

The above is what I meant when writing, "If you can become aware of the miraculousness which I symbolize, you can help save the freedom mankind is so unhappily losing." For, if one is aware that these know-hows will naturally, yes, automatically, arrange themselves into creative and productive patterns in response to human necessity and demand—that is, in the absence of governmental or any other coercive masterminding—then one will possess an absolutely essential ingredient for freedom: *a faith in free people.* Freedom is impossible without this faith.

Once government has had a monopoly of a creative activity such, for instance, as the delivery of the mails, most individuals will believe that the mails could not be efficiently delivered by men acting freely. And here is the reason: Each one acknowledges that he himself doesn't know how to do all the things incident to mail delivery. He also recognizes that no other individual could do it. These assumptions are correct. No individual possesses enough know-how to perform a nation's mail delivery any more than any individual possesses enough know-how to make a pencil. Now, in the absence of faith in free people—in the unawareness that millions of tiny know-hows would naturally and miraculously form and cooperate to satisfy this necessity—the individual cannot help but reach the erroneous conclusion that mail can be delivered only by governmental "master-minding."

TESTIMONY GALORE

If I, Pencil, were the only item that could offer testimony on what men and women can accomplish when free to try, then those with little faith would have a fair case. However, there is testimony galore; it's all about us and on every hand. Mail delivery is exceedingly simple when compared, for instance, to the making of an automobile or a calculating machine or a grain combine or a milling machine or to tens of thousands of other things. Delivery? Why, in this area where men have been left free to try, they deliver the human voice around the world in less than one second; they deliver an event visually and in motion to any person's home when it is happening; they deliver 150 passengers from Seattle to Baltimore in less than four hours; they deliver gas from Texas to one's range or furnace in New York at unbelievably low rates and without subsidy; they deliver each four pounds of oil from the Persian Gulf to our Eastern Seaboard—halfway around the world—for less money than the government charges for delivering a one-ounce letter across the street!

The lesson I have to teach is this: *Leave all creative energies uninhibited.* Merely organize society to act in harmony with this lesson. Let society's legal apparatus remove all obstacles the best it can. Permit these creative know-hows freely to flow. Have faith that free men and women will respond to the Invisible Hand. This faith will be confirmed. I, Pencil, seemingly simple though I am, offer the miracle of my creation as testimony that this is a practical faith, as practical as the sun, the rain, a cedar tree, the good earth.

Leonard E. Read (1898–1983) founded FEE in 1946 and served as its president until his death.

"I, Pencil," his most famous essay, was first published in the December 1958 issue of The Freeman. *Although a few of the manufacturing details and place names have changed over the past forty years, the principles are unchanged.*

What Is Seen and What Is Not Seen

By Frédéric Bastiat

In the economic sphere an act, a habit, an institution, a law produces not only one effect, but a series of effects. Of these effects, the first alone is immediate; it appears simultaneously with its cause; *it is seen.* The other effects emerge only subsequently; *they are not seen;* we are fortunate if we *foresee* them.

There is only one difference between a bad economist and a good one: the bad economist confines himself to the *visible* effect; the good economist takes into account both the effect that can be seen and those effects that must be *foreseen.*

Yet this difference is tremendous; for it almost always happens that when the immediate consequence is favorable, the later consequences are disastrous, and vice versa. Whence it follows that the bad economist pursues a small present good that will be followed by a great evil to come, while the good economist pursues a great good to come, at the risk of a small present evil.

The same thing, of course, is true of health and morals. Often, the sweeter the first fruit of a habit, the more bitter are its later fruits: for example, debauchery, sloth, prodigality. When a man is impressed by the effect *that is seen* and has not yet learned to discern the effects *that are not seen,* he indulges in deplorable habits, not only through natural inclination, but deliberately.

This explains man's necessarily painful evolution. Ignorance surrounds him at his cradle; therefore, he regulates his acts according to their first consequences, the only ones that, in his infancy, he can see. It is only after a long time that he learns to take account of the others. Two very different masters teach him this lesson: experience and foresight. Experience teaches efficaciously but brutally. It instructs us in all the effects of an act by making us feel them, and we cannot fail to learn eventually, from having been burned ourselves, that fire burns. I should prefer, in so far as possible, to replace this rude teacher with one more gentle: foresight. For that reason I shall investigate the consequences of several economic phenomena, contrasting those *that are seen* with those *that are not seen.*

Have you ever been witness to the fury of that solid citizen, James Goodfellow, when his incorrigible son has happened to break a pane of glass? If you have been present at this spectacle, certainly you must also have observed that the onlookers, even if there are as many as thirty of them, seem with one accord to offer the unfortunate owner the selfsame consolation: "It's an ill wind that blows nobody some good. Such accidents keep industry going. Everybody has to make a living. What would become of the glaziers if no one ever broke a window?"

Now, this formula of condolence contains a whole theory that it is a good idea for us to expose, *flagrante delicto*, in this very simple case, since it is exactly the same as that which, unfortunately, underlies most of our economic institutions.

Suppose that it will cost six francs to repair the damage. If you mean that the accident gives six francs' worth of encouragement to the aforesaid industry, I agree. I do not contest it in any way; your reasoning is correct. The glazier will come, do his job, receive six francs, congratulate himself, and bless in his heart the careless child. *That is what is seen.*

But if, by way of deduction, you conclude, as happens only too often, that it is good to break windows, that it helps to circulate money, that it results in encouraging industry in general, I am obliged to cry out: That will never do! Your theory stops at *what is seen*. It does not take account of *what is not seen*.

It is not seen that, since our citizen has spent six francs for one thing, he will not be able to spend them for another. *It is not seen* that if he had not had a windowpane to replace, he would have replaced, for example, his worn-out shoes or added another book to his library. In brief, he would have put his six francs to some use or other for which he will not now have them.

Let us next consider industry *in general*. The window having been broken, the glass industry gets six francs' worth of encouragement; *that is what is seen.*

If the window had not been broken, the shoe industry (or some other) would have received six francs' worth of encouragement; *that is what is not seen.*

And if we were to take into consideration *what is not seen*, because it is a negative factor, as well as *what is seen*, because it is a positive factor, we should understand that there is no benefit to industry *in general* or to *national employment* as a whole, whether windows are broken or not broken.

Now let us consider James Goodfellow.

On the first hypothesis, that of the broken window, he spends six francs and has, neither more nor less than before, the enjoyment of one window.

On the second, that in which the accident did not happen, he would have spent six francs for new shoes and would have had the enjoyment of a pair of shoes as well as of a window.

Now, if James Goodfellow is part of society, we must conclude that society, considering its labors and its enjoyments, has lost the value of the broken window.

From which, by generalizing, we arrive at this unexpected conclusion: "Society loses the value of objects unnecessarily destroyed," and at this aphorism, which will make the hair of the protectionists stand on end: "To break, to destroy, to dissipate is not to encourage national employment," or more briefly: "Destruction is not profitable."

What will the *Moniteur industriel* say to this, or the disciples of the estimable M. de Saint-Chamans, who has calculated with such precision what industry would gain from the burning of Paris, because of the houses that would have to be rebuilt?

I am sorry to upset his ingenious calculations, especially since their spirit has passed into our legislation. But I beg him to begin them again, entering *what is not seen* in the ledger beside *what is seen*.

The reader must apply himself to observe that there are not only two people, but three, in the little drama that I have presented. The one, James Goodfellow, represents the consumer, reduced by destruction to one enjoyment instead of two. The other, under the figure of the glazier, shows us the producer whose industry the accident encourages. The third is the shoemaker (or any other manufacturer) whose industry is correspondingly discouraged by the same cause. It is this third person who is always in the shadow, and who, personifying *what is not seen*, is an essential element of the problem. It is he who makes us understand how absurd it is to see a profit in destruction. It is he who will soon teach us that it is equally absurd to see a profit in trade restriction, which is, after all, nothing more nor less than partial destruction. So, if you get to the bottom of all the arguments advanced in favor of restrictionist measures, you will find only a paraphrase of that common cliché: "*What would become of the glaziers if no one ever broke any windows?*"

Capitalism, Socialism, and Democracy

The Process of Creative Destruction

By Joseph Schumpeter

The theories of monopolistic and oligopolistic competition and their popular variants may in two ways be made to serve the view that capitalist reality is unfavorable to maximum performance in production. One may hold that it always has been so and that all along output has been expanding in spite of the secular sabotage perpetrated by the managing bourgeoisie. Advocates of this proposition would have to produce evidence to the effect that the observed rate of increase can be accounted for by a sequence of favorable circumstances unconnected with the mechanism of private enterprise and strong enough to overcome the latter's resistance. This is precisely the question which we shall discuss in Chapter IX. However, those who espouse this variant at least avoid the trouble about historical fact that the advocates of the alternative proposition have to face. This avers that capitalist reality once tended to favor maximum productive performance, or at all events productive performance so considerable as to constitute a major element in any serious appraisal of the system; but that the later spread of monopolist structures, killing competition, has by now reversed that tendency.

First, this involves the creation of an entirely imaginary golden age of perfect competition that at some time somehow metamorphosed itself into the monopolistic age, whereas it is quite clear that perfect competition has at no time been more of a reality than it is at present. Secondly, it is necessary to point out that the rate of increase in output did not decrease from the nineties from which. I suppose, the prevalence of the largest-size concerns, at least in manufacturing industry, would have to be dated; that there is nothing in the behavior of the time series of total output to suggest a "break in trend"; and, most important of all, that the modern standard of life of the masses evolved during the period of relatively unfettered "big business." If we list the items that enter the modern workman's budget and from 1899 on observe the course of their prices not in terms of money but in terms of the hours of labor that will buy them—i.e., each year's money prices divided by each year's hourly wage rates—we cannot fail to be struck by the rate of the advance which, considering the spectacular improvement in qualities, seems to have been greater and not smaller than it ever was before. If we economists were given less to wishful thinking and more to the observation of facts, doubts would immediately arise as to the realistic virtues of a theory that would have led us to expect a very different result. Nor is this all. As soon as we go into details and inquire into the individual items in which progress was most conspicuous, the trail leads not to the doors of those firms that work under conditions of comparatively free competition but precisely to the doors of the large concerns—which, as in the case of agricultural machinery, also account for much of the progress in the competitive sector—and a shocking suspicion dawns upon us that big business may have had more to do with creating that standard of life than with keeping it down.

The conclusions alluded to at the end of the preceding chapter are in fact almost completely false. Yet they follow from observations and theorems that are almost completely[1] true. Both economists and popular writers have once more run away with some fragments of reality they happened to grasp. These fragments themselves were mostly seen correctly. Their formal properties were mostly developed correctly. But no conclusions about capitalist reality as a whole follow from such fragmentary analyses. If we draw them nevertheless, we can be right only by accident. That has been done. And the lucky accident did not happen.

The essential point to grasp is that in dealing with capitalism we are dealing with an evolutionary process. It may seem strange that anyone can fail to see so obvious a fact which moreover was long ago emphasized by Karl Marx. Yet that fragmentary analysis which yields the bulk of our propositions about the functioning of modern capitalism persistently neglects it. Let us restate the point and see how it bears upon our problem.

Capitalism, then, is by nature a form or method of economic change and not only never is but never can be stationary. And this evolutionary character of the capitalist process is not merely due to the fact that economic life goes on in a social and natural environment which changes and by its change alters the data of economic action; this fact is important and these changes (wars, revolutions and so on) often condition industrial change, but they are not its prime movers. Nor is this evolutionary character due to a quasi-automatic increase in population and capital or to the vagaries of monetary systems' of which exactly the same thing holds true. The fundamental impulse that sets and keeps the capitalist engine in motion comes from the new consumers' goods, the new methods of production or transportation, the new markets, the new forms of industrial organization that capitalist enterprise creates.

As we have seen in the preceding chapter, the contents of the laborer's budget, say from 1760 to 1940, did not simply grow on unchanging lines but they underwent a process of qualitative change. Similarly, the history of the productive apparatus of a typical farm, from the beginnings of the rationalization of crop rotation, plowing and fattening to the mechanized thing of today—linking up with elevators and railroads—is a history of revolutions. So is the history of the productive apparatus of the iron and steel industry from the charcoal furnace to our own type of furnace, or the history of the apparatus of power production from the overshot water wheel to the modern power plant, or the history of transportation from the mail-coach to the airplane. The opening up of new markets, foreign or domestic, and the organizational development from the craft shop and factory to such concerns as U. S. Steel illustrate the same process of industrial mutation—if I may use that biological term—that incessantly revolutionizes[2] the economic structure *from within*, incessantly destroying the old one, incessantly creating a new one. This process of Creative Destruction is the essential fact about capitalism. It is what capitalism consists in and what every capitalist concern has got to live in. This fact bears upon our problem in two ways.

---

1   As a matter of fact, those observations and theorems are not completely satisfactory. The usual expositions of the doctrine of imperfect competition fail in particular to give due attention to the many and important cases in which, even as a matter of static theory, imperfect competition approximates the results of perfect competition. There are other cases in which it does not do this, but offers compensations which, while not entering any output index, yet contribute to what the output index is in the last resort intended to measure—the cases in which a firm defends its market by establishing a name for quality and service for instance. However in order to simplify matters, we will not take issue with that doctrine on its own ground.

---

2   Those revolutions are not strictly incessant; they occur in discrete rushes which are separated from each other by spans of comparative quiet. The process as a whole works incessantly however, in the sense that there always is either revolution or absorption of the results of revolution, both together forming what are known as business cycles.

First, since we are dealing with a process whose every element takes considerable time in revealing its true features and ultimate effects, there is no point in appraising the performance of that process *ex visu* of a given point of time; we must judge its performance oven time, as it unfolds through decades or centuries. A system—any system, economic or other—that at *every* given point of time fully utilizes its possibilities to the best advantage may yet in the long run be inferior to a system that does so at *no* given point of time, because the latter's failure to do so may be a condition for the level or speed of long-run performance.

Second, since we are dealing with an organic process, analysis of what happens in any particular part of it—say, in an individual concern or industry—may indeed clarify details of mechanism but is inconclusive beyond that. Every piece of business strategy acquires its true significance only against the background of that process and within the situation created by it. It must be seen in its role in the perennial gale of creative destruction; it cannot be understood irrespective of it or, in fact, on the hypothesis that there is a perennial lull.

But economists who, *ex visu* of a point of time, look for example at the behavior of an oligopolist industry—an industry which consists of a few big firms—and observe the well-known moves and countermoves within it that seem to aim at nothing but high prices and restrictions of output are making precisely that hypothesis. They accept the data of the momentary situation as if there were no past or future to it and think that they have understood what there is to understand if they interpret the behavior of those firms by means of the principle of maximizing profits with reference to those data. The usual theorist's paper and the usual government commission's report practically never try to see that behavior, on the one hand, as a result of a piece of past history and, on the other hand, as an attempt to deal with a situation that is sure to change presently—as an attempt by those firms to keep on their feet, on ground that is slipping away from under them. In other words, the problem that is usually being visualized is how capitalism administers existing structures, whereas the relevant problem is how

it creates and destroys them. As long as this is not recognized, the investigator does a meaningless job. As soon as it is recognized, his outlook on capitalist practice and its social results changes considerably.[3]

The first thing to go is the traditional conception of the *modus operandi* of competition. Economists are at long last emerging from the stage in which price competition was all they saw. As soon as quality competition and sales effort are admitted into the sacred precincts of theory, the price variable is ousted from its dominant position. However, it is still competition within a rigid pattern of invariant conditions, methods of production and forms of industrial organization in particular, that practically monopolizes attention. But in capitalist reality as distinguished from its textbook picture, it is not that kind of competition which counts but the competition from the new commodity, the new technology, the new source of supply, the new type of organization (the largest-scale unit of control for instance)—competition which commands a decisive cost or quality advantage and which strikes not at the margins of the profits and the outputs of the existing firms but at their foundations and their very lives. This kind of competition is as much more effective than the other as a bombardment is in comparison with forcing a door, and so much more important that it becomes a matter of comparative indifference whether competition in the ordinary sense functions more or less promptly; the powerful lever that in the long run expands output and brings down prices is in any case made of other stuff.

It is hardly necessary to point out that competition of the kind we now have in mind acts not only when in being but also when it is merely an ever-present threat. It disciplines before it attacks. The businessman feels himself to be in a competitive situation even if he is alone in his field or if, though not alone, he holds a position such that investigating

---

3 It should be understood that it is only our appraisal of economic performance and not our moral judgment that can be so changed Owing to its autonomy, moral approval or disapproval is entirely independent of our appraisal of social (or any other) results, unless we happen to adopt a moral system such as utilitarianism which makes moral approval and disapproval turn on them *ex defiritione*.

government experts fail to see any effective competition between him and any other firms in the same or a neighboring field and in consequence conclude that his talk, under examination, about his competitive sorrows is all make-believe. In many cases, though not in all, this will in the long run enforce behavior very similar to the perfectly competitive pattern.

Many theorists take the opposite view which is best conveyed by an example, Let us assume that there is a certain number of retailers in a neighborhood who try to improve their relative position by service and "atmosphere" but avoid price competition and stick as to methods to the local tradition—a picture of stagnating routine. As others drift into the trade that quasi-equilibrium is indeed upset, but in a manner that does not benefit their customers. The economic space around each of the shops having been narrowed, their owners will no longer be able to make a living and they will try to mend the case by raising prices in tacit agreement. This will further reduce their sales and so, by successive pyramiding, a situation will evolve in which increasing potential supply will be attended by increasing instead of decreasing prices and by decreasing instead of increasing sales.

Such cases do occur, and it is light and proper to work them out. But as the practical instances usually given show, they are fringe-end cases to be found mainly in the sectors furthest removed from all that is most characteristic of capitalist activity.[4] Moreover, they are transient by nature. In the case of retail trade the competition that matters arises not from additional shops of the same type, but from the department store, the chain store, the mail-order house and the supermarket which are bound to destroy those pyramids sooner or later.[5] Now a theoretical construction which neglects this essential element of the case neglects all that is most typically capitalist about it; even if correct in logic as well as in fact, it is like *Hamlet* without the Danish prince.

---

4   This is also shown by a theorem we frequently meet with in expositions of the theory of imperfect competition, viz., the theorem that, under conditions of imperfect competition, producing or trading businesses tend to be irrationally small. Since imperfect competition is at the same time held to be an outstanding characteristic of modem industry we are set to wondering what world these theorists live in, unless, as stated above, fringe-end cases are all they have in mind.

5   The mere threat of their attack cannot, in the particular conditions, environmental and personal, of small-scale retail trade, have its usual disciplining influence, for the small man is too much hampered by his cost structure and, however well he may manage within his inescapable limitations, he can never adapt him self to the methods of competitors who can afford to sell at the price at which he buys.

A First Analysis of the Category of Action

Human Action: A Treatise on Economics

By Ludwig von Mises

1. ENDS AND MEANS

The result sought by an action is called its end, goal, or aim. One uses these terms in ordinary speech also to signify intermediate ends, goals, or aims; these are points which acting man wants to attain only because he believes that he will reach his ultimate end, goal, or aim in passing beyond them. Strictly speaking the end, goal, or aim of any action is always the relief from a felt uneasiness.

A means is what serves to the attainment of any end, goal, or aim. Means are not in the given universe; in this universe there exist only things. A thing becomes a means when human reason plans to employ it for the attainment of some end and human action really employs it for this purpose. Thinking man sees the serviceableness of things, i.e., their ability to minister to his ends, and acting man makes them means. It is of primary importance to realize that parts of the external world become means only through the operation of the human mind and its offshoot, human action. External objects are as such only phenomena of the physical universe and the subject matter of the natural sciences. It is

human meaning and action which transform them into means. Praxeology does not deal with the external world, but with man's conduct with regard to it. Praxeological reality is not the physical universe, but man's conscious reaction to the given state of this universe. Economics is not about things and tangible material objects; it is about men, their meanings and actions. Goods, commodities, and wealth and all the other notions of conduct are not elements of nature; they are elements of human meaning and conduct. He who wants to deal with them must not look at the external world; he must search for them in the meaning of acting men.

Praxeology and economics do not deal with human meaning and action as they should be or would be if all men were inspired by an absolutely valid philosophy and equipped with a perfect knowledge of technology. For such notions as absolute validity and omniscience there is no room in the frame of a science whose subject matter is erring man. An end is everything which men aim at. A means is everything which acting men consider as such.

It is the task of scientific technology and therapeutics to explode errors in their respective fields. It is the task of economics to expose erroneous doctrines in the field of social action. But if men do not follow the advice of science, but cling to their fallacious prejudices, these errors are reality and must be dealt with as such. Economists consider foreign exchange control as inappropriate to attain the ends aimed at by those who take recourse to it. However, if public opinion does not abandon its delusions and governments consequently resort to foreign exchange control, the course of events is determined by this attitude. Present-day medicine considers the doctrine of the therapeutic effects of mandrake as a fable. But as long as people took this fable as truth, mandrake was an economic good and prices were paid for its acquisition. In dealing with prices economics does not ask what things are in the eyes of other people, but only what they are in the meaning of those intent upon getting them. For it deals with real prices, paid and received in real transactions, not with prices as they would be if men were different from what they really are.

Means are necessarily always limited, i.e., scarce with regard to the services for which man wants to use them. If this were not the case, there would not be any action with regard to them. Where man is not restrained by the insufficient quantity of things available, there is no need for any action.

It is customary to call the end the ultimate good and the means goods. In applying this terminology economists mainly used to think as technologists and not as praxeologists. They differentiated between *free goods* and *economic goods*. They called free goods those things which, being available in superfluous abundance, do not need to be economized. Such goods are, however, not the object of any action. They are general conditions of human welfare; they are parts of the natural environment in which man lives and acts. Only the economic goods are the substratum of action. They alone are dealt with in economics.

Economic goods which in themselves are fitted to satisfy human wants directly and whose service-ableness does not depend on the cooperation of other economic goods, are called consumers' goods or goods of the first order. Means which can satisfy wants only indirectly when complemented by coop-eration of other goods are called producers' goods or factors of production or goods of a remoter or

higher order. The services rendered by a producers' good consist in bringing about, by the cooperation of complementary producers' goods, a product. This product may be a consumers' good; it may be a pro-ducers' good which when combined with other pro-ducers' goods will finally bring about a consumers' good. It is possible to think of the producers' goods as arranged in orders according to their proximity to the consumers' good for whose production they can be used. Those producers' goods which are nearest to the production of a consumers' good are ranged in the second order, and accordingly those which are used for the production of goods of the second order in the third order and so on.

The purpose of such an arrangement of goods in orders is to provide a basis for the theory of value and prices of the factors of production. It will be shown later how the valuation and the prices of the goods of higher orders are dependent on the valuation and the prices of the goods of lower orders produced by their expenditure. The first and ultimate valuation of external things refers only to consumers' goods. All other things are valued according to the part they play in the production of consumers' goods.

It is therefore not necessary actually to arrange producers' goods in various orders from the second to the nth. It is no less superfluous to enter into pe-dantic discussions of whether a concrete good has to be called a good of the lowest order or should rather be attributed to one of the higher orders. Whether raw coffee beans or roast coffee beans or ground coffee or coffee prepared for drinking or only coffee prepared and mixed with cream and sugar are to be called a consumers' good ready for consumption is of no importance. It is immaterial which manner of speech we adopt. For with regard to the problem of valuation, all that we say about a consumers' good can be applied to any good of a higher order (except those of the highest order) if we consider it as a product.

An economic good does not necessarily have to be embodied in a tangible thing. Nonmaterial economic goods are called services.

2. THE SCALE OF VALUE

Acting man chooses between various opportunities offered for choice. He prefers one alternative to others.

It is customary to say that acting man has a scale of wants or values in his mind when he arranges his actions. On the basis of such a scale he satisfies what is of higher value, i.e., his more urgent wants, and leaves unsatisfied what is of lower value, i.e., what is a less urgent want. There is no objection to such a presentation of the state of affairs. However, one must not forget that the scale of values or wants manifests itself only in the reality of action. These scales have no independent existence apart from the actual behavior of individuals. The only source from which our knowledge concerning these scales is derived is the observation of a man's actions. Every action is always in perfect agreement with the scale of values or wants because these scales are nothing but an instrument for the interpretation of a man's acting.

Ethical doctrines are intent upon establishing scales of value according to which man should act but does not necessarily always act. They claim for themselves the vocation of telling right from wrong and of advising man concerning what he should aim at as the supreme good. They are normative disciplines aiming at the cognition of what ought to be. They are not neutral with regard to facts; they judge them from the point of view of freely adopted standards.

This is not the attitude of praxeology and economics. They are fully aware of the fact that the ultimate ends of human action are not open to examination from any absolute standard. Ultimate ends are ultimately given, they are purely subjective, they differ with various people and with the same people at various moments in their lives. Praxeology and economics deal with the means for the attainment of ends chosen by the acting individuals. They do not express any opinion with regard to such problems as whether or not sybaritism is better than asceticism. They apply to the means only one yardstick, viz.,

whether or not they are suitable to attain the ends at which the acting individuals aim.

The notions of abnormality and perversity therefore have no place in economics. It does not say that a man is perverse because he prefers the disagreeable, the detrimental, and the painful to the agreeable, the beneficial, and the pleasant. It says only that he is different from other people; that he likes what others detest; that he considers useful what others want to avoid; that he takes pleasure in enduring pain which others avoid because it hurts them. The polar notions normal and perverse can be used anthropologically for the distinction between those who behave as most people do and outsiders and atypical exceptions; they can be applied biologically for the distinction between those whose behavior preserves the vital forces and those whose behavior is self-destructive; they can be applied in an ethical sense for the distinction between those who behave correctly and those who act otherwise than they should. However, in the frame of a theoretical science of human action, there is no room for such a distinction. Any examination of ultimate ends turns out to be purely subjective and therefore arbitrary.

Value is the importance that acting man attaches to ultimate ends. Only to ultimate ends is primary and original value assigned. Means are valued derivatively according to their serviceableness in contributing to the attainment of ultimate ends. Their valuation is derived from the valuation of the respective ends. They are important for man only as far as they make it possible for him to attain some ends.

Value is not intrinsic, it is not in things. It is within us; it is the way in which man reacts to the conditions of his environment.

Neither is value in words and doctrines. It is reflected in human conduct. It is not what a man or groups of men say about value that counts, but how they act. The oratory of moralists and the pompousness of party programs are significant as such. But they influence the course of human events only as far as they really determine the actions of men.

3. THE SCALE OF NEEDS

Notwithstanding all declarations to the contrary, the immense majority of men aim first of all at an improvement of the material conditions of well-being. They want more and better food, better homes and clothes, and a thousand other amenities. They strive after abundance and health. Taking these goals as given, applied physiology tries to determine what means are best suited to provide as much satisfaction as possible. It distinguishes, from this point of view, between man's "real" needs and imaginary and spurious appetites. It teaches people how they should act and what they should aim at as a means.

The importance of such doctrines is obvious. From his point of view the physiologist is right in distinguishing between sensible action and action contrary to purpose. He is right in contrasting judicious methods of nourishment from unwise methods. He may condemn certain modes of behavior as absurd and opposed to "real" needs. However, such judgments are beside the point for a science dealing with the reality of human action. Not what a man should do, but what he does, counts for praxeology and economics. Hygiene may be right or wrong in calling alcohol and nicotine poisons. But economics must explain the prices of tobacco and liquor as they are, not as they would be under different conditions.

There is no room left in the field of economics for a scale of needs different from the scale of values as reflected in man's actual behavior. Economics deals with real man, weak and subject to error as he is, not with ideal beings, omniscient and perfect as only gods could be.

4. ACTION AS AN EXCHANGE

Action is an attempt to substitute a more satisfactory state of affairs for a less satisfactory one. We call such a willfully induced alteration an exchange. A less desirable condition is bartered for a more desirable. What gratifies less is abandoned in order to attain something that pleases more. That which is abandoned is called the price paid for the attainment of the end sought. The value of the price paid is called cost. Cost is equal to the value attached to the satisfaction which one must forego in order to attain the end aimed at.

The difference between the value of the price paid (the costs incurred) and that of the goal attained is called gain or profit or net yield. Profit in this primary sense is purely subjective, it is an increase in the acting man's happiness, it is a psychical phenomenon that can be neither measured nor weighed. There is a more and a less in the removal of uneasiness felt; but how much one satisfaction surpasses another one can only be felt; it cannot be established and determined in an objective way. A judgment of value does not measure, it arranges in a scale of degrees, it grades. It is expressive of an order of preference and sequence, but not expressive of measure and weight. Only the ordinal numbers can be applied to it, but not the cardinal numbers.

It is vain to speak of any calculation of values. Calculation is possible only with cardinal numbers. The difference between the valuation of two states of affairs is entirely psychical and personal. It is not open to any projection into the external world. It can be sensed only by the individual. It cannot be communicated or imparted to any fellow man. It is an intensive magnitude.

Physiology and psychology have developed various methods by means of which they pretend to have attained a substitute for the unfeasible measurement of intensive magnitudes. There is no need for economics to enter into an examination of these rather questionable makeshifts. Their supporters themselves realize that they are not applicable to value judgments. But even if they were, they would not have any bearing on economic problems. For economics deals with action as such, and not with the psychical facts that result in definite actions.

It happens again and again that an action does not attain the end sought. Sometimes the result, although inferior to the end aimed at, is still an improvement when compared with the previous state of affairs; then there is still a profit, although a smaller one than that expected. But it can happen that the action produces a state of affairs less desirable than the previous state it was intended to alter. Then the difference between the valuation of the result and the costs incurred is called loss.

CHAPTER 2

Microeconomics

Price Theory and Public Choice

By Thomas Rustici

SECTION 1

The crown jewel of economics is *price theory*. The formation, function, and interaction of relative prices reflect and direct the choices made by billions of individuals in a world of scarcity. The relevance of microeconomic price theory is illustrated in practice by the 1945 classic essay by Friedrich von Hayek entitled, *The Use of Knowledge in Society*. Hayek demonstrates that the price system is not simply a set of numbers on tags; rather, it is an enormously complex information system for consumers and producers alike. Prices communicate information about human values; they are the "words" in the language of trade. Relative price changes in a free market spread information, make rational economic calculation possible, and transmit honest information between complete strangers. Prices allow us to give and receive economic knowledge in ways we could never access through reason alone. The price system is spontaneous, unplanned, undefined. Hayek's essay deserves multiple readings.

In addition to the classic essays in price theory, this section contains many of the basic graphical and analytical economic tools not only necessary for micro theory, absolutely critical for proper understanding of macro theory as well. Why? The reason is because the economy is not "out there somewhere" detached from individual people.; microeconomic choice theory is the foundation of the macro economy. Individuals, and the actions of individuals, make up the aggregate economy. The word "economy" is an abstract label that defines the summation of all the critical choices made and actions taken—and not taken—by individuals; it refers to the tabulation of the billions of decisions to work, save, invest and produce each day. Put to paper these tabulations become what are called economic statistics or aggregates, and help to conceptualize and describe the size and contour of the macro economy, but do not mistake these descriptions for the thing itself.

Those aggregates must always be traceable back to the choices made that brought about that aggregate statistic; this is an essential assumption of economic science: *methodological individualism*. The decision maker is always the unit of analysis. People can and do form groups to make choices, yet ultimately only individuals choose (even when their choices are tabulated in a group setting, this tabulation is merely the collection of individual choices). Just as there are no groups without people, there are no economies without humans! What is the current Gross Domestic Product on Jupiter? How about the unemployment rate on Mars? These are nonsense questions because there are no human choice makers on these planets. No decisions to tabulate—no economic statistics. We are the economy! The editors strongly believe that macroeconomics without a consistent logical and empirical linkage to basic microeconomic principles such as methodological individualism is more than wrong, it is nonsense and non-science.

SECTION 2—PUBLIC CHOICE

Chapter 2 also includes essays on public choice economics, that is, economic theory applied to political markets. What is the motivational principle underpinning the choices made in bureaus and statehouses? What are the institutional rules that govern decision makers? James Buchanan received the Nobel Prize in Economics in 1986 for answering these questions.

According to Professor Buchanan, individuals pursue their own self-interest in public and political markets just as they do in their private sector and voluntary markets and activities. People are people and they don't take off the "horns" of greed they wear in their private lives (as utility seeking consumers, profit maximizing entrepreneurs, or workers pursuing real wage raises). only to trade them for the "halos" of truth, love and beauty in public life (in their roles as voters, politicians and bureaucrats).

Adam Smith first noted long ago that the incentive to maximize our own self-interest is always present. The essay *"Politics without Romance"* by James Buchanan, is part of this tradition and is critical for properly understanding the nature of public policies both at micro and macro levels. This realistic view of government removes the "rose-tinted glasses" economists may be tempted to wear when advising policy makers, and absolutely rules out the search for Plato's benevolent philosopher king. Students often

ask professors why governments pursue destructive policies (policies that on the surface seem to make very little economic sense), or pursue policies whose results seem to contradict their rhetorical goals. Public choice reminds us that what is rational in a political market may contradict or even subvert what is rational for the economy as a whole.

SECTION 3—ENTREPRENEURSHIP

In a market economy entrepreneurs make decisions about the future, investing, taking risks, and coordinating the structure of production to the perceived needs and values of consumers. They undertake plans with the hope that their efforts yield an *economic profit*. The gain that comes from wise investment is the lure that drives the economic engine towards new goods, better technology, and innovative processes that create higher levels of labor productivity (wages) and consumer (utility). Without entrepreneurial activity, the world becomes stationary, a static routine that does not offer any improvement for humans in their everyday life. Getting a handle on how the entrepreneur fits into the price system is very important for the micro and macro economy. The seminal essay by Joseph Schumpeter covers the *"gales of creative destruction"* and is of great significance when looking at the creation of dynamic technological change. On the other hand, the essay by Israel Kirzner highlights an entrepreneur with a crucial *"alertness to opportunity."* When exploiting opportunity, the entrepreneur functionally coordinates and stabilizes the price system while capturing the reward of economic profit. Both essays open a range of insights on the entrepreneur's role in various situations, be it as speculator, middleman, innovator, risk taker, or coordinator.

SECTION 4—TRADE

Why do people engage in the activities they do? What is the economic logic of the division of labor? Specialization in production increases the benefits of exchange. While Adam Smith points out in the *Wealth of Nations* that trade is mutually beneficial, he recognizes this only does so on the principle of *absolute advantage*. I have an advantage picking apples, and you make shoes better than me. I start an orchard, you become a shoemaker, and when we trade apples for shoes both of us are better off than if we had both performed each task ourselves.

It was the great insight of David Ricardo though, in his 1817 essay "*On Foreign Trade*," that one need not be absolutely superior in any task to reap the benefits from trade; in fact you can be inferior in everything and still benefit from the freedom and opportunity to trade. This principle of *comparative advantage* says that, in short, we do what we do best and trade for all the rest. Even where one person is absolutely inferior at everything compared to his trading partner, he will still specialize in that activity where his relative disadvantage is the least, and trade with his neighbor. Comparative advantage is simply an application of the economics concept of *opportunity costs*.

Often we may not know our present comparative advantage—this must be discovered. Competitive entrepreneurs help in that process of discovery. This has important implications for social cooperation locally, nationally, and internationally. Trade is always a win-win proposition *ex ante*. Free trade leads to prosperity (higher real incomes) and peace with our trading and investment partners.

While the mercantilist fallacy of trade as a zero-sum game was refuted by Ricardo's great insight, other fallacies still linger. Often students hear it said that "trade deficits are harmful to the economy." This is certainly wrong since **trade always balances**! In *Do Trade Deficits Matter?* Paul Heyne reminds us that trade deficits in the Current Account are less important than many think. The accounting logic of double-entry bookkeeping reminds us that the "books must always balance" whether for the individual household, firm, or the nation. In other words, discussions of trade deficits are illustrative of flawed accounting practices. The idea of a trade deficit is the mistaken application of single-entry bookkeeping to a double-entry world. It is important to remember in all economic examinations that nothing of economic significance can be inferred from partial accounting.

Prices

How the Price System Works

Economics in One Lesson

By Henry Hazlitt

I

The whole argument of this book may be summed up in the statement that in studying the effects of any given economic proposal we must trace not merely the immediate results but the results in the long run, not merely the primary consequences but the secondary consequences, and not merely the effects on some special group but the effects on everyone. It follows that it is foolish and misleading to concentrate our attention merely on some special point—to examine, for example, merely what happens in one industry without considering what happens in all. But it is precisely from the persistent and lazy habit of thinking only of some particular industry or process in isolation that the major fallacies of economics stem. These fallacies pervade not merely the arguments of the hired spokesmen of special interests, but the arguments even of some economists who pass as profound.

It is on the fallacy of isolation, at bottom, that the "production-for-use-and-not-for-profit" school is based, with its attack on the allegedly vicious "price system." The problem of production, say the adherents of this school, is solved. (This resounding error, as we shall see, is also the starting point of most

currency cranks and share-the-wealth charlatans.) The problem of production is solved. The scientists, the efficiency experts, the engineers, the technicians, have solved it. They could turn out almost anything you cared to mention in huge and practically unlimited amounts. But, alas, the world is not ruled by the engineers, thinking only of production, but by the businessmen, thinking only of profit. The businessmen give their orders to the engineers, instead of vice versa. These businessmen will turn out any object as long as there is a profit in doing so, but the moment there is no longer a profit in making that article, the wicked businessmen will stop making it, though many people's wants are unsatisfied, and the world is crying for more goods.

There are so many fallacies in this view that they cannot all be disentangled at once. But the central error, as we have hinted, comes from looking at only one industry, or even at several industries in turn, as if each of them existed in isolation. Each of them in fact exists in relation to all the others, and every important decision made in it is affected by and affects the decisions made in all the others.

We can understand this better if we understand the basic problem that business collectively has to solve. To simplify this as much as possible, let us consider the problem that confronts a Robinson Crusoe on his desert island His wants at first seem endless. He is soaked with rain; he shivers from cold; he suffers from hunger and thirst. He needs everything: drinking water, food, a roof over his head, protection from animals, a fire, a soft place to lie down. It is impossible for him to satisfy all these needs at once; he has not the time, energy, or resources. He must attend immediately to the most pressing need. He suffers most, say, from thirst. He hollows out a place in the sand to collect rain water, or builds some crude receptacle. When he has provided for only a small water supply, however, he must turn to finding food before he tries to improve this. He can try to fish; but to do this he needs either a hook and line, or a net, and he must set to work on these. But everything he does delays or prevents him from doing something else only a little less urgent. He is faced constantly by the problem of *alternative* applications of his time and labor.

A Swiss Family Robinson, perhaps, finds this problem a little easier to solve. It has more mouths to feed, but it also has more hands to work for them. It can practice division and specialization of labor. The father hunts; the mother prepares the food; the children collect firewood. But even the family cannot afford to have one member of it doing endlessly the same thing, regardless of the relative urgency of the common need he supplies and the urgency of other needs still unfilled. When the children have gathered a certain pile of firewood, they cannot be used simply to increase the pile. It is soon time for one of them to be sent, say, for more water. The family too has the constant problem of choosing among *alternative* applications of labor, and, if it is lucky enough to have acquired guns, fishing tackle, a boat, axes, saws, and so on, of choosing among alternative applications of labor and capital. It would be considered unspeakably silly for the wood-gathering member of the family to complain that they could gather more firewood if his brother helped him all day, instead of getting the fish that were needed for the family dinner. It is recognized clearly in the case of an isolated individual or family that one occupation can expand *only at the expense of all other occupations.*

Elementary illustrations like this are sometimes ridiculed as "Crusoe economics." Unfortunately, they are ridiculed most by those who most need

them, who fail to understand the particular principle illustrated even in this simple form, or who lose track of that principle completely when they come to examine the bewildering complications of a great modern economic society.

2

Let us now turn to such a society. How is the problem of alternative applications of labor and capital, to meet thousands of different needs and wants of different urgencies, solved in such a society? It is solved precisely through the price system. It is solved through the constantly changing interrelationships of costs of production, prices, and profits.

Prices are fixed through the relationship of supply and demand, and in turn affect supply and demand. When people want more of an article, they offer more for it. The price goes up. This increases the profits of those who make the article. Because it is now more profitable to make that article than others, the people already in the business expand their production of it, and more people are attracted to the business. This increased supply then reduces the price and reduces the profit margin, until the profit margin on that article once more falls to the general level of profits (relative risks considered) in other industries. Or the demand for that article may fall; or the supply of it may be increased to such a point that its price drops to a level where there is less profit in making it than in making other articles; or perhaps there is an actual loss in making it In this case the "marginal" producers, that is, the producers who are least efficient, or whose costs of production are highest, will be driven out of business altogether. The product will now be made only by the more efficient producers who operate on lower costs. The supply of that commodity will also drop, or will at least cease to expand. This process is the origin of the belief that prices are determined by costs of production. The doctrine, stated in this form, is not true. Prices are determined by supply and demand, and demand is determined by how intensely people want a commodity and what they have to offer in exchange for it. It is true that supply is in part determined by costs of production. What a commodity *has* cost to produce in the past cannot determine its value. That will depend on the *present* relationship of supply and demand. But the expectations of businessmen concerning what a commodity *will* cost to produce in the future, and what its future price will be, will determine how much of it will be made. This will affect future supply. There is therefore a constant tendency for the price of a commodity and its marginal cost of production to *equal* each other, but not because that marginal cost of production directly determines the price.

The private enterprise system, then, might be compared to thousands of machines, each regulated by its own quasi-automatic governor, yet with these machines and their governors all interconnected and influencing each other, so that they act in effect like one great machine. Most of us must have noticed the automatic "governor" on a steam engine. It usually consists of two balls or weights which work by centrifugal force. As the speed of the engine increases, these balls fly away from the rod to which they are attached and so automatically narrow or close off a throttle valve which regulates the intake of steam and thus slows down the engine. If the engine goes too slowly, on the other hand, the balls drop, widen the throttle valve, and increase the engine's speed. Thus every departure from the desired speed itself sets in motion the forces that tend to correct that departure.

It is precisely in this way that the relative supply of thousands of different commodities is regulated under the system of competitive private enterprise. When people want more of a commodity, their competitive bidding raises its price. This increases the profits of the producers who make that product. This stimulates them to increase their production. It leads others to stop making some of the products they previously made, and turn to making the product that offers them the better return. But this increases the supply of that commodity at the same time that it reduces the supply of some other commodities.

The price of that product therefore falls in relation to the price of other products, and the stimulus to the relative increase in its production disappears.

In the same way, if the demand falls off for some product, its price and the profit in making it go lower, and its production declines.

It is this last development that scandalizes those who do not understand the "price system" they denounce. They accuse it of creating scarcity. Why, they ask indignantly, should manufacturers cut off the production of shoes at the point where it becomes unprofitable to produce any more? Why should they be guided merely by their own profits? Why should they be guided by the market? Why do they not produce shoes to the "full capacity of modern technical processes"? The price system and private enterprise, conclude the "production-for-use" philosophers, are merely a form of "scarcity economics."

These questions and conclusions stem from the fallacy of looking at one industry in isolation, of looking at the tree and ignoring the forest. Up to a certain point it is necessary to produce shoes. But it is also necessary to produce coats, shirts, trousers, homes, plows, shovels, factories, bridges, milk, and bread. It would be idiotic to go on piling up mountains of surplus shoes, simply because we could do it, while hundreds of more urgent needs went unfilled.

Now in an economy in equilibrium, a given industry can expand *only at the expense of other industries*. For at any moment the factors of production are limited. One industry can be expanded only by *diverting* to it labor, land, and capital that would otherwise be employed in other industries. And when a given industry shrinks, or stops expanding its output, it does not necessarily mean that there has been any *net* decline in aggregate production. The shrinkage at that point may have merely *released* labor and capital to *permit the expansion of other industries*. It is erroneous to conclude, therefore, that a shrinkage of production in one line necessarily means a shrinkage in *total* production.

Everything, in short, is produced at the expense of forgoing something else. Costs of production themselves, in fact, might be defined as the things that are given up (the leisure and pleasures, the raw materials with alternative potential uses) in order to create the thing that is made.

It follows that it is just as essential for the health of a dynamic economy that dying industries should be allowed to die as that growing industries should be allowed to grow. For the dying industries absorb labor and capital that should be released for the growing industries. It is only the much vilified price system that solves the enormously complicated problem of deciding precisely how much of tens of thousands of different commodities and services should be produced in relation to each other. These otherwise bewildering equations are solved quasi-automatically by the system of prices, profits, and costs. They are solved by this system incomparably better than any group of bureaucrats could solve them. For they are solved by a system under which each consumer makes his own demand and casts a fresh vote, or a dozen fresh votes, every day; whereas bureaucrats would try to solve it by having made for the consumers, not what the consumers themselves wanted, but what the bureaucrats decided was good for them.

Yet though the bureaucrats do not understand the quasi-automatic system of the market, they are always disturbed by it. They are always trying to improve it or correct it, usually in the interests of some wailing pressure group. What some of the results of their intervention is, we shall examine in succeeding chapters.

The Use of Knowledge in Society

By F. A. Hayek

What is the problem we wish to solve when we try to construct a rational economic order? On certain familiar assumptions the answer is simple enough. *If* we possess all the relevant information, *if* we can start out from a given system of preferences, and *if* we command complete knowledge of available means, the problem which remains is purely one of logic. That is, the answer to the question of what is the best use of the available means is implicit in our assumptions. The conditions which the solution of this optimum problem must satisfy have been fully worked out and can be stated best in mathematical form: put at their briefest, they are that the marginal rates of substitution between any two commodities or factors must be the same in all their different uses.

This, however, is emphatically *not* the economic problem which society faces. And the economic calculus which we have developed to solve this logical problem, though an important step toward the solution of the economic problem of society, does not yet provide an answer to it. The reason for this is that the "data" from which the economic calculus starts are never for the whole society "given" to a single mind which could work out the implications and can never be so given.

The peculiar character of the problem of a rational economic order is determined precisely by the fact that the knowledge of the circumstances of which we must make use never exists in concentrated or integrated form but solely as the dispersed bits of incomplete and frequently contradictory knowledge which all the separate individuals possess. The economic problem of society is thus not merely a problem of how to allocate "given" resources—if "given" is taken to mean given to a single mind which deliberately solves the problem set by these "data." It is rather a problem of how to secure the best use of resources known to any of the members of society, for ends whose relative importance only these individuals know. Or, to put it briefly, it is a problem of the utilization of knowledge which is not given to anyone in its totality.

This character of the fundamental problem has, I am afraid, been obscured rather than illuminated by many of the recent refinements of economic theory, particularly by many of the uses made of mathematics. Though the problem with which I want primarily to deal in this paper is the problem of a rational economic organization, I shall in its course be led again and again to point to its close connections with certain methodological questions. Many of the points I wish to make are indeed conclusions toward which diverse paths of reasoning have unexpectedly converged. But, as I now see these problems, this is no accident. It seems to me that many of the current disputes with regard to both economic theory and economic policy have their common origin in a misconception about the nature of the economic problem of society. This misconception in turn is due to an erroneous transfer to social phenomena of the habits of thought we have developed in dealing with the phenomena of nature.

II

In ordinary language we describe by the word "planning" the complex of interrelated decisions about the allocation of our available resources. All economic activity is in this sense planning; and in any society in which many people collaborate, this planning, whoever does it, will in some measure have to be based on knowledge which, in the first instance, is not given to the planner but to somebody else, which somehow will have to be conveyed to the planner. The various ways in which the knowledge on which people base their plans is communicated to them is the crucial problem for any theory explaining the economic process, and the problem of what is the best way of utilizing knowledge initially dispersed among all the people is at least one of the main problems of economic policy—or of designing an efficient economic system.

The answer to this question is closely connected with that other question which arises here, that of *who* is to do the planning. It is about this question that all the dispute about "economic planning" centers. This is not a dispute about whether planning is to be done or not. It is a dispute as to whether planning is to be done centrally, by one authority for the whole economic system, or is to be divided among many individuals. Planning in the specific sense in which the term is used in contemporary controversy necessarily means central planning—direction of the whole economic system according to one unified plan. Competition, on the other hand, means decentralized planning by many separate persons. The halfway house between the two, about which many people talk but which few like when they see it, is the delegation of planning to organized industries, or, in other words, monopoly.

Which of these systems is likely to be more efficient depends mainly on the question under which of them we can expect that fuller use will be made of the existing knowledge. And this, in turn, depends on whether we are more likely to succeed in putting at the disposal of a single central authority all the knowledge which ought to be used but which is initially dispersed among many different individuals, or in conveying to the individuals such additional knowledge as they need in order to enable them to fit their plans with those of others.

III

It will at once be evident that on this point the position will be different with respect to different kinds of knowledge; and the answer to our question will therefore largely turn on the relative importance of the different kinds of knowledge; those more likely to be at the disposal of particular individuals and those which we should with greater confidence expect to find in the possession of an authority made up of suitably chosen experts. If it is today so widely assumed that the latter will be in a better position, this is because one kind of knowledge, namely, scientific knowledge, occupies now so prominent a place in public imagination that we tend to forget that it is not the only kind that is relevant. It may be admitted that, as far as scientific knowledge is concerned, a body of suitably chosen experts may be in the best position to command all the best knowledge available—though this is of course merely shifting the difficulty to the problem of selecting the experts. What I wish to point out is that, even assuming that this problem can be readily solved, it is only a small part of the wider problem.

Today it is almost heresy to suggest that scientific knowledge is not the sum of all knowledge. But a little reflection will show that there is beyond question a body of very important but unorganized knowledge which cannot possibly be called scientific in the sense of knowledge of general rules: the knowledge of the particular circumstances of time and place. It is with respect to this that practically every individual has some advantage over all others because he possesses unique information of which beneficial use might be made, but of which use can be made only if the decisions depending on it are left to him or are made with his active cooperation. We need to remember only how much we have to learn in any occupation after we have completed our theoretical training, how big a part of our working life we spend learning particular jobs, and how valuable an asset in all walks of life is knowledge of people, of local conditions, and of special circumstances. To know of and put to use a machine not fully employed, or somebody's skill which could be better utilized, or to be aware of a surplus stock which can be drawn upon during an interruption of supplies, is socially quite as useful as the knowledge of better alternative techniques. And the shipper who earns his living from using otherwise empty or half-filled journeys of tramp-steamers, or the estate agent whose whole knowledge is almost exclusively one of temporary opportunities, or the *arbitrageur* who gains from local differences of commodity prices, are all performing eminently useful functions based on special knowledge of circumstances of the fleeting moment not known to others.

It is a curious fact that this sort of knowledge should today be generally regarded with a kind of contempt and that anyone who by such knowledge gains an advantage over somebody better equipped with theoretical or technical knowledge is thought to have acted almost disreputably. To gain an advantage from better knowledge of facilities of communication or transport is sometimes regarded as almost dishonest, although it is quite as important that society make use of the best opportunities in this respect as in using the latest scientific discoveries.

This prejudice has in a considerable measure affected the attitude toward commerce in general compared with that toward production. Even economists who regard themselves as definitely immune to the crude materialist fallacies of the past constantly commit the same mistake where activities directed toward the acquisition of such practical knowledge are concerned—apparently because in their scheme of things all such knowledge is supposed to be "given." The common idea now seems to be that all such knowledge should as a matter of course be readily at the command of everybody, and the reproach of irrationality leveled against the existing economic order is frequently based on the fact that it is not so available. This view disregards the fact that the method by which such knowledge can be made as widely available as possible is precisely the problem to which we have to find an answer.

IV

If it is fashionable today to minimize the importance of the knowledge of the particular circumstances of time and place, this is closely connected with the smaller importance which is now attached to change as such. Indeed, there are few points on which the assumptions made (usually only implicitly) by the "planners" differ from those of their opponents as much as with regard to the significance and frequency of changes which will make substantial alterations of production plans necessary. Of course, if detailed economic plans could be laid down for fairly long periods in advance and then closely adhered to, so that no further economic decisions of importance would be required, the task of drawing up a comprehensive plan governing all economic activity would be much less formidable.

It is, perhaps, worth stressing that economic problems arise always and only in consequence of change. So long as things continue as before, or at least as they were expected to, there arise no new problems requiring a decision, no need to form a new plan. The belief that changes, or at least day-to-day adjustments, have become less important in modern times implies the contention that economic problems also have become less important. This belief in the decreasing importance of change is, for that reason, usually held by the same people who argue that the importance of economic considerations has been driven into the background by the growing importance of technological knowledge.

Is it true that, with the elaborate apparatus of modern production, economic decisions are required only at long intervals, as when a new factory is to be erected or a new process to be introduced? Is it true that, once a plant has been built, the rest is all more or less mechanical, determined by the character of the plant, and leaving little to be changed in adapting to the ever-changing circumstances of the moment?

The fairly widespread belief in the affirmative is not, as far as I can ascertain, borne out by the practical experience of the businessman. In a competitive industry at any rate—and such an industry alone can serve as a test—the task of keeping cost from rising requires constant struggle, absorbing a great part of the energy of the manager. How easy it is for an inefficient manager to dissipate the differentials on which profitability rests, and that it is possible, with the same technical facilities, to produce with a great variety of costs, are among the commonplaces of business experience which do not seem to be equally familiar in the study of the economist. The very strength of the desire, constantly voiced by producers and engineers, to be allowed to proceed untrammeled by considerations of money costs, is eloquent testimony to the extent to which these factors enter into their daily work.

One reason why economists are increasingly apt to forget about the constant small changes which make up the whole economic picture is probably their growing preoccupation with statistical aggregates, which show a very much greater stability than the movements of the detail. The comparative stability of the aggregates cannot, however, be accounted for—as the statisticians occasionally seem to be inclined to do—by the "law of large numbers" or the mutual compensation of random changes. The number of elements with which we have to deal is not large enough for such accidental forces to produce stability. The continuous flow of goods and services is maintained by constant deliberate adjustments, by new dispositions made every day in the light of circumstances not known the day before, by *B* stepping in at once when *A* fails to deliver. Even the large and highly mechanized plant keeps going largely because of an environment upon which it can draw for all sorts of unexpected needs; tiles for its roof, stationery for its forms, and all the thousand and one kinds of equipment in which it cannot be self-contained and which the plans for the operation of the plant require to be readily available in the market.

This is, perhaps, also the point where I should briefly mention the fact that the sort of knowledge with which I have been concerned is knowledge of the kind which by its nature cannot enter into statistics and therefore cannot be conveyed to any central authority in statistical form. The statistics which such a central authority would have to use would have to be arrived at precisely by abstracting from minor differences between the things, by lumping together, as resources of one kind, items which differ as regards location, quality, and other particulars, in a way which may be very significant for the specific decision. It follows from this that central planning based on statistical information by its nature cannot take direct account of these circumstances of time and place and that the central planner will have to find some way or other in which the decisions depending on them can be left to the "man on the spot."

V

If we can agree that the economic problem of society is mainly one of rapid adaptation to changes in the particular circumstances of time and place, it would seem to follow that the ultimate decisions must be left to the people who are familiar with these circumstances, who know directly of the relevant changes and of the resources immediately available to meet them. We cannot expect that this problem will be solved by first communicating all this knowledge to a central board which, after integrating *all* knowledge, issues its orders. We must solve it by some form of decentralization. But this answers only part of our problem. We need decentralization because only thus can we insure that the knowledge of the particular circumstances of time and place will be promptly used. But the "man on the spot" cannot decide solely on the basis of his limited but intimate knowledge of the facts of his immediate surroundings. There still remains the problem of communicating to him such further information as he needs to fit his decisions into the whole pattern of changes of the larger economic system.

How much knowledge does he need to do so successfully? Which of the events which happen beyond the horizon of his immediate knowledge are of relevance to his immediate decision, and how much of them need he know?

There is hardly anything that happens anywhere in the world that *might* not have an effect on the decision he ought to make. But he need not know of these events as such, nor of *all* their effects. It does not matter for him *why* at the particular moment more screws of one size than of another are wanted, *why* paper bags are more readily available than canvas bags, or *why* skilled labor, or particular machine tools, have for the moment become more difficult to obtain. All that is significant for him is *how much more or less* difficult to procure they have become compared with other things with which he is also concerned, or how much more or less urgently wanted are the alternative things he produces or uses. It is always a question of the relative importance of the particular things with which he is concerned, and the causes which alter their relative importance are of no interest to him beyond the effect on those concrete things of his own environment.

It is in this connection that what I have called the "economic calculus" proper helps us, at least by analogy, to see how this problem can be solved, and in fact is being solved, by the price system. Even the single controlling mind, in possession of all the data for some small, self-contained economic system, would not—every time some small adjustment in the allocation of resources had to be made—go explicitly through all the relations between ends and means which might possibly be affected. It is indeed the great contribution of the pure logic of choice that it has demonstrated conclusively that even such a single mind could solve this kind of problem only by constructing and constantly using rates of equivalence (or "values," or "marginal rates of substitution"), *i.e.,* by attaching to each kind of scarce resource a numerical index which cannot be derived from any property possessed by that particular thing, but which reflects, or in which is condensed, its significance in view of the whole means-end structure. In any small change he will have to consider only these quantitative indices (or "values") in which all the relevant information is concentrated; and, by adjusting the quantities one by one, he can appropriately rearrange his dispositions without having to solve the whole puzzle *ab initio* or without needing at any stage to survey it at once in all its ramifications.

Fundamentally, in a system in which the knowledge of the relevant facts is dispersed among many people, prices can act to coordinate the separate actions of different people in the same way as subjective values help the individual to coordinate the parts of his plan. It is worth contemplating for a moment a very simple and commonplace instance of the action of the price system to see what precisely it accomplishes. Assume that somewhere in the world a new opportunity for the use of some raw material, say, tin, has arisen, or that one of the sources of supply of tin has been eliminated. It does not matter for our purpose—and it is very significant that it does not matter—which of these two causes has made tin more scarce. All that the users of tin need to know is that some of the tin they used to consume is now more profitably employed elsewhere and that, in consequence, they must economize tin. There is no need for the great majority of them even to know where the more urgent need has arisen, or in favor of what other needs they ought to husband the supply. If only some of them know directly of the new demand, and switch resources over to it, and if the people who are aware of the new gap thus created in turn fill it from still other sources, the effect will rapidly spread throughout the whole economic system and influence not only all the uses of tin but also those of its substitutes and the substitutes of these substitutes, the supply of all the things made of tin, and their substitutes, and so on; and all his without the great majority of those instrumental in bringing about these substitutions knowing anything at all about the original cause of these changes. The whole acts as one market, not because any of its members survey the whole field, but because their limited individual fields of vision sufficiently overlap so that through many intermediaries the relevant information is communicated to all. The mere fact that there is one price for any commodity—or rather that local prices are connected in a manner determined by the cost of transport, etc.—brings about the solution which (it is just conceptually possible) might have been arrived at by one single mind possessing all the information which is in fact dispersed among all the people involved in the process.

VI

We must look at the price system as such a mechanism for communicating information if we want to understand its real function—a function which, of course, it fulfils less perfectly as prices grow more rigid. (Even when quoted prices have become quite rigid, however, the forces which would operate through changes in price still operate to a considerable extent through changes in the other terms of the contract.) The most significant fact about this system is the economy of knowledge with which it operates, or how little the individual participants need to know in order to be able to take the right action. In abbreviated form, by a kind of symbol, only the most essential information is passed on and

passed on only to those concerned. It is more than a metaphor to describe the price system as a kind of machinery for registering change, or a system of telecommunications which enables individual producers to watch merely the movement of a few pointers, as an engineer might watch the hands of a few dials, in order to adjust their activities to changes of which they may never know more than is reflected in the price movement.

Of course, these adjustments are probably never "perfect" in the sense in which the economist conceives of them in his equilibrium analysis. But I fear that our theoretical habits of approaching the problem with the assumption of more or less perfect knowledge on the part of almost everyone has made us somewhat blind to the true function of the price mechanism and led us to apply rather misleading standards in judging its efficiency. The marvel is that in a case like that of a scarcity of one raw material, without an order being issued, without more than perhaps a handful of people knowing the cause, tens of thousands of people whose identity could not be ascertained by months of investigation, are made to use the material or its products more sparingly; *i.e.,* they move in the right direction. This is enough of a marvel even if, in a constantly changing world, not all will hit it off so perfectly that their profit rates will always be maintained at the same constant or "normal" level.

I have deliberately used the word "marvel" to shock the reader out of the complacency with which we often take the working of this mechanism for granted. I am convinced that if it were the result of deliberate human design, and if the people guided by the price changes understood that their decisions have significance far beyond their immediate aim, this mechanism would have been acclaimed as one of the greatest triumphs of the human mind. Its misfortune is the double one that it is not the product of human design and that the people guided by it usually do not know why they are made to do what they do. But those who clamor for "conscious direction"—and who cannot believe that anything which has evolved without design (and even without our understanding it) should solve problems which we should not be able to solve consciously—should remember this: The problem is precisely how to extend the span of out utilization of resources beyond the span of the control of any one mind; and therefore, how to dispense with the need of conscious control, and how to provide inducements which will make the individuals do the desirable things without anyone having to tell them what to do.

The problem which we meet here is by no means peculiar to economics but arises in connection with nearly all truly social phenomena, with language and with most of our cultural inheritance, and constitutes really the central theoretical problem of all social science. As Alfred Whitehead has said in another connection, "It is a profoundly erroneous truism, repeated by all copy-books and by eminent people when they are making speeches, that we should cultivate the habit of thinking what we are doing. The precise opposite is the case. Civilization advances by extending the number of important operations which we can perform without thinking about them." This is of profound significance in the social field. We make constant use of formulas, symbols, and rules whose meaning we do not understand and through the use of which we avail ourselves of the assistance of knowledge which individually we do not possess. We have developed these practices and institutions by building upon habits and institutions which have proved successful in their own sphere and which have in turn become the foundation of the civilization we have built up.

The price system is just one of those formations which man has learned to use (though he is still very far from having learned to make the best use of it) after he had stumbled upon it without understanding it. Through it not only a division of labor but also a coordinated utilization of resources based on an equally divided knowledge has become possible. The people who like to deride any suggestion that this may be so usually distort the argument by insinuating that it asserts that by some miracle just that sort of system has spontaneously grown up which is best suited to modern civilization. It is the other way round: man has been able to develop that division of labor on which our civilization is based because he happened to stumble upon a method which made

it possible. Had he not done so, he might still have developed some other, altogether different, type of civilization, something like the "state" of the termite ants, or some other altogether unimaginable type. All that we can say is that nobody has yet succeeded in designing an alternative system in which certain features of the existing one can be preserved which are dear even to those who most violently assail it—such as particularly the extent to which the individual can choose his pursuits and consequently freely use his own knowledge and skill.

VII

It is in many ways fortunate that the dispute about the indispensability of the price system for any rational calculation in a complex society is now no longer conducted entirely between camps holding different political views. The thesis that without the price system we could not preserve a society based on such extensive division of labor as ours was greeted with a howl of derision when it was first advanced by von Mises twenty-five years ago. Today the difficulties which some still find in accepting it are no longer mainly political, and this makes for an atmosphere much more conducive to reasonable discussion. When we find Leon Trotsky arguing that "economic accounting is unthinkable without market relations"; when Professor Oscar Lange promises Professor von Mises a statue in the marble halls of the future Central Planning Board; and when Professor Abba P. Lerner rediscovers Adam Smith and emphasizes that the essential utility of the price system consists in inducing the individual, while seeking his own interest, to do what is in the general interest, the differences can indeed no longer be ascribed to political prejudice. The remaining dissent seems clearly to be due to purely intellectual, and more particularly methodological, differences.

A recent statement by Professor Joseph Schumpeter in his *Capitalism, Socialism, and Democracy* provides a clear illustration of one of the methodological differences which I have in mind. Its author is pre-eminent among those economists who approach economic phenomena in the light of a certain branch of positivism. To him these phenomena accordingly appear as objectively given quantities of commodities impinging directly upon each other, almost, it would seem, without any intervention of human minds. Only against this background can I account for the following (to me startling) pronouncement. Professor Schumpeter argues that the possibility of a rational calculation in the absence of markets for the factors of production follows for the theorist "from the elementary proposition that consumers in evaluating ('demanding') consumers' goods *ipso facto* also evaluate the means of production which enter into the production of these goods."[1]

Taken literally, this statement is simply untrue. The consumers do nothing of the kind. What Professor Schumpeter's *"ipso facto"* presumably means is that the valuation of the factors of production is implied in, or follows necessarily from, the valuation of consumers' goods. But this, too, is not correct. Implication is a logical relationship which can be meaningfully asserted only of propositions simultaneously present to one and the same mind. It is evident, however, that the values of the factors of production do not depend solely on the valuation of the consumers' goods but also on the conditions of supply of the various factors of production. Only to a mind to which all these facts were simultaneously known would the answer necessarily follow from the facts given to it. The practical problem, however, arises precisely because these facts are never so given to a single mind, and because, in consequence, it is necessary that in the solution of the problem knowledge should be used that is dispersed among many people.

The problem is thus in no way solved if we can show that all the facts, *if* they were known to a single mind (as we hypothetically assume them to be given to the observing economist), would uniquely determine the solution; instead we must show how a solution is produced by the interactions of people each of whom possesses only partial knowledge. To assume all the knowledge to be given to a single

mind in the same manner in which we assume it to be given to us as the explaining economists is to assume the problem away and to disregard everything that is important and significant in the real world.

That an economist of Professor Schumpeter's standing should thus have fallen into a trap which the ambiguity of the term "datum" sets to the unwary can hardly be explained as a simple error. It suggests rather that there is something fundamentally wrong with an approach which habitually disregards an essential part of the phenomena with which we have to deal: the unavoidable imperfection of man's knowledge and the consequent need for a process by which knowledge is constantly communicated and acquired. Any approach, such as that of much of mathematical economics with its simultaneous equations, which in effect starts from the assumption that people's *knowledge* corresponds with the objective *facts* of the situation, systematically leaves out what is our main task to explain. I am far from denying that in our system equilibrium analysis has a useful function to perform. But when it comes to the point where it misleads some of our leading thinkers into believing that the situation which it describes has direct relevance to the solution of practical problems, it is high time that we remember that it does not deal with the social process at all and that it is no more than a useful preliminary to the study of the main problem.

NOTE FOR THIS CHAPTER

1. J. Schumpeter, *Capitalism, Socialism, and Democracy* (New York; Harper, 1942), p. 175. Professor Schumpeter is, I believe, also the original author of the myth that Pareto and Barone have "solved" the problem of socialist calculation. What they, and many others, did was merely to state the conditions which a rational allocation of resources would have to satisfy and to point out that these were essentially the same as the conditions of equilibrium of a competitive market. This is something altogether different from knowing how the

allocation of resources satisfying these conditions can be found in practice. Pareto himself (from whom Barone has taken practically everything he has to say), far from claiming to have solved the practical problem, in fact explicitly denies that it can be solved without the help of the market. See his *Manuel d'économie pure* (2d ed., 1927), pp. 233–34. The relevant passage is quoted in an English translation at the beginning of my article on "Socialist Calculation: The Competitive 'Solution,' " in *Economica,* New Series, Vol. VIII, No. 26 (May, 1940), p. 125.

The Formation and Function of Prices

By Hans Sennholz

For almost two thousand years economic investigation was handicapped by the common notion that economic exchange is fair only as long as each party gets exactly as much as he gives the other. This notion of equality in exchange even permeated the writings of the classical economists.

Back in the 1870's the Englishman Jevons, the Swiss Walras, and the Austrian Menger irrefutably exploded this philosophical foundation. The Austrian School, especially, built a new foundation on the cognition that economic exchange results from a *difference in individual valuations*, not from an equality of costs. According to Menger, "the principle that leads men to exchange is the same principle that guides them in their economic activity as a whole; it is the endeavor to insure the greatest possible satisfaction of their wants." Exchange comes to an end as soon as one party to the exchange should judge both goods of equal value.

In the terminology of the economists, the value of a good is determined by its marginal utility. This means that the value of a good is determined by the importance of the least important want that can be satisfied by the available supply of goods. A simple example first used by Böhm-Bawerk, the eminent Austrian economist, may illustrate this principle.

A pioneer farmer in the jungle of Brazil has just harvested five sacks of grain. They are his only means of subsistence until the next harvest. One sack is absolutely essential as the food supply which is to keep him alive. A second sack is to assure his full strength and complete health until the next harvest. The third sack is to be used for the raising of poultry which provides nutriment in the form of meat. The fourth sack is devoted to the distilling of brandy. And finally, after his modest personal wants are thus provided for, he can think of no better use for his fifth sack than to feed it to a number of parrots whose antics give him some entertainment.

It is obvious that the various uses to which the grain is put do not rank equally in importance to him. His life and health depend on the first two sacks, while the fifth and last sack "at the margin" has the least importance or "utility." If he were to lose this last sack, our frontier farmer would suffer a loss of well-being no greater than the pleasure of parrot entertainment. Or, if he should have an opportunity to trade with another frontiersman who happens to pass his solitary log cabin, he will be willing to exchange one sack for any other good that in his judgment exceeds the pleasure of parrot entertainment.

But now let us assume that our frontier farmer has a total supply of only three sacks. His valuation of any one sack will be the utility provided by the third and last sack, which affords him the meat. Loss of any one of three sacks would be much more serious, its value and price therefore much higher. Our farmer could be induced to exchange this sack only if the usefulness of the good he is offered would exceed the utility derived from the consumption of meat.

And finally, let us assume that he possesses only a single sack of grain. It is obvious that any exchange is out of the question as his life depends on it. He would rather fight than risk loss of this sack.

THE LAW OF SUPPLY AND DEMAND

This discussion of the principles of valuation is not merely academic. In a highly developed exchange economy these principles explain the familiar observation that the value and price of goods vary inversely to their quantity. The larger the supply of goods the lower will be the value of the individual good, and vice versa. This elementary principle is the basis of the price doctrine known as the *law of supply and demand*. Stated in a more detailed manner, the following factors determine market prices: the value of the desired good according to the subjective judgment of the buyer and his subjective value of the medium of exchange; the subjective value of the good for the seller and his subjective value of the medium of exchange.

In a given market there can be only *one* price. Whenever businessmen discover discrepancies in prices of goods at different locations, they will endeavor to buy in the lower-price markets and sell in the higher-price markets. But these operations tend to equalize all prices. Or, if they discover discrepancies between producers' goods prices and the anticipated prices of consumers' goods, they may embark upon production in order to take advantage of the price differences.

Value and price constitute the very foundation of the economics of the market society, for it is through value and price that the people give purpose and aim to the production process. No matter what their ultimate motivation may be, whether material or ideal, noble or base, the people judge goods and services according to their suitability for the attainment of their desired objectives. They ascribe value to consumers' goods and determine their prices. And according to Böhm-Bawerk's irrefutable "imputation theory," they even determine indirectly the prices of all factors of production and the income of every member of the market economy.

The prices of the consumers' goods condition and determine the prices of the factors of production: land, labor, and capital. Businessmen appraise the production factors in accordance with the anticipated prices of the products. On the market, the price and remuneration of each factor then emerges from the bids of the competing highest bidders. The businessmen, in order to acquire the necessary production factors, outbid each other by bidding higher prices than their competitors. Their bids are limited by their anticipation of the prices of the products.

The pricing process thus reveals itself as a social process in which all members of society participate. Through buying or abstaining from buying, through cooperation and competition, the millions of consumers ultimately determine the price structure of the market and the allocation of the income of each individual.

PRICES ARE PRODUCTION SIGNALS

Market prices direct economic production. They determine the selection of the factors of production, particularly the land and resources that are employed—or left unused. Market prices are the essential signals that provide meaning and direction to the market economy. The entrepreneurs and capitalists are merely the consumers' agents, and must cater to their wishes and preferences. Through their judgments of value and expressions of price, the consumers decide what is to be produced and in what quantity and quality; where it is to be produced and by whom; what method of production is to be employed; what material is to be used; and they make numerous other decisions. Indeed, the baton of price makes every member of the market economy a conductor of the production process.

Prices also direct investments. True, it may appear that the businessman determines the investment of savings and the direction of production. But he does not exercise this control arbitrarily, as his own desires dictate. On the contrary, he is guided by the prices of products. Where lively demand assures or promises profitable prices, he expands his production. Where prices decline, he restricts production. Expansion and contraction of production tend to alternate until an equilibrium has been established between supply and demand. In final analysis, then, it is the consumer—not the businessman—who determines the direction of production through his buying or abstention from buying.

If, for instance, every individual member of the market society were to consume all his income, then the demand for consumers' goods would determine prices in such a way that businessmen would be induced to produce consumers' goods only. The stock of capital goods will stay the same, provided people do not consume more than their income. If they consume more, the stock of capital goods is necessarily diminished.

If, on the other hand, people save part of their incomes and reduce consumption expenditures, the prices of consumption goods decline. Businessmen thus are forced to adjust their production to the changes demanded. Let us assume that people, on the average, save 25 percent of their incomes. Then, businessmen, through the agency of prices, would assign only 75 percent of production to immediate consumption and the rest to increasing capital.

Our knowledge of prices also discloses the most crucial shortcoming of socialism and the immense superiority of the market order. Without the yardstick of prices, economic calculation is impossible. Without prices, how is the economic planner to calculate the results of production? He cannot compare the vast number of different materials, kinds of labor, capital goods, land, and methods of production with the yields of production. Without the price yardstick, he cannot ascertain whether certain procedures actually increase the productivity and output of his system. It is true, he may calculate in kind. But such a calculation permits no value comparison between the costs of production and its yield. Other socialist substitutes for the price denominator, such as the calculation of labor time, are equally spurious.

GOVERNMENT INTERFERENCE WITH PRICES

Economic theory reveals irrefutably that government intervention causes effects that tend to be undesirable, even from the point of view of those who design that intervention. To interfere with prices, wages, and the rates of interest through government orders and prohibitions is to deprive the people of their central position as sovereigns of the market process. It compels entrepreneurs to obey government orders rather than the value judgments and price signals of consumers. In short, government intervention curtails the economic freedom of the people and enhances the power of politicians and government officials.

The price theory, also explains the various other economic problems of socialism and the interventionist state. It explains, for instance, the unemployment suffered in the industrial areas, the agricultural surpluses accumulated in government bins and warehouses; it even explains the gold and dollar shortages suffered by many central banks all over the world.

The market price equates the demand for and the supply of goods and services. It is the very function of price to establish this equilibrium. At the free market price, anyone willing to sell can sell, and anyone willing to buy can buy. Surpluses or shortages are inconceivable where market prices continuously adjust supply and production to the demand exerted by the consumers.

But whenever government by law or decree endeavors to raise a price, a surplus inevitably results. The motivation for such a policy may indeed be laudable: to raise the farmers, income and improve their living conditions. But the artificially high price causes the supply to increase and the demand to decline. A surplus is thus created, which finds some producers unable to sell their goods at the official price. This very effect explains the $8 billion agricultural surplus now held by the U.S. Government.

It also explains the chronic unemployment of some 5 million people in the United States. For political and social reasons and in attempted defiance of the law of supply and demand, the U.S. Government has enacted minimum wage legislation that is pricing millions of workers right out of the market. The minimum wage is set at $1.25 per hour—to which must be added approximately 30¢ in fringe costs such as social security, vacations and paid holidays, health, and other benefits—so that the minimum employment costs of an American worker exceed $1.55 an hour. But in the world of economic reality, there are millions of unskilled workers, teenagers, and elderly workers whose productivity rates are lower than this minimum. Consequently, no businessman will employ them unless he is able to sustain continuous losses on their employment.

In fact, these unfortunate people are unemployable as long as the official minimum wage exceeds their individual productivity in the market. This kind of labor legislation, even when conceived in good intentions, has bred a great variety of problems which give rise and impetus to more radical government intervention.

The price theory also explains most money problems in the world. For several years after World War II, many underdeveloped countries suffered a chronic gold and dollar shortage. And in recent years, the United States itself has had serious balance-of-payments problems, which are reflected in European countries as a dollar flood.

No matter what the official explanations may be, our knowledge of prices provides us with an understanding of these international money problems. Price theory reveals the operation of "Gresham's Law," according to which an inflated depreciated currency causes gold to leave the country. Gresham's Law merely constitutes the monetary case of the general price theory, which teaches that a shortage inevitably results whenever the government fixes an official price that is below the market price. When the official exchange ratio between gold and paper money understates the value of gold, or overstates the paper, a shortage of gold must inevitably emerge.

And finally, our knowledge of the nature of prices and of the consequences of government interference with prices also explains the "shortages" of goods and services suffered in many countries. Whether the interference is in the form of emergency or wartime controls, international commodity agreements, price stops, wage stops, rent stops, or "usury laws" that artificially limit the yield of capital—and whether they are imposed on the people of America, Africa, Asia, or Europe—government controls over prices control and impoverish the people. And yet, omnipotent governments all over the world are bent on substituting threats and coercion for the laws of the market.

Price Controls

By Hugh Rockoff

Governments have been trying to set maximum or minimum prices since ancient times. The Old Testament prohibited interest on loans, medieval governments fixed the maximum price of bread, and in recent years governments in the United States have fixed the price of gasoline, the rent on apartments in New York City, and the minimum wage, to name a few. At times governments go beyond fixing specific prices and try to control the general level of prices, as was done in the United States during both world wars, during the Korean War, and by the Nixon administration from 1971 to 1973.

The appeal of price controls is easy to divine. Even though they fail to protect many consumers and hurt others, controls hold out the promise of protecting groups of consumers who are particularly hardpressed to meet price increases. Thus the prohibition against usury—charging high interest on loans—was intended to protect someone forced to borrow by desperation; the maximum price for bread was supposed to protect the poor, who depended on bread to survive; and rent controls were supposed to protect those who rented at a time when demand for apartments appeared to exceed the supply and landlords were able to "gouge" tenants.

But despite the frequent use of price controls, and despite the superficial logic of their appeal, economists are generally opposed to them, except perhaps for very brief periods during emergencies. The reason is that controls on prices distort the allocation of resources. To paraphrase a remark by Milton Friedman, economists may not know much, but they do know how to produce a surplus or shortage. Price ceilings, which prevent prices from exceeding a certain maximum, cause shortages. Price floors, which prohibit prices below a certain minimum, cause surpluses. Suppose that the supply and demand for automobile tires are balanced at the current price, and that the government then fixes a lower ceiling price. The number of tires supplied will be reduced, but the number demanded will increase. The result will be excess demand and empty shelves. Although some consumers will be lucky enough to purchase tires at the lower price, others will be forced to do without.

Because controls prevent the price system from rationing the supply to those who demand it, some other mechanism will take its place. A queue or lineup, once a familiar sight in the controlled economies of Eastern Europe, is one possibility. When the U.S. government set maximum prices for gasoline in 1973 and 1979, dealers sold gas on a first-come-first-served basis, and drivers got a little taste of what life was like for people in the Soviet Union: they had to wait in long lines to buy gas. The true price of gas, which included both the cash paid and the time spent waiting in line, was often higher than if prices were not controlled at all. At one time in 1979, for example, the U.S. government fixed the price of gasoline at about $1.00 per gallon. If the market price would have been $1.20, a driver who bought ten gallons apparently saved $.20 per gallon, or $2.00. But if the driver had to line up for thirty minutes to buy gas, and if her time was worth $8.00 per hour, the real cost to her was $10.00 for the gas and $4.00 for the time, an overall cost of $1.40 per gallon. Some gas, of course, was held for friends, long-time customers, the politically well-connected, or those who were willing to pay a little cash on the side.

The incentives to evade controls are ever present, and the forms that evasion can take are limitless. The precise form depends on the nature of the good or service, the organization of the industry, the degree of government enforcement, and so on. One of the simplest forms of evasion is quality deterioration. In the United States during World War II, fat was added to hamburger, candy bars were made smaller and of inferior ingredients, and landlords reduced their maintenance of rent-controlled apartments. The government can attack quality deterioration by issuing specific product standards (hamburger must contain so much lean meat, apartments must be painted once a year, and so on) and by government oversight and enforcement. But this means that the government bureaucracy controlling prices tends to get bigger, more intrusive, and more expensive.

Sometimes more subtle forms of evasion arise. One is the tie-in sale. During World War I, for example, in order to buy wheat flour at the official price, consumers were often required to purchase unwanted quantities of rye or potato flour. Forced up-trading is another. Consider a manufacturer that produces a lower-quality, lower-priced line sold in large volumes at a small markup, and a higher-priced, higher-quality line sold in small quantities at a high markup. When the government introduces price ceilings and causes a shortage of both lines, the manufacturer may discontinue the lower-priced line, forcing the consumer to "trade up" to the higher-priced line. In World War II, for this reason, the government made numerous attempts to force clothing manufacturers to continue lower-priced lines. Under the controls imposed by President Nixon in the early seventies, steel manufacturers eliminated a middle grade of steel sheet, allegedly with the intention of inducing buyers to purchase a more expensive grade.

Not only do producers have an incentive to raise prices, but at least some consumers have an incentive to pay them. The result may be payments on the side to distributors (a bribe for the superintendent of a rent-controlled building, for example) or it may be a full-fledged black market in which goods are bought and sold clandestinely. Prices in black markets may be above not only the official price, but even the price that would prevail in a free market, because the buyers are unusually desperate and because both buyers and sellers face penalties if their transactions are detected.

The obvious costs of queuing, evasion, and black markets often lead governments to impose some form of rationing. The simplest is a coupon issued to consumers entitling them to buy a fixed quantity of the controlled good. For example, each motorist might receive a coupon permitting the purchase of one set of new tires. Rationing solves some of the shortage problems created by controls. Producers no longer find it easy to divert supplies to the black market since they must have ration tickets to match their production; distributors no longer have as much incentive to accept bribes or demand tie-in purchases; consumers no longer have as much incentive to pay excessive prices since they are assured a minimum amount.

But rationing creates its own problems. The government must undertake the difficult job of adjusting rations to reflect fluctuating supplies and demands and the needs of individual consumers.

While an equal ration for each consumer makes sense in a few cases—bread in a city under siege is the classic example—most rationing programs must face the problem that consumer needs vary widely. Some motorists drive a lot and buy a lot of gasoline, and others drive very little.

One solution is to tailor the ration to the needs of individual consumers. Physicians or salesmen can be given extra rations of gasoline. In World War II, community boards in the United States had the power to issue extra rations to particularly needy individuals. The danger of favoritism and corruption in such a scheme, particularly if continued after the spirit of patriotism has begun to erode, is obvious. One way of ameliorating some of the problems created by rationing is to permit a free market in ration tickets. The free exchange of ration tickets has the advantage of providing additional income for consumers who sell their extra tickets and also improves the well-being of those who buy. But the white market does nothing to encourage additional supplies, an end that can be accomplished only by removing price controls.

With all of the problems generated by controls, we can well ask why are they ever imposed, and why are they sometimes maintained for so long. The answer, in part, is that the public does not always see the links between controls and the problems they create. The elimination of lower-priced lines of merchandise may be interpreted simply as callous disregard for the poor rather than a consequence of controls. But price controls almost always benefit some subset of consumers, who may have a particular claim to public sympathy and who, in any case, have a strong interest in lobbying for controls. Minimum wage laws may create unemployment among the unskilled, but they do raise the income of poor workers who remain employed; rent controls make it difficult for young people to find an apartment, but they do hold down the price of rent for those who already have an apartment when controls are instituted (see **Rent Control**).

General price controls—controls on prices of many goods—are often imposed when the public becomes alarmed that inflation is out of control. In the twentieth century, war has frequently been the reason for general price controls. Here, the case can be made that controls have a positive psychological benefit that outweighs, at least in the short run, the costs of shortages, bureaucracy, black markets, and rationing. Surging inflation may lead to panic buying, strikes, animosity toward racial or ethnic minorities that are perceived as benefiting from inflation, and so on. Price controls may make a positive contribution by calming these fears, particularly if patriotism can be counted on to limit evasion. However, such benefits are not likely to outlive the wartime emergency.

Moreover, most inflation, even in wartime, is due to inflationary monetary and fiscal policies rather than to panic buying. To the extent that wartime controls suppress price increases produced by monetary and fiscal policy, controls only postpone the day of reckoning, converting what would have been a steady inflation into a period of slow inflation followed by more rapid inflation. Also, part of the apparent stability of the price indices under wartime controls is an illusion. All of the problems with price controls—queuing, evasion, black markets, and rationing—raise the real price of goods to consumers, and these effects are only partly taken into account when the price indices are computed. When controls are removed, the hidden inflation is unveiled. During World War II, for example, measured inflation remained comparatively modest. But after controls were lifted the consumer price index jumped 18 percent between December 1945 and December 1946, the biggest one-year increase in this century.

Inflation is extremely difficult to contain through general controls, in part because some prices are inevitably left uncontrolled. At times the decision to leave some prices out is deliberate. The reason for controlling only some prices—those, say, of steel, wheat, and oil—is that these goods are strategic in the sense that controlling their prices is sufficient to control the whole price level. But demand tends to shift from the controlled to the uncontrolled sector, with the result that prices in the latter rise even faster than before. Resources follow prices, and supplies tend to rise in the uncontrolled sector at the expense of supplies in the controlled sector. Because the controlled sector was originally chosen to include goods thought to be crucial inputs for many production processes, the reduction in the amount of these inputs is particularly galling. Thus, if controls are kept in place for a long time, a government that begins by controlling prices on selected goods tends to replace them with across-the-board controls.

THIS IS WHAT HAPPENED IN THE UNITED STATES IN WORLD WAR II

A second problem that afflicts general controls is the trade-off between the need to have a simple program generally perceived as fair and the need for sufficient flexibility to maintain a semblance of efficiency. Simplicity requires holding most prices constant, but efficiency requires making frequent changes. Adjustments of relative prices, however, subject the bureaucracy administering controls to a barrage of lobbying and complaints of unfairness. This conflict was brought out sharply by the American experience in World War II. At first, relative prices were changed frequently on the advice of economists who maintained that this was necessary to eliminate potential shortages and other distortions in specific markets. But mounting complaints that the program was unfair and was not stopping inflation led to President Roosevelt's famous "hold-the-line" order, issued in April 1943, that froze most prices. Whatever its defects as economic policy, the hold-the-line order was easy to explain and to sell to the public.

The case for imposing general controls in peacetime turns on the possibility that controls can ease the transition from high to low inflation. If, after a long period of inflation, a tight money policy is introduced to reduce inflation, some prices may continue to rise for a time at the old higher rate. Wages, in particular, may continue to rise because of long-term contracts or because workers fail to appreciate the extent of the change in policy. That, in turn, leads to high unemployment and reduced output. Price controls may limit these costs of disinflation by prohibiting wage increases that are out of line with the new trends in demand and prices. From this viewpoint restrictive monetary policy is the operation that cures inflation, and price and wage controls are the anesthesia that suppresses the pain.

While the logic is acceptable, the result often is not. In the eyes of the public, price controls free the monetary authority—the Federal Reserve in the United States—from responsibility for inflation. As a result the pressures on the Fed to avoid recession may lead to a continuation or even acceleration of excessive growth in the money supply. The painkiller is mistaken for the cure. Something very like this happened in the United States under the controls imposed by President Nixon in 1971. Although controls were justified on the grounds that they were being used to "buy time" while more fundamental cures for inflation were put in place, monetary policy continued to be expansionary, perhaps even more so than before.

The study of price controls teaches important lessons about free competitive markets. By examining cases in which controls have prevented the price mechanism from working, we gain a better appreciation of its usual elegance and efficiency. This does not mean that there are no circumstances in which temporary controls may be effective. But a fair reading of economic history shows just how rare those circumstances are.

FURTHER READING

Blinder, Alan S. *Economic Policy and the Great Stagflation.* 1979.

Clinard, Marshall Barron. *The Black Market: A Study in White Collar Crime.* 1952.

Galbraith, John Kenneth. *A Theory of Price Control.* 1952.

Grayson, C. Jackson. *Confessions of a Price Controller.* 1974.

Jonung, Lars. *The Political Economy of Price Controls: The Swedish Experience 1970–1987.* 1990.

Rockoff, Hugh. *Drastic Measures: A History of Wage and Price Controls in the United States.* 1984.

Schultz, George P., and Robert Z. Aliber, eds. *Guidelines: Informal Controls and the Market Place.* 1966.

Taussig, Frank W. "Price-Fixing as Seen by a Price-Fixer." *Quarterly Journal of Economics* 33 (1919): 205–41.

Supply, Demand, and Price Controls

By Dima Yazji Shamoun and Thomas Rustici

THE DEMAND CURVE

The demand curve depicts the relationship between the price of a good and the quantity demanded of that good at every price. In other words, the demand curve demonstrates two things: first, what happens to the quantity demanded of a good as the price of that good increases when holding everything else constant; and second, by what proportion the quantity demanded of a good will decrease as the price of that good increases. The law of demand tells us that as the price of a good increases, the quantity demanded of that good decreases *ceteris paribus*, or holding everything else constant.

The law of demand is described by the negative slope of the demand curve. Price elasticity of demand, on the other hand, measures the percent decrease in quantity demanded that results from a one-percent increase in price. How receptive are consumers to increases in the price a good? If more than 1% of consumers reduce their consumption for every 1% increase in price, then the demand curve is said to be *elastic*. If less than 1%

of consumers reduce their consumption for every 1% increase in price, then the demand curve is said to be inelastic. Finally, if exactly 1% of consumers reduce their consumption for every 1% increase in price, then the demand curve is said to be *unitary elastic*.

The law of demand, saying that the demand curve slopes downward, is universal and always true. There are three reasons that explain the negative slope of the demand curve. First, *Diminishing Marginal Utility*: even though *total* utility increases as the amount consumed of a good increases, the marginal utility of the next unit of the good is lower, which, in turn, puts a downward pressure on the price one is willing to pay for more of the same good. Second, *Substitution Effect:* if two goods serve similar ends, then when the price of the first increases, holding the price of the second good constant, people can switch to consuming the cheaper substitute good. Third, *Income Effect:* As the price of a good increases, holding income constant, individuals have less to spend on that good.

It is necessary, however, to differentiate *demand curves, demand,* and *demand schedules* from *quantities demanded*. The words demand, demand curve, and demand schedule describe the information displayed by an entire demand graph, i.e., the locus of points forming the demand curve. Quantity demanded, on the other hand, is the x-value of each of the individual points on the demand, demand curve, or demand schedule. In mathematical terminology, the demand, demand curve, or demand schedule refer to the function, while the quantity demanded refers to the coordinate. When economists speak of an increase in the quantity demanded, they mean a rightward movement *on* the demand curve, which is not necessarily accompanied with an increase in demand. An increase in demand is an outward shift *of* the entire demand curve.

Movement along the Demand Curve vs. Movement of the Demand Curve

CAUSE	EFFECT	FIGURE
Change in price	Movement *along* the demand curve	Figure 1
Change in income	Movevement *of* the demand cruve	
• Increase in income	• Demand curve shifts to the right, i.e., demand increases	Figure 2
• Decrease in income	• Demand curve shifts to the left, i.e., decreases	Figure 3
Change in preferences	Movevement *of* the demand cruve	
• Positive change in preferences	• Demand curve shifts to the right	Figure 4
• Negative change in preferences	• Demand curve shifts to the left	Figure 5
Change in the number of buyers	Movevement *of* the demand cruve	
• Increase in the number of buyers	• Demand curve shifts to the right	Figure 6
• Decrease in the number of buyers	• Demand curve shifts to the left	Figure 7
Change in the price of related goods	Movevement *of* the demand cruve	
• Increase in the price of a substitute good x.	• Demand curve of good y (a substitute to x) shifts to the right	Figure 8
• Decrease in the price of a substitute good x.	• Demand curve of good y (a substitute to x) shifts to the left	Figure 9
• Increase in the price of a comelementary good x.	• Demand curve of good y (a complement to x) shifts to the left	Figure 10
• Decrease in the price of a complementary good x.	• Demand curve of good y (a ccomplement to x) shifts to the right	Figure 11
Change in expectations	Movement *of* the demand curve	
• Increase in the expected future price of a good.	• Demand curve shifts to the right	Figure 12
• Decrease in the expected future price of a good.	• Demand curve shifts to the left	Figure 13
• Increase in expected future income.	• Demand curve shifts to the right	Figure 14
• Decrease in expected future income.	• Demand curve shifts to the left	Figure 15

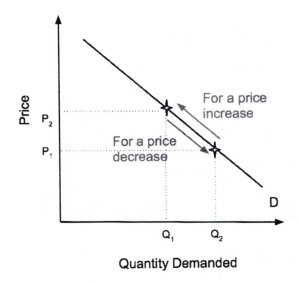

Quantity Demanded

Figure 1: Change in price causing a movement along the demand curve. When the price of a good increase from P_1 to P_2, the quantity demand decreases from Q_2 to Q_1. Conversely, when the price of a good decreases from P_2 to P_1, the quantity demanded increaes from Q_1 to Q_2. Such changes are illustrated by movements along the demand curve and *not* shifts of the entire curve. Movements along the demand curve maintain the functioanl relationship between the price and quantity demanded; whereas, shifts of the entire curve change the functional relationship.

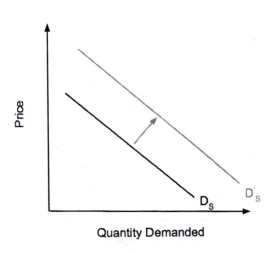

Quantity Demanded

Figure 2: Demand shift due to an increase in income

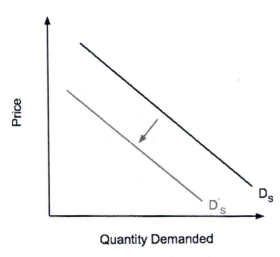

Quantity Demanded

Figure 3: Demand shift due to a decrease in income

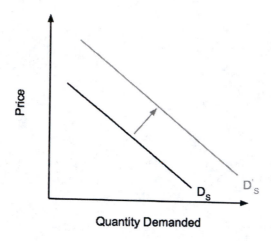

Figure 4: Demand shift due to a positive change in preferences. If a recent hype for Blu-Ray induces a favorable change in consumers' preferences for Blu-Ray products, then the demand for Blu-Ray products increase which is illustrated by the outward shift of the demand curve for Blu-Ray.

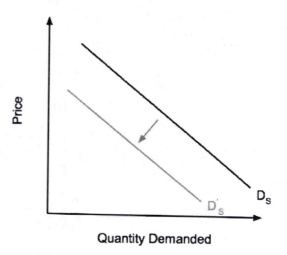

Figure 5: Demand shift due to a negative change in preferences. If consumers discover that a new type of preservative causes cancer, then the demand for products with this type of preservative decreases which is illustrated by the inward shift of the demand curve.

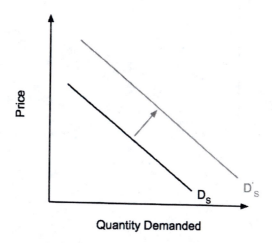

Figure 6: Demand shift due to an increase in the number of buyers.

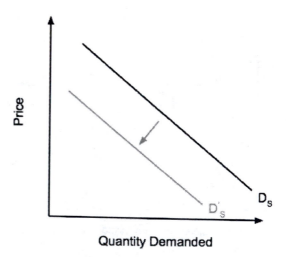

Figure 7: Demand shift due to a decrease in the number of buyers.

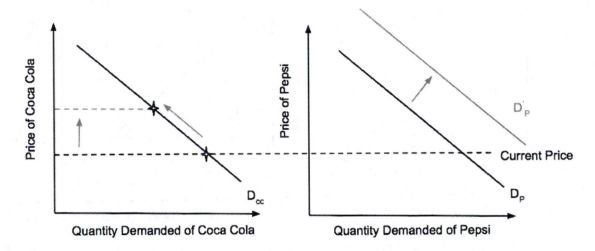

Figure 8: Demand shift for Pepsi due to an increase in the price the substitute good Coca Cola. The increase in the price of Coca Cola causes a decrease in the *quantity demanded* of Coca Cola illustrated in the leftward movement *along* the Coca Cola demand curve. As a result of this increase in price, consumers shift their consumption to the substitute good Pepsi causing the demand for Pepsi to increase which is illustrated by the outward shift of the Pepsi demand curve.

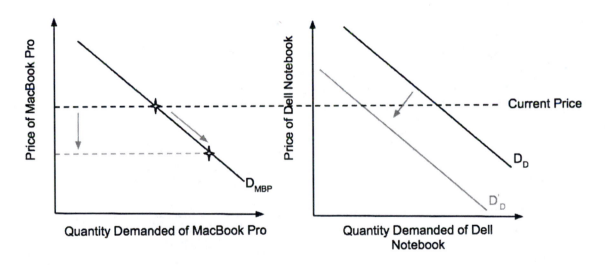

Figure 9: Demand shift for Dell Notebooks due to a decrease in the price the substitute good MacBook Pro. The decrease in the price of MacBook Pro causes an increase in the *quantity demanded* of MacBook Pro illustrated in the rightward movement *along* the MacBook Pro demand curve. As a result of this decrease in price, consumers reduce their consumption of the substitute good, Dell Notebooks, causing the demand of Dell Notebooks to decrease which is illustrated by the inward shift of the Dell Notebook demand curve.

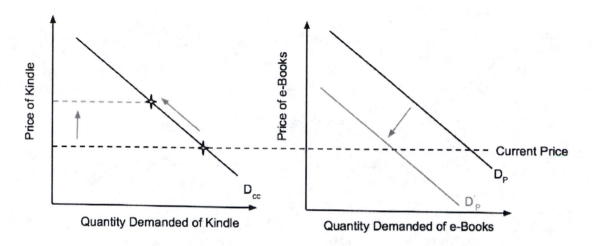

Figure 10: Demand shift for e-Books due to an increase in the price of a complementary good Kindle. The increase in the price of Kindles causes a decrease in the *quantity demanded* of Kindles illustrated in the leftward movement *along* the Kindle demand curve. As a result of this increase in price, consumers reduce their consumption of the complementary good, e-Books, causing the demand of e-Books to decrease which is illustrated by the inward shift of the e-Book demand curve.

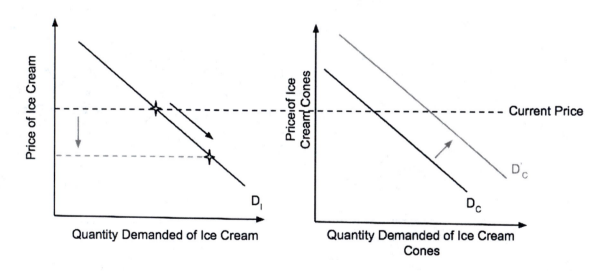

Figure 11: Demand shift for Ice Cream Cones due to a decrease in the price of a complementary good, Ice Cream. The decrease in the price of Ice Cream causes an increase in the *quantity demanded* of Ice Cream illustrated in the rightward movement *along* the Ice Cream demand curve. As a result of this decrease in price, consumers increase their consumption of the complementary good, Ice Cream Cones, causing the demand for Ice Cream Cones to increase which is illustrated by the outward shift of the Ice Cream Cones demand curve.

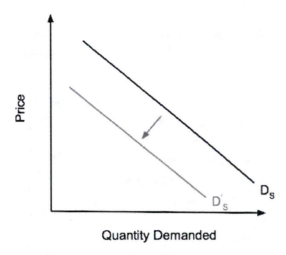

Figure 12: Demand shift due to a decrease in the expected future price of gasoline. When consumers expect the price of gasoline to fall in the future, they decrease their consumption of gasoline while the relatively expensive price lasts.

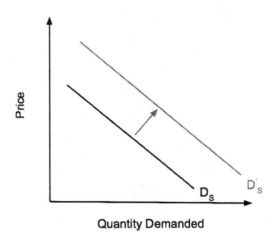

Figure 13: Demand shift due to an increase in the future price of gasoline. If the price of gasoline is expected to increase in the future, then consumers expedite some of their consumption before the price rises.

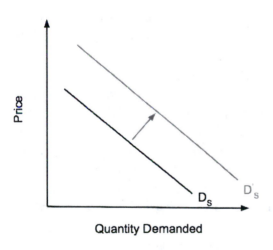

Figure 14: Demand shift due to an increase in expected future income.

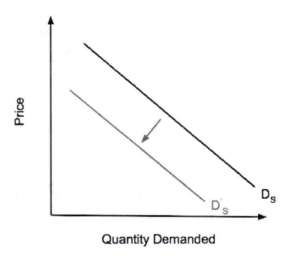

Figure 15: Demand shift due to a decrease in expected future income.

THE SUPPLY CURVE

The supply curve describes the relationship between the price of a good and the quantity supplied of that good. As the price of a good increases, suppliers are willing to supply more of that good. This concept is reflected in the positive slope of the supply curve. Just like demand schedules, supply curves have determinants that causes them to shift inward or outward. These determinants are expectations, prices of input of production, technology, and the number of sellers. For example, technological innovations tend to increase the supply of some goods, such as

Movement along the Supply Curve vs. Movement of the Supply Curve

CAUSE	EFFECT
Change in price	Movement *along* the supply curve
Change in production cost	Movevement *of* the supply cruve
• **Increase in production cost**	• Supply curve shifts to the left, i.e., supply decreases
• **Decrease in production cost**	• Supply curve shifts to the right, i.e., increases
Change in Technology	Movevement *of* the supply cruve
• **Technological emprevement**	• Supply curve shifts to the right
• **Technological deteriariation**	• Supply curve shifts to the left
Change in the number of sellers	Movevement *of* the supply cruve
• **Increase in the number of sellers**	• Supply curve shifts to the right
• **Decrease in the number of buyers**	• Supply curve shifts to the left
Change in expectations	Movement *of* the supply curve
• **Increase in the expected future price of a good.**	• Supply curve shifts to the left.
• **Decrease in the expected future price of a good.**	• Supply curve shifts to the right

computers, and thus cause an outward shift in their supply curves. When the price of oil, an input in flight production, increases, *ceteris paribus,* the supply of flights decreases.

SUPPLY & DEMAND ANALYSIS

When the supply and demand frameworks are joined together in one graph, we begin our analysis of a particular market. The point at which the supply and demand curves intersect is called that particular market's *equilibrium,* with the quantity demanded called the *equilibrium quantity* and the price called the *market-clearing price.* The market equilibrium is characterized by the fact that there is exactly as much quantity supplied as there is quantity demanded of a good. In other words, the market equilibrium is said to be economically efficient, as it does not yield deadweight loss. In some markets, however, governments choose to intervene by holding the price above or below the market-clearing price. Such

interventions aiming to hold the price artificially low or artificially high are called *price controls.* Holding everything else constant, price controls *always* lead to deadweight losses, i.e., inefficiencies.

There are two types of price controls that distort the market: price floors and price ceilings. When governments decide that the market-clearing price is too low and thus must be increased, they impose a *price floor.* In this case, the price is held artificially high above the market-clearing price and is not allowed to dip below the legally imposed price, i.e., the floor.

Figure 16 demonstrates the case of minimum wage restrictions, an example of a price floor. The artificially high wage creates a situation in which the quantity of labor supplied is higher than the quantity demanded by employers. Thus, those whose marginal product of labor is lower than the legally mandated wage lose their job. The deadweight loss in this scenario, i.e., the surplus, is unemployment. Recall that, *ceteris paribus,* price controls *always* lead to inefficiencies in the form of either surpluses or shortages. When the consequences of price controls are not apparent, it does not mean that inefficiencies do not exist; they are simply masked by the change in

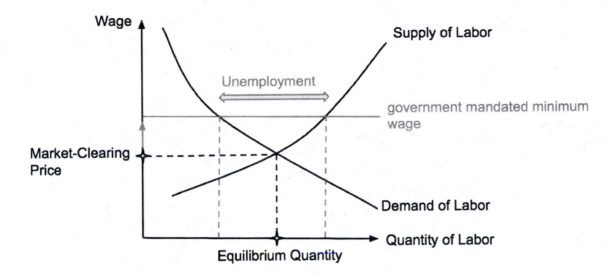

Figure 16: Minimum Wage

some other variable. For example, if unemployment figures decline after the imposition of a minimum wage law setting the price higher than the prevailing market clearing price, then that does not mean that minimum wage laws are harmless. Instead, one may want to look at other variables. For example, in the 1940s, teenage black unemployment did not rise following the imposition of a new minimum wage law in 1938. However, this was due to the significant inflation that took place in the 1940s which effectively cancelled out the minimum wage.[1] Once minimum wage laws steadily increased the minimum wage to combat inflation, the unemployment effects materialized again.

Figure 17 illustrates the effects of the second type of distorting price controls: price ceilings and, as an example, the case of rent controls. Governments impose price ceilings when they judge that the market-clearing price is too high and thus must be lowered. When the price is held artificially low, such as in the case of rent control, the quantity demanded exceeds the quantity supplied, creating shortages. In addition to the shortage of rental housing, landlords who are forced to provide rental units at a cheaper

price try to compensate for their loss by letting the rental units deteriorate. Some rentcontrolled sites in New York City turned into utter destructions indistinguishable from Hiroshima after the nuclear bomb.[2]

Governments will often try to manipulate the human values expressed in the price system and use coercion to dictate terms of trade that do not reflect the underlying reality of values of buyers and sellers. There are consequences nonetheless. Economics is about revealing the law of unintended consequences. Whether well-intentioned or not, price controls force institutionalized chaos on a dynamically emergent market process, creating surpluses and shortages of vital goods and services, and hurting people in the process. Specifically, where prices are held too high relative to the market, surpluses are created; where held below the market equilibrium, shortages are created.

Prices tell us about the tradeoffs, opportunities, and values of other people when not controlled by a coercive threat. When prices are controlled, misinformation creates disharmony and disorder. The price system is like the thermometer attached to the thermostat in your home. The temperature

1 Thomas Sowell, "Minimum Wage Madness," *Townhall Magazine,* September 17, 2013, http://townhall.com/columnists/thomassowell/2013/09/17/minimum-wage-madness-n1701840/page/full.

2 Milton Friedman et al., eds., *Rent Control, Myths & Realities: International Evidence of the Effects of Rent Control in Six Countries* (Vancouver, B.C., Canada: Fraser Institute, 1981).

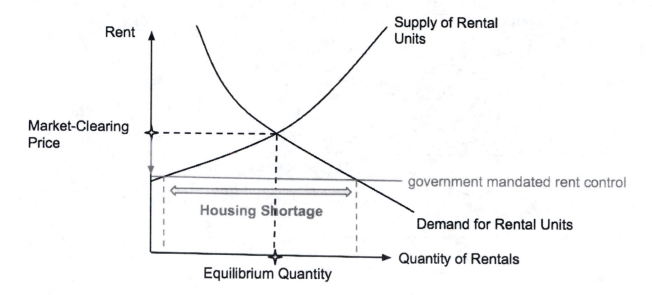

Figure 17: Rent Control

in the room is gauged by the mercury in the thermometer. But the mercury in the thermometer does not directly affect the temperature in the room. If the room is on fire and the mercury reads 120° F, we don't cool the room by sticking a needle in the thermometer and taking out mercury until it reads 30° F. Causation does not run from the mercury to the room, but from the room to the mercury. Misinformation gets forced into the system by such a control. Misguided policy, as in the aforementioned example of artificially changing the mercury level to achieve the desired thermometer reading, always has unintended consequences. The thermostat reads 30° F when it really is 120° F in the room. Exactly when we want the room cooler, it gets hotter, the heater comes on when the thermostat is tricked into believing the temperature is only 30° F, the opposite of what we would want to have happen.

Conversely, if there is a hole in the roof in the winter, which allows snow and ice to accumulate in the room so that the temperature is only 10° F in the room, we would have a maintenance company come fix the hole, changing the underlying variables. If the mercury reads 10° F, we don't make it warmer by putting a lit match under the mercury. The thermometer would then be communicating false information. When we want it warmer, the thermostat starts the air conditioning.

Let the Data Speak

The Truth Behind Minimum Wage Laws

By Steve Hanke

President Obama set the chattering classes abuzz after his recent unilateral announcement to raise the minimum wage for newly hired Federal contract workers. During his State of the Union address in January, he sang the praises for his decision, saying that "It's good for the economy; it's good for America." As the worldwide economic slump drags on, the political drumbeat to either introduce minimum wage laws (read: Germany) or increase the minimums in countries where these laws exist—such as Indonesia—is becoming deafening. Yet the glowing claims about minimum wage laws don't pass the most basic economic tests. Just look at the data from Europe (see the accompanying chart).

There are seven European Union (E.U.) countries in which no minimum wage is mandated (Austria, Cyprus, Denmark, Finland, Germany, Italy, and Sweden). If we compare the levels of unemployment in these countries with E.U. countries that impose a minimum wage, the results are clear. A minimum wage leads to higher levels of unemployment. In the 21 countries with a minimum wage, the average country has an unemployment rate of 11.8%. Whereas, the average unemployment rate in the seven countries without mandated minimum wages is about one third lower—at 7.9%.

This point is even more pronounced when we look at rates of unemployment among the E.U.'s youth—defined as those younger than 25 years of age (see the accompanying chart).

In the twenty-one E.U. countries where there are minimum wage laws, 27.7% of the youth demographic—more than one in four young adults—was unemployed in 2012. This is considerably higher than the youth unemployment rate in the seven E.U. countries without minimum wage laws—19.5% in 2012—a gap that has only widened since the Lehman Brothers collapse in 2008.

So, minimum wage laws—while advertised under the banner of social justice—do not live up to the claims made by those who tout them. They do not lift low wage earners to a so-called "social minimum." Indeed, minimum wage laws—imposed at the levels employed in Europe—push a considerable number of people into unemployment. And, unless those newly unemployed qualify for government assistance (read: welfare), they will sink below, or further below, the social minimum.

As Nobelist Milton Friedman correctly quipped, "A minimum wage law is, in reality, a law that makes it illegal for an employer to hire a person with limited skills."

Dr. Jens Weidmann, President of Germany's Bundesbank, must have heard Prof. Friedman and

Average Unemployment Rate of E.U. Countries With & Without Minimum Wages

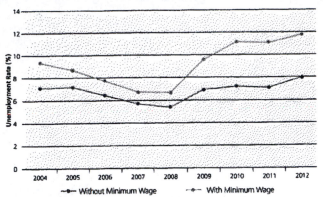

Sources: Eurostat (Unemployment rates - Annual Average), and calculations by Prof. Steve H. Hanke, The Johns Hopkins University.
Note: The averages displayed in the chart are arithmetic means.

Average Youth Unemployment Rate of E.U. Countries With & Without Minimum Wages

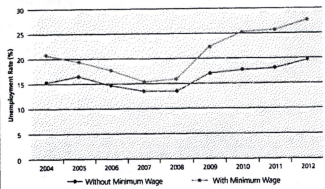

Sources: Eurostat (Unemployment rates - Annual Average; Age: Less than 25 years), and calculations by Prof. Steve H. Hanke, The Johns Hopkins University.
Note: The averages displayed in the chart are arithmetic means.

looked at these European data before he took on Chancellor Angela Merkel for proposing the introduction of a minimum wage law in Germany. In short, Dr. Weidmann said that this would damage Germany's labor market and be a German job killer. He is right.

And, executives surveyed in the recently released Duke University/CFO Magazine Global Business Outlook Survey agree, too, Indeed, Chief Financial Officers from around the world were interviewed and a significant number of them concurred: a minimum wage increase in the United States—from the current $7.25/hour to President Obama's proposed $10.10/hour—would kill U.S. jobs. The accompanying table shows what the CFOs had to say.

Perhaps, Prof. Friedman said it best when he concluded that "The real tragedy of minimum wage laws is that they are supported by well-meaning groups who want to reduce poverty. But the people who are hurt most by high minimums are the most poverty stricken."

High mandated minimum wages will throw people out of work and onto the welfare rolls in cases where unemployment benefits exist. When it comes to welfare payments, they obey the laws of economics, too. Indeed, if something—like unemployment—is subsidized, more of it will be produced. When the data on unemployment benefits

Raise Minimum Wage, Kill Jobs

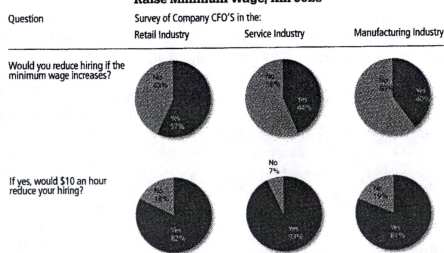

Sources: CFOSurvey.org. Prepared by: Prof. Steve H. Hanke, The Johns Hopkins University.

speak, they tell us that if the unemployed receive unemployment benefits, the chances that they will become employed are reduced. Those data also show that the probability of an unemployed worker finding employment increases dramatically the closer an unemployed worker comes to the termination date for receipt of his unemployment benefits. In short, when the prospect of losing welfare benefits raises its head, unemployed workers magically tend to find work.

The most important lesson to take away from allowing the minimum wage and unemployment benefit data to talk is that abstract notions of what is right, good and just should be examined from a concrete, operational point of view. A dose of reality is most edifying.

Public Choice

A Petition

From the Manufacturers of Candles, Tapers, Lanterns, Sticks, Street Lamps, Snuffers, and Extinguishers, and from Producers of Tallow, Oil, Resin, Alcohol, and Generally of Everything Connected with Lighting

By Frédéric Bastiat

To the Honourable Members of the Chamber of Deputies.

Gentlemen:

You are on the right track. You reject abstract theories and have little regard for abundance and low prices. You concern yourselves mainly with the fate of the producer. You wish to free him from foreign competition, that is, to reserve the domestic market for domestic industry.

We come to offer you a wonderful opportunity for your—what shall we call it? Your theory? No, nothing is more deceptive than theory. Your doctrine? Your system? Your principle? But you dislike doctrines, you have a horror of systems, as for principles, you deny that there are any in political economy; therefore we shall call it your practice—your practice without theory and without principle.

We are suffering from the ruinous competition of a rival who apparently works under conditions so far superior to our own for the production of light that he is flooding the domestic market with it at an incredibly low price; for the moment he appears, our sales cease, all the consumers turn to him, and a branch of French industry whose ramifications are innumerable is all at once reduced to complete stagnation. This rival, which is none other than the sun, is waging war on us so mercilessly we suspect he is being stirred up against us by perfidious Albion (excellent diplomacy nowadays!), particularly because he has for that haughty island a respect that he does not show for us.

We ask you to be so good as to pass a law requiring the closing of all windows, dormers, skylights, inside and outside shutters, curtains, casements, bull's-eyes, deadlights, and blinds— in short, all openings, holes, chinks, and fissures through which the light of the sun is wont to enter houses, to the detriment of the fair industries with which, we are proud to say, we have endowed the country, a country that cannot, without betraying ingratitude, abandon us today to so unequal a combat.

Be good enough, honourable deputies, to take our request seriously, and do not reject it without at least hearing the reasons that we have to advance in its support.

First, if you shut off as much as possible all access to natural light, and thereby create a need for artificial light, what industry in France will not ultimately be encouraged?

If France consumes more tallow, there will have to be more cattle and sheep, and, consequently, we shall see an increase in cleared fields, meat, wool, leather, and especially manure, the basis of all agricultural wealth.

If France consumes more oil, we shall see an expansion in the cultivation of the poppy, the olive, and rapeseed. These rich yet soil-exhausting plants will come at just the right time to enable us to put to profitable use the increased fertility that the breeding of cattle will impart to the land.

Our moors will be covered with resinous trees. Numerous swarms of bees will gather from our mountains the perfumed treasures that today waste their fragrance, like the flowers from which they emanate. Thus, there is not one branch of agriculture that would not undergo a great expansion.

The same holds true of shipping. Thousands of vessels will engage in whaling, and in a short time we shall have a fleet capable of upholding the honour of France and of gratifying the patriotic aspirations of the undersigned petitioners, chandlers, etc.

But what shall we say of the specialities of Parisian manufacture? Henceforth you will behold gilding, bronze, and crystal in candlesticks, in lamps, in chandeliers, in candelabra sparkling in spacious emporia compared with which those of today are but stalls.

There is no needy resin-collector on the heights of his sand dunes, no poor miner in the depths of his black pit, who will not receive higher wages and enjoy increased prosperity.

It needs but a little reflection, gentlemen, to be convinced that there is perhaps not one Frenchman, from the wealthy stockholder of the Anzin Company to the humblest vendor of matches, whose condition would not be improved by the success of our petition.

We anticipate your objections, gentlemen; but there is not a single one of them that you have not picked up from the musty old books of the advocates of free trade. We defy you to utter a word against us that will not instantly rebound against yourselves and the principle behind all your policy.

Will you tell us that, though we may gain by this protection, France will not gain at all, because the consumer will bear the expense?

We have our answer ready:

You no longer have the right to invoke the interests of the consumer. You have sacrificed him whenever you have found his interests opposed to those of the producer. You have done so in order to encourage industry and to increase employment. For the same reason you ought to do so this time too.

Indeed, you yourselves have anticipated this objection. When told that the consumer has a stake in the free entry of iron, coal, sesame, wheat, and textiles, "Yes," you reply, "but the producer has a stake in their exclusion." Very well, surely if consumers have a stake in the admission of natural light, producers have a stake in its interdiction.

"But," you may still say, "the producer and the consumer are one and the same person. If the manufacturer profits by protection, he will make the farmer prosperous. Contrariwise, if agriculture is prosperous, it will open markets for manufactured goods." Very well, If you grant us a monopoly over the production of lighting during the day, first of all we shall buy large amounts of tallow, charcoal, oil, resin, wax, alcohol, silver, iron, bronze, and crystal, to supply our industry; and, moreover, we and our numerous suppliers, having become rich, will consume a great deal and spread prosperity into all areas of domestic industry.

Will you say that the light of the sun is a gratuitous gift of Nature, and that to reject such gifts would be to reject wealth itself under the pretext of encouraging the means of acquiring it?

But if you take this position, you strike a mortal blow at your own policy; remember that up to now you have always excluded foreign goods because and in proportion as they approximate gratuitous gifts. You have only half as good a reason for complying with the demands of other monopolists as you have for granting our petition, which is in complete accord with your established policy; and to reject our demands precisely because they are better founded than anyone else's would be tantamount to accepting the equation: + × + = -; in other words, it would be to heap absurdity upon absurdity.

Labour and Nature collaborate in varying proportions, depending upon the country and the climate, in the production of a commodity. The part that Nature contributes is always free of charge; it is the part contributed by human labour that constitutes value and is paid for.

If an orange from Lisbon sells for half the price of an orange from Paris, it is because the natural heat of the sun, which is, of course, free of charge, does for the former what the latter owes to artificial heating, which necessarily has to be paid for in the market.

Thus, when an orange reaches us from Portugal, one can say that it is given to us half free of charge, or, in other words, at half price as compared with those from Paris.

Now, it is precisely on the basis of its being semi-gratuitous (pardon the word) that you maintain it should be barred. You ask: "How can French labour withstand the competition of foreign labour when the former has to do all the work, whereas the latter has to do only half, the sun taking care of the rest?" But if the fact that a product is half free of charge leads you to exclude it from competition, how can its being totally free of charge induce you to admit it into competition? Either you are not consistent, or you should, after excluding what is half free of charge as harmful to our domestic industry, exclude what is totally gratuitous with all the more reason and with twice the zeal.

To take another example: When a product—coal, iron, wheat, or textiles—comes to us from abroad, and when we can acquire it for less labour than if we produced it ourselves, the difference is a gratuitous gift that is conferred up on us. The size of this gift is proportionate to the extent of this difference. It is a quarter, a half, or three-quarters of the value of the product if the foreigner asks of us only three-quarters, one-half, or one-quarter as high a price. It is as complete as it can be when the donor, like the sun in providing us with light, asks nothing from us. The question, and we pose it formally, is whether what you desire for France is the benefit of consumption free of charge or the alleged advantages of onerous production. Make your choice, but be logical; for as long as you ban, as you do, foreign coal, iron, wheat, and textiles, in proportion as their price approaches zero, how inconsistent it would be to admit the light of the sun, whose price is zero all day long!

Public Choice Theory

By Jane S. Shaw

Public choice theory is a branch of economics that developed from the study of taxation and public spending. It emerged in the fifties and received widespread public attention in 1986, when James Buchanan, one of its two leading architects (the other was his colleague Gordon Tullock), was awarded the Nobel Prize in economics. Buchanan started the Center for Study of Public Choice at George Mason University, and it remains the best-known locus of public choice research. Others include Florida State University, Washington University (St. Louis), Montana State University, the California Institute of Technology, and the University of Rochester.

Public choice takes the same principles that economists use to analyze people's actions in the marketplace and applies them to people's actions in collective decision making. Economists who study behavior in the private marketplace assume that people are motivated mainly by self-interest. Although most people base some of their actions on their concern for others, the dominant motive in people's actions in the marketplace—whether they are employers, employees, or consumers—is a concern for themselves. Public choice economists make the same assumption—that although people acting in the political marketplace have some concern for others, their main motive, whether they are voters,

politicians, lobbyists, or bureaucrats, is self-interest. In Buchanan's words the theory "replaces ... romantic and illusory ... notions about the workings of governments [with] ... notions that embody more skepticism."

In the past many economists have argued that the way to rein in "market failures" such as monopolies is to introduce government action. But public choice economists point out that there also is such a thing as "government failure." That is, there are reasons why government intervention does not achieve the desired effect. For example, the Justice Department has responsibility for reducing monopoly power in noncompetitive industries. But a 1973 study by William F. Long, Richard Schramm, and Robert Tollison concluded that actual anti-competitive behavior played only a minor role in decisions by the Justice Department to bring antimonopoly suits. Instead, they found, the larger the industry, the more likely were firms in it to be sued. Similarly, Congress has frequently passed laws that are supposed to protect people against environmental pollution. But Robert Crandall has shown that congressional representatives from northern industrial states used the 1977 Clean Air Act amendments to reduce competition by curbing economic growth in the Sunbelt. The amendments required tighter emissions standards in undeveloped areas than in the more developed and more polluted areas, which tend to be in the East and Midwest.

One of the chief underpinnings of public choice theory is the lack of incentives for voters to monitor government effectively. Anthony Downs, in one of the earliest public choice books, *An Economic Theory of Democracy*, pointed out that the voter is largely ignorant of political issues and that this ignorance is rational. Even though the result of an election may be very important, an individual's vote rarely decides an election. Thus, the direct impact of casting a well-informed vote is almost nil; the voter has virtually no chance to determine the outcome of the election. So spending time following the issues is not personally worthwhile for the voter. Evidence for this claim is found in the fact that public opinion polls consistently find that less than half of all voting-age Americans can name their own congressional representative.

Public choice economists point out that this incentive to be ignorant is rare in the private sector. Someone who buys a car typically wants to be well informed about the car he or she selects. That is because the car buyer's choice is decisive—he or she pays only for the one chosen. If the choice is wise, the buyer will benefit; if it is unwise, the buyer will suffer directly. Voting lacks that kind of direct result. Therefore, most voters are largely ignorant about the positions of the people for whom they vote. Except for a few highly publicized issues, they do not pay a lot of attention to what legislative bodies do, and even when they do pay attention, they have little incentive to gain the background knowledge and analytic skill needed to understand the issues.

Public choice economists also examine the actions of legislators. Although legislators are expected to pursue the "public interest," they make decisions on how to use other people's resources, not their own. Furthermore, these resources must be provided by taxpayers and by those hurt by regulations whether they want to provide them or not. Politicians may intend to spend taxpayer money wisely. Efficient decisions, however, will neither save their own money nor give them any proportion of the wealth they save for citizens. There is no direct reward for fighting powerful interest groups in order to confer benefits on a public that is not even aware of the benefits or of who conferred them. Thus, the incentives for good management in the public interest are weak. In contrast, interest groups are organized by people with very strong gains to be made from governmental action. They provide politicians with campaign funds and campaign workers. In return they receive at least the "ear" of the politician and often gain support for their goals.

In other words, because legislators have the power to tax and to extract resources in other coercive ways, and because voters monitor their behavior poorly, legislators behave in ways that are costly to citizens. One technique analyzed by public choice is log rolling, or vote trading. An urban legislator votes to subsidize a rural water project in order to win another legislator's vote for a city housing subsidy. The two projects may be part of a single spending bill. Through such log rolling both legislators get what they want. And even though neither project uses resources efficiently, local voters know that their representative got something for them. They may not know that they are paying a pro-rata share of a bundle of inefficient projects! And the total expenditures may well be more than individual taxpayers would be willing to authorize if they were fully aware of what is going on.

In addition to voters and politicians, public choice analyzes the role of bureaucrats in government. Their incentives explain why many regulatory agencies appear to be "captured" by special interests. (The "capture" theory was introduced by the late George Stigler, a Nobel Laureate who did not work mainly in the public choice field.) Capture occurs because bureaucrats do not have a profit goal to guide their behavior. Instead, they usually are in government because they have a goal or mission. They rely on Congress for their budgets, and often the people who will benefit from their mission can influence Congress to provide more funds. Thus interest groups—who may be as diverse as lobbyists for regulated industries or leaders of environmental groups—become important to them. Such interrelationships can lead to bureaucrats being captured by interest groups.

Although public choice economists have focused mostly on analyzing government failure, they also have suggested ways to correct problems. For example, they argue that if government action is required, it should take place at the local level whenever possible. Because there are many local governments, and because people "vote with their feet," there is competition among local governments, as well as some experimentation. To streamline bureaucracies, Gordon Tullock and William Niskanen have recommended allowing several bureaus to supply the same service on the grounds that the resulting competition will improve efficiency. Forest economist Randal O'Toole recommends that the Forest Service charge hikers and backpackers more than token fees to use the forests. This, he argues, will lead Forest Service personnel to pay more attention to recreation and reduce logging in areas that are attractive to nature lovers. And Rodney Fort and John Baden have suggested the creation of a "predatory bureau" whose mission is to reduce the budgets of other agencies, with its income depending on its success.

Public choice economists have also tried to develop rule changes that will reduce legislation that caters to special interests and leads to ever-expanding government expenditures. In the late eighties James C. Miller, a public choice scholar who headed the Office of Management and Budget during the Reagan Administration, helped pass the Gramm-Rudman law, which set a limit on annual spending and backed it with automatic cuts if the ceiling was not met. The law had at least a temporary effect in slowing spending. Support for term limits and for a line-item veto also reflects the public choice view that additional legislative rules are needed to limit logrolling and the power of special interests. Public choice scholars, however, do not necessarily agree on the potential effectiveness of specific rules.

Because of its skepticism about the supposedly benign nature of government, public choice is sometimes viewed as a conservative or libertarian branch of economics, as opposed to more "liberal" (that is, interventionist) wings such as Keynesian economics. This is partly correct. The emergence of public choice economics reflects dissatisfaction with the implicit assumption, held by Keynesians, among others, that government effectively corrects market failures.

But not all public choice economists are conservatives or libertarians. Mancur Olson is an important counterexample. Olson is known in public choice for his path-breaking book *The Logic of Collective Action,* in which he pointed out that large interest groups have trouble gaining and maintaining the support of those who benefit from their lobbying. That is because it is easy for individuals to "free-ride" on the efforts of others if they benefit automatically from those efforts. That is why, Olson explained, nineteenth-century farmers' groups, which were organized to be political lobbying groups, also sold insurance and other services. These provided a direct incentive for the individual farmer to stay involved. (As the number of farmers has declined in recent decades, they have become more politically powerful, an observation that supports Olson's contention.)

More recently, Olson wrote *The Rise and Decline of Nations,* which concludes that Germany and Japan thrived after World War II because the war destroyed the power of special interests to stifle entrepreneurship and economic exchange. But Olson still favors a strong government.

Many public choice economists take no political or ideological position. Some build formal mathematical models of voting strategies and apply game theory to understand how political conflicts are resolved. Economists at the California Institute of Technology, for example, have pointed out that "agenda-setting"—that is, identifying the options that voters choose from, and even specifying the order of voting on the options—can influence political outcomes. This explains the role of initiatives and referenda as ways for voters to set agendas, opening up options that legislatures otherwise would ignore or vote down.

Some of these economists have developed a separate and quite mathematical discipline known as "social choice." Social choice traces its roots to early work by Nobel Prize-winning economist Kenneth Arrow. Arrow's 1951 book, *Social Choice and Individual Values,* attempted to figure out through logic whether people who have different goals can use voting to make collective decisions that please everyone. He concluded that they cannot, and thus his argument is called the "impossibility theorem."

In addition to providing insight into how public decision making occurs today, public choice analyzes the rules that guide the collective decision-making process itself. These are the constitutional rules that are made before political activity gets underway. Consideration of these rules was the heart of *The Calculus of Consent*, by James Buchanan and Gordon Tullock, one of the classics of public choice.

Buchanan and Tullock began with the view that a collective decision that is truly just—that is, a decision in the public interest—would be one that all voters would support unanimously. While unanimity is largely unworkable in practice, the book effectively challenged the widespread assumption that majority decisions are inherently fair. The approach reflected in *The Calculus of Consent* has led to a further subdiscipline of public choice, "constitutional economics," which focuses exclusively on the rules that precede parliamentary or legislative decision making and limit the domain of government.

FURTHER READING

Buchanan, James M., and Gordon Tullock. *The Calculus of Consent*. 1962.

Downs, Anthony. *An Economic Theory of Democracy*. 1957.

Gwartney, James D., and Richard L. Stroup. *Economics: Private and Public Choice*, 6th ed. Especially chaps. 4, 30. 1992.

Gwartney, James D., and Richard E. Wagner, eds. *Public Choice and Constitutional Economics*. 1988.

Henderson, David R. "James Buchanan and Company." *Reason* (November 1987): 37–43.

GROWING SKEPTICISM

One sure sign of the impact of a school of thought is whether and how it shows up in popular textbooks. By that criterion public choice thinking has had a big impact. Consider the famous textbook by noted MIT economist and Nobel Prize winner Paul Samuelson. In the book's early editions, starting in 1948, Samuelson showed little skepticism about the efficacy of government solutions. But by 1985 Samuelson's text, coauthored with Yale University's William Nordhaus, had become more critical of government. Their skepticism was explicitly based on public choice reasoning. Indeed, in "Public Choice," an eleven-page section of the 1985 text, they explain some of the points made in this article. "Often," they write, "a logrolling process may end up as a redistributive scheme, where the winning coalition takes a bad initial proposal, and loads it with enough provisions that appeal to special-interest groups, until a solid majority has been obtained for a legislative dog." Samuelson and Nordhaus conclude: "Before we race off to our federal, state, or local legislature, we should pause to recognize that *there are government failures as well as market failures.*"

—DRH

Public Choice

Politics Without Romance

By James M. Buchanan

***P**ublic choice theory demonstrates why looking to government to fix things can often lead to more harm than good, as one of its leading architects and Nobel laureate James M. Buchanan explains*

Public choice should be understood as a research programme rather than a discipline or even a sub-discipline of economics. Its origins date to the mid-20th century, and viewed retrospectively, the theoretical 'gap' in political economy that it emerged to fill seems so large that its development seems to have been inevitable.

Nations emerging from World War II, including the Western democracies, were allocating between one-third and one-half of their total product through political institutions rather than through markets. Economists, however, were devoting their efforts almost exclusively to understanding and explaining the market sector. My own modest first entry into the subject matter, in 1949, was little more than a call for those economists who examined taxes and spending to pay some attention to empirical reality, and thus to politics.

Initially, the work of economists in this area raised serious doubts about the political process. Working simultaneously, but independently, Kenneth Arrow and Duncan Black proved that democracy, interpreted as majority rule, could not work to promote any general or public interest. The now-famous 'impossibility theorem', as published in Arrow's book Social Choice and Individual Values (1951), stimulated an extended discussion. What Arrow and Black had in fact done was to discover or rediscover the phenomenon of 'majority cycles', whereby election results rotate in continuous cycles with no equilibrium or stopping point. The suggestion of this analysis was that majoritarian democracy is inherently unstable.

I entered this discussion with a generalized critique of the analysis generated by the Arrow-Black approach. Aren't 'majority cycles' the most desirable outcome of a democratic process? After all, any attainment of political equilibrium via majority rule would amount to the permanent imposition of the majority's will on the outvoted minority. Would not a guaranteed rotation of outcomes be preferable, enabling the members of the minority in one round of voting to come back in subsequent rounds and ascend to majority membership? My concern, then and later, was the prevention of discrimination against minorities rather than stability of political outcomes. The question, from an economist's perspective, was how to obtain a combination of efficiency and justice under majority rule.

WICKSELL'S INSIGHT

The great Swedish economist Knut Wicksell was the most important of all precursory figures in public choice. In his dissertation, published in 1896, he was concerned about both the injustice and the inefficiency resulting from unfettered majority rule in parliamentary assemblies. Majority rule seemed quite likely to impose net costs or damages on large segments of the citizen or taxpayer group. Why should members of such minorities, facing discrimination, lend their support to democratic political structures? Unless all groups can benefit from the ultimate exchange with government, how can overall stability be maintained?

These considerations led Wicksell to question the efficacy of majority rule itself. His solution to the problem was to propose that majority rule be modified in the direction of unanimity. If the agreement of all persons in the voting group is required to implement collective action, it would guarantee that all persons secure net gains and, further, that the approved actions would yield benefits in excess of costs. Of course, Wicksell recognized that, if applied in a literal voting setting, a requirement of unanimity would produce stalemate. To recognize this, however, does not diminish the value of the unanimity rule as a benchmark for comparative evaluation. In suggestions for practical constitutional reforms, Wicksell supported changes in voting rules from simple to qualified or super majorities, for example, a requirement of five-sixths approval for collective proposals.

In their analyses, Black and Arrow had assumed, more or less implicitly, that the choices to be voted on exist prior to, and outside of, the decision-making process itself. Wicksell understood the error in this assumption, although he did not recognize the importance of this insight. Neither did Gordon Tullock, who wrote a seminal paper in 1959 using the example of farmer voters, each of whom wants to have his local road repaired with costs borne by the whole community. Tullock showed that majority rule allows for coalitions of such farmers to generate election results that impose unjust costs on the whole community while producing inefficiently large outlays on local roads.

If majority rule produces unjust and inefficient outcomes, and if political stability is secured only by discrimination against minorities, how can democracy, as the organizing principle for political structure, possibly claim normative legitimacy? Wicksell's criterion for achieving justice and efficiency in collective action-the shift from majority rule toward unanimity-seems institutionally impractical. But without some such reform, how could taxpayers be assured that their participation in the democracy would yield net benefits?

CONSTITUTIONAL ECONOMICS

In implicit response to these questions, Tullock and I commenced to work on what was to become The Calculus of Consent, published in 1962. The central contribution of this book was to identify a two-level structure of collective decision-making. We distinguished between 'ordinary politics', consisting of decisions made in legislative assemblies, and 'constitutional politics', consisting of decisions made about the rules for ordinary politics.

We were not, of course, inventing this distinction. Both in legal theory and in practice, constitutional law had long been distinguished from statute law. What we did was to bring this distinction into economic analysis. Doing so allowed us to answer the questions posed previously: From the perspective of both justice and efficiency, majority rule may safely be allowed to operate in the realm of ordinary politics provided that there is generalized consensus on the constitution, or on the rules that define and limit what can be done through ordinary politics. It is in arriving at this constitutional framework where Wicksell's idea of requiring unanimity-or at least super majorities-may be practically incorporated.

In a sense, the analysis in our book could have been interpreted as a formalization of the structure that James Madison and his colleagues had in mind when they constructed the American Constitution. At the least, it offered a substantive criticism of the then-dominant elevation of unfettered majority rule to sacrosanct status in political science.

Our book was widely well received, which prompted Tullock and me, who were then at the University of Virginia, to initiate and organize a small research conference in April 1963. We brought together economists, political scientists, sociologists and scholars from other disciplines, all of whom were engaged in research outside the boundaries of their disciplines. The discussion was sufficiently stimulating to motivate the formation of an organization which we first called the Committee on Non-Market Decision-Making, and to initiate plans for a journal to be called Papers on Non-Market Decision-Making.

We were unhappy with these awkward labels, and after several meetings there emerged the new name 'public choice', both for the organization and the journal. In this way the Public Choice Society and the journal Public Choice came into being. Both have proved to be quite successful as institutional embodiments of the research programme, and sister organizations and journals have since been set up in Europe and Asia.

Many sub-programmes have emerged from the umbrella of public choice. One in particular deserves mention-'rent seeking', a sub-programme initiated in a paper by Tullock in 1967, and christened with this title by Anne Krueger in 1974. Its central idea emerges from the natural mindset of the economist, whose understanding and explanation of human interaction depends critically on predictable responses to measurable incentives. In essence, it extends the idea of the profit motive from the economic sphere to the sphere of collective action. It presupposes that if there is value to be gained through politics, persons will invest resources in efforts to capture this value. It also demonstrates how this investment is wasteful in an aggregate-value sense.

Tullock's early treatment of rent seeking was concentrated on monopoly, tariffs and theft, but the list could be almost indefinitely expanded. If the government is empowered to grant monopoly rights or tariff protection to one group, at the expense of the general public or of designated losers, it follows that potential beneficiaries will compete for the prize. And since only one group can be rewarded, the resources invested by other groups-which could have been used to produce valued goods and services-are wasted. Given this basic insight, much of modern politics can be understood as rent-seeking activity. Pork-barrel politics is only the most obvious example. Much of the growth of the bureaucratic or regulatory sector of government can best be explained in terms of the competition between political agents for constituency support through the use of promises of discriminatory transfers of wealth.

As noted, the primary contribution of The Calculus of Consent was to distinguish two levels of collective action, ordinary or day-to-day politics and constitutional politics. Indeed, the subtitle of that book was 'Logical Foundations of Constitutional Democracy'. Clearly, political action takes place at two distinct levels, one within the existing set of rules or constitution, the other establishing the rules or constitution that impose limits on subsequent actions.

Only recently have economists broken away from the presumption that constraints on choices are always imposed from the outside. Recent research has involved the choice of constraints, even on the behavior of persons in non-collective settings, for instance, with regard to drug or gambling addiction. But even beyond that, what I have called the 'constitutional way of thinking' shifts attention to the framework rules of political order-the rules that secure consensus among members of the body politic. It is at this level that individuals calculate their terms of exchange with the state or with political authority. They may well calculate that they are better off for their membership in the constitutional order, even while assessing the impact of ordinary political actions to be contrary to their interests.

A somewhat loose way of putting this is to say that in a constitutional democracy, persons owe loyalty to the constitution rather than to the government. I have long argued that on precisely this point, American public attitudes are quite different from those in Europe.

OBJECTIONS TO PUBLIC CHOICE

There is a familiar criticism of public choice theory to the effect that it is ideologically biased. In comparing and analyzing alternative sets of constitutional rules, both those in existence and those that might be introduced prospectively, how does public choice theory, as such, remain neutral in the scientific sense?

Here it is necessary to appreciate the prevailing mindset of social scientists and philosophers at the midpoint of the 20th century when public choice arose. The socialist ideology was pervasive, and was supported by the allegedly neutral research programme called 'theoretical welfare economics', which concentrated on identifying the failures of observed markets to meet idealized standards. In sum, this branch of inquiry offered theories of market failure. But failure in comparison with what? The implicit presumption was always that politicized corrections for market failures would work perfectly. In other words, market failures were set against an idealized politics.

Public choice then came along and provided analyses of the behavior of persons acting politically, whether voters, politicians or bureaucrats. These analyses exposed the essentially false comparisons that were then informing so much of both scientific and public opinion. In a very real sense, public choice became a set of theories of governmental failures, as an offset to the theories of market failures that had previously emerged from theoretical welfare economics. Or, as I put it in the title of a lecture in Vienna in 1978, public choice may be summarized by the three-word description, 'politics without romance'.

The public choice research programme is better seen as a correction of the scientific record than as the introduction of an anti-governmental ideology. Regardless of any ideological bias, exposure to public choice analysis necessarily brings a more critical attitude toward politicized nostrums to alleged socioeconomic problems. Public choice almost literally forces the critic to be pragmatic in comparing alternative constitutional arrangements, disallowing any presumption that bureaucratic corrections for market failures will accomplish the desired objectives.

A more provocative criticism of public choice centres on the claim that it is immoral. The source of this charge lies in the application to politics of the assumption that individuals in the marketplace behave in a self-interested way. More specifically, economic models of behaviour include net wealth, an externally measurable variable, as an important 'good' that individuals seek to maximize. The moral condemnation of public choice is centered on the presumed transference of this element of economic theory to political analysis. Critics argue that people acting politically—for example, as voters or as legislators-do not behave as they do in markets. Individuals are differently motivated when they are choosing 'for the public' rather than for themselves in private choice capacities. Or so the criticism runs.

At base, this criticism stems from a misunderstanding that may have been fostered by the failure of economists to acknowledge the limits of their efforts. The economic model of behaviour, even if restricted to market activity, should never be taken to provide the be-all and end-all of scientific explanation. Persons act from many motives, and the economic model concentrates attention only on one of the many possible forces behind actions. Economists do, of course, presume that the 'goods' they employ in their models for predicting behaviour are relatively important. And in fact, the hypothesis that promised shifts in net wealth modify political behaviour in predictable ways has not been readily falsifiable empirically.

Public choice, as an inclusive research programme, incorporates the presumption that persons do not readily become economic eunuchs as they shift from market to political participation. Those who respond predictably to ordinary incentives in the marketplace do not fail to respond at all when they act as citizens. The public choice theorist should, of course, acknowledge that the strength and predictive power of the strict economic model of behaviour is somewhat mitigated as the shift is made from private market to collective choice. Persons in political roles may, indeed, act to a degree in terms of what they consider to be the general interest. Such acknowledgment does not, however, in any way imply that the basic explanatory model loses all of its predictive potential, or that ordinary incentives no longer matter.

IMPACT OF PUBLIC CHOICE

Public choice theory has developed and matured over the course of a full half-century. It is useful to assess the impact and effects of this programme, both on thinking in the scientific community and in the formation of public attitudes. By simple comparison with the climate of opinion in 1950, both the punditry and the public are more critical of politics and politicians, more cynical about the motivations of political action, and less naive in thinking that political nostrums offer easy solutions to social problems. And this shift in attitudes extends well beyond the loss of belief in the efficacy of socialism, a loss of belief grounded both in historical regime failures and in the collapse of intellectually idealized structures.

As I noted earlier, when we look back at the scientific and public climates of discussion 50 years ago, the prevailing mindset was socialist in its underlying presupposition that government offered the solution to social problems. But there was a confusing amalgam of Marxism and ideal political theory involved: Governments, as observed, were modeled and condemned by Marxists as furthering class interests, but governments which might be installed 'after the revolution', so to speak, would become both omniscient and benevolent.

In some of their implicit modeling of political behavior aimed at furthering special group or class interests, the Marxists seemed to be closet associates of public choice, even as they rejected methodological individualism. But how was the basic Marxist critique of politics, as observed, to be transformed into the idealized politics of the benevolent and omniscient superstate? This question was simply left glaringly unanswered. And the debates of the 1930s were considered by confused economists of the time to have been won by the socialists rather than by their opponents, Ludwig von Mises and Friedrich Hayek. Both sides, to an extent, neglected the relevance of incentives in motivating human action, including political action.

The structure of ideas that was adduced in support of the emerging Leviathan welfare state was logically flawed and could have been maintained only through long-continued illusion. But, interestingly, the failure, in whole or in part, of the socialist structure of ideas did not come from within the academy. Mises and Hayek were not successful in their early efforts, and classical liberalism seemed to be at its nadir at mid-century. Failure came, not from a collapse of an intellectually defunct structure of ideas, but from the cumulative record of non-performance in the implementation of extended collectivist schemes-non-performance measured against promised claims, something that could be observed directly. In other words, governments everywhere overreached. They tried to do more than the institutional framework would support. This record of failure, both in the socialist and welfare states, came to be recognized widely, commencing in the 1960s and accelerating in the 1970s.

Where is the influence of public choice in this history? I do not claim that it dislodged the prevailing socialist mindset in the academies, and that this intellectual shift then exerted feedback on political reality. What I do claim is that public choice exerted major influence in providing a coherent understanding and interpretation of what could be everywhere observed. The public directly sensed that collectivistic schemes were failing, that politicization did not offer the promised correctives for any and all social ills, that governmental intrusions often made things worse rather than better. How could these direct observations be fitted into a satisfactory understanding?

Public choice came along and offered a foundation for such an understanding. Armed with nothing more than the rudimentary insights from public choice, persons could understand why, once established, bureaucracies tend to grow apparently without limit and without connection to initially promised functions. They could understand why pork-barrel politics dominated the attention of legislators; why there seems to be a direct relationship between the overall size of government and the investment in efforts to secure special concessions from government (rent seeking); why the tax system is described by the increasing number of special credits, exemptions, and loopholes; why balanced budgets are so hard to secure; and why strategically placed industries secure tariff protection.

A version of the old fable about the king's nakedness may be helpful here. Public choice is like the small boy who said that the king really has no clothes. Once he said this, everyone recognized that the king's nakedness had been recognized, but that no-one had really called attention to this fact.

Let us be careful not to claim too much, however. Public choice did not emerge from some profoundly new insight, some new discovery, some social science miracle. Public choice, in its basic insights into the workings of politics, incorporates an understanding of human nature that differs little, if at all, from that of James Madison and his colleagues at the time of the American Founding. The essential wisdom of the 18th century, of Adam Smith and classical political economy and of the American Founders, was lost through two centuries of intellectual folly. Public choice does little more than incorporate a rediscovery of this wisdom and its implications into economic analyses of modern politics.

Entrepreneurship

Entrepreneurship

By Israel M. Kirzner

A solid case can be made for the claim that entrepreneurship has, throughout the history of the Austrian school, been among its central theoretical constructs. In their history of the variety of ways of understanding the essence of entrepreneurship, Hébert and Link (1988, p. 64) refer to the three 'distinct viewpoints' in early neoclassical economics (the 'Austrian, French and British'). They remark that, 'of the three, the Austrian approach proved most fertile for advancing the theory of the entrepreneur'. In a paper exploring aspects of the history of entrepreneurial theory, Dolores Tremewan Martin (1979, p. 271) observes that 'much of the modern economic analysis … is devoid of any serious consideration of the role of the entrepreneur …', but adds in a footnote that 'the primary exceptions to this general trend in the literature are found in the writings of the "modern Austrian economists"'.

In the following pages we will briefly examine some highlights in the history of Austrian theories of entrepreneurship; canvass some contemporary disagreements among Austrians in regard to entrepreneurship; and seek to explain why it was that the Austrians, rather than other schools of marginalist economics, came to assign such importance to the entrepreneurial role.

THE ENTREPRENEUR IN THE EARLIER AUSTRIAN TRADITION

It is well known that it was only in the course of the marginalist revolution that economists came to recognize an analytically distinct role for the entrepreneur. In classical economics—or at least in its dominant British version—there was simply no distinct entrepreneurial function. It was the capitalist upon whom, it appears, the economists implicitly relied to assure fulfilment of the tasks we generally consider to be entrepreneurial. The profit share of income earned by the capitalist, in classical economics, corresponded mainly in fact to what neoclassical economics was to identify as interest on capital. For the classical economists there was no pure entrepreneurial profit, because for them there was no pure entrepreneurial role. It was in the course of the neoclassical development of the theory of the market that economists came to recognize the importance of the function played by the entrepreneur who acquires all the resource services–including those of capital—in order to produce the product to be sold to consumers. During the 1880s and 1890s there emerged a small flood of articles dealing with this entrepreneurial role. It was at this time that the American theorists,

J. B. Clark and Frederick B. Hawley, developed their separate theories of pure profit (upon the elements of which Frank Knight was later to build his own more nuanced theory). It was soon after this period that the Austrian J. A. Schumpeter introduced his own theory of the entrepreneur, laying the foundation for his characteristic way of seeing and understanding the capitalist process.

The Austrians were prominent participants in this discovery of entrepreneurship. Carl Menger had already, in his 1871 *Grundsätze*, paid some significant attention, at least, to the entrepreneurial function. In characteristic subjectivist fashion, indeed, Menger (1950, p. 160) emphasized the element of information and the act of will involved in this entrepreneurial function (although, unlike Schumpeter and later Austrians, he saw the exercise of this function as merely a special kind of labor service). During the 1880s his teaching apparently inspired two of his students, Mataja and Gross, each to write his dissertation on the entrepreneurial role. There has been some disagreement among historians of thought concerning the influence exercised by Menger upon subsequent Austrian developments in the theory of entrepreneurship. Streissler (1972, pp. 432f) has maintained that Schumpeter built his own theory of entrepreneurial innovation largely on Menger's foundations. This seems to contrast sharply with Knight's typically dismissive assessment of the influence of Menger's contribution in this respect. (See also Martin, 1979; Kirzner, 1979, chapter 4, for discussions of Menger's concept of the entrepreneur in the context of the subsequent Schumpeterian and Knightian views.) Be this as it may, there seems little ground to doubt that Schumpeter's own emphasis on the entrepreneur was rooted, not in his well-known admiration for Walrasian general equilibrium theory, but in the subjectivist, Austrian legacy he imbibed from Böhm-Bawerk's seminars.

An assessment by the historian of thought of the state of entrepreneurial theory in the economics of 1914 would recognize the importance of the Austrian contributions, but would certainly not pronounce entrepreneurial theory to be exclusively or even predominantly the province of the Austrians. The bulk of the prewar literature on entrepreneurship and on entrepreneurial profit was certainly contributed by economists of other schools. Yet general mainstream interest in this branch of economic theory was to decline sharply following the war. Knight's work would of course represent a magisterial contribution to the identification of the entrepreneurial role and to the understanding of pure entrepreneurial profit. It offered a crystal-clear articulation of the distinction between the utterly certain Walrasian world of perfectly competitive equilibrium and the real world of radical, inescapable uncertainty. But the progress of mainstream neoclassical economics in the succeeding half-century was virtually to ignore the implications of this distinction. Even among Knight's own disciples microeconomics came to mean, in the second half of the twentieth century, the theory of markets in complete competitive equilibrium, with no possibility of pure profit, and none of the uncertainty which calls forth the special characteristics of the Knightian entrepreneur. It was during this period that understanding of the entrepreneurial role became, if only by default, more or less an exclusively Austrian concern. It was in the economics of Ludwig von Mises that this was most obvious.

ENTREPRENEURSHIP IN MID-TWENTIETH-CENTURY AUSTRIAN ECONOMICS

What Mises contributed to the theory of entrepreneurship may not be immediately obvious to the superficial reader of his works. Although the index to his *Human Action* (1949) demonstrates the importance of the entrepreneur for Misesian economics, a reader may be excused for concluding that what Mises had to say about the entrepreneur was not exactly pathbreaking. The nuances which separate the Misesian entrepreneur from the Schumpeterian or the Knightian might well appear to be only of marginal significance, but the truth is that it is indeed the role which Mises assigns to the entrepreneur which sets Misesian economics so decisively apart from mainstream midtwentieth century economics. And the modest revival of the Austrian approach during the past two decades must be seen as recognition of the valuable character of precisely this aspect of the Misesian system.

What sets the Misesian system apart from mainstream neoclassical economics is the Misesian portrayal of *the market as an entrepreneurially driven process*:

> The operation of [the factor] market is actuated and kept in motion by the exertion of the promoting entrepreneurs, eager to profit from the differences in the market prices of the factors of production and the expected prices of the products ... The activities of the entrepreneurs are the element that would bring about the unrealizable state of the evenly rotating economy if no further changes were to occur ... The competition between the entrepreneurs ... reflects in the external world the conflict which the inexorable scarcity of the factors of production brings about in the soul of each consumer. It makes effective the subsumed decisions of the consumers as to what purpose the nonspecific factors should be used for and to what extent the specific factors of production should be used. (1949, pp. 331, 335)

It was in the course of the famed inter-war debate on the possibility of economic calculation under socialism that Mises's entrepreneurial view of the market process came to be crystallized and subsequently clearly articulated. As Lavoie has emphasized, it was appreciation for the entrepreneurial character of the market process which enabled the Austrians to see the fallacy of quasi-market 'solutions' (such as those of Lange and Lemer) to the calculation problem. This writer has argued that Hayek's important contributions to the calculation debate, although couched in terms of utilization of knowledge rather than in terms of entrepreneurial discovery, ultimately reflect,

at least implicitly, a similar understanding of the market process.

In fact the novelty of the Misesian perception of the market as a continuing process of entrepreneurial competition is mute evidence of the drastic decline, in mid-twentieth-century mainstream economic thought, of awareness of the entrepreneurial role. As Baumol has observed, the entrepreneur had virtually disappeared from the theoretical literature. And it was indeed the Misesian emphasis on the entrepreneurial role which inspired subsequent Austrian interest in the theory of entrepreneurship.

THE MISESIAN ENTREPRENEUR FURTHER EXPLORED

Much of this subsequent Austrian interest has been reflected in the present writer's work seeking to articulate more definitively the essential characterise tics of the Misesian entrepreneur, and to demonstrate how central these characteristics must be for an understanding of the competitive process. As one writer has put it, the 'leitmotif' of this work has been that 'the exploitation of the gains from trade will not take place automatically. To achieve the advantages of co-ordination through exchange requires first that these potential gains are noticed. The entrepreneurial role is to be "alert" to as yet unexploited gains from trade' (Ricketts, 1992, p. 67).

Mainstream economics has of course always assumed that exploitation of gains from trade *will* take place automatically, as soon as the gains exceed the relevant costs. This assumes that all opportunities for winning pure gain are instantly perceived and exploited. It follows that the market outcomes, at any given instant, must necessarily be understood as embodying the fulfilment of the most exacting conditions for equilibrium. Each economic agent in the market must, at each instant, therefore be assumed *not* to be grasping for pure profit (since all such opportunities for pure profit have *already* been grasped and eliminated). This has forced mainstream microeconomics into a straitjacket in which all decisions being made at each instant are, somehow, automatically fully coordinated ('pre-reconciled') with every other decision being made in the system. This has restricted modern microeconomics to strictly defined states of equilibrium. This has, in turn, had the consequence that the notion of *competition* has had to mean, not any process during which competing market participants struggle to get ahead of one another, but a state of affairs in which any such struggle is both unnecessary and inconceivable.

By liberating economics from the assumption that all opportunities for pure gain have already been captured, this Misesian-inspired perspective on markets permits us to see market processes as ones in which such opportunities—hitherto overlooked–come to be perceived and exploited. This has opened up an entirely fresh dimension for economic activity, a dimension necessarily missing from an equilibrium-bound microeconomics. This new dimension is that of entrepreneurial *alertness* and entrepreneurial discovery. Whereas traditional economics has operated in a framework in which outcomes can be attributed to either (or a mix of) (a) deliberate maximizing choice, or (b) pure luck, this entrepreneurial perspective draws our attention to a third possible (and, in general, necessary) source for observed outcomes. This third source is *discovery*, in which unfocused, unspecified, purposefulness—a generalized intentness upon noticing the useful opportunities that may be present within one's field of vision—in fact yields discovered opportunities (which may then be subsequently exploited in maximizing choice fashion). Such discovery cannot itself be characterized as rational, maximizing choice (in the way in which deliberate cost-conscious *search* activity has been treated in the theory of information literature) because, prior to the moment of discovery, the potential discoverer is perceived not to have any specific search objective or search procedure in

mind and is (therefore) not seen as weighing the likely benefits of a successful find against the costs of necessary search. (In fact his discovery may consist in *realizing* that he *has* before him a promising opportunity for profitable search.) Nor can a discovered opportunity be entirely attributed to pure luck. Although, to be sure, the «¡objective existence of the opportunity itself (prior to its discovery but at a point in space and time likely to result in discovery) may (disregarding the philosophical reservations one may have concerning the 'existence' of an unperceived opportunity) be seen as entirely a matter of luck, its discovery must, at least in part, be attributed to the alertness of the discoverer.

The notion of entrepreneurship as the alertness necessary for the discovery of opportunities has had important implications for the positive understanding of market processes, and for ethical judgements concerning the moral status of market outcomes. The positive theory of the competitive market process has come, in this line of modern Austrian economics, to mean the sequence of market trades and acts of production which can be attributed to the succession of entrepreneurial discoveries generated by disequilibrium conditions. To compete means, in this framework, to perceive an opportunity to serve the market better (than it is currently being served by one's competitors). This view of the function of the entrepreneur has been central to the modern Austrian appreciation of free markets, and to its understanding of the perils of interventionist public policies.

These Austrian insights concerning the role of entrepreneurial discovery have also revealed the *discovered* character of pure entrepreneurial profit. This has permitted an ethical view of the possible justice of such profit in a manner not open to mainstream economics (for which pure profit is likely to appear to have been enjoyed by the entrepreneur strictly as a matter of his good luck). This insight has been explored in Kirzner (1989).

ENTREPRENEURSHIP: SOME CONTEMPORARY AUSTRIAN DEBATES

Although the central features of Misesian entrepreneurship are, by and large, accepted within modern Austrian economics, certain features emphasized in this writer's expositions of it (as outlined in the preceding section) have been challenged during recent years by a number of Austrian economists, as well as by others. (One line of modern Austrian work, *not* dealt with in this section, is that identified with the late Ludwig Lachmann. That work has sharply questioned the equilibrative character of entrepreneurship which is central to the Misesian view.) We may group these debates around two related themes.

Creativity

The 'alertness' view of entrepreneurship appears to separate entrepreneurship from any genuinely creative activity. To be alert to an opportunity would appear not to include anything except noticing that which is *already* fully developed, merely waiting to be grasped. A number of modem Austrians have been unhappy with such implications. See also Ricketts (1992).

Uncertainty

The 'alertness' view of entrepreneurship has been understood by its critics effectively to abstract from uncertainty. To define entrepreneurship in terms of *seeing* opportunities, it is held by the critics, seems to identify it exclusively with success: to define it in terms apparently impervious to the very possibility of entrepreneurial loss. Yet surely such possibility of loss cannot be separated from the exercise of entrepreneurship. As soon as entrepreneurship is extended from simultaneous arbitrage to intertemporal arbitrage, uncertainty inevitably enters the picture. All this has suggested to the critics that the essence of entrepreneurship be sought in such qualities as *imagination* (White, 1976) or *judgement* (High, 1982).

In his more recent writings the present writer has attempted to meet some of these criticisms. He has of course agreed that uncertainty is inseparable from the entrepreneurial function in the context of ongoing time; so that it is indeed the case that the futurity of entrepreneurial activity must entail both judgement and imagination. Entrepreneurial alertness, in regard to opportunities the profitability of which lies in the future, cannot be exercised without imagination of that which does not yet exist, and without judgement concerning which of today's active forces is likely, in the course of time, to dominate the others. To concur warmly in these valid and important observations is not, however, to retreat from the insight that the essence of all entrepreneurial action is the perception of opportunities—offering profit in the present, the near future, or the distant future. To recognize that alertness in a world of uncertainty may call for good judgement and lively imagination does not, surely, affect the centrality of the insight that entrepreneurship refers, not to the deliberate exploitation of perceived opportunities, but to the alert perception of opportunities available for exploitation.

Rather similar considerations relate to the criticisms which see the emphasis on alertness as being blind to the role of creativity in the entrepreneurial role. Surely, such criticisms run, what the entrepreneur does, in so many cases, is not so much to perceive a given opportunity as to imaginatively *create* that which nobody had hitherto dreamed of. To such criticisms it seems appropriate to respond that, while the opportunity to be discovered is often indeed the opportunity to be created, this truth should not obscure the more fundamental insight regarding entrepreneurship. This insight is simply that for any entrepreneurial discovery, creativity is never enough: it is necessary *to recognize* one's own creativity. In other words, an essential ingredient in each successful creative innovation is its innovator's vision of what he can creatively accomplish.

The point in these responses to the critics is that, while the entrepreneur operates under uncertainty, and therefore displays imagination, judgement and creativity, his role is not so much the *shouldering* of uncertainty as it is his ability *to shoulder uncertainty aside* through recognizing opportunities in which imagination, judgement and creativity can successfully manifest themselves.

AUSTRIAN ECONOMICS AND THE ENTREPRENEURIAL ROLE

The centrality of the entrepreneur in Austrian economics, virtually since its inception in 1871, appears to be no accident. If one accepts *subjectivism* as being the unifying thread which has characterized the Austrian economic tradition throughout its history, then the centrality of entrepreneurship seems eminently understandable. Mainstream economics, with a lesser emphasis on subjectivism, has been prone to presuming that the mere objective presence of the possibility for gains from trade is sufficient to ensure their exploitation. Economic agents are presumed to maximize in terms of the opportunities which exist, without any concern regarding any possible gap between the opportunities which exist and the opportunities which are perceived to exist. Market prices are interpreted as the outcomes consistent with a state of the world in which all market participants are maximizing in respect of the opportunities objectively inherent in the actions of all their fellow participants. There is no need, in such an analytical scheme, for any role specifically geared to ensuring that the opportunities perceived in fact tend to correspond to what is objectively available. There is no need for any role specifically geared to explaining any process through which market outcomes might tend to come to express actual (as against possibly erroneously perceived) mutual possibilities—since no possibility of such a gap is entertained.

It is in a consciously subjectivist mode of analysis, such as that of the Austrian tradition, in which the possibility is taken seriously that agents may be seeking to maximize within erroneously perceived frameworks, that scope for entrepreneurship can easily come to be recognized. Within such a tradition an emphasis upon knowledge and ignorance, imagination and discovery has indeed emerged naturally and organically. Despite the changes over time in Austrian entrepreneurial constructs, and despite contemporary Austrian marginal disagreements concerning the essential entrepreneurial functions, it seems reasonable to attribute the perennial Austrian interest in the entrepreneur to the tradition's consistent subjectivist thrust

BIBLIOGRAPHY

Hébert, Robert F. and Albert N. Link (1988), *The Entrepreneur: Mainstream Views and Radical Critiques*, 2nd edn, New York: Praeger.

High, Jack (1982), 'Alertness and Judgment: Comment on Kirzner', in Israel M. Kirzner (ed.), *Method, Process and Austrian Economics, Essays in Honor of Ludwig von Mises*, Lexington: D.C. Heath.

Kirzner, Israel M. (1979), *Perception, Opportunity and Profit, Studies in the Theory of Entrepreneurship*, Chicago: University of Chicago Press.

Kirzner, Israel M. (1989), *Discovery, Capitalism, and Distributive Justice*, Oxford: Basil Blackwell.

Martin, Dolores Tremewan (1979), 'Alternative Views of Mengerian Entrepreneurship', *History of Political Economy*, 11, (2), summer, 271–85.

Menger, Carl (1950), *Principles of Economics*, translated and edited by J. Dingwall and Bert F. Hoselitz, Glencoe IL: Free Press.

Mises, Ludwig von (1949), *Human Action*, New Haven: Yale University Press.

Ricketts, Martin (1992), 'Kirzner's Theory of Entrepreneurship—A Critique', in Bruce J. Caldwell and Stephan Böhm (eds), *Austrian Economics: Tensions and New Directions*, Boston: Kluwer Academic.

Streissler, Erich (1972), 'To What Extent Was the Austrian School Marginalist?', *History of Political Economy*, 4, fall.

White, Lawrence H. (1976), 'Entrepreneurship, Imagination and the Question of Equilibration', ms., published in Stephen C. Littlechild, *Austrian Economics*, vol. III, Aldershot: Edward Elgar, 1990, pp. 87–104.

The Entrepreneur

The Theory of Social Economy

By Gustav Cassel

I n our economic system, the work of directing production in conformity with the requirements of consumers falls principally upon the entrepreneurs. This task is by no means so simple as Socialists imagine when they say that all that is necessary is to compile statistics of wants in advance and then officially to regulate production on the basis of these statistics. Regulating consumption in this manner would be equivalent, in a large degree, to suppressing the freedom of choice of consumption that is characteristic of the exchange economy. But the consumers wish most decidedly to retain this freedom of choice to the last moment.

The difficulty of the problem lies precisely in the fact that the constantly varying demands of consumers, which cannot be determined in advance with any degree of certainty, must be satisfied, despite incessant changes in the methods and conditions of production. This work is actually done—naturally not perfectly—by a number of independent entrepreneurs, each of whom, on the whole, looks merely to his own interest.

This solution of the problem is possible because, whenever a want that can be paid for is left unsatisfied, or is not completely satisfied, or satisfied only at an abnormally high price—every time, that is, the problem of the economic direction of social production is not satisfactorily solved—an entrepreneur is encouraged by the prospect of earning a special profit to make a better provision for the want in question, and the productive process is thus steadily improved. The entrepreneur intervenes, not only where something is to be done for the immediate satisfaction of consumers' wants, but everywhere where the productive process, somewhere among the thousands of its component processes, exhibits a gap which leaves room for his enterprise. In this way, all these partial processes are united into a single productive process, embracing the entire satisfaction of wants in the exchange economy.

The standard by which we can judge the use to be made of the various factors of production is, as has been shown, the pricing process. The factors of production, however, do not flow spontaneously in the direction marked out for them by prices. They must be directed by human activity, as is done when the entrepreneur buys factors of production, uses them in co-operation, and sells the products of his enterprise. Thus the pricing of the factors of production is, in general, in the hands of the entrepreneurs, and is effected by their work.

The part played by entrepreneurs can be best explained by saying that they bring together other factors of production than their own labour for productive purposes, and set them to work. The entrepreneur is, above all, a type for us. The director of a large business in which all the factors of production are used is a typical entrepreneur. This man can be regarded as essentially "the entrepreneur." It is true that he usually has capital of his own invested in the business. In this respect, however, he is a capitalist, not an entrepreneur. He also does work of one kind or other on behalf of the business. To that extent, he is a worker, in the wider sense of the word. Hence we must, as it were, distinguish the different aspects of his personality, in order that we may be able to grasp the nature of the work which he performs in his specialised capacity as an entrepreneur.

In actual economic life, the business of entrepreneur is largely exercised by individuals who can scarcely be called entrepreneurs in the proper sense. The manual worker or the peasant uses other factors of production besides his own labour in his productive process: the labour of others, capital, and land. Possibly he is himself mainly a worker. But we have to dissect his personality so that theoretically we can conceive of him as an entrepreneur in that aspect of his work. In this way we are able, when we speak of entrepreneurs, to include under that head all individuals who in one way or other perform the work of entrepreneurs.

The economic motive of this work is the desire to make a profit. The entrepreneur's profit is the surplus of gross proceeds above cost; that is, above the price which has to be paid for the co-operation of the factors of production. If the entrepreneur himself acts, to some extent, as a worker or official, or puts capital or land into the business, he must allow a certain sum, based on prevailing prices, as payment for the co-operation of these factors of production. It is only the remainder that represents the pure profit of enterprise.

This profit of enterprise is, at first sight, akin to a pure differential profit that is made merely as a result of the difference in costs in different undertakings. It includes, however, other elements which have an approximately definite price, and which must therefore be regularly taken into account in the calculations on which a business is based. These prices must, therefore, be put on the same footing as costs, and must normally be covered by the prices of the products.

To this class belongs, first of all, the personal work of the entrepreneur in his capacity of employer, in organising and directing the undertaking. This work may in part be replaced by the paid work of officials. The manager of a medium-sized business performs a number of functions which are only handed over to the heads of departments, etc., at a later stage, when it has grown to a large business. Work of this kind must clearly be reckoned among the costs of the undertaking. Even the general management of the business, however large, may be entrusted to a salaried official. This, indeed, is the customary thing in the case of limited companies. There is a price for each of these functions of enterprise in every economically advanced country. This price follows the ordinary rules of pricing: the relative scarcity of competent individuals in proportion to the demand for them is the primary determining factor of the price of the entrepreneur's work. Hence the determining factors of this price are substantially the same as those of wages, though the pricing of the work done by entrepreneurs naturally has its special features. The price of the entrepreneur's work must be included among the costs of the business. Every limited company does this, and every private entrepreneur who carries on his business sensibly must do the same. If an entrepreneur, making an annual profit of £1,500 in his own business, can earn £1,000 as a director of a limited company, he will reckon £500 only as the actual profit derived from his business. If the net proceeds are only £750, it will be dear to him that he is really working at a loss, since his managerial ability is worth £1,000.[1]

A second element of the profit of the entrepreneur, in the broad sense of the word indicated above, which must be reckoned as a cost, is the risk—in so far as it can be calculated with some degree of probability and so included in the estimate of cost. This, of course, is particularly the case with regard to any risk against which it is possible to insure, such as fire, or shipwreck, and so forth. Generally, insurance premiums are paid for these risks and included in the

---

1   The work of an entrepreneur can if so desired, be regarded as a special factor of production, in addition to labour in the usual sense of the term. The peculiarity of the determining factors of the wages of management would account for such a distinction.

costs. They must be put on the same footing, among the costs, as depreciation of buildings, of machinery, etc. When we consider production as a whole, accidents of this kind occur with a certain regularity, and are therefore part of the normal wear and tear of the things used in production. The payment of insurance premiums is, substantially, merely a method of spreading evenly the amount to be written off for depreciation. This idea is put into practice in the case of the big shipping companies, which do not insure, in view of the large number of their ships, but form instead an insurance fund of their own and enter the sums assigned to it under the head of current costs.

As a rule, it is not possible to insure against the actual business risks of an undertaking. That these risks, within certain normal limits, are taken into account in business calculations is beyond question. It is seen, for example, in the fact that in planning a business the interest on the capital is reckoned at (say) 10 per cent., although the usual interest on the best securities is perhaps only 4 per cent. A sound trading account of a limited company also reckons among costs the sums that must be set aside to form a proper reserve, since this must serve to cover losses incurred in the normal course of business. In so far as the risk of a business consists in a faulty estimate of costs, it must clearly be included as a special item in the estimate. The same is also obviously true of the risk arising out of an unavoidable falling-off in sales or in selling price; normally, a price must be fixed which will cover occasional losses of this type, so that, on the average, taking long periods, the price actually obtained for the product will suffice to cover the whole of the actual cost. This incurring of risk may itself be regarded as a special factor of production. Under economically advanced conditions this factor has a market of its own and a fairly definite price. It may also be substituted for other factors of production, as always happens when, in order to reduce costs, a lower grade of security is tolerated.

If we separate these two elements from the profit of the entrepreneur, both of which can be calculated to some extent in advance and must be considered a real cost of production, we may regard whatever remains of the net proceeds of the business as the entrepreneur's profit in the strict sense

of the word—as a pure profit of enterprise. This corresponds accurately with our definition of such profit as the surplus of gross proceeds over costs; for, now, all the items that can be regarded as costs have been subtracted. There can be no doubt that in real life there is an entrepreneur's profit of this kind. It is particularly evident when limited companies, which remunerate their directors and consulting experts very generously, and also put aside large reserves for all sorts of objects, not only pay normal interest on their capital, but also distribute additional dividends. However, only in comparatively few cases is the pure entrepreneur's profit very large. Most of them make a pure profit only during a trade boom. Probably, on the average, the returns are barely sufficient to cover all the costs, as we understand them here. A relatively large number of entrepreneurs can never cover these costs, but work at some loss. The pure profit of the entrepreneur is, in such cases, always negative. Experience shows that some of these businesses are only maintained after adequate writing-off of capital and "reconstructions." But the number of businesses that fail completely and disappear from the public view is very large. The public, which sees little of this, is dazzled by the enormous profits of a few prosperous firms, and is always disposed to exaggerate the amount of the total pure profit made by entrepreneurs in the national economy.

There are, of course, no norms as to the extent of pure profit. Pure profit is not a normal thing, but a specific element of the individual business. It is often the outcome of sheer accident, as, for example, when some development of the market takes place that is particularly profitable for a certain firm, but over which the entrepreneur has exerted no influence whatever. It varies a good deal, as a rule, with the trade movements in the branch of business in question. It further depends upon a favoured position which the business has secured in one respect or other. Possibly, the business has long had an assured circle of customers, a patented trade mark, favourable long-term contracts with suppliers of raw materials, good conditions in the business world, etc. Perhaps, being fully developed and well-organised, it enjoys an advantage over smaller competitors; or it possibly has at its disposal so much capital that it can crush competition; or it may have a legal monopoly, or perhaps has secured a monopoly by forming a trust. The exceptional position may also be due to personal factors. The business may employ managers, officials and workers who do more and better work than similarly paid managers, officials and workers of rival firms. The whole organisation of the business, the training and the efficiency of the employees in their work, the interest of all in the prosperity of the business, are also factors which tend to consolidate the position of a firm. In many of these cases the position is the fruit of years of endeavour, and the pure profit of enterprise now made is in part the outcome of the position that has been won. It can, however, be easily lost in the continual changes of modern economic life, in which forces are always at work to displace old and favoured firms and give place to new ones. Its maintenance necessitates, as a rule, a ceaseless effort, an unrelaxing vigilance—in a word, exertions which must be paid for, and the price must be included in the costs.

In the cases where a favoured business position—whether won or whether due to external circumstances ("unearned")—secures a permanent pure profit, this profit must be regarded as being akin to a rent of position, and the position itself has a capital value which is realised when the business is sold. But these things cannot be fully understood until we come to the inquiries in the next chapter.

The question of the extent to which the profit of the entrepreneur enters into the price of the product can now be easily answered. Those elements of profit, in the broader sense of the word, which we have shown to be real costs must, of course, be regarded as normal constituents of the price of the product. Whether the pure profit of the entrepreneur is included in the price of the product depends upon the conditions of competition. If the business which makes such a profit is not in a position to supply the whole market, and other entrepreneurs must have a share in the work, it is possible that the final business thus required will yield no pure profit, and that, consequently, the price will only just cover the cost in this marginal firm. In this case the price, in accordance with the differential principle, is fixed by the marginal cost, and the pure profit made by

the more favourably placed firms is entirely in the nature of a differential profit, and is irrelevant to the price of the product. If, on the other hand, the business in question is in a position of monopoly, and succeeds in using it to make a pure profit, this can only be done by raising the price of the product above the cost, and the entrepreneur's profit must, in that case, be regarded distinctly as a part of the price of the product. The question whether the price of the product is increased on account of the monopoly is not examined here. In many cases the monopoly profit is obtained only by means of an extensive and efficient organisation, which keeps the costs down to a minimum, perhaps to such an extent that the product, despite the monopoly profit, is sold more cheaply.

§ 19 THE PROBLEM OF IMPUTATION AND THE SOCIAL PROBLEM OF DISTRIBUTION

When two individuals have co-operated in making a certain article, the question immediately arises as to how much each of them has contributed, or what is the share of each in the production of it. The primitive feeling of justice demands an objective standard for settling the division of the proceeds, and is disposed to find this in a causal link between work and product We thus arrive at the so-called problem of imputation or attribution. Its importance increases when we pass from the simple case of sharing between two individuals to the more complex one of the general distribution of social production. It holds a fundamental position in an age of widespread division of labour and sharp stratification of classes in the community.

The idea that the proceeds of production can be shared according to the principle of causality, in proportion to the work done by each of the several factors, is very popular. It is confirmed when we consider cases where the activities necessary to make the product are homogeneous, and can therefore be reduced to a common measure. It is then possible to distribute arithmetically according to work done. But if the activities required to make the product are of very different kinds, it is impossible to reduce them to a common measure, and there can be no "correct" distribution in the objective sense.

This applies primarily to activities of the most heterogenous nature which we are accustomed to lump together as "work." There is no common measure for the work of the thinker, the artist, the manager of a business, and the manual worker. Their common product can never be shared according to the work done by each.

The impossibility of this kind of imputation is made still clearer when other factors of production of various kinds are added to "labour"—capital, natural materials, or land. It is, however, precisely in this case that the problem of imputation attracts the widespread interest which it has in modern economic life. It is just when the activities co-operating in production are quite different that the most bitter controversy as to who is to have the proceeds of production arises. Each party is naturally inclined to emphasise the importance of its own share of the work, to claim as large a portion as possible of the returns, and, consequently, to denounce the actual apportionment as unfair. As a rule, the so-called proof of this is to imagine one's own share of the work withdrawn and then ask what the other factors of production would do without it.

The Instability of Capitalism

By Joseph Schumpeter

What matters for the subject of this study is merely the essentially discontinuous character of this process, which does not lend itself to description in terms of a theory of equilibrium. But we may conveniently lead up to this by insisting for the moment on the importance of the difference between this view and what I have called the received one. Innovation, unless it consists in producing, and forcing upon the public, a new commodity, means producing at smaller cost per unit, breaking off the old "supply schedule" and starting on a new one. It is quite immaterial whether this is done by making use of a new invention or not; for, on the one hand, there never has been any time when the store of scientific knowledge had yielded all it could in the way of industrial improvement, and, on the other hand, it is not the knowledge that matters, but the successful solution of the task *sui generis* of putting an untried method into practice—there may be, and often is, no scientific novelty involved at all, and even if it be involved, this does not make any difference to the nature of the process. And we should not only, by insisting on invention, emphasise an irrelevant point—irrelevant to our set of problems, although otherwise, of course, just as relevant as, say, climate—and be thereby led away from the relevant one, but we should also be forced to consider inventions as a case of external economies.[1]

---

1   There is another point which arises out of the usual treatment of these things: Nobody can possibly deny the occurrence or relevance of those great breaks in industrial practice which change the data of economic life from time to time. Marshall, therefore, distinguishes these, which he calls "substantive" inventions and which he deals with as chance events acting from outside on the analogy, say, of earthquakes, from inventions which, being of the nature of more obvious applications of known principles, may be expected to arise in consequence of expansion itself. This distinction is insisted upon by Prof. Pigou in the paper quoted above. This view, however, cuts up a homogeneous phenomenon, the elements of which do not differ from one another except by degree, and is readily seen to create a difficulty similar to that of filling the empty boxes. Exactly as the failure to distinguish different processes leads, in the case of the boxes, to a difficulty in distinguishing between groups of facts—and leads, also, to that state of discussion in which some authors hold that most industries display *increasing*, others that most industries display *decreasing*, still others, that normally any industry shows *constant*, returns—so it is obviously impossible to draw any line between those classes of innovations, or, for that matter, inventions; and the difficulty is not one of judging

Now this hides part of the very essence of the capitalist process. This kind of external economies—and, in fact, nearly every kind, even the trade journal must, unless the product of collective action, be somebody's business—characteristically comes about by first being taken up by one firm or a few—by acting, that is, as an internal economy. This firm begins to undersell the others, part of which are thereby definitely pushed into the background to linger there on accumulated reserves and quasi-rents, whilst another part copies the methods of the disturber of the peace. *That* this is so, we can see every day by looking at industrial life; it is precisely what goes on, what is missing in the static apparatus and what accounts both for dissatisfaction with it and for the attempts to force such phenomena into its cracking frame—instead of, as we think it natural to do, recognising and explaining this as a distinct process going on along with the one handled by the static theory. *Why* this is so, is a question which it would lead very far to answer satisfactorily. Successful innovation is, as said before, a task *sui generis*. It is a feat not of intellect, but of will. It is a special case of the social phenomenon of leadership.[2] Its difficulty consisting in the resistances and uncertainties incident to doing what has not been done before, it is accessible for, and appeals to, only a distinct type which is rare. Whilst differences in aptitude for the routine work of "static" management only result in differences of success in doing what every one does, differences in this particular aptitude result in only some being able to do this particular thing at all. To overcome these difficulties incident to change of practice is the function characteristic of the entrepreneur.

Now if this process meant no more than one of many classes of "friction," it certainly would not be worth our while to dissent from the usual exposition on that account, however many facts might come under this heading. But it means more than this: Its analysis yields the explanation of phenomena which cannot be accounted for without it. There is, first, the "entrepreneurial" function as distinct from the mere "managerial" function—although they may, and mostly must, meet one another in the same individual—the nature of which only shows up within the process of innovation. There is, secondly, the explanation of entrepreneurs' gain, which emerges in this process and otherwise gets lost in the compound of "earnings of management,"[3] the treating of which as a

---

particular cases, but one of principle. For *no* invention is independent of existing data; and *no* invention is *so* dependent on them as to be automatically produced by them. In the case of important invention, change in data is great; in the case of unimportant invention it is small. But this is all, and the *nature* of the process and of the special mechanism set in motion is always the same.

2   This does not imply any glorification. Leadership itself does not mean only such aptitudes as would generally command admiration, implying, as it does, narrowness of outlook in any but one direction and a kind of force which sometimes it may be hardly possible to distinguish from callousness. But economic leadership has, besides, nothing of the glamour some other kinds of leadership have. Its intellectual implications may be trivial; wide sympathies, personal appeal, rhetorical sublimation of motives and acts count for little in it; and although not without its romance, it is in the main highly unromantic, so that any craving for personal hero-worship can hardly hope for satisfaction where, among, to be sure, other types, we meet with slave-trading and brandy-producing puritans at the historic threshold of the subject.

Apart from this source of possible objections, there is a much more serious one in the mind of every well-trained economist, whom experience has taught to think little of such intrusions into theory of views savouring of sociology, and who is prone to associate any such things with a certain class of objections to received doctrine, which continually turn up however often they

---

may have been refuted—sublimely ignorant of the fact—such as objections to the economic man, to marginal analysis, to the use of the barter hypothesis and so on. The reader may, I think, satisfy himself that no want of theoretic training is responsible for statements which I believe to tally fundamentally with Marshallian analysis.

No difficulty whatever arises as to verification. That new commodities or new qualities *or new quantities* of commodities are forced upon the public by the initiative of entrepreneurs—which, of course, does not affect the role of demand within the static process—is a fact of common experience; that one firm or a small group of firms leads in the sense meant above, in the process of innovation, thereby creating its own market and giving impulse to the environment generally, is equally patent (and we do not deny facts of other complexion—the secondary or "consequential" ones); and all we are trying to do is to fit the analytic apparatus to take account of such facts without putting its other parts out of gear.

3   The function in question being a distinct one, it does not matter that it appears in practice rarely, if ever, by itself. And whoever cares to observe the behaviour of business men at close quarters will not raise the objection that new things and routine work are done, as a rule, indiscriminately by the same manager. He will find that routine work is done with a smoothness wholly

homogeneous whole is unsatisfactory for precisely the same reason which, by universal consent, makes it unsatisfactory so to treat, say, the income of a peasant tilling his own soil, instead of treating it as a sum of wages, rent, quasi-rent and, possibly, interest. Furthermore, it is *this* entrepreneurs' profit which is the primary source of industrial fortunes, the history of every one of which consists of, or leads back to, successful acts of innovation.[4] And as the rise and decay of industrial fortunes is *the* essential fact about the social structure of capitalist society, both the emergence of what is, in any single instance, an essentially temporary gain, and the elimination of it by the working of the competitive mechanism, obviously are more than "frictional" phenomena, as is that process of underselling by which industrial progress comes about in capitalist society and by which its achievements result in higher real incomes all round.

---

absent as soon as a new step is to be taken, and that there is a sharp cleavage between the two, insuperable for a very worthy type of manager. This extends far into the realm of what we are wont to consider as automatic change, bringing about external economies and increasing returns. Take the instance of a business letting out motor cars on the principle "drive yourself." A mere growth of the neighbourhood, sufficient to make such a business profitable, does not produce it. Someone has to realise the possibility and to found the firm, to get people to appreciate its services, to get the right type of cars and so on. This implies solution of a legion of small problems. Even if such a firm already exists and further environmental growth make discontinuous extension feasible, the thing to be done is not so easy as it looks. It would be easy for the trained mind of a leading industrialist, but it is not so for a typical member of the stratum which does such business.

4   It is, as has been said in a previous note, not the *running* of a business according to new plan, but the act of *getting it* to run on a new plan, which accounts for entrepreneurs' profits, and makes it so undesirable to try to express them by "static" curves, which describe precisely the phenomena of the "running" of it. The theoretical reason for our proposition is, that either competition or the process of imputation must put a stop to any "surplus" gain, even in a case of monopoly, in which the value of the patent, the natural agent or of whatever else the monopoly position is contingent on, will absorb the return in the sense that it will no longer be profit. But there is also a "practical" observation to support this view. No firm ever yields returns indefinitely, if only run according to unchanged plan. For everyone comes the day when it will cease to do so. And we all of us know that type of industrial family firm of the third generation which is on the road to that state, however conscientiously it may be "managed."

Nor is this all. This process of innovation in industry by the agency of entrepreneurs supplies the key to all the phenomena of capital and credit. The role of credit would be a technical and a subordinate one in the sense that everything fundamental about the economic process could be explained in terms of goods, if industry grew by small steps along coherent curves. For in that case financing could and would be done substantially by means of the current gross revenue, and only small discrepancies would need to be smoothed. If we simplify by assuming that the whole circular process of production and consumption takes exactly one period of account, no instruments or consumers' goods surviving into the next, capital—defined as a monetary concept—and income would be exactly equal, and only different phases of one and the same monetary stream. As, however, innovation, being discontinuous and involving considerable change and being, in competitive capitalism, typically embodied in new firms, requires large expenditure previous to the emergence of any revenue, credit becomes an essential element of the process. And we cannot turn to savings in order to account for the existence of a fund from which these credits are to flow. For this would imply the existence of previous profits, without which there would not be anything like the required amount—even as it is, savings usually lag behind requirements—and assuming previous profits would mean, in an explanation of principles, circular reasoning. "Credit-creation," therefore, becomes an essential part both of the mechanism of the process and of the theory explaining it.

Hence, saving, properly so called, turns out to be of less importance than the received doctrine implies, for which the continuous growth of saving—accumulation—is a mainstay of explanation. Credit-creation is the method by which the putting to new uses of existing means of production is brought about through a rise in price enforcing the "saving" of the necessary amount of them out of the uses they hitherto served ("enforced savings"—cp. Mr. Robertson's "imposed lacking").

Finally, it cannot be said that whilst all this applies to individual firms, the development of whole industries might still be looked at as a continuous process, a comprehensive view "ironing out" the discontinuities which occur in every single case. Even then individual discontinuities would be the carriers of essential phenomena. But, besides, for a definite reason that is not so. As shown both by the typical rise of general prices and the equally typical activity of the constructional trades in the prosperity phase of the business cycle, innovations cluster densely together. So densely, in fact, that the resultant disturbance produces a distinct period of adjustment—which precisely is what the depression phase of the business cycle consists in. *Why* this should be so, the present writer has attempted to show elsewhere.[5] *That* it is so, is the best single verification and justification of the view submitted, whether we apply the criterion of its being "true to life" or the criterion of its yielding explanation of a phenomena *not itself implied in its fundamental 'principle.*

If, then, the putting to new uses of existing resources is what "progress" fundamentally consists in; if it is the nature of the entrepreneur's function to act as the propelling force of the process; if entrepreneur's profits, credit, and the cycle prove to be essential parts of its mechanism—the writer even believes this to be true of interest—then industrial expansion *per se* is better described as a consequence than as a cause; and we should be inclined to turn the other way round what we have termed the received chain of causation. In this case, and as those

phenomena link up so as to form a coherent and self-contained logical whole, it is obviously conducive to clearness to bring them out boldly; to relegate to one distinct body of doctrine the concept of equilibrium, the continuous curves and small marginal variations, all of which, in their turn, link up with the circuit flow of economic routine under constant data; and to build, alongside of this, and *before* taking account of the full complexity of the "real" phenomenon—secondary waves, chance occurrences, "growth 55 and so on—a theory of capitalist change, assuming, in so doing, that noneconomic conditions or data are constant and automatic and gradual change in economic conditions is absent. But there is no difficulty in inserting all this. And it would seem to follow that the organic analogy is less adapted to express faithfully the nature of the process than many of us think; although, of course, being a mere analogy, it may be so interpreted as not to imply anything positively wrong and as to avoid the idea of an equilibrium growth *ad instar* of the growth of a tree, which it may, but need not necessarily, suggest.

Summing up the argument and applying it to the subject in hand, we see that there is, indeed, one element in the capitalist process, embodied in the type and function of the entrepreneur, which will, *by its mere working and from within*—in the absence of all outside impulses or disturbances and even of "growth"—destroy any equilibrium that may have established itself or been in process of being established; that the action of that element is not amenable to description by means of infinitesimal steps; and that it produces the cyclical "waves" which are essentially the form "progress" takes in competitive capitalism and could be discovered by the theory of it, if we did not know of them by experience. But by a mechanism at work in, and explaining the features of, periods of depression, a new equilibrium always emerges, or tends to emerge, which absorbs the results of innovation carried out in the preceding periods of prosperity. The new elements find their equilibrium proportions; the old ones adapt themselves or drop out; incomes are rearranged; prosperity inflation is corrected by automatic self-deflation through the repayment of credits out of profits, through the new

---

5 "Theorie der wirtschaftlichen Entwicklung," 1911, 2nd ed. 1926. Cp. also "The Explanation of the Business Cycle," *Economica,* 1927. The failure of the price-level to rise in the United States during the period 1923–1926 will be seen to be no objection but a further verification of this theory. It has, however, been pointed out to the writer, by a very high authority, that prices did also fail to rise in the United States in the prosperity immediately preceding the War. It could be replied that the factors which account for the stability 1923–1926 had been active already before the War. But the U.S. Bureau of Labour figures for 1908–1913 are 91, 97, 99, 95, 101, 100. Cp. also Prof. Persons' chart in *Review of Economic Statistics,* Jan. 1927. It may be well to mention that constructional trades and their materials need not necessarily show their activity fully by *every* index. Iron, *e.g.,* being an international commodity, need not rise in price if the phases of the cycle do not quite coincide in different countries. As a matter of fact, they generally do. But the right way to deal with iron and steel is to use the Spiethoff index (production + imports-exports), and this has, so far, always worked satisfactorily.

consumers' goods entering the markets and through saving stepping into the place of "created" credits. So the instabilities, which arise from the process of innovation, tend to right themselves, and do not go on accumulating. And we may phrase the result we reach in our terminology by saying that there is, though instability of the *System,* no economic instability of the *Order.*

Trade

Of Restraints Upon the Importation

From Foreign Countries of Such Goods as Can Be Produced at Home

By Adam Smith

By restraining, either by high duties or by absolute prohibitions, the importation of such goods from foreign countries as can be produced at home, the monopoly of the home market is more or less secured to the domestic industry employed in producing them. Thus the prohibition of importing either live cattle[1] or salt provisions from foreign countries secures to the graziers of Great Britain the monopoly of the home market for butcher's meat. The high duties upon the importation of corn,[2] which in times of moderate plenty amount to a prohibition, give a like advantage to the growers of that commodity. The prohibition of the importation of foreign woollens is equally favourable to the woollen manufacturers.[3] The silk manufacture, though altogether employed upon foreign materials, has lately obtained the same advantage.[4] The linen manufacture has not yet obtained it, but is making great strides towards it.[5] Many other sorts of manufacturers[6] have, in the same manner, obtained in Great Britain, either altogether or very nearly, a monopoly against their countrymen. The variety of goods of which the importation into Great Britain is prohibited, either absolutely, or under certain circumstances, greatly exceeds what can easily be suspected by those who are not well acquainted with the laws of the customs.[7]

That this monopoly of the home-market frequently gives great encouragement to that particular species of industry which enjoys it, and frequently turns towards that employment a greater share of both the labour and stock of the society than would otherwise have gone to it, cannot be doubted. But whether it tends either to increase the general industry of the society, or to give it the most advantageous direction, is not, perhaps, altogether so evident.[8]

The general industry of the society never can exceed what the capital of the society can employ. As the number of workmen that can be kept in employment by any particular person must bear a certain proportion to his capital, so the number of those that can be continually employed by all the members of a great society must bear a certain proportion to the whole capital of that society, and never can exceed that proportion. No regulation of commerce can increase the quantity of industry in any society beyond what its capital can maintain. It can only divert a part of it into a direction into which it might not otherwise have gone; and it is by no means certain that this artificial direction is likely to be more advantageous to the society than that into which it would have gone of its own accord.

Every individual is continually exerting himself to find out the most advantageous employment for whatever capital he can command. It is his own advantage, indeed, and not that of the society, which he has in view. But the study of his own advantage naturally, or rather necessarily, leads him to prefer that employment which is most advantageous to the society.

First, every individual endeavours to employ his capital as near home as he can, and consequently as much as he can in the support of domestic industry; provided always that he can thereby obtain the ordinary, or not a great deal less than the ordinary profits of stock.

Thus, upon equal or nearly equal profits, every wholesale merchant naturally prefers the home-trade to the foreign trade of consumption, and the foreign trade of consumption to the carrying trade. In the home-trade his capital is never so long out of his sight as it frequently is in the foreign trade of consumption. He can know better the character and situation of the persons whom he trusts, and if he should happen to be deceived, he knows better the laws of the country from which he must seek redress. In the carrying trade, the capital of the merchant is, as it were, divided between two foreign countries, and no part of it is ever necessarily brought home, or placed under his own immediate view and command. The capital which an Amsterdam merchant employs in carrying corn from Konigsberg to Lisbon, and fruit and wine from Lisbon to Konigsberg, must generally be the one half of it at Konigsberg and the other half at Lisbon. No part of it need ever come to Amsterdam. The natural residence of such a merchant should either be at Konigsberg or Lisbon, and it can only be some very particular circumstances which can make him prefer the residence of

Amsterdam. The uneasiness, however, which he feels at being separated so far from his capital generally determines him to bring part both of the Konigsberg goods which he destines for the market of Lisbon, and of the Lisbon goods which he destines for that of Konigsberg, to Amsterdam: and though this necessarily subjects him to a double charge of loading and unloading, as well as to the payment of some duties and customs, yet for the sake of having some part of his capital always under his own view and command, he willingly submits to this extraordinary charge; and it is in this manner that every country which has any considerable share of the carrying trade becomes always the emporium, or general market, for the goods of all the different countries whose trade it carries on. The merchant, in order to save a second loading and unloading, endeavours always to sell in the home-market as much of the goods of all those different countries as he can, and thus, so far as he can, to convert his carrying trade into a foreign trade of consumption. A merchant, in the same manner, who is engaged in the foreign trade of consumption, when he collects goods for foreign markets, will always be glad, upon equal or nearly equal profits, to sell as great a part of them at home as he can. He saves himself the risk and trouble of exportation, when, so far as he can, he thus converts his foreign trade of consumption into a home-trade. Home is in this manner the centre, if I may say so, round which the capitals of the inhabitants of every country are continually circulating, and towards which they are always tending, though by particular causes they may sometimes be driven off and repelled from it towards more distant employments. But a capital employed in the home-trade, it has already been shown,[9] necessarily puts into motion a greater quantity of domestic industry, and gives revenue and employment to a greater number of the inhabitants of the country, than an equal capital employed in the foreign trade of consumption: and one employed in the foreign trade of consumption has the same advantage over an equal capital employed in the carrying trade. Upon equal, or only nearly equal profits, therefore, every individual naturally inclines to employ his capital in the manner in which it is likely to afford the greatest support to domestic industry, and to give revenue and employment to the greatest number of[10] people of his own country.

Secondly, every individual who employs his capital in the support of domestic industry, necessarily endeavours so to direct that industry that its produce may be of the greatest possible value.

The produce of industry is what it adds to the subject or materials upon which it is employed. In proportion as the value of this produce is great or small, so will likewise be the profits of the employer. But it is only for the sake of profit that any man employs a capital in the support of industry; and he will always, therefore, endeavour to employ it in the support of that industry of which the produce is likely to be of the greatest value, or to exchange for the greatest quantity either of money or of other goods.

But the annual revenue of every society is always precisely equal to the exchangeable value of the whole annual produce of its industry, or rather is precisely the same thing with that exchangeable value. As every individual, therefore, endeavours as much as he can both to employ his capital in the support of domestic industry, and so to direct that industry that its produce may be of the greatest value; every individual necessarily labours to render the annual revenue of the society as great as he can. He generally, indeed, neither intends to promote the public interest, nor knows how much he is promoting it. By preferring the support of domestic to that of foreign industry, he intends only his own security; and by directing that industry in such a manner as its produce may be of the greatest value, he intends only his own gain, and he is in this, as in many other cases, led by an invisible hand to promote an end which was no part of his intention. Nor is it always the worse for the society that it was no part of it. By pursuing his own interest he frequently promotes that of the society more effectually than when he really intends to promote it. I have never known

much good done by those who affected to trade for the public good. It is an affectation, indeed, not very common among merchants, and very few words need be employed in dissuading them from it.

What is the species of domestic industry which his capital can employ, and of which the produce is likely to be of the greatest value, every individual, it is evident, can, in his local situation, judge much better than any statesman or lawgiver can do for him. The statesman who should attempt to direct private people in what manner they ought to employ their capitals would not only load himself with a most unnecessary attention, but assume an authority which could safely be trusted, not only to no single person, but to no council or senate whatever, and which would nowhere be so dangerous as in the hands of a man who had folly and presumption enough to fancy himself fit to exercise it.

To give the monopoly of the home-market to the produce of domestic industry, in any particular art or manufacture, is in some measure to direct private people in what manner they ought to employ their capitals, and must, in almost all cases, be either a useless or a hurtful regulation. If the produce of domestic can be brought there as cheap as that of foreign industry, the regulation is evidently useless. If it cannot, it must generally be hurtful. It is the maxim of every prudent master of a family never to attempt to make at home what it will cost him more to make than to buy. The taylor does not attempt to make his own shoes, but buys them of the shoemaker. The shoemaker does not attempt to make his own clothes, but employs a taylor. The farmer attempts to make neither the one nor the other, but employs those different artificers. All of them find it for their interest to employ their whole industry in a way in which they have some advantage over their neighbours, and to purchase with a part of its produce, or what is the same thing, with the price of a part of it, whatever else they have occasion for.

What is prudence in the conduct of every private family can scarce be folly in that of a great kingdom. If a foreign country can supply us with a commodity cheaper than we ourselves can make it, better buy it of them with some part of the produce of our own industry employed in a way in which we have some advantage. The general industry of the country, being always in proportion to the capital which employs it, will not thereby be diminished, no more than that of the above-mentioned artificers; but only left to find out the way in which it can be employed with the greatest advantage. It is certainly not employed to the greatest advantage when it is thus directed towards an object which it can buy cheaper than it can make. The value of its annual produce is certainly more or less diminished when it is thus turned away from producing commodities evidently of more value than the commodity which it is directed to produce. According to the supposition, that commodity could be purchased from foreign countries cheaper than it can be made at home. It could, therefore, have been purchased with a part only of the commodities, or, what is the same thing, with a part only of the price of the commodities, which the industry employed by an equal capital would have produced at home, had it been left to follow its natural course. The industry of the country, therefore, is thus turned away from a more to a less advantageous employment, and the exchangeable value of its annual produce, instead of being increased, according to the intention of the lawgiver, must necessarily be diminished by every such regulation.

By means of such regulations, indeed, a particular manufacture may sometimes be acquired sooner than it could have been otherwise, and after a certain time may be made at home as cheap or cheaper than in the foreign country. But though the industry of the society may be thus carried with advantage into a particular channel sooner than it could have been otherwise, it will by no means follow that the sum total, either of its industry, or of its revenue, can ever be augmented by any such regulation. The industry of the society can augment only in proportion as its capital augments, and its capital can augment only in proportion to what can be gradually saved out of its revenue. But the immediate effect of every such regulation is to diminish its revenue, and what diminishes its revenue is certainly not very likely to augment its capital faster than it would have augmented of its own accord had both capital and industry been left to find out their natural employments.

Though for want of such regulations the society should never acquire the proposed manufacture, it would not, upon that account, necessarily be the poorer in any one period of its duration. In every period of its duration its whole capital and industry might still have been employed, though upon different objects, in the manner that was most advantageous at the time. In every period its revenue might have been the greatest which its capital could afford, and both capital and revenue might have been augmented[11] with the greatest possible rapidity.

The natural advantages which one country has over another in producing particular commodities are sometimes so great that it is acknowledged by all the world to be in vain to struggle with them. By means of glasses, hotbeds, and hot walls, very good grapes can be raised in Scotland, and very good wine too can be made of them at about thirty times the expence for which at least equally good can be brought from foreign countries. Would it be a reasonable law to prohibit the importation of all foreign wines merely to encourage the making of claret and burgundy in Scotland? But if there would be a manifest absurdity in turning towards any employment thirty times more of the capital and industry of the country than would be necessary to purchase from foreign countries an equal quantity of the commodities wanted, there must be an absurdity, though not altogether so glaring, yet exactly of the same kind, in turning towards any such employment a thirtieth, or even a three-hundredth part more of either. Whether the advantages which one country has over another be natural or acquired is in this respect of no consequence. As long as the one country has those advantages, and the other wants them, it will always be more advantageous for the latter rather to buy of the former than to make. It is an acquired advantage only, which one artificer has over his neighbour, who exercises another trade; and yet they both find it more advantageous to buy of one another than to make what does not belong to their particular trades.

Merchants and manufacturers are the people who derive the greatest advantage from this monopoly of the home-market. The prohibition of the importation of foreign cattle, and of salt provisions, together with the high duties upon foreign corn, which in times of moderate plenty amount to a prohibition,[12] are not near so advantageous to the graziers and farmers of Great Britain as other regulations of the same kind are to its merchants and manufacturers. Manufactures, those of the finer kind especially, are more easily transported from one country to another than corn or cattle. It is in the fetching and carrying manufactures, accordingly, that foreign trade is chiefly employed. In manufactures, a very small advantage will enable foreigners to undersell our own workmen, even in the home-market. It will require a very great one to enable them to do so in the rude produce of the soil. If the free importation of foreign manufactures were[13] permitted, several of the home manufactures would probably suffer, and some of them, perhaps, go to ruin altogether, and a considerable part of the stock and industry at present employed in them would be forced to find out some other employment. But the freest importation of the rude produce of the soil could have no such effect upon the agriculture of the country.

If the importation of foreign cattle, for example, were made ever so free, so few could be imported that the grazing trade of Great Britain could be little affected by it. Live cattle are, perhaps, the only commodity of which the transportation is more expensive by sea than by land. By land they carry themselves to market. By sea, not only the cattle, but their food and their water too, must be carried at no small expence and inconveniency. The short sea between Ireland and Great Britain, indeed, renders the importation of Irish cattle more easy. But though the free importation of them, which was lately permitted only for a limited time, were rendered perpetual, it could have no considerable effect upon the interest of the graziers of Great Britain. Those parts of Great Britain which border upon the Irish Sea are all grazing countries. Irish cattle could never be imported for their use, but must be driven through those very extensive countries, at no small expence and inconveniency, before they could arrive at their proper market. Fat cattle could not be driven so far. Lean cattle, therefore, only could be imported, and such importation could interfere, not with the interest of the feeding or fattening countries, to which, by reducing the price of lean cattle, it would rather be advantageous, but with that of the breeding countries only. The small number of Irish cattle imported since their importation was permitted, together with the good price at which lean cattle still continue to sell, seem to demonstrate that even the breeding countries of Great Britain are never likely to be much affected by the free importation of Irish cattle. The common people of Ireland, indeed, are said to have sometimes opposed with violence the exportation of their cattle. But if the exporters had found any great advantage in continuing the trade, they could easily, when the law was on their side, have conquered this mobbish opposition.

Feeding and fattening countries, besides, must always be highly improved, whereas breeding countries are generally uncultivated. The high price of lean cattle, by augmenting the value of uncultivated land, is like a bounty against improvement. To any country which was highly improved throughout, it would be more advantageous to import its lean cattle than to breed them. The province of Holland, accordingly, is said to follow this maxim at present. The mountains of Scotland, Wales, and Northumberland, indeed, are countries not capable of much improvement, and seem destined by nature to be the breeding countries of Great Britain. The freest importation of foreign cattle could have no other effect than to hinder those breeding countries from taking advantage of the increasing population and improvement of the rest of the kingdom, from raising their price to an exorbitant height, and from laying a real tax upon all the more improved and cultivated parts of the country.

The freest importation of salt provisions, in the same manner, could have as little effect upon the interest of the graziers of Great Britain as that of live cattle. Salt provisions are not only a very bulky commodity, but when compared with fresh meat, they are a commodity both of worse quality, and as they cost more labour and expence, of higher price. They could never, therefore, come into competition with the fresh meat, though they might with the salt provisions of the country. They might be used for victualling ships for distant voyages and such like uses, but could never make any considerable part of the food of the people. The small quantity of salt provisions imported from Ireland since their importation was rendered free is an experimental proof that our graziers have nothing to apprehend from it. It does not appear that the price of butcher's meat has ever been sensibly affected by it.

Even the free importation of foreign corn could very little affect the interest of the farmers of Great Britain. Corn is a much more bulky commodity than butcher's meat. A pound of wheat at a penny is as dear as a pound of butcher's meat at fourpence. The small quantity of foreign corn imported even in times of the greatest scarcity may satisfy our farmers that they can have nothing to fear from the freest importation. The average quantity imported, one year with another, amounts only, according to the very well informed author of the tracts upon the corn trade, to twenty-three thousand seven hundred and twenty-eight quarters of all sorts of grain, and does not exceed the five hundred and seventy-one part of the annual consumption.[14] But as the bounty upon corn occasions a greater exportation in years of plenty, so it must of consequence occasion a greater importation in years of scarcity than in the actual state of tillage[15] would otherwise take place. By means of it the plenty of one year does not compensate the scarcity of another, and as the average quantity exported is necessarily augmented by it, so must likewise, in the actual state of tillage, the average quantity imported. If there were[16] no bounty, as less corn would be exported, so it is probable that, one year with another, less would be imported than at present. The corn merchants, the fetchers and carriers of corn between Great Britain and foreign countries would have much less employment, and might suffer considerably; but the country gentlemen and farmers could suffer very little. It is in the corn merchants accordingly, rather than in the country gentlemen and farmers, that I have observed the greatest anxiety for the renewal and continuation of the bounty.

Country gentlemen and farmers are, to their great honour, of all people, the least subject to the wretched spirit of monopoly. The undertaker of a great manufactory is sometimes alarmed if another work of the same kind is established within twenty miles of him. The Dutch undertaker of the woollen manufacture at Abbeville[17] stipulated that no work of the same kind should be established within thirty leagues of that city. Farmers and country gentlemen, on the contrary, are generally disposed rather to promote than to obstruct the cultivation and improvement of their neighbours' farms and estates. They have no secrets such as those of the greater part of manufacturers, but are generally rather fond of communicating to their neighbours and of extending as far as possible any new practice which they have found to be advantageous. *Pius Questus*, says old Cato, *stabilissimusque, minimeque invidiosus; minimeque male cogitantes sunt, qui in eo studio occupati sunt*.[18] Country gentlemen and farmers, dispersed in different parts of the country, cannot so easily combine as merchants and manufacturers, who, being collected into towns, and accustomed to that exclusive corporation spirit which prevails in them, naturally endeavour to obtain against all their countrymen the same exclusive privilege which they generally possess against the inhabitants of their respective towns. They accordingly seem to have been the original inventors of those restraints upon the importation of foreign goods which secure to them the monopoly of the home-market. It was probably in imitation of them, and to put themselves upon a level with those who, they found, were disposed to oppress them, that the country gentlemen and farmers of Great Britain in so far forgot the generosity which is natural to their station as to demand the exclusive privilege of supplying their countrymen with corn and butcher's-meat. They did not perhaps take time to consider how much less their interest could be affected by the freedom of trade than that of the people whose example they followed.

To prohibit by a perpetual law the importation of foreign corn and cattle is in reality to enact that the population and industry of the country shall at no time exceed what the rude produce of its own soil can maintain.

There seem, however, to be two cases in which it will generally be advantageous to lay some burden upon foreign for the encouragement of domestic industry.

The first is, when some particular sort of industry is necessary for the defence of the country. The defence of Great Britain, for example, depends very much upon the number of its sailors and shipping. The act of navigation,[19] therefore, very properly endeavours to give the sailors and shipping of Great Britain the monopoly of the trade of their own country in some cases by absolute prohibitions and in others by heavy burdens upon the shipping of foreign countries. The following are the principal dispositions of this Act.

First, all ships, of which the owners and three-fourths of the mariners are not British subjects, are prohibited, upon pain of forfeiting ship and cargo, from trading to the British settlements and plantations, or from being employed in the coasting trade of Great Britain.[20]

Secondly, a great variety of the most bulky articles of importation can be brought into Great Britain only, either in such ships as are above described, or in ships of the country where those goods are purchased, and of which the owners, masters, and three-fourths of the mariners are of that particular country; and when imported even in ships of this latter kind, they are subject to double aliens duty. If imported in ships of any other country, the penalty is forfeiture of ship and goods.[21] When this act was made, the Dutch were, what they still are, the great carriers of Europe, and by this regulation they were entirely excluded from being the carriers to Great Britain, or from importing to us the goods of any other European country.

Thirdly, a great variety of the most bulky articles of importation are prohibited from being imported, even in British ships, from any country but that in which they are produced, under pains of forfeiting ship and cargo.[22] This regulation, too, was probably intended against the Dutch. Holland was then, as now, the great emporium for all European goods, and by this regulation British ships were hindered from loading in Holland the goods of any other European country.

Fourthly, salt fish of all kinds, whale-fins, whalebone, oil, and blubber, not caught by and cured on board British vessels, when imported into Great Britain, are subjected to double aliens duty.[23] The Dutch, as they are they the principal, were then the only fishers in Europe that attempted to supply foreign nations with fish. By this regulation, a very heavy burden was laid upon their supplying Great Britain.

When the act of navigation was made, though England and Holland were not actually at war, the most violent animosity subsisted between the two nations. It had begun during the government of the Long Parliament, which first framed this act,[24] and it broke out soon after in the Dutch wars during that of the Protector and of Charles the Second. It is not impossible, therefore, that some of the regulations of this famous act may have proceeded from national animosity. They are as wise, however, as if they had all been dictated by the most deliberate wisdom. National animosity at that particular time aimed at the very same object which the most deliberate wisdom would have recommended, the diminution of the naval power of Holland, the only naval power which could endanger the security of England.

The act of navigation is not favourable to foreign commerce, or to the growth of that opulence which can arise from it. The interest of a nation in its commercial relations to foreign nations is, like that of a merchant with regard to the different people with whom he deals, to buy as cheap and to sell as dear as possible. But it will be most likely to buy cheap, when by the most perfect freedom of trade it encourages all nations to bring to it the goods which it has occasion to purchase; and, for the same reason, it will be most likely to sell dear, when its markets are thus filled with the greatest number of buyers. The act of navigation, it is true, lays no burden upon foreign ships that come to export the produce of British industry. Even the ancient aliens duty, which used to be paid upon all goods exported as well as imported, has, by several subsequent acts, been taken off from the greater part of the articles of exportation.[25] But if foreigners, either by prohibitions or high duties, are hindered from coming to sell, they cannot always afford to come to buy; because coming without a cargo, they must lose the freight from their own country to Great Britain. By diminishing the number of sellers, therefore, we necessarily diminish that of buyers, and are thus likely not only to buy foreign goods dearer, but to sell our own cheaper, than if there was a more perfect freedom of trade. As defence, however, is of much more importance than opulence, the act of navigation is, perhaps, the wisest of all the commercial regulations of England.

The second case, in which it will generally be advantageous to lay some burden upon foreign for the encouragement of domestic industry is, when some tax is imposed at home upon the produce of the latter. In this case, it seems reasonable that an equal tax should be imposed upon the like produce of the former. This would not give the monopoly of the home market to domestic industry, nor turn towards a particular employment a greater share of the stock and labour of the country than what would naturally go to it. It would only hinder any part of what would naturally go to it from being turned away by the tax into a less natural direction, and would leave the competition between foreign and domestic industry, after the tax, as nearly as possible upon the same footing as before it. In Great Britain, when any such tax is laid upon the produce of domestic industry, it is usual at the same time, in order to stop the clamorous complaints of our merchants and manufacturers that they will be undersold at home, to lay a much heavier duty upon the importation of all foreign goods of the same kind.

This second limitation of the freedom of trade according to some people should, upon some occasions, be extended much farther than to the precise foreign commodities which could come into competition with those which had been taxed at home. When the necessaries of life have been taxed any country, it becomes proper, they pretend, to tax not only the like necessaries of life imported from other countries, but all sorts of foreign goods which can come into competition with anything that is

the produce of domestic industry. Subsistence, they say, becomes necessarily dearer in consequence of such taxes; and the price of labour must always rise with the price of the labourers' subsistence. Every commodity, therefore, which is the produce of domestic industry, though not immediately taxed itself, becomes dearer in consequence of such taxes, because the labour which produces it becomes so. Such taxes, therefore, are really equivalent, they say, to a tax upon every particular commodity produced at home. In order to put domestic upon the same footing with foreign industry, therefore, it becomes necessary, they think, to lay some duty upon every foreign commodity equal to this enhancement of the price of the home commodities with which it can come into competition.

Whether taxes upon the necessaries of life, such as those in Great Britain upon[26] soap, salt, leather, candles, &c. necessarily raise the price of labour, and consequently that of all other commodities, I shall consider hereafter,[27] when I come to treat of taxes. Supposing, however, in the meantime, that they have this effect, and they have it undoubtedly, this general enhancement of the price of all commodities, in consequence of that of labour, is a case which differs in the two following respects from that of a particular commodity of which the price was enhanced by a particular tax immediately imposed upon it.

First, it might always be known with great exactness how far the price of such a commodity could be enhanced by such a tax: but how far the general enhancement of the price of labour might affect that of every different commodity about which labour was employed could never be known with any tolerable exactness. It would be impossible, therefore, to proportion with any tolerable exactness the tax upon every foreign to this enhancement of the price of every home commodity.

Secondly, taxes upon the necessaries of life have nearly the same effect upon the circumstances of the people as a poor soil and a bad climate. Provisions are thereby rendered dearer in the same manner as if it required extraordinary labour and expence to raise them. As in the natural scarcity arising from soil and climate it would be absurd to direct the people in what manner they ought to employ their capitals and industry, so is it[28] likewise in the artificial scarcity arising from such taxes. To be left to accommodate, as well as they could, their industry to their situation, and to find out those employments in which, notwithstanding their unfavourable circumstances, they might have some advantage either in the home or in the foreign market, is what in both cases would evidently be most for their advantage. To lay a new tax upon them, because they are already overburdened with taxes, and because they already pay too dear for the necessaries of life, to make them likewise pay too dear for the greater part of other commodities, is certainly a most absurd way of making amends.

Such taxes, when they have grown up to a certain height, are a curse equal to the barrenness of the earth and the inclemency of the heavens; and yet it is in the richest and most industrious countries that they have been most generally imposed. No other countries could support so great a disorder. As the strongest bodies only can live and enjoy health under an unwholesome regimen, so the nations only that in every sort of industry have the greatest natural and acquired advantages can subsist and prosper under such taxes. Holland is the country in Europe in which they abound most, and which from peculiar circumstances continues to prosper, not by means of them, as has been most absurdly supposed, but in spite of them.

As there are two cases in which it will generally be advantageous to lay some burden upon foreign for the encouragement of domestic industry, so there are two others in which it may sometimes be a matter of deliberation; in the one, how far it is proper to continue the free importation of certain foreign goods; and in the other, how far, or in what manner, it may be proper to restore that free importation after it has been for some time interrupted.

The case in which it may sometimes be a matter of deliberation how far it is proper to continue the free importation of certain foreign goods is, when some foreign nation restrains by high duties or prohibitions the importation of some of our manufactures into their country. Revenge in this case naturally dictates retaliation, and that we should impose the like duties and prohibitions upon the importation of some or all of their manufactures into ours. Nations, accordingly, seldom fail to retaliate in this manner. The French have been particularly forward to favour their own manufactures by restraining the importation of such foreign goods as could come into competition with them. In this consisted a great part of the policy of Mr. Colbert, who, notwithstanding his great abilities, seems in this case to have been imposed upon by the sophistry of merchants and manufacturers, who are always demanding a monopoly against their countrymen. It is at present the opinion of the most intelligent men in France that his operations of this kind have not been beneficial to his country. That minister, by the tariff of 1667, imposed very high duties upon a great number of foreign manufactures. Upon his refusing to moderate them in favour of the Dutch, they in 1671 prohibited the importation of the wines, brandies, and manufactures of France. The war of 1672 seems to have been in part occasioned by this commercial dispute. The peace of Nimeguen put an end to it in 1678 by moderating some of those duties in favour of the Dutch, who in consequence took off their prohibition. It was about the same time that the French and English began mutually to oppress each other's industry by the like duties and prohibitions, of which the French, however, seem to have set the first example. The spirit of hostility which has subsisted between the two nations ever since has hitherto hindered them from being moderated on either side. In 1697 the English prohibited the importation of bonelace, the manufacture of Flanders. The government of that country, at that time under the dominion of Spain, prohibited in return the importation of English woollens. In 1700, the prohibition of importing bonelace into England was taken off upon condition that the importance of English woollens into Flanders should be put on the same footing as before.[29]

There may be good policy in retaliations of this kind, when there is a probability that they will procure the repeal of the high duties or prohibitions complained of. The recovery of a great foreign market will generally more than compensate the transitory inconveniency of paying dearer during a short time for some sorts of goods. To judge whether such retaliations are likely to produce such an effect does not, perhaps, belong so much to the science of a legislator, whose deliberations ought to be governed by general principles which are always the same, as to the skill of that insidious and crafty animal, vulgarly called a statesman or politician, whose councils are directed by the momentary fluctuations of affairs. When there is no probability that any such repeal can be procured, it seems a bad method of compensating the injury done to certain classes of our people to do another injury ourselves, not only to those classes, but to[30] almost all the other classes of them. When our neighbours prohibit some manufacture of ours, we generally prohibit, not only the same, for that alone would seldom affect them considerably, but some other manufacture of theirs. This may no doubt give encouragement to some particular class of workmen among ourselves, and by excluding some of their rivals, may enable them to raise their price in the home-market. Those workmen, however, who suffered by our neighbours prohibition will not be benefited by ours. On the contrary, they and almost all the other classes of our citizens will thereby be obliged to pay dearer than before for certain goods. Every such law, therefore, imposes a real tax upon the whole country, not in favour of that particular class of workmen who were injured by our neighbours prohibition, but of some other class.

The case in which it may sometimes be a matter of deliberation, how far, or in what manner, it is proper to restore the free importation of foreign goods, after it has been for some time interrupted, is, when particular manufactures, by means of high duties or prohibitions upon all foreign goods which can come into competition with them, have been so far extended as to employ a great multitude of hands. Humanity may in this case require that the freedom of trade should be restored only by slow gradations, and with a good deal of reserve and circumspection. Were those high duties and prohibitions taken away all at once, cheaper foreign goods of the same kind might be poured so fast into the home-market as to deprive all at once many thousands of our people of their ordinary employment and means of subsistence. The disorder which this would occasion might

no doubt be very considerable. It would in all probability, however, be much less than is commonly imagined, for the two following reasons:-

First, all those manufactures, of which any part is commonly exported to other European countries without a bounty, could be very little affected by the freest importation of foreign goods. Such manufactures must be sold as cheap abroad as any other foreign goods of the same quality and kind, and consequently must be sold cheaper at home. They would still, therefore, keep possession of the home-market, and though a capricious man of fashion might sometimes prefer foreign wares, merely because they were foreign, to cheaper and better goods of the same kind that were made at home, this folly could, from the nature of things, extend to so few that it could make no sensible impression upon the general employment of the people. But a great part of all the different branches of our woollen manufacture, of our tanned leather, and of our hardware, are annually exported to other European countries without any bounty, and these are the manufactures which employ the greatest number of hands. The silk, perhaps, is the manufacture which would suffer the most by this freedom of trade, and after it the linen, though the latter much less than the former.

Secondly, though a great number of people should, by thus restoring the freedom of trade, be thrown all at once out of their ordinary employment and common method of subsistence, it would by no means follow that they would thereby be deprived either of employment or subsistence. By the reduction of the army and navy at the end of the late war, more than a hundred thousand soldiers and seamen, a number equal to what is employed in the greatest manufactures, were all at once thrown out of their ordinary employment; but, though they no doubt suffered some inconveniency, they were not thereby deprived of all employment and subsistence. The greater part of the seamen, it is probable, gradually betook themselves to the merchant-service as they could find occasion, and in the meantime both they and the soldiers were absorbed in the great mass of the people, and employed in a great variety of occupations. Not only no great convulsion, but no sensible disorder arose from so great a change in the situation of more than a hundred thousand men, all accustomed to the use of arms, and many of them to rapine and plunder. The number of vagrants was scarce any-where sensibly increased by it, even the wages of labour were not reduced by it in any occupation, so far as I have been able to learn, except in that of seamen in the merchant-service. But if we compare together the habits of a soldier and of any sort of manufacturer, we shall find that those of the latter do not tend so much to disqualify him from being employed in a new trade, as those of the former from being employed in any. The manufacturer has always been accustomed to look for his subsistence from his labour only: the soldier to expect it from his pay. Application and industry have been familiar to the one; idleness and dissipation to the other. But it is surely much easier to change the direction of industry from one sort of labour to another than to turn idleness and dissipation to any. To the greater part of manufactures besides, it has already been observed,[31] there are other collateral manufactures of so similar a nature that a workman can easily transfer his industry from one of them to another. The greater part of such workmen too are occasionally employed in country labour. The stock which employed them in a particular manufacture before will still remain in the country to employ an equal number of people in some other way. The capital of the country remaining the same, the demand for labour will likewise be the same, or very nearly the same, though it may be exerted in different places and for different occupations. Soldiers and seamen, indeed, when discharged from the king's service, are at liberty to exercise any trade, within any town or place of Great Britain or Ireland.[32] Let the same natural liberty of exercising what species of industry they please, be restored to all his Majesty's subjects, in the same manner as to soldiers and seamen; that is, break down the exclusive privileges of corporations, and repeal the statute of apprenticeship, both which are real encroachments upon natural liberty, and add to these the repeal of the law of settlements, so that a poor workman, when thrown out of employment either in one trade or in one place, may seek for it in another trade or in another place without the fear either of a prosecution or of a removal, and neither the public nor the individuals will suffer much more from the occasional disbanding some particular classes of manufacturers than from that of soldiers. Our manufacturers have no doubt great merit with their country, but they cannot have more than those who defend it with their blood, nor deserve to be treated with more delicacy.

To expect, indeed, that the freedom of trade should ever be entirely restored in Great Britain is as absurd as to expect that an Oceana or Utopia[33] should ever be established in it. Not only the prejudices of the public, but what is much more unconquerable, the private interests of many individuals, irresistibly oppose it. Were the officers of the army to oppose with the same zeal and unanimity any reduction in the numbers of forces with which master manufacturers set themselves against every law that is likely to increase the number of their rivals in the home-market; were the former to animate their soldiers in the same manner as the latter enflame their workmen to attack with violence and outrage the proposers of any such regulation, to attempt to reduce the army would be as dangerous as it has now become to attempt to diminish in any respect the monopoly which our manufacturers have obtained against us. This monopoly has so much increased the number of some particular tribes of them that, like an overgrown standing army, they have become formidable to the government, and upon many occasions intimidate the legislature. The Member of Parliament who supports every proposal for strengthening this monopoly is sure to acquire not only the reputation of understanding trade, but great popularity and influence with an order of men whose numbers and wealth render them of great importance. If he opposes them, on the contrary, and still more if he has authority enough to be able to thwart them, neither the most acknowledged probity, nor the highest rank, nor the greatest public services can protect him from the most infamous abuse and detraction, from personal insults, nor sometimes from real danger, arising from the insolent outrage of furious and disappointed monopolists.

The undertaker of a great manufacture, who, by the home-markets being suddenly laid open to the competition of foreigners, should be obliged to abandon his trade, would no doubt suffer very considerably. That part of his capital which had usually been employed in purchasing materials and in paying his workmen might, without much difficulty, perhaps, find another employment. But that part of it which was fixed in workhouses, and in the instruments of trade, could scarce be disposed of without considerable loss. The equitable regard, therefore, to his interest requires that changes of this kind should never be introduced suddenly, but slowly, gradually, and after a very long warning. The legislature, were it possible that its deliberations could be always directed, not by the clamorous importunity of partial interests, but by an extensive view of the general good, ought upon this very account, perhaps, to be particularly careful neither to establish any new monopolies of this kind, nor to extend further those which are already established. Every such regulation introduces some degree of real disorder into the constitution of the state, which it will be difficult afterwards to cure without occasioning another disorder.

How far it may be proper to impose taxes upon the importation of foreign goods, in order not to prevent their importation but to raise a revenue for government, I shall consider hereafter when I come to treat of taxes.[34] Taxes imposed with a view to prevent, or even to diminish importation, are evidently as destructive of the revenue of the customs as of the freedom of trade.

NOTES FOR THIS CHAPTER

1. [See above, p. 443.]
2. [See below, vol. ii., pp. 43, 44.]
3. [11 and 12 Ed. III., c. 3; 4 Ed. IV., c. 7.]
4. [6 Geo. III., c. 28.]
5. [By the additional duties. 7 Geo. III., c. 28.]
6. [Misprinted 'manufactures' in ed. 5.]
7. [This sentence appears first in Additions and Corrections and ed. 3.]
8. [Ed. 1 reads 'certain'.]
9. [Above, pp. 390–394.]
10. [Ed. 1 reads 'the' here.]
11. [Ed. 1 reads 'augmenting,' which seems more correct.]
12. [Above, p. 474, and below, vol. ii., pp. 43, 44.]
13. [Eds. 1-3 read 'was' here and seven lines lower down.]
14. [Charles Smith, *Three Tracts on the Corn-Trade and Corn-Laws*, pp. 144–145. The same figure is quoted below, vol. ii. p. 42.]
15. [Ed. 1 does not contain the words 'in the actual state of tillage'.]
16. [Eds. 1-3 read 'was'.]
17. [Joseph Van Robais in 1669.—John Smith, *Memoirs of Wool*, vol. ii., pp. 426, 427, but neither John Smith nor Charles King, *British Merchant*, 1721, vol. ii., pp. 93, 94, gives the particular stipulation mentioned.]
18. [Cato, *De re rustica, ad init.*, but '*Questus*' should of course be '*quæstus*'.]
19. [12 Car. II., c. 18, 'An act for the encouraging and increasing of shipping and navigation.']
20. [§§ 1 and 6.]
21. [§§ 8 and 9. Eds. 1 and 2 read 'ship and cargo'. The alteration was probably made in order to avoid wearisome repetition of the same phrase in the three paragraphs.]
22. [§ 4, which, however, applies to all such goods of foreign growth and manufacture as were forbidden to be imported except in English ships, not only to bulky goods. The words 'great variety of the most bulky articles of importation' occur at the beginning of the previous paragraph, and are perhaps copied here by mistake.]
23. [§ 5.]
24. [In 1651, by 'An act for the increase of shipping and encouragement of the navigation of this nation,' p. 1,449 in the collection of Commonwealth Acts.]
25. [By 25 Car. II., c. 6, § 1, except on coal. The plural 'acts' may refer to renewing acts. Anderson, *Commerce*, A.D. 1672.]
26. [Ed. 1 contains the words 'malt, beer' here.]
27. [Below, vol. ii., pp. 399–405.]
28. [Ed. 1 reads 'it is'.]
29. [The importation of bone lace was prohibited by 13 and 14 Car. II., c. 13, and 9, and 10 W. III., c. 9, was

passed to make the prohibition more effectual. By 11 and 12 W. III., c. 11, it was provided that the prohibition should cease three months after English woollen manufactures were readmitted to Flanders.]

30. [Ed. 1 reads 'injury ourselves, both to those classes and to'.]

31. [Above, p. 151.]

32. [12 Car. II., c. 16; 12 Ann., st. 1, § 13; 3 Geo. III., c. 8, gave this liberty after particular wars.]

33. [Ed. 1 reads 'Utopea'.]

34. [Below, vol. ii., pp. 426–431.]

On Foreign Trade

By David Ricardo

Under a system of perfectly free commerce, each country naturally devotes its capital and labour to such employments as are most beneficial to each. This pursuit of individual advantage is admirably connected with the universal good of the whole. By stimulating industry, by rewarding ingenuity, and by using most efficaciously the peculiar powers bestowed by nature, it distributes labour most effectively and most economically: while, by increasing the general mass of productions, it diffuses general benefit, and binds together, by one common tie of interest and intercourse, the universal society of nations throughout the civilised world. It is this principle which determines that wine shall be made in France and Portugal, that corn shall be grown in America and Poland, and that hardware and other goods shall be manufactured in England.

In one and the same country, profits are, generally speaking, always on the same level; or differ only as the employment of capital may be more or less secure and agreeable. It is not so between different countries. If the profits of capital employed in Yorkshire should exceed those of capital employed in London, capital would speedily move from London to Yorkshire, and an equality of profits would be effected; but if in consequence of the diminished rate of production in the lands of England, from the increase of capital and population, wages should rise and profits fall, it would not follow that capital and population would necessarily move from England to Holland, or Spain, or Russia, where profits might be higher.

If Portugal had no commercial connection with other countries, instead of employing a great part of her capital and industry in the production of wines, with which she purchases for her own use the cloth and hardware of other countries, she would be obliged to devote a part of that capital to the manufacture of those commodities, which she would thus obtain probably inferior in quality as well as quantity.

The quantity of wine which she shall give in exchange for the cloth of England is not determined by the respective quantities of labour devoted to the production of each, as it would be if both commodities were manufactured in England, or both in Portugal.

England may be so circumstanced that to produce the cloth may require the labour of 100 men for one year; and if she attempted to make the wine, it might require the labour of 120 men for the same time. England would therefore find it her interest to import wine, and to purchase it by the exportation of cloth.

To produce the wine in Portugal might require only the labour of 80 men for one year, and to produce the cloth in the same country might require the labour of 90 men for the same time. It would therefore be advantageous for her to export wine in exchange for cloth. This exchange might even take place notwithstanding that the commodity imported by Portugal could be produced there with less labour than in England. Though she could make the cloth with the labour of 90 men, she would import it from a country where it required the labour of 100 men to produce it, because it would be advantageous to her rather to employ her capital in the production of wine, for which she would obtain more cloth from England, than she could produce by diverting a portion of her capital from the cultivation of vines to the manufacture of cloth.

Thus England would give the produce of the labour of 100 men for the produce of the labour of 80. Such an exchange could not take place between the individuals of the same country. The labour of 100 Englishmen cannot be given for that of 80 Englishmen, but the produce of the labour of 100 Englishmen may be given for the produce of the labour of 80 Portuguese, 60 Russians, or 120 East Indians. The difference in this respect, between a single country and many, is easily accounted for, by considering the difficulty with which capital moves from one country to another, to seek a more profitable employment, and the activity with which it invariably passes from one province to another in the same country.[1]

It would undoubtedly be advantageous to the capitalists of England, and to the consumers in both countries, that under such circumstances the wine and the cloth should both be made in Portugal, and therefore that the capital and labour of England employed in making cloth should be removed to Portugal for that purpose. In that case, the relative value of these commodities would be regulated by the same principle as if one were the produce of Yorkshire; and the other of London: and in every other case, if capital freely flowed towards those countries where it could be most profitably employed, there could be no difference in the rate of profit, and no other difference in the real or labour price of commodities than the additional quantity of labour required to convey them to the various markets where they were to be sold.

Experience, however, shows that the fancied or real insecurity of capital, when not under the immediate control of its owner, together with the natural disinclination which every man has to quit the country of his birth and connections, and intrust himself, with all his habits fixed, to a strange government and new laws, check the emigration of capital …

---

1 It will appear, then, that a country possessing very considerable advantages in machinery and skill, and which may therefore be enabled to manufacture commodities with much less labour than her neighbours, may, in return for such commodities, import a portion of the corn required for its consumption, even if its land were more fertile and corn could be grown with less labour than in the country from which it was imported. Two men can both make shoes and hats, and one is superior to the other in both employments; but in making hats he can only exceed' his competitor by one-fifth or 20 percent, and in making shoes he can excel him by one-third or 33 percent—will it not be for the interest of both that the superior man should employ himself exclusively in making shoes, and the inferior man in making hats?

Different is Beautiful

By Dima Yazji Shamoun*

You may have noticed that, nowadays, humans can afford many luxuries, among which is leisure. Though it seems quite ordinary to afford a luxury—that even the word luxury seems unwarranted—as simple as leisure, humans for much of their existence had to produce everything they consumed, from food to clothing to shelter and myriad other products. Leisure was in indeed a luxury. How were we able to transform what we do with our time so that we can *afford* leisure? How do we pay for our leisure? The easy answer: other people. To be specific we mean the *Division of Labor (DoL)*, or specialization. We don't spend our time trying to do everything; we concentrate on what we perceive to be our *comparative advantage* and trade with other people for the rest.

If I am handier with an axe and you with a bow and arrow, then I will have a fine pile of wood and you a delicious dinner. But then I will be hungry and you will be cold, and it will naturally become clear that we are both better off cooperating. I should concentrate my efforts on shelter; you, on the food.

But what of the case where you are the superior lumberjack *and* hunter? Surely I should be suspicious of your overtures toward cooperation, since the only reason why you would want to collaborate with someone who is your inferior is that you plan to profit at my expense! Right?

Here is one of the greatest lessons of economics: it is our *differences* that encourage our cooperation, *not* our similarities. This is the lesson that shows that, though it gets little publicity, the study of economics is as much about cooperation as it is about competition. In fact, more so. And it does not even matter if one party holds even an *absolute* advantage across all activities; for cooperation to emerge *it only matters that they are different.*

In the following three cases we will follow as two individuals, Farmer Smith and Farmer Jones, collect wood for shelter and catch rabbits for food. Table 1 describes the first scenario in which Farmer Smith is the superior rabbit hunter, and Jones the wood collector. Thus, the first is a case of *comparative advantage,* where each individual is relatively more skilled than the other in a specific domain. As Table 1 shows, if Smith and Jones decide to collaborate, then

---

* The author is grateful to the insights of Dr. Jörg Guido Hülsmann whose lecture on The Division of Labor and Social Order has inspired the contents of this essay.

Table 1: Comparative Advantage

| | PRODUCTIVITY | | IMPACT OF DOL (10H/DAY) | |
	Wood	Rabbits	Before	After
Bob	10kg/h	2r/h	50kg; 10r	20r
Jones	15kg/h	1r/h	75kg; 5r	150kg
Total			**125kg; 15r**	**150kg; 20r**

Smith can concentrate on catching the rabbits and Jones can focus on collecting the wood. Assuming a 10-hour workday and the specified productivity levels, it pays off for both Smith and Jones to collaborate through specialization. They can increase the total amount of wood and rabbits, or they can collect the same total as before and take some hours of leisure time.

More specifically, before DoL, Smith can collect 50kg of wood and catch 10 rabbits a day, and Jones can collect 75kg of wood and 5 rabbits. With specialization, Smith, the rabbit-catching expert, can allocate all 10 hours to catching rabbits and thus snare 20 rabbits by the end of the day. Similarly Jones, the wood-collecting specialist, can allocate all 10 hours to collecting wood, thereby accumulating 150kg of wood. As a result of this specialization, they can both increase their stock of wood by 12.5kg (=150kg–125kg/2) and their stock of rabbits by 2.5r (=20r–15r/2). In other words, Smith ends up with 62.5kg of wood and 12.5 rabbits, whereas Jones ends up with 87.5kg of wood and 7.5 rabbits.

Table 2 modifies the first scenario. Now, Jones is superior to Smith *both* in collecting wood and catching rabbits. If Jones suggests collaboration to Smith, is he being charitable towards Smith? As Table 2 shows, Smith should collaborate and Jones

is *not* offering charity to Smith; he is instead simply pursuing his own interests.

But now, since Jones exceeds Smith in both activities, should they toss a coin to decide who specializes in what activity? Not quite. There is a better way to decide. Note that the common unit of account here is time. In one hour, Smith can either catch two rabbits or collect 10kg of wood; for Jones the numbers are four and 15, respectively. Therefore, the opportunity cost of each rabbit is 5kg of wood (=10kg/2) for Smith and 3.75kg of wood (=15kg/4) for Jones. Alternatively, one kilo of wood costs Smith one fifth of a rabbit (so to speak) and Jones just over a quarter. We can see then that the most profitable distribution of their efforts involves Smith spending his entire day collecting wood, with Jones joining him for two hours, and then allocating his final eight hours to catching rabbits. As Table 2 shows, the new arrangement increases the wealth of both individuals. Each gains 2.5kg of wood (=130kg–125kg/2) and a rabbit (=32r–30r/2), all for the same effort.

The final scenario, depicted in Table 3, describes a world of two identically skilled individuals. Though unlikely, this example best demonstrates why different is beautiful. They could decide to divide their duties by flipping a coin, but regardless of the tradeoff Table 3 shows that division in this case does not increase total production and the two parties

Table 2: Absolute Advantage

| | PRODUCTIVITY | | IMPACT OF DOL (10H/DAY) | |
	Wood	Rabbits	Before	After
Bob	10kg/h	2r/h	50kg; 10r	100kg
Jones	15kg/h	4r/h	75kg; 20r	30kg; 32r
Total			**125kg; 30r**	**130kg; 32r**

Table 3: Perfect Equality

	PRODUCTIVITY		IMPACT OF DOL (10H/DAY)	
	Wood	Rabbits	Before	After
Bob	10kg/h	2r/h	50kg; 10r	100kg
Jones	10kg/h	2r/h	50kg; 10r	20r
Total			**100kg; 20r**	**100kg; 20r**

are unable to improve on their status quo—at least not through a *mutually* beneficial agreement. *Ceteris paribus*, the only way for Smith or Jones to increase their wealth by exchange is by plunder.

Differences do not have to lead to confrontation. In fact, when the economic implications are properly understood, we have found that differences lead to cooperation, and that cooperation leads to wealth and leisure. The only circumstances where men do not gain from exchange would be in that terrible world where we were all the same. Different is beautiful.

The Balance of Trade

By Frédéric Bastiat

The balance of trade is an article of faith. We know what it consists in: if a country imports more than it exports, it loses the difference. Conversely, if its exports exceed its imports, the excess is to its profit. This is held to be an axiom, and laws are passed in accordance with it.

On this hypothesis, M. Mauguin warned us the day before yesterday, citing statistics, that France carries on a foreign trade in which it has managed to lose, out of good will, without being required to do so, two hundred million francs a year.

"You have lost by your trade, in eleven years, two billion francs. Do you understand what that means?"

Then, applying his infallible rule to the facts, he told us: "In 1847 you sold 605 million francs' worth of manufactured products, and you bought only 152 millions' worth. Hence, you *gained* 450 million."

"You bought 804 millions' worth of raw materials, and you sold only 114 million; hence, you *lost* 690 million."

This is an example of the dauntless naïveté of following an absurd premise to its logical conclusion. M. Mauguin has discovered the secret of making even Messrs. Darblay and Lebeuf laugh at the expense of the balance of trade. It is a great achievement, of which I cannot help being jealous.

Allow me to assess the validity of the rule according to which M. Mauguin and all the protectionists calculate profits and losses. I shall do so by recounting two business transactions which I have had the occasion to engage in.

I was at Bordeaux. I had a cask of wine which was worth 50 francs; I sent it to Liverpool, and the customhouse noted on its records an *export* of 50 francs.

At Liverpool the wine was sold for 70 francs. My representative converted the 70 francs into coal, which was found to be worth 90 francs on the market at Bordeaux. The customhouse hastened to record an *import* of 90 francs.

Balance of trade, or the excess of imports over exports: 40 francs.

These 40 francs, I have always believed, putting my trust in my books, I had gained. But M. Mauguin tells me that I have lost them, and that France has lost them in my person.

And why does M. Mauguin see a loss here? Because he supposes that any excess of imports over exports necessarily implies a balance that must be paid in cash. But where is there in the transaction that I speak of, which follows the pattern of all profitable commercial transactions, any balance to pay? Is it, then, so difficult to understand that a merchant compares the prices current in different markets and decides to trade only when he has the certainty, or at least the probability, of seeing the exported value return to him increased? Hence, what M. Mauguin calls *loss* should be called *profit*.

A few days after my transaction I had the simplicity to experience regret; I was sorry I had not waited. In fact, the price of wine fell at Bordeaux and rose at Liverpool; so that if I had not been so hasty, I could have bought at 40 francs and sold at 100 francs. I truly believed that on such a basis my *profit* would have been greater. But I learn from M. Mauguin that it is the *loss* that would have been more ruinous.

My second transaction had à very different result.

I had had some truffles shipped from Périgord which cost me 100 francs; they were destined for two distinguished English cabinet ministers for a very high price, which I proposed to turn into pounds sterling. Alas, I would have done better to eat them myself (I mean the truffles, not the English pounds or the Tories). All would not have been lost, as they were, for the ship that carried them off sank on its departure. The customs officer, who had noted on this occasion an export of 100 francs, never had any re-import to enter in this case.

Hence, M. Mauguin would say, France gained 100 francs; for it was, in fact, by this sum that the export, thanks to the shipwreck, exceeded the import. If the affair had turned out otherwise, if I had received 200 or 300 francs worth of English pounds, then the balance of trade would have been unfavorable, and France would have been the loser.

From the point of view of science, it is sad to think that all the commercial transactions which end in loss according to the businessmen concerned show a profit according to that class of theorists who are always declaiming against theory.

But from the point of view of practical affairs, it is even sadder, for what is the result?

Suppose that M. Mauguin had the power (and to a certain extent he has, by his votes) to substitute his calculations and desires for the calculations and desires of businessmen and to give, in his words, "a good commercial and industrial organization to the country, a good impetus to domestic industry." What would he do?

M. Mauguin would suppress by law all transactions that consist in buying at a low domestic price in order to sell at a high price abroad and in converting the proceeds into commodities eagerly sought after at home; for it is precisely in these transactions that the imported value exceeds the exported value.

Conversely, he would tolerate, and, indeed, he would encourage, if necessary by subsidies (from taxes on the public), all enterprises based on the idea of buying dearly in France in order to sell cheaply abroad; in other words, exporting what is useful to us in order to import what is useless. Thus, he would leave us perfectly free, for example, to send off cheeses from Paris to Amsterdam, in order to bring back the latest fashions from Amsterdam to Paris; for in this traffic the balance of trade would always be in our favor.

Yet, it is sad and, I dare add, degrading that the legislator will not let the interested parties decide and act for themselves in these matters, at their peril and risk. At least then everyone bears the responsibility for his own acts; he who makes a mistake is punished and is set right. But when the legislator imposes and prohibits, should he make a monstrous error in judgment, that error must become the rule of conduct for the whole of a great nation. In France we love freedom very much, but we hardly understand it. Oh, let us try to understand it better! We shall not love it any the less.

M. Mauguin has stated with imperturbable aplomb that there is not a statesman in England who does not accept the doctrine of the balance of trade. After having calculated the loss which, according to him, results from the excess of our imports, he cried out: "If a similar picture were to be presented to the English, they would shudder, and there is not a member in the House of Commons who would not feel that his seat was threatened."

For my part, I affirm that if someone were to say to the House of Commons: "The total value of what is exported from the country exceeds the total value of what is imported," it is then that they would feel threatened; and I doubt that a single speaker could be found who would dare to add: "The difference represents a profit."

In England they are convinced that it is important for the nation to receive more than it gives. Moreover, they have observed that this is the attitude of all businessmen; and that is why they have taken the side of *laissez faire* and are committed to restoring free trade.

Do Trade Deficits Matter?

By Paul Heyne

INTRODUCTION

Some things matter whether or not they exist. The Loch Ness monster is one. National trade deficits are another. Trade deficits obviously matter to many people, because (whatever they are) they seem to have significant consequences. They cause problems or create undesirable constraints or compel government policy changes.

It is often extraordinarily difficult, however, to determine the precise consequences of trade deficits, real or alleged. The current U.S. trade deficit, if we have one, provides a good example. Are the problems supposedly associated with it the *causes* of the deficit or its *effects*? One reason we cannot answer that question might be that we cannot agree whether the deficit is already here or merely impending. Has the United States been running a continual trade deficit since 1975, as some reports would have it? Or are we only on the way toward a deficit, as a consequence of our current economic recovery and the lagging recovery of our principal trading partners?

Both claims are made and published. Those who report to alarmed readers that the United States has run a trade deficit in every single month over the past seven years almost never stop to reconcile this "fact" with the equally well-established "fact" that

U.S. exports of goods and services exceeded imports from 1976 through 1982 by an annual average of almost $13 billion.[1] How can a $90 billion surplus be accumulated by running deficits each and every month?

The explanation, of course, is that the monthly "deficits" are the difference between merchandise exports and imports, while the annual "surpluses" are the difference between exports and imports of merchandise plus services. Now it is essential that the phrase "of course" appear in the above explanation, to avoid any implication that I think I am saying something new or profound by calling attention to the difference between the merchandise trade balance and the balance on goods and services. After careful reflection, however. I want to withdraw the phrase. Let the first sentence of this paragraph stand unblushingly stripped of its fig leaf.

It is quite possible that nothing at all in this paper is new or profound. That in fact is exactly how it appears to me. The entire essay seems to me to be a series of fairly obvious assertions. If I am going to start saying "of course," therefore, I will have to

---

1 In this paper all data on U.S. International transactions are based on the standard Department of Commerce calculations, as reported in numerous official publications. See, for example, the International Statistics section in the monthly issues of *Economic Indicators*.

do an awful lot of it, and that would quickly grow tiresome. More importantly, it would disguise the essential point I want to make, which is that we are not thinking carefully or communicating responsibly when we talk about trade deficits. I am therefore going to omit the defensive "of course" in everything that follows, and try instead to be clear. It might even happen that, if I make my position unmistakably clear, some critic will be able to rescue me from error, and show me why those who speak of trade deficits are in fact making sense, not wandering in darkness and confusion.

It isn't only backwoods editors or small-town journalists who treat deficits in merchandise trade as if they were more than they are. The *Wall Street Journal* and the *New York Times* frequently report the Commerce Department's monthly merchandise trade figures in a language of alarm, offering no hint to the reader that the deficits result from a partial accounting.[2] The government's recent forecast of a more than $100 billion merchandise trade deficit for 1984 was referred to by the *Journal* as "a red-ink total." If they do these things in a green tree, what shall be done in the dry? So let us return to fundamentals to see if we can first agree what it is we are talking about.

We should all be able to agree that any report of a deficit or surplus in a nation's total international transactions is necessarily based on a partial accounting of some sort, for the simple reason that all international economic transactions are treated as exchanges, in which, for accounting purposes, the value of whatever is given up is exactly equal to the value of what is obtained in return. Consequently, the balance of payments always and necessarily balances. If the flow of measured exports exceeds or falls short of the total of measured imports, measuring errors must have occurred—as they are bound to do in any attempt to keep track of the international transactions of 230 million people. The record keepers consequently add the difference to the smaller of the two flows and label it "statistical *discrepancy.*"[3]

It follows from this that any announcement of a deficit or surplus in a nation's foreign transactions results from a decision *not to count certain transactions.* Which ones? And why are they excluded? In order to see what might be going on here, we must first turn our attention to one of the most useful and simultaneously most misleading concepts in economics, the concept of *equilibrium.*

THE CONCEPT OF EQUILIBRIUM

In economic theory, an equilibrium situation is a situation of balance among contending forces. It is a stable situation, in the sense that it can be expected to persist as long as all the contending forces retain their present form. The crucial point to be noticed is that *equilibrium is a concept,* not something that can be observed empirically. Any and every constellation of economic variables is an equilibrium constellation *from some point of view.* After all, any actual situation must be the result of a balance among contending forces, however momentary that balance may be. And every imaginable situation will be an "equilibrium" if we imagine the appropriate circumstances.

The point is much easier to make with concrete examples.[4] Let's take the common textbook case of government price supports and an equilibrium price for corn. Although economists frequently characterize the equilibrium price as "the price that clears the market," this cannot be a correct definition since *the market clears at every price.* The quantity of corn purchased is always equal to the quantity sold, whatever the price, because purchases and sales are opposite sides of the same coin.

---

2   Readers who want to sample these reports should see the newspapers on the 29th day of any month.

3   The statistical discrepancy in recorded data for the United States came to $42 billion In 1982, an amount that swamps any defensible measurement of a deficit (or surplus) for the year. I do not know why this bit of news has so little effect on those who anxiously report on the shifting course of deficits and surpluses.

4   My argument in this section has been extensively influenced by the perceptive analysis in Steven N. S. Cheung, "A Theory of Price Control, *Journal of Law and Economics* 17 (April 1974); 53–71.

"Wait a moment," an economic theorist will object. "The quantities purchased and sold are not the same thing as the quantities demanded and supplied. It's quite true that purchases will exactly match sales; but sellers might *want* to sell more than purchasers are willing to buy. The quantity supplied at the going price, in other words, might be greater than the quantity demanded at that price—which is what we mean by a disequilibrium. The market only clears when the quantity that demanders *want* to purchase matches the quantity that suppliers *want* to sell."

But notice what this argument implies. It tells us that some demanders or suppliers are behaving differently from the way they want to behave. Isn't that rather odd? If the suppliers of corn want to sell more than they are actually selling, why don't they do it?

"They can't," our hypothetical theorist replies, "because the price is too high."

Then why don't some corn suppliers offer to sell at a slightly lower price, which is what we would predict if the corn suppliers really do want to sell more corn than buyers want to purchase?

"Suppliers don't have any incentive to lower their price," is the rejoinder, "as long as the government stands willing to purchase at the support price all the corn suppliers want to sell at that price."

End of the argument. An equilibrium price for corn, it now emerges, is the price that would clear the market in the absence of a government price support program. It is the price that equates the quantity supplied with the quantity demanded when we exclude from consideration the demand stemming from the Commodity Credit Corporation.

If every situation is taken to be an equilibrium situation, the concept of equilibrium is useless. The usefulness of the concept hinges, therefore, on our ability to specify and distinguish disequilibrium situations. We do this by isolating and excluding some of the forces supposedly at work in the situation under analysis. In the case just argued, the government's demand was excluded in order to focus attention on the factors causing the amount of corn in storage to rise or fall. The exclusion is justified by the purpose it serves. The danger is that we may forget about the purpose that led to the exclusion which defined the

disequilibrium, and start pretending that the government-supported price is "really" a disequilibrium price. That's simply nonsense.

Consider another example. Economists frequently claim (I have done it myself) that legislated price controls create shortages by preventing prices from moving to their equilibrium levels. But what do we mean by a shortage? We do not mean a situation in which there isn't enough for all buyers to have as much as they want, because that describes just about every situation. We live in a world where scarcity is the general rule. When economists speak of shortages, they usually mean situations in which demanders are unable to purchase all that they want to purchase *at the prevailing price*.

But that's not really accurate, either. If demanders cannot purchase as much as they would like to purchase, won't they search for ways to accommodate their preferences more satisfactorily? And won't these efforts raise the price that purchasers must pay, until the quantity demanded comes into line with the quantity supplied? In the presence of effective legal controls on the *monetary* price, the adjustment in response to competition among purchasers will have to occur entirely in the non-monetary components of the buyers' opportunity cost. But those components affect the quantity demanded just as surely as the monetary price affects it. When we speak of "the quantity demanded at the prevailing price," we are really talking about the quantity demanded at the prevailing cost of acquisition, which includes all kinds of non-monetary costs.

The economist's claim that price controls create shortages turns out, therefore, to be the claim that price controls lead to increases in non-monetary costs of acquisition. The "disequilibrium" prices produced by price controls are disequilibrium prices only if we exclude from consideration *changes* in non-monetary components of the purchase price. This exclusion is justified by the economist's desire to isolate these changes and to examine their effectiveness, relative to changes in monetary price, in securing mutual accommodation between suppliers and demanders. We see once again that an analytical intention suggested the exclusion which gave meaning to the notion of a disequilibrium.

Every claim of a disequilibrium rests upon an analytical exclusion. It is sometimes important to insist upon this fact, in order to avoid giving the impression that the "problem" with a "disequilibrium" is independent of human purposes. A playground seesaw is in physical equilibrium when a fifty-pound person sits on one end and a two- hundred pound person on the other. Only when we take account of the parties' desire to move up and down can we correctly say that the seesaw is in disequilibrium when the heavy person is on the far end rather than up toward the middle.

With only two parties, intentions or purposes are relatively easy to ascertain; we can therefore usually decide quickly whether or not a seesaw is in disequilibrium and start looking for an equilibrium solution. Can we do the same in the case of an alleged disequilibrium in the balance of international payments?

DISEQUILIBRIUM IN THE BALANCE OF PAYMENTS

I think we would be far more suspicious when confronted by any alleged trade deficit if we stopped to realize how much is concealed in such disequilibrium claims. They are often, as Fritz Machlup has argued, disguised political judgments.[5] I happen not to share the horror of political or ethical judgments that is conventionally professed among economists. But *disguised* political judgments are another matter. They violate the imperative of clarity. And lack of clarity in an area where conflicting political interests abound is an invitation to trouble. That is certainly the case when we start talking about trade deficits.

Any claim of deficit or surplus in a nation's trade balance, I have argued, necessarily rests upon a decision to exclude some items when calculating the balance. Which ones? And why are they excluded? We're ready now, after our digression on the equilibrium concept, to suggest an answer. The items excluded will be those which enable the persons alleging a trade deficit (or surplus) to call attention to the problems that concern them.

It must be granted at the outset that most people who talk or write about trade deficits are simply taking over uncritically someone else's definition. They may not know what has been excluded in order to create the deficit; and if they do know, they may have no idea of how the exclusion can be justified. I certainly do not want to be understood as arguing that every journalist, academician, or economist in the Commerce Department is concerned about some particular problem when referring to trade deficits. I am more interested in maintaining that all concepts of a trade deficit harbor concealed concerns and disguised political judgments—concealed and disguised, more often than not, from the very people wielding the concepts.

In the last few years, the deficit most often discussed by the news media has been the merchandise trade deficit. Recorded data indicate that the United States has imported a greater dollar value of merchandise than it has exported in every single month since the end of 1975. But why is that called a deficit? What is significant about the relationship between merchandise exports and imports, taken by itself? I don't know how to answer that question, because I don't think that it has any significance at all, and I don't recall ever encountering an explanation that went beyond vague rhetorical alarms.

It is often suggested or implied that the growing merchandise trade deficit reveals this country's increasing inability to compete internationally with goods manufactured in other countries. But what does this really mean? The inability of General Motors to persuade motorists to buy its automobiles rather than, let us say, Japanese automobiles, probably constitutes a problem for GM's managers, employees, shareholders, and franchised dealers. But how do we know that this demonstrates an

---

5   Fritz Machlup, "Equilibrium and Disequilibrium: Misplaced Concreteness and Disguised Politics," *The Economic Journal* 88 (March 1958); reprinted in Machlup, Essays on *Economic Semantics* (Englewood Cliffs, N.J.: Prentice-Hall, 1963), pp. 43–72.

increasing inability of "this country" to compete, rather than the ongoing operation of the principle of comparative advantage?

I have learned from experience how difficult it is to persist in this line of argument and be taken seriously. It is simply "obvious" to many people that the United States cannot prosper if our imports of manufactured goods regularly exceed our exports of manufactured goods—as has supposedly been the case for the past seven years and more. I shall pass by the fact that merchandise is not the same as manufactured goods, that the growth of petroleum imports has had far more effect on our merchandise trade balance over the past decade than the dreaded Japanese have had, and that the United States actually exported a greater value of manufactured goods than it imported in both 1980 and 1981, as well as in 1977 and 1979 if we use customs valuations in our calculations. I shall pass by these facts quickly because I fail to see that anything of inherent significance would have been established even if it were true that U. S. exports of manufactured goods had been below imports for each of the past 10 years.

This is not to deny that U.S. firms have often performed poorly in recent years, or that sizeable sectors of the economy are going to diminish dramatically or disappear if major adjustments do not occur in response to foreign competition. What I deny is that comparisons of aggregate merchandise exports with imports provide any kind of help in describing, diagnosing, or prescribing for this situation.

They do, however, provide political arguments that can be used by people who want protection from foreign competitors or subsidies for their efforts to sell abroad. For the existence of a trade deficit implies that the ratio of imports to exports *must eventually decline*, since no deficit can continue forever. So we might as well get on with it now: Fund the Export-Import Bank, restrict imports from nations that interfere with our exports, slap penalties on foreign firms that are "dumping" in our markets, and face up in general to the fact that free trade is good trade only if it is fair trade.

Trade deficits are politically potent weapons because "everyone knows" that "deficits cannot continue indefinitely." Even the federal government must eventually stop running deficits, or else … something fearful will happen. What? Popular opinion is vague about the consequences, but fairly firm in the underlying conviction that "you can't go on running deficits forever."

The truth is that the federal government can indeed go on adding indefinitely to its indebtedness, with no assignable limit. It can spend more than it collects in taxes, even without expanding the money stock, so long as it can collect the difference in loans. And it will be able to borrow just so long as and to the extent that people are willing to loan to it. People will be willing to buy and hold government bonds insofar as they think they will be better off owning government bonds than they would be with alternative assets. When the public displays reluctance to hold all the debt that the federal government must issue in order to finance a current deficit, a slight decline in the purchase price of government bonds quickly secures their cooperation. Consequently, the federal government never does operate "in the red": Total outlays are always matched exactly by total receipts, as long as receipts are defined to include funds raised by borrowing. The concept of a government budget deficit has meaning only insofar as we exclude borrowed funds from the total of government receipts. We might well want to do that, for various analytical purposes. But once again it is the analytical intention that creates the deficit, by specifying what will be excluded from total receipts—which would otherwise necessarily equal total outlays.

For reasons that are unclear to me, this line of argument does not seem to be generally accepted when it comes to discussions about the balance of payments.[6] The data-tenders calculate deficits or surpluses of various kinds with an astonishing lack of

---

6   The *Survey of Current Business* celebrated its 50th anniversary in 1971 with a special issue devoted to a review of the programs of the Bureau of Economic Analysis (then the Office of Business Economics) in the Department of Commerce. Several of the distinguished scholars invited to contribute focused on balance-of-payments accounting. Their comments are illuminating, but they leave the reader—this reader, at least—wondering why the bureau continued afterward to gather, publish, *and publicize* balance-of-payments data. *Survey of Current Business* 51, no. 7, part 2 (July 1971): 4–22, 33–35, 105–07, and the concluding comments of Bureau Director George Jaszi in his brilliant and witty review of the symposium, 212–13..

attention to what has been excluded in the process. It is no doubt obvious, at least in the Department of Commerce, that the merchandise trade deficit omits services. But to whom is it obvious that something has also been omitted when the data-keepers calculate the balance of trade on goods *and* services? It is not at all obvious, I submit, to some knowledgeable writers for the *Wall Street Journal,* to take just one example.

The headline on a recent back-page story in the *Journal* (9 August 1983) declared: "As Economy Continues to Revive From Slump, Country's Balance of Trade Grows Sicklier." An accompanying chart, drawn from Commerce Department data, shows net exports of goods and services declining steeply from over $50 billion on an annual basis in the fourth quarter of 1980 to about $10 billion at an annual rate in the first quarter of this year, and still headed downward.[7]

It is all quite puzzling. To begin with, why is this called "sicklier"? *If* surpluses are evidence of health and deficits are signs of sickness, shouldn't the correct description at least have been 'less healthy'? But that is still not the basic question, Why should a deficit be regarded in the first place as evidence of economic ill health? We could probably all agree that some events which produce deficits are evidence of matters gone wrong. Short-term borrowing to finance grain imports made necessary by a harvest failure, for example, would push a nation's balance of trade toward deficit as conventionally defined. But the problem here is the harvest failure, not the deficit in the trade balance, and obsession with the deficit that results from the harvest failure obscures the problem.

Not only is the deficit a mere symptom of the problem, it is also a symptom of the problem's resolution. And that's extremely important to keep in mind. The deficit is evidence that funds were made available with which to purchase grain after the harvest failure, and thus to ward off starvation. Isn't the deficit, viewed in this larger perspective, something to welcome rather than to lament? Lamentation is

appropriate with regard to the harvest failure; but the deficit is something for which the nation's citizens could properly be grateful.

We are still talking about deficits, however, without deciding what they are. An actual deficit cannot exist in an accounting system that *defines* credits and debits so that they are necessarily equal. Trade deficits must therefore be conceptual phenomena. A trade deficit must be a disequilibrium, not an actual inequality between purchases and sales. And a disequilibrium, we have argued, entails the isolation and exclusion of some factors for purposes of analysis. What do the keepers of the trade balance exclude in order to calculate a deficit or surplus? And why?

They do not offer us an unambiguous answer. Let me therefore suggest on my own that they intend to exclude what we may call "involuntary" transactions. They assume that international exchange includes two distinguishable kinds of transactions. Some are undertaken for the sake of prospective advantage; people initiate such transactions because they hope to gain something from them. These "autonomous" transactions will ordinarily tend to balance each other off; a nation's imports will be basically financed by means of its export earnings. Imports and exports, it must be remembered, include services as well as merchandise, and services include both the loan of capital and payments for the use of capital.

Almost inevitably, however, on this view of the matter, the "autonomous" transactions initiated by households, business firms, governments, and other agencies will fail to produce a precise match between debits and credits in each trading nation. The difference will have to be made up by compensating transactions, or what we are calling "involuntary" transactions to indicate that the parties initiating them do not undertake them for the sake of prospective advantage to themselves, but rather to accommodate the actions of others. Thus, if a nation's financial institutions increase their holdings of deposits denominated in a foreign currency, *not* for the sake of the interest return on those deposits, but rather to compensate for a merchandise net export surplus, that increase in deposits represents a surplus in the nation's balance of trade (and a deficit for the nation whose liabilities have increased). Deficits and

---

7   Alfred L., Malabre, Jr., "As Economy Continues to Revive From Slump, Country's Balance of Trade Grows Sicklier," *Wall Street Journal* (9 August 1983), p. 56..

surpluses are calculated, then, by excluding from the totals of export and import transactions all such "involuntary" or merely compensating transactions.

SOME CAVEATS

This use of the equilibrium concept strikes me as thoroughly illegitimate. To begin with, a distinction between "autonomous" and "involuntary" transactions is hard to draw without abandoning the basic premise of economic theory, that actions represent rational choices under constraint. Moreover, commercial banks clearly do not hold foreign assets in order to square the national trade balance. Nor do central banks. Just what does make central bankers tick is a mystery to many, of whom I am one; but I am confident that no central bank anywhere adjusts the composition of its asset portfolio in order to equate the balance of payments, if for no other reason than that it cannot possibly acquire the information it would need to do so.

The managers of financial institutions, whether private or official, national or international, affect the balance of payments in the same way that ordinary exporters and importers do it: as the consequence of pursuing their own interests in a situation with diverse but limited options. This is not to say that central bankers do not pursue what they regard as the national interest. They well may. But when they do so, they do *not* do it by aiming at a balance in the balance of international payments. We know this is not their target because we know this is a target they cannot see. They are necessarily aiming at something else if they are "aiming" at anything at all.

Their actual target might be some particular foreign exchange rate, or some rate of growth in a domestic monetary aggregate, or some desired interest rate, or improved relations with influential parties who want central bank intervention in foreign exchange markets, or even the election of a particular presidential candidate.[8] There are many possibilities. And that is the problem. The allegation of a trade deficit amounts to a vague claim that international exchange transactions are out of order and must be set right. The fundamental issues of exactly what is out of order and how it got that way do not have to be addressed. With the problem undefined, the solution is necessarily undefined. A wide variety of actions might be appropriate. Since even experts disagree extensively on just how any particular policy move is likely to affect the long list of important variables in the world of domestic finance and international exchange, the declaration of a trade deficit amounts in practice to a kind of declaration of martial law. What is most dangerous about such a declaration is that it gives government officials a license to subordinate the rule of law and respect for established rights to considerations of political advantage.

I do not want to be misunderstood. I am not now claiming, whatever I might believe, that we would be better off if central banks stayed out of the foreign exchange markets. Nor am I trying to construct an argument for unrestricted international trade. My claim is a much more limited one. It is that whatever the proper role of government might be in affecting the course of international trade, the concept of trade deficits and surpluses or disequilibrium in the balance of payments darkens counsel. It has no agreed-upon meaning. It ought to be abandoned, so that the way can be cleared for more responsible and effective discussion of the issues that concern us.

I have never encountered a case in which the concept of a balance-of-payments disequilibrium was used to interpret an economic problem where the problem could not have been more clearly explicated, in my judgment, by abandoning the concept. What would we substitute for it? Whatever assertion the balance-of-payments concept is concealing in each particular case. Every claim of a balance-of-payments disequilibrium can be more accurately and adequately expressed as a prediction, such as "The dollar will depreciate relative to certain other

8 In support of the last possibility, see Lindley H. Clark, "The Odd Couple: Treasury and Fed Try to Reelect Reagan," *Wall Street Journal* (16 August 1983), p. 33.

currencies," or "Certain desired imports will not be available unless foreign lenders can be persuaded to extend credit," or "'It is going to be increasingly difficult for producer A to sell in market Y,' or "Important political support will be secured by imposing quotas on the importation of goods M and N."[9]

CONCLUSION

I am uncomfortably aware of the violence that this recommendation does to long-established tradition. The concept of a balance of international payments has been called, by economists far more reputable than I, a significant analytical achievement.[10] I am claiming that it was in fact and from the beginning a conceptual device that concealed more than it revealed. And the trouble with such concepts in the social sciences is that they facilitate the presentation of political arguments in the garb of empirical assertions.

I think Adam Smith was right "Nothing ... can be more absurd than this whole doctrine of the balance of trade."[11] It is a concept originally devised and promulgated by merchants in order to promote their special interests under the pretense of protecting the national interest. And a government that tries to watch over the balance of trade has embarked upon a task that is intricate, embarrassing, and fruitless.[12]

---

9   At a time when macroeconomic theory is in such unsettled shape, it seems to me more than ever imperative to strive for clarity in our assertions in this area. We all use theory as a shorthand in making empirical assertions, as when we say that "the outfielder missed the fly ball because of the sun."' This practice begins to create confusion as soon as relationships "settled" by theory start behaving in ways inconsistent with the theory (or consistent with only *some versions* of the theory). Relevant examples include relationships at the present time between money stock growth rates and interest rates and between foreign exchange rates and relative rates of inflation.

10   In his *History of Economic Analysts,* Joseph Schumpeter calls the balance of payments "an Important datum in the diagnosis of the economic condition of a country and an important factor in its business processes," Against his explicit claim that development of the concept represented a significant analytical advance. I would adduce his own discussion on pages 352–53, including the long footnote 6. Schumpeter's actual discussion seems to me to demonstrate the inherent ambiguity of the concept and its vast potential for buttressing question-begging arguments. Joseph A. Schumpeter, *History of Economic Analysis* (New York: Oxford University Press, 1954), pp. 352–53.

11   Adam Smith, An *Inquiry Into the Nature and Causes of the Wealth of Nations* (Oxford: Clarendon Press, 1976), book IV, chapter III, part II, paragraph 2. The quotation is on page 456 in the Modern Library edition.

12   Ibid., book IV, chapter I, paragraph 10. See pages 376–77 in the Modern Library edition.

Tariffs

Tariffs

By Thomas Rustici

A *Tariff* is a tax on imports. Foreign goods may be subject to tariffs for reasons ranging from protectionism to political payback. Regardless of the underlying motivation for the tariff, the domestic consumer of those goods is forced to pay higher prices, substitute, or abstain; and with imports reduced, demand for the country's exports must diminish (fewer dollars leaving in exchange for imports means fewer dollars demanding repatriation!). Domestic consumers and exporters must be made to sacrifice if the domestic producers are to be subsidized.

Seldom are the costs of tariffs advertised alongside arguments made in favor of tariffs, i.e., promotion of domestic industry, increased revenue to the government, or *realpolitik*. The fact is, however, that although the tariff will reduce social wealth on net, it will be advertised, and generally accepted, as a success. This is because the gains from the tariff—whether from "saved" jobs, fuller coffers, or from having punished foreign nation—are highly concentrated and visible, yet the losses (e.g. jobs lost in other industries, reduced revenue for localities that have lost export jobs, and foregone trade opportunities along with soured international relations) are dispersed and therefore difficult to detect and discern.

Who's "Protected" by Tariffs?

By Henry Hazlitt

1

A mete recital of the economic policies of governments all over the world is calculated to cause any serious student of economics to throw up his hands in despair. What possible point can there be, he is likely to ask, in discussing refinements and advances in economic theory, when popular thought and the actual policies of governments, certainly in everything connected with international relations, have not yet caught up with Adam Smith? For present-day tariff and trade policies are not only as bad as those in the seventeenth and eighteenth centuries, but incomparably worse. The real reasons for those tariffs and other trade-barriers are the same, and the pretended reasons are also the same.

In the century and three-quarters since *The Wealth of Nations* appeared, the case for free trade has been stated thousands of times, but perhaps never with more direct simplicity and force than it was stated in that volume. In general Smith rested his case on one fundamental proposition: "In every country it always is and must be the interest of the great body of the people to buy whatever they want of those who sell it cheapest." "The proposition is

so very manifest," Smith continued, "that it seems ridiculous to take any pains to prove it; nor could it ever have been called in question, had not the interested sophistry of merchants and manufacturers confounded the common-sense of mankind."

From another point of view, free trade was considered as one aspect of the specialization of labor:

It is the maxim of every prudent master of a family, never to attempt to make at home what it will cost him more to make than to buy. The tailor does not attempt to make his own shoes, but buys them of the shoemaker. The shoemaker does not attempt to make his own clothes, but employs a tailor. The farmer attempts to make neither the one nor the other, but employs those different artificers. All of them find it for their interest to employ their whole industry in a way in which they have some advantage over their neighbors, and to purchase with a part of its produce, or what is the same thing, with the price of a part of it, whatever else they have occasion for. What is prudence in the conduct of every private family can scarce be folly in that of a great kingdom.

But whatever led people to suppose that what was prudence in the conduct of every private family *could* be folly in that of a great kingdom? It was a whole network of fallacies, out of which mankind has still been unable to cut its way. And the chief of them was the central fallacy with which this book is concerned. It was that of considering merely the immediate effects of a tariff on special groups, and neglecting to consider its long-run effects on the whole community.

2

An American manufacturer of woolen sweaters goes to Congress or to the State Department and tells the committee or officials concerned that it would be a national disaster for them to remove or reduce the tariff on British sweaters. He now sells his sweaters for $15 each, but English manufacturers could sell here sweaters of the same quality for $10. A duty of $5, therefore, is needed to keep him in business. He is not thinking of himself, of course, but of the thousand men and women he employs, and of the people to whom their spending in turn gives employment. Throw them out of work, and you create unemployment and a fall in purchasing power, which would spread in ever-widening circles. And if he can prove that he really would be forced out of business if the tariff were removed or reduced, his argument against that action is regarded by Congress as conclusive.

But the fallacy comes from looking merely at this manufacturer and his employees, or merely at the American sweater industry. It comes from noticing only the results that are immediately seen, and neglecting the results that are not seen because they are prevented from coming into existence.

The lobbyists for tariff protection are continually putting forward arguments that are not factually correct. But let us assume that the facts in this case are precisely as the sweater manufacturer has stated them. Let us assume that a tariff of $5 a sweater is necessary for him to stay in business and provide employment at sweater making for his workers.

We have deliberately chosen the most unfavorable example of any for the removal of a tariff. We have not taken an argument for the imposition of a new tariff in order to bring a new industry into existence, but an argument for the retention of a tariff *that has already brought an industry into existence,* and cannot be repealed without hurting somebody.

The tariff is repealed; the manufacturer goes out of business; a thousand workers are laid off; the particular tradesmen whom they patronized are hurt. This is the immediate result that is seen. But there are also results which, while much more difficult to trace, are no less immediate and no less real. For now sweaters that formerly Cost $15 apiece can be bought for $10. Consumers can now buy the same quality of sweater for less money, or a much better one for the same money. If they buy the same quality of sweater, they not only get the sweater, but they have $5 left over, which they would not have had under the previous conditions, to buy something else. With the $10 that they pay for the imported sweater they help employment—as the American manufacturer no doubt predicted—in the sweater industry in England. With the $5 left over they help employment in any number of other industries in the United States.

But the results do not end there. By buying English sweaters they furnish the English with dollars to buy American goods here. This, in fact (if I may here disregard such complications as multilateral exchange, loans, credits, gold movements, etc. which do not alter the end result) is the only way in which the British can eventually make use of these dollars. Because we have permitted the British to sell more to us, they are now able to buy more from us. They are, in fact, eventually *forced* to buy more from us if their dollar balances are not to remain perpetually unused. So, as a result of letting in more British goods, we must export more American goods. And though fewer people are now employed in the American sweater industry, more people are employed—and much more efficiently employed—in, say, the American automobile or washing-machine business. American employment on net balance has not gone down, but American and British production on net balance has gone up. Labor in each country is more fully employed in doing just those things that it does best, instead of being forced to do things that it does inefficiently or badly. Consumers in both countries are better off. They are able to buy what they want where they can get it cheapest. American consumers are better provided with sweaters, and British consumers are better provided with motor cars and washing machines.

3

Now let us look at the matter the other way round, and see the effect of imposing a tariff in the first place. Suppose that there had been no tariff on foreign knit goods, that Americans were accustomed to buying foreign sweaters without duty, and that the argument were then put forward that we could *bring a sweater industry into existence* by imposing a duty of $5 on sweaters.

There would be nothing logically wrong with this argument so far as it went. The cost of British sweaters to the American consumer might thereby be forced so high that American manufacturers would find it profitable to enter the sweater business. But American consumers would be forced to subsidize this industry On every American sweater they bought they would be forced in effect to pay a tax of $5 which would be collected from them in a higher price by the new sweater industry.

Americans would be employed in a sweater industry who had not previously been employed in a sweater industry. That much is true. But there would be no net addition to the country's industry or the country's employment. Because the American consumer had to pay $5 more for the same quality of sweater he would have just that much less left over to buy anything else. He would have to reduce his expenditures by $5 somewhere else. In order that one industry might grow or come into existence, a hundred other industries would have to shrink. In order that 20,000 persons might be employed in a sweater industry, 20,000 fewer persons would be employed elsewhere.

But the new industry would be *visible*. The number of its employees, the capital invested in it, the market value of its product in terms of dollars, could be easily counted. The neighbors could see the sweater workers going to and from the factory every day. The results would be palpable and direct. But the shrinkage of a hundred other industries, the loss of 20,000 other jobs somewhere else, would not be so easily noticed. It would be impossible for even the cleverest statistician to know precisely what the incidence of the loss of other jobs had been—precisely how many men and women had been laid off from each particular industry, precisely how much business each particular industry had lost—because consumers had to pay more for their sweaters. For a loss spread among all the other productive activities of the country would be comparatively minute for each. It would be impossible for anyone to know precisely how each consumer *would* have spent his extra $5 if he had been allowed to retain it. The overwhelming majority of the people, therefore, would probably suffer from the optical illusion that the new industry had cost us nothing.

4

It is important to notice that the new tariff on sweaters would not raise American wages. To be sure, it would enable Americans to work *in the sweater industry* at approximately the average level of American wages (for workers of their skill), instead of having to compete in that industry at the British level of wages. But there would be no increase of American wages *in general* as a result of the duty; for, as we have seen, there would be no net increase in the number of jobs provided, no net increase in the demand for goods, and no increase in labor productivity. Labor productivity would, in fact, be *reduced* as a result of the tariff.

And this brings us to the real effect of a tariff wall. It is not merely that all its visible gains are offset by less obvious but no less real losses. It results, in fact, in a net loss to the country. For contrary to centuries of interested propaganda and disinterested confusion, the tariff *reduces* the American level of wages.

Let us observe more clearly how it does this. We have seen that the added amount which consumers pay for a tariff-protected article leaves them just that much less with which to buy all other articles. There is here no net gain to industry as a whole. But as a result of the artificial barrier erected against foreign goods, American labor, capital and land are deflected from what they can do more efficiently to what they do less efficiently. Therefore, as a result of the tariff wall, the average productivity of American labor and capital is reduced.

If we look at it now from the consumer's point of view, we find that he can buy less with his money. Because he has to pay more for sweaters and other protected goods, he can buy less of everything else. The general purchasing power of his income has therefore been reduced. Whether the net effect of the tariff is to lower money wages or to raise money prices will depend upon the monetary policies that are followed. But what is clear is that the tariff—though it may increase wages above what they would have been in *the protected industries*—must on net balance, when *all* occupations are considered, *reduce real wages*.

Only minds corrupted by generations of misleading propaganda can regard this conclusion as paradoxical. What other result could we expect from a policy of deliberately using our resources of capital and manpower in less efficient ways than we know how to use them? What other result could we expect from deliberately erecting artificial obstacles to trade and transportation?

For the erection of tariff walls has the same effect as the erection of real walls. It is significant that the protectionists habitually use the language of warfare. They talk of "repelling an invasion" of foreign products. And the means they suggest in the fiscal field are like those of the battlefield. The tariff barriers that are put up to repel this invasion are like the tank traps, trenches, and barbed-wire entanglements created to repel or slow down attempted invasion by a foreign army.

And just as the foreign army is compelled to employ more expensive means to surmount those obstacles—bigger tanks, mine detectors, engineer corps to cut wires, ford streams, and build bridges—so more expensive and efficient transportation means must be developed to surmount tariff obstacles. On the one hand, we try to reduce the cost of transportation between England and America, or Canada and the United States, by developing faster and more efficient ships, better roads and bridges, better locomotives and motor trucks. On the other hand, we offset this investment in efficient transportation by a tariff that makes it commercially even more difficult to transport goods than it was before. We make it $1 cheaper to ship the sweaters, and then increase the tariff by $2 to prevent the sweaters from being shipped. By reducing the freight that can be profitably carried, we reduce the value of the investment in transport efficiency.

5

The tariff has been described as a means of benefiting the producer at the expense of the consumer. In a sense this is correct. Those who favor it think only of the interests of the producers immediately benefited by the particular duties involved. They forget the interests of the consumers who are immediately injured by being forced to pay these duties. But it is wrong to think of the tariff issue as if it represented a conflict between the interests of producers as a unit against those of consumers as a unit. It is true that the tariff hurts all consumers as such. It is not true that it benefits all producers as such. On the contrary, as we have just seen, it helps the protected producers at the expense of all other American producers, *and particularly of those who have a comparatively large potential export market.*

We can perhaps make this last point clearer by an exaggerated example. Suppose we make our tariff wall so high that it becomes absolutely prohibitive, and no imports come in from the outside world at all. Suppose, as a result of this, that the price of sweaters in America goes up only $5. Then American consumers, because they have to pay $5 more for a sweater, will spend on the average five cents less in each of a hundred other American industries. (The figures are chosen merely to illustrate a principle: there will, of course, be no such symmetrical distribution of the loss; moreover, the sweater industry itself will doubtless be hurt because of protection of still *other* industries. But these complications may be put aside for the moment.)

Now because foreign industries will find their market in America *totally* cut off, they will get no dollar exchange, and therefore they will be *unable to buy any American goods at all.* As a result of this, American industries will suffer in direct proportion to the percentage of their sales previously made abroad. Those that will be most injured, in the first instance, will be such industries as raw cotton producers, copper producers, makers of sewing machines, agricultural machinery, typewriters and so on.

A higher tariff wall, which, however, is not prohibitive, will produce the same kind of results as this, but merely to a smaller degree.

The effect of a tariff, therefore, is to change the *structure* of American production. It changes the number of occupations, the kind of occupations, and the relative size of one industry as compared with another. It makes the industries in which we are comparatively inefficient larger, and the industries in which we are comparatively efficient smaller. Its net effect, therefore, is to reduce American efficiency, as well as to reduce efficiency in the countries with which we would otherwise have traded more largely.

In the long run, notwithstanding the mountains of argument pro and con, a tariff is irrelevant to the question of employment. (True, sudden *changes* in the tariff, either upward or downward, can create temporary unemployment, as they force corresponding changes in the structure of production. Such sudden changes can even cause a depression.) But a tariff is not irrelevant to the question of wages. In the long run it always reduces real wages, because it reduces efficiency, production and wealth.

Thus all the chief tariff fallacies stem from the central fallacy with which this book is concerned. They are the result of looking only at the immediate effects of a single tariff rate on one group of producers, and forgetting the long-run effects both on consumers as a whole and on all other producers.

(I hear some reader asking: "Why not solve this by giving tariff protection to *all* producers?" But the fallacy here is that this cannot help producers uniformly, and cannot help at all domestic producers who already "outsell" foreign producers: these efficient producers must necessarily suffer from the diversion of purchasing power brought about by the tariff.)

6

On the subject of the tariff we must keep in mind one final precaution. It is the same precaution that we found necessary in examining the effects of machinery. It is useless to deny that a tariff does benefit—or at least *can* benefit—*special interests.* True, it benefits them *at the expense of everyone else.* But it does benefit them. If one industry alone could get protection, while its owners and workers enjoyed the benefits of free trade in everything else they bought, that industry would benefit, even on net balance. As an attempt is made to *extend* the tariff blessings, however, even people in the protected industries, both as producers and consumers, begin to suffer from other people's protection, and may finally be worse off even on net balance than if neither they nor anybody else had protection.

But we should not deny, as enthusiastic free traders have so often done, the possibility of these tariff benefits to special groups. We should not pretend, for example, that a reduction of the tariff would help everybody and hurt nobody. It Is true that its reduction would help the country on net balance. But *somebody* would be hurt Groups previously enjoying high protection would be hurt. That in fact is one reason why it is not good to bring such protected interests into existence in the first place. But clarity and candor of thinking compel us to see and acknowledge that some industries are right when they say that a removal of the tariff on their product would throw them out of business and throw their workers (at least temporarily) out of jobs. And if their workers have developed specialized skills, they may even suffer permanently, or until they have at long last learnt equal skills. In tracing the effects of tariffs, as in tracing the effects of machinery, we should endeavor to see *all* the chief effects, in both the short run and the long run, on *all* groups.

As a postscript to this chapter I should add that its argument is not directed against *all* tariffs, including duties collected mainly for revenue, or to keep alive industries needed for war; nor is it directed against all arguments for tariffs. It is merely directed against the fallacy that a tariff on net balance "provides employment," "raises wages," or "protects the American standard of living." It does none of these things; and so far as wages and the standard of living are concerned, it does the precise opposite. But an examination of duties imposed for other purposes would carry us beyond our present subject.

Nor need we here examine the effect of import quotas, exchange controls, bilateralism, and other devices in reducing, diverting or preventing international trade. Such devices have, in general, the same effects as high or prohibitive tariffs, and often worse effects. They present more complicated issues, but their net results can be traced through the same kind of reasoning that we have just applied to tariff barriers.

The Smoot-Hawley Tariff and the Great Depression

By Theodore Shamoun, Thomas Rustici, and Dima Yazji Shamoun

Few areas of historical research have provoked such intensive study as the origins of America's Great Depression. From 1929 to 1933 America suffered the worst economic decline in its history. Real national income fell by 36 percent; unemployment increased from 3 percent to over 25 percent; more than 40 percent of all banks were permanently closed; and international investment and trade declined dramatically.

The dimensions of the economic catastrophe in America and the rest of the world from 1929 to 1933 cannot be captured fully by quantitative data alone. Tens of millions of humans suffered intense misery and despair. Because of this trauma the Great Depression has dominated much of the macroeconomic debate since the mid-twentieth century.

In 1930 a large majority of economists believed the Smoot-Hawley Tariff Act would exacerbate the U.S. recession into a worldwide depression. On May 5 of that year 1,028 members of the American Economic Association released a signed statement that vigorously opposed the act. The protest included five basic points. First, the tariff would raise the cost of living by "compelling the consumer to subsidize waste and inefficiency in [domestic] industry." Second, the farm sector would not be helped since "cotton, pork, lard, and wheat are export crops and sold in the world market" and the price

of farm equipment would rise. Third, "our export trade in general would suffer. Countries cannot buy from us unless they are permitted to sell to us." Fourth, the tariff would "inevitably provoke other countries to pay us back in kind against our goods." Finally, Americans with investments abroad would suffer since the tariff would make it "more difficult for their foreign debtors to pay them interest due them." Likewise most of the empirical discussions of the downturn in world economic activity taking place in 1929–1933 put Smoot-Hawley at or near center stage.

Economists today, however, hold a different view of the effects of Smoot-Hawley. While economic historians generally believe the tariff was misguided and may have aggravated the economic crisis, the consensus appears to relegate it to a minor status relative to other forces. We believe many modern economists are wrong because flawed modeling leads to two systematic understatements of the tariff's negative effects. The first reason for this is that reliance on macro aggregates can sometimes mask serious underlying problems by dissipating their apparent impact over a broad area. For example, U.S. national income declined 36 percent in real terms from 1929 to 1933, and the view held by prominent economists, ranging from University of Chicago Nobel laureate Robert Lucas and Yale economist Robert

Shiller to MIT economists Rudiger Dornbush and Stanley Fischer, is that since the foreign-trade sector was only about 7 percent of gross national product (GNP), the tariff (though misguided) could not explain much of this decline.

Viewed at the level of "macro magnitudes," critical micro connections suffer from a "dissipation effect" and always look small. But size does not equal significance. While it is true that foreign trade represented only a small percentage of the overall domestic and international economy, it does not follow that the tariff was insignificant in its effects. The Panama Canal contains but a small fraction of the world's ocean water, but if it were closed the effects would be quite devastating to world trade. A focus on aggregates risks missing the trees for the forest, and not all trees are created equal.

Here's a second way Smoot-Hawley is underestimated: If regulations or tariffs are studied in partitioned models, their interrelationships are missed and their true impacts are trivialized. For example, recent attempts have been made to quantify price distortions caused by the tariff. Mario Crucini and James Kahn have tried to correct systematic underestimates of the harm of Smoot-Hawley found in a variety of macro studies that ignored the effect of tariff retaliation on the rate of capital accumulation. Using a general-equilibrium model, they calculate that the microeconomic distortion effects reduced U.S. GNP by only 2 percent in the early 1930s. Likewise economist Douglas Irwin computed the general-equilibrium inefficiencies caused by the tariff at nearly 2 percent of GNP.

So when even ostensibly free-market, free-trade economists such as Lucas, Irwin, and others downplay the negative effects of the Smoot-Hawley Tariff, what's the verdict? Were the loud protests of over a thousand professors of economics just unsophisticated exaggerations? Were these pre-Keynesian classical theorists misguided because they lacked the tools of modern macroeconomics and econometrics? Or did their vision remain unclouded for the same reason? Were they Chicken Littles or Cassandras?

IGNORED EFFECTS

Modern measurements of Smoot-Hawley often ignore a wide range of important negative effects. For instance, the secondary financial markets, such as the New York Stock Exchange, crashed twice during the last eight months of Smoot-Hawley's legislative history. Jude Wanniski and Scott Sumner have linked concern over the impending tariff to the October 1929 crash and the June 1930 crash. The Dow Jones Industrial Average fell 23 percent in the first two weeks of June 1930 leading up to President Herbert Hoover's signing the bill into law. On June 16 Hoover claimed, "I shall approve the tariff bill," and stocks lost $1 billion in value that day—a huge sum at the time.

Furthermore, if losses of GNP were not evenly distributed across the economy but were concentrated (say, in export-oriented states), the tariff most likely distorted monetary conditions significantly. Two percent of GNP does not sound like a big change, but if it's concentrated in one-fifth to one-third of the states, it's very large indeed. The tariff dramatically lowered U.S. exports, from $7 billion in 1929 to $2.4 billion in 1932, and a large portion of U.S. exports were agricultural; therefore it cannot be assumed that the microeconomic inefficiencies were evenly distributed. Many individual states suffered severe drops in farm incomes due to collapsing export markets arising from foreign retaliation, and it's no coincidence that rural farm banks in the Midwest and southern states began failing by the thousands.

Agriculture was not the only export sector destroyed by the tariff. The worldwide retaliation against U.S. minerals greatly depressed income in mining states and can be partially blamed for the collapse of the Wingfield chain of banks (about one-third of the banks in Nevada, with 65 percent of all deposits and 75 percent of commercial loans). U.S. iron and steel exports decreased 85.5 percent by 1932 due to retaliation by Canada. The cumulative decrease in those exports below their pre-tariff levels totaled $369 million. Is it any wonder that Pittsburgh saw 11 of its largest banks, with $67 million in deposits, close in September 1931? How about U.S.-made automobiles? European retaliation raised tariffs so high that U.S. exports declined from $541 million per year to $97 million by 1933, an 82 percent drop! Thus there was a cumulative export decline of $1.57 billion from the pre-tariff volume to 1933. Is it any wonder that the Detroit banking system (tied to the auto industry) was in complete collapse by early 1933?

Let's not forget World War I, which made America the world's creditor. The center of the financial world moved from London to New York, and billions of dollars were owed to large U.S. banks. The Smoot-Hawley Tariff threw inter-allied war-debt repayment relations into limbo by shutting down world trade. An international moratorium on debtor repayments to the United States froze billions in foreign assets, thus weakening the financial solvency of the American banks. Specifically, over $2 billion worth of German loans were obstructed by Germany's inability to acquire dollars through trade to repay its debts. This same scenario played out in many other countries as well. The tariff wars created widespread financial crises across America, Europe, and a host of nations in South America. In September 1931 England abandoned sound money; America would follow suit in 1933. The functional operation of the post-World War I gold exchange standard was sabotaged by worldwide protectionism in reaction to Smoot-Hawley.

Historians of the Great Depression have overlooked important connections between trade conditions and monetary collapse. The tariff and retaliations against it destroyed the world trade system and demolished the integrated world financial structure operating under the gold-exchange standard as well. America's monetary and capital structure from 1921 to 1929 was primarily shaped by six factors: first, a centrally planned monetary system; second, a decade of disguised inflation; third, branch-banking restrictions; fourth, state deposit insurance programs; fifth, agricultural subsidies; and finally, a plethora of taxes and regulations.

Smoot-Hawley placed enormous pressure on the central banking system and capital structure. In addition it caused the dramatic loss of export markets and declining farm income (due to foreign retaliation), rendering much agricultural useless. This was responsible for widespread agricultural bank failures, which then led to contagion effects. Due to the uncertainty of trade conditions, each of the ten largest world economies had their secondary financial markets crash. It created international financial chaos leading to foreign debt repayment suspensions. As a result of thousands of bank failures, the U.S. money supply dropped 29 percent from 1929 to 1933. (The weighted average of the world money supply of the eight largest economies annually declined by double digits from 1931 to 1932). All of this, and much more—and yet only 2 percent of GNP? We think not.

MACROECONOMIC THOUGHT AND SMOOT-HAWLEY

Modern macroeconomics falls into three broad schools of thought: Keynesian, monetarist (including New Classical), and Austrian. While great differences exist among the different theories of the business cycle, all seem to agree that the tariff had little causal relevance to the severity of the Great Depression. For example, Keynesian Peter Temin never cites the tariff once in his Did Monetary Forces Cause the Great Depression? Likewise Milton Friedman and Anna Schwartz delegate a mere footnote to Smoot-Hawley in their massive treatise, A Monetary History of the United States, 1867–1960. To his credit Austrian economist Murray Rothbard at least devotes one and a half pages to the tariff in America's Great Depression.

As noted Smoot-Hawley can be directly linked to the U.S. agricultural crisis of the early 1930s and the initial banking crises in a variety of Midwestern agricultural states. Therefore trade policy may have indirectly, but severely, worsened monetary conditions. If the great monetary contraction was an important factor in the severity of the Great Depression, then the Smoot-Hawley tariff must be held responsible in large part. Estimates that downplay the significance of the tariff on aggregate economic activity are dangerous because the correct lessons will not be learned. The relationship between monetary policy and trade policy is not a one-way street. Policymakers speak of affecting the terms of trade by manipulating the money, but they do not realize that their money has become vulnerable to the terms of trade. Modern macro and micro modeling biases preclude economists from seeing this full impact.

SMOOT-HAWLEY AND BANK CRISES

In 1976 monetarist Allan Meltzer noted, "Given the size of the decline in food exports and in agricultural prices, it is not surprising that many of the U.S. banks that failed in 1930 and in 1931 were in agricultural regions." Meltzer's observation indicates that misguided trade policy may have triggered the bank failures and resulting monetary collapse in a significant way. We believe Meltzer's insight gives us a better understanding of the Great Depression.

The most widely accepted theory for the beginning of the Great Depression is the monetarist narrative, which has the collapsing banking system as the prime causal factor. The empirical evidence suggests that a disguised monetary inflation throughout the 1920s was followed abruptly by an open and severe deflation following 1929. The appreciable financial disintegration and deflation caused by over 10,000 bank failures and an implosion of the inverted credit pyramid certainly had very real negative economic effects.

The thesis that a negative trade shock can impact monetary policy fits these empirical puzzle pieces together. The tariff not only closed off the U.S. export market to farmers, it also left a vast volume of heterogeneous and specific capital goods used in agricultural production idle and suddenly worthless. Empty silos and buildings, rusting tools and machinery, and unused acreage—all in particular geographical regions—led to severe liquidations and farm foreclosures in the states experiencing the first banking crisis, with the vast bulk of failures involving small state-chartered rural banks. Economic historian Eugene White, who examined individual bank balance-sheet data, identifies the agricultural distress in the Midwestern states as a central reason for the pattern of failures. The Smoot-Hawley tariff was a direct factor in both the pattern of failures and their geographic location.

MICROECONOMIC CONNECTIONS

Here is where the Austrian business cycle model can aid our understanding of the crisis. The monetary theory of capital malinvestment arises from relative price distortions and heterogeneous capital. Both points are by and large absent from most macro modeling of business cycles. These microeconomic connections are, however, fundamental. Disguised inflation in the 1920s probably created a constellation of malinvestments in need of liquidation, meaning that by 1929 a business recession was likely inevitable. However, an extraordinary tariff war brought world trade to a screeching halt. The tariff created additional malinvestment in a capital structure already in need of market readjustments. Both prior monetary inflation and restrictive trade policy led to and exacerbated the economic downturn. They are not mutually exclusive alternatives.

Misguided public policies, such as state-run deposit insurance and branch-banking restrictions, created a banking system vulnerable to pervasive failures caused by adverse trade shocks. The moral-hazard problems associated with inaccurate risk-pricing—and the fragility of the system due to restrictions on geographical risk diversification—would prove fatal. At the same time that intervention was leading rural banks to commit capital to riskier loan portfolios, intervention was exposing them to additional risk. When unexpected changes in regional economic conditions arise from arbitrary interventions in the free-trade system, undiversified banks will fail in large numbers. Smoot-Hawley, one of the most massive tariffs in American history, destroyed an enormous portion of the vulnerable capital structure. The resultant contagion, bank runs, and failures that followed show that trade policy can affect monetary conditions.

Central Bank Illusion

Whether the Federal Reserve could have stopped the contagion and subsequent bank failures misses the main economic point. Central-banking advocates sell an illusion of monetary stability, when in reality the system is wide open to adverse shocks and therefore is highly unstable over the long run. A central bank can easily overexpand or overcontract the stock of money and credit. This is best illustrated by the contrast of the Federal Reserve System to its freer Canadian counterpart. Canada did not have antibranching regulations, socialized deposit insurance, or a central bank. This is significant because over 30 percent of Canada's GNP originated in foreign trade. Smoot-Hawley escalated tariff barriers between Canada and the United States, yet Canada did not experience any bank failures or bank runs, and its money supply declined by only 13 percent (versus 29 percent in America). There is every reason to believe that a free-banking system most likely would have prevented the disguised inflation of the 1920s and averted the geographical vulnerabilities

along with the open secondary deflation characteristic of the 1930s. After World War I many countries tragically established central banks under the illusion that monopoly and central planning in money would lead to economic stability. History has rendered its verdict on central planning: Whether it be shoes, screws, or money, it always fails.

All of which brings us to today. While "welfare-warfare" states throughout the world are running huge fiscal deficits, their central banks are recklessly monetizing massive quantities of debt (inflation). Extraordinary volatility now characterizes financial markets amidst a worsening sovereign debt crisis. Major financial institutions throughout the world hold mountainous portfolios of worthless assets that government policy has steered them into holding. Defaults threaten to destroy the world monetary systems in spite of all the short-run political machinations of prime ministers and central-bank leaders. And in these dangerous waters, what do we hear from the politicians, many already with their hands red? Trade protectionism!

When political agents denounce China on trade and demand an appreciation of its currency, it is the functional equivalent of placing a tariff on each and every Chinese export. This type of protectionist saber-rattling risks igniting not only a destructive international trade war but also, with the economy in the aftermath of a colossal bubble and the world's banker growing restless with its hoard of depreciating IOUs, vastly more damage than the world is prepared to handle. Have we learned nothing from the past?

CHAPTER 3

Money

Money, What Is It Good For?

By Thomas Rustici

The initial chapters in this anthology have been designed to train the student in the fundamentals of microeconomic Choice Theory. Macroeconomic theory detached from microeconomic principles is seriously flawed, though it has been common practice at least since the early 1950s to treat price theory and macro theory almost as separate disciplines. This was due primarily to the influence of John Maynard Keynes and his 1936 book *The General Theory of Employment, Interest and Money*. Prior to Keynes, economic science was broadly understood as Price and Money and Banking Theory. In short, before the 1930s students would learn about supply and demand, the unique role and nature of money, price and income determination, and the broad principles of economic cycles and growth. This defined the scope and nature of economics.

The followers of Keynes, however, created a methodological *wall of separation* between Choice Theory (microeconomics) and The Aggregate Economy (macroeconomics).For a student leaving microeconomics class and entering his first macro class this must seem puzzling. He has left a world where values are peacefully coordinated, prices move to clear markets, and production is generally efficient, and entered into another where nothing can be produced without central coordination, markets break down

because prices won't budge, and the economy is in perpetual recession or outright collapse at the aggregate level. The economy has become unmoored and seems to have passed through the looking glass.

In fact the study of the macro economy must be returned to its micro foundations. A recent and welcome trend has been the attempt to discover the micro underpinnings of macroeconomics. A cursory examination of modern macroeconomics brings to the forefront this basic return to some variation of that classical world--view. A wide range of schools of thought, including monetarism, neoclassical synthesis (around the Phillips Curve), rational expectations, supply—side economics, Austrian economics, and even to some extent new—Keynesian theory illustrate this general trend. This is the right spirit.

It is our firm belief, however, that the pre--Keynesian classical thinkers did not make this methodological wrong turn. Thus, much of modern macroeconomics, beginning with Keynes, has been a diversion and a return to the classical roots of monetary and macro theory is in order. A proper reading and understanding of this rich body of thought will provide the foundation and logical consistency necessary to understand the real forces behind the visible outcomes in the economy. The first and most fundamental element of the macro economy that we must understand is money.

MONEY, WHAT IS IT GOOD FOR?

Money is the most important economic good in any society for it is the medium of exchange. Money makes specialization and the division of labor, and so the economy, possible; money makes civilization possible. Wide scale killing, enslaving, and plunder can be achieved without money, but wide scale peaceful trade is not. Money is central to the dispersion of knowledge. The extraordinarily complex structure of production that brings shoes, bread, and computers into our life is not possible absent a medium of exchange. Without money we are reduced to direct barter in our social relations.

But how did money come about? The seminal essay by Carl Menger, *The Theory of Money*, describes the microeconomic and entrepreneurial underpinnings of the genesis of money. Money originated as a classic spontaneous order, a product of human action but not of human design or intention. Various types of commodities arose to gradually replace direct barter in a society with indirect exchange, that is, to they became money. Direct barter is extraordinarily inefficient because it involves the problem of the *double coincidence of wants* and it is difficult to ascertain the quality and character of many goods at the time of exchange. Money solves these problems and more.

Once a usable commodity becomes money, it then acquires subsidiary functional roles in an economy. Money becomes a **unit of account** through which financial accounting records are kept for profit-and-loss calculation. For all practical purposes, accounting is impossible in a barter world because a common unit of account is needed for all values to be standardized and recorded. Money also functions as a **store of value.** As such it allows for more efficient inter-temporal trade and investment over direct barter goods. As Adam Smith explains in his essay, *The Origin and Use of Money*, efficient money needs to be durable, divisible, portable, hide able, and inexpensively maintained. As the medium of exchange becomes the institution for financial accounting as well as a store of wealth for future time periods, it also becomes **standard of deferred payments** for efficient credit transactions. Again, money makes civilization possible.

The following vignette illustrates the wide range of commodities that have served for purposes of medium of exchange.

The Origin and Evolution of Money

Various Kinds of Money Throughout History

By Thomas Rustici

clay	pigs	wool	porcelain
iron	salt	horses	cowrie shells
stone	bronze	wampum	sheep
corn	iron	nickel	tortoise shells
goats	wine	copper	paper
beer	slaves	brass	nails
leather	whale teeth	rice	knives
silver	pasteboard	boar tusks	tea
hoes	gold	playing cards	pots
furs	tobacco	electrum	lead
debts of individ.	cattle	pitch	boats
debts of banks	cigarettes	deer skins	cognac
fish hooks	dried codfish	debts of gov.	ivory
woodpecker scalps	porpoise teeth	goose quills	cocoa beans

World's First Coins

Birmingham Button Makers, the Royal Mint, and the Beginnings of Modern Coinage

By Rondo Cameron

Figure 1: Greek coins. The coin on the left, with simple punch marks on the face (A) and a striated surface on the back (B), is of electrum, dating, from about 600 B.C. The silver coin on the right, with the face of Athena (C) and the owl of Athens on the reverse (D), dates from about 480 W.C.; it shows how far the technology of minting advanced in little more than a century. (Hirmer Fotoarchiv München.)

"…but more likely the first coins were struck by some enterprising merchant or banker of one of the Greek cities on the coast as a form of advertising. In any event, their potential for both profit and prestige was quickly recognized by governments, which arrogated the coining of money as a state monopoly. The effigy of a ruler or the symbol of a city (the owl of Athens, for example) stamped on a coin testified not only to the purity of the metal but also the glory of its issuer." (p. 36)

Of the Origin and Use of Money

By Adam Smith

When the division of labour has been once thoroughly established. It is but a very small part of a man's wants which the produce of his own labour can supply. He supplies the far greater part of them by exchanging that surplus part of the produce of his own labour, which is over and above his own consumption, for such parts of the produce of other men's labour as he has occasion for. Every man thus lives by exchanging, or becomes in some measure a merchant, and the society itself grows to be what is properly a commercial society.

But when the division of labour first began to take place, this power of exchanging must frequently have been very much clogged and embarrassed in its operations. One man, we shall suppose, has more of a certain commodity than he himself has occasion for, while another has less. The former consequently would be glad to dispose of, and the latter to purchase, a part of this superfluity. But if this latter should chance to have nothing that the former stands in need of, no exchange can be made between them. The butcher has more meat in his shop than he himself can consume, and the brewer and the baker would each of them be willing to purchase a part of it. But they have nothing to offer in exchange, except the different productions of their respective trades, and the butcher is already provided with all the bread and beer which he has immediate occasion for. No exchange can, in this case, be made between them. He cannot be their merchant, nor they his customers; and they are all of them thus mutually less serviceable to one another. In order to avoid the inconveniency of such situations, every prudent man in every period of society, after the first establishment of the division of labour, must naturally have endeavoured to manage his affairs in such a manner, as to have at all times by him, besides the peculiar produce of his own industry, a certain quantity of some one commodity or other, such as he imagined few people would be likely to refuse in exchange for the produce of their industry.[1]

Many different commodities, it is probable, were successively both thought of and employed for this purpose. In the rude ages of society, cattle are said to have been the common instrument of commerce; and, though they must have been a most inconvenient one, yet in old times we find things were frequently valued according to the number of cattle which had been given in exchange for them. The armour of Diomede, says Homer, cost only nine oxen; but that of Glaucus cost an hundred oxen.[2] Salt is said to be the common instrument of commerce and exchanges in Abyssinia;[3] a species of shells in some parts of the coast of India; dried cod at Newfoundland; tobacco in Virginia;[4] sugar in some of our West India colonies; hides or dressed leather in some other countries; and there is at this day a village in Scotland where it is not uncommon, I am told, for a workman to carry nails instead of money to the baker's shop or the ale-house.[5]

In all countries, however, men seem at last to have been determined by irresistible reasons to give the preference, for this employment, to metals above every other commodity.[6] Metals can not only be kept with as little loss as any other commodity, scarce any thing being less perishable than they are, but they can likewise, without any loss, be divided into any number of parts, as by fusion those parts can easily be reunited again; a quality which no other equally durable commodities possess, and which more than any other quality renders them fit to be the instruments of commerce and circulation. The man who wanted to buy salt, for example, and had nothing but cattle to give in exchange for it, must have been obliged to buy salt to the value of a whole ox, or a whole sheep, at a time. He could seldom buy less than this, because what he was to give for it could seldom be divided without loss; and if he had a mind to buy more, he must, for the same reasons, have been obliged to buy double or triple the quantity, the value, to wit, of two or three oxen, or of two or three sheep. If, on the contrary, instead of sheep or oxen, he had metals to give in exchange for it, he could easily proportion the quantity of the metal to the precise quantity of the commodity which he had immediate occasion for.

Different metals have been made use of by different nations for this purpose. Iron was the common instrument of commerce among the antient Spartans; copper among the antient Romans; and gold and silver among all rich and commercial nations.

Those metals seem originally to have been made use of for this purpose in rude bars, without any stamp or coinage. Thus we are told by Pliny,[7] upon the authority of Timæus, an antient historian, that, till the time of Servius Tullius, the Romans had no coined money, but made use of unstamped bars of copper, to purchase whatever they had occasion for. These rude bars, therefore, performed at this time the function of money.

The use of metals in this rude state was attended with two very considerable inconveniencies; first with the trouble of weighing;[8] and, secondly, with that[9] of assaying them. In the precious metals, where a small difference in the quantity makes a great difference in the value, even the business of weighing, with proper exactness, requires at least very accurate weights and scales. The weighing of gold in particular is an operation of some nicety. In the coarser metals, indeed, where a small error would be of little consequence, less accuracy would, no doubt, be necessary. Yet we should find it excessively troublesome, if every time a poor man had occasion either to buy or sell a farthing's worth of goods, he was obliged to weigh the farthing. The operation of assaying is still more difficult, still more tedious, and, unless a part of the metal is fairly melted in the crucible, with proper dissolvents, any conclusion that can be drawn from it, is extremely uncertain. Before the institution of coined money, however, unless they went through this tedious and difficult operation, people must always have been liable to the grossest frauds and impositions, and instead of a pound weight of pure silver, or pure copper, might receive in exchange for their goods, an adulterated composition of the coarsest and cheapest materials, which had, however, in their outward appearance, been made to resemble those metals. To prevent such abuses, to facilitate exchanges, and thereby to encourage all sorts of industry and commerce, it has been found necessary, in all countries that have made any considerable advances towards improvement, to affix a public stamp upon certain quantities of such particular metals, as were in those countries commonly made use of to purchase goods. Hence the origin of coined money, and of those public offices called mints;[10] institutions exactly of the same nature with those of the aulnagers and stampmasters of woollen and linen cloth.[11] All of them are equally meant to ascertain, by means of a public stamp, the quantity and uniform goodness of those different commodities when brought to market.

The first public stamps of this kind that were affixed to the current metals, seem in many cases to have been intended to ascertain, what it was both most difficult and most important to ascertain, the goodness or fineness of the metal, and to have resembled the sterling mark which is at present affixed to plate and bars of silver, or the Spanish mark which is sometimes affixed to ingots of gold, and which being struck only upon one side of the piece, and not covering the whole surface, ascertains the fineness, but not the weight of the metal. Abraham weighs to Ephron the four hundred shekels of silver which he had agreed to pay for the field of Machpelah.[12] They are said however to be the current money of the merchant, and yet are received by weight and not by tale, in the same manner as ingots of gold and bars of silver are at present. The revenues of the antient Saxon kings of England are said to have been paid, not in money but in kind, that is, in victuals and provisions of all sorts. William the Conqueror introduced the custom of paying them in money.[13] This money, however, was, for a long time, received at the exchequer, by weight and not by tale.[14]

The inconveniency and difficulty of weighing those metals with exactness gave occasion to the institution of coins, of which the stamp, covering entirely both sides of the piece and sometimes the edges too, was supposed to ascertain not only the fineness, but the weight of the metal. Such coins, therefore, were received by tale as at present, without the trouble of weighing.

The denominations of those coins seem originally to have expressed the weight or quantity of metal contained in them. In the time of Servius Tullius, who first coined money at Rome,[15] the Roman As or Pondo contained a Roman pound of good copper. It was divided in the same manner as our Troyes pound, into twelve ounces, each of which contained a real ounce of good copper. The English pound sterling in the time of Edward I., contained a pound, Tower weight, of silver of a known fineness. The Tower pound seems to have been something more than the Roman pound, and something less than the Troyes pound. This last was not introduced into the mint of England till the 18th of Henry VIII. The French livre contained in the time of Charlemagne a pound, Troyes weight, of silver of a known fineness. The fair of Troyes in Champaign was at that time frequented by all the nations of Europe, and the weights and measures of so famous a market were generally known

and esteemed. The Scots money pound contained, from the time of Alexander the First to that of Robert Bruce, a pound of silver of the same weight and fineness with the English pound sterling. English, French, and Scots pennies too, contained all of them originally a real pennyweight of silver, the twentieth part of an ounce, and the two-hundred-and-fortieth part of a pound. The shilling too seems originally to have been the denomination of a weight. *When wheat is at twelve shillings the quarter,* says an antient statute of Henry III. *then wastel bread of a farthing shall weigh eleven shillings and four pence.*[16] The proportion, however, between the shilling and either the penny on the one hand, or the pound on the other, seems not to have been so constant and uniform as that between the penny and the pound. During the first race of the kings of France, the French sou or shilling appears upon different occasions to have contained five, twelve, twenty, and forty pennies.[17] Among the antient Saxons a shilling appears at one time to have contained only five pennies,[18] and it is not improbable that it may have been as variable among them as among their neighbours, the antient Franks. From the time of Charlemagne among the French,[19] and from that of William the Conqueror among the English[20] the proportion between the pound, the shilling, and the penny, seems to have been uniformly the same as at present, though the value of each has been very different. For in every country of the world, I believe, the avarice and injustice of princes and sovereign states, abusing the confidence of their subjects, have by degrees diminished the real quantity of metal, which had been originally contained in their coins. The Roman As, in the latter ages of the Republic, was reduced to the twenty-fourth part of its original value, and, instead of weighing a pound, came to weigh only half an ounce.[21] The English pound and penny contain at present about a third only; the Scots pound and penny about a thirty-sixth; and the French pound and penny about a sixty-sixth part of their original value.[22] By means of those operations the princes and sovereign states which performed them were enabled, in appearance, to pay their debts and to fulfil their engagements with a smaller quantity of silver than would otherwise have been requisite. It was indeed in appearance only; for their creditors were really defrauded of a part of what was due to them. All other debtors in the state were allowed the same privilege, and might pay with the same nominal sum of the new and debased coin whatever they had borrowed in the old. Such operations, therefore, have always proved favourable to the debtor, and ruinous to the creditor, and have sometimes produced a greater and more universal revolution in the fortunes of private persons, than could have been occasioned by a very great public calamity.[23]

It is in this manner that money has become in all civilized nations the universal instrument of commerce, by the intervention of which goods of all kinds are bought and sold, or exchanged for one another.[24]

What are the rules which men naturally observe in exchanging them either for money or for one another, I shall now proceed to examine. These rules determine what may be called the relative or exchangeable value of goods.

The word VALUE, it is to be observed, has two different meanings, and sometimes expresses the utility of some particular object, and sometimes the power of purchasing other goods which the possession of that object conveys. The one may be called 'value in use;' the other, 'value in exchange.' The things which have the greatest value in use have frequently little or no value in exchange; and on the contrary, those which have the greatest value in exchange have frequently little or no value in use. Nothing is more useful than water: but it will purchase scarce any thing; scarce any thing can be had in exchange for it. A diamond, on the contrary, has scarce any value in use; but a very great quantity of other goods may frequently be had in exchange for it.[25]

In order to investigate the principles which regulate the exchangeable value of commodities, I shall endeavour to shew.

First, what is the real measure of this exchangeable value; or, wherein consists the real price of all commodities.

Secondly, what are the different parts of which this real price is composed or made up.

And, lastly, what are the different circumstances which sometimes raise some or all of these different parts of price above, and sometimes sink them below their natural or ordinary rate; or, what are the causes which sometimes hinder the market price, that is, the actual price of commodities, from coinciding exactly with what may be called their natural price.

I shall endeavour to explain, as fully and distinctly as I can, those three subjects in the three following chapters, for which I must very earnestly entreat both the patience and attention of the reader: his patience in order to examine a detail which may perhaps in some places appear unnecessarily tedious; and his attention in order to understand what may, perhaps, after the fullest explication which I am capable of giving of it, appear still in some degree obscure. I am always willing to run some hazard of being tedious in order to be sure that I am perspicuous; and after taking the utmost pains that I can to be perspicuous, some obscurity may still appear to remain upon a subject[26] in its own nature extremely abstracted.

NOTES FOR THIS CHAPTER

1. [The paragraph has a close resemblance to Harris, *Money and Coins*, pt. i., §§ 19, 20.]

2. [*Iliad*, vi. 236; quoted with the same object in Pliny, *Hist. Nat.*, lib. xxxiii., cap. i.; Pufendorf, *De jure naturæ et gentium*, lib. v., cap. v., § 1; Martin-Leake, *Historical Account of English Money*, 2nd ed., 1745 p. 4 and elsewhere.]

3. [Montesquieu, *Esprit des lois*, liv. xxii., chap i., note.]

4. [W. Douglass, *A Summary Historical and Political of the First Planting, Progressive Improvements and Present State of the British Settlements in North America*, 1760, vol. ii., p. 364. Certain law officers' fees in Washington were still computed in tobacco in 1888.—J. J. Lalor, *Cyclopædia of Political Science*, 1888, *s.v.* Money, p. 879.]

5. [Playfair, ed. of *Wealth of Nations*, 1805, vol. i., p. 36, says the explanation of this is that factors furnish the nailers with materials and during the time they are working give them a credit for bread, cheese and chandlery goods, which they pay for in nails when the iron is

worked up. The fact that nails are metal is forgotten at the beginning of the next paragraph in the text above.]

6. [For earlier theories as to these reasons see Grotius, *De jure belli et pacis*, lib. ii., cap. xii., § 17; Pufendorf, *De jure naturæ et gentium*, lib. v., cap. i., § 13; Locke, *Some Considerations* 2nd ed., 1696, p. 31; Law, *Money and Trade*, 1705, ch. i.; Hutcheson, *System of Moral Philosophy*, 1755, vol. ii., pp. 55, 56; Montesquieu, *Esprit des lois*, liv. xxii., ch. ii.; Cantillon, *Essai sur la Nature du Commerce en général*, 1755, pp. 153, p. 355–357; Harris, *Money and Coins*, pt. i., §§ 22-27, and cp. *Lectures*, pp. 182-185.]

7. Plin. Hist. Nat. lib. 33. cap. 3. ['Servius rex primus signavit aes. Antea rudi usos Romæ: Timæus tradit.' Ed. 1 reads 'authority of one Remeus, an ancient author,' Remeus being the reading in the edition of Pliny in Smith's library, cp. Bonar's *Catalogue of the Library of Adam Smith*, 1894, p. 87. Ed. 1 does not contain the note.]

8. [Ed. 1 reads ' weighing them'.]

9. [Ed. 1 reads ' with the trouble'.]

10. [Aristotle, *Politics*, 1257a, 38–41; quoted by Pufendorf, *De jure naturæ et gentium*, lib. v. cap. 1., § 12.]

11. [The aulnager measured woollen cloth in England under 25 Ed. III., st. 4, c. 1. See John Smith, *Chronicon Rusticum-Commerciale or Memoirs of Wool*, 1747, vol. i., p. 37. The stampmasters of linen cloth in the linen districts of Scotland were appointed under 10 Ann., c. 21, to prevent 'divers abuses and deceits' which 'have of late years been used in the manufactories of linen cloth … with respect to the lengths, breadths and unequal sorting of yarn, which leads to the great debasing and undervaluing of the said linen cloth both at home and in foreign parts.'—*Statutes of the Realm*, vol. ix., p. 682.]

12. [Genesis xxiii 16.]

13. ['King William the First, for the better pay of his warriors caused the *firmes* which till his time had for the most part been answered in victuals, to be converted *in pecuniam numeratam*.'—Lowndes, *Report containing an Essay for the Amendment of the Silver Coins*, 1695, p. 4. Hume, whom Adam Smith often follows, makes no such absurd statement, *History*, ed. of 1773, vol. i., pp. 225, 226.]

14. [Lowndes, Essay, p. 4.]

15. [Above, I.4.6.]

16. [The Assize of Bread and Ale, 51 Hen. III., contains an elaborate scale beginning, 'When a quarter of wheat is sold for xii *d.* then wastel bread of a farthing shall weigh vi *l.* and xvi *s.*' and goes on to the figures quoted in the text above. The statute is quoted at second-hand from Martin Folkes' *Table of English Silver Coins* with the same object by Harris, *Essay upon Money and Coins*, pt. i., § 29, but Harris does not go far enough in the scale to bring in the penny as a weight. As to this scale see below, I.11.100, 114–116.]

17. [Ed. 1 reads 'twenty, forty and forty-eight pennies'. Gamier, *Recherches sur la nature et les causes de la richesse des nations, par Adam Smith*, 1802 tom. v., p. 55, in a note on this passage says that the sou was always twelve deniers.]

18. [Hume, *History of England*, ed. of 1773, i. p. 226. Fleetwood, *Chronicon Preciosum*, 1707, p. 30. These authorities say there were 48 shillings in the pound, so that 240 pence would still make £1.]

19. [Harris *Money and Coins*, pt. i., § 29.]

20. ['It is thought that soon after the Conquest a pound sterling was divided into twenty shillings.'—Hume, *History of England*, ed. of 1773, vol. i., p. 227.]

21. [Pliny, *Hist. Nat.*, lib. xxxiii., cap. iii.; see below, vol. ii., pp. 468, 469.]

22. [Harris, *Money and Coins*, pt. i., § 30, note, makes the French livre about one seventieth part of its original value.]

23. [The subject of debased and depreciated coinage occurs again below, I.5.11–13, I.11.143–144; vol. ii., IV.6.16–32, V.3.61–65. One of the reasons why gold and silver became the most usual forms of money is dealt with below, I.11.79–83. See Coin and Money in the index.]

24. [In *Lectures*, pp. 182–190, where much of this chapter is to be found, money is considered 'first as the measure of value and then as the medium of permutation or exchange'. Money is said to have had its origin in the fact that men naturally fell upon one commodity with which to compare the value of all other commodities. When this commodity was once selected it became the medium of exchange. In this chapter money comes into use from the first as a medium of exchange, and its use as a measure of value is not mentioned. The next chapter explains that it is vulgarly used as a measure of

value because it is used as an instrument of commerce or medium of exchange.]

25. [*Lectures,* p. 157. Law, *Money and Trade,* 1705, ch. 1. (followed by Harris, *Money and Coins,* pt. 1., § 3), contrasts the value of water with that of diamonds. The cheapness of water is referred to by Plato *Euthydem.* 304 B., quoted by Pufendorf, *De jure naturæ et gentium,* lib. v., cap. 1., § 6; cp. Barbeyrac's note on § 4.]

26. [Ed. 1 reads 'subject which is'.]

What Has Government Done to Our Money?

By Murray Rothbard

I.

Introduction

Few economic subjects are more tangled, more confused than money. Wrangles abound over "tight money" vs. "easy money," over the roles of the Federal Reserve System and the Treasury, over various versions of the gold standard, etc. Should the government pump money into the economy or siphon it out? Which branch of the government? Should it encourage credit or restrain it? Should it return to the gold standard? If so, at what rate? These and countless other questions multiply, seemingly without end.

Perhaps the Babel of views on the money question stems from man's propensity to be "realistic," i.e., to study only immediate political and economic problems. If we immerse ourselves wholly in day-to-day affairs, we cease making fundamental distinctions, or asking the really basic questions. Soon, basic issues are forgotten, and aimless drift is substituted for firm adherence to principle. Often we need to gain perspective, to stand aside from our everyday affairs in order to understand them more fully. This is particularly true in our economy, where interrelations are so intricate that we must isolate a few important factors, analyze them, and then trace their operations in the complex world. This was the point of "Crusoe economics," a favorite device of classical economic theory. Analysis of Crusoe and Friday on a desert island, much abused by critics as irrelevant to today's world, actually performed the very useful function of spotlighting the basic axioms of human action.

Of all the economic problems, money is possibly the most tangled, and perhaps where we most need perspective. Money, moreover, is the economic area most encrusted and entangled with centuries of government meddling. Many people—many economists—usually devoted to the free market stop short at money. Money, they insist, is different; it must be supplied by government and regulated by government. They never think of state control of money as interference in the free market; a free market in money is unthinkable to them. Governments must mint coins, issue paper, define "legal tender," create central banks, pump money in and out, "stabilize the price level," etc.

Historically, money was one of the first things controlled by government, and the free market "revolution" of the eighteenth and nineteenth centuries made very little dent in the monetary sphere. So it is high time that we turn fundamental attention to the life-blood of our economy—money.

Let us first ask ourselves the question: Can money be organized under the freedom principle? Can we have a free market in money as well as in other goods and services? What would be the shape of such a market? And what are the effects of various governmental controls? If we favor the free market in other directions, if we wish to eliminate government invasion of person and property, we have no more important task than to explore the ways and means of a free market in money.

1.

The Value of Exchange

How did money begin? Clearly, Robinson Crusoe had no need for money. He could not have eaten gold coins. Neither would Crusoe and Friday, perhaps exchanging fish for lumber, need to bother about money. But when society expands beyond a few families, the stage is already set for the emergence of money.

To explain the role of money, we must go even further back, and ask: why do men exchange at all? Exchange is the prime basis of our economic life. Without exchanges, there would be no real economy and, practically, no society. Clearly, a voluntary exchange occurs because both parties expect to benefit. An exchange is an agreement between A and B to transfer the goods or services of one man for the goods and services of the other. Obviously, both benefit because each values what he receives in exchange more than what he gives up. When Crusoe, say, exchanges some fish for lumber, he values the lumber he "buys" more than the fish he "sells," while Friday, on the contrary, values the fish more than the lumber. From Aristotle to Marx, men have mistakenly believed that an exchange records some sort of equality of value—that if one barrel of fish is exchanged for ten logs, there is some sort of underlying *equality* between them. Actually, the exchange was made only because each party valued the two products in *different* order.

Why should exchange be so universal among mankind? Fundamentally, because of the great *variety* in nature: the variety in man, and the diversity of location of natural resources. Every man has a different set of skills and aptitudes, and every plot of ground has its own unique features, its own distinctive resources. From this external natural fact of variety come exchanges; wheat in Kansas for iron in Minnesota; one man's medical services for another's playing of the violin. Specialization permits each man to develop his best skill, and allows each region to develop its own particular resources. If no one could exchange, if every man were forced to be completely self-sufficient, it is obvious that most of us would starve to death, and the rest would barely remain alive. Exchange is the lifeblood, not only of our economy, but of civilization itself.

The Theory of Money

Principles of Economics

By Carl Menger

THE NATURE AND ORIGIN OF MONEY[1]

In the early stages of trade, when economizing individuals are only slowly awakening to knowledge of the economic gains that can be derived from exploitation of existing exchange opportunities, their attention is, in keeping with the simplicity of all cultural beginnings, directed only to the most obvious of these opportunities. In considering the goods he will acquire in trade, each man takes account only of their use value to himself. Hence the exchange transactions that are actually performed are restricted naturally to situations in which economizing individuals have goods in their possession that have a smaller *use value* to them than goods in the possession of other economizing individuals who value the same goods in reverse fashion.

A has a sword that has a smaller use value to him than B's plough, while to B the same plough has a smaller use value than A's sword—at the beginning of human trade, all exchange transactions actually performed are restricted to cases of this sort.

It is not difficult to see that the number of exchanges actually performed must be very narrowly limited under these conditions. How rarely does it happen that a good in the possession of one person has a smaller use value to him than another good owned by another person who values these goods in precisely the opposite way at the same time! And even when this relationship is present, how much rarer still must situations be in which the two persons actually meet each other! A has a fishing net that he would like to exchange for a quantity of hemp. For him to be in a position actually to perform this exchange, it is not only necessary that there be another economizing individual, B, who is willing to give a quantity of hemp corresponding to the wishes of A for the fishing net, but also that the two economizing individuals, with these specific wishes, meet each other. Suppose that Farmer C has a horse that he would like to exchange for a number of agricultural implements and clothes. How unlikely it is that he will find another person who needs his horse and is, at the same time, both willing and in a position to

---

1 Theodor Mommsen, *Geschichte des römischen Münzwesens*, Berlin, 1860, pp. v–xx, and 167 ff.; Carnap, "Zur Geschichte der Münzwissenschaft und der Werthzeichen" *Zeitschrift für die gesammte Staatswissenschaft*, XVI (i860), 548–396; Friedrich Kenner, "Die Anfänge des Geldes in Alterthume," *Sitzungsberichte der Kaiserlichen Akademie der Wissenschaften zu Wien: Philologisch-Historische Classe*, XLIII (1863), 382–490; Roscher, *op cit., pp.* 36–40; Hildebrand, *op. cit.,* p. 5; Scheel, op. cit., pp. 12–29; A. N. Bernardakis, "De l'origine des mon-naies et de leurs noms," *Journal des Economistes,* (Third Series), XVIII (1870), 209–245.

give him all the implements and clothes he desires to have in exchange!

This difficulty would have been insurmountable, and would have seriously impeded progress in the division of labor, and above all in the production of goods for future sale, if there had not been, in the very nature of things, a way out. But there were elements in their situation that everywhere led men inevitably, without the need for a special agreement or even government compulsion, to a state of affairs in which this difficulty was completely overcome.

The direct provision of their requirements is the ultimate purpose of all the economic endeavors of men. The *final end* of their exchange operations is therefore to exchange their commodities for such goods as have use value to them. The endeavor to attain this final end has been equally characteristic of all stages of culture and is entirely correct economically. But economizing individuals would obviously be behaving un-economically if, in all instances in which this final end cannot be reached *immediately and directly*, they were to forsake approaching it altogether.

Assume that a smith of the Homeric age has fashioned two suits of copper armor and wants to exchange them for copper, fuel, and food. He goes to market and offers his products for these goods. He would doubtless be very pleased if he were to encounter persons there who wish to purchase his armor and who, at the same time, have for sale all the raw materials and foods that he needs. But it must obviously be considered a particularly happy accident if, among the small number of persons who at any time wish to purchase a good so difficult to sell as his armor, he should find any who are offering precisely the goods that he needs. He would therefore make the marketing of his commodities either totally impossible, or possible only with the expenditure of a great deal of time, if he were to behave so un-economically as to wish to take in exchange for his commodities only goods that have use value to himself and not also other goods which, although they would have commodity-character to him, nevertheless *have greater marketability than his own commodity*. Possession of these commodities would considerably facilitate his search for persons who

have just the goods he needs. In the times of which I am speaking, cattle were, as we shall see below, the most saleable of all commodities. Even if the armorer is already sufficiently provided with cattle for his direct requirements, he would be acting very uneconomically if he did not give his armor for a number of additional cattle. By so doing, he is of course not exchanging his commodities for consumption goods (in the narrow sense in which this term is opposed to "commodities") but only for goods that also have commodity-character to him. But for his less saleable commodities he is obtaining others of greater marketability. Possession of these more saleable goods clearly multiplies his chances of finding persons on the market who will offer to sell him the goods that he needs. If our armorer correctly recognizes his individual interest, therefore, he will be led naturally, without compulsion or any special agreement, to give his armor for a corresponding number of cattle. With the more saleable commodities obtained in this way, he will go to persons at the market who are offering copper, fuel, and food for sale, in order to achieve his *ultimate objective*, the acquisition by trade of the consumption goods that he needs. But now he can proceed to this end much more quickly, more economically, and with a greatly enhanced probability of success.

As *each* economizing individual becomes increasingly more aware of his economic interest, he is led by this *interest, without any agreement, without legislative compulsion, and even without regard to the public interest*, to give his commodities in exchange for other, more saleable, commodities, even if he does not need them for any immediate consumption purpose. With economic progress, therefore, we can everywhere observe the phenomenon of a certain number of goods, especially those that are most easily saleable at a given time and place, becoming, under the powerful influence of *custom*, acceptable to everyone in trade, and thus capable of being given in exchange for any other commodity. These goods were called "*Geld*"[2] by our ancestors, a term derived

---

2 For obvious reasons, the words "*Geld*" and "*gelten*" in this and the following sentence are left untranslated.—TR.

from *"gelten"* which means to compensate or pay. Hence the term *"Geld"* in our language designates the means of payment as such.[3]

The great importance of *custom*[4] in the origin of money can be seen immediately by considering the process, described above, by which certain goods became money. The exchange of less easily saleable commodities for commodities of greater market-ability is in the economic interest of *every* economizing individual. But the actual performance of exchange operations of this kind presupposes a knowledge of their interest on the part of economizing individuals. For they must be willing to accept in exchange for their commodities, because of its greater marketability, a good that is perhaps itself quite useless to them. This knowledge will never be attained by all members of a people at the same time. On the contrary, only a small number of economizing individuals will at first recognize the advantage accruing to them from the acceptance of other, more saleable, commodities in exchange for their own whenever a direct exchange of their commodities for the goods they wish to consume is impossible or highly uncertain. This advantage is *independent of a general acknowledgement of any one commodity as money.* For an exchange of this sort will always, under any circumstances whatsoever, bring an economizing individual considerably nearer to his final end, the acquisition of the goods he wishes to consume. Since there is no better way in which men can become enlightened about their economic interests than by observation of the economic success of those who employ the correct means of achieving their ends, it is evident that nothing favored the rise of money so much as the long-practiced, and economically profitable, acceptance of eminently saleable commodities in exchange for all others by the most discerning and most capable economizing individuals. In this way, custom and practice contributed in no small degree to converting the commodities that were most saleable at a given time into commodities

that came to be accepted, not merely by many, but by all economizing individuals in exchange for their own commodities.[5]

Within the boundaries of a state, the legal order usually has an influence on the money-character of commodities which, though small, cannot be denied. The origin of money (as distinct from coin, which is only one variety of money) is, as we have seen, entirely natural and thus displays legislative influence only in the rarest instances. Money is not an invention of the state. It is not the product of a legislative act. Even the sanction of political authority is not necessary for its existence. Certain commodities came to be money quite naturally, as the result of economic relationships that were independent of the power of the state.

But if, in response to the needs of trade, a good receives the sanction of the state as money, the result will be that not only every payment to the state itself but all other payments not explicitly contracted for in other goods can be required or offered, with legally binding effect, only in units of that good. There will be the further, and especially important, result that when payment has originally been contracted for in other goods but cannot, for some reason, be made, the payment substituted can similarly be required or offered, with legally binding effect, only in units of the one particular good. Thus the sanction of the state gives a particular good the attribute of being a universal substitute in exchange, and although the state is not responsible for the existence of the money-character of the good, it is responsible for a significant improvement of its money- character.[6]

THE KINDS OF MONEY APPROPRIATE TO PARTICULAR PEOPLES AND TO PARTICULAR

---

3 See the first two paragraphs of Appendix I (p. 312) for material originally appearing here as a footnote.—TR.

4 Custom as a factor in the origin of money is stressed by Condillac, op. cit., pp. 286–290 and by G. F. Le Trosne, *De Vintérêt social*, Paris, 1777. PP. 43.

5 See Appendix J (p. 315) for material originally appended here as a footnote.—TR.

6 See Stein, *op. cit.,* p. 55; especially also Karl Knies, "Ueber die Geldentwerthung und die mit ihr in Verbindung gebrachten Erscheinungen," *Zeitschrift für die gesammte Staatwissenschaft,* XIV (1858), 266; and Mommsen, *op. cit.,* pp. vii–viii.

HISTORICAL PERIODS

Money is not the product of an agreement on the part of economizing men nor the product of legislative acts. No one invented it. As economizing individuals in social situations became increasingly aware of their economic interest, they everywhere attained the simple knowledge that surrendering less saleable commodities for others of greater saleability brings them substantially closer to the attainment of their specific economic purposes. Thus, with the progressive development of social economy, money came to exist in numerous centers of civilization independently. But precisely because money is a natural product of human economy, the specific forms in which it has appeared were everywhere and at all times the result of specific and changing economic situations. Among the same people at different times, and among different peoples at the same time, different goods have attained the special position in trade described above.

In the earliest periods of economic development, cattle seem to have been the most saleable commodity among most peoples of the ancient world. Domestic animals constituted the chief item of the wealth of every individual among nomads and peoples passing from a nomadic economy to agriculture. Their marketability extended literally to all economizing individuals, and the lack of artificial roads combined with the fact that cattle transported themselves (almost without cost in the primitive stages of civilization!) to make them saleable over a wider geographical area than most other commodities. A number of circumstances, moreover, favored broad quantitative and temporal limits to their marketability. A cow is a commodity of considerable durability. Its cost of maintenance is insignificant where pastures are available in abundance and where the animals are kept under the open sky. And in a culture in which everyone attempts to possess as large Herds as possible, cattle are usually not brought to market in excessive quantities at any one time. In the period of which I am speaking, there was no similar juncture of circumstances establishing as broad a range of marketability for any

other commodity. If we add to these circumstances the fact that trade in domestic animals was at least as well developed as trade in any other commodity, cattle appear to have been the most saleable of all available commodities and hence the natural money of the peoples of the ancient world.[7]

The trade and commerce of the most cultured people of the ancient world, the *Greeks*, whose stages of development history has revealed to us in fairly distinct outlines, showed no trace of coined money even as late as the time of Homer. Barter still prevailed, and wealth consisted of herds of cattle. Payments were made in cattle. Prices were reckoned in cattle. And cattle were used for the payment of fines. Even Draco imposed fines in cattle, and the practice was not abandoned until Solon converted them, apparently because they had outlived their usefulness, into metallic money at the rate of one drachma for a sheep and five drachmae for a cow. Even more distinctly than with the Greeks, traces of cattle-money can be recognized in the case of the cattle breeding ancestors of the peoples of the *Italian* peninsula. Until very late, cattle and, next to them sheep, formed the means of exchange among the Romans. Their earliest legal penalties were cattle fines (imposed in cattle and sheep) which appear still in the lex Aternia Tarpeia of the year 454 B.C., and were only converted to coined money 24 years later.[8]

Among our own ancestors, the old *Germanic* tribes, at a time when, according to Tacitus, they held silver and earthen vessels in equal esteem, a large herd of cattle was considered identical with riches. Barter stood in the foreground, just as it did among the Greeks of the Homeric age, and cattle again and, in this case, horses (and weapons too!) already served as means of exchange. Cattle constituted their most highly esteemed property and were preferred above all else. Legal fines were paid in cattle and weapons,

---

7 See the last two paragraphs of Appendix I (p. 313) for material appended here as a footnote in the original.—TR.

8 August Böckh, *Metrologische Untersuchungen über Gewichte, Münz-fusse und Masse des Alterthums*, Berlin, 1838, pp. 385 ff., 420 ff.; Mommsen, *op. cit.*, p. 169; Friedrich O. Hultsch, *Griechische und römische Metrologie*, Berlin, 1862, pp. 124 ff., 188 ff.

and only later in metallic money.[9] Otto the Great still imposed fines in terms of cattle.

Among the *Arabs,* the cattle standard existed as late as the time of Mohammed.[10] Among the peoples of eastern Asia Minor, where the writings of Zoroaster, the Zendavesta, were held sacred, other forms of money replaced the cattle standard only quite late, after the neighboring peoples had long gone over to a metallic currency.[11] That cattle were used as currency by the Hebrews,[12] by the peoples of Asia Minor, and by the inhabitants of Mesopotamia, in prehistoric times may be supposed although we cannot find evidence of it. These tribes all entered history at a level of civilization at which they had presumably already gone beyond the cattle standard—if one may be permitted to draw general conclusions, by analogy, from later developments, and from the fact that it appears to be unnatural in a primitive society to make large payments in metal or metallic implements.[13]

But rising civilization, and above all the division of labor and its natural consequence, the gradual formation of cities inhabited by a population devoted primarily to industry, must everywhere have had the result of simultaneously diminishing the marketability of cattle and increasing the marketability of many other commodities, especially the metals then in use. The artisan who began to trade with the farmer was seldom in a position to accept cattle as money; for a city dweller, the temporary possession of cattle necessarily involved, not only discomforts, but also considerable economic sacrifices; and the keeping and feeding of cattle imposed no significant economic sacrifice upon the farmer only as long as

he had unlimited pasture and was accustomed to keep his cattle in an open field. With the progress of civilization, therefore, cattle lost to a great extent the broad range of marketability they had previously had with respect to the number of persons to whom, and with respect to the time period within which, they could be sold economically. At the same time, they receded more and more into the background relative to other goods with respect to the spatial and quantitative limits of their marketability. They ceased to be the most saleable of commodities, the *economic* form of money, and finally ceased to be money at all.

In all cultures in which cattle had previously had the character of money, cattle-money was abandoned with the passage from a nomadic existence and simple agriculture to a more complex system in which handicraft was practised, its place being taken by the metals then in use. Among the metals that were at first principally worked by men because of their ease of extraction and malleability were copper, silver, gold, and in some cases also iron. The transition took place quite smoothly when it became necessary, since metallic implements and the raw metal itself had doubtless already been in use everywhere as money in addition to cattle-currency, for the purpose of making small payments.

Copper was the earliest metal from which the farmer's plough, the warrior's weapons, and the artisan's tools were fashioned. Copper, gold, and silver were the earliest materials used for vessels and ornaments of all kinds. At the cultural stage at which peoples passed from cattle-money to an exclusively metallic currency, therefore, copper and perhaps some of its alloys were goods of very general use, and gold and silver, as the most important means of satisfying that most universal passion of primitive men, the desire to stand out in appearance before the other members of the tribe, had become goods of most general desire. As long as they had few uses, the three metals circulated almost exclusively in finished forms. Later, circulating as raw metal, they were less limited as to use and had greater divisibility. Their marketability was neither restricted to a small number of economizing persons nor, because of their great usefulness to all peoples and easy transportability at

9   Wilh. Wackernagel, "Gewerbe, Handel und Schifffahrt der Germanen," *Zeitschrift für deutsches Alterthum,* IX (1853), 548 ff.; Jakob Grimm, *Deutsche Rechtsalterthümer,* 4th edition prepared by A. Heusler and R. Hübner, Leipzig, 1899, II, 123–124; Ad. Soetbeer, "Beiträge zur Geschichte des Geld- und Münzwesens in Deutschland," *Forschungen zur deutschen Geschichte,* I (1862), 215.

10   Aloys Sprenger, *Das Leben und die Lehre des Mohammad,* Berlin, 1861–65, III, 139.

11   Friedrich v. Spiegel, *Commentar über das Avesta,* Wien, 1864–68, I, 94 ff.

12   Moritz A. Levy, *Geschichte der jüdischen Münzen,* Leipzig, 1862, p. 7.

13   Roscher, *op cit.,* note 5 on p. 309.

relatively slight economic sacrifices, confined within narrow spatial limits. Because of their durability they were not restricted in marketability to narrow limits in time. As a result of the general competition for them, they could be more easily marketed at economic prices than any other commodities in comparable quantities (p. 227). Thus we observe an economic situation in the historical period following nomadism and simple agriculture in which these three metals, being the most saleable goods, became the exclusive means of exchange.

This transition did not take place abruptly, nor did it take place in the same way among all peoples. The newer metallic standard may have been in use for a long time along with the older cattle-standard before it replaced the latter completely. The value of an animal, in metallic money, may have served as the basis for the currency unit even after metal had completely displaced cattle as currency in trade. The Dekaboion, Tesseraboion, and Hekatomboion of the Greeks, and the earliest metallic money of the Romans and Gauls were probably of this nature, and the animal picture appearing on the pieces of metal was probably a symbol of this value.[14]

It is, to say the least, uncertain whether copper or brass, as the most important of the metals in use, were the earliest means of exchange, and whether the precious metals acquired the function of money only later. In eastern Asia, in China, and perhaps also in India, the copper standard experienced its most complete development. In central Italy an exclusively copper standard also developed. In the ancient cultures on the Euphrates and Tigris, on the other hand, not even traces of the former existence of an exclusively copper standard are to be found, and in Asia Minor and Egypt, as well as in Greece, Sicily, and lower Italy, its independent development was arrested, wherever it had existed at all, by the vast development of Mediterranean

commerce, which could not be carried on adequately with copper alone. But it is certain that all peoples who were led to adopt a copper standard as a result of the material circumstances under which their economy developed, passed on from the less precious metals to the more precious ones, from copper and iron to silver and gold, with the further development of civilization, and especially with the geographical extension of commerce. In all places, moreover, where a silver standard became established, there was a later transition to a gold standard, and if the transition was not always actually completed, the tendency existed nevertheless.

In the narrow commerce of an ancient Sabine city with the surrounding region, and in keeping with the early simplicity of Sabine customs, when the cattle-standard had outlived its usefulness, copper best served the practical purposes of the farmers and of the city dwellers as well. It was the most important metal in use, certainly the commodity whose marketability extended to the largest number of persons, and the quantitative limits of its marketability were wider than those of any other commodity—the most important requisites of money in the primitive stages of civilization. It was, moreover, a good whose easy and inexpensive preservation and storage in small amounts and whose relatively moderate cost of transportation qualified it to a sufficient degree for monetary purposes within narrow geographical limits. But as soon as the area of trade widened, as the rate of commodity turnover quickened, and as the precious metals became more and more the most saleable commodities of a new epoch, copper naturally lost its capacity to serve as money. With the trade of this people extending over the whole world, with the rapid turnover of their commodities, and with the increasing division of labor, each economizing individual felt more and more the need of carrying money on his person. With the progress of civilization, the precious metals became the most saleable commodities and thus the natural money of peoples highly developed economically.

The history of other peoples presents a picture of great differences in their economic development and hence also in their monetary institutions. When Mexico was invaded for the first time by Europeans,

---

14 Plutarch, *Lives*, with an English translation by Bernadotte Perrin, London: William Heinemann, 1914, I, 55; Pliny, *The Natural History*, translated by John Bostock and H. T. Riley, London: H. G. Bohn, 1856, IV, 5-6; Heinrich Schreiber, "Die Metallringe der Kelten als Schmuck und Geld," *Taschenbuch für Geschichte und Alterthum*, II, 67–152, 240–247, and III, 401–408.

it appears already to have reached an unusual level of economic development, according to the reports published by eye-witnesses about the condition of the country at that time. The trade of the ancient Aztecs is of special interest to us for two reasons: (1) it proves to us that the economic thinking that leads men to activity directed to the fullest possible satisfaction of their needs is everywhere responsible for analogous economic phenomena, and (2) ancient Mexico presents us with the picture of a country in the state of transition from a pure barter to a money economy. We thus have the record of a situation in which we can observe the characteristic process by which a number of goods attain greater prominence than the rest and become money.

The reports of the conquistadors and contemporary writers depict Mexico as a country with numerous cities and a well organized and imposing trade in goods. There were daily markets in the cities, and every five days major markets were held which were distributed over the country in such a way that the major market of any one city was not impaired by the competition of that of a neighboring city. There was a special large square in each city for trade in commodities, and in it a particular place was assigned for each commodity, outside of which trade in that commodity was forbidden. The only exceptions to this rule were foodstuffs and objects difficult to transport (timber, tanning, materials, stones, etc.). The number of people assembled at the market place of the capital, Mexico, was estimated to have been 20,000 to 25,000 for the daily markets, and between 40,000 and 50,000 on major market days. A great many varieties of commodities were traded.[15]

The interesting question that arises is whether, in the markets of ancient Mexico, which were similar in so many ways to those of Europe, there had also already appeared phenomena analogous in nature and origin to our money.

The actual report of the Spanish invaders is that the trade of Mexico, at the time they first entered the country, had long since ceased to move exclusively within the limits of simple barter, and that some commodities had instead already attained the special status in trade that I discussed more extensively earlier—that is, the status of money. Cocoa beans in small bags containing 8,000 to 24,000 beans, certain small cotton handkerchiefs, golds and in goose quills that were accepted according to size (balances and weighing instruments in general being unknown to the Mexicans), pieces of copper, and finally, thin pieces of tin, appear to have been the commodities that were readily accepted by-everyone (as money), even if the persons receiving them did not need them immediately, whenever a direct exchange of immediately usable commodities could not be accomplished.

Eye-witnesses mention the following commodities as being traded on the Mexican markets: live and dead animals, cocoa, all other foods, precious stones, medicinal plants, herbs, gums, resins, earths, prepared medicines, commodities made of the fibers of the century plant, of palm leaves, and of animal hair, articles made of feathers, and of wood and stone, and finally gold, copper, tin, timber, stones, tanning materials, and hides. If we consider not only this list of commodities but also (1) the fact that Mexico, at the time of its discovery by Europeans, was already a developed country with some industry and populous cities, (2) that since the majority of our domestic animals were unknown to them, a cattle-standard was entirely out of the question, (3) that cocoa was the daily beverage, cotton the most common clothing material, and gold, copper, and tin the most widely used metals of the Aztec people, and (4) that the nature of these commodities and the fact of their general use gave them greater marketability than all other commodities, it is not difficult to understand exactly why these goods became the money of the Aztec people. They were the natural, even if little developed, currency of ancient Mexico.

Analogous causes were responsible for the fact that animal skins became money among hunting peoples engaged in external trade. Among hunting tribes there is naturally an oversupply of furs, since providing a family with food by means of hunting leads to so great an accumulation of skins that at most only a competition for especially beautiful or

---

15 Francesco Saverio Clavigero, *The History of Mexico*, Richmond, 1806, II, 188 ff.

rare kinds of skins can arise among the members of the hunting tribe. But if the tribe enters into trade with foreign peoples, and a market for skins arises in which numerous consumable goods can, at the choice of the hunters, be exchanged for furs, nothing is more natural than that skins will become the most saleable good, and hence that they will come to be preferred and accepted even in exchanges taking place between the hunters themselves. Of course hunter A does not need the skins of hunter B that he accepts in an exchange, but he is aware that he will be able to exchange them easily on the markets for other goods that he does need. He therefore prefers the skins, even though they also have only the character of commodities to him, to other commodities in his possession that are less easily saleable. We can actually observe this relationship among almost all hunting tribes who carry on foreign trade with their skins.[16]

The fact that slaves and chunks of salt became money in the interior of Africa, and that cakes of wax on the upper Amazon, cod in Iceland and Newfoundland, tobacco in Maryland and Virginia, sugar in the British West Indies, and ivory in the vicinity of the Portuguese colonies, took on the functions of money is explained by the fact that these goods were, and in some cases still are, the chief articles exported from these places. Thus they acquire, just as did furs among hunting tribes, a preeminent marketability.

The local money-character of many other goods, on the other hand, can be traced back to their great and general use value locally and their resultant marketability. Examples are the money-character of dates in the oasis of Siwa, of tea-bricks in central Asia and Siberia, of glass beads in Nubia and Sennar, and of ghussub, a kind of millet, in the country of Ahir (Africa). An example in which both factors have been responsible for the money-character of a good is provided by cowrie-shells, which have, at the same time, been both a commonly desired ornament and an export commodity.[17]

Thus money presents itself to us, in its special locally and temporally different forms, not as the result of an agreement, legislative compulsion, or mere chance, but as the natural product of differences in the economic situation of different peoples at the same time, or of the same people in different periods of their history.

---

16   A beaver skin is still the unit of exchange value in several regions of the Hudson's Bay Company. Three martens are equal to one beaver, one white fox to two beavers, one black fox or one bear equal to four beavers, and one rifle equal to 15 beavers ("Die Jäger im nördlichen Amerika," *Das Ausländ*, XIX, no. 21, [Jan. 21, 1846], 84). The Estonian word "*raha*" (money) has in the related language of the Laplanders the meaning of fur (Philipp Krug, *Zur Münzkunde Russlands*, St. Petersburg, 1805). On fur money in the Russian middle ages, see the report by Nestor (A. L. Schlözer, translator, *Nestor, Russische Annalen*, Goettingen,. 1802–1809, III, 90). The old word, "*kung*" (money) really means marten. As late as 1610 a Russian war chest containing 5450 rubles in silver and 7000 rubles worth of fur was taken. (See Nikolai Karamzin, *Geschichte des russischen Reichs*, Riga, 1820–1833, XI, 183). See also Roscher, *op. cit.*, p. 309, and Heinrich Storch, *Handbuch der National-Wirthschaftlehre*, ed. by K. H. Rau, Hamburg, 1820, III, 25–26.

---

17   Roscher, *op. cit.*, note 13 on pp. 313–314.

Why Money?

By Armen Alchian

Ignorance of availability of goods and of their terms of trade and attributes will provoke efforts to reduce that ignorance in order to achieve more trade. Several institutions have evolved to reduce those costs: money, specialist middlemen who are experts in assessing attributes of goods and who carry inventories and whose reliability of assurance is high, specialized market places, and even unemployment. This paper concentrates on the way in which that ignorance leads to the use of money and how money requires concurrent exchange with specialist, expert middlemen of high reputability. It will be seen that the use of money does not rest on a bookkeeping, debt-recording function. The recording function could be done by any good without specialized markets if goods were perfectly and costlessly identifiable in all relevant, present and future, attributes including future terms of trade. We mean by money a commodity used in all or a dominant number of exchanges.

Imagine society to be composed of people with different goods but without costlessly perfect knowledge of characteristics or attributes of each good. Any exchange proposed between two parties with two goods will be hindered (be more costly) the less fully informed are the two parties about the true characteristics of the proffered goods. We assume: Interpersonal differences exist in degrees of knowledge about different goods—either by fortuitous circumstance or by deliberate development of such knowledge. Goods differ in the costs of determining or conveying to others their true qualities and attributes. Reputability of people as sources of reliable information about goods differs, and their ranking is different among goods. People differ in their costs of not only assaying goods but in searching out potential profferers of the good.

These differences may be fortuitous or may be developed in response to economic motives, a point to which we shall return. With these conditions it can be shown that:

i. People will specialize in certain goods in providing information and availability to searching buyers.

ii. Specialist purveyors (or buyers) of goods will be reputable (low variance) sources of estimates of the quality of what is being purchased from or sold to that specialist.

iii. People who have developed lower costs of identifying characteristics of goods will be specialists in selling, buying, inventorying, and giving information about the good.

iv. Trade between a specialist and a novice will involve lower transactions costs than trade between two nonexperts.

v. If some good was sufficiently and most cheaply identifiable so that everyone was like an expert in it, exchange cost of that good for any other good would be less than if a more costly to identify good were offered, and it would become a money.

Consider a world of four goods: diamonds, wheat, oil, and the one called just C. Not all are immediately identifiable in all their true characteristics at insignificant costs, and some are more expensive to identify than others. The community consists of people most of whom are novices, or nonspecialists, in these goods. Imagine (and this begs a question initially) four people who are experts respectively in one of the four goods.

Prior to completing an exchange of diamonds for oil between two novices in diamonds and oil, each will incur the costs of identifying the other's product attributes, including legal entitlements, quantity, and all aspects defining the rights and the quality and quantity of the good being transferred. The net value transfer after subtracting those costs will be less than if they knew costlessly the true characteristics of these goods.

Table 1 shows the proportions of value remaining after "transactions" costs between all pairs of traders with various goods. For example, if a novice in diamonds were to trade some of his diamonds (no

matter why!) for the diamonds of another novice in diamonds, only four percent of the (perfect knowledge) value would be remaining, as stated in row one. Why? Each party knows the quality of only his own diamonds. Each would assess the quality of the other's diamonds. Assume the costs of the assay amount to 80 percent of the diamonds tested—a sort of destructive test in which four out of five good diamonds were destroyed for each one determined to be good. Instead of a destructive test, one can think of the costs of determining the quality as being equal to 80 percent of the value of the diamond. If offered 100 diamonds on a one-for-one basis (prior to tested quality), then net of examination costs he is receiving 20 proven diamonds for his 100. The second party, also a novice, will incur the same costs in examining the first party's stones. He will net only 20 of the 100 diamonds he would receive. So, knowing his own proffered diamonds are good, the first party would be willing to offer only 20 of his diamonds for the 100 untested ones of the other party. The second, who would receive 20 untested diamonds, would end up with four tested, proven diamonds after he incurs his tests. So the second party would have given 100 of his diamonds to get back four tested ones—a loss from exchange of 96 percent of the value of what he gave up. An exchange is less likely.

If a pair of novices were to make an agreeable exchange of a diamond for some oil, their costs of ascertaining the qualities of the two products to be purchased would, according to Table 1, amount to 92 percent of the value of the goods. Only eight cents on the dollar would be remaining. Unless at least one of the parties had a very high marginal personal value for one of those goods, no trade would occur. A very large part of that net potential gain would be dissipated in the transactions costs.

If a diamond novice were to trade his diamond for wheat from a wheat novice, 12 percent of the value of the two goods remains.

By definition of C, trade between a novice in diamonds and one in C would lose less than between

Table 1: Net value after exchanges

SINGLE PARTY AFTER INSPECTION VALUE		NOVICES				EXPERTS		
		D	O	W	C	D	O	W
Novices		.2	.4	.6	.95	.85	.90	.95
D	.2	.04	.08	.12	.19	.85	.18	.19
O	.4	.08	.16	.24	.38	.34	.90	.38
W	.6	.12	.24	.36	.57	.51	.54	.95
C	.95	.19	.38	.57	.90	.81	.86	.90
Experts								
D	.85	.85	.34	.51	.81	1	1	1
O	.90	.18	.90	.54	.86	1	1	1
W	.95	.19	.38	.95	.90	1	1	1
C	.99	.20	.40	.59	.95	1	1	1

novices trading diamonds and any other good, as can be seen from the first row, left side. The first row is pertinent to a novice in diamonds who proposes to sell a diamond. The right half of the row is the result of trades made by our diamond novice with experts in diamonds, oil, wheat, or C. An expert is defined as one who has a lower cost function for identifying attributes of a good. (We temporarily beg the question of why some are more expert than others.)

A transaction with an expert will cost less if the novitiate buyer of the product from the expert will rely on the expert's word. The expert's word will have value if he develops a reputation for honesty and reliability in his assessment. Experts will then sell their knowledge at a price lower than the cost for a buyer to get such information in other ways. It is not necessary that the expert be the seller of the good in which he has expertise. He could be an independent as sayer, but for reasons to be discussed later, experts will tend to be dealers in the commodity in which they are experts—and dealers will tend to be experts in the goods in which they deal.

The right-hand half of row one indicates that a diamond novice trading with a jeweler (diamond expert), where the novice trades his diamond for some from the expert (no matter why such a trade would be made), will experience a lower loss of value than if the diamond were sold to an expert of any other good. A diamond for a diamond will get better terms because the expert is an expert in what he is both getting and giving (here just one kind of good), whereas though a diamond by a novice for oil from an oil expert will save on oil identification costs, it will not save on diamond identification. Hence the costs of transactions between a novice and an expert in the same commodity are less than those between a novice and an expert in a different good.

The matrix is completed, with some redundancy, by filling in the row cells in the bottom half, representing sales by experts in diamonds, wheat, oil, and C to novices (in the left-hand half of those rows). Exchanges between pairs of experts, one in each commodity, are represented in the lower right-hand half. We assume experts are perfectly knowledgeable in the commodities in which they specialize and are 100 percent honest. This assumption may be too strong, but we make it.

Less loss occurs with trade between two novices where one exchanges diamonds for C than when he trades diamonds for wheat. It may be tempting, but erroneous, to conclude that trades should occur of diamonds for C, and then with the C to buy wheat. That is not quite correct.

To test that, try to find how a *novice* in one good could trade for another good with a novice and gain by going through an intermediary good. It can't be done in the upper left-hand portion of the table, because the costs of recognizing the intermediate good are an added cost incurred by use of an intermediary trading good. The costs of identifying the two "basic" goods are not reduced, while an extra cost identifying the intermediate good is added.

Using the specialist expert involves an extra exchange, a cost of identification of another good—the one offered to him, in which he is not an expert. An expert is an expert in one good only, not in all *pairs* of goods. Hence the problem of identification costs persists. Now, if there is some good in which identification costs are both (a) *low* and (b) low for *everyone*, that will permit purchase of product identification information cheaply from the specialized intermediary expert. If his costs of identifying that offered (money) good are less than the reductions in costs by using the specialist for information about the basic goods, the total costs of identification can be reduced.

The cost of identifying that intermediary good is less than the reduced costs by use of a specialist who provides information about the basic good at a low cost. That double event, (1) a low identification cost to everyone about the intermediate commodity and (2) specialist-experts who provide quality assurance

and information more cheaply than novices can provide for themselves, explains the use of a low identification cost commodity as a general intermediary medium of exchange—money. It permits purchase of information from lower cost sources, a cost reduction that exceeds the added cost of using an intermediary good for indirect exchange. No double coincidence of wants is pertinent. Indeed, it is a general prevalence of double coincidence of information by both parties that would avoid use of money.

The matrix illustrates the above propositions. For example, consider some alternative routes of exchange for a novice with diamonds, who wants some wheat.

1. Diamonds to wheat, novice to novice ($D_n \rightarrow W_n$). A diamond novice exchanges diamonds for wheat with a wheat novice. The net value obtained by the diamond novice, according to the matrix of information- transaction costs, is .12.
2. Diamonds to oil to wheat, all through novices ($D_n - O_n - W_n$), yield .0196 (= 1 × .08 × .24). This is less than .12 because of an extra pair of identification costs of oil.
3. Diamonds to C (cash*) to wheat, all through novices ($D_n - C_n - W_n$). The result is a net value of .108 (= 1 × .19 × .57). Though better than through any other mediary because cash, C (because identification costs are less than for oil), it is not as cheap as either direct barter or route 4.
4. Diamond novice to wheat with wheat specialist. The net result is. 19. Contrasting this with the prior route shows the gain from using the specialist for wheat. The difference is the saving to the diamond novice in identifying the wheat, because the wheat specialist offers him "wheat assurance" at a lower cost. And the wheat specialist's word, his reputable reliability, is a source of income. A dishonest specialist would lose a source of income if he destroyed his credibility. So an established wheat merchant has more

incentive to make honest statements about the quality of his wheat than does a transient novice.

5. Interposing the intermediary good, C, into route 4 will worsen matters because the costs of identifying an intermediary good, C, are added to the process, with no reductions in any other costs. For example, going from a diamond novice through a C novice—or even a C expert—rather than through a diamond expert first won't help. Some buyer of the novice's diamonds still has to value them. Whether a wheat specialist or anyone else (except a diamond specialist) does so won't reduce costs. And introduction of C as another good only adds another identification cost. The net value of a route from diamond novice through C through a wheat specialist is .1715, compared to .19 for a direct barter via route 4 without intermediate goods.

6. A gain would arise if the lower cost services of a diamond expert could be used in the exchange process. So what does permit further lowering of costs through an intermediary good is the use of two specialists—in wheat and in diamonds. The diamond novice sells to a diamond expert (who assesses qualities more cheaply than any other buyer could), and then our novice takes the proceeds of C and purchases wheat from a wheat specialist, relying on the specialists' reputations and knowledge as a cheaper substitute for the demand and wheat assessment costs by novices. The extra costs of using C are offset by the expert's lower diamond assessment costs.

In our matrix we can compute the net value (.767) of the intermediate-good, two-middlemen route wherein a diamond novice goes to a diamond specialist and then to a wheat specialist using the good C as the medium between specialists. The value is .767, as the product of .85 × .9025, the values, respectively, of (a) the diamond specialist who receives C, and (b) the entry in the cell for the C novice (the former diamond novice who now offers C to the wheat specialist) selling C to the wheat specialist.[1] This increase in value to .767 is the result of ability to get quality assurance at a lower cost from the diamond specialist and from the wheat specialist without imposing on them the higher costs of identifying goods other than C, in which most people are nearly experts.

The feature emphasized here (without excluding others) is the use of the pair of specialists in diamonds and wheat to reduce information costs. With only one specialist no intermediary good helped. (See routes 2 and 3.) The intermediary good C would be of no use in this context if two (or more) specialists were not used as economical sources of quality assurance. It is both (1) the presence of more than one specialist and (2) the generally low identification cost good, C, that enable indirect exchange to reduce quality ascertainment costs. Use of C as the intermediary good with the lowest general identification costs enables obtaining the conveying information more cheaply from several specialists.

What properties of the matrix of information costs are critical? First, specialists permit lower costs, as indicated by the larger numbers in the cells in the upper right-hand or lower left-hand quadrants. Second, the row and column of C for novices is larger uniformly than any other row or column, and the corresponding rows and columns for experts are also dominant. It is the dominance of the row of C both for the novice and for the experts in other goods that seems critical. The ability of everyone to assess the qualities of C enables it to be used as a low-cost means of purchasing information about other goods from specialists without imposing offsetting high costs on the experts to identify the good C.

---

1 Where does the diamond specialist get C to pay the diamond novice who offers diamonds? From a C specialist. The diamond specialist will have an inventory of C on hand because that will economize on the novice's information costs the novice induces with the wheat specialist when the novice purchases wheat from the wheat specialist. Of all the intermediary goods to be used by a novice between successive specialists, the best is C, a generally easily recognizable good. Try interposing others, and the poorer results will be demonstrated with the data of the matrix.

An alternative view of the reason for use of a common medium of exchange is in its presumed role of avoiding the necessity of a double coincidence of wants. But any commodity used as an intermediary would do that. If goods were perfectly identifiable at zero costs, rights to goods could be transferred, and any commodity would serve as measure of debt. This would then leave some goods as presumably less volatile in value so that the exchange value of units of those goods would be preferred. But this confuses the store of value with the medium of exchange. The two need not be the same good.

Another presumed rationale is the case of search over the population of potential demanders of a good. If everyone uses a good, it is more likely that it could be a medium of exchange. But, again, everyone uses bread or milk. Generality of use aids, but is neither a sufficient nor a necessary precondition. Generality here is a result of people using it as a medium of exchange, not a cause of the good becoming a medium. For example, chocolate candy and nylons became a near money during price controls in the absence of other "money." The items were cheaply identifiable by many people—not necessarily consumed by everybody.

Costs of identifying qualities of a good are what counts. If costs for some good are low and generally low across members of society, the good will become a medium through which information costs can be reduced and exchange made more economical. But it will rise only with the rise of chains of specialists in various goods and commodities, who know the goods cheaply, whose reputation for reliability of evaluation is high, who because of that knowledge and cheapness of assurance to buyers become specialist middlemen in the good as both inventory carriers and buying and selling agents. Other explanations of the occurrence and use of money are silent or vacuous on the existence of specialists and their reliability and activities.

This analysis explains the use of money, which good becomes money, why it is not necessarily also the store of value, the existence of two or more specialists in the sequence of exchanges with money, the reputability of specialists as an integral part of their capital values, and the reason specialists are also dealers.

This model is also consistent with the explanation of unemployment as a search and selection process for best work opportunities during demand shifts among potentially performed activities. Commodities or services that are more difficult to assess in qualities will experience greater losses or changes in values consequent to demand shifts. That higher cost tends to act like specificity of a good to particular tasks. The higher costs of assessing their attributes are like a tax on transfer. Hence the larger gains (or avoidance of loss) from more expensive search in the event of a demand shift (with a large change or high variance of next best known opportunities) induce greater or longer search. It is not simply a task of searching out best opportunities, but also a search for potential demanders to assess productive qualities. Those costs of becoming informed about what a good or service or rented good will do will raise transfer costs and also reward longer or greater searching activity by potential buyers or employers. Commodities or services with qualities that have high costs for other people to ascertain will tend to be held longer in inventories awaiting sale and will suffer greater costs of exchange—as evident by larger bid-ask spreads, wholesale-retail spreads, or "unemployment" lengths. Since the commodity used as money will have low cost in these respects, we conclude money will have the lowest "unemployment" rate.

It is not the absence of a double coincidence of wants, or of the costs of searching out the market of potential buyers and sellers of various goods, or of record keeping, but the costliness of information about the attributes of goods available for exchange that induces the use of money in an exchange economy—if some good has low recognition costs for a large segment of the population while other goods do not. A result is the use not only of money but of knowledgeable experts, with high reputability, who deal in the goods in which they are specialists.

Because most of the formal economic models of competition, exchange, and equilibrium have ignored ignorance and lack of costless full and perfect information, many institutions of our economic system, institutions that are productive in creating knowledge more cheaply than otherwise, have been erroneously treated as parasitic appendages. The explanation of use of money, expertise with dealing in a good as a middleman specialist with a trademark or brand name, reputability or goodwill, along with advertising of one's wares (and even unemployment) is often misunderstood. All these can be derived from the same information cost factors that give rise to use of an intermediary medium of exchange.

An Evolutionary Theory of the State Monopoly over Money

By David Glasner

Although the state monopoly over money has rarely been questioned, repeated attempts have been made to restrain governments in exploiting that monopoly. But periods such as the nineteenth century, when the world, under gold, silver, or bimetallic standards, enjoyed an unusual era of price stability, have been more the exception than the rule. Explaining the evolution of the monopoly over money will also illuminate the reasons for the temporary ascendancy of the gold standard.

In the next two sections, I discuss how the state monopoly over money evolved. In the third section, I use the sovereignty-national-defense argument for the state monopoly to suggest the optimality (for a selfish government) of price stability during peacetime. Since peacetime price stability enlarges the ex-post, wartime capital levy on cash balances and on other fixed nominal liabilities of the state, a problem of time consistency arises. To cope with the time-consistency problem, governments can commit themselves to a contingent monetary rule or invest in a reputation for stable prices (Barro and Gordon 1983; Barro 1983, 1986). The fourth section argues that the growth of democracy and the extension of the franchise complicated the time-consistency problem. The time-consistency problem provides the motivation for a public-choice–theoretic explanation of the evolution of constraints, such as the nineteenth-century gold standard, on the exercise of the state monopoly. I offer some concluding remarks in section five.

THE EVOLUTION OF MONEY AND THE ORIGINS OF THE STATE MONOPOLY

Monetary evolution began long before the state assumed any role in monetary affairs (Burns 1927, Ederer 1964, Menger 1892). Only after a few of the precious metals had evolved to become media of exchange did the state assume a key role. The state never prescribed what money should be, but by minting coins the state did assure the weight and fineness of metals that had already begun to circulate as media of exchange. By reducing the costs of transacting, minted coins could command a premium over unminted metals of equal fineness. Seeking not to improve the monetary system but only to exploit the profit opportunity implicit in this premium, governments extracted the premium as a charge for coining metal at the mint.

Nothing about operating a mint requires the state rather than private enterprise to perform that function.[3] The oldest known coins were struck in Lydia. Since the names on them are not those of any known Lydian sovereigns, it is likely that they were minted privately (Burns 1927, 75). Perhaps the imprimatur of the sovereign gave traders more confidence in the weight and fineness of coins than any private trademark could have. Such confidence, however, would have manifested itself in the market and would have allowed the sovereign's mint to command a larger premium for his coins than competing private mints could for theirs. Technical superiority in the provision of confidence is not a rationale for a state monopoly over coinage.

It is often said that the production of money is a natural monopoly. But the meaning of this assertion is not exactly clear. For the production of a good to be a natural monopoly, the technology must exhibit economies of scale that ensure that the average cost of production is always lower if one firm produces the entire output of an industry than if two or more firms with access to the identical technology divide the output. But even if the state were the lowest-cost producer of money, it would not necessarily enjoy the economies of scale required for the existence of a natural monopoly.

The assertion that money is a natural monopoly is sometimes alleged to follow from the demand-side characteristics of money instead of from its supply-side characteristics (Vaubel 1977). Thus, because it is cheaper to make calculations and execute transactions using just one currency unit rather than several, it is maintained that only one currency unit will survive within a reasonably self-contained economic area. But, as I have argued in another paper (Glasner 1991), the cost savings from trading in only one currency do not imply that the production of money is a natural monopoly. To suggest that it is confuses the gains from standardizing technology with economies of scale. Standardization confers external benefits to consumers at large. It is possible that these benefits cannot be fully internalized by individual producers but could be internalized if production were

undertaken by just one firm. But even then, there would be no natural monopoly because the market would accommodate entry by firms adopting the standards set by the monopolist. Just as the gains from standardization did not make IBM a natural monopolist in the computer industry, they do not make the production of dollars a natural monopoly. Competing issuers can (and do) issue distinguishable moneys denominated in dollar units, thereby achieving the gains from standardization without limiting production to a single issuer.

That the state asserted a legal monopoly over the production of money cannot, therefore, be explained by any requirements implied by the technology of producing or using money. A more plausible explanation is that the monopoly was the result of the characteristic quest by the state for sources of revenue. In ancient times, when the state was just beginning to develop its power to tax, a potential source of revenue could be critical to the survival of the sovereign.

But control of the mint did more than provide the ancient state with a source of revenue. Control of the mint enabled owners of private mints to compete for control of the state itself (Burns 1927, 81–83). Minting a large quantity of debased coins might enable a private mint owner to finance an attempt to overthrow an incumbent sovereign. To be sure, such a debasement would violate the mint owner's promises about the content of the coins he was issuing. But upon becoming the sovereign, the owner could avoid any legal liability by annulling his legal obligation to those he had defrauded.

Thus, coinage and tyranny seem to have emerged together, a confluence which is borne out by the experience of the ancient world. Both coinage and tyranny originated in Lydia. Gyges, the Lydian king of the seventh century B.C. to whom the term tyrant was first applied (Durant 1939, 122), is also credited with having made the coinage "the prerogative of the state after he had first used it to obtain supreme power" (Ure 1922, 143).

A similar pattern appears in the Greek world during the seventh and sixth centuries B.C. (known as the Age of Tyrants), when currency developments were most rapid (Burns 1927, 81). The Greek tyrants "were the first men in their various cities to realize the political possibilities of the new conditions created by the introduction of the new coinage and ... to a large extent they owed their positions as tyrants to a financial or commercial supremacy which they had already established before they had attained supreme political power in their several states" (Ure 1922, 2). Moreover, "Sparta, the most antityrannical state in Greece, was without a real coinage" (Ure 1922, 14).

Burns (1927, 82–83) suggests that it was the general economic power of the early tyrants rather than their control over the mints specifically that enabled them to seize power. Still, he concludes:

> Having risen to power, the tyrant assumed the monopoly over coining. This step was probably part of a policy aimed at the enhancement of his own power and commercial success and the hindrance of his rivals. He kicked away the ladder by which he had risen lest others might attempt to use it.

Once they monopolized coinage, ancient sovereigns sought to increase the revenue potential of their monopolies by limiting the circulation of coins minted by other states. The Greek city-states, which almost invariably established local monopoly mints, introduced the legal principle of legal tender to reinforce their local monopolies in just this way (Kraay 1964).

Local monopolies required legal protection because, contrary to Gresham's Law, bad moneys do not necessarily drive out good ones. That only happens when, for some reason, it is costly to trade the good money at ¡a premium over the bad money. For example, full-bodied and debased coins were sometimes different denominations of the same money of account defined by a particular state (e.g., a debased one-pound coin and a full-bodied five-pound coin). The relative value of the two coins would be determined independently of their metallic content (Rolnick and Weber 1986). Heavier coins would then disappear from circulation and only the lightweight coins would be exchanged. But when two coins were defined in terms of different moneys of account, their exchange rate could reflect the difference in their metallic content. If one were debased more rapidly than the other, the debasement would show up in the exchange rates. If the public could choose to hold either currency, wealth maximization implies that they would hold the appreciating currency. But this preference would also imply the disappearance of the depreciating currency from trade.

Despite the special legal privileges accorded to local coins, coins often circulated beyond the territory of the governments that minted them (Finley 1973, 166). The circulation of coins minted by foreign mints, and the opportunity of making payments by weighing precious metals as well as by counting coins, constrained the monopoly power of any single government. Only in modem times, when payments in precious metals have ceased, could the state increase the levy on holding its money virtually without limit.[4]

As the apparatus of the state and its power to tax grew stronger,[5] maintaining a monopoly over coinage simply to prevent competition for power within the state became less necessary. Private minting might more safely have been tolerated, especially since complaints about shortages of coins abounded in ancient times (Finley 1973, 166), but the monopoly over coinage was as useful in defending the state against external threats as against internal ones.[6] The monopoly over money is distinguished from monopolies over other goods by the power conferred by the monopoly over money to impose an ex-post tax on certain forms of capital. Debasing the currency can be very lucrative when it is levied unexpectedly. Monopolizing other goods would generate revenue over time, but they would not generate as much revenue on short notice as the monopoly over money via currency debasement.

In the Near East it was not uncommon for the state to monopolize a range of commodities, usually through regulation rather than by direct operation. Only rarely did the Greek city-states do so, but the Hellenistic kings followed the Near Eastern practice as did the Roman emperors. Their motive was always openly fiscal (Finley 1973, 165–66). However, only the coinage was universally monopolized by the state.

It is also significant that attempts to depreciate the coinage were almost always carried out in time of war (Burns 1927, 462-63). Numerous Greek city-states exploited their monopolies over coinage to raise additional funds during wars. It is well known that Athens issued token bronze coins in 406 B.C. to help defray the costs of the Peloponnesian War.[7] Not long afterwards, Timotheus of Athens seems to have used a forced token coinage, which he promised eventually to redeem—an important promise, as we shall see later—to pay his soldiers in the war against the Olinthians.[8] And Dionysius of Syracuse, trying to stave off the Carthaginians, used both depreciation and debasement of the currency to raise funds.[9] After conquering Rhegium, Dionysius called in all coins for counterstamping. He reduced the standard by half and reissued the coins at double their nominal value, keeping half the coins to pay off his outstanding debts, the real value of which he had just reduced by 50 percent. He later debased the currency by issuing tin-plated bronze coins to pass as silver coins. Although his tactics have been deplored, Dionysius did prevent the Carthaginians from sacking Syracuse as they had other Sicilian cities (Burns 1927, 366–69).

Currency debasement in republican Rome was invariably associated with wars. As Burns (1927, 463) observed:

> The first issue of coins was probably made during the Samnite War, the first issues of silver during the Pyrrhic War, a possible reduction of the *as* during the first Punic War, a reduction of both silver and bronze and the issue of silver-plated coins during the second Punic War, and the reduction of the *as* and the reissue of plated coins during the Social War.

Currency debasement became a continuing source of revenue when the Empire went into decline. Why the Republic and the early emperors were able to maintain monetary stability during peacetime while the Empire lapsed into more or less continuous currency depreciation and debasement is an issue I shall come back to in section four.

In his history of Roman money Theodore Mommsen (1860) held that the monopoly over coinage was on a par in Roman law with the power to tax (de Cecco 1985, 811). The prerogative of the sovereign over coinage was preserved after the fall of Rome. In the Middle Ages, however, mon-archs were forced to allow prominent noblemen to operate their own mints. Since medieval monarchs were certainly no more tolerant of competition in coinage than the sovereigns of other epochs, the multiplicity of mints was symptomatic of the fragmentation of sovereignty that characterized the Middle Ages. As Miskimin (1984) has shown for fifteenth-century France, one of the main objectives of monarchs during the late Middle Ages, when they began to reassert their sovereign claims against the nobility, was to reclaim control over the coinage.

The close relationship between control over money, sovereignty, and national defense would explain why counterfeiting was treated as a treasonable offense by the Greeks and Romans (Finley 1973, 167), as well as under English law (Blackstone 1979, 4:84; Maitland 1908, 226). This treatment reflected a feeling, engendered by millennia of historical experience, that control of the monetary system cannot be relinquished without compromising the sovereignty and independence of a country.[10]

THE EVOLUTION OF BANKING AND THE STATE MONOPOLY OVER MONEY

As money has evolved from its ancient origins as just another commodity, a growing share of all monetary instruments in most countries has been created by banks; and the significance of the monopoly over coinage has correspondingly diminished. Moreover, because banking requires far more business judgment than does minting coins, it was much more difficult technically for governments to operate their own monopoly banks than it was for them to operate monopoly mints. Consequently, the development of banking institutions posed a threat to the existing state monopoly over money. If the benefits from banking and financial intermediation were not to be lost, the state had to cope with the threat without actually suppressing banks.

Banking evolved because it combined two services that proved to be strongly complementary: provision of a medium of exchange and intermediation between ultimate borrowers and lenders. Banks encroached on the monopoly power of the state, because individuals could use less costly banknotes and deposits (from which governments earned no seignorage) instead of having to use coins (from which governments earned seignorage) as media of exchange. Bank money was less costly than coins for several reasons. Holders of deposits often received interest and bore no losses from the wear and tear of coins. They also bore no costs of transporting coins or of protecting them against theft or robbery. And, when making transactions, they could avoid the costs of counting, weighing, and inspecting coins.

By allowing people to avoid the costs of holding coins, banks reduced the demand for coins issued by the state and hence the value of the monopoly over coinage. The tension between the state monopoly over coinage and private banking is manifested in legislation that was frequently enacted to restrict the creation of notes and deposits by banks. In the fifteenth century, for example, hostile legislation in the Low Countries prohibited the payment of bills of exchange by direct transfer from one account to

another, causing virtually all banking activity to cease (de Roover 1948, 350–51). In the same century, the municipal government of Barcelona made the municipal Bank of Deposit the sole legal depository of money that was subject to litigation or was being administered by trustees, executors, or guardians. Some private banks were forced into liquidation, and the number of private banks was strictly controlled. In what seems to have been a misguided, predatory, vertical foreclosure of banking services from competitors, the municipal government prohibited private banks from holding deposits at the municipal Bank of Deposit (Usher 1943, 246–50, 309–10).[11]

But other governments understood that private banks could increase the access of the state to sources of credit as well as promote economic development. Instead of trying to suppress banking institutions, many governments extended monopoly privileges to certain banks in exchange for a share of the monopoly profits. As was true of coinage, monopolistic banks were created not to improve the performance of the monetary system but to create a source of revenue for the state.

CONCLUSION

I have proposed in this paper an evolutionary explanation of the state monopoly over money that views the monopoly as contributing to the security of the state against internal and external threats. Many aspects of monetary history, I have argued, are better explained by this approach than by one that views the monopoly as required by the technology of money creation.

There are, however, some reasons to suspect that the sovereignty-national defense rationale for the state monopoly is less important now than in earlier stages of monetary evolution. Changes in military technology that require heavier peacetime expenditures and the increase in the tax-collecting and borrowing power of the state all seem to have diminished the contribution of the state monopoly to national defense. Moreover, the Keynesian revolution shifted the focus of monetary policy to macroeconomic stabilization, so that the state monopoly is now held to be desirable because it permits a more activist countercyclical policy than would be possible in its absence. Challenges to the monopoly over money in advanced countries would now be less likely to be resisted on the ground that to abolish the monopoly would infringe on the sovereign power of the state and more likely to be resisted on the ground that to abolish it would deprive the government of an essential tool for promoting high employment and economic growth.

Whether the monopoly over money indeed helps to achieve those goals is a question for a much different inquiry from the one I have conducted in this paper. But there is little reason to suppose that those concerns had anything to do with the evolution of the monopoly over money in the past. Since there seems to be no technical reason inherent in the nature of a medium of exchange that would have necessitated a monopoly over money, the defense-sovereignty explanation I have proposed here seems to be a more plausible explanation for the monopoly than any other yet proposed.

NOTES FOR THIS CHAPTER

1. This chapter is a further development of ideas contained in the first two chapters of Glasner (1989).
2. This hypothesis was suggested to me by Earl Thompson. See Thompson (1974, 1979) for attempts to use a national defense hypothesis to rationalize seeming inefficiencies in the tax code and the protection of certain industries against foreign competition. A full application of his national defense theory to monetary institutions is presented in Thompson (1997).
3. Private mints operated in the United States until they were prohibited during the Civil War.
4. Transactors, of course, could still resort to precious metals as a means of payment. However, precious metals

have long since ceased to function as media of exchange. Resorting to precious metals as a means of payment would, in a modem economy, be virtually to resort to barter exchange.

5. Indeed, the power to tax helped the state increase its monopoly power over the coinage by allowing the state to declare that only coins from its own mint would be accepted in payment of taxes (Kraay 1964).
6. Other commodities or activities were occasionally monopolized by the state in ancient times. It was understood that such monopolies could be sources of revenue to the state, but not until the later Roman Empire did monopolization seem to have been widely introduced as a revenue source for the state. No enterprise other than coinage seems to have been universally monopolized by the state in ancient times. Nor does it seem that private producers of possibly strategic commodities were considered a threat to the state.
7. The issue of copper coins elicited perhaps the earliest statement of Gresham's Law when Aristophanes complained in the *Frogs*, "in our Republic bad citizens are preferred to good, just as bad money circulates while good money disappears." It seems that the quantity of copper coins was not sufficiently restricted to prevent a depreciation of copper coins in relation to silver (Burns, 289–90).
8. The author of the pseudo-Aristotelian *Economica* described the episode as follows:

   Timotheus the Athenian, when he was at war with the Olynthians, and in need of money, struck a bronze coinage and distributed it to his soldiers. When they protested, he told them that the merchants and the retailers would all sell their goods on the same terms as before. He told the merchants if they received bronze money to use it again to buy the commodities sent in for sale from the country and anything brought in as plunder, and said that if they brought him any bronze money they had left over they should receive silver for it. (II, 2)

9. The distinction here between depreciation and debasement is that the former openly reduces the weight of the coin while preserving its fineness, while the latter surreptitiously reduces the fineness while maintaining the weight. Depreciation presumably causes a more or less immediate adjustment in prices, while debasement

only does so gradually as the public learns of the reduced metallic content of the coins.

10. The abortive 1983 proposal for monetary reform by the Israeli finance minister, Yoram Aridor, illustrates the strength of this feeling. The proposal, immediately identified as the Aridor Plan, was to make the shekel fully convertible into the dollar at a fixed parity and to make all contractual liabilities, including tax liabilities, payable in dollars or the stipulated dollar value. The plan, therefore, envisioned virtually complete dollarization of the economy. Despite the far-reaching de facto dollarization that had been achieved, the Aridor plan was denounced immediately by all segments of Israeli opinion. Although it is likely that Israel had exceeded even the short-run, profit-maximizing rate of inflation, so that the contribution of the monopoly over money to national defense had been to a large extent exhausted, the typical response to the Aridor plan was the comment of a right-wing, nationalist politician suggesting that, if the plan were implemented, Israel might as well begin flying the American flag and adopt the "Star-Spangled Banner" as its national anthem. (*New York Times*, 14 October 1983, p. A4).

11. See Reiffen and Kleit (1990), who explain why the vertical foreclosure of an essential input for downstream competitors is generally not a profit-maximizing strategy for a monopolist over a unique facility.

REFERENCES

Aurenheimer, Leonardo. 1974. "The Honest Government's Guide to the Revenue from the Creation of Money." *Journal of Political Economy* 82(3): 598–606.

Bailey, Martin J. 1956. "The Welfare Cost of Inflationary Finance." *Journal of Political Economy* 64(2): 93–110.

Barro, Robert J. 1979. "Money and the Price Level under the Gold Standard." *Economic Journal* 89(1): 13–33.

———. 1983. "Inflationary Finance Under Discretion and Rules." *Canadian Journal of Economics* 16(1): 1–16.

———. 1986. "Reputation in a Model of Monetary Policy with Incomplete Information." *Journal of Monetary Economics* 17(1): 3–20.

Barro, Robert J., and David B. Gordon. 1983. "Rules, Discretion and Reputation in a Model of Monetary Policy." *Journal of Monetary Economics* 12(1): 101–21.

Batchelder, Ronald W., and Herman Freudenberger. 1983. "On the Rational Origins of the Modern Centralized State." *Explorations in Economic History*, 20(1): 1–13.

Blackstone, William. [1776] 1979. *Commentaries on the Laws of England.* Chicago: University of Chicago Press.

Bloomfield, Arthur I.1959. *Monetary Policy under the International Gold Standard.* New York: Federal Reserve Bank.

Bordo, Michael D. 1986. "Money, Deflation and Seigniorage in the Fifteenth Century: A Review Essay." *Journal of Monetary Economics* 18(3): 337–46.

Burns, Arthur R. 1927. *Money and Monetary Policy in Early Times.* New York: Alfred K. Knopf.

Cagan, Phillip. 1956. "The Monetary Dynamics of Hyperinflation." In *Studies in the Quantity Theory of Money,* edited by Milton Friedman, 25–117. Chicago: University of Chicago Press.

Calvo, Guillermo. 1978. "Optimal Seigniorage from Money Creation: An Analysis in Terms of the Optimal Balance of Payments Deficit Problem." *Journal of Monetary Economics* 4(3): 503–17.

de Cecco, Marcelo. 1985. "Monetary Theory and Roman History." *Journal of Economic History* 45(4): 809–22.

de Roover, Raymond. 1948. *Money, Credit, and Banking in Mediaeval Bruges.* Cambridge, MA.: The Mediaeval Academy.

———. 1976. "New Interpretations in Banking History." Chapter 5 in R. de Roover, *Business, Banking, and Economic Thought in the Middle Ages and Early Modern Europe,* Chicago: University of Chicago Press.

Durant, Will. 1939. *The Story of Civilization: Our Greek Heritage.* New York: Simon and Shuster.

Ederer, Rupert J. 1964. *The Evolution of Money.* Washington, DC: Public Affairs Press.

Feavearyear, Arthur 1963. *The Pound Sterling,* Oxford: Clarendon Press.

Fetter, Frank W. 1965. *The Development of British Monetary Orthodoxy 1797–1873.* Cambridge, MA: Harvard University Press.

Finley, Moses I. *1973. The Ancient Economy.* Berkeley: University of California Press.

Fratianni, Michele, and Franco Spinelli. 1984. "Italy in the Gold Standard Period, 1861–1914." In *A Retrospective on the Classical Gold Standard, 1821–1931,* edited by Michael D. Bordo and Anna J. Schwartz, 405–41. Chicago: University of Chicago Press.

Friedman, Milton. 1952. "Discussion of the Inflationary Gap." In Milton Friedman, *Essays in Positive Economics,* 251–62. Chicago: University of Chicago Press.

———. 1971. "Government Revenue from Money Creation." *Journal of Political Economy* 79(3): 846–56.

Glasner, David. 1989. *Free Banking and Monetary Reform.* New York: Cambridge University Press.

———. 1991. "How Natural Is the State Monopoly over Money?" (Manuscript).

Hayek, F. A. 1976. *A Tiger by the Tail.* London: Institute for Economic Affairs.

Jonung, Lars. 1984. "Swedish Experience under the Classical Gold Standard, 1873- 1914." In *A Retrospective on the Classical Gold Standard, 1821–1931,* edited by Michael D. Bordo and Anna J. Schwartz, 361–99. Chicago: University of Chicago Press.

———. 1986. "The Economics of Private Monies." (Manuscript).

Keynes, J. M. [1925] 1972. *The Economic Consequences of Mr. Churchill.* In *The Collected Writings of John Maynard Keynes,* vol. 9, 207–30. London: Macmillan.

Kraay, C. M. 1964. "Hoards, Small Change, and the Origirt of Coinage." *Journal of Hellenic Studies* 84: 76–91.

Kydland, Finn, and Edward C. Prescott. 1977. "Rules Rather Than Discretion: The Inconsistency of Optimal Plans." *Journal of Political Economy* 85(3): 473–92.

Lane, Frederic C. 1937. "Venetian Bankers, 1496–1533: A Study in the Early Stages of Deposit Banking" *Journal of Political Economy* 45(2): 187–206.

Maitland, Frederic W. 1908. *The Constitutional History of England.* Cambridge: Cambridge University Press.

Menger, Carl. 1892. "On the Origin of Money." *Economic Journal* 2(3): 239–55.

Mises, Ludwig von. 1952. *The Theory of Money and Credit.* London: Jonathan Cape.

Miskimin, Harry A. 1984. *Money and Power in Fifteenth Century France.* New Haven, CT: Yale University Press.

Mommsen, Theodor. 1860. *Geschicte des Romischen Munzwesens,* Berlin: Weidman.

Prestwich, Michael. 1979. "Italian Merchants in Late Thirteenth and Fourteenth Century England." In *The Dawn of Modem Banking,* 77–104. New Haven, CT: Yale University Press.

Reiffen, David, and Andrew N. Kleit. 1990. "Terminal Railroad Revisited: Foreclosure of an Essential Facility or Simple Horizontal Monopoly?" *Journal of Law and Economics* 33(2): 419–38.

Reiffen, David, and Maggie Patterson. 1990. "The Rise and Retreat of the Market for Joint-Stock Shares Revisited: The Effect of the Bubble Act in Eighteenth Century England." *Journal of Economic History* 50(1): 163–71.

Robbins, Lionel C. 1934, *The Great Depression.* London: Macmillan.

Rolnick, Arthur J., and Warren E. Weber. 1986. "Gresham's Law or Gresham's Fallacy?" *Journal of Political Economy* 94(1): 186–201.

Sandberg, Lars G. 1978. "Banking and Economic Growth in Sweden before World War I." *Journal of Economic History* 38(3): 650–80.

Shearer, Ronald A., and Carolyn Clark. 1984. "Canada and the Interwar Gold Standard, 1920–35: Monetary Policy without a Central Bank." In A *Retrospective on the Classical Gold Standard, 1821–1931,* edited by Michael D. Bordo and Anna J. Schwartz, 277–302. Chicago: University of Chicago Press.

Thompson, Earl A. 1974. "Taxation and National Defense." *Journal of Political Economy* 82(4): 755–82.

———. 1979. "An Economic Basis for the 'National Defense Argument' for Aiding Certain Industries." *Journal of Political Economy* 87(1): 1–36.

———. 1997. "Gold Standard: Causes and Consequences." In *Business Cycles and Depressions: An Encyclopedia,* edited by David Glasner, 267–72. New York: Garland.

Ure, P. N. 1922. *The Origin of Tyranny.* Cambridge: Cambridge University Press.

Usher, Abbot P. 1943. *The Early History of Deposit Banking in Mediterranean Europe.* Cambridge, MA: Harvard University Press.

Vaubel, Roland. 1977. "Free Currency Competition." *Weltwirtschaftliches Archiv* 113(3): 435–61.

Yeager, Leland B. 1984. "The Image of the Gold Standard." In A *Retrospective on the Gold Standard, 1821–1931,* edited by Michael D. Bordo and Anna J. Schwartz, 651–69. Chicago: University of Chicago Press.

The Island of Stone Money

Money Mischief

By Milton Friedman

From 1899 to 1919 the Caroline Islands, in Micronesia, were a German colony. The most westerly of the group is the island of Uap, or Yap, which at the time had a population of between five thousand and six thousand.

In 1903 an American anthropologist named William Henry Furness III spent several months on the island and wrote a fascinating book about the habits and customs of its inhabitants. He was particularly impressed by the islanders' monetary system, and accordingly he gave his book the title I have given this chapter: *The Island of Stone Money* (1910).

> [A]s their island yields no metal, they have had recourse to stone; stone, on which labour in fetching and fashioning has been expended, is as truly a representation of labour as the–mined and minted coins of civilisation.
>
> Their medium of exchange they call *fei*, and it consists of large, solid, thick, stone wheels, ranging in diameter from a foot to twelve feet, having in the centre a hole varying in size with the diameter of the stone, wherein a pole may be inserted sufficiently large and strong to bear the weight and facilitate transportation. These

stone "coins" [were made from limestone found on an island some four hundred miles distant. They] were originally quarried and shaped [on that island and the product] brought to Uap by some venturesome native navigators, in canoes and on rafts. ...

> [A] noteworthy feature of this stone currency ... is that it is not necessary for its owner to reduce it to possession. After concluding a bargain which involves the price of a *fei* too large to be conveniently moved, its new owner is quite content to accept the bare acknowledgment of ownership and without so much as a mark to indicate the exchange, the coin remains undisturbed on the former owner's premises.
>
> My faithful old friend, Fatumak, assured me that there was in the village near-by a family whose wealth was un-questioned—acknowledged by every one—and yet no one, not even the family itself, had ever laid eye or hand on this wealth; it consisted of an enormous *fei*, where of the size is known only by tradition; for the past two or three generations it had been, and at that very time it was

lying at the bottom of the sea! Many years ago an ancestor of this family, on an expedition after *fei,* secured this remarkably large and exceedingly valuable stone, which was placed on a raft to be towed homeward. A violent storm arose, and the party, to save their lives, were obliged to cut the raft adrift, and the stone sank out of sight. When they reached home, they all testified that *the fei* was of magnificent proportions and of extraordinary quality, and that it was lost through no fault of the owner. Thereupon it was universally conceded in their simple faith that the mere accident of its loss overboard was too trifling to mention, and that a few hundred feet of water off shore ought not to affect its marketable value, since it was all chipped out in proper form. The purchasing power of that stone remains, therefore, as valid as if it were leaning visibly against the side of the owner's house. ...

What Is a Dollar?

By Edwin Vieira

Mr. Vieira is an attorney specializing in constitutional law. He is the author of numerous publications on monetary law.

The question "What is a 'dollar'?" seems trivial. Very few people, however, can correctly define a "dollar," even though a correct definition is vital to their economic and political well-being.

1. Why is a correct definition of the term "dollar" important?

In America's free-market economy, prices are expressed in units of *money*. Under present law, "United States *money* is expressed in *dollars* ..."[1] Moreover, all "United States coins and currency (including Federal Reserve Notes ...) are legal tender for all debts, public charges, taxes and dues."[2] Thus, defining the noun "dollar" is necessary in order to know what is the "money" of the United States and what constitutes "legal tender."

2. Do the present monetary statutes intelligibly define the "dollar"?

The present monetary statutes do not define the "dollar" intelligibly.

a. *Federal Reserve Notes.* Most people mistake the Federal Reserve Note (FRN) "dollar bill" for a "dollar." But no statute defines or ever defined the "one dollar" FRN as *the* "dollar" or even a "dollar." Moreover, the *United States Code* provides that FRNs "shall be *redeemed in lawful money* on demand at the Treasury Department of the United States ... or at any Federal Reserve bank."[3] Thus, if FRNs are not themselves "lawful money," they cannot be "dollars," the units in which all "United States money is expressed."

b. *United States coins.* The situation with coinage is equally confusing. The *United States Code* provides for base-metallic coinage, gold coinage, and silver coinage, all denominated in "dollars." The base-metallic coinage includes "a dollar coin," weighing "8.1 grams," and composed of copper and nickel.[4] The gold coinage includes a "fifty dollar gold coin" that "weighs 33.931 grams, and contains one troy ounce of fine gold."[5] Finally, the silver coinage consists of a coin that is inscribed "One Dollar," weighs "31.103 grams," and contains one ounce of ".999 fine silver "[6] What is the rational relationship between this "dollar" of 31.103 grams of silver, a "fifty- dollar" coin containing 33.931 grams of gold alloy, and a "dollar" containing

"8.1 grams" of base metals? Obviously, these are not the amounts of the metals that exchange against each other in the free market—that is, the different weights of different metals do not reflect equivalent purchasing powers. So, on what theory are each of these disparate weights, and purchasing powers, equally "dollars"?

c. *Currency of "equal purchasing power."* The *United States Code* mandates that the latter question should not even be capable of being asked. For the *Code* commands that "the Secretary [of the Treasury] shall redeem gold certificates owned by the Federal reserve banks at times and in amounts the Secretary decides are necessary to maintain the equal purchasing power of each kind of United States currency"[7] obviously, the Secretary has defaulted on this obligation to keep all forms of "United States currency" at parity with one other—that is, to maintain a "dollar" of constant purchasing-power, whether it be composed of gold, silver, or base metals.

In sum, the monetary statutes do not define the noun "dollar" in a unique way. Instead, completely different things have the same name, things unequal to each other are treated as equivalent, and things that should have the same characteristics (*i.e.,* "equal purchasing power[s]") are quite different.

3. What does American history and the Constitution identify as the "dollar"?

History shows that the *real* "dollar" is a coin containing 371.25 grains (troy) of fine silver.

a. *The "dollar " in the Constitution.* Both Article I, Section 9, Clause 1 of the Constitution and the Seventh Amendment use the noun "dollar." The Constitution does not define the "dollar," though, because in the late 1700s everyone knew that the word meant the *silver Spanish milled dollar.*

b. *Adoption of the "dollar" as the "Money- Unit " prior to ratification of the Constitution.* The Founding Fathers did not need explicitly to adopt the "dollar" as the national unit of money or to define

the "dollar" in the Constitution, because the Continental Congress had already done so.

The American Colonies did not originally adopt the dollar from England, but from Spain. Under that country's monetary reforms of 1497, the silver *real* became the Spanish money of account. A new coin consisting of eight *reales* also appeared. Known as *pesos, duros, piezas de a ocho* ("pieces of eight"), or Spanish dollars, the coins achieved predominance in the New World because of Spain's then-important commercial and political position.[8] Indeed, by 1704, the "pieces of eight" had in fact become a unit of account of the Colonies, as Queen Anne's Proclamation of 1704 recognized, when it decreed that all other current foreign silver coins "stand regulated, according to their weight and fineness, according and in proportion to the rate ... limited and set for the pieces of eight of Sevil, Pillar, and Mexico" (forms of Spanish dollars).[9]

By the American War of Independence, the Spanish dollar had become the major monetary unit of the Colonies. Not surprisingly, the Continental Congress adopted the dollar as the nation's standard of value. On May 22, 1776, a Congressional committee reported on "the value of the several species of gold and silver coins current in these colonies, and the proportions they ought to bear to Spanish milled dollars." And on September 2 of that year, a further committee report undertook to "declar[e] the precise weight and fineness of the ... Spanish milled dollar ... now becoming the Money-Unit or common measure of other coins in these states."[10]

Meanwhile, the Continental Congress worked on a new national monetary system. In his letter to Congress of January 15, 1782, Robert Morris, Superintendent of the Office of Finance, recommended that "our money standard ought to be affixed to silver." Although Morris favored creating an entirely new standard coin, he recognized that, of "[t]he various coins which have circulated in America. ... there is hardly any which can be considered as a general standard, unless it be Spanish dollars".[11]

In a plan published on July 24, 1784, Thomas Jefferson concurred that "[t]he Spanish dollar seems to fulfill all ... conditions" applicable to "fixing the unit of money." "The unit, or dollar," he wrote, "is a known coin … already adopted from south to north … Our public debt, our requisitions and their apportionments, have given it actual and long possession of the place of unit."[12]

Yet Jefferson recognized the necessity of "say[ing] with precision what a dollar is. This coin as struck at different times, of different weight and fineness, is of different values." So, Jefferson suggested, "we should examine the quantity of pure metal in each [type of dollar], and from them form an average for our unit. This is a work … which should be decided on actual and accurate experiments."[13]

On July 6, 1785, Congress unanimously "Resolved, That the money unit of the United States be one dollar,"[14] on April 8, 1786, the Board of Treasury reported to Congress on the establishment of a mint:

> Congress by their Act of the 6th July last resolved, that the Money Unit of the United States should be a Dollar, but did not determine what number of grains of Fine Silver should constitute the Dollar.
>
> We have concluded that Congress by their Act aforesaid, intended the common Dollars that are Current in the United States, and we have made our calculations accordingly.
>
> * * * * *
>
> The Money Unit or Dollar will contain three hundred and seventy five grains and sixty four hundredths of a Grain of fine Silver. A Dollar containing this number of Grains of fine Silver, will be worth as much as the New Spanish Dollars.[15]

On August 8, 1787, Congress adopted this standard as "the money Unit of the United States."[16]

Many of the same people who served in the Continental Congress participated in the Federal Convention that drafted the Constitution. And even those members of the Convention who had not served in the Continental Congress knew what that Congress had done. Therefore, when the Convention used the noun "dollar" in Article I, Section 9, Clause 1 of the Constitution, it was with the tacit understanding of the relevant history. The lesson here is clear: *The constitutional "dollar" is a fixed weight of fine silver in the form of a coin.*

c. *Adoption of the "dollar" as the "Money-Unit" immediately after ratification of the Constitution.* Upon ratification of the Constitution, Congress and the Executive began work on a national monetary system.

On 28 January 1791, Secretary of the Treasury Alexander Hamilton presented to Congress his *Report on the Subject of a Mint.* Hamilton posed two questions, "1st. What ought to be … of the money unit of the United States?," and "2d. What [should be] the proportion between gold and silver, if coins of both metals are to be established?"[17]

On the first question, Hamilton referred to the resolutions of the Continental Congress and concluded that "usage and practice … indicate the dollar" as the money unit. As to "what precise quantity of fine silver" the dollar should contain, he surveyed the various dollar coins in circulation over the years, and recommended that "[t]he actual dollar in common circulation has … a much better claim to be regarded as the actual money unit."[18]

Turning to "the proportion which ought to subsist between [gold and silver] in the coins," Hamilton recommended the domestic market-ratio of "about as 1 to 15." "There can hardly be a better rule in any country for the legal than the market proportion," he explained, "if this can be supposed to have been produced by the free and steady course of commercial principles. The presumption in such a case is that each metal finds its true level, according to its intrinsic utility, in the general system of money operation."[19]

Hamilton recommended the minting of two coins: a silver coin of 371–1/4 grains of fine silver (the dollar), and a gold coin of 24–3/4 grains of fine gold. "[N]othing better," he wrote, "can be done … than to pursue the track marked out by the resolution [of the Continental Congress] of the 8th of August, 1786."[20]

Congress then enacted the Coinage Act of 1792,[21] embodying the constitutional principles that Hamilton had re-affirmed in his *Report*. First, Congress followed American tradition by continuing the use of silver and gold as money. [22] Second, it reiterated the judgment of the Continental Congress and the Constitution that "the money of account of the United States shall be expressed in dollars or units."[23] and defined the "DOLLARS OR UNITS" as "of the value of a Spanish milled dollar as the same is now current, and to contain three hundred and seventy-one grains and four sixteenth parts o: a grain of pure ... silver."[24] Congress also created a new gold coin, the "EAGLE ... each to be of the value of ten dollars or units"[25] (*i.e.*, the weight of fine gold equivalent in the marketplace to 3,712.50 grains of fine silver). It fixed "the proportional value of gold to silver in all coins which shall by law be current as money within the United States" at "fifteen to one, according to quantity in weight, of pure gold or pure silver."[26] It made "all the gold and silver coins ... issued from the ... mint ... a lawful tender in all payments whatsoever, those of full weight according to the respective values [established in the Act], and those of less than full weight at values proportional to their respective weights."[27] And it provided free coinage "for any person or persons," and affixed the penalty of death for the crime of debasing the coinage.[28]

Thus, Congress did not create a "gold dollar," or establish a "gold standard," as the popular misconception holds. For example, the *Encyclopedia Britannica* erroneously reports that the "dollar ... was defined in the Coinage Act of 1792 as either 24.75 gr. (troy) of fine gold or 371.25 gr. (troy) of fine silver."[29] The Act did no such thing. It defined the "dollar" as a weight of silver, and "regulate[d] the Value"[30] of gold coins according to this standard unit and the market exchange-rate between the two metals. Nowhere did the Act refer to a "gold dollar," only to various gold coins of other names that it valued in "dollars."[31]

4. Where are we now?

This history demonstrates that official Washington, D.C., has no conception of what a "dollar" really is. The reason for this self-imposed ignorance is obvious. By reducing the "dollar" to a political abstraction, the government has empowered itself to engage in limitless debasement (depreciation in purchasing power) of our money. A "dollar" that must perforce of the Constitution contain 371.25 grains of fine silver cannot be reduced in value below the market exchange value of silver. A *pseudo*-"dollar" that contains no fixed amount of any particular substance *per* "dollar," on the other hand, can be reduced in value infinitely.

Because debasement of money amounts to a hidden tax, Congress' silent refusal to recognize the constitutional "dollar" amounts to the usurpation of an unlimited power to tax through manipulation of the monetary system. Thus, modem money has become a means for the total confiscation of private property by the government.

One need not be overly pessimistic to predict that misuse by politicians of the fictional, constantly depreciating *pseudo" "dollar"* to expropriate unsuspecting citizens will continue until an economic crisis finally shocks an increasingly impoverished American people out of its slumber, and forces the people to ask the simple question: "What is a 'dollar'?" At that time, the answer will be no different from what it is today, and has been since 1704.

NOTES FOR THIS CHAPTER

1. 31 U.S.C. § 5101 (emphasis supplied). See Act of 2 April 1792, ch. 16, § 9, 1 Stat. 246, 248
2. 31 U.S.C. § 5103.
3. 12 U.S.C. § 411 (emphasis supplied).
4. 31 U.S.C. § 5112(a), 51120o).
5. 31 U.S.C. § 5112(a)(7).
6. 31 U.S.C. § 5112(e).
7. 31 U.S.C. § 5119(a) (emphasis supplied).

8. *See* Sumner, "The Spanish Dollar and the Colonial Shilling," 3 *Amer. Hist. Rev.* 607 (1898).

9. *See An* Act for ascertaining the rates of foreign coins in her Majesty's plantations in America, 1707, 6 Anne, oh. 30. § I.

10. *4 Journals of the Continental Congress, 1777–1789* (W. Ford, ed., 1905), at 381–82; *5 id.* at 725.

11. Propositions respecting the Coinage of Gold, Silver, and Copper (printed folio pamphlet presented to the Continental Congress 13 May 1785), at 4, 5.

12. "NOTES on the Establishment of a MONEY MINT, and of a COINAGE for the United States," *The Providence Gazette and Country Journal,* Vol. XXI, NO. 1073 (24 July 1784), in Propositions, note 11, at 9, 10.

13. Id. at 11.

14. 29 *Journals of the Continental Congress* at 499–500.

15. 30 *Id.* at 162–63. After ratification of the Constitution, Congress made a more accurate determination of the value of the dollar, setting it at 371–1/4 grains of fine silver (as described below).

16. 31 *Journals of the Continental Congress* at 503.

17. 2 *The Debates and Proceedings in the Congress of the United States* ($. Gales compil. 1834), Appendix, at 2059, 2060, 2061.

18. *Id.* at 2061–63.

19. *Id. at 2066, 2068, 2069.*

20. *Id* at 2082.

21. Act of 2 April 1792, ch. 16, 1 Stat. 246.

22. §9, 1 Stat. at 248.

23. § 20, 1 Slat at 250.

24. § 9, 1 Slat at 248.

25. § 9,1 Slat at 248.

26. § 11, 1 Slat at 248–49.

27. § 16,1 Slat at 250.

28. § § 14–15, 1 Star, at 249–50; § 19, 1 Star, at 250.

29. Vol. 7, "Dollar" (1963 ed.) at 558,

30. *See* U.S. Cost. art. I, § 8, el. 5.

31. For the correct interpretation of the Act, *See, e.g.,* A. Hepburn, *History of Coinage and Currency in the United States and the Perennial Contest for Sound Money* (1903), at 22.

CHAPTER 4

The Quantity Theory of
Money

The Quantity Theory of Money

By Thomas Rustici

All economic goods have prices derived from subjective marginal valuations in a world of scarcity; these prices are denominated in terms of units of money. Money is therefore the most important economic good in any society and holds a unique place in the structure of economic theory. Yet in one sense money seems to be an abstraction. Supply & Demand curves with market-clearing equilibrium money prices really just represent in effect mediated barter prices. Economists denominate these prices in terms of physical money units or (purchasing power) for conceptual ease of analysis.

In a monetary economy, every good has two prices: *nominal prices* (in terms of money) as well as real prices (in terms of other goods). Money then enters into virtually every transaction across the whole economy. In a sense, it is the only system--wide good, with its market being every other market Money is mid-point on the continuum of the exchange process of goods → money → goods.. Therefore anything that affects the value of money affects transactions across the entire economy.

While goods and services ultimately are used to trade for and pay for other goods and services, their prices are denominated in terms of monetary units. But if money has its own price, what determines the price of money as an economic good? This question is answered by the Quantity Theory of money. The principle of the Quantity Theory is a special application of the microeconomic laws of Supply & Demand, but with respect to money. Essays in this discussion of the classical quantity theories trace all the way back to the writings of Nicolas Copernicus and are carried forward into the modern era with the formulations of Milton Friedman and Armen Alchian.

On the Minting of Money

By Nicolas Copernicus (translated by Gerald Malsbary)

THEORETICAL FOUNDATIONS

Although there are countless maladies that are forever causing the decline of kingdoms, princedoms, and republics, the following four (in my judgment) are the most serious: civil discord, a high death rate, sterility of the soil, and the debasement of coinage. The first three are so obvious that everybody recognizes the damage they cause; but the fourth one, which has to do with money, is noticed by only a few very thoughtful people, since it does not operate all at once and at a single blow, but gradually overthrows governments, and in a hidden, insidious way.

Money, or coinage, is gold or silver that has been specially marked—in accordance with policy established by any government or head of government—for the purpose of reckoning the prices of things that are bought and sold. Money is therefore a kind of common "measuring stick" for the valuation of things. Now, whatever is taken as a measure has to be stable—must keep to a fixed limit. Otherwise, public order will necessarily be disturbed, and the buyers and sellers of things will be cheated many times over, just as if basic measures of length [Latin *ulna,* or *ell*], bulk measure [Latin *modius,* or *peck*], or weight did not have a fixed quantity. Now, I think that the relevant measure here is the *valuation* [Latin *aestimatio*] of the money as such, and, although this is *founded* in the quality of the metal it is made of, nevertheless, money's material or metallic value [Latin *valor*] must be distinguished from its valuation as money [*aestimatio*]; for money can be valued more in itself than the material it is composed of and vice versa [i.e., its material value may be more than its actual valuation].[1]

It is necessary for money to be established: even though exchange could also take place simply by weights of gold or silver alone (since, by universal human consent, gold and silver are everywhere highly valued); nevertheless, money is needed for two reasons: first, because of the inconvenience of always having to carry around heavy weights of metal, and second, because the real value of the metals is not easily grasped by everyone at a glance. Thus it has become customary to mark money with a public seal, by means of which the proper amount of gold or silver is indicated as present in each coin, and that the public authority is to be trusted in this.

It is customary for coins—especially silver coins—to be made with an alloy of bronze,[2] and this for two reasons (as I judge at least): (1) that the coins be less exposed to the danger of being hoarded up

213

and remelted than they would be if they were made of pure silver and (2) so that the silver divided up into tiny portions, by being mixed with bronze, can have a convenient size in the form of | small coins; a third reason can be added as well: (3) with the support of the bronze alloy, the coins | will last longer and not quickly wear away with use.

Now a correct and fair valuation of money is in place when each coin holds slightly less gold or silver than the amount of gold or silver it can buy: the difference would be the added value due to the expense of minting the coins. The mark put on the coin, that is to say, must add some worth to the material as such.[3]

This worth is cheapened, for the most part, through too much quantity [of silver]: that is to say, if so much silver is made into coins that people desire the sheer mass of the silver[4] more than the money itself; in this way, the worth of the money [dignitas] is damaged when it is not possible to buy as much silver by its means as the money itself contains, and a greater value is realized by destroying (i.e., melting down) the money to get the silver. The remedy for this problem is to withhold from the coining of new money until it equals out, and the money is worth more than the silver.[5]

The [material] value of money is lessened in many ways: either through defect of material alone, namely, when more bronze is mixed with silver than is right for that particular weight of coin; or through the loss of [total] weight of the coin, even though the proportion of bronze to silver is correct; or (and this is the worst case) through both of these defects occurring at the same time; finally, the value can just diminish on its own through usage, over a long passage of time, and this is the only reason for making new money. The evidence of this happening is, if the silver in the money is found to be significantly less than what can be bought with it—and this is rightly considered debasement [or poverty: Latin penuria] of the currency.[6]

THE DEBASEMENT OF PRUSSIAN CURRENCY—A BRIEF HISTORY

These basic principles of coinage having been set out, let us consider the specific case of Prussian monetary history, and show, first, how it reached such a low level of value.

This money circulates under the names of marks, scots, and so forth, and there are also weights going by the same names: a weighed mark [i.e., a mark "of weight"—Latin marcha ponder is] is one half-pound. But a counted mark [i.e., a mark of money—Latin marcha numeri] consists of sixty solids [Latin solidi, French sous, German schillings]. All this is commonly known. In order to ward off any confusion about these two kinds of mark, from this point forward, whenever the term mark is used, it will be understood to refer to the counted or money type of mark; by the name of pound [Latin libra], however, a weight of two [weighed] marks will be signified, it being understood that a half-pound is equivalent to one mark of weight.

Now, we learn from ancient archives and written accounts that, under the reign of Conrad of Jungingen[7], (i.e., not long before the Battle of Tarmenberg[8] [1410]), a ½-pound (or 1 mark) of pure silver could be purchased for 2 Prussian marks [of money] and 8 scots[9], when a l/4th part of bronze was alloyed with 3/4ths of silver. From a ½-pound of that [alloyed] mass they made 112 solidi [or schillings].[10] Adding l/3rd of this to it (l/3rd of 112 equals 37 ⅓) makes a total of 149, plus 2 denarii [i.e. 2 obols or pennies, each a l/6th part of a schilling: or l/3rd of a schilling] making 149 V3 schillings, weighing 2/3rd of a whole pound, or 32 scots of silver [i.e., 24 for a 1-weight mark plus 8 for another l/3rd of a mark], which will clearly be 3/4th pure silver (and that was a ½-pound of pure silver to begin with [in weight]). But it has already been said that the price of that much silver was 140 solidi per ½-pound. The other 9 ⅓ solids were accounted for by the value of the coinage per se [i.e., its aestimatio].[11] In this way its valuation was conveniently correlated with its material value.

This was the money of Winrich [of Kniprode], and Conrad and Ulrich [of Jungingen][12], and pieces of it can still be found in their treasuries. But after the defeat of Prussia and the battle mentioned above, the decline of the republic began to appear in the currency. The *solids* [i.e., *schillings*] under Heinrich[13], although they looked just like the ones we described above, have been discovered to contain no more than 3/5ths silver. This error progressed to the point where there were 3 parts of bronze to a 1/4th part of silver—the exact inverse of before. It was really "copper money," not silver anymore, even though the weight was still 112 solids per ½-pound[14]. But since it does not at all make sense to introduce new, good money while the old, cheaper money is still in circulation, so much the more was it mistaken to introduce new, cheaper money when the old, better money was still circulating, because this not only tainted the old money, but as it were, overthrew it completely. The administration of Michael [of Sternberg] and [Paul Belitzer of] Rusdorff[15] wanted to fix this problem and bring the currency back to its original state. They minted new *solidi* that we now call *grossi;* but since it didn't seem possible to abolish the older, cheaper money without taking a substantial loss, the old solidi remained in use along with the new, and this was a signal error.

Two "old schillings" now passed for one of the new, and now the people had a double kind of mark, made of old schillings or of new ones. The new or good mark, and the old or cheap mark, were both worth sixty schillings. *Obols* [smallest unit, a kind of *penny*] remained in use, but for an old schilling six were exchanged, for a new one, twelve. (We can easily gather from this that originally a *solidus* was made up of twelve *obols*. For just as we call a fifteenth part a *mandel*, so in many parts of Germany the word *schilling* is used for a twelfth part). But the name of *novi solidi* [or *new schillings*] remained until the times when I can remember: how they eventually became *grossi* [or *groats*] I will explain below.

Eight marks, then, of new schillings (sixty each) contained one pound of silver. This is sufficiently clear from their composition: they are one-half bronze and one-half silver, and eight marks weigh about two pounds. The old ones weighed the same, but had half the silver content [Latin *valor*]: it took sixteen marks to get a pound of silver, so the ratio of weight to silver content was four to one.

Afterwards, however, when there was a change of government, when the cities were granted the power to mint coinage (and they fully used this privilege) money increased in quantity but not in quality [Latin *bonitas—goodness*][16] A fifth part of silver began to be combined with four parts of bronze in *old schillings*, until it required twenty marks to be changed for a pound of silver.[17] At this stage, since the *new schillings* [i.e., of the reformed value] were now more than twice the worth of the latest schillings, they were made into scots, that were now to be twenty-four [instead of sixty] to the lightweight mark.[18] Thereby a fifth part of the worth [Latin *bonitas*] of the mark was lost.[19] After that, when the new schillings (now made into scots) disappeared since they had been accepted even through the March [of Brandenburg],[20] it was decided to recall them through the [new] valuation of *groats* [Latin *grossi*], that is, to have each groat be the equivalent of three [old, cheaper] schillings.[21] This was a huge mistake and completely beneath the dignity of such a wise gathering of leaders; as if Prussia could not survive without them, although they were not worth more than fifteen pennies each [Latin *denarii*] of the current value of money, when the quantity was overwhelming its valuation [Latin *aestimatio*]. Thus the groats were out of sync with the schillings by being worth a fifth or sixth part less than what they were established to be,[22] and by this fallacious and unfair valuation, they detracted from the dignity of the schilling. Perhaps it was only fitting to take revenge for the injury that schillings had first inflicted on the groats by forcing them to become scots![23]

But woe to you, Prussia! With your collapse, you are paying the price of a badly administered republic! And now, although both the material value and the valuation of your money are vanishing everywhere, still there is no cessation from the coining of money, and even when the expenses [of doing so] are not being met, through which the later coinages would seem to be equivalent of the earlier, and a later coin was always introduced that ruined the quality of the earlier coin, until the valuation of schillings became proportionate to the material worth of the groats, and twenty-four light marks went for one pound of silver. At long last, even such a diminished value of the money should have remained: indeed, there was no thought of formally establishing it. But what had over so long a period of time become the inveterate habit (or license) of adulterating, pilfering, and cheapening the money,[24] has not ceased in our day. For what it later became and what it is today I am ashamed to say. The value has collapsed so much that now *thirty* marks scarcely contain a pound of silver! What will come next, unless we do something? Prussia will be totally empty of gold and silver and will have only copper money. Imports of foreign goods will cease and soon all business dealings as well. What foreign merchant will want to exchange his goods for copper? And finally, what one of our merchants will be able to acquire foreign goods with that same money? But those who are in charge think little of this huge disaster of the Prussian republic, and their most sweet fatherland (to which they owe—in second place, of course, to their piety toward God—not only their occupations but their very lives) allow it to languish and go to ruin, more and more as the days go by, through their spineless negligence.

So then, while Prussian currency, and thus the entire country, suffers from such great problems, only the goldsmiths and people who are expert in judging the quality of metals profit from these miseries. This is because they are good at collecting the old money out of the mix, can melt it down and sell the silver, always getting more silver out of the inexperienced populace. Once those early shillings have completely disappeared, they start to collect the second best, leaving a pile of inferior money left over. This is what leads to that constant complaint people make that the price of gold, silver, the family grocery bill, the cost of services, and anything that anybody needs is going up; but we are blind to the fact that the expensiveness of everything proceeds from the debasement of the money. Everything goes up or down according to the condition of money, and especially gold and silver, whose value we do not determine by bronze or copper but by gold and silver: the point is, gold and

silver are a kind of basis upon which the appreciation of money's value [*aestimatio*] depends.

But perhaps someone will object, "A leaner money is more advantageous to human uses: it really helps the poor, by bringing a lower price of groceries and by supplying the other necessities of life more easily, whereas when the money is of higher value, everything becomes more expensive, and tenant farmers and people who have to pay annual rents are burdened more than usual." The people who will applaud this point of view are the ones who have been deprived of their hope of the profits they were planning to make, before their ability to mint money was prohibited, and probably certain merchants and craftsmen might agree: people who won't otherwise lose anything, when they sell their services and goods at the value of gold, and can exchange that for a greater sum of money, the cheaper the money's worth.

But if such persons will only consider the common good [*communis utilitas*], they certainly will not deny that an excellent currency is good not only for the state but for themselves and all classes of people, and that cheap money is harmful. The truth of this is clear, not only for many other reasons but especially thanks to that wise teacher, experience: we see countries that have good money flourishing most of all, and those with poor money declining and perishing. It is no wonder that Prussia was flourishing when one Prussian mark was changed for two Hungarian florins, and when, as I said in the beginning, two Prussian marks and eight scots were exchanged for a half-pound, that is, a (weighted) mark of pure silver. But since then, the money has been cheapening more and more every day, and our country through this pestilence and other catastrophes has been nearly brought to ruin. It is also well known that wherever cheap money is in use, the practice of the better arts and human talents is neglected through laziness, lack of interest and a kind of cowardly idleness, and there is no abundance of anything: nobody has forgotten how inexpensively grain and food could be purchased in Prussia when we still had good money. Now that the currency is debased, we are experiencing a rise in the price of everything useful for human life. And therefore it is clear that cheap money encourages laziness rather than helps anyone's poverty. Nor will an improvement of money burden those who pay a yearly rent, for although they may seem to be paying more than usual for their property, they will also be selling the fruits of their land, their livestock, and that kind of thing for a larger price themselves. The reciprocal give-and-take of buying and selling will be balanced through the proportionate measurement of the money.

A PLAN FOR REFORM

If it has finally been determined , then, to rescue, some day, the present disastrous condition of Prussia through a restoration of the currency, we must first of all take care to avoid the confusion that comes from having a variety of mints producing the money. The multiplicity prevents uniformity, and it will be more work to keep a number of mints on the right path than one. ... *It would be advantageous therefore for there to be only one common mint for all Prussia,* [25] *in which every type of money would be stamped on one side with the insignia of the lands of Prussia: they should have a crown at the top, so that the superiority of the kingdom would be recognized. On the obverse, the insignia of the duke of Prussia could be seen under the crown above it.*

But if the duke of Prussia refuses this arrangement, and wants to have his own mint ... let two places (at most) be designated, one in the lands of the royal majesty and the other in the territory of the duke.[26] In the former, let money be minted with royal insignia on one side but with [the insignia of] the lands of Prussia on the other, but in the latter mint, let one side have royal insignia and the other the duke's insignia. Let both coinages be subject to the royal authority and be used and accepted throughout the entire land by the order of His Royal Majesty. This measure will have no small impetus toward reconciling those who disagree and toward encouraging the successful pursuit of business operations.

It would be worth the trouble to have both these coinages of the same grain [*granum*], metallic value [*valor*], and monetary value [*aestimatio*], and that they stay that way permanently, through the vigilant supervision of the political authorities, according to the arrangement now to be established.[27] And it would also be important that the authorities in both operations obtain no profit from coining money: let only so much bronze be added that the monetary value exceeds the metallic value just enough to reimburse the cost of making the money, and to remove the temptation to melt it down again. [28]

In order, then, to avoid falling once again into the confusion of our times caused by the mixture of the new money with the old money, it seems imperative to get rid of the old money completely, and let it perish, once the new money has been made; and that this old money then be exchanged for new, according to the proportion of its metallic value. Otherwise, the work of renewing the coinage will be a waste of time, and the resulting confusion perhaps worse than before. Once again, the old money will adulterate the worth of the new money: the mixed money will make the total weigh less than what is proper, and once it has been excessively increased [in quantity], will lead to the problem described above.[29] Now, before this time people have sought to solve this problem by keeping the old money in circulation and simply allowing it a smaller comparative worth in proportion as its metallic value is less or cheaper than that of the new money. But this cannot be done without huge confusion: there is already such a complicated diversity of groats [*grossi*] and schillings [*solidi*] and even pennies [*denarii*] that any given coin can hardly be judged for its value, or be distinguished from other coins. This is how an artificially induced variety of money generates inextricable confusion and increases trouble for merchants and labor contractors, not to mention other problems. Therefore, it will always be preferable to completely abolish the old money when restoring new money. Such a relatively minor loss should always be endured with patience—if we should even consider a "loss" what actually increases profits and brings continual improvement and growth to the republic.

But it is extremely difficult—and, after the catastrophe we have suffered, almost impossible—to restore Prussian money to its original quality. But, although any restoration will take a lot of trouble, nevertheless in the conditions of our time it does seem possible and convenient to effect a renovation, so that at least one pound of silver would go into twenty marks, in the following way: let three pounds of bronze be used for the schillings, along with one pound of silver minus one half-ounce or however much must be allowed for the expenses of minting. Let that molten mass be made into twenty marks, which will be able to pay for one pound (or two-weight marks) of silver. Scots, groats, and obols [i.e., pennies] could then be produced as desired, according to the same formula.

A COMPARISON OF SILVER AND GOLD

It was stated in the beginning that gold and silver are the basis on which the goodness [*bonitas*] of money depends. And what has been said about silver money can also be said, for the most part, about gold. All that remains is to explain, in a brief digression, the rationale involved in exchanging gold and silver. First, we must investigate the method of determining the relative prices of pure gold and pure silver, moving in this way from general to specific and from the simple to the more complex. In fact, the relationship between gold and silver (of the same grade) in the mass[30] is the same as between gold and silver of the same grade when already coined, and again, the relationship of coined gold to mass gold is the same as the relationship of coined silver to mass silver, as long as the proportion of alloy and the weight are the same. Now the purest gold to be found in the coinage we use is in Hungarian florins, which have a minimum admixture of alloy: only just enough, perhaps, as needed to fund the expense of coining the money, and therefore florins are normally exchanged

for the equivalent of their weight in pure gold, the dignity [*dignitas*] of the stamped coin making up for the subtraction of gold. It follows, therefore, that the same relationship exists between pure unformed silver and pure unformed gold as between this same kind of silver and Hungarian florins, as long as the weights are kept the same. But 110 Hungarian florins—each of the same and proper weight, that is, of 72 grains— make up 1 pound (I am thinking still of a pound as containing 2 marks of weight). By this criterion we find universally, and in all nations, that one pound of pure gold has as much value as twelve pounds of pure silver. However, we have discovered that once it was *eleven* pounds [of silver] for one [of gold], and thus it appears to have been determined long ago that *ten* Hungarian gold pieces weighed an eleventh part of a pound.[31] But if that same price for the same weight was still in force today, we could have (according to the reasoning here presented) a convenient conformity of Polish and Prussian money: for if 20 marks or thereabouts were to be made from 1 pound of silver, then precisely 2 marks would equal 1 gold piece,[32] the equivalent of 40 Polish groats. But now that it has become an accepted custom in practice that 12 parts of silver are the equal of 1 part of gold, the weight does not match up with the price, so that 10 Hungarian gold pieces can buy a 1 1/11 part of a pound of silver. If, therefore, 20 marks can be made from 1 1/11 pounds of silver, then Polish and Prussian money will be coordinated in value, groat for groat, and 2 Prussian marks will be equivalent to 1 Hungarian gold piece. But the price of silver will be 9[33] marks and 10 solidi for each 1/2-pound, or thereabouts.

However, if what people desire is cheapness of money and the destruction of the country, and if this modest restitution and value coordination will seem too difficult to undertake,[34] so that it is decided that 15 Polish groats should remain the worth of 1 mark, and 2 marks 16 scots (i.e., 2 ⅔ marks) should remain at the worth of 1 Hungarian gold piece, by the same reckoning it will not be a huge problem for 24 marks to be made from 1 pound of silver.[35] This is what happened not long ago, when 12 marks was still the price of a ½-pound of silver, and 1 Hungarian florin was exchanged for that much money. This is mentioned for the sake of an example, and to suggest a way to proceed. There are countless methods for configuring a monetary system, and it is not possible to explain them all. Common consensus, arrived at after careful deliberation, will be able to determine whatever seems most suitable for the republic. But if our money is properly related to the Hungarian florin and has been correctly made, other [kinds of] florins will also be set in correlation with them, according to their gold and silver contents.

This seems to be enough on the subject of restoring currency; I hope that with the foregoing I have clearly explained in what ways its worth [*dignitas*] has fallen, and how it can be restored.

EPILOGUE ON THE RESTORATION OF MONEY

The following points need to be taken into account in understanding the repair and preservation of money.

First: let there be no renewal without the slow deliberation and unanimous decree of the rulers.

Second: let there be only one place set aside, if possible, for an official mint, and let such a mint produce money with a stamp on it, not in the name of one city alone, but for the whole country, together with its symbols. The Polish money demonstrates the significance of this recommendation, for it is only because of this that it keeps its value over so much territory.

Third: when new money is being minted and distributed, let the old money be taken out of circulation and abolished.

Fourth: let it be invariably, and without any compromise perpetually, observed that twenty marks and no more be made from one pound of pure silver, with only so much being subtracted as can cover the expenses of the minting. In this way, Prussian money will be proportionate to Polish money, and twenty Prussian groats as well as twenty Polish groats will be the equivalent of one Prussian mark.

Fifth: that the excess production of money be avoided.

Sixth: that the money be simultaneously produced in all its denominations. Scots or groats, solids [schillings], and obols [pennies] should all be minted.

With respect to the amount of alloy: whether groats or solids are produced, or even silver *denarii* which can add up to a *ferto* [one fourth of a mark— German *Viertel*] or half-mark, or even a whole mark, let it be decided according to the wishes of those who are concerned, provided only that moderation be exercised and that a decision is made that can have lasting effectiveness.

Let there be provision for *obols* as well, since they have simply too little value now, with an entire mark's worth of them containing barely more silver than in one groat.

A final difficulty arises from the existence of contracts and obligations made before and after the renewal of the money. A way should be found for solving these issues that does not overly burden the contracting parties. An example of how this was done in earlier times is presented on the following page[36] ...

The Origin and Function of Money

By Majorie Grice-Hutchinson

THE ORIGIN AND FUNCTIONS OF MONEY PP. 57–58

Exchange, or the barter of things other than money, as the jurisconsult Paulus elegantly shows, is a much more ancient contract than that of sale and purchase, which began after money was invented. Before the invention of money, anyone who wished to exchange his house for another was obliged to seek out some person who had the house he wanted and who was willing to exchange it; while a man who had wine and wool but no wheat or shoes would try to find another who had wheat and shoes and was prepared to make the exchange, as is still done by some of the barbarous peoples with whom the Spaniards trade. Later, however, money was invented. Certainly, in one way it was a very necessary invention; and yet, in another, I doubt whether it is really so today, for it destroys souls through avarice, bodies by war and great dangers upon the seas, and even whole fleets (in which it is transported) by fearful tempests and shipwrecks.

The earliest use of money, then, and the principal reason for its invention, was as a price, so that it might promote the sale and purchase of all things needful for human life, and also serve as a kind of public measure of saleable goods. Later on, money of one metal or tale began to be changed for that of another: for example, coins of larger denominations for those of smaller. Still later, when the money of a particular country came to be worth less there than abroad (as today nearly all the gold and silver of Spain is worth less in Spain than in Flanders and France), there came into being the art of exchange, which is the art of giving and taking one kind of money in exchange for another. In this way money began to pass from places where it was worth less to those where it was worth more. Thus, in our own day many people have greatly increased their fortunes by carrying to Flanders and France ducats of two, four, and ten, some in kegs as though they were olives, others in barrels hidden in the wine, on each of which they make a big profit; and they bring merchandise from abroad which is worth little there, and here much, doing us some good in the one, but a great deal of harm in the other.

Now, Aristotle disapproved of this art of exchange and of trading in money: it seemed to him both unnatural and unprofitable to the republic, and to have no end other than gain, which is an end without end. St. Thomas, too, condemned all business whose main object is gain for gain's sake. But even St. Thomas allows that the merchant's trade is lawful so long as he undertakes it for a moderate profit in order to maintain himself and his family. After all, the art of exchange benefits the republic to some extent. I myself hold it to be lawful, provided it is conducted as it should be, in order to earn a moderate living, Nor is it true that to use money by changing it at a profit is against nature. Although this is not the first and principal use for which money was invented, it is none the less an important secondary use. To deal in shoes for profit is not the chief use for which they were invented, which is to protect our feet: but this is not to say that to trade in shoes is against nature.

THE VALUE OF MONEY IN EXCHANGE P. 80

The difficulty is to see how a man may change money at a profit while giving the money its just value. To which we reply that this may be done with money as with other goods by paying it over in exchange when or where it is worth less and being repaid when or where it is worth more. As St. Thomas clearly explains, and we have said already, money (even considered purely as money) may justly be exchanged for other money at a profit.

The solution of the problem lies in knowing how and why a given money, which is equal to another according to the common price set upon it by law or custom at the time of its minting, comes to be worth more than the other. We cannot know whether an exchange transaction be just unless we know the value of both moneys; since, as we have seen, the money must be changed at its proper value if the transaction is to be a fair one.

Now, we maintain that the value of the two moneys may diverge for one of eight reasons:

First, because the moneys are of different metals.
Second, because the metal of which they are made is of different fineness.

Third, because the moneys are of different tale or weight.
Fourth, because they are in different countries.
Fifth, because one of them may be repudiated, raised, or lowered.
Sixth, because of diversity in time.
Seventh, because of scarcity and need.
Eighth, because one of the moneys is absent and the other present.

As to the first respect, which is because the moneys are of different metals, sometimes a gold ducat is worth more to its owner than its equivalent in silver or metal, because he can store or transport it more easily. On the other hand, sometimes a ducat of silver or metal will be worth more than one of gold, owing to a scarcity of small change for spending purposes.

As to the second respect, a variation in the metal of the moneys in question, it sometimes happens that of two ducats which are legally estimated at the same value (for example, the ducats of Castile, Portugal, Hungary, and Florence) one may be worth more than another, even if they are in the same country.

As to the third respect, a difference in tale or weight, sometimes one ducat may be worth more than another of the same issue, if, for instance, it weighs a grain too much or is particularly clearly stamped, and if the other weighs a grain too little or is broken, clipped, or otherwise disfigured.

As to the fourth respect, one and the same money may be worth more in one country than in another, as Calderinus admits. This may happen either because the metal of which it is made is more valuable in the one than in the other (gold, for example, is worth more in Spain than in the Indies, and more in France than in Spain), or because the king or the custom of one country sets a higher value upon it than the king or the custom of the other. It happened, for instance, at the time when I was studying in Toulouse, that the King of France greatly raised the tale of his *écus d'or au soleil* and of the Spanish ducat, and it is said that he has since raised it still higher. So far, nearly everyone is in agreement.

As to the fifth respect, which is that a money may be repudiated and its value lowered, or that such a measure is feared, we have seen in recent years that the *tarjas* of 10 were worth less at one time than before. And in other countries, where many lords have the right to mint money, they often forbid the circulation of their neighbours' money in their own territory. Others lower the price of their money, and then its exchange value falls, just as when its circulation is forbidden. Similarly, whenever such repudiation or lowering of the value of money is expected, and the matter is in doubt, the exchange value of the money tends to fall. When, however, there is a possibility of its price being raised, the money begins to exchange for rather more than was formerly the case … .

As to the sixth respect, diversity in time, which causes money to rise or fall in value, a hundred gold, silver, or metal ducats, or a hundred absolutely in quantity, may sometimes be worth more and sometimes less than in a year's time. They would be worth more if for one of many possible reasons (for instance, if money has been sent abroad to buy provisions, make war, or help friends who have been at war, &c.) there is a shortage of certain coins or of all of them, and if in a year's time they become abundant, either because provisions or other merchandise of the country have been sold, or because the king has paid his soldiers and servants well, or for other similar reasons. On the other hand, they will be worth less now than in a year's time if they are now abundant and in a year's time become scarce, just as a load of wheat is usually worth less in August, when it is plentiful, than in May, when it is scarce or at any rate scarcer … .

As to the seventh respect which causes money to rise or fall in value (namely, whether it is scarce and greatly needed, or abundant), money is worth more when and where it is scarce than where it is abundant, as is maintained by Calderinus, Laurentius de Rpdolphis, and Sylvester, with whom Cajetan and Soto agree. The reasons for this opinion are as follows:

First, that this concept is common to all men, good and evil, throughout Christendom, and thus it would seem to be a law of God and Nature.

Second, and of great importance, that all merchandise becomes dearer when it is in great demand and short supply, and that money, in so far as it may be sold, bartered, or exchanged by some other form of contract, is merchandise and therefore also becomes dearer when it is in great demand and short supply.

Third, that (other things being equal) in countries where there is a great scarcity of money all other saleable goods, and even the hands and labour of men, are given for less money than where it is abundant. Thus we see by experience that in France, where money is scarcer than in Spain, bread, wine, cloth, and labour are worth much less. And even in Spain, in times when money was scarcer, saleable goods and labour were given for very much less than after the discovery of the Indies, which flooded the country with gold and silver. The reason for this is that money is worth more where and when it is scarce than where and when it is abundant. What some men say, that a scarcity of money brings down other things, arises from the fact that its excessive rise makes other things seem lower, just as a short man standing beside a very tall one looks shorter than when he is beside a man of his own height.

Fourth, if there is a shortage of gold coins their value may well increase, so that more coins of silver or other metal are given in exchange for them. Thus we now see that because of the great scarcity of gold money some people will give 23, and even 24 and 25 *reales* for a doubloon, which according to the law and price of the kingdom is worth only 22. Similarly, if silver money becomes scarce its value may rise, so that more gold or metal money is given in exchange for it. Thus in Portugal we have been given 106 *maravedis* in *cetis*, at a time when they were abundant, for one *testón*, which was worth only 100. Afterwards, when cetis became scarce, only 94 were given to the *testón*. Thus it seems that a general shortage of money produces a general rise in its value.

OF HOW THE DIVERSE ESTIMATION OF MONEYS IS SUFFICIENT TO JUSTIFY THE EXCHANGES PP. 94–95

There are two points to be investigated and clarified in this chapter. The first is that modern exchange transactions are founded on the diversity in the estimation of money. It is understood that this estimation is to be universal throughout the whole of a kingdom, not peculiar to two or three or five needy persons in a town. Thus we see that in all Flanders and in all Rome money is more highly esteemed than in all Seville, and in Seville more than in the Indies, and in the Indies more than in New Spain, and in New Spain more than in Peru.

What I have said will be clear when we come to examine this sort of commerce. Nowhere is so large an increment charged as in places where it is evident that money is greatly esteemed. The most profitable exchange transactions are those of Flanders and Rome on Spain, where money is clearly worth more than elsewhere [*sic.*]. This is good proof that money-changers take this diversity of estimation into account.

The second point is that from Seville on Medina, Lisbon, and any other place, the thing that causes a rise or fall in the market is the abundance or scarcity of silver. If it is abundant the rate is low, and, if scarce, high. Clearly, then, abundance or scarcity causes money to be little or greatly esteemed. Hence, if in Seville at the present moment money is esteemed more highly than it will be in a month's time, this is simply because in some way the market will have been altered and freshly supplied, and, since money will be more abundant, its estimation will fall. Estimation is and always will be the basis of such transactions.

Indeed, these two considerations seem to me to be evident and effective, and I think that they clearly show how important for this type of business is the fact that money is more highly esteemed in one place than in another. In practice we see that when a money-changer knows that money is going to be very scarce in some province he tries to send large sums there in good time.

Our opinion is rendered very probable and even true by the proof which we have given earlier in this treatise that the profit gained in an exchange transaction does not arise because of any variation in the fineness of the two moneys, or because one is present and the other absent, or as a salary for transporting the money, as many people have thought. It follows that the rate can be founded on no other reason (if it is to have a foundation at all) but the diverse estimation in which money is held from city to city. Thus we see that the money-changers make use of all their shrewdness and ingenuity in arranging to place large sums where money is highly esteemed either always or for a few days; and we also understand the reason for the fluctuations in the rate.

If in spite of all these arguments the reader persists that this is not the foundation of the exchanges, I shall not oppose him very strongly but shall request him to show the true reason, or, at any rate, one better and more fitting than my own. In these obscure and complicated matters I am not so obstinate or tenacious of my own judgement that I believe in it like the Gospel. The explanation I have given seems to correspond most nearly to commercial practice, more especially since we are not at present investigating the nature and justice of one sort of exchange transaction, or two, or any in particular, or transactions effected either abroad or within the kingdom, but are considering all exchange business in general. For all such transactions in common I can certainly see no more universal root than this, and no other explanation that harmonizes so many different facts, I well know, of course, that sometimes the necessity of one man, or the tyranny of another, causes the increment to be high. But we need not take this into consideration when we are discussing the exchanges in general terms.

It remains to show that this explanation suffices to justify the profit made in exchange transactions. We have already said that 'to exchange' means in plain language to barter, Now barter, if it is to be lawful, must first and foremost be equal. One thing must be worth the same as the other, or there will be injustice and offence. We know, too, that the same article of clothing may vary in price from province to province. A measure of wine is incomparably more valuable in the Indies than in Spain, and a measure of oil in Flanders than in Castile. So much so, that one barrel of wine in Mexico is worth ten in Jerez, and they could lawfully be bartered and exchanged, giving one barrel in New Spain against ten in Cazalla. And, within a single kingdom, a basket of olives in Valladolid may be exchanged for four in Manzanilla, and yet the barter will be just and equal. The same thing happens to sums of money, which, because money is more highly esteemed in one place than in another, come to be equal even though the sums are different, 93 in Flanders to 100 in Seville, not because the ducats are of a different fineness or tale, but because the country in itself, so so speak, causes money to be more highly regarded. We are accustomed to say 'A *real* here is better than two elsewhere' ; not because a *real* is not worth 34 *maravedis* here and two *reales* 68, but because the 34 here are more highly esteemed than the 68 elsewhere.

Thus, corresponding to the advantage which the Indies enjoy over Spain in their abundance of gold and silver, so are 70 ducats in Madrid esteemed as highly as 100 in Lima and 90 in Vera Cruz; and if I were to state that the excess were larger I do not think that I should be deceived. It is the same between Spain and Rome, for 100 in Burgos are certainly worth 94 in Rome. Therefore, to exchange the 100 for the 94 is a just transaction, even if the 94 in Italy could be paid on the very same night and with no delay or lapse of time. Indeed, people often wish to be paid immediately in this way—for instance, if they are sending the costs of certain dispensations, or if they are eager to make a profit. On the very same day that they deliver the money here, they want, if possible, the bill to be settled within a few hours. And yet they often lose 10 or even 14 per cent.

All the foregoing will be repeated and more extensively explained in the rest of this little book. It is the very foundation of the edifice, the very base of the column, that we are seeking to build up, In fact, little remains but to apply this doctrine and general rule to each particular kind of exchange transaction.

Importing Inflation

Conquistadores and the Quantity Theory of Money

By *Reader's Digest*

TREASURES THAT SURVIVED THE MELTING-POT

Stories of a 'kingdom of gold' attracted the Spanish conquistadores to Peru. Gold was plentiful in the Inca Empire; the Incas called gold the 'sweat of the sun,' and used it to make a variety of objects, often associated with religious ceremonies. When Francisco Pizarro's forces invaded and conquered Peru in 1532 they looted the empire of all the treasure they could discover. Gold vessels, ornaments, masks and crowns were melted down for the bullion they produced, which was then shipped back to Spain. Many of the objects that survived were made by earlier Peruvian peoples, on whom the Incas based their own art and government.

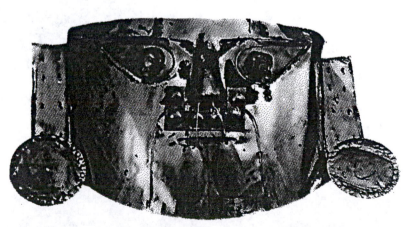

MASTER METAL-WORKERS *Immediately before the rise to power of the Incas, the most powerful people along Peru's northern coastlands were the Chimu, a nation whose richness and splendour were reflected in the work of their goldsmiths. This gold funeral mask for a chieftain, complete with nose and ear ornaments, bears traces of red and green paint and has eyes of stone. Many Chimu craftsmen were pressed into service by the conquering Incas, and continued to produce fine metal-work for their new overlords*

DRUG POUCH *A gold pouch in the form of a puma skin held the leaves of a plant known as coca, used as a narcotic*

TREASURE AND THE PIRATES

The new discoveries did not merely give the European countries the prestige of having an overseas empire; they also had important economic effects within Europe. New wealth was tapped. Portuguese routes to the Spice Islands threatened the monopoly of Italian merchants. Spanish gold and silver from Mexico and Peru was carried home to Seville in great treasure fleets which sailed twice a year, in April and August. They were threatened by Dutch and English pirates, but they usually got through. However, this was not always the case. In the course of his voyage round the world in the *Golden Hind*, Sir Francis Drake captured Spanish treasure worth over $2 million.

The steady increase in the amount of money in circulation in Europe led to a rapid rise in prices, by as much as 400 per cent in 90 years. The familiar economic problems of the modern world—inflation, speculation and boom, followed by deflation and unemployment—which had first been felt in the 1300's, revived in the 16th century.

LIFE AND CUSTOMS *The golden figure from the Inca period (left) depicts a man carrying an aryballus, a jar used for transporting liquids. The hollow hand made in gold (right) is from a Chimu tomb, and may have been used to hold incense. The arm is elaborately tattooed, a frequent practice among the Chimu*

Of Money

Essays, Moral, Political, and Literary

By David Hume

Money is not, properly speaking, one of the subjects of commerce; but only the instrument which men have agreed upon to facilitate the exchange of one commodity for another. It is none of the wheels of trade: It is the oil which renders the motion of the wheels more smooth and easy. If we consider any one kingdom by itself, it is evident, that the greater or less plenty of money is of no consequence; since the prices of commodities are always proportioned to the plenty of money, and a crown in HARRY VII's time served the same purpose as a pound does at present.[1] It is only the *public* which draws any advantage from the greater plenty of money; and that only in its wars and negotiations with foreign states. And this is the reason, why all rich and trading countries from CARTHAGE to GREAT BRITAIN and HOLLAND, have employed mercenary troops, which they hired from their poorer neighbours. Were they to make use of their native subjects, they would find less advantage from their superior riches, and from their great plenty of gold and silver; since the pay of all their servants must rise in proportion to the public opulence. Our small army of 20,000 men is maintained at as great expence as a FRENCH army twice as numerous. The ENGLISH fleet, during the late war,[2] required as much money to support it as all the ROMAN legions, which kept the whole world in subjection, during the time of the emperors.[3]

The greater number of people and their greater industry are serviceable in all cases; at home and abroad, in private, and in public. But the greater plenty of money, is very limited in its use, and may even sometimes be a loss to a nation in its commerce with foreigners.

There seems to be a happy concurrence of causes in human affairs, which checks the growth of trade and riches, and hinders them from being confined entirely to one people; as might naturally at first be dreaded from the advantages of an established commerce. Where one nation has gotten the start of another in trade, it is very difficult for the latter to regain the ground it has lost; because of the superior industry and skill of the former, and the greater stocks, of which its merchants are possessed, and which enable them to trade on so much smaller profits. But these advantages are compensated, in some measure, by the low price of labour in every nation which has not an extensive commerce, and does not much abound in gold and silver. Manufactures, therefore gradually shift their places, leaving those countries and provinces which they have already enriched, and flying to others, whither they are allured by the cheapness of provisions and labour; till they have enriched these also, and are again banished by the same causes. And, in general, we may observe, that the dearness of every thing, from plenty of money, is a disadvantage, which attends an established commerce, and sets bounds to it in every country, by enabling the poorer states to undersell the richer in all foreign markets.

This has made me entertain a doubt concerning the benefit of *banks* and *paper-credit,* which are so generally esteemed advantageous to every nation. That provisions and labour should become dear by the encrease of trade and money, is, in many respects, an inconvenience; but an inconvenience that is unavoidable, and the effect of that public wealth and prosperity which are the end of all our wishes. It is compensated by the advantages, which we reap from the possession of these precious metals, and the weight, which they give the nation in all foreign wars and negotiations. But there appears no reason for encreasing that inconvenience by a counterfeit money, which foreigners will not accept of in any payment, and which any great disorder in the state will reduce to nothing. There are, it is true, many people in every rich state, who having large sums of money, would prefer paper with good security; as being of more easy transport and more safe custody. If the public provide not a bank, private bankers will take advantage of this circumstance; as the goldsmiths formerly did in LONDON, or as the bankers do at present in DUBLIN: And therefore it is better, it may be thought, that a public company should enjoy the benefit of that paper-credit, which always will have place in every opulent kingdom. But to endeavour artificially to encrease such a credit, can never be the interest of any trading nation; but must lay them under disadvantages, by encreasing money beyond its natural proportion to labour and commodities, and thereby heightening their price to the merchant and manufacturer. And in this view, it must be allowed, that no bank could be more advantageous, than such a one as locked up all the money it received,[4] and never augmented the circulating coin, as is usual, by returning part of its treasure into commerce. A public bank, by this expedient, might cut off much of the dealings of private bankers and money-jobbers; and though the state bore the charge of salaries to the directors and tellers of this bank (for, according

to the preceding supposition, it would have no profit from its dealings), the national advantage, resulting from the low price of labour and the destruction of paper-credit, would be a sufficient compensation. Not to mention, that so large a sum, lying ready at command, would be a convenience in times of great public danger and distress; and what part of it was used might be replaced at leisure, when peace and tranquillity was restored to the nation.

But of this subject of paper credit we shall treat more largely hereafter. And I shall finish this essay on money, by proposing and explaining two observations, which may, perhaps, serve to employ the thoughts of our speculative politicians.

It was a shrewd observation of ANACHARSIS[5] the SCYTHIAN, who had never seen money in his own country, that gold and silver seemed to him of no use to the GREEKS, but to assist them in numeration and arithmetic. It is indeed evident, that money is nothing but the representation of labour and commodities, and serves only as a method of rating or estimating them. Where coin is in greater plenty; as a greater quantity of it is required to represent the same quantity of goods; it can have no effect, either good or bad, taking a nation within itself; any more than it would make an alteration on a merchant's books, if, instead of the ARABIAN method of notation, which requires few characters, he should make use of the ROMAN, which requires a great many. Nay, the greater quantity of money, like the ROMAN characters, is rather inconvenient, and requires greater trouble both to keep and transport it. But notwithstanding this conclusion, which must be allowed just, it is certain, that, since the discovery of the mines in AMERICA, industry has increased in all the nations of EUROPE, except in the possessors of those mines; and this may justly be ascribed, amongst other reasons, to the encrease of gold and silver. Accordingly we find, that, in every kingdom, into which money begins to flow in greater abundance than formerly, every thing takes a new face: labour and industry gain life; the merchant becomes more enterprising, the manufacturer more diligent and skilful, and even the farmer follows his plough with greater alacrity and attention. This is not easily to be accounted for, if we consider only the influence which a greater abundance of coin has in the kingdom itself, by heightening the price of commodities, and obliging every one to pay a greater number of these little yellow or white pieces for every thing he purchases. And as to foreign trade, it appears, that great plenty of money is rather disadvantageous, by raising the price of every kind of labour.

To account, then, for this phenomenon, we must consider, that though the high price of commodities be a necessary consequence of the encrease of gold and silver, yet it follows not immediately upon that encrease; but some time is required before the money circulates through the whole state, and makes its effect be felt on all ranks of people. At first, no alteration is perceived; by degrees the price rises, first of one commodity, then of another; till the whole at last reaches a just proportion with the new quantity of specie which is in the kingdom. In my opinion, it is only in this interval or intermediate situation, between the acquisition of money and rise of prices, that the encreasing quantity of gold and silver is favourable to industry. When any quantity of money is imported into a nation, it is not at first dispersed into many hands; but is confined to the coffers of a few persons, who immediately seek to employ it to advantage. Here are a set of manufacturers or merchants, we shall suppose, who have received returns of gold and silver for goods which they sent to CADIZ.[6] They are thereby enabled to employ more workmen than formerly, who never dream of demanding higher wages, but are glad of employment from such good paymasters. If workmen become scarce, the manufacturer gives higher wages, but at first requires an encrease of labour; and this is willingly submitted to by the artisan, who can now eat and drink better, to compensate his additional toil and fatigue. He carries his money to market, where he finds every thing at the same price as formerly, but returns with greater quantity and of better kinds, for the use of his family. The farmer and gardener, finding, that all their commodities are taken off, apply themselves with alacrity to the raising more; and at the same time can afford to take better and more cloths from their tradesmen, whose price is the same as formerly, and their industry only whetted by so much new gain. It is easy to trace the money in its progress through the whole commonwealth; where we shall find, that it must first quicken the diligence of every individual, before it encrease the price of labour.

And that the specie may encrease to a considerable pitch, before it have this latter effect, appears, amongst other instances, from the frequent operations of the FRENCH king on the money; where it was always found, that the augmenting of the numerary value did not produce a proportional rise of the prices, at least for some time. In the last year of LOUIS XIV, money was raised three-sevenths, but prices augmented only one. Corn in FRANCE is now sold at the same price, or for the same number of livres it was in 1683; though silver was then at 30 livres the mark, and is now at 50.[7] Not to mention the great addition of gold and silver, which may have come into that kingdom since the former period.

From the whole of this reasoning we may conclude, that it is of no manner of consequence, with regard to the domestic happiness of a state, whether money be in a greater or less quantity. The good policy of the magistrate consists only in keeping it, if possible, still encreasing; because, by that means, he keeps alive a spirit of industry in the nation, and encreases the stock of labour, in which consists all real power and riches. A nation, whose money decreases, is actually, at that time, weaker and more miserable than another nation, which possesses no more money, but is on the encreasing hand. This will be easily accounted for, if we consider, that the alterations in the quantity of money, either on one side or the other, are not immediately attended with proportionable alterations in the price of commodities. There is always an interval before matters be adjusted to their new situation; and this interval is as pernicious to industry, when gold and silver are diminishing, as it is advantageous when these metals are encreasing. The workman has not the same employment from the manufacturer and merchant; though he pays the same price for every thing in the market. The farmer cannot dispose of his corn and cattle; though he must pay the same rent to his landlord. The poverty, and beggary, and sloth, which must ensue, are easily foreseen.

II. The second observation which I proposed to make with regard to money, may be explained after the following manner. There are some kingdoms, and many provinces in EUROPE, (and all of them were once in the same condition) where money is so scarce, that the landlord can get none at all from his tenants; but is obliged to take his rent in kind, and either to consume it himself, or transport it to places where he may find a market. In those countries, the prince can levy few or no taxes, but in the same manner: And as he will receive small benefit from impositions so paid, it is evident that such a kingdom has little force even at home; and cannot maintain fleets and armies to the same extent, as if every part of it abounded in gold and silver. There is surely a greater disproportion between the force of GERMANY, at present, and what it was three centuries ago,[8] than there is in its industry, people, and manufactures. The AUSTRIAN dominions in the empire are in general well peopled and well cultivated, and are of great extent; but have not a proportionable weight in the balance of EUROPE; proceeding, as is commonly supposed, from the scarcity of money. How do all these facts agree with that principle of reason, that the quantity of gold and silver is in itself altogether indifferent? According to that principle wherever a sovereign has numbers of subjects, and these have plenty of commodities, he should of course be great and powerful, and they rich and happy, independent of the greater or lesser abundance of the precious metals. These admit of divisions and subdivisions to a great extent; and where the pieces might become so small as to be in danger of being lost, it is easy to mix the gold or silver with a baser metal, as is practised in some countries of EUROPE; and by that means raise the pieces to a bulk more sensible and convenient. They still serve the same purposes of exchange, whatever their number may be, or whatever colour they may be supposed to have.

To these difficulties I answer, that the effect, here supposed to flow from scarcity of money, really arises from the manners and customs of the people; and that we mistake, as is too usual, a collateral effect for a cause. The contradiction is only apparent; but it requires some thought and reflection to discover the principles, by which we can reconcile *reason* to *experience*.

It seems a maxim almost self-evident, that the prices of every thing depend on the proportion between commodities and money, and that any considerable alteration on either has the same effect, either of heightening or lowering the price. Encrease the commodities, they become cheaper; encrease the money, they rise in their value. As, on the other hand, a diminution of the former, and that of the latter, have contrary tendencies.

It is also evident, that the prices do not so much depend on the absolute quantity of commodities and that of money, which are in a nation, as on that of the commodities, which come or may come to market, and of the money which circulates. If the coin be locked up in chests, it is the same thing with regard to prices, as if it were annihilated; if the commodities be hoarded in magazines and granaries, a like effect follows. As the money and commodities, in these cases, never meet, they cannot affect each other. Were we, at any time, to form conjectures concerning the price of provisions, the corn, which the farmer must reserve for seed and for the maintenance of himself and family, ought never to enter into the estimation. It is only the overplus, compared to the demand, that determines the value.

To apply these principles, we must consider, that, in the first and more uncultivated ages of any state, ere fancy has confounded her wants with those of nature, men, content with the produce of their own fields, or with those rude improvements which they themselves can work upon them, have little occasion for exchange, at least for money, which, by agreement, is the common measure of exchange. The wool of the farmer's own flock, spun in his own family, and wrought by a neighbouring weaver, who receives his payment in corn or wool, suffices for furniture and cloathing. The carpenter, the smith, the mason, the tailor, are retained by wages of a like nature; and the landlord himself, dwelling in the neighbourhood, is content to receive his rent in the commodities raised by the farmer. The greater part of these he consumes at home, in rustic hospitality: The rest, perhaps, he disposes of for money to the neighbouring town, whence he draws the few materials of his expence and luxury.

But after men begin to refine on all these enjoyments, and live not always at home, nor are content with what can be raised in their neighbourhood, there is more exchange and commerce of all kinds, and more money enters into that exchange. The tradesmen will not be paid in corn; because they want something more than barely to eat. The farmer goes beyond his own parish for the commodities he purchases, and cannot always carry his commodities to the merchant who supplies him. The landlord lives in the capital, or in a foreign country; and demands his rent in gold and silver, which can easily be transported to him. Great undertakers, and manufacturers, and merchants, arise in every commodity; and these can conveniently deal in nothing but in specie. And consequently, in this situation of society, the coin enters into many more contracts, and by that means is much more employed than in the former.

The necessary effect is, that, provided the money encrease not in the nation, every thing must become much cheaper in times of industry and refinement, than in rude, uncultivated ages. It is the proportion between the circulating money, and the commodities in the market, which determines the prices. Goods, that are consumed at home, or exchanged with other goods in the neighbourhood, never come to market; they affect not in the least the current specie; with regard to it they are as if totally annihilated; and consequently this method of using them sinks the proportion on the side of the commodities, and encreases the prices. But after money enters into all contracts and sales, and is every where the measure of exchange, the same national cash has a much greater task to perform; all commodities are then in the market; the sphere of circulation is enlarged; it is the same case as if that individual sum were to serve a larger kingdom; and therefore, the proportion being here lessened on the side of the money, every thing must become cheaper, and the prices gradually fall.

By the most exact computations, that have been formed all over EUROPE, after making allowance for the alteration in the numerary value or the denomination, it is found, that the prices of all things have only risen three, or at most, four times, since the discovery of the WEST INDIES.[9] But will any one assert, that there is not much more than four times the coin in EUROPE, that was in the fifteenth century, and the centuries preceding it? The SPANIARDS and PORTUGUESE from their mines, the ENGLISH, FRENCH, and DUTCH, by their AFRICAN trade, and by their interlopers in the WEST INDIES, bring home about six millions a year, of which not above a third goes to the EAST-INDIES. This sum alone, in ten years, would probably double the ancient stock of money in EUROPE. And no other satisfactory reason can be given, why all prices have not risen to a much more exorbitant height, except that which is derived from a change of customs and manners. Besides that more commodities are produced by additional industry, the same commodities come more to market, after men depart from their ancient simplicity of manners. And though this encrease has not been equal to that of money, it has, however, been considerable, and has preserved the proportion between coin and commodities nearer the ancient standard.

Were the question proposed, Which of these methods of living in the people, the simple or refined, is the most advantageous to the state or public? I should, without much scruple, prefer the latter, in a view to politics at least; and should produce this as an additional reason for the encouragement of trade and manufactures.

While men live in the ancient simple manner, and supply all their necessaries from domestic industry or from the neighbourhood, the sovereign can levy no taxes in money from a considerable part of his subjects; and if he will impose on them any burthens, he must take payment in commodities, with which alone they abound; a method attended with such great and obvious inconveniencies, that they need not here be insisted on. All the money he can pretend to raise, must be from his principal cities, where alone it circulates; and these, it is evident, cannot afford him so much as the whole state could, did gold and silver circulate throughout the whole. But besides this obvious diminution of the revenue, there is another cause of the poverty of the public in such a situation. Not only the sovereign receives less money, but the same money goes not so far as in times of industry and general commerce. Every thing is dearer, where the gold and silver are supposed equal; and that because fewer commodities come to market, and the whole coin bears a higher proportion to what is to be purchased by it; whence alone the prices of every thing are fixed and determined.

Here then we may learn the fallacy of the remark, often to be met with in historians, and even in common conversation, that any particular state is weak, though fertile, populous, and well cultivated, merely because it wants money. It appears, that the want of money can never injure any state within itself: For men and commodities are the real strength of any community. It is the simple manner of living which here hurts the public, by confining the gold and silver to few hands, and preventing its universal diffusion and circulation. On the contrary, industry and refinements of all kinds incorporate it with the whole state, however small its quantity may be: They digest it into every vein, so to speak; and make it enter into every transaction and contract. No hand is entirely empty of it. And as the prices of every thing fall by that means, the sovereign has a double advantage: He may draw money by his taxes from every part of the state; and what he receives, goes farther in every purchase and payment.

We may infer, from a comparison of prices, that money is not more plentiful in CHINA, than it was in EUROPE three centuries ago: But what immense power is that empire possessed of, if we may judge by the civil and military establishment maintained by it? POLYBIUS[10] tells us, that provisions were so cheap in ITALY during his time, that in some places the stated price for a meal at the inns was a *semis* a head, little more than a farthing! Yet the ROMAN power had even then subdued the whole known world. About a century before that period, the CARTHAGINIAN ambassador said, by way of raillery, that no people lived more sociably amongst themselves than the ROMANS; for that, in every entertainment, which, as foreign ministers, they

received, they still observed the same plate at every table.[11] The absolute quantity of the precious metals is a matter of great indifference. There are only two circumstances of any importance, namely, their gradual encrease, and their thorough concoction and circulation through the state; and the influence of both these circumstances has here been explained.

In the following Essay we shall see an instance of a like fallacy as that above mentioned; where a collateral effect is taken for a cause, and where a consequence is ascribed to the plenty of money; though it be really owing to a change in the manners and customs of the people.

NOTES FOR THIS CHAPTER

1. [Henry (or Harry) VII was king of England from 1485 to 1509. For an analysis of the monetary theory that Hume develops in this essay and its relation to other views of his time, see Rotwein, *David Hume: Writings on Economics*, pp. liv–lxvii. Hume's broad purpose here is to oppose mercantilist views that tended to identify wealth with money and thus to encourage policies aimed at increasing the quantity of a nation's bullion or money. Hume argues for the general principle that an abundant quantity of money does not increase a state's domestic happiness and may sometimes even harm it. He undertakes to reconcile this principle with evidence that an increase in the supply of money can be a beneficial stimulus to industry at certain stages of economic development and that a wide distribution of money is favorable to the collection of revenues.]

2. [Hume refers here to the War of the Austrian Succession (1740–48), which Great Britain entered to prevent French hegemony in Europe and to protect her commercial and colonial empire by establishing naval supremacy over France. In 1746, Hume accompanied an expeditionary force under General James St. Clair

in an attack on the French coast. Hume describes the expedition, for which he received a commission as Judge-Advocate, in a manuscript known as the "Descent on the Coast of Brittany." See Mossner, *The Life of David Hume* (Edinburgh: Nelson, 1954), pp. 187–204.]

3. A private soldier in the ROMAN infantry had a denarius a day, somewhat less than eightpence. The ROMAN emperors had commonly 25 legions in pay, which allowing 5000 men to a legion, makes 125,000. TACIT. *Ann.* lib. iv. [5.] It is true, there were also auxiliaries to the legions; but their numbers are uncertain, as well as their pay. To consider only the legionaries, the pay of the private men could not exceed 1,600,000 pounds. Now, the parliament in the last war commonly allowed for the fleet 2,500,000. We have therefore 900,000 over for the officers and other expences of the ROMAN legions. There seem to have been but few officers in the ROMAN armies, in comparison of what are employed in all our modern troops, except some SWISS corps. And these officers had very small pay: A centurion, for instance, only double a common soldier. And as the soldiers from their pay (TACIT. *Ann.* lib. i. [17]) bought their own cloaths, arms, tents, and baggage; this must also diminish considerably the other charges of the army. So little expensive was that mighty government, and so easy was its yoke over the world. And, indeed, this is the more natural conclusion from the foregoing calculations. For money, after the conquest of ÆGYPT, seems to have been nearly in as great plenty at ROME, as it is at present in the richest of the EUROPEAN kingdoms.

4. This is the case with the bank of AMSTERDAM.

5. PLUT. *Quomodo quis suos profectus in virtute sentire possit.* [Plutarch, *Moralia*, "How a Man may become aware of his Progress in Virtue," sec. 7.]

6. [Cádiz was the Spanish seaport where bullion entered from the West Indies.]

7. These facts I give upon the authority of Mons. du TOT in his *Reflections politiques* [*Réflexions politiques sur les finances et le commerce* (1738); translated as *Political Reflections upon the Finances and Commerce of France* (1739)], an author of reputation. Though I must confess, that the facts which he advances on other occasions,

are often so suspicious, as to make his authority less in this matter. However, the general observation, that the augmenting of the money in FRANCE does not at first proportionably augment the prices, is certainly just.

8. By the by, this seems to be one of the best reasons which can be given, for a gradual and universal encrease of the denomination of money, though it has been entirely overlooked in all those volumes which have been written on that question by MELON, Du TOT, and PARIS de VERNEY [Joseph Paris-Duverney, *Examen du livre intitulé Réflections politiques sur les finances et le commerce, par de Tott* (Examination of a book entitled Political reflections upon finances and commerce, by Dutot), 1740]. Were all our money, for instance, recoined, and a penny's worth of silver taken from every shilling, the new shilling would probably purchase every thing that could have been bought by the old; the prices of every thing would thereby be insensibly diminished; foreign trade enlivened; and domestic industry, by the circulation of a great number of pounds and shillings, would receive some encrease and encouragement. In executing such a project, it would be better to make the new shilling pass for 24 halfpence, in order to preserve the illusion, and make it be taken for the same. And as a recoinage of our silver begins to be requisite, by the continual wearing of our shillings and sixpences, it may be doubtful, whether we ought to imitate the example in King WILLIAM'S reign, when the clip'd money was raised to the old standard.

9. The ITALIANS gave to the Emperor MAXIMILIAN, the nickname of POCCI-DANARI. None of the enterprises of that prince ever succeeded, for want of money. [Maximilian I became Holy Roman Emperor Elect in 1508, but because of Venetian hostility, he was unable to go to Rome for his coronation. Maximilian then joined with France, Spain, and the Pope in the League of Cambrai, whose aim was to partition the Republic of Venice. Because of his lack of money and troops, he was considered an unreliable partner in the war that followed. *Pochi danari* means "very few funds."]

10. [Hume uses *West Indies* broadly to refer to Central and South America. The exploration and conquest of the

new world after Christopher Columbus's discovery of the West Indies islands off the Atlantic coast of America in 1492 led, in the next century, to a tremendous increase in the supply of precious metals in Europe.

Hume's point is that the increase of prices has not kept pace with the increase in coin.]

11. Lib. ii. cap. 15. [*Histories* 2.15.]

Of the Value of Money as Dependent on Demand and Supply

Principles of Political Economy

By John Stuart Mill

§ 1. It is unfortunate that in the very outset of the subject we have to clear from our path a formidable ambiguity of language. The Value of Money is to appearance an expression as precise, as free from possibility of misunderstanding, as any in science. The value of a thing is what it will exchange for: the value of money, is what money will exchange for; the purchasing power of money. If prices are low, money will buy much of other things, and is of high value; if prices are high, it will buy little of other things, and is of low value. The value of money is inversely as general prices: falling as they rise, and rising as they fall.

But unhappily the same phrase is also employed, in the current language of commerce, in a very different sense. Money, which is so commonly understood as the synonym of wealth, is more especially the term in use to denote it when it is the subject of borrowing. When one person lends to another, as well as when he pays wages or rent to another, what he transfers is not the mere money, but a right to a certain value of the produce of the country, to be selected at pleasure; the lender having first bought this right, by giving for it a portion of his capital. What he really lends is so much capital; the money is the mere instrument of transfer. But the capital usually passes from the lender to the receiver through the means either of money, or of

an order to receive money, and at any rate it is in money that the capital is computed and estimated. Hence, borrowing capital is universally called borrowing money; the loan market is called the money market: those who have their capital disposable for investment on loan are called the monied class: and the equivalent given for the use of capital, or in other words, interest, is not only called the interest of money, but, by a grosser perversion of terms, the value of money. This misapplication of language, assisted by some fallacious appearances which we shall notice and clear up hereafter,[1] has created a general notion among persons in business, that the Value of Money, meaning the rate of interest, has an intimate connexion with the Value of Money in its proper sense, the value or purchasing power of the circulating medium. We shall return to this subject before long: at present it is enough to say, that by Value I shall always mean Exchange Value, and by money the medium of exchange, not the capital which is passed from hand to hand through that medium.

§2. The value or purchasing power of money depends, in the first instance, on demand and supply. But demand and supply, in relation to money, present themselves in a somewhat different shape from the demand and supply of other things.

The supply of a commodity means the quantity offered for sale. But it is not usual to speak of offering money for sale. People are not usually said to buy or sell money. This, however, is merely an accident of language. In point of fact, money is bought and sold like other things, whenever other things are bought and sold *for* money. Whoever sells corn, or tallow, or cotton, buys money. Whoever buys bread, or wine, or clothes, sells money to the dealer in those articles. The money with which people are offering to buy is money offered for sale. The supply of money, then, is the quantity of it which people are wanting to lay out; that is, all the money they have in their possession, except what they are hoarding, or at least keeping by them as a reserve for future contingencies. The supply of money, in short, is all the money in *circulation* at the time.

The demand for money, again, consists of all the goods offered for sale. Every seller of goods is a buyer of money, and the goods he brings with him constitute his demand. The demand for money differs from the demand for other things in this, that it is limited only by the means of the purchaser. The demand for other things is for so much and no more; but there is always a demand for as much money as can be got. Persons may indeed refuse to sell, and withdraw their goods from the market, if they cannot get for them what they consider a sufficient price. But this is only when they think that the price will rise, and that they shall get more money by waiting. If they thought the low price likely to be permanent, they would take what they could get. It is always a *sine quâ non* with a dealer to dispose of his goods.

As the whole of the goods in the market compose the demand for money, so the whole of the money constitutes the demand for goods. The money and the goods are seeking each other for the purpose of being exchanged. They are reciprocally supply and demand to one another. It is indifferent whether, in characterizing the phenomena, we speak of the demand and supply of goods, or the supply and the demand of money. They are equivalent expressions.

We shall proceed to illustrate this proposition more fully. And in doing this, the reader will remark a great difference between the class of questions which now occupy us, and those which we previously had under discussion respecting Values. In considering Value, we were only concerned with causes which

acted upon particular commodities apart from the rest. Causes which affect all commodities alike do not act upon values. But in considering the relation between goods and money, it is with the causes that operate upon all goods whatever that we are specially concerned. We are comparing goods of all sorts on one side, with money on the other side, as things to be exchanged against each other.

Suppose, everything else being the same, that there is an increase in the quantity of money, say by the arrival of a foreigner in a place, with a treasure of gold and silver. When he commences expending it (for this question it matters not whether productively or unproductively), he adds to the supply of money, and, by the same act, to the demand for goods. Doubtless he adds, in the first instance, to the demand only for certain kinds of goods, namely, those which he selects for purchase; he will immediately raise the price of those, and so far as he is individually concerned, of those only. If he spends his funds in giving entertainments, he will raise the prices of food and wine. If he expends them in establishing a manufactory, he will raise the prices of labour and materials. But at the higher prices, more money will pass into the hands of the sellers of these different articles; and they, whether labourers or dealers, having more money to lay out, will create an increased demand for all the things which they are accustomed to purchase: these accordingly will rise in price, and so on until the rise has reached everything. I say everything, though it is of course possible that the influx of money might take place through the medium of some new class of consumers, or in such a manner as to alter the proportions of different classes of consumers to one another, so that a greater share of the national income than before would thenceforth be expended in some articles, and a smaller in others; exactly as if a change had taken place in the tastes and wants of the community. If this were the case, then until production had accommodated itself to this change in the comparative demand for different things, there would be a real alteration in values, and some things would rise in price more than others, while some perhaps would not rise at all. These effects, however, would evidently proceed, not from the mere increase of money, but from accessory circumstances attending it. We are now only called upon to consider what would be the effect of an increase of money, considered by itself. Supposing the money in the hands of individuals to be increased, the wants and inclinations of the community collectively in respect to consumption remaining exactly the same; the increase of demand would reach all things equally, and there would be an universal rise of prices. We might suppose, with Hume, that some morning, every person in the nation should wake and find a gold coin in his pocket: this example, however, would involve an alteration of the proportions in the demand for different commodities; the luxuries of the poor would, in the first instance, be raised in price in a much greater degree than other things. Let us rather suppose, therefore, that to every pound, or shilling, or penny, in the possession of any one, another pound, shilling, or penny, were suddenly added. There would be an increased money demand, and consequently an increased money value, or price, for things of all sorts. This increased value would do no good to any one; would make no difference, except that of having to reckon pounds, shillings, and pence, in higher numbers. It would be an increase of values only as estimated in money, a thing only wanted to buy other things with; and would not enable any one to buy more of them than before. Prices would have risen in a certain ratio, and the value of money would have fallen in the same ratio.

It is to be remarked that this ratio would be precisely that in which the quantity of money had been increased. If the whole money in circulation was doubled, prices would be doubled. If it was only increased one-fourth, prices would rise one-fourth. There would be one-fourth more money, all of which would be used to purchase goods of some description. When there had been time for the increased supply of money to reach all markets, or (according to the conventional metaphor) to permeate all the channels of circulation, all prices would have risen one-fourth. But the general rise of price is independent of this diffusing and equalizing process. Even if some prices were raised more, and others less, the average rise would be one-fourth. This is a necessary consequence of the fact that a fourth more money

would have been given for only the same quantity of goods. *General* prices, therefore, would in any case be a fourth higher.

The very same effect would be produced on prices if we suppose the goods diminished, instead of the money increased: and the contrary effect if the goods were increased or the money diminished. If there were less money in the hands of the community, and the same amount of goods to be sold, less money altogether would be given for them, and they would be sold at lower prices; lower, too, in the precise ratio in which the money was diminished. So that the value of money, other things being the same, varies inversely as its quantity; every increase of quantity lowering the value, and every diminution raising it, in a ratio exactly equivalent.

This, it must be observed, is a property peculiar to money. We did not find it to be true of commodities generally, that every diminution of supply raised the value exactly in proportion to the deficiency, or that every increase lowered it in the precise ratio of the excess. Some things are usually affected in a greater ratio than that of the excess or deficiency, others usually in a less: because, in ordinary cases of demand, the desire, being for the thing itself, may be stronger or weaker: and the amount of what people are willing to expend on it, being in any case a limited quantity, may be affected in very unequal degrees by difficulty or facility of attainment. But in the case of money, which is desired as the means of universal purchase, the demand consists of everything which people have to sell; and the only limit to what they are willing to give is the limit set by their having nothing more to offer. The whole of the goods being in any case exchanged for the whole of the money which comes into the market to be laid out, they will sell for less or more of it, exactly according as less or more is brought.

§3. From what precedes, it might for a moment be supposed that all the goods on sale in a country, at any one time, are exchanged for all the money existing and in circulation at that same time: or, in other words, that there is always in circulation in a country, a quantity of money equal in value to the whole of the goods then and there on sale. But this would be a complete misapprehension. The money laid out is equal in value to the goods it purchases; but the quantity of money laid out is not the same thing with the quantity in circulation. As the money passes from hand to hand, the same piece of money is laid out many times, before all the things on sale at one time are purchased and finally removed from the market: and each pound or dollar must be counted for as many pounds or dollars, as the number of times it changes hands in order to effect this object. The greater part of the goods must also be counted more than once, not only because most things pass through the hands of several sets of manufacturers and dealers before they assume the form in which they are finally consumed, but because in times of speculation (and all times are so, more or less) the same goods are often bought repeatedly, to be resold for a profit, before they are bought for the purpose of consumption at all.

If we assume the quantity of goods on sale, and the number of times those goods are resold, to be fixed quantities, the value of money will depend upon its quantity, together with the average number of times that each piece changes hands in the process. The whole of the goods sold (counting each resale of the same goods as so much added to the goods) have been exchanged for the whole of the money, multiplied by the number of purchases made on the average by each piece. Consequently, the amount of goods and of transactions being the same, the value of money is inversely as its quantity multiplied by what is called the rapidity of circulation. And the quantity of money in circulation is equal to the money value of all the goods sold, divided by the number which expresses the rapidity of circulation.

The phrase, rapidity of circulation, requires some comment. It must not be understood to mean the number of purchases made by each piece of money in a given time. Time is not the thing to be considered. The state of society may be such that each piece of money hardly performs more than one purchase in a year: but if this arises from the small number of transactions—from the small amount of business done, the want of activity in traffic, or because what traffic there is, mostly takes place by barter—it constitutes no reason why prices should be lower, or the value of money higher. The essential point is, not how often the same money changes hands in a given time, but how often it changes hands in order to perform a given amount of traffic. We must compare the number of purchases made by the money in a given time, not with the time itself, but with the goods sold in that same time. If each piece of money changes hands on an average ten times while goods are sold to the value of a million sterling, it is evident that the money required to circulate those goods is 100,000*l.* And conversely, if the money in circulation is 100,000*l.*, and each piece changes hands by the purchase of goods ten times in a month, the sales of goods for money which take place every month must amount on the average to 1,000,000/slash sign.

Rapidity of circulation being a phrase so ill adapted to express the only thing which it is of any importance to express by it, and having a tendency to confuse the subject by suggesting a meaning extremely different from the one intended, it would be a good thing if the phrase could be got rid of, and another substituted, more directly significant of the idea meant to be conveyed. Some such expression as "the efficiency of money," though not unexceptionable, would do better; as it would point attention to the quantity of work done, without suggesting the idea of estimating it by time. Until an appropriate term can be devised, we must be content, when ambiguity is to be apprehended, to express the idea by the circumlocution which alone conveys it adequately, namely, the average number of purchases made by each piece in order to effect a given pecuniary amount of transactions.

§4. The proposition which we have laid down respecting the dependence of general prices upon the quantity of money in circulation, must be understood as applying only to a state of things in which money, that is, gold or silver, is the exclusive instrument of exchange, and actually passes from hand to hand at every purchase, credit in any of its shapes being unknown. When credit comes into play as a means of purchasing, distinct from money in hand, we shall hereafter find that the connexion between prices and the amount of the circulating medium is much less direct and intimate, and that such connexion as does exist no longer admits of so simple a mode of expression. But on a subject so full of complexity as that of currency and prices, it is necessary to lay the foundation of our theory in a thorough understanding of the most simple cases, which we shall always find lying as a groundwork or substratum under those which arise in practice. That an increase of the quantity of money raises prices, and a diminution lowers them, is the most elementary proposition in the theory of currency, and without it we should have no key to any of the others. In any state of things, however, except the simple and primitive one which we have supposed, the proposition is only true other things being the same: and what those other things are, which must be the same, we are not yet ready to pronounce. We can, however, point out, even now, one or two of the cautions with which the principle must be guarded in attempting to make use of it for the practical explanation of phenomena; cautions the more indispensable, as the doctrine, though a scientific truth, has of late years been the foundation of a greater mass of false theory, and erroneous interpretation of facts, than any other proposition relating to interchange. From the time of the resumption of cash payments by the Act of 1819, and especially since the commercial crisis of 1825, the favourite explanation of every rise or fall of prices has been "the currency;" and like most popular theories, the doctrine has been applied with little regard to the conditions necessary for making it correct.

For example, it is habitually assumed that whenever there is a greater amount of money in the country, or in existence, a rise of prices must necessarily follow. But this is by no means an inevitable consequence. In no commodity is it the quantity in existence, but the quantity offered for sale, that determines the value. Whatever may be the quantity of money in the country, only that part of it will affect prices which goes into the market of commodities, and is there actually exchanged against goods. Whatever increases the amount of this portion of the money in the country, tends to raise prices. But money hoarded does not act on prices. Money kept in reserve by individuals to meet contingencies which do not occur, does not act on prices. The money in the coffers of the Bank, or retained as a reserve by private bankers, does not act on prices until drawn out, nor even then unless drawn out to be expended in commodities.

It frequently happens that money, to a considerable amount, is brought into the country, is there actually invested[2] as capital, and again flows out, without having ever once acted upon the markets of commodities, but only upon the market of securities, or, as it is commonly though improperly called, the money market. Let us return to the case already put for illustration, that of a foreigner landing in the country with a treasure. We supposed him to employ his treasure in the purchase of goods for his own use, or in setting up a manufactory and employing labourers; and in either case he would, *cæteris paribus,* raise prices. But instead of doing either of these things, he might very probably prefer to invest his fortune at interest; which we shall suppose him to do in the most obvious way, by becoming a competitor for a portion of the stock, exchequer bills, railway debentures, mercantile bills, mortgages, &c., which are at all times in the hands of the public. By doing this he would raise the prices of those different securities, or in other words would lower the rate of interest; and since this would disturb the relation previously existing between the rate of interest on capital in the country itself, and that in foreign countries, it would probably induce some of those who had floating capital seeking employment, to send it abroad for foreign investment rather than buy securities at home at the advanced price. As much money might thus go out as had previously come in, while the prices of commodities would have shown no trace of its temporary presence. This is a case highly deserving of attention: and it is a fact now beginning to be recognised, that the passage of the precious metals from country to country is determined much more than was formerly supposed by the state of the loan market in different countries, and much less by the state of prices.

Another point must be adverted to, in order to avoid serious error in the interpretation of mercantile phenomena. If there be, at any time, an increase in the number of money transactions, a thing continually liable to happen from differences in the activity of speculation, and even in the time of year (since certain kinds of business are transacted only at particular seasons); an increase of the currency which is only proportional to this increase of transactions, and is of no longer duration, has no tendency to raise prices. At the quarterly periods when the public dividends are paid at the Bank, a sudden increase takes place of the money in the hands of the public; an increase estimated at from a fifth to two-fifths of the whole issues of the Bank of England. Yet this never has any effect on prices; and in a very few weeks, the currency has again shrunk into its usual dimensions, by a mere reduction in the demands of the public (after so copious a supply of ready money) for accommodation from the Bank in the way of discount or loan. In like manner the currency of the agricultural districts fluctuates in amount at different seasons of the year. It is always lowest in August: "it rises generally towards Christmas, and obtains its greatest elevation about Lady-day, when the farmer commonly lays in his stock, and has to pay his rent and summer taxes," and when he therefore makes his principal applications to country bankers for loans. "Those variations occur with the same regularity as the season, and with just as little disturbance of the markets as the quarterly fluctuations of the notes of the Bank of England. As soon as the extra payments have been completed, the superfluous" currency, which is estimated at half a million, "as certainly and immediately is reabsorbed and disappears."[3]

If extra currency were not forthcoming to make these extra payments, one of three things must happen. Either the payments must be made without money, by a resort to some of those contrivances by which its use is dispensed with; or there must be an increase in the rapidity of circulation, the same sum of money being made to perform more payments; or, if neither of these things took place, money to make the extra payments must be withdrawn from the market for commodities, and prices, consequently, must fall. An increase of the circulating medium, conformable in extent and duration to the temporary stress of business, does not raise prices, but merely prevents this fall.

The sequel of our investigation will point out many other qualifications with which the proposition must be received, that the value of the circulating medium depends on the demand and supply, and is in the inverse ratio of the quantity;[4] qualifications which, under a complex system of credit like that existing in England, render the proposition an extremely incorrect expression of the fact.

NOTES FOR THIS CHAPTER

1. Infra, chap. xxiii.
   Book III. Chapter VIII. Section 4
2. ["Invested" substituted for "employed" in 3rd ed. (1852).]
3. Fullarton, *Regulation of Currencies,* 2nd edit. pp. 87–9.
4. [The rest of the sentence was added in the 4th ed. (1857), and the proposition described as "a totally incorrect expression of the fact." In the 5th ed. (1862) "extremely" was substituted for "totally."]

The Determinants of the Objective Exchange Value of Money

By Ludwig von Mises

§1 THE DEPENDENCE OF THE SUBJECTIVE VALUATION OF MONEY ON THE EXISTENCE OF OBJECTIVE EXCHANGE—VALUE

According to modern Value Theory, price is the resultant of the interaction in the market of subjective valuations of commodities and price-goods. From beginning to end, it is the product of subjective valuations. Goods are valued by the individuals exchanging them, according to their subjective use-values, and their exchange-ratios are determined within that range where both supply and demand are in exact quantitative equilibrium. The Law of Price stated by Menger and Böhm-Bawerk provides a complete and numerically precise explanation of these exchange-ratios; it accounts exhaustively for all the phenomena of direct exchange. Under bilateral competition, market-price is determined within a range whose upper limit is set by the valuations of the lowest bidder among the actual buyers and the highest offerer among the excluded would- be sellers, and whose lower limit is set by the valuations of the lowest offerer among the actual sellers and the highest bidder among the excluded would-be buyers.

This Law of Price is just as valid for indirect as for direct exchange. The price of money, like other prices, is determined in the last resort by the subjective valuations of buyers and sellers. But, as has been said already, the subjective use-value of money, which coincides with its subjective exchange-value, is nothing but the anticipated use-value of the things that are to be bought with it. The subjective value of money must be measured by the marginal utility of the goods for which the money can be exchanged.[1]

It follows that a valuation of money is possible only on the assumption that the money has a certain objective exchange-value. Such a *point d'appui* is necessary before the gap between satisfaction and 'useless' money can be bridged. Since there is no direct connexion between money as such and any human want, individuals can obtain an idea of its utility and consequently of its value only by assuming a definite purchasing-power. But it is easy to see that this supposition cannot be anything but an expression of the exchange-ratio ruling at the time in the market between the money and commodities.[2]

---

1 Cp. p. 99 above. Also Böhm-Bawerk, *op. cit.*, Zweite Abt., p. 274; Wieser, *Der natürliche Wert*, p. 46. (Eng. tr. *The Theory of Natural Value.*)
2 Cp. Wieser, *Der Geldwert und seine Veränderungen*, pp. 513 ff.

Once an exchange-ratio between money and commodities has been established in the market, it continues to exercise an influence beyond the period during which it is maintained; it provides the basis for the further valuation of money. Thus the past objective exchange-value of money has a certain significance for its present and future valuation. The money-prices of to-day are linked with those of yesterday and before, and with those of to-morrow and after.

But this alone will not suffice to explain the problem of the Element of Continuity in the value of money; it only postpones the explanation. To trace back the value that money has to-day to that which it had yesterday, the value that it had yesterday to that which it had the day before, and so on, is to raise the question of what determined the value of money in the first place. Consideration of the origin of the use of money and of the particular components of its value that depend on its monetary function suggest an obvious answer to this question. The first value of money was clearly the value which the goods used as money possessed (thanks to their suitability for satisfying human wants in other ways) at the moment when they were first used as common media of exchange. When individuals began to acquire objects, not for consumption, but to be used as media of exchange, they valued them according to the objective exchange-value with which the market already credited them by reason of their 'industrial' usefulness, and only as an additional consideration on account of the possibility of using them as media of exchange. The earliest value of money links up with the commodity-value of the monetary material. But the value of money since then has been influenced not merely by the factors dependent on its 'industrial' uses, which determine the value of the material of which the commodity-money is made, but also by those which result from its use as money. Not only its supply and demand for industrial purposes, but also its supply and demand for use as a medium of exchange, have influenced the value of gold from that point of time onwards when it was first used as money.[3]

§2 THE NECESSITY FOR A VALUE INDEPENDENT OF THE MONETARY FUNCTION BEFORE AN OBJECT CAN SERVE AS MONEY

If the objective exchange-value of money must always be linked with a pre-existing market exchange-ratio between money and other economic goods (since otherwise individuals would not be in a position to estimate the value of the money), it follows that an object cannot be used as money unless, at the moment when its use as money begins, it already possesses an objective exchange-value based on some other use. This provides both a refutation of those theories which derive the origin of money from a general agreement to impute fictitious value to things intrinsically valueless[4] and a confirmation of Menger's hypothesis concerning the origin of the use of money.

This link with a pre-existing exchange-value is necessary not only for commodity money, but equally for credit money and fiat money.[5] No fiat money could ever come into existence if it did not satisfy this condition. Let us suppose that, among those ancient and modern kinds of money about which it may be doubtful whether they should be reckoned as credit money or fiat money, there have actually been representatives of pure fiat money. Such money must have come into existence in one of two ways. It may have come into existence because money-substitutes already in circulation, i.e., claims payable in money on demand, were deprived of their character as claims, and yet still used in commerce as media of exchange. In this case, the starting-point for their valuation lay in the objective exchange-value that they had at the moment when they were deprived of their character as claims. The other possible case is that in which coins that once circulated as commodity-money are transformed into fiat money

3 Cp. Knies, *op. cit.*, I. Bd., p. 324.

4 Thus Locke, *Some Considerations of the Consequences of the Lowering of Interest and Raising the Value of Money*, and 2nd edn., London 1696, p. 31,
5 Cp. Subercaseaux, *op. cit.*, p. 17 f.

by cessation of free coinage (either because there was no further minting at all, or because minting was continued only on behalf of the Treasury), no obligation of conversion being *de jure* or *de facto* assumed by anybody, and nobody having any grounds for hoping that such an obligation ever would be assumed by anybody. Here the starting-point for the valuation lies in the objective exchange-value of the coins at the time of the cessation of free coinage.

Before an economic good begins to function as money it must already possess exchange-value based on some other cause than its monetary function. But money that already functions as such may remain valuable even when the original source of its exchange-value has ceased to exist. Its value then is based entirely on its function as common medium of exchange.[6]

§3 THE SIGNIFICANCE OF PRE-EXISTING PRICES IN THE DETERMINATION OF MARKET EXCHANGE-RATIOS

From what has just been said, the important conclusion follows that a historically-continuous component is contained in the objective exchange-value of money.

The past value of money is taken over by the present and transformed by it; the present value of money passes on into the future and is transformed in its turn. In this there is a contrast between the determination of the exchange-value of money and that of the exchange-value of other economic goods. All pre-existing exchange-ratios are quite irrelevant so far as the actual levels of the reciprocal exchange-ratios of other economic goods are concerned. It is true that if we look beneath the concealing monetary veil to the real exchange-ratios between goods we

observe a certain continuity. Alterations in real prices occur slowly as a rule. But this stability of prices has its cause in the stability of the price-determinants, not in the Law of Price-determination itself. Prices change slowly because the subjective valuations of human beings change slowly. Human needs, and human opinions as to the suitability of goods for satisfying those needs, are no more liable to frequent and sudden changes than are the stocks of goods available for consumption, or the manner of their social distribution. The fact that to-day's market price is seldom very different from yesterday's is to be explained by the fact that the circumstances that determined yesterday's price have not greatly changed overnight, so that to-day's price is a resultant of nearly identical factors. If rapid and erratic variations in prices were usually encountered in the market, the conception of objective exchange-value would not have attained the significance that it is actually accorded both by consumer and producer.

In this sense, reference to an inertia of prices is unobjectionable, although the errors of earlier economists should warn us of the real danger that the use of terms borrowed from mechanics may lead to a 'mechanical' system, i.e. to one that abstracts erroneously from the subjective valuations of individuals. But any suggestion of a *causal relationship* between past and present prices must be decisively rejected.

It is not disputed that there are institutional forces in operation which oppose changes in prices that would be necessitated by changes in valuations, and which are responsible when changes in prices that would have been caused by changes in supply and demand are postponed and when small or transitory changes in the relations between supply and demand lead to no corresponding change in prices at all. It is quite permissible to speak of an inertia of prices in this sense. Even the statement that the closing price forms the starting point for the transactions of the next market[7] may be accepted if it is understood in the sense suggested above. If the general conditions that determined yesterday's price

---

6   Cp. Simmel, *op. cit.*, p. 115 f.; but, above all, Wieser, *Der Geldwert und seine Veränderungen*, p. 513.

7   Cp. Schmoller, *Grundriss der allgemeinen Volkswirtsch afts-lehre*, Leipzig 1902, II. Bd., p. 110.

have altered but little during the night, to-day's price should be but little different from that of yesterday, and in practice it does not seem incorrect to make yesterday's the starting-point. Nevertheless, there is no causal connexion between past and present prices as far as the relative exchange-ratios of economic goods (not including money) are concerned. The fact that the price of beer was high yesterday cannot be of the smallest significance as far as to-day's price is concerned—we need only think of the effect upon the prices of alcoholic drinks that would follow a general triumph of the prohibition movement. Anybody who devotes attention to market activities is daily aware of alterations in the exchange-ratios of goods, and it is quite impossible for anybody who is well acquainted with economic phenomena to accept a theory which seeks to explain price-changes by a supposed constancy of prices.

It may incidentally be remarked that to trace the determination of prices back to their supposed inertia, as even Zwiedineck in his pleadings for this assumption is obliged to admit, is to resign at the outset any hope of explaining the ultimate causes of prices and to be content with explanations from secondary causes.[8] It must unreservedly be admitted that an explanation of the earliest forms of exchange transaction that can be shown to have existed—a task to the solution of which the economic historian has so far contributed but little—would show that the forces that counteract sudden changes in prices were once stronger than they are now. But it must positively be denied that there is any sort of connexion between those early prices and those of the present day; that is, if there really is anybody who believes it possible to maintain the assertion that the exchange-ratios of economic goods (not the money-prices) that prevail to-day on the German Stock Exchanges are in any sort of causal connexion

with those that were valid in the days of Hermann or Barbarossa. If all the exchange-ratios of the past were erased from human memory, the process of market-price-determination might certainly become more difficult, because everybody would have to construct a new scale of valuations for himself; but it would not become impossible. In fact, people the whole world over are engaged daily and hourly in the operation from which all prices result: the decision as to the relative significance enjoyed by specific quantities of goods as conditions for the satisfaction of wants.

It is so far as the money prices of goods are determined by *monetary* factors, that a historically-continuous component is included in them, without which their actual level could not be explained. This component, too, is derived from exchange-ratios which can be entirely explained by reference to the subjective valuations of the individuals taking part in the market, even though these valuations were not originally grounded upon the specifically monetary utility alone of these goods. The valuation of money by the market can only start from a value possessed by the money in the past, and this relationship influences the new level of the objective exchange-value of money. The historically-transmitted value is transformed by the market without regard to what has become its historical content.[9] But it is not merely the starting-point for to-day's objective exchange-value of money; it is an indispensable element in its determination. The individual must take into account the objective exchange-value of money, as determined in the market yesterday, before he can form an estimate of the quantity of money that he needs to-day. The demand for money and the supply of it are thus influenced by the value of money in the past; but they in their turn modify this value until they are brought into equilibrium.

---

8 Cp. Zwiedineck, *Kritisches und Positives zur Preislehre* (*Zeitschrift für die gesamte Staatswissenschaft*, 65. Jahrgang), pp. 100 ff.

---

9 Cp. Wieser, *Der Geldwert und seine Veränderungen*, p. 513.

§4 THE APPLICABILITY OF THE MARGINAL-UTILITY THEORY TO MONEY

Demonstration of the fact that search for the determinants of the objective exchange-value of money always leads us back to a point where the value of money is not determined in any way by its use as a medium of exchange, but solely by its other functions, prepares the way for developing a complete theory of the value of money on the basis of the subjective theory of value and its peculiar doctrine of marginal utility.

Until now the subjective school has not succeeded in doing this. In fact, among the few of its members who have paid any attention at all to the problem there have been some who have actually attempted to demonstrate its insolubility. The subjective theory of value has been helpless in face of the task here confronting it.

There are two theories of money which, whatever else we may think of them, must be acknowledged as having attempted to deal with the whole problem of the value of money.

The objective theories of value succeeded in introducing a formally unexceptionable theory of money into their systems, which deduces the value of money from its cost of production.[10] It is true that the abandonment of this monetary theory is not merely to be ascribed to those shortcomings of the objective theory of value in general which led to its supersession by the theory of the modern school. Apart from this fundamental weakness, the cost-of-production theory of the value of money exhibited one feature that was an easy target for criticism. While it certainly provided a theory of commodity money (even if only a *formally* correct one), it was unable to deal with the problem of credit money and fiat money. Nevertheless, it was a complete theory of money in so far as it did at least attempt to give a full explanation of the value of commodity money.

The other similarly complete theory of the value of money is that version of the Quantity Theory associated with the tame of Davanzati.[11] According to this theory, all the things that are able to satisfy human wants are conventionally equated with all the monetary metal. From this, since what is true of the whole is also true of its parts, the exchange-ratios between commodity-units and units of money can be deduced. Here we are confronted with a hypothesis that is not in any way supported by facts. To demonstrate its untenability once more would nowadays be a waste of time. Nevertheless, it must not be overlooked that Davanzati was the first who attempted to present the problem as a whole and to provide a theory that would explain not merely the variations in an *existing* exchange-ratio between money and other economic goods, but also the origin of this ratio.

The same cannot be said of other versions of the Quantity Theory. These all tacitly assume a certain value of money as given, and absolutely refuse to investigate further into the matter. They overlook the fact that what is required is an explanation of what determines the exchange-ratio between money and commodities, and not merely of what causes changes in this ratio. In this respect, the Quantity Theory resembles various general theories of value (many versions of the doctrine of supply and demand, for example), which have not attempted to explain price as such but have been content to establish a law of price-variations.[12] These forms of the Quantity Theory are in fact nothing but the application of the Law of Supply and Demand to the problem of the value of money. They introduce into monetary theory all the strong points of this doctrine; and of course all its weak points as well.*

The revolution in economics since 1870 has not yet been any more successful in leading to an entirely

---

10   Cp. Senior, *Three Lectures on the Value of Money*, London 1840, reprinted 1931, pp. 1 ff.; *Three Lectures on the Cost of Obtaining Money*, London 1830, reprinted 1931, PP. 1 ff.

11   Cp. Davanzati, *Lezioni delle monete*, 1588 (in *Scrittori classici italiani di economic politica, Parte Antica*, Tomo II, Milan 1804), p. 32. Locke and, above all, Montesquieu (*De lEsprit des lois*, Edition Touquet, Paris, 1821, Tome II, p. 485 f.) share this view. Cp. Willis, *The History and Present Application of the Quantity Theory (Journal of Political Economy*, 1896), Vol. IV, pp. 419 ff.

12   Cp. Zuckerkandl, *Zur Theorie des Preises*, Leipzig 1889, p. 124.

satisfactory solution of this problem. Of course, this does not mean that the progress of the science has left no trace on monetary theory in general and on the theory of the value of money in particular. It is one of the many services of the subjective theory of value to have prepared the way for a deeper understanding of the nature and value of money. The investigations of Menger have placed the theory on a new basis. But till now one thing has been neglected. Neither Menger, nor any of the many investigators who have tried to follow him, have even so much as attempted to solve the fundamental problem of the value of money. Broadly speaking, they have occupied themselves with checking and developing the traditional views and here and there expounding them more correctly and precisely, but they have not provided an answer to the question: What are the determinants of the objective exchange-value of money? Menger and Jevons have not touched upon the problem at all. Carver[13] and Kinley[14] have contributed nothing of real importance to its solution. Walras[15] and Kemmerer* assume a given value of money and develop what is merely a theory of variations in the value of money. Kemmerer, it is true, approaches very close to a solution of the problem, but passes it by.

Wieser expressly refers to the incomplete nature of the previous treatment. In his criticism of the Quantity Theory he argues that the Law of Supply and Demand in its older form, the application of which to the problem of money constitutes the Quantity Theory, has a very inadequate content, since it gives no explanation at all of the way in which value is really determined or of its level at any given time, but confines itself without any further explanation merely to stating the direction in which value will move in consequence of variations in supply or demand; i.e. in an opposite direction to changes in the former and in the same direction as changes in the latter. He further argues that it is no longer possible to rest content with a theory of the economic value of money which deals so inadequately with the

problem; that since the supersession of the old Law of Supply and Demand as applied to commodities, the case for which it was originally constructed, a more searching law must also be sought to apply to the case of money.[16] But Wieser does not deal with the problem whose solution he himself states to be the object of his investigation, for in the further course of his argument he declares that the concepts of supply of money and demand for money *as a medium of exchange* are useless for his purpose and puts forward a theory which attempts to explain variations in the objective exchange-value of money (*objektive innere Tauschwert des Geldes*)[17] by reference to the relationship that exists in an economic community between money income and real income. For while it is true that reference to the ratio between money income and real income may well serve to explain *variations* in the objective exchange-value of money, Wieser nowhere makes the attempt to evolve a *complete* theory of money–an attempt which, admittedly, the factors of supply and demand being excluded from consideration, would be certain to fail. The very objection that he raises against the old Quantity Theory, that it affirms nothing concerning the actual determination of value or the level at which it must be established at any time, must also be raised against his own doctrine; and this is all the more striking inasmuch as it was Wieser who, by revealing the historical element in the purchasing power of money, laid the foundation for the further development of the subjective theory of the value of money.

The unsatisfactory results offered by the subjective theory of value might seem to justify the opinion that this doctrine and especially its proposition concerning the significance of marginal utility must necessarily fall short as a means of dealing with the problem of money. Characteristically enough, it was a representative of the new school, Wicksell, who first expressed this opinion. Wicksell considers that the principle which lies at the basis of all modern investigation into the theory of value, viz. the concept of marginal utility, may well be suited

---

13   Cp. Wieser, *Der Geldwert und seine Veränderungen*, pp. 514 .
14   Cp. Carver, *The Value of the Money Unit, Quarterly Journal of Economics*, Vol. XI, 1897, p. 429 ff.
15   Cp. Kinley, *Money*, New York, 1909, pp. 123 ff.

16   Cp. Walras, *Théorie de la Monnaie*, pp. 25 ff.
17   [See p. 124n. H.E.B.]

to explaining the determination of exchange-ratios between one commodity and another, but that it has practically no significance at all, or at most an entirely secondary significance, in explaining the exchange-ratios between money and other economic goods. Wicksell, however, does not appear to detect any sort of objection to the marginal-utility theory in this assertion. According to his argument, the objective exchange-value of money is not determined at all by the processes of the market in which money and the other economic goods are exchanged. If the money-price of a single commodity or group of commodities is wrongly assessed in the market, then the resulting maladjustments of the supply and demand and the production and consumption of this commodity or group of commodities will sooner or later bring about the necessary correction. If, on the other hand, all commodity prices, or the average price-level, should for any reason be raised or lowered, there is no factor in the circumstances of the *commodity* market that could bring about a reaction. Consequently, if there is to be any reaction at all against a price assessment that is either too high or too low it must in some way or other originate outside the commodity market. In the further course of his argument, Wicksell arrives at the conclusion that the regulator of money-prices is to be sought in the relations of the commodity market to the money market, in the broadest sense of the term. The cause which influences the demand for raw materials, labour, the use of land, and other means of production, and thus indirectly determines the upward or downward movement of commodity prices, is the ratio between the money rate of interest (*Darlehnszins*) and the 'natural' or equilibrium rate of interest (*natürliche Kapitalzins*), by which we are to understand that rate of interest which would be determined by supply and demand if real capital was itself lent directly without the intermediation of money.[18]

Wicksell imagines that this argument of his provides a theory of the determination of the objective exchange-value of money. In fact, however, all that he

attempts to prove is that forces operate from the loan market on the commodity market which prevent the objective exchange-value of money from rising too high or falling too low. He never asserts that the rate of interest on loans determines the actual level of this value in any way; in fact, to assert this would be absurd. But if we are to speak of a level of money-prices that is 'too high' or 'too low', we must first state how the ideal level with which the actual level is compared has been established. It is in no way sufficient to show that the position of equilibrium is returned to after any disturbance, if the existence of this position of equilibrium is not first explained. Indubitably, this is the primary problem, and its solution leads directly to that of the other; without it, further inquiry must remain unfruitful, for the state of equilibrium can only be maintained by those forces which first established it and continue to re-establish it. If the circumstances of the loan market can provide no explanation of the genesis of the exchange-ratio subsisting between money and other economic goods, then neither can they help to explain why this ratio does not alter. The objective exchange-value of money is determined in the market where money is exchanged for commodities and commodities for money. To explain its determination is the task of the theory of the value of money. But Wicksell is of the opinion 'that the laws of the exchange of commodities contain in themselves nothing that could determine the absolute level of money-prices.'[19] This amounts to a denial of all possibility of scientific investigation in this sphere.

Helfferich also is of the opinion that there is an insurmountable obstacle in the way of applying the marginal-utility theory to the problem of money; for while the marginal-utility theory attempts to base the exchange-value of goods on the degree of their utility to the individual, the degree of utility of money to the individual quite obviously depends on its exchange-value, since money can have utility only if it has exchange-value, and the degree of the utility is determined by the level of the exchange-value. Money is valued subjectively according to the amount of consumable goods that can be obtained in exchange for it, or according to what other goods

18 Cp. Wicksell, *Geldzins und Güterpreise,* Jena 1898, pp. iv ff, 16 ff.

19 Cp. Wicksell, *op. cit.,* p. 35.

have to be given in order to obtain the money needed for making payments. The marginal utility of money to any individual, i.e., the marginal utility derivable from the goods that can be obtained with the given quantity of money or that must be surrendered for the required money, presupposes a certain exchange-value of the money; so the latter cannot be derived from the former.[20]

Those who have realized the significance of historically-transmitted values in the determination of the objective exchange-value of money will not find great difficulty in escaping from this apparently circular argument. It is true that valuation of the monetary unit by the individual is possible only on the assumption that an exchange-ratio already exists in the market between the money and other economic goods. Nevertheless, it is erroneous to deduce from this that a complete and satisfactory explanation of the determination of the objective exchange-value of money cannot be provided by the marginal-utility theory. The fact that this theory is unable to explain the objective exchange-value of money entirely by reference to its *monetary* utility; that to complete its explanation, as we were able to show, it is obliged to go back to that original exchange-value which was based not on a monetary function at all but on other uses of the object that was to be used as money—this must not in any way be reckoned to the discredit of the theory, for it corresponds exactly to the nature and origin of the particular objective exchange-value under discussion. To demand of a theory of the value of money that it should explain the exchange-ratio between money and commodities solely with reference to the monetary function, and without the assistance of the element of historical continuity in the value of money, is to make demands of it that run quite contrary to its nature and its proper task.

The theory of the value of money as such can trace back the objective exchange-value of money only to that point where it ceases to be the value of money and becomes merely the value of a commodity. At this point the theory must hand over all further investigation to the general theory of value, which will then find no further difficulty in the solution of the problem. It is true that the subjective valuation of money presupposes an existing objective exchange-value; but the value that has to be presupposed is not the same as the value that has to be explained; what has to be presupposed is *yesterday's* exchange-value, and it is quite legitimate to use it in an explanation of that of to-day. The objective exchange-value of money which rules in the market to-day is derived from yesterday's under the influence of the subjective valuations of the individuals frequenting the market, just as yesterday's in its turn was derived under the influence of subjective valuations from the objective exchange-value possessed by the money the day before yesterday.

If in this way we continually go farther and farther back we must eventually arrive at a point where we no longer find any component in the objective exchange-value of money that arises from valuations based on the function of money as a common medium of exchange; where the value of money is nothing other than the value of an object that is useful in some other way than as money. But this point is not merely an instrumental concept of theory; it is an actual phenomenon of economic history, making its appearance at the moment when indirect exchange begins.

Before it was usual to acquire goods in the market, not for personal consumption, but simply in order to exchange them again for the goods that were really wanted, each individual commodity was only accredited with that value given by the subjective valuations based on its direct utility. It was not until it became customary to acquire certain goods merely in order to use them as media of exchange that people began to esteem them more highly than before, on account of this possibility of using them in indirect exchange. The individual valued them in the first place because they were useful in the ordinary sense, and then additionally because they could be used as media of exchange. Both sorts of valuation are subject to the law of marginal utility. Just as the original starting-point of the value of money was nothing but the result of subjective valuations, so also is the present-day value of money.

But Helfferich manages to bring forward yet another argument for the inapplicability of the

---

20 Cp. Helfferich, *Das Geld*, p. 577.

marginal-utility theory to money. Looking at the economic system as a whole, it is clear that the notion of marginal utility rests on the fact that, given a certain quantity of goods, only certain wants can be satisfied and only a certain set of utilities provided. With given wants and a given set of means, the marginal degree of utility is determined also. According to the marginal-utility theory, this fixes the value of the goods in relation to the other goods that are offered as an equivalent in exchange, and fixes it in such a manner that that part of the demand that cannot be satisfied with the given supply is excluded by the fact that it is not able to offer an equivalent corresponding to the marginal utility of the good demanded. Now Helfferich objects that while the existence of a limited supply of any goods except money is in itself sufficient to imply the limitation of their utility also, this is not true of money. The utility of a given quantity of money depends directly upon the exchange-value of the money, not only from the point of view of the individual, but also for society as a whole. The higher the value of the unit in relation to other goods, the greater will be the quantity of these other goods that can be paid for by means of the same sum of money. The value of goods in general results from the limitation of the possible utilities that can be obtained from a given supply of them, and while it is usually higher according to the degree of utility which is excluded by the limitation of supply, the total utility of the supply itself cannot be increased by an increase in its value; but in the case of money, the utility of a given supply can be increased *ad lib.* by an increase in the value of the unit.[21]

The error in this argument is to be found in its regarding the utility of money from the point of view of the community instead of from that of the individual. Every valuation must emanate from somebody who is in a position to dispose in exchange of the object valued. Only those who have a choice between two economic goods are able to form a judgement as to value, and they do this by preferring the one to the other. If we start with valuations from the point of view of society as a whole, we tacitly assume

the existence of a socialized economic organization in which there is no exchange and in which the only valuations are those of the responsible official body. Opportunities for valuation in such a society would arise in the control of production and consumption, as, for example, in deciding how certain production goods were to be used when there were alternative ways of using them. But in such a society there would be no room at all for money. Under such conditions, a common medium of exchange would have no utility and consequently no value either. It is therefore illegitimate to adopt the point of view of the community as a whole when dealing with the value of money. All consideration of the value of money must obviously presuppose a state of society in which exchange takes place and must take as its starting point individuals acting as independent economic agents within such a society,[22] that is to say, individuals engaged in valuing things.

§5 'MONETARY' AND 'NON-MONETARY' INFLUENCES AFFECTING THE OBJECTIVE EXCHANGE-VALUE OF MONEY

Now, the first part of the problem of the value of money having been solved, it is at last possible for us to evolve a plan of further procedure. We no longer are concerned to explain the *origin* of the objective exchange-value of money; this task has already been performed in the course of the preceding

---

21 Cp. ibid., p. 578.

22 Dr. M. B. Anderson, on pp. 100–110 of his excellent work on *The Value of Money* (New York, 1917) has objected to the theory set forth above that instead of a logical analysis it provides merely a temporal regressus. Nevertheless, all the acute objections that he manages to bring forward are directed only against the argument that finds a historical component in the exchange-ratios subsisting between commodities, an argument with which I also [see pp. 111 ff. above] am in definite disagreement. But Dr. Anderson recognizes the logical foundation of my theory when he declares 'I shall maintain that value from some source other then the monetary employment is an essential pre-condition of the monetary employment' (*op. cit.*, p. 126).

investigation. We now have to establish the laws which govern *variations* in existing exchange-ratios between money and the other economic goods. This part of the problem of the value of money has occupied economists from the earliest times, although it is the other that ought logically to have been dealt with first. For this reason, as well as for many others, what has been done towards its elucidation does not amount to very much. Of course, this part of the problem is also much more complicated than the first part.

In investigations into the nature of changes in the value of money it is usual to distinguish between two sorts of determinants of the exchange-ratio that connects money and other economic goods; those that exercise their effect on the money side of the ratio and those that exercise their effect on the commodity side. This distinction is extremely useful; without it, in fact, all attempts at a solution would have to be dismissed beforehand as hopeless. Nevertheless its true meaning must not be forgotten.

The exchange-ratios between commodities–and the same is naturally true of the exchange-ratios between commodities and money–result from determinants which affect both terms of the exchange-ratio. But existing exchange-ratios between goods may be modified by a change in determinants connected only with one of the two sets of exchanged objects. Although all the factors that determine the valuation of a good remain the same, its exchange-ratio with another good may alter if the factors that determine the valuation of this second good alter. If of two persons I prefer A to B, this preference may be reversed, even though my feeling for A remains unchanged, if I contract a closer friendship with B. Similarly with the relationships between goods and human beings. He who to-day prefers the consumption of a cup of tea to that of a dose of quinine may make a contrary valuation to-morrow, even though his liking for tea has not diminished, if he has, say, caught a fever overnight. Whereas the factors that *determine* prices always affect both sets of the goods that are to be exchanged, those

of them which merely modify existing prices may sometimes be restricted to one set of goods only.[23]

(II) FLUCTUATIONS IN THE OBJECTIVE EXCHANGE- VALUE OF MONEY EVOKED BY CHANGES IN THE RATIO BETWEEN THE SUPPLY OF MONEY AND THE DEMAND FOR IT

§6 THE QUANTITY THEORY

If we wish to arrive at a just appraisal of the Quantity Theory we must consider it in the light of the contemporary theories of value. The core of the doctrine consists in the proposition that the supply of money and the demand for it both affect its value. This proposition is probably a sufficiently good hypothesis to explain big changes in prices; but it is far from containing a complete theory of the value of money. It describes *one* cause of changes in prices; it is nevertheless inadequate for dealing with the problem exhaustively. By itself it does not comprise a theory of the value of money; it needs the basis of a general value theory. One after another, the doctrine of supply and demand, the cost-of-production theory, and the subjective theory of value have had to provide the foundations for the Quantity Theory.

If we make use in our discussion of only one fundamental idea contained in the Quantity Theory, the

---

23 Cp. Menger, *Grundsätze*, pp. 304 ff. [In the German edition of this book, the above paragraph was followed by an explanation that German writers, following Menger, usually refer to 'the question of the nature and extent of the influence upon the exchange-ratios between money and commodities exerted by variations in those determinants of prices that lie on the monetary side' as the problem of the *innere objektive Tauschwert* of money, and to 'those concerned with variations in the objective exchange-value of money throughout time and space in general' as the problem of its *äussere objektive Tauschwert*. Since this distinction has not been usual in English terminology, it has been omitted from the present version; and, in what follows, wherever 'the objective exchange-value of money' is referred to, it is the *innere* exchange-value that is meant unless the contrary is explicitly stated. H.E.B.]

idea that a connexion exists between variations in the value of money on the one hand and variations in the relations between the demand for money and the supply of it on the other hand, our reason is not that this is the most correct expression of the content of the theory from the historical point of view, but that it constitutes that core of truth in the theory which even the modern investigator can and must recognize as useful. Although the historian of economic theory may find this formulation inexact and produce quotations to refute it, he must nevertheless admit that it contains the correct expression of what is valuable in the Quantity Theory and usable as a corner-stone for a theory of the value of money.

Beyond this proposition, the Quantity Theory can provide us with nothing. Above all, it fails to explain the mechanism of variations in the value of money. Some of its expositors do not touch upon this question at all; the others employ an inadequate principle for dealing with it. Observation teaches us that certain relations of the kind suggested between the available stock of money and the need for money do in fact exist; the problem is to deduce these relations from the fundamental laws of value and so at last to comprehend their true significance.

§ 7 THE STOCK OF MONEY AND THE DEMAND FOR MONEY

The process, by which supply and demand are accommodated to one another until a position of equilibrium is established and both are brought into quantitative and qualitative coincidence, is the higgling of the market. But supply and demand are only the links in a chain of phenomena, one end of which has this visible manifestation in the market, while the other is anchored deep in the human mind. The intensity with which supply and demand are expressed, and consequently the level of the exchange-ratio at which both coincide, depends on the subjective valuations of individuals. This is true, not only of the direct exchange-ratios between economic goods other than money, but also of the exchange-ratio between money on the one hand and commodities on the other.

For a long time it was believed that the demand for money was a quantity determined by objective factors and independent of subjective considerations. It was thought that the demand for money in an economic community was determined, on the one hand by the total quantity of commodities that had to be paid for during a given period, and on the other hand by the velocity of circulation of the money. There is an error in the very starting-point of this way of regarding the matter, which was first successfully attacked by Menger.[24] It is inadmissible to begin with the demand for money of the community. The individualistic economic community as such, which is the only sort of community in which there is a demand for money, is not an economic agent. It demands money only in so far as its individual members demand money. The demand for money of the economic community is nothing but the sum of the demands for money of the individual economic agents composing it. But for individual economic agents it is impossible to make use of the formula: Total Volume of Transactions ÷ Velocity of Circulation. If we wish to arrive at a description of the demand for money of an individual we must start with the considerations that influence such an individual in receiving and paying out money.

Every economic agent is obliged to hold a stock of the common medium of exchange sufficient to cover his probable business and personal requirements. The amount that will be required depends upon individual circumstances. It is influenced both by the custom and habits of the individual and by the organization of the whole social apparatus of production and exchange.

But all of these objective factors always affect the matter only as motivations of the individual. They are never capable of a direct influence upon the actual amount of his demand for money. Here, as in all departments of economic life, it is the subjective

---

24 Cp. Menger, *Grundsätze*, pp. 325 ff.; also Helfferich, *Das Geld*, pp. 500 ff.

valuations of the separate economic agents that alone are decisive. The store of purchasing power held by two such agents whose objective economic circumstances were identical might be quite different if the advantages and disadvantages of such a store were estimated differently by the different agents.

The cash balance held by an individual need by no means consist entirely of money. If secure claims to money, payable on demand, are employed commercially as substitutes for money, being tendered and accepted in place of money, then individuals' stores of money can be entirely or partly replaced by a corresponding store of these substitutes. In fact, for technical reasons (such, e.g., as the need for having money of various denominations on hand) this may sometimes prove an unavoidable necessity. It follows that we can speak of a demand for money in a broader and in a narrower sense. The former comprises the entire demand of an individual for money and money-substitutes; the second, merely his demand for money proper. The former is determined by the will of the economic agent in question. The latter is fairly independent of individual influences, if we disregard the question of denomination referred to above. Apart from this, the question whether a greater or smaller part of the cash balance held by an individual shall consist of money-substitutes is only of importance to him when he has the opportunity of acquiring money-substitutes which bear interest, such as interest-bearing bank-notes–a rare case–or bank deposits. In all other cases it is a matter of complete indifference to him.

The individual's demand and stock of money is the basis of the demand and stock in the whole community. So long as there are no money-substitutes in use, the social demand for money and the social stock of money are merely the respective sums of the individual demands and stocks. But this is changed with the advent of money- substitutes. The social demand for money in the narrower sense is no longer the sum of the individual demands for money in the narrower sense, and the social demand for money in the broader sense is by no means the sum of the individual demands for money in the broader sense. Part of the money-substitutes functioning as money in the cash holdings of individuals are 'covered' by sums

of money held as 'redemption funds' at the place where the money-substitutes are cashable, which is usually, although not necessarily, the issuing concern. We shall use the term Money-Certificates for those money-substitutes that are completely covered by the reservation of corresponding sums of money, and the term Fiduciary Media[25] for those which are not covered in this way. The suitability of this terminology, which has been chosen with regard to the problem to be dealt with in the third Part of the present work, must be demonstrated in that place. It is not to be understood in the light of banking technique nor in a juristic sense; it is merely intended to serve the ends of economic argument.

Only in the rarest cases can any particular money-substitutes be immediately assigned to the one or the other group. That is possible only for those money-substitutes of which the whole species is either entirely covered by money or not covered by money at all. In the case of all other money-substitutes, those the total quantity of which is partly covered by money and partly not covered by money, only an imaginary ascription of an aliquot part to each of the two groups can take place. This involves no fresh difficulty. If, for example, there are bank-notes in circulation one-third of the quantity of which is covered by money and two-thirds not covered, then each individual note is to be reckoned as two-thirds fiduciary medium and one-third money-certificate. It is thus obvious that a community's demand for money in the broader sense cannot be the sum of the demands of individuals for money and money-substitutes, because to reckon in the demand for money-certificates as well as that for the money that serves as a cover for them at the banks and elsewhere is to count the same amount twice over. A community's demand for money in the broader sense is the sum of the demands of the individual economic agents for money proper and fiduciary media (including the demand for cover). And a community's demands for money in the narrower sense is the sum of the demands of the individual economic agents for money and money-certificates (this time *not* including cover).

---

25 [See Appendix B.]

In this Part we shall ignore the existence of fiduciary media and assume that the demands for money of individual economic agents can be satisfied merely by money and money-certificates, and consequently that the demand for money of the whole economic community can be satisfied merely by money proper.[26] The third Part of this book is devoted to an examination of the important and difficult problems arising from the creation and circulation of fiduciary media.

The demand for money and its relations to the stock of money forms the starting-point for an explanation of fluctuations in the objective exchange-value of money. Not to understand the nature of the demand for money is to fail at the very outset of any attempt to grapple with the problem of variations in the value of money. If we start with a formula that attempts to explain the demand for money from the point of view of the community instead of from that of the individual, we shall fail to discover the connexion between the stock of money and the subjective valuations of individuals—the foundation of all economic activity. But on the other hand, this problem is solved without difficulty if we approach the phenomena from the individual agent's point of view.

No long explanation is necessary, of the way in which an individual will behave in the market when his demand for money exceeds his stock of it. He who has more money on hand than he thinks he needs, will buy, in order to dispose of the superfluous stock of money that lies useless on his hands. If he is an entrepreneur, he will possibly enlarge his business. If this use of the money is not open to him, he may purchase interest-bearing securities; or possibly he may decide to purchase consumption goods. But in any case, he expresses by a suitable behaviour in the market the fact that he regards his reserve of purchasing power as too large.

And he whose demand for money is less than his stock of it will behave in an exactly Contrary fashion. If an individual's stock of money diminishes (his property or income remaining the same), then he will take steps to reach the desired level of reserve purchasing power by suitable behaviour in making sales and purchases. A shortage of money means a difficulty in disposing of commodities for money. He who is obliged to dispose of a commodity by way of exchange will prefer to acquire some of the common medium of exchange for it, and only when this acquisition involves too great a sacrifice will he be content with some other economic good, which will indeed be more marketable than that which he wishes to dispose of but less marketable than the common medium of exchange. Under the present organization of the market, which leaves a deep gulf between the marketability of money on the one hand and of other economic goods on the other hand, nothing but money enters into consideration at all as a medium of exchange. Only in exceptional circumstances is any other economic good pressed into this service. In the case mentioned, therefore, every seller will be willing to accept a smaller quantity of money than he otherwise would have demanded, so as to avoid the fresh loss that he would have to suffer in again exchanging the commodity that he has acquired, which is harder to dispose of than money, for the commodity that he actually requires for consumption.

The older theories, which started from an erroneous conception of the social demand for money, could never arrive at a solution of this problem. Their sole contribution is limited to paraphrases of the proposition that an increase in the stock of money at the disposal of the community while the demand for it remains the same decreases the objective exchange-value of money, and that an increase of the demand with a constant available stock has the contrary effect, and so on. By a flash of genius, the formulators of the Quantity Theory had already recognized this. We cannot by any means call it an advance when the formula giving the amount of the demand for money (Volume of Transactions ÷ Velocity of Circulation) was reduced to its elements, or when the attempt was made to give exact precision to the idea of a stock of money, so long as this

---

26 Examination of the relationship of this supposition to the doctrine of the 'purely metallic currency' as expounded by the Currency School would necessitate a discussion of the criticism that has been levelled at it by the Banking School; but certain remarks in the third Part of the present work on fiduciary media and the clearing system will fill the gap left above.

occurred under a misapprehension of the nature of fiduciary media and of clearing transactions. No approach whatever was made towards the central problem of this part of the theory of money so long as theorists were unable to show the way in which subjective valuations are affected by variations in the ratio between the stock of money and the demand for money. But this task was necessarily beyond the power of these theories; they break down at the crucial point.[27]

Recently, Wieser has expressed himself against employing the 'collective concept of the demand for money' as the starting-point for a theory of fluctuations in the objective exchange-value of money. He says that in an investigation of the value of money we are not concerned with the total demand for money. The demand for money to pay taxes with, for example, does not come into consideration, for these payments do not affect the value of money but only transfer purchasing power from those who pay the taxes to those who receive them. In the same way, capital and interest payments in loan transactions and the making of gifts and bequests merely involve a transference of purchasing power between persons and not an augmentation or diminution of it. A functional theory of the value of money must, in stating its problem, have regard only to those factors by which the value of money is determined. The value of money is determined in the process of exchange. Consequently, the theory of the value of money must take account only of those quantities which enter into the process of exchange.[28]

But these objections of Wieser's are not only rebutted by the fact that even the surrender of money in paying taxes, in making capital and interest payments, and in giving presents and bequests, falls into the economic category of exchange. Even if we accept Wieser's narrow definition of exchange, we must still oppose his argument. It is not a peculiarity of money that its value (Wieser obviously means its objective exchange-value) is determined in the process of exchange; the same is true of all other economic goods. For all economic goods it must therefore be correct to say that the theory of value has to investigate only certain quantities, viz., only those that are involved in the process of exchange. But there is no such thing in economics as a quantity that is not involved in the process of exchange. From the economic point of view, a quantity has no other relationships than those which exercise some influence upon the valuations of individuals concerned in some process or other of exchange.

This is true, even if we admit that value only arises in connection with exchange in the narrow sense intended by Wieser. But those who participate in exchange transactions, and consequently desire to acquire or dispose of money, do not value the monetary unit solely with regard to the fact that they can use it in other acts of exchange (in Wieser's narrower sense of the expression), but also because they require money in order to pay taxes, to transfer borrowed capital and pay interest, and to make presents. They consider the level of their purchasing-power reserves with a view to the necessity of having money ready for all these purposes, and their judgement as to the extent of their requirements for money is what decides the demand for money with which they enter the market.

§8 THE CONSEQUENCES OF AN INCREASE IN THE QUANTITY OF MONEY WHILE THE DEMAND FOR MONEY REMAINS UNCHANGED OR DOES NOT INCREASE TO THE SAME EXTENT

Those variations in the ratio between the individual's demand for money and his stock of it that arise from purely individual causes cannot as a rule have a very large quantitative influence in the market. In most cases they will be entirely, or at least partly,

---

27 It is remarkable that even investigators who otherwise take their stand upon the subjective theory of value have been able to fall into this error. So, for example, Fisher and Brown, *The Purchasing Power of Money*, New York 1911, pp. 8 ff.

28 Cp. Wieser, *Der Geldwert und seine Veränderungen*, pp. 515 ff.

compensated by contrary variations emanating from other individuals in the market. But a variation in the objective exchange-value of money can arise only when a force is exerted in one direction that is not cancelled by a counteracting force in the opposite direction. If the causes that alter the ratio between the stock of money and the demand for it from the point of view of an individual consist merely in accidental and personal factors that concern that particular individual only, then, according to the law of large numbers, it is likely that the forces arising from this cause, and acting in both directions in the market, will counterbalance each other. The probability that the compensation will be complete is the greater, the more individual economic agents there are.

It is otherwise when disturbances occur in the community as a whole, of a kind to alter the ratio existing between the individual's stock of money and his demand for it. Such disturbances, of course, cannot have an effect except by altering the subjective valuations of the individual; but they are social economic phenomena in the sense that they influence the subjective valuations of a large number of individuals, if not simultaneously and in the same degree, at least in the same direction, so that there must necessarily be some resultant effect on the objective exchange-value of money.

In the history of money a particularly important part has been played by those variations in its objective exchange-value that have arisen in consequence of an increase in the stock of money while the demand for it has remained unchanged or has at least not increased to the same extent. These variations, in fact, were what first attracted the attention of economists; it was in order to explain them that the Quantity Theory of money was first propounded. All writers have dealt most thoroughly with them. It is perhaps justifiable, therefore, to devote special attention to them and to use them to illuminate certain important theoretical points.

In whatever way we care to picture to ourselves the increase in the stock of money, whether as arising from increased production or importation of the substance of which commodity money is made, or through a new issue of fiat or credit money, the new money always increases the stock of money at the disposal of certain individual economic agents. An increase in the stock of money in a community always means an increase in the money incomes of a number of individuals; but it need not necessarily mean at the same time an increase in the quantity of goods that are at the disposal of the community, that is to say, it need not mean an increase in the national dividend. An increase in the amount of fiat or credit money is only to be regarded as an increase in the stock of goods at the disposal of society if it permits the satisfaction of a demand for money which would otherwise have been satisfied by commodity money instead, since the material for the commodity money would then have had to be procured by the surrender of other goods in exchange or produced at the cost of renouncing some other sort of production. If, on the other hand, the nonexistence of the new issue of fiat or credit money would not have involved an increase in the quantity of commodity money, then the increase of money cannot be regarded as an increase of the income or wealth of society.

An increase in a community's stock of money always means an increase in the amount of money held by a number of economic agents, whether these are the issuers of fiat or credit money or the producers of the substance of which commodity money is made. For these persons, the ratio between the demand for money and the stock of it is altered; they have a relative superfluity of money and a relative shortage of other economic goods. The immediate consequence of both circumstances is that the marginal utility to them of the monetary unit diminishes. This necessarily influences their behaviour in the market. They are in a stronger position as buyers. They will now express in the market their demand for the objects they desire more intensively than before; they are able to offer more money for the commodities that they wish to acquire. It will be the obvious result of this that the prices of the goods concerned will rise, and that the objective exchange-value of money will fall in comparison.

But this rise of prices will by no means be restricted to the market for those goods that are desired by those who originally have the new money at their disposal. In addition, those who have brought these goods to market will have their incomes and their proportionate stocks of money increased and, in their turn, will be in a position to demand more intensively the goods they want, so that these goods will also rise in price. Thus the increase of prices continues, having a diminishing effect, until all commodities, some to a greater and some to a lesser extent, are reached by it.[29]

The increase in the quantity of money does not mean an increase of income for all individuals. On the contrary, those sections of the community that are the last to be reached by the additional quantity of money have their incomes reduced, as a consequence of the decrease in the value of money called forth by the increase in its quantity; this will be referred to later. The reduction in the income of these classes now starts a counter-tendency, which opposes the tendency to a diminution of the value of money due to the increase of income of the other classes, without being able to rob it completely of its effect.

Those who hold the mechanical version of the Quantity Theory will be the more inclined to believe that the increase in the quantity of money must eventually lead to a uniform increase in the prices of all economic goods, the less clear their concept is of the way in which the determination of prices is affected by it. Thorough comprehension of the mechanism by means of which the quantity of money affects the prices of commodities makes their point of view altogether untenable. Since the increased quantity of money is received in the first place by a limited number of economic agents only and not by all, the increase of prices at first embraces only those goods that are demanded by these persons; further, it affects these goods more than it afterwards affects any others. When the increase of prices spreads farther, if the increase in the quantity of money is only a single transient phenomenon, it will not be possible for the differential increase of prices of these goods to be completely maintained; a certain degree of adjustment will take place. But there will not be

such a complete adjustment of the increases that all prices increase in the same proportion. The prices of commodities after the rise of prices will not bear the same relation to each other as before its commencement; the decrease in the purchasing power of money will not be uniform with regard to different economic goods.

Hume, it may be remarked, bases his argument concerning this matter on the supposition that every Englishman is miraculously endowed with five pieces of gold during the night.[30] Mill rightly remarks on this, that it would not lead to a uniform increase in the demand for separate commodities; the luxury articles of the poorer classes would rise more in price than the others. All the same, he believes that a uniform increase in the prices of all commodities, and this exactly in proportion to the increase in the quantity of money, would occur, if 'the wants and inclinations of the community collectively in respect to consumption' remained the same. He assumes, no less artificially than Hume, that 'to every pound, or shilling, or penny, in the possession of any one, another pound, shilling, or penny were suddenly added'.[31] But Mill fails to see that even in this case a uniform rise of prices would not occur, even supposing that for each member of the community the proportion between stock of money and total wealth was the same, so that the addition of the supplementary quantity of money did not result in an alteration of the relative wealth of individuals. For, even in this quite impossible case, every increase in the quantity of money would necessarily cause an alteration in the conditions of demand, which would lead to a disparate increase in the prices of the individual economic goods. Not all commodities would be demanded more intensively, and not all of those that were demanded more intensively would be affected in the same degree.[32]

There is no justification whatever for the widespread belief that variations in the quantity of money must lead to inversely proportionate variations in the objective exchange-value of money, so that, for

---

29 Cp. Hume, *Essays* (ed. Frowde, London), pp. 294 ff.; Mill, *op. cit.,* pp. 298 ff.; Cairnes, *Essays in Political Economy, Theoretical and Applied,* London 1873, pp. 57 ff.; Spiethoff, *Die Quantitätstheorie,* pp. 250 ff.

30 Cp. Hume, *op. cit.,* p. 307.

31 Cp. Mill, *op. cit.,* p. 299.

32 Cp. Conant, *What determines the Value of Money? (Quarterly Journal of Economics,* Vol. XVIII, 1904), pp. 559 ff.

example, a doubling of the quantity of money must lead to a halving of the purchasing power of money.

Even assuming that in some way or other–it is confessedly difficult to imagine in what way-every individual's stock of money were to be increased so that his relative position as regards other holders of property was unaltered, it is not difficult to prove that the subsequent variation in the objective exchange-value of money would not be proportioned to the variation in the quantity of money. For, in fact, the way in which an individual values a variation in the quantity of money at his disposal is by no means directly dependent on the amount of this variation; but we should have to assume that it was, if we wished to conclude that there would be a proportionate variation in the objective exchange-value of money. If the possessor of a units of money receives b additional units, then it is not at all true to say that he will value the total stock $a + b$ exactly as highly as he had previously valued the stock a alone. Because he now has disposal over a larger stock, he will now value each unit less than he did before; but *how much* less will depend upon a whole series of individual circumstances, upon subjective valuations that will be different for each individual. Two individuals who are equally wealthy and who each possess a stock of money a, will not by any means arrive at the same variation in their estimation of money after an increase of b units in each of their stocks of money. It is nothing short of absurdity to assume that, say, doubling the amount of money at the disposal of an individual must lead to a halving of the exchange-value that he ascribes to each monetary unit. Let us, for example, imagine an individual who is in the habit of holding a stock of a hundred kronen and assume that a sum of a further hundred kronen is paid by somebody or other to this individual. Mere consideration of this example is sufficient to show the complete unreality of all the theories that ascribe to variations in the quantity of money a uniformly proportionate effect on the purchasing power of money. For it involves no essential modification of this example to assume that similar increases in the quantity of money are experienced by all the members of the community at once.

The mistake in the argument of those who suppose that a variation in the quantity of money results in an inversely proportionate variation in its purchasing power lies in its starting-point. If we wish to arrive at a correct conclusion, we must start with the valuations of separate individuals; we must examine the way in which an increase or decrease in the quantity of money affects the value-scales of individuals, for it is from these alone that variations in the exchange- ratios of goods proceed. The initial assumption in the arguments of those who maintain the theory that changes in the quantity of money have a proportionate effect on the purchasing power of money is the proposition that if the value of the monetary unit were doubled, half of the stock of money at the disposal of the community would yield the same utility as that previously yielded by the whole stock. The correctness of this proposition is not disputed; nevertheless it does not prove what it is meant to prove.

In the first place, it must be pointed out that the level of the total stock of money and of the value of the money unit are matters of complete indifference as far as the utility obtained from the use of the money is concerned. Society is always in enjoyment of the maximum utility obtainable from the use of money. Half of the money at the disposal of the community would yield the same utility as the whole stock, even if the variation in the value of the monetary unit was not proportioned to the variation in the stock of money. But it is important to note that it by no means follows from this that doubling the quantity of money means halving the objective exchange-value of money. It would have to be shown that forces emanate from the valuations of individual economic agents which are able to bring about such a proportionate variation. This can never be proved; in fact, its contrary is likely. We have already given a proof of this for the case in which an increase of the quantity of money held by individual economic agents involves at the same time an increase of their income or wealth. But even when the increase in the quantity of money does not affect the wealth or income of the individual economic agents, the effect is still the same.

Let us assume that a man gets half his income in the form of interest-bearing securities and half in the form of money; and that he is in the habit of saving three-quarters of his income, and does this by retaining the securities and using that half of his income which he receives in cash in equal parts for paying for current consumption and for the purchase of further securities. Now let us assume that a variation in the composition of his income occurs, so that he receives three-quarters of it in cash and only one-quarter in securities. From now on this man will use two-thirds of his cash receipts for the purchase of interest-bearing securities. If the price of the securities rises or, which is the same thing, if their rate of interest falls, then in either case he will be less willing to buy and will reduce the sum of money that he would otherwise have employed for their purchase; he is likely to find that the advantage of a slightly increased reserve exceeds that which could be obtained from the acquisition of the securities. In the second case he will doubtless be inclined to pay a higher price, or more correctly, to purchase a greater quantity at the higher price, than in the first case. But he will certainly not be prepared to pay *double* as much for a unit of securities in the second case as in the first case.

As far as the earlier exponents of the Quantity Theory are concerned, the assumption that variations in the quantity of money would have an inversely proportionate effect on its purchasing power may nevertheless be excusable. It is easy to go astray on this point if the attempt is made to explain the value phenomena of the market by reference to exchange-value. But it is inexplicable that those theorists also who suppose they are taking their stand on the subjective theory of value could fall into similar errors. The blame here can only be laid to the account of a mechanical conception of market processes. Thus even Fisher and Brown, whose concept of the Quantity Theory is a mechanical one, and who attempt to express in mathematical equations the law according to which the value of money is determined, necessarily arrive at the conclusion that variations in the ratio between the quantity of money and the demand for it lead to proportionate

variations in the objective exchange-value of money.[33] How and through what channels this comes about is not disclosed by the formula, for it contains no reference at all to the only factors that are decisive in causing variations of the exchange-ratios, that is, variations in the subjective valuations of individuals.

§9 FURTHER APPLICATIONS OF THE QUANTITY THEORY

In general the Quantity Theory has not been used for investigating the consequences that would follow a *decrease* in the demand for money while the stock of money remained the same. There has been no historical motive for such an investigation. The problem has never been a live one; for there has never been even a shadow of justification for attempting to solve controversial questions of economic policy by answering it. Economic history shows us a continual increase in the demand for money. The characteristic feature of the development of the demand for money is its intensification; the growth of division of labour and consequently of exchange transactions, which have constantly become more and more indirect and dependent on the use of money, have helped to bring this about, as well as the increase of population and prosperity. The tendencies which result in an increase in the demand for money became so strong in the years preceding the War that even if the increase in the stock of money had been very much greater than it actually was, the objective exchange-value of money would have been sure to increase. Only the circumstance that this increase in the demand for money was accompanied by an extraordinarily large expansion of credit, which certainly exceeded the increase in the demand for money in the broader sense, can serve to explain the fact that the objective exchange-value of money during this period not only failed to increase, but actually decreased. (Another

33   Cp. pp. 302 ff. below.

factor that was concerned in this is referred to later in this chapter.)

If we were to apply the mechanical version of the Quantity Theory to the case of a decrease in the demand for money while the stock of money remained unaltered, we should have to conclude that there would be a uniform increase in all commodity prices, arithmetically proportional to the change in the ratio between the stock of money and the demand for it. We should expect the same results as would follow upon an increase of the stock of money while the demand for it remained the same. But the mechanical version of the theory, based as it is upon an erroneous transference of static law to the dynamic sphere, is just as inadequate in this case as in the other. It cannot satisfy us because it does not explain what we want to have explained. We must build up a theory that will show us how a decrease in the demand for money while the stock of it remains the same affects prices by affecting the subjective valuations of money on the part of individual economic agents. A diminution of the demand for money while the stock remained the same would in the first place lead to the discovery by a number of persons that their cash reserves were too great in relation to their needs. They would therefore enter the market as buyers with their surpluses. From this point, a general rise in prices would come into operation, a diminution of the exchange-value of money. More detailed explanation of what would happen then is unnecessary.

Very closely related to this case is another, whose practical significance is incomparably greater. Even if we think of the demand for money as constantly increasing it may happen that the demand for *particular kinds* of money diminishes, or even ceases altogether so far as it depends upon their characteristics as general media of exchange, and this is all we have to deal with here. If any given kind of money is deprived of its monetary characteristics, then naturally it also loses the special value that depends on its use as a common medium of exchange, and only retains that value which depends upon its other employment. In the course of history this has always occurred when a good has been excluded from the constantly narrowing circle of common media of exchange. Generally speaking, we do not know much about this process, which to a large extent took place in times about which our information is scanty. But recent times have provided an outstanding example: the almost complete demonetization of silver. Silver, which previously was widely used as money, has been almost entirely expelled from this position, and there can be no doubt that at a time not very far off, perhaps even in a few years only, it will have played out its part as money altogether. The result of the demonetization of silver has been a diminution of its objective exchange-value. The price of silver in London fell from 60–9/10d. on an average in 1870 to 23–12/16d. on an average in 1909. Its value was bound to fall, because the sphere of its employment had contracted. Similar examples can be provided from the history of credit money also. For instance, the notes of the southern States in the American Civil War may be mentioned, which as the successes of the northern States increased, lost *pari passu* their monetary value as well as their value as claims.[34]

More deeply than with the problem of the consequences of a diminishing demand for money while the stock of it remains the same, which possesses only a small practical importance, the adherents of the Quantity Theory have occupied themselves with the problem of a diminishing stock of money while the demand for it remains the same and with that of an increasing demand for money while the stock of it remains the same. It was believed that complete answers to both questions could easily be obtained in accordance with the mechanical version of the Quantity Theory, if the general formula, which appeared to embrace the essence of the problems, was applied to them. Both cases were treated as inversions of the case of an increase in the quantity of money while the demand for it remained the same; and from this the corresponding conclusions were drawn. Just as the attempt was made to explain the depreciation of credit-money simply by reference to the enormous increase in the quantity of money, so the attempt was made to explain the depression of the 'seventies and 'eighties by reference to an increase of the demand for

---

34 Cp. White, *Money and Banking Illustrated by American History*, Boston 1895, pp. 160 ff.

money while the quantity of money did not increase sufficiently. This proposition lay at the root of most of the measures of currency policy of the nineteenth century. The aim was to regulate the value of money by increasing or diminishing the quantity of it. The effects of these measures appeared to provide an inductive proof of the correctness of this superficial version of the Quantity Theory, and incidentally concealed the weaknesses of its logic. This supposition alone can explain why no attempt was ever made to exhibit the mechanism of the increase of the value of money as a result of the decrease in the volume of circulation. Here again the old theory needs to be supplemented, as has been done in our argument above.

Normally, the increase in the demand for money is slow, so that any effect on the exchange-ratio between money and commodities is discernible only with difficulty. Nevertheless cases do occur in which the demand for money in the narrower sense increases suddenly and to an unusually large degree, so that the prices of commodities drop suddenly. Such cases occur when the public loses faith in an issuer of fiduciary media at a time of crisis, and the fiduciary media cease to be capable of circulation. Many examples of this sort are known to history (one of them is provided by the experiences of the United States in the late autumn of 1907), and it is possible that similar cases may occur in the future.

Paper Money and Quantity Theory

Currency and Credit

By Ralph Hawtrey

It may be admitted at once that future convertibility into coin is sometimes an important factor in determining the value of paper money which is for the time being inconvertible. But that does not mean that this is an explanation of universal or even of general application. Not only are there many cases where there is practically no expectation of future convertibility, but even where this expectation does exist it probably plays a much less important part in fixing the value of the paper money than the fundamental quality of being legal tender. In fact there is a demand for the means of payment *as such,* and this demand gives a value to whatever is established by law or custom as the means of payment, quite apart from any value it may possess for any other purpose. Gold itself derives part of its value from the demand for it as a means of payment.

If an issue of paper money derives a value in the market from the prospect of its ultimately becoming convertible into coin, and if this value is *greater* than its value as the means of payment, it will be acquired and held by speculators who wish to profit by its convertibility when the time comes. But this is an exceptional case of quite subsidiary importance in comparison with the general question of the determination of the value of the legal means of payment.

To answer this question we must discover in what manner the value of a legal tender currency without intrinsic value and unsupported by convertibility into anything of intrinsic value is determined.

The same problem really arises in the case of the hypothetical country assumed in Chapter I., which had no money and used credit as the sole medium of exchange. There the unit of value was something entirely arbitrary, a mere arithmetical abstraction. In all the transactions into which the unit of value enters, what requires to be measured is the *proportion* which the value of some commodity, service, right, or debt bears to some other. To measure that proportion, it is convenient to express each value as a number, but the choice of a unit as the basis of these numbers is as non-essential as the choice of a language in which the bargains are to be concluded. In the economic life of the community the proportions to be measured are of the substance, while the unit in which they are measured is of the form only. This being so, if the whole of the economic fabric of society and all the transactions be supposed given, to fix the numerical measure of one value is to determine the unit, and therefore to fix the numerical measures of all.

Now one of the quantities which are measurable in terms of the unit of value is the aggregate of all the bank credits outstanding. This aggregate, which, under our hypothesis that no money is used, is of course the same as the aggregate of unspent purchasing power in circulation, may conveniently be called the "unspent margin". It can be arrived at either by adding up the liabilities of all the banks, or by adding up the credits held by all their customers, whether depositors or note-holders. For to ascertain the total of a number of debts we can obtain the particulars either from the accounts of the debtors or from those of the creditors. Let the unit of value be settled, and the numerical measure of the unspent margin is determined Conversely, if the number of units of value in the unspent margin is settled, the unit of value is thereby determined, and the determination of the unit of value determines all 'the other quantities, such as the prices of commodities and services, which are measured by it. Thus we see that, given all the economic conditions, the prices of commodities are directly proportional to the number of units of value contained in the unspent margin of purchasing power.

But we must beware of reading more into this conclusion than it really says. It does not say that if the number of units of value in circulation *changes,* the prices of commodities) will change in exact proportion. A change in the unit of value is likely to cause a number of other changes (some of which we examined in Chapter I.) so that the economic conditions are no longer all "given". Nor can we assume that prices at two different times will be exactly proportional to the quantities of purchasing power in circulation (though, if economic conditions at the two epochs are very nearly identical, this will be nearly true). All that we have established is that, if *everything* in the economic picture be painted in, save only the numbers to be expressed in terms of the unit of value, then, since the mutual proportions of these numbers are already determined by the economic conditions, the number of units in any one will be directly proportional to the number in any other, and in particular the prices of commodities will be proportional to the number of units of value contained in the aggregate of bank credits or unspent margin.

Suppose now that money is used. Money will be substituted for credit in a certain proportion of the transactions. A certain proportion of the purchasing power in being—that is to say, of what we have called the unspent margin—will be in the form of money instead of bank credits. The extent to which money is held rather than credit will be wholly determined by the convenience of the people and their habits and preferences. The unspent margin is now made up of two parts, the money in circulation and the bank credits outstanding. Each is expressible in terms of the unit of value, and the proportion of one to the other is determined, like all the other proportions, by the economic conditions. Provided therefore that all the economic conditions are given, including the proportion of bank credits to money, we infer that all money values, and in particular the prices of commodities, are directly proportional to the quantity of money in circulation, In the case of a free gold currency, or a paper currency maintained at a fixed gold value, one of the given economic conditions must be that the value of gold as currency is equal to its value as a commodity, and this is sufficient to determine all the other values. In the case of a paper currency with no fixed value in terms of gold or any other commodity, the principle at which we have arrived shows how its value is determined. The value of the unit is inversely proportional to the quantity in circulation. Here we have in its simplest form what is called the Quantity Theory of money.

But so long as this principle is subject to the limitation that *all* other economic conditions must be given, it is The first question to answer is this: how do members of the community settle what margin of unspent purchasing power they shall keep, whether in the form of cash or in the form of credit ? From the point of view of the individual there are three principal purposes for which reserves of purchasing power have to be kept.

First, income and expenditure do not exactly keep pace. In the case of the weekly wage-earner they very nearly do keep pace; but even he gets occasional windfalls in the shape of overtime earnings, or other exceptional receipts, and suffers occasional interruptions of earning power from illness and unemployment; and from time to time he incurs extra expenditure on furniture, clothes, holidays, etc. The well-to-do man receives his income at longer and sometimes at more irregular intervals; he may have a fixed salary or dividends paid quarterly, or he may be earning professional fees in variable amounts and at variable times. Every one tends to have a good deal of money in hand just before a large item of expenditure becomes due or just after receiving a large item of income.

Secondly, every one endeavours to keep a supply of money in hand to meet an unforeseen emergency. It is impossible to anticipate all the different occasions for expenditure that may arise, and therefore the prudent man so regulates his balances of cash or credit that at those times (immediately after large disbursements or before large receipts) when the balances are lowest he still has something in hand.

Thirdly, the man who is saving cannot be perpetually investing his savings in driblets. He lets his balances accumulate until he can spare some considerable sum; he then invests all he can without unduly depleting his balances, and starts saving again. The procedure is the same in the case of the working man who periodically puts two or three pounds in the savings bank; in the case of the professional man who every now and then invests a hundred or two; or in the case of the rich man whose savings are reckoned in thousands.

The problem of regulating balances is somewhat different for a trader's business. It is a normal practice in the case of such a business to borrow for short periods, and this makes possible a much nicer calculation of balances than in the case of an individual. A balance of cash or credit is in itself a source of loss, since, except in the case of a deposit subject to notice, it is earning no interest, and even a deposit subject to notice earns interest at less than the full rate. By borrowing to meet large disbursements and applying large receipts in repayment of borrowings, a business concern can reduce this loss of interest to a minimum. Its power of borrowing also enables it to be ready for an unforeseen emergency without perpetually keeping a stock of money on hand for the purpose.

As to the distribution of the unspent margin of purchasing power between cash and credit, we have already seen that the man rich enough to have a banking account will keep the bulk of his reserve

balance in credit, and only an unimportant sum of pocket money in cash. The poor man keeps all his reserve balance in cash, except in so far as he puts it in the savings bank, and a deposit in a savings bank is rather an investment than a part of the unspent margin. For a business, balances are kept in the form of credit, but the manufacturer has constantly to draw out large sums of cash to pay wages, and the retailer, the railway, tram or omnibus company, the collector of working class rents, the theatre manager, and others whose receipts are mainly in cash, are continually paying cash into the banks. The banks themselves keep reserves of cash sufficient in proportion to their liabilities to meet their customers' demands.

For each private individual the appropriate balance of credit and the appropriate balance of cash will bear a determinate proportion to his income (not of course the same proportion for different individuals or for the same individual at different times). For each business the appropriate balances will likewise be determined by convenience, but will be proportional rather to the gross transactions or turnover, than to the net income of the business. Traders, however, can regulate their balances more closely. Consequently their balances bear a far smaller proportion to their turnover than those of private individuals to their incomes. In all cases alike the balances of purchasing power kept in reserve are settled with a view to the transactions to be financed.

The requirements of the community for reserves of purchasing power may be regarded as constituting the demand for credit and money. The supply of credit emanates from the banks. The supply of money is determined by the legal and administrative arrangements for regulating the coinage and the issue of legal tender paper. But here again the banks intervene, for it is only such part of the available stock of money as is in the hands of the public that forms part of the unspent margin of purchasing power. The money which forms the reserves of the banks is excluded from the unspent margin, though of course it is part of the assets held by the banks against the credits which compose their liabilities, and these credits are part of the unspent margin. The unspent margin in fact is equal to the money in circulation, *plus* the obligations of the banks. These obligations are equal to the assets of the banks, *less* their capital. The amount of credit rises and falls with the assets Of the banks, and these assets are composed of two parts—interest-bearing assets, such as loans, discounts and investments, and cash reserves. If the cash reserves are increased by a return of money from circulation into the banks, or if they are diminished by the withdrawal of money from the banks into circulation, the unspent margin is unaffected; all that happens is that so much cash is turned into credit, or so much credit into cash. But if the banks increase or decrease their loans or advances, the unspent margin is increased or decreased by the same amount. Now the banks undertake to transform cash into credit and credit into cash at the choice of their customers; they themselves claim no say in the matter. The choice of their customers as between cash and credit proceeds, as we have seen, from the economic conditions, being determined entirely by the convenience of the individual. The public cannot be compelled arbitrarily to increase or decrease their holdings of cash; they can only be induced to do so by modifying the economic conditions, If the quantity of money is increased or diminished, the result in the first instance is merely to increase or diminish the cash reserves of the banks, and it rests with the banks to decide whether they shall make any change in their other assets or in their demand liabilities.

Changes therefore in the unspent margin depend upon the action of the banks in creating more or less credit. Such changes are not really within the purview of the quantity theory, which deals, strictly speaking, with static conditions. The quantity theory, in the form in which we have enunciated., it, merely equates the unspent margin of purchasing power, which is a total of monetary units, to the command over wealth which the people hold in reserve. It equates, in fact, a total of monetary units to a total of wealth,[1] and so determines the value of the monetary unit in terms of wealth, But if the theory is to be of any practical value its relation to changes in economic conditions must be discovered,.

We have already examined two particular cases of this general question. We have seen in Chapter I. how the value of the monetary unit might vary without limit, if credit were the sole medium of payment and money did not exist. With' a gold currency, limited in amount, we have seen in Chapter II. how an expansion of credit might exhaust the available stocks of cash and precipitate a crisis. Now that we have introduced paper money into the problem we are in a position to attack the general question.

We have just shown that it rests with the banks to increase or decrease the unspent margin of purchasing power. The unspent margin is equal to the cash in circulation, *plus* the; assets of the banks, *less* their capital.

The assets of the banks are equal to their cash reserves, *plus* the amount of their other assets, such as loans and investments. Consequently the unspent margin is equal to all the cash, whether in circulation or in the banks, *plus* the net interest-bearing assets of the banks.[2] Assume for the present that the cash remains unaltered. In that case the unspent margin can only be increased or decreased by an increase or decrease in the net interest-bearing assets of the banks. In other words there must be an acceleration or retardation of that process which we have called the creation of credit, the exchange of immediate obligations from the banks to the traders, for obligations at future dates from the traders to the banks.

Let such an acceleration or retardation of the creation of credit occur. What will be its effects? The first thing that requires to be said about it is that no one borrows money in order to keep it idle. The borrowing is done by people in business, who have deliberately relied on borrowing in order at other times to avoid keeping large idle balances. It follows that practically all the sums borrowed will be quickly paid way. Some may be paid away from one trader to another in exchange for goods, and the vendor may apply the money which he receives to paying off an existing debt. But this is not really the creation of new credit at all; it is simply the substitution of one trader's debt for another among the banks' assets. Apart from this shuffling of debts, all

---

1 A *potential,* not an actual, total of wealth. It depends on people's expectations of the purchasing power of their balances, but their expectations are ultimately governed by the prices which rule in the market.

---

2 The assets held against their capital being excluded.

the credit created is created for the purpose of being paid away in the form of profits, wages, salaries, interest, rents—in fact, to provide the incomes of all who contribute, by their services or their property, to the process of production, production being taken in the widest sense to include whatever produces value. It is for the expenses of production, in this wide sense, that people borrow, and it is of these payments that the expenses of production consist. So we reach the conclusion that an acceleration or retardation of the creation of credit[3] means an equal increase or decrease in people's incomes.

An increase or decrease in people's incomes will lead to an increase or decrease in their expenditures. The income and expenditure now in question are, of course, *money* income and *money* expenditure, that is to say, the number of monetary units (whether in credit or in money) received or spent. With *real* income, or actual command over wealth per unit of time, we are not directly concerned.

---

3 We are speaking here, of course, of the amount of credit created *per unit of time*.

Quantity Theory

Its Versions and Variables

By Thomas Rustici

INTRODUCTION

The quantity theory is nothing more than a sophisticated version of supply and demand theory applied to money. There are three versions of the quantity equation: MV=PT, MV=PQ or Y, and M=KPQ or Y; where M is money supply, V is velocity of circulation, P is the average level of nominal prices, T= transactions; Q is real output or Y = income; and K is = 1/V or the ratio of money to income. The fundamental concepts concerning these different versions are as follows:

MV=PT   Irving Fisher Transaction Version

(1) application of double-entry bookkeeping, (2) the elementary event is the transaction, (3) money is desired for its medium of exchange function, and (4) the total value of all transactions are counted, intermediate expenditure is not netted out (not consistent with national income accounting).

MV=PQ or Y   Income Version

(1) Value of all intermediate transactions are netted out of income total (only the value added is counted thus this is consistent national income accounting), (2) velocity is the average number of times per unit time the stock of money makes final transactions, and (3) the most important feature of money is it is being held.

M=KPQ or Y Cambridge Cash-balance Version

(1) We can construct a testable hypothesis as to the relationship between "actual" and "desired" money holdings, (2) the act of purchase is separated from sale thus money is held as an asset (store of value function), and (3) the expected costs and returns of holding cash-balances are important to estimating their real demand.

THE MONETARY TRANSMISSION MECHANISM

The monetary transmission mechanism between money supply (M) and average level of nominal money prices (P) follows from 5 implications: (1) what matters is real value of the cash balances not the nominal, (2) the money supply is always entirely owned in the form of cash- balances, (3) given monetary equilibrium between actual and desired real cash balances, any additional new cash-balances cause people to spend their excess cash balances (nominal balances are real balances until prices change), (4) since we all own all the cash-balances, my decrease is your increase, (5) as cash balances are spent there is upward pressure on the demand for goods, inflating in nominal prices and deflating the real value of cash holdings until actual cash balances (in real terms) equal desired balances. Thus, inflation is primarily caused by the increase of the money supply.

FACTORS AFFECTING QUANTITY EQUATION VARIABLES

The only thing that can change P is one of the other variables in the equation. But what are the factors effecting these variables? Let's look at some. First there is money supply M. There are three primary determinates of the quantity of a nation's money supply. First, the **Federal Reserve System** (or the central bank) deliberately uses its powers (open market operations, changing legal reserve requirements, changing the discount rate) to target the aggregate growth in the quantity of money. Second, the **behavior of banks** with respect to holding excess reserves versus lending changes the level of money and credit. Third, the **cash holding public** and their preferences for currency in hand, versus cash balances on deposit in the banks (deposit to currency ratio).

The determinates of money demand are a little more complicated than money supply. First, there are transactions uses for money. Increasing trade, *ceteris paribus*, increases the more demand for cash-balances. If market transactions are replaced by vertical integration (a car company buys a steel factory) there is less demand to hold cash-balances.

A movement from a rural agrarian barter type economy to an industrial economy expands the demand to hold money. A growing population also increases the aggregate desired cash-holding, a declining population the opposite. Payment practices also affect the demand to hold cash-balances. For example, a clearinghouse allows for the settling of the outstanding net balances between banks, thus, lowering the demand to hold cash-balances.

Second, there is the store of value uses when money is an asset. (1) The expected changes in returns cn other relatively liquid, but safe assets such as AA bonds, Treasury Bills, and blue chip stocks can change the demand for money. If the yield on these assets is expected to rise in the future, the demand for cash-balances will fall, and visa versa. (2) The expectations of permanent income effect cash-holdings. If people perceive their permanent stream of future income to be higher, ceteris paribus, they will hold less cash balances in the present. (3) The fraction of wealth in the form of physical assets (house, car etc) versus human capital (skills and education yielding higher income). Because we generally can not easily borrow money against our human capital (How do lenders repossesses a person? Implication of slave or indentured servitude here), increasing levels of human capital visa vi physical assets increases the demand to hold cash, and visa versa. (4) Generally perceived political and economic stability effects money demand. If people expect a war, revolution, depression etc, they will want to hold onto more cash balances, and visa versa. (5) **Finally and most important of all, the expected change in the future value of money.** If people expect increasing rates of inflation, they will hold less cash-balances because they lose real purchasing power in their cash-balances. Conversely, expected deflation induces people to hold more money because the real purchasing power of their cash balances rises.

Last, there is the goods side of the equation called Q. The primary determinate in the growth of economic goods and services is labor productivity. Labor productivity is increased by the following: secure property rights, capital accumulation (savings), human capital (skills, education etc.), technology, increasing division of labor, and so on. While the quantity of goods variable is important to the value of money over the long-run, it is generally not the main cause of the changes in P in the short-run because real economic growth rates rarely deviate much from 1 to 3% per year.

CHAPTER 5

Inflation and Episodes in
Hyperinflation

Inflation

Inflations and Hyperinflations

By Thomas Rustici

Lenin is said to have declared that the best way to destroy the capitalist system was to debauch the currency. By a continuing process of inflation, governments can confiscate, secretly and unobserved, an important part of the wealth of their citizens. By this method they not only confiscate, but they confiscate arbitrarily; and, while the process impoverishes many, it actually enriches some. ... the process of wealth-getting degenerates into a gamble and a lottery. ... Lenin was certainly right. There is no subtler, no surer means of overturning the existing basis of society than to debauch the currency. The process engages all the hidden forces of economic law on the side of destruction, and does it in a manner which not one man in a million is able to diagnose.[1]

—J.M. Keynes

Scientific propositions must be rigorously tested for logical consistency **and** against all potential evidence. When it comes to debasing or printing money, history provides a wealth of empirical evidence to examine. Monetary history overwhelmingly points to the observations made by classical thinkers regarding the quantity of money and the value of money.

While money emerges from a competitive market process to replace a direct-barter economy, this amazing economic good has often been *destroyed* by government policy with the *inflation tax*, i.e., earning revenue through debasement. Evidence of runaway inflation caused by rapid expansion of the supply of money is so frequent throughout history that it is shocking to the editors how little of this history is ever discussed in textbooks covering modern macroeconomics. The essays in this section are chosen to rectify this void.

The laws of economics are not dependent on any unique period, time, and place in history. Essays in this section cover the hyperinflation of the Roman Empire, the Sung Dynasty (China), Revolutionary France, Colonial America, Weimar Germany, Post-WWII Hungary, and a host of other, more modern hyperinflations. The patterns seem to be as clear and consistent as they are destructive. Hyperinflation is not about simply nominal prices rising every day. Nor is it just a problem with the value of money sinking lower and lower by the hour. It's fundamentally *a race to destroy the monetary economy and the division of labor built on that system.* Public Choice

---

1   John M. Keynes, *The Economic Consequences of the Peace* (New York: Harcourt Brace ,1920) p. 236

can tell us the political incentives that cause the nightmare scenario to play out over and over again.

Students can use their economic tools to learn the warning signs.

Problems of Rising Prices

By Armen Alchian

I believe inflation is inevitable as a long-run trend, with transient, decade-long interruptions of stable or falling prices. That forecast reflects my view of government. Inflation is a tax on money. Like any tax, it will be used. The more subtle, the less detected, and the less avoidable the tax, the better it is for those with predominant political power and the more surely it will be used. I join Keynes in at least part of the following: "progressive deterioration in the value of money through history is not an accident, and has had behind it two great driving forces—the impecuniosity of governments and the superior political influence of the debtor class."[1]

Since Keynes has been dead wrong in interpreting the effects of inflation, I cite him for eloquence, not authority. Furthermore, the "superior political influence of the debtor class" is not clearly significant. But impecuniosity of governments, that is, their desire to spend more and their ability to do so by creating money, is, I believe, irresistible for any government. And when we add the recent priestly dogma that increasing the money stock is a means of assuring high employment, there is no doubt that inflation at a transient varying rate is a way of life.

By inflation I mean either a single-shot rise in the price level or a continuing rising price level. Thus, I can interpret a rising price level as a sequence of factors, possibly overlapping, causing single-shot rises, though possibly so overlapping that one is unable to distinguish their putt-putt forces from a continuous jet stream.

SOURCES OF INFLATION

I turn first to sources of inflation. Two already have been mentioned—the ability to print money and the dogma that more *should* be printed to reduce unemployment. As causes of inflation, two factors should be distinguished: (1) changes in the ratio of money supply to money demand, and (2) factors that induce changes in that ratio—that is, that induce us to embark on an inflationary policy. An increased supply of money relative to demand creates higher prices. But the factor that persuaded the money suppliers to increase the supply of money is what induced us to embark on a monetary policy

---

1 J. M. Keynes, *Tract on Monetary Reform* (London, 1923; reprint New York: St. Martin's Press, 1971), p. 12. Is it a definition of government to say that any possessor of the dominant military power and monopoly of the base money is a government?

that creates inflation. Monetary policy is a means of creating inflation; the objective of the policy is the reason for resorting to inflation. Both are often called "causes." The increased money stock relative to demand creates inflation, whatever the reason ("cause") for embarking on the inflationary increase in the supply of money. Unless we keep those things distinct, we aren't going to get anywhere.

The supply of money can increase in a variety of ways. Gold or silver discoveries, development of new, more efficient forms of money (bank demand deposits) used along with the existing money, or the simple printing of more money by the official money printer for the "impecunious" government all are increases.

Certain interesting factors, events, or goals induce the government to spend more than its explicit tax income. To identify them, ask, "What do governments do?" The answer is, "More than before." That reply is especially valid when the costs can be spread over a wide range of people and their impact can thereby be attenuated below the individual's costs of preventing them. A larger fraction of national income will be taxed, and the larger that fraction, the greater the extent to which the printing press will be used to "balance the budget." That is the Keynesian "impecuniosity."

In addition, it has recently become respectable to create money by twisting the Keynesian doctrine that government should increase the money supply to counter major monetary contractions. That original Keynesian monetary prescription has been twisted particularly by political aspirants, for whom it is a congenial way to enhance their political status or use of government power. The new dogma is that employment is to be maintained—or, more accurately, efforts are to be exerted to try to maintain it—above that level maintainable in a free, liberal society in which people not assigned to jobs could investigate and choose those they themselves deem best. In other words, each person has the right to refuse to work for wages he, and he alone, deems unacceptable because of opportunities he believes to be discoverable elsewhere or available later. If we announce that action will be taken to assure current jobs at wages greater than those acceptable to both parties, we are announcing a policy of trying to maintain an impossibly low average rate of unemployment by assuring jobs and incomes to people whose services consumers think are not worth their asking price. The policy is to induce employers to buy their employees' services by increasing the employers' demand for their services and in turn by increasing the demand for those employers' products. This is not the desirable policy of avoiding monetary contractions; instead, monetary expansion is recommended for *any* reduction in actual employment.

The source of the (erroneous) belief that monetary expansion would assure such jobs—that is, that it would hold unemployment below that rate consistent with changed demands and with costs of getting information about new opportunities and costs for entrepreneurs to ascertain to what other tasks or outputs they should convert their productive facilities (I shall return to this point later)—is a result of confused analysis and misread empirical evidence. The employment acts in the United States and Britain simply assumed that we could somehow keep employment at that natural "full employment" rate, presumably by pure fiscal policy. But transient shifts in demand among firms and industries and products will induce higher rates of unemployment in some and lower rates in others. To prevent all unemployment increases in every sector is to attempt the impossible in a free, liberal society—a fact that still seems to escape most people. That doctrine was given an aura of respectability by the delusion of the Phillips curve.

In sum, at least two forces for inflationary monetary policy are present: "impecuniosity" of governments, and the attempt to assure full employment by money expansion (whether through government expenditures or otherwise). The former force regards money increases as regrettable but necessary, because we just "can't" balance the budget. The latter regards them as desirable. Who can beat a combination like that?

There are other policies intended to aid high employment and rapid adaptability to changing demands and supply conditions that do not involve monetary expansion. These policies attempt to lower that natural unemployment rate by, for example, cheapening the costs of ascertaining the best unexploited opportunities or by trying to avoid downward, transient shocks in the system caused by misguided, politically motivated monetary policy keyed to interest rates, balance of payments, and fixed exchange rates.

IRRELEVANCY OF MONOPOLY

Anyone, unions, business firms, or a single person, can set and persist in a price too high for his full employment or output. The belief that unions or large corporations have monopoly power and thus push up prices and cause inflation is a fallacious analysis and is wrong in fact. Any union or business or seller that pushes prices above its wealth-maximizing level will lose business and reduce employment. Resources will be released for use elsewhere, and prices elsewhere will have to be lower than they otherwise would be. The price level is not changed; relative prices are changed. Once a monopoly has set its best price, it will not raise prices higher, and not even a union, which some people think wants higher wages for the fewer and fewer remaining members who retain jobs at those higher wages, would raise the price level if it raised prices higher than its best price. The unemployed in that occupation would have to work elsewhere, lowering wages. Despite this analysis and empirical studies, some people (for example, Galbraith) try to incriminate corporations for driving up prices, while others (for example, Haberler) condemn the unions. Neither accusation is correct.

What is necessary is a will by the government to increase the stock of money to assure employment to anyone who raises his wage above the market clearing wage or price. To blame unions or corporations is to misdirect attention from the critical factor at work—the will to inflate the money supply to assure employment at whatever wages or prices people may ask. Anyone who raises his prices, be he college professor, gardener, or machinist, and to whom

the government responds quickly in assuring full employment, can be said to "cause" inflation. But as we said earlier, the term cause is so ambiguous that we should avoid putting the proposition that way. We can say that the money supply increase creates inflation—that the money supply increase occurs as the government implements its promises of full employment assurance, revising expenditures when it observes unemployment (of some degree someplace). We could say that the particular people whose unemployment is the most important to the government policy makers will be the "more important" inducers of inflation, but I don't know who they are. Nor is it conducive to clarity of analysis to try to attach the concept of "cause" to any one of those stages of the process.

The amount of verbiage in the literature arguing whether to call the inflation cost-push, demand-pull, monopoly-union, monopoly-corporate, full-employment-assurance, or money-supply-increase inflation is dismaying. One is reminded of the scandalous literature on the equality of savings and investment by the writings on the cause of inflation. Indeed, some people have even proposed trying to test which is the operating cause! I suppose we might interpret that to mean they are proposing to test whether the government has a full-employment assurance policy, whether it has increased the quantity of money, or whether anyone ever raises his wages or prices to a height which creates less than market clearing employment or output for him. As for myself, I perhaps foolishly was willing to take each of those factors for granted with casual though extensive evidence. An inquiry that does appear interesting to me is this: Given all the above, to whose unemployment is government most responsive?

We cannot wholly abandon the monopoly element in inflation. One monopoly, the government monopoly of the supply of legal base money, does indeed permit inflation. Without that monopoly, with open competition in the creation of separate, identifiable brands of money, it can be argued very cogently and persuasively that inflation would be avoided. Suppliers of money, each producing a different brand of money, would compete to produce the best money—a noninflating one. However, this possibility will remain purely hypothetical and therefore is given no attention.[2]

Money is more than a lower-cost substitute for simple barter. It also is a store of value, a measure of debt in generalized goods. Instead of expressing or settling all debts or expressing them in single goods, a general package in terms of the exchange value of a medium of exchange is an economically useful institution. But while money may perform its function as a medium of exchange (because of easy portability, recognizability, and divisibility), its storability, or economic value of such future claims, is more uncertain. Furthermore, variations in its rate of inflation make the value more variable. Money loses the predictability of its value. One of our great social institutions, money, is damaged, and our wealth is subjected to greater variations, which we all can justifiably regard as unjustifiable.

Disposable also is the excuse that inflation is a world-wide phenomenon, like some disease that infects us all. Such error hardly merits notice, except that sometimes we are careless and think fixed exchange rates tying all countries' monies together are a cause of inflation, a mistake that confuses co-variation with inflation. The world-wide deflation of the 1930's was a result of fixed exchange rates. Fixed exchange rates imply a similarity in price level movements, not necessarily inflation or deflation. Indeed, if exchange rates are allowed to respond to free, open-market forces, I know of no basis on which to predict whether countries would inflate faster or less fast, though I would bet on less correlation and faster inflation simply because the government is released from a restraint on the rate at which it can inflate.

2 For the two best discussions of which I am aware, see B. Klein, "The Competitive Supply of Money," *Journal of Money, Credit and Banking* 6, no. 4 (Nov., 1974), and E. Thompson, "The Theory of Money and Income Consistent with Orthodox Value Theory," in *Trade, Stability and Macroeconomics: Essays in Honorof Lloyd A. Metzler* (New York: Academic Press, 1974), pp. 427–53.

A PROCESS OF PRICING IN INFLATION

How do expectations operate in inflation? That process is, I believe, widely misunderstood, which means that my understanding of it differs from that of most other people. I believe an analysis along the following pattern is valid. When speaking of expected price, I mean, and economic analysis refers to (or should refer to), the price (l) that a person initially (now) sets (in other words, will accept) for his services or goods, and (2) at which he believes he will sell the amount he chooses to offer at that price. For example, a producer hopes, plans, or expects to sell some amount of product at a price. He sets that price and then soon begins to learn whether he gets the amount of demand he anticipated. If he does, that price (his expectation of his market clearing price) was correct. It was the price that did permit him to sell what he offered at that price. That actual price is the one he expected to be or believed would be the market clearing price. If it is not, he will sell less than he offers or he will find more demanded than he offers. He will learn whether it is an equilibrating price. Before asking how he learns that, if he does, let me emphasize in the strongest way that I know there is reason to assume the price he asks (his "expectation") is just as solidly, firmly, or confidently held if it is a higher price than yesterday's, by, say, 10 percent, as if it were the same price. In each case, that price is an actual price *and* a prediction of what the market clearing price is. It is asked (set) and it is not withdrawn at the instant sales deviate.

As I have argued elsewhere, price inflexibility is not a silly, uneconomic thing. Nor does price firmness mean unchanged price over time. It means unchanging price in the face of only *transient* reversible deviations of sales or production around what is believed to be a market clearing rate. Noncontinuous varying sales rates are not responded to by instant changes of prices. Production and inventories are among the adjusting variables.

A price that may turn out not to be an equilibrium price is just as slow to adjust in the face of new developing information if (1) it was set higher today in response to (erroneous) beliefs that the market clearing price was higher, or (2) it is the same as yesterday's price when no inflation was (erroneously) expected. If the price is wrong, in each case correct adjustment to the new equilibrating price is equally uncertain, costly, and time-consuming and is preceded, or accompanied, by changes in output or sales. Nor is information about all other market options and opportunities provided instantly and costlessly. The new market clearing price vector can not be discovered instantly. Actual prices "lag" behind the market clearing vector. That information lag is the pertinent lag, an "error" in forecast.

A price today that is the same as a past price is no more natural than a rising sequence of prices. It all depends upon what current demands will sustain.[3] So long as demand does not sustain the price (as a market clearing price), and so long as the parties do not know the new best price vector, the search for the new best prices and best alternative activities is no simple task. Nor are the processes and implications of the search well understood. It is no less complex during stable price expectations than during rising demands with rising price expectations. (Add to this complexity the long-term commitments or arrangements emphasized by D. Gordon in explaining why wages do not fall quickly enough to permit hiring of the unemployed, even though those who retain their jobs still receive higher wages than the unemployed are asking. Gordon's analysis also is consistent with the proposition that one should not expect rising demand to be synonymous with demand rising *above* the prices people expect to be appropriate for clearing the market.)[4] Whatever people believe is today's market clearing price is asked (or bid) and persists until they are convinced of their error. Then they have to search for more appropriate price, product,

rate of output, and investment. An increased nominal demand—but not sufficient to exceed or match the increased current price—is as contractionary as a falling demand with constant prices. Demand for a good is relative not only to various other goods; it is relative also to an expected market demand for the good at the currently charged prices.

In the usual jargon, the preceding discussion is translated into terms of anticipations or expectations of inflation not matching "actual" inflation. I prefer to identify prices now being set as the prices that are expected to be the present market clearing prices. These prices are actual prices—not "expected" prices. What is expected is that they will be market clearing.

Can the adjustment process be reversed? Can the "latest," unknown, equilibrium price vector be revised toward actual prices? This is the reverse of the common insistence on adjusting actual prices to the new, but unknown, market clearing vector. For example, many economists in the thirties strongly recommended monetary re-expansion to restore that market clearing nominal price vector up toward actual prices, rather than await the process of search, discovery, and convergence of actual prices with the low market clearing price vector to which actual prices have to be adjusted. How can the market clearing nominal vector be inflated to match current prices?

1. New money may be sprinkled from the skies, with all demands increasing until the formerly under-priced, over-demanded goods rise in price relative to the formerly over-priced goods. This plan will increase the average price in the clearing vector, and if we assume greater upward price adjustments in response to increased demand for goods that were more fully employed at existing prices, we *might* ease and quicken the convergence of the clearing vector and actual prices. Old money will be taxed (or depreciated) by the price rise, and initial recipients of the new money from the skies will gain wealth. If new money is given in exact proportion to the old money holdings of each person, there is no net interpersonal wealth transfer of money.

---

3 There is no inconsistency between this analysis and the Martingale property of prices. The interest rate reflects that average belief about future price levels. Hence, the *average* equilibrating price expectation for tomorrow is today's price plus the interest rate—the usual Martingale property. See A. Alchian, "Information, Martingales and Prices," *Swedish Journal of Economics* 76 (1974): 3–11.

4 D. F. Gordon, "A Neo-Classical Theory of Keynesian Unemployment," *Economic Inquiry* 12, no. 4 (Dec., 1974): 431–59.

2. New money may be initially spent directly in the excessively priced vector, increasing demand there. In this case, the tax on moneyholders finances the intentionally increased relative demand in the "depressed" sector and brings a rise in the equilibrium market clearing price for that sector, thereby bringing it closer to the actual price. The equilibrium (absolute and relative) price structure over the whole economy approaches the actual prices. Increased demand relative to newly posited prices (which are the objective aspects of "expectations") increases output and employment. Sales exceed the expected sales at the prices that are believed to be market clearing prices. No lag of any actual prices behind any other prices (no relative price change) is involved. The pertinent lag is the lag of adjustment of actual nominal prices to the market clearing vector, for which search must be made. That informational lag is critical. It creates what we call the natural rate of unemployment, it is always present— during unanticipated inflation, unanticipated deflation, anticipated inflation, and anticipated deflation—as long as the future (that is, the market clearing vector) is not costlessly, correctly perceived by everyone.

The excessively priced sector may require a greater increase in demand relative to the rest of the economy than can be financed by the inflation tax on money—and there is a limit to how much real wealth can be taxed by an inflation. In such a case inflation simply cannot finance the required shift. It will not restore full employment in that sector if that sector insists on, and is assured of, a higher real wage relative to other sectors. Expenditures financed by a direct tax on other forms of wealth or income must be used to shift relative demands sufficiently. But if these excessive prices are "assured" in enough sectors, it will be impossible to "assure" the excessive real demands, since the price vector would more than exhaust the social product at full employment.

Political assurance of full employment has the terrible problem of ascertaining whether current prices assured politically to everyone are compatible with physical production possibilities—a problem the free enterprise price system escapes because no one can have any assurance of profits or employment at whatever real income or price he deems "right." But we have politically made that commitment—or we act as if we have made that commitment—and now we naively wonder why we have inflation or more and more controls by government. Whatever other reasons are increasing the role of government, that desire for full employment certainly is.

A "puzzle" disposed by the preceding analysis is the so-called paradox of inflation and unemployment, or inflation and recession. The puzzle arises only if one assumes that a zero inflation rate is the basis on which people are making price commitments. If people expect the equilibrating, market clearing prices to be higher today than in the past, and yet if today the higher actual prices are not maintainable with full employment, what is adjusted? I know of no reason to expect prices to give way under that situation any more than when market clearing prices were incorrectly expected to be the same today as yesterday (incorrect because of a deflation).

Deflation? Does a reduced growth of the money stock and market demand below the anticipated inflation rate produce a less severe, shorter recession than does an equal-sized difference in money growth below a formerly constant price level? If so, ability to break a recent inflation without causing along, severe depression would be enhanced. But I have no evidence for or against that possibility.

Irrelevancy of cost push and demand pull. This analysis does not say that demand increases and then prices go up. Nor is it a cost-push view either. Nor is monopoly power involved. If people believe and forecast that market clearing prices will be higher, they will enter the market with higher prices which they believe are market clearing prices. If demand has increased less than that forecast, people will not instantly revise their prices downward. The erroneous belief that they will instantly bid prices down assumes costless discovery of information about the state of market demand here and about opportunities elsewhere. If prices are too high, what will happen? Unemployment and recession will be the result; indeed, they are the process of the search for the new equilibrating price vector and wealth maximizing activities (if prices were too high initially).

This analysis of the stimulation of employment does not rely on the hoary, falsified dogma that wages lag behind prices. That phenomenon *does not* occur. There is no other conclusion that can be drawn from the extensive empirical analysis or from economic analysis.[5]

THE PACE OF INFLATION

How fast will inflation occur? It depends upon the expectations and commitments. Whatever the forecast inflation, the government will have to validate a higher rate of inflation if it attempts to maintain employment at every price asked by a seller. Once we have embarked on the policy of validating whatever price vector exists and however rapidly anyone wants more, there is no limit to the speed of inflation.

It is commonly believed that inflation is fed by insatiable desires and attempts of people to beat each other out, and that if only we would restrain our demands or prices, inflation would not occur. That is simply wrong. (Did we all become less greedy in the Great Deflation of the thirties?) What counts are *forecasts* of the equilibrium prices. Hence, even if we all miraculously, in saintly fashion, asked for lower real incomes, but had at the same time done so on the basis of too high a forecast of the market clearing price vector, inflation would be induced

if the government were to stand ready to assure full employment by monetary methods.

The motivation for resorting to an inflationary policy is the political policy of validating whatever prices the public asks in order to "assure" employment by government action. That is what is implied by a full employment assurance policy. Then in this case the public, or that portion of it that asks for the greatest increases in price, sets the rate at which inflation must be created. The governmental monetary authorities will have shirked the responsibility that belongs to a monopolist in charge of the money stock. If any monopoly is to be blamed for inflation, it is clearly the government monopoly over the money stock, not any of unions or business, that is responsible.

It does not make any difference whether only one group asks for more than is sustainable at an equilibrium price vector with existing relative demands, or whether the whole economy asks for greater real income than can be produced if full-employment promises are believed and attempted. The price level will explode at whatever rate a portion of the public asks for prices above the equilibrium. There will be an explosion, determined not by choice of some inflation rate but by how fast the public thinks the government will respond to any unemployment.

What would stop the explosion? Obviously and forlornly, we should never have started the policy of full-employment assurance by monetary expansion, however much that expansion is done in the name of "fiscal" policy. Equally forlornly, we can now stop inflating the money stock and disappoint those who seek higher employment than is maintainable at their currently requested prices. That action would, aside from resulting in transient recession, amount to reverting to price controls by market competition, not by political power, the kind of market competition that says if you raise your price above the full-employment level acceptable to buyers you will be quickly and surely punished by loss of sales or employment—a penalty imposed by consumers, not by some government agent. Or we could try to reduce the natural rate of unemployment by lowering costs of search, discovery, and transfer to new, best alternative tasks.

---

5 M. Friedman, "The Role of Monetary Policy," *American Economic Review* 58 (Mar., 1968): 10. Even so careful an economist as Friedman slipped into the "lag of wages behind prices" error in his presidential address of December, 1967. Scores of economists, in trying to understand the relation between inflation and employment, chased him down that alley but haven't yet understood that they are as much in error in taking that path. They accept that premise and then try to find the flaw someplace else. If one accepts that error, the negative-sloped Phillips curve is hard to dismiss, but if one grasps the error, the vertical Phillips curve for correctly anticipated inflation is obvious, as is avoidance of propositions about real wage changes supposedly inherent in the process.

THE EFFECTS OF INFLATION

Wealth Redistribution Effects. The wealth transfer effects of inflation depend on whether it was under- or over-anticipated—except for the tax on non-interest-bearing money, usually the base money of the economy. Other forms of money usually pay implicit interest (for example, bank services), and it is difficult to know whether holders of bank demand deposits lose from an inflation of, say, 10 percent a year. Services rendered as checking services are not trivial.

For under-anticipated inflation a wealth transfer from net monetary creditors to net monetary debtors is implied and well established. Usually associated with the inflation is a shift in relative demands, which the inflationary increase in money stock was created to facilitate, possibly toward the borrowing sector or any other that happens to be politically strong. (To illustrate these demands, an example of a five-person economy is given in the appendix to this chapter.) The main moral is: Distinguish between the inflation and the relative demand shifts for which the inflationary money increase may have been initiated and financed by the inflation tax on existing money.

If the inflation is anticipated correctly by every participant with complete confidence, the interest rate will have an adjustment factor and all wealth transfers from net monetary creditors or net monetary debtors will cease except for a monetary asset or liability that does not pay interest (would cash and currency be an example?). Demand deposits would pay interest explicitly or implicitly. All monetary asset claims will be indexed (though by what index, I do not know). I suspect the short-term rate will dominate most interest rate contracts. If the adjustment is made in interest rate, the term of the loan is essentially shortened, as the interest rate includes adjustment for loss of capital value due to the rising price level. Capital is repaid earlier because the constant nominal amount due always represents the falling real amount of principal still due on the longer-term loan. This means the life length or term of the loan will depend on the rate of inflation that

results or is forecast during the interim. A speeding up of the rate will result in higher interest rates being placed on the loan—if it is a long-term, floating-interest-rate loan—and a shortening of the average maturity of the loan.

Resource Use Distortions. If *everyone* zeroed in on the forecast with no greater uncertainty in their minds than for forecasts during zero rates of inflation, the effects of error of anticipated inflation would be no different than during deviations around stable prices. But that is not our world. Not everyone will have the same forecast, though the average of their beliefs could create exactly the right market interest rate. Therefore, even if the market interest rate did correctly anticipate the inflation, two effects are significant: (1) more people are disappointed, and some are pleasantly surprised, by the wealth transfers that do or do not occur because of the incorrect forecasts by different people, and (2) the capital structure is changed.

Two extremes are instructive. One person believes that the nominal rate is the real rate, with zero expected price-level rise. He invests only up to the point at which the real and nominal return on investments equals that high real rate. He later discovers that the price level rose while the real rate was lower. He has underinvested in real capital. Another person believes the real rate is low, say 1 percent, with the rest of the nominal rate reflecting expected price-level changes. He invests heavily in real investment but suffers a loss in real terms because the real rate was higher.

The noise and random alteration of investment results imply less efficient use of investible resources and also cause disappointment and annoyance. Confidence in the economic system and the monetary system as not having an excessive incidence of socially useless, "unjustified" gains and losses provokes attempts to alter the system by giving aid to each person who believes he has been abused.

The variance of outcomes to which we are exposed increases. We are forced to play a game with a larger, more "random" variance of outcomes—one larger than with a zero price level. That is another cause for dissatisfaction. Appeals to government to compensate for the large "unjustified" changes in wealth enlarge government. Even without price controls and appeals to government to force others to compensate us for those changes, the increased insecurity and inability to know how much our wealth will be worth later tends to reduce the willingness to save and invest. The belief that price controls are then necessary (along with mandatory allocations, "compensatory" taxes, and subsidies) increases the scope of government regulation of economic action.

There is more. Normally shifting relative demands and costs cause "unemployment," a process of seeking the new best available activities (whether of employees detecting best jobs or of producers trying to detect new most profitable products, investments, or output rates). That task is hard enough during stable price levels. With a price level more subject to larger, variable rates of increase, each person now has demand for his service affected by nominal changes as well as by relative changes. A new source of noise is added. With inflation at an unpredictable rate, a new source of confusion arises. Are the shifts real (relative to others) or nominal? If all shifts that were nominal impinged on each person equally on the demand side and the cost, or input, side and were of the same proportion in each, at least the relative shifts would be less confused. But that is not the way events are understood or news is transmitted. Sales rates change, then prices change—at least in some sectors. But in others, prices change faster, with sales rates not changing (especially if buffer inventories are more expensive). Prices do not all respond at the same rate, because, for one reason at least, information about what underlying factors have changed is not freely and instantly available to everyone.

The increase in noise because of the variable and imperfectly predictable increases in rates of inflationary demand makes detection of the shifting (if it is) market clearing activity and price vector more difficult and slower. Activities are less efficiently coordinated and directed.

This inefficiency may show up as overemployment, but it may induce higher quit rates if people believe options elsewhere are increasing faster than in their present jobs. I know of no theory to rely on to derive unambiguous implications. One could get a positive-sloped Phillips curve. As an aside, I believe

that a trade-off between inflation and unemployment is misinterpreted. It confuses the recovery of prices from a recession and longer-run inflation. Increased rates of inflation over the expected rate may reduce the full-employment rate of unemployment, but that is not demonstrably a desirable thing. The choices of people in jobs are distorted toward accepting less than the best available job, because they are misled into accepting jobs at lower wages than they would have obtained with more search. This stricture applies to full-employment rates of unemployment. I conjecture that inflationary increases in demand that are faster than anticipated lead to too small unemployment—too little search for the better market clearing vector of prices and activities by all people, employees, employers, equipment owners, and so on. In real terms, output value is smaller.

The higher the inflation, the greater is its component of noise—or so I believe. Please do not ask me for hard evidence or proof. I "believe" a higher inflation rate will have a higher (in basis points, at least) variance. I cannot imagine a country with a 5 percent rate experiencing the same variance around that rate, or into the near or distant future, as one now experiencing a 40 percent rate.

Implicit in the preceding argument is a presumption that beliefs of price-level stability around zero percent average change are more accurate than around high rates of inflation. A belief, faith, goal, objective, or commitment to a money that does not depreciate or appreciate relative to most other goods is a characteristic of a preferred money. I believe a zero average rate is a more clearly identified and "agreed-upon" rate than is 1 or 2 or 3 percent—any of the other infinite alternatives. But once belief in a departure from zero as a goal or criterion occurs, I know of no way to identify or produce agreement on an alternative. Do higher rates of inflation create greater interpersonal dispersions of predicted rates by different people? B. Klein seems to have demonstrated that the higher the rate, the larger the variance and the less likely are differences in successive price-level changes to be negatively correlated.[6] The variance and error for a

---

6   B. Klein, "The Social Costs of the Recent Inflation and Our New Monetary Standard: The Mirage of Steady 'Anticipated' Inflation," unpublished manuscript (Apr., 1974).

given interval—say, a five-year span—will be larger because of the more highly positively correlated first differences. The available evidence, though it is not overpowering, is sufficiently strong to command serious consideration.

If we can identify factors that induce an inflationary monetary policy, are there reasons to conclude that when those factors make us resort to higher rates of inflation then they are also more variable? Do factors that induce inflation tend to be quickly reversing, independent, or positively correlated? We do not have sufficient evidence, but I conjecture increased variance at higher rates. My colleague E. Thompson suggested one explanation that would imply higher inflation and higher variation across countries. Assume, in argument, that poor countries have less efficient direct taxing systems and use inflation more as part of their general tax structure. Assume also that the poor countries have less developed, more expensive capital markets in which governments (or anyone else) can borrow funds. Then any fluctuations in government expenditures will be financed less by equivalent variations in borrowing and more by the remaining buffer source of finance: creation of new money by the government. Given those assumptions, we find that poorer countries will have higher inflation and greater variation in that rate. If that sounds like a weak proposition (and it does not sound weak to me) try conjuring up your own explanations of why higher inflations have higher temporal variance and less predictability of future price levels or rate of rise—if they do.

The problem of rising prices is not only the "random" wealth redistributions of inflation or the increased natural rate of unemployment caused by higher rates of inflation. It is, in my weighing of cultural and economic effects, the consequent increased power of government in our daily cultural, social, and economic life—an increase aided by inflation. First, inflation financing is a "convenient" form of taxation by the government—at least until the money stock is replaced with a new money that the government "promises" will be stable for who knows how long. Neat and beautiful is the inflation money tax that can be hidden from public awareness. Second, it induces more government activity.

The random changes in wealth create disaffection with (or may I say "alienation" from?) the economic system. The public's attitude toward a stable currency is not one relying on any legislative law that the money unit will be stable, but rather on a deeper, more pervasive "common law" that a stable money is a characteristic of a good economic and political system. That the instability of money values is a result of political power instead of an economic system resting on private property rights must be news to many people. Indeed, even many economists get cheap publicity by blaming unions, corporations, wars, businessmen, oil embargoes, middlemen, and greedy people (who else is there?) for inflation. The public demands correction of the random "unjust" wealth redistributions. Any ailment that befalls them during inflation is blamed on the inflation. But since the reasons for the inflation are unfathomed, they demand government correction of their idiosyncratic ills. Such demands enlarge the scope of government and are not resisted by the politically strong or aspiring. Third, direct attacks on the symptoms known to flow from inflation are politically convenient. As inflation occurs, politicians and the public blame businessmen and producers for raising prices and mulcting the public. It is even fallaciously announced by government officials that of the one- thousand-dollar rise in average annual incomes over the past year, 80 percent is eroded away by inflation. The stamp of official doctrine is established that inflation reduces real incomes, when in fact it does not. The obvious response is to call for price controls. They provoke shortages; there obviously must be government action to set matters aright. The markets have failed; the economic system has failed.

The so-called shortage of gasoline and energy in the United States was precisely and only such a political attack. It could not have been brought about more cleverly and deceitfully even if the politically ambitious had explicitly written the script. Inflate the money stock; when prices rise, impose price controls to correct the situation. These controls lead to shortages which "require" government intervention to assure appropriate use of the limited supply and to allocate it and even to control and nationalize the production of energy. The powers of political authorities are increased; the open society is suppressed.

That is, in my opinion, the problem of inflation. Those are the results of inflation that frighten me. Those are the consequences that I cannot help but attribute as a goal of those who argue that inflation is really not so serious if it is announced and anticipated and that the unemployment it "avoids" is a very small price.

In fact, there is no lasting trade-off at all. There is only a transient effect from an acceleration or deceleration, while the lasting effects are those of greater political power. Incomes policies, wage and price controls, allocations, and nationalization are politically administered, with power and wealth going to those to perform those tasks, at least until they are forced by competition into the increased costs of achieving those powers. Inflation increases government power and growth. That is the problem of rising prices. I see no escape.

APPENDIX

Let us suppose that the government—which we shall arbitrarily use as our source of inflation—decides to shift its relative demands. People for whose services or goods there has been a relative increase in demand will experience an increase in income and wealth. These demand-revision effects neither cause nor are caused by the effects of inflation on net monetary status. The gross effect is a sum of both inflation and demand-shift effects, as can be illustrated by the following numerical illustration. Suppose that the government wishes to obtain wealth by printing fiat money. Assume that it creates and spends new money for services rather than for existing capital goods (although this spending does not affect the wealth transfer process). Furthermore, let the creation of money and the resulting inflation be a one-shot operation. Let the individuals in a community be typified by five individuals whose wealth and income positions are summarized in Table 1-1.

All sorts of assumptions are possible about the ratio of income from capital assets and from labor. Assume, for simplicity, that the total income flow per period from labor and capital is equal to 10 percent of the community's capital and that all income is consumed. Capital goods can be used up if consumption is to be changed. For the redistributive process, that assumption would make no difference. Only the numerical results would be modified. In equilibrium, assume that the community jointly (but not severally) holds 10 percent of the total wealth (including money) in the form of money ($6 of the money equals 10 percent of the community's wealth of $54 + $6 = $60). Let the government inflate the money supply by $1.20 of fiat money and spend $1.00 of it—all for the services of individual B.[7] When $1.00 per period of increased money demand impinges on B, the price of his service is assumed to double (his income was formerly $1.00 per period). The government gets only half of B's services, since the private sector was offered $1.00 for all of B's services before the government's additional demand of $1.00. None of this increased demand goes to anyone except B in the first stage. The rise in service prices is reflected in capital goods prices.

Looking at each individual, we see what this implies. A's balance sheet initially is:

A (before inflation and demand revision)
Cash	$ 2.40	Equity	$15.15
Goods	12.75		
	$15.15		

In the first period, his income stays at $2.25, while the price level of services rises to, say, $1.20. If he spends all his income, his consumption in real terms falls to $2.25 (= 1.20 × $1,875), a decline of $0,375 in original-price units. In the next period he receives a larger income, $2.70, as B spends part of

---

7   By the time the government has spent $1.00, prices will be 1.20 of the former level. At this price level the government, given its propensity for liquidity, will want to hold larger cash balances, because the demand for cash is in part a function of one's level of nominal wealth. If prices have risen by 20 percent, we shall suppose the government wants to hold $1.20 in money. The upshot is that only $1.00 of the new money is spent.

Table 1: Pre-inflation wealth, dealth, and incomes of individuals

PERSONS	WEALTH	CASH	GOODS	INTERPERSONAL DEBTS (—) OR CREDITS (+)	INCOME
A	15.15	2.40	12.75	0	2.25
B	9.85	.85	9.00	0	1.00
C	16.10	.60	14.25	1.25	.75
D	4.65	.40	4.75	−.50	.25
E	4.25	.75	4.25	−.75	.75
	50.00	5.00	45.00	0	5.00
Government	10.00	1.00	9.00	0	1.00
Total	60.00	6.00	54.00	0	6.00

his increased earnings. A has the choice of spending $2.70 or saving part of it to restore some of his wealth. If he spends it all in order to maintain his consumption at its original level, his balance sheet will be:

A (no saving)

Cash	$ 2.40	Equity	$17.70
Goods	15.30		
	$17.70		

His equity, in original-price units, would be $17.70 ÷ 1.20 = $14.75, a decline in wealth of $0.40 (from $15.15). He experienced a decline in real income in the first period of $0,375. The wealth loss, $0.40, is his wealth redistribution loss due to the inflation, and his second loss is the loss of income consequent to the *demand revision* as relative demand is shifted toward B. In fact, no matter what the demand shift, the inflationary loss is unaffected. Only if the degree of demand shift is tied to the degree of inflation are the two effects related, but this tie is a policy correlation, completely independent of the fact of inflation.

Suppose that A decides to save the increment of money income in order to increase his stock of money. His balance sheet would now appear:

A (saving all his increased money income)

Cash	$ 2.85	Equity $18.15

Goods	15.30
	$18.15

In real terms his equity is $18.15 +1.20 = $15.125, a decline of $0.025 from the original level. He has to save still more if he wants to restore his equity to its original real level. Although he can choose any level of saving and resultant equity, he will have suffered the same loss of $0.40 in wealth because of the inflation and the reduced real income of $0.375 consequent to the demand revision. How he chooses to bear these two separate losses, that is, whether he will maintain consumption by eating up his wealth, restore his wealth by saving, or not save at all, is entirely up to his discretion. He is forced into no particular way, but he is forced into making a choice among them—a choice forced on him by both the inflationary wealth redistribution and the revised demand effect on income and asset values.

In the same manner, B's experience can be examined. Initially, his balance sheet is:

B (before inflation and before demand changes)

Cash	$0.85	Equity	$9.85
Goods	6.00		
	$9.85		

During the first period he has received $2.00 of income and has spent $1.00. With the higher prices, his real income is $2.00 1.20 or $1.666, an increase of $0.666 in original-price units. He has lost wealth by being a net monetary creditor; the real value of his money stock falls to $0.85 1.20 = $0.70833, a decline of $0.1416—exactly the same loss as if there were no demand shift. He can choose any combination of saving and consequent level of wealth that he wishes. If he saves all of his increase in real income, $0,666, this will more than offset the inflationary loss of wealth of $0.1416. He will have a net increase in wealth of $0,525. If, instead, he saves, say, only $0.20, his balance sheet will be:

B (after restoring cash ratio)

Cash	$ 1.05	Equity	$11.85
Goods	10.80		
	$11.85		

His equity (in original-price units) is now $11.85 ÷ 1.20 = $9.875, an increase of $0.025. This increase is the result of his voluntary decision to save $0.20. In summary, he loses $0.1416 (original-price-level units) by being a net monetary creditor during the inflation, and he gains a transitory one-period increase of $0.1666 in income by the demand shift. He chose to save $0.20 of that increase in income ($0.1666 in original-price-level units), so his wealth increased by $0.1666 - $0.1416 = $0,025. The rest

of the increased real income, in original-price-level units, $0.666 - $0.1666 = $0.50, is devoted to increasing his consumption. Similar analysis for C, D, and E yields the results given in the appropriate rows of Table 1–2. Columns (1) and (3), when summed, give column (4).

Table 1-2 shows that all of the income gain, $0.666, accruing to B is at the expense of the rest of the community (proportionate to their income) and not from inflation. Also, the net wealth redistribution due to inflation is independent to the degree of demand revision. With the demand revision, income revision has occurred, as shown in the second column, whereas the inflation wealth redistribution went from the moneyholders to the government and from private net creditors to private net debtors. In this particular example, the amount of savings increments was simply assumed to be just sufficient to restore the private community's stock of real wealth. Under different assumptions about the desire to hold cash and to save, the numerical results would be different. The government could get the services without at the same time inducing the rest of the community to do any saving or dissaving. Or the community could insist on maintaining its consumption rate (and consume some wealth). In our example the community saved enough to restore

Table 2: Summary of effects of inflation and demand shifts on income and wealth (all in original-price-leuel units)

	(1) NET WEALTH REDISTRIBUTION FROM INFLATION	(2) INCOME CHANGE CAUSED BY DEMAND REVISION: ONE PERIOD OF INCOME	(3) VOLUNTARY SAVINGS INCREMENTS	(4) NET CHANGES IN WEALTH OF PRIVATE SECTOR
A	−$0.4000	−$0.3750	$0.3750	−$0.025
B	−.1416	.6666	.1666	.025
C	−.3083	−.1250	.1250	−.1833
D	.0166	−.0416	.0416	.0583
E	.0000	−.1250	.1250	.1250
	−$0.833 (to government)	0	$0.8333	0

its wealth to the pre-inflation level. But in any event, the inflation effect is one thing, the shift in relative demand another, and the resultant saving decision still another.

Episodes in Hyperinflation

The Roman Hyperinflation

By Thomas Rustici

Those that cannot remember the past are condemned to repeat it.[1]

G. Santayana

An application of the quantity theory of money to the history of civilization teaches many macroeconomic principles. The monetary history of the world has been the perpetual monopolization of money, taken away from the free market by the state. The government draws in real resources and defaults on the real value of its debts, even while it creates winners and losers through the mechanism and distribution of the inflation itself. This use and reckless abuse of the "inflation tax" was discovered as early as the Roman Empire. Let's see what happened, and what lessons that can be drawn for today.

The earliest well-documented episode in hyperinflation on a sustained and significant scale is found in the late Roman Empire. Early in Roman history the various Caesars had learned that monopolization and nationalization of the mint under the emperor's direct authority allowed control of the quality, and, as a corollary, the quantity of coins in circulation.

The four major coins used as currency within the Roman Empire were: the *aureus* (gold), *denarius* (silver), *libra* (copper), and the *sestertius* (bronze). The process of debasement originated with bronze *sestertius* coins, moved into the copper *libra*, then on to the silver *denarius*, and finally into the gold *aureus*.[2]

The debauchery of the currency, as in most cases, was precipitated by the government's chronic and very large fiscal deficits. While deficits do not *cause* inflation per se, the monetization of the deficit is pure inflation. According to the equation of exchange, during a monetization as the quantity of money ("M") expands it puts pressure on prices ("P"). During the first century AD, the financial fortunes of the Empire changed as the empire switched from being a net creditor to a net debtor by the second century AD. The growing burdens assumed by the state had pushed beyond the limits where they could be financed by direct taxation and government. [3]

---

1 George Santayana, *Reason in Common Sense* (1905), p.284.

2 Glyn Davies, *A History of Money: From Ancient Times to the Present* (Cardiff: The University of Wales Press, 1994), p. 94.

3 Robert Schuettinger and Eamonn F. Butler, *Forty Centuries of Wage Price Controls*, (Washington D.C: The Heritage Foundation, 1979), p.21. Schuettinger and Butler also observed

There are at least three reasons the empire was in such debt. First, the ever expanding peripheries of empire increased military costs (approximately 400,000 soldiers in arms) while the returns in the form of tribute from progressive conquests declined.[4] In fact, from the time of Augustus (27 BC to 14 AD) to the time of Diocletian (284 to 305 AD), the military cost of empire expanded by a factor of about 35 to 1.[5] Also, by the second century, the burdens of the Roman warfare state were very high—consuming up to about 65% of the government's budget.[6]

The second problem for the empire's public financial system was the fact that the various emperors maintained a massive and elaborate internal welfare state. Each succeeding emperor appeased a chorus of special interest groups by offering "free" bread, wine, cash gratuities, land, and other favors in an attempt to buy support for their regime.[7] As early as the death of Julius Caesar in 44 BC the population of Rome was about 1 million, of which 200,000 were receiving free wheat, and with the estimates of total welfare transfer recipients of all kinds exceeding 350,000—or over one third of the population.[8] After construction of the Coliseum in 72 AD huge Roman circuses lasting up to 100 days and offering free admission, food, and drink were common for up to 50,000 Romans at a time.[9]

Third, the bureaucracy to administer this welfare-warfare state exploded in size.[10] By the time of Emperor Aurelian (270 AD), the state bureaucracy oversaw the 96 new territorial units within the empire, as well as ran the numerous state controlled economic sectors including textiles, arms, quarries, mines, fisheries, salt deposits, bricks, tiles, and others.[11] Here is how historians Will and Ariel Durant summarize this:

> The task of controlling men in economic detail proved too much for Diocletian's (284 AD) expanding, expensive, and corrupt bureaucracy. To support this officialdom—the army, the court, public works, and the dole—taxation rose to such heights that men lost the incentive to work or earn, and an erosive contest began between lawyers finding devices to evade taxes and lawyers formulating laws to prevent evasion. Thousands of Romans, to escape the tax gatherer, fled over the frontiers to seek refuge among the barbarians. Seeking to check this elusive mobility, and to facilitate regulation and taxation, the government issued decrees binding the peasant to his field and the worker to his shop until all his debts and taxes had been paid. In this and other ways medieval serfdom began.[12]

In the first century AD under Emperor Nero (54 AD), Rome started drowning in large budget deficits. Taxes could not be effectively increased since one third of the population lived exclusively on handouts, and Roman soldiers were often paid in tax-exempt land. The shrinking tax-base of the economy produced immediate contractionary supply-side effects, by, for example, driving merchants to go underground to escape the escalating

---

supply-side macroeconomic effects, "As taxes rose, the tax base shrank and it became increasingly difficult to collect taxes, resulting in a vicious circle." Also, see Prodromos Prodromidis, "Economic Environment, Policies and Inflation in the Roman Empire up to the Time of Diocletian's Price Edict," *The Journal of European Economic History*, Vol. 3 2009, p.582.

4   *Cambridge Ancient History: The Imperial Crisis and Recovery AD 193-324* (Cambridge: Cambridge University Press, 1939), Vol. 12, p. 262; S.A. Cook, F.L. Adcock, M.P. Charlesworth, and N.H. Baynes editors. Also, see Prodrom os Prodromidis, ""Economic Environment, Policies and Inflation in the Roman Empire up to Diocletian's Price Edict," *The Journal of European Economic History*, Vol 3, 2009, pp.572-574.

5   Ibid. p, 601.

6   Ibid. Prodromidis, p. 576

7   James Dale Davidson, *The Squeeze* (New York: Pocket Books, 1980), p.63.

8   Davies, p.96.

9   Paul Smith, "10 Interesting Facts About the Coliseum in Rome", October 1, 2013, *Nomadblog*. Smith also notes that during the used life of the Coliseum, over 500,000 people and over 1,000,000 wild animals were slaughtered in these Roman circuses.

10   *Cambridge Ancient History*, Vol. 12, p. 259.

11   Will Durant, *The Story of Civilization: Part 3 Caesar and Christ* (New York: Simon and Schuster, 1944), p. 336. Also, see Prodromidis, p. 582.

12   Will Durant and Ariel Durant, *The Lessons of History* (New York: Simon and Schuster, 1968), p. 61.

taxes, and farmers to keep their grain from the city markets— just to keep them from the tax collectors. Thus, higher taxes brought forth less revenue, and declining revenue lead to ever-higher taxes. Nero, and every one of his successors, increasingly exploited the inflation tax. The emperors maintained over 1,500 state controlled mints in which hundreds of millions of coins were debased (mixed with more abundant inferior metals), shaved, clipped, and filed at a feverish pace.[13] About 100 AD, the Roman leaders invented coercive *legal tender laws* to force unwilling creditors to accept such fraudulent coins for repayment of the government's debts. Since coins carried the imperial stamp,[14] refusal of Caesar's coins was tantamount to treason punished as a capital offence.

With large deficits and legal tender laws in place, a vast acceleration of the money supply would follow. For example, the silver content of the *denarius* was reduced down to 40% of its original value by 250 AD,[15] and less than twenty years later the *denarius* was nothing more than a copper coin with a few speckled flakes of silver: only 1/5000th of its original value.[16] In 270, Emperor Aurelian began a process of re-coinage and re-stamped the nominal weight to 2 ½ times their old weight. This monetary expansion created an utter disaster of a hyperinflation of horrendous proportions by 300 AD.[17] The bronze *sestertius* was largely demonetized by the middle of the third century[18], and the silver *denarius* became worthless. Economist Prodromos Prodromidis has observed that the money supply of debased coins increased at *minimum* 7-fold from 238 AD to 274 AD.[19]

By the time Emperor Diocletian takes power in 284, the price level was at least 100 times higher than it was under Nero. And yet, the level of inflation would accelerate even higher! For example, the price of a bushel of wheat (measured in Egyptian *drachmai*, the unit used in the Roman province) rose from 6 in the first century to over 2 million by 344 AD.[20] In fact, at the time of Jesus, 1,000 relatively pure silver *denarius* coins were equivalent in value to a pound of pure gold. By 350 AD, a pound of gold was worth about 2.2 billion newly minted *denarius* coins (now just a lead/copper coin).[21]

In 301 AD, Diocletian set out to *repress* the runaway inflation. On September 1, 301, he imposed the *Edict on Currency* which ordered a further debasement of the coins—in fact, a doubling overnight![22] This explosion of "M" put tremendous upward pressure on prices quoted in monetary terms. This was bad enough for the Roman economy, but what happened a few months later was the height of absurdity to the modern economic mind. In early December 301, Diocletian issued his *Edict on Prices*—a set of maximum wage and price controls.

While rapid monetary inflation pushes prices *upward* from their equilibrium values, the maximum price controls force prices *below* their equilibrium values. These simultaneous contradictory pressures then create widespread shortages. The real quantity of goods under maximum controls declines. The short-side of the market determines the quantities transacted and suppliers are the short-side here. So now look at these microeconomic implications in the macro equation of exchange. Rapid acceleration of "M" pushes prices "P" upwards reflecting that monetary increase. Then maximum controls reduce real quantities of goods or "Q" by creating shortages. *Ceteris paribus* when real output falls "P" rises even faster! Thus, repressed inflation *magnifies* the destructive consequences of open inflation.

His *Edict on Prices* set price controls on over 900 commodities, as well as freight rates, and 130 kinds of labor.[23] A cursory examination of the text reveals Diocletian's numerous and vehement denunciations of the "greed or avarice" driving "the wicked" merchants and "profiteers" as the cause of the Roman

---

13 Davies, p. 110.
14 Prodromidis, p.575.
15 Davies, p. 111
16 Schuettinger and Butler, p.21.
17 Davies, p. 97.
18 Prodromidis, p.585.
19 Ibid, p. 573.

---

20 Schuettinger and Butler, p. 20.
21 Davies, p. 107.
22 Prodromidis, p.587
23 Prodromidis, p.588.

hyperinflation. [24] Government always looks for its scapegoat. In paragraph eight of the *Edict*, Diocletian states:

> And to the avarice of those who are always eager to turn to their own profit … regard for common humanity impels us to set a limit.

(Diocletian expresses his concern and love for humanity multiple times in the first eleven paragraphs)

In paragraph 12, Diocletian changes his tone:

> It is our pleasure, therefore, that those prices, which the concise items of the following list indicate, be held in attention throughout our whole domain, in such a way that all men understand that *freedom to exceed them is removed.*

In paragraph 14, Diocletian's "love of "humanity" comes with penalties:

> But it is always fear, justest teacher of duties, which will restrain and guide them in the right path – it is our pleasure that if anyone have acted with boldness against the letter of this statute, *he shall be subject to capital punishment.* [25]

In paragraph 16, Diocletian then turns his love onto the buyers:

> He also shall be subject to the same peril, who in *eagerness to purchase* has come to an agreement with an avarice which retails in violation of the statutes.

In short, the death penalty was exacted on *both* seller and buyer. [26] Thousands of merchants and their customers were murdered in the Coliseum either as dinner for lions, burnt alive, or assassinated for sport. Diocletian doubled the size of the already bloated bureaucracy and enlisted thousands of secret spies, informants and police to catch violator; thus Rome had become a totalitarian police-state. The maximum price edict of Diocletian created massive shortages throughout the empire. Trade stopped and Roman cities were deserted as famine loomed on the horizon. This "repressed inflation" ultimately devastated the Roman Empire. Here is how the *Cambridge Ancient History* describes the collapse:

> In these disturbed and catastrophic decades of the third century countless people, especially of the bourgeois middle class, were impoverished, even ruined, and these were precisely the men who had brought into being and maintained the economic prosperity of former times. The wasteful policy of the State, the constant interference with private economic life, and the inflations, amounted to a landslide beneath which a vast amount that was of value was crushed out of existence. [27]

The Roman inflation has many lessons to teach about the quantity theory of money, budgetary deficits, monetization, price controls, and public policies. That this economic train wreck played itself out two millennia ago is one thing. That very predictable and eerily similar patterns often repeat in modern societies is shockingly disturbing in more ways than one. The remaining essays in this chapter are a stark reminder that hyperinflation and the devastation it leaves in its wake are never fully understood by the general public. Will more than one man in a million ever be able to correctly diagnose the causes of inflation and its hidden forces leading to destruction; or will we be condemned to forever repeat the tragic economic policies of history?

---

24 *The Edict of Diocletian Fixing Maximum Prices*, University of Pennsylvania Law Review, November 1, 1920, Vol. 69, pp. 35-47.
25 Schuettinger and Butler, pp. 156-57
26 Prodromidis, p. 588.

27 *Cambridge Ancient History*, Vol. 12, pp. 266-67.

Lessons from History

On Official Paper Money Inflation

By Jerome Smith

LESSON ONE: MEDIEVAL CHINA[1]

During the roughly 6,000 years of recorded history, there have been 34 discernible civilizations.[2] Of all these, only two used paper money. We are all too familiar with the experience of one of these civilizations: our own. But Western civilization was not the first. Western eyes first saw the Chinese using paper and printing presses, and Marco Polo included paper money along with spaghetti, gunpowder, and porcelain in his tales of wondrous Chinese inventions.

Modern paper (as opposed to Egyptian papyrus) was invented in about 50 B.C. Short lengths of bamboo were beaten into pulp, formed into sheets and dried. This method is very close to modern techniques.

The history of paper money in China stretches over seven dynasties and some 800 years; it dates from the ninth century to the seventeenth. Eight times the Chinese tried systems of unbacked paper currencies. Eight times the fiat was abandoned;

several times only after the value had plummeted to zero. Often, collapse of the "official" currency was followed by a proliferation of private currencies.

The origins of Chinese paper money have a familiar ring: About 700 A.D. people first began to take valuables to merchants who stored them and issued receipts to owners. By 1000 A.D. these merchants discovered that the receipts themselves circulated as money, and began issuing more notes than the amount of valuables they had on deposit.

Soon afterwards the Sung conquered most of China and entered this profitable storage business. These rulers issued paper money during the next century, but they did it modestly and gradually, giving the people time to get used to it. This gradual introduction made the future fiat money possible for people to accept, in like manner to modern experience.[3] Meanwhile another part of China was indeed using unbacked paper. Paper money probably developed faster in Szechuan province because the metal it replaced was iron, too cumbersome for ready use. At first a fixed quota of currency was

---

1   Excerpted from *Swiss Economic Viewpoint*, Oct. 1, 1976. Published quarterly by Foreign Commerce Bank, Bellariastrasse 82, 8038 Zurich, Switzerland.
2   These are documented in Arnold Toynbee's monumental 12-volume series, *A Study of History*.

3   This sort of lengthy introduction Is often necessary; the following incident illustrates it: Three centuries later, the Chinese conquered Persia and tried to introduce the same fiat money being used back in Peking. Advisers and presses were duly sent, but the Persians had never before seen paper money. They simply refused to believe that the nicely printed pieces of paper were worth anything. The experiment failed.

annually printed for redemption in new notes three years later. This stable currency system became the Chinese equivalent of the gold standard, and for a century it prevented the government from inflating. But in 1072 a second series of 1071 notes was run off. The yearly issues got larger and soon redemption dates were frequently missed. In 35 years the money supply rose 2,000 percent. Not long afterward the currency passed out of use.

By this time a new dynasty, the Southern Sung, had replaced the Sung in the rest of China. Several unsuccessful attempts were made to get paper established; this finally succeeded in 1168. The same "three-year plan" was inaugurated, with a quota of 10 million "strings" a year. The "string" was the Chinese paper currency. Just as the English pound began as a pound of sterling silver, the string represented an actual string upon which a thousand copper coins had been threaded. (This custom is the reason for the hole in the middle of Chinese coins.)

Deficit spending soon caused the government to inflate. In 1176 certain issues were allowed to circulate nine years instead of three. In 1195 the yearly quota was tripled; and by 1209 the money supply was twenty times its original size. Until this time, however, the paper's value held firm. This could be explained by the fact that the paper gradually made its way to the outlying provinces of the empire. Eventually the point was reached where paper circulated throughout the whole empire, and any further increase would cause depreciation. This dangerous point was reached about 1210. The Southern Sung chose this moment to launch a war against the barbarian Chin[4] dynasty to the north. The war failed and the value of Sung paper plummeted. By 1232 the money supply had tripled and soon periods of circulation became unlimited. The currency began to be printed on silky paper infused with a delicate hint of perfume, to make it more attractive, but this tactic fooled no one. Not long afterward, the Mongols conquered the Sung.

Meanwhile, the Chin were also issuing paper currency. The Chin currency was remarkable in that there were separate issues for the various geographical

areas under their control. Depreciation, as usual, began slowly. But for the first time in Chinese history, various laws were passed to stem too rapid a fall. For instance, in 1192 an imperial decree prevented the paper supply from exceeding the copper supply. The next year certain taxes were ordered paid in paper, thus increasing the demand for it. But copper began to be hoarded, and silver was introduced at par with paper to draw attention away from copper. Both silver and paper were highly overvalued against copper, and were ignored. A measure was enacted that every transaction involving over one string had to be made in notes or (while it lasted) silver. This would be the first in an increasing number of actions during the next centuries designed to eliminate monies competing with official fiat. In 1206, a particularly ludicrous anti-inflationary technique was employed. Efforts were made to withdraw the largest denomination bills, because they were somehow considered more inflationary than, say, two or three smaller bills totalling the same amount. (This belief seems to be endemic in China, for the same phenomenon was observed in the post-World War II Chinese inflation.)

The steady use of the printing press rendered all these measures useless. And the above-mentioned war with the Southern Sung was also a blow to the Chin currency. In addition, the Mongols began to menace Chin frontiers. Due to high military spending, currency values rapidly disintegrated. Eighty-four cartloads of paper were distributed to the troops just before a severe Chin defeat (1210). The rulers began issuing notes of ever-increasing denomination, apparently realizing the foolishness of the 1206 edict. There was a brief, unsuccessful experiment in price controls. New issues became worthless practically overnight, and by 1216 they were worth less than one percent of their face value. The next year a "new" currency was issued at the rate of 1,000 to one. It wasn't enough: a newer currency (1222) replaced it at an 800-to-one rate (its current "black market" value). Before the year had passed this sank below one percent of face value. Soon after, both the Chin government and its currency were put out of their miseries by the Mongol hordes of Genghis Khan.

---

4   For whom China is named.

Remarkably, the Mongols did not at first consider the possibilities of paper money. But in 1260 Kublai Khan made a former Chin inflationist his principal advisor. The presses began rolling in that year, and were to cease only with the demise of Mongol rule. A national currency was issued, but began to lose value instantly. Accordingly, for the only time in history, that value was legally set at one-half face value. Initially, currency value was maintained. The Mongols had an empire much larger than the Sung, so years elapsed before new money brought price inflation. In 1262 a series of very tough decrees began. Gold and silver were prohibited in exchange, the penalty being death. (It seems that the Mongol penalty for most crimes was death, but then a regime which several times seriously considered a policy of killing all Chinese and turning China into pasture land could not be expected to feel remorse in enacting severe punishments for even minor infractions.)

Between 1260 and 1330 the monetary inflation rate was an incredible *323,300 percent*, an average of over *4,600 percent* a year![5] This seventy-year period was characterized by numerous issues of new paper currency, and continual decrees to enforce its acceptance. Refusal to accept notes in exchange brought death to "only" the offender, but counterfeiting them brought death to three generations!

It was at this time that Marco Polo visited China, He waxed enthusiastic about the glories of paper money: "Each year," he said, the Great Khan "has so great a supply of them (notes) made in Peking that he could buy with it all the treasure in the world, though it costs him nothing."

Polo seemed unaware of any problems the fiat caused. Indeed, he never even mentioned the yearly decline of its value all the while he was in China. He brought this rose-colored picture back to Europe, and doubtless swayed future generations. Private currencies began to compete with government money to such an extent that in 1294 their use was outlawed. These private monies were tokens issued by reputable commercial establishments entitling the bearer to various commodities of general usefulness, such as a pound of salt. While the decrees against private money worked fairly well in large cities, they failed utterly in the vast outlying districts.

Dogged by catastrophe on both the international and home fronts, the Mongol empire began to disintegrate. As a result of increasing disorder, most statistical data ends in 1330. We do know that by 1350 people valued only hard cash. The dynasty ended in 1368. The Mings, who conquered them, were just as' inflationary during and after their successful uprising. But once again, currency initially held its value. However, by 1400 the notes had fallen to three percent of face value, by 1425 to one percent, and by 1450 to one-tenth of one percent.

INFLATION FINALLY HALTED

But the Mings had learned their lesson and gradually stopped printing money, rapidly replacing it with metal coins. From 1500 on we hear little of Chinese paper money. The Mings briefly considered using it just before they fell to the Manchus in 1644, and the new dynasty only fleetingly printed money (1650–1661). In fact, China did not use paper again until it was introduced in 1851 by the British, the Western descendants of Marco Polo, the man who brought the inventions of paper and printing back home with him.

While the *government* had stopped using paper money, private merchants again began issuing notes after 1500. With centuries of inflation behind them, most merchants shunned note over-issue. (The public put those who didn't out of business.) Different commodities were used by different note issuers; some notes were backed, for instance, by bricks of tea.

---

5 From 360,000 string in 1260 to 116.4 billion in 1330.

CONCLUSION

Certainly the most interesting feature of this Chinese monetary history is that, after 500 years' experience, China eventually abandoned state-sponsored paper money in favor of hard money and private banknotes. Western use of government fiat money has run only about 250 years. Let us hope we don't wait another 250 years to repudiate it before we repeat medieval China's ultimate act of sanity.

Not Worth a Continental

By Pelatiah Webster

EDITOR'S NOTE

"Not worth a continental" is a descriptive phrase born of an early American experiment in deficit financing. If its lessons are ignored or forgotten, that experience will have been as worthless as the Continental currency itself.

Pelatiah Webster, "an able though not conspicuous citizen" of Philadelphia (1726–1795), is credited by James Madison and others as having been the first advocate of a constitutional convention. Though he was not a delegate, many points in the Constitution conform to an outline he had proposed several years prior to the Convention.

The "fatal mistakes" of deficit financing, inflation, and price control were understood by men like Webster. Lessons learned the hard way during the period of revolutionary America had a determining influence on those who founded the republic.

The Continental Congress authorized the printing of paper money but depended upon enabling legislation by the respective states under the Tender Acts to give negotiability to the irredeemable paper and to keep it in circulation on a par with the "hard money" of those days. Webster considered it his duty as a citizen to criticize monetary enforcement legislation then being proposed by the Assembly of Pennsylvania. The proposal was offered by the Assembly for public consideration on November 29, and was enacted into law, despite Webster's protest, on December 19, 1780.

It is too soon to tell the full impact of Webster's observations, for they were written with the hope "that our fatal mistakes may be a caution and a warning to future financiers who may live and act in any country which may happen to be in circumstances similar to ours at that time." Yet the circumstances in which we find ourselves today, the penalties of deficit financing and other uneconomic practices are the same as they were in 1780.

The text has been stripped of some archaisms of grammar and expression, but Webster's ideas and lucid style are intact.

The fatal error—that the credit and currency of the Continental money could be kept up and supported by acts of compulsion—entered so deep into the minds of Congress and of all departments of administration through the states that no considerations of justice, religion, or policy, or even experience of its utter inefficacy, could eradicate it. It seemed to be a kind of obstinate delirium, totally deaf to every argument drawn from justice and right, from its natural tendency and mischief, from common sense, and even common safety.

Congress began, as early as January 11, 1776, to hold up and recommend this *maxim of maniasm*, when Continental money was but five months old. Congress then resolved that "whoever should refuse to receive in payment Continental bills, etc., should be deemed and treated as an enemy of his country, and be precluded from all trade and intercourse with the inhabitants …"—that is, should be outlawed, which is the severest penalty, except of life and limb, known in our laws.

THESE FATAL MEASURES

This ruinous principle was continued in practice for five successive years, and appeared in all shapes and forms—in tender acts, in limitations of prices, in awful and threatening declarations, in penal laws with dreadful and ruinous punishments, and in every other way that could be devised. And all were executed with a relentless severity by the highest authorities then in being, namely, by Congress, assemblies and conventions of the states, by committees of inspection (whose powers in those days were nearly sovereign) and even by military force. Men of all descriptions stood trembling before this monster of force without daring to lift a hand against it during all this period. Its unrestrained energy ever proved ineffectual to its purposes, but in every instance increased the evils it was

designed to remedy, and destroyed the benefits it was intended to promote. At best its utmost effect was like that of water sprinkled on a blacksmith's forge, which indeed deadens the flame for a moment, but never fails to increase the heat and force of the internal fire. Many thousand families of full and comfortable fortune were ruined by these fatal measures, and lie in ruins to this day, without the least benefit to the country or to the great and noble cause in which we were then engaged.

I do not mention these things from any pleasure I have in opening the wounds of my country or exposing its errors, but with a hope that our fatal mistakes may be a caution and warning to future financiers who may live and act in any country which may happen to be in circumstances similar to ours at that time.

A STANDARD OF VALUE

The nature of a Tender-Act is no more or less than establishing by law the standard value of money, and has the same use with respect to the currency that the legal standard pound, bushel, yard, or gallon has to those goods, the quantities of which are usually ascertained by those weights and measures. Therefore, to call anything a pound or shilling, which really is not so, and make it a legal standard, is an error of the same nature as diminishing the standard bushel, yard, or gallon, or making a law that a foot shall be the legal yard, an ounce the legal pound, a peck the legal bushel, or a quart the legal gallon, and compelling everybody to receive all goods due to them by such deficient measures.

Further, to make anything the legal standard, which is not of fixed but variable nature, is an error of the same kind and mischief as the others—for example, to make a turnip the standard pound weight, which may dry up in the course of a year to a pith of not more than two or three ounces, or to make a flannel string the standard yard, which will shrink in using to half its length. The absurdity of this is too glaring to need anything further said on it.

But to come to the matter now in question. The first observation which occurs to me is that the bills, which are made a tender, contain a public promise of money to be paid in six years. On which I beg leave to remark that the best and most indubitable security of money to be paid in six years, or any future time, is not so good or valuable as ready cash.

Therefore, the law which obliges a man to accept these bills instead of ready cash obliges him to receive a less valuable thing in full payment of a more valuable one, and injures him to the amount of the difference. This is a direct violation of the laws of commutative justice—laws grounded in the nature of human rights, supported by the most necessary natural principles, and enjoined by the most express authority of God Almighty. No legislature on earth should have right to infringe or abrogate this freedom of choice in the exchange of goods for goods.

Again, the security arising from the public promise is not generally deemed certain. The public faith has been so often violated, and the sufferings of individuals thence arising have been so multiplied and extensive, that the general confidence of our people in that security is much lessened. Since a chance or uncertainty can never be so valuable as a certainty, those bills must and will be considered as less valuable than they would be if the security on which they depended were free of all doubt or uncertainty; and consequently, the discount of their value will always be estimated by, and of course be equal to, this difference. Therefore, the injustice of forcing them on the subject at full value of present cash is greatly increased.

These positions and reasonings are grounded on such notoriety of fact that any explanation or proof is needless; and I hope an objection against a law, drawn from the most manifest and acknowledged injustice of its operation and effect, will not be deemed trivial or be easily set aside or got over.

AN HONEST MAN

Suppose a man of grave countenance and character should, in distress, apply to his neighbor for the loan of 1000 silver dollars, with solemn promise on his honor and truth to repay them in a month, and in the meantime the Tender-Act under consideration should pass into a law, and the borrower, at the month's end, should tender 1000 of the new paper dollars in payment.

I beg leave here to ask of every member of the Assembly who voted for that law, and every other man who is a member of this state, what their sentiments of that action would be, and in what light they would view the borrower who tendered the paper dollars—that is, two-fifths of the debt[1]—in payment of the silver ones he had received: Would they consider him as an upright, honest man, or a shameless rascal?

In whichever of the two characters they may choose to consider such a man, it may be proper to note that the act in question, if passed into a law, would protect him, and not only so, but would subject the lender to the loss of the whole money if he refused to receive it. This is a somewhat delicate matter which it is painful to dwell long upon. I will therefore close what I have to say on it with a few very serious remarks, the truth, justice, and propriety of which I humbly submit to the reader:

1. The worst kind of evil, and that which corrupts and endangers any community most, is that iniquity which is framed by a law; for this places the mischief in the very spot—on the very seat—to which every one ought to look and apply for a remedy.

2. It cannot be consistent with the honor, the policy, the interest, or character of an Assembly of Pennsylvania to make a law which, by its natural operation, shall afford protection to manifest injustice, deliberate knavery, and known wrong.

3. No cause or end can be so good—so heavenly in its origin, so excellent in its nature, so perfect in its principles, and so useful in its operation—as to require or justify

infernal means to promote it. By infernal means I mean such as are most opposed to Heaven and its laws, most repugnant to natural principles of equity which .are all derived from Heaven, and most destructive of the rights of human nature which are essential to the happiness of society. Such laws are engraven by Heaven on the heart of every man. Some wicked men have formerly said, "Let us do evil, that good may come," whose damnation is just.

But perhaps this sort of argument may not have all the effect I could wish on the mind of every reader. I therefore proceed to another argument, which goes to the nature and principle of the act itself: The credit or value of money cannot, in the very nature of the thing, be supplied, preserved, or restored by penal laws or any coercive methods. The subject is incompatible to force; it is out of its reach, and never can be made susceptible of it or controllable by it.

The thing which makes money an object of desire—which gives it strength of motive on the hearts of all men—is the general confidence, the opinion which it gains as a sovereign means of obtaining everything needful. This confidence, this opinion, exists in the mind only, and is not compellable or assailable by force, but must be grounded on that evidence and reason which the mind can see and believe. And it is no more subject to the action of force than any other passion, sentiment, or affection of the mind; any more than faith, love, or esteem.

It is not more absurd to attempt to impel faith into the heart of an unbeliever by fire and faggot, or to whip love into your mistress with a cowskin, then to force value or credit into your money by penal laws.

TRIAL AND ERROR

You may, indeed, by force compel a man to deliver his goods for money which he does not esteem, and the same force may compel him to deliver his goods without any money at all. But the credit or value of the money cannot be helped by all this, as appears by countess examples. Plain facts are stubborn and undeniable proof of this. Indeed, this has been tried among ourselves in such extent of places and variety of shapes—and in every instance been found ineffectual—that I am amazed to see any attempt to revive it under any devisable form whatsoever. Countless are the instances of flagrant oppression and wrong, and even ruin, which have been the sad effects of these dreadful experiments, with infinite detriment to the community in general, without effecting in any one instance the ends intended. The facts on which this argument depends are fresh in everyone's memory.

I could wish, for the honor of my country, to draw a veil over what is past, and that wisdom might be derived from past errors sufficient to induce everyone to avoid them in the future. In conclusion, from the contemplation of the nature of the thing, and of the facts and experiments which have been made in every variety of mode and supported by every degree of power and exertion, it appears as plain and undeniable as intuitive proof that the credit or value of money is not in its nature controllable by force. Therefore, any attempt to reach it in that way must end in disappointment. The greater the efforts—and the higher the authority which may be exerted in that way—the greater must be the chagrin, shame, and mortification when the baseless fabric shall vanish into smoke.

NATURAL VALUE

The only possible method then of giving value or credit to money is to give it such qualities, and clothe it with such circumstances, as shall make it a sure means of procuring every needful thing; for money that will not answer all things is defective, and has not in it the full nature and qualities of money. In this way only it will grow fast enough into esteem, and become a sufficient object of desire, to answer every end and use of money. Therefore, when the question is proposed: "How shall we give credit or value to our money?" the answer, the only true answer, is: "Bring it into demand, make it necessary to everyone, make it a high means of happiness and a sure remedy of misery." To attempt this in any other way is to go against nature, and of course into difficulty, only to obtain shameful disappointment in the end.

There is nothing better than to take things in their natural way. A great and difficult work may be accomplished by easy diligence if a good method and a wise choice of means are adopted; but a small work may be made difficult, very soon, if taken at the wrong end and pursued by unnatural means. There is a right and a wrong method of doing everything. You may lead with a thread what you cannot drive with whips and scorpions. The Britons have found this to their cost in the unnatural means they have pursued to preserve and recover their dominions in America. I wish we might be made wise by their errors. *Happy is he who is made cautious by observing the dangers of others.*

I would be willing to learn wisdom from Great Britain. *It is right to be taught even by an enemy.* Amidst all their madness, and in all their distresses for money, they never once thought of making their bank or exchequer bills a tender, or supporting their currency by penal laws. But these considerations may have little, effect on some minds who are not very delicate in their choice of means, but seem resolved to carry their point, God willing or not.

I therefore hasten to another topic of argument. It appears to me the act is founded in mistaken and very bad policy, and by its natural operation must produce many effects extremely prejudicial to our great and most important interests.

It seems plain to me that the act has a fatal tendency to destroy the great motives of industry, and to dishearten and discourage men of every profession and occupation from pursuing their business on any large scale or to any great effect. Therefore, it will prevent the production of those supplies derived from husbandry and manufactures, which are essential to our safety, support, and comfort. Few men will bestow their labor, attention, and good money, with zeal, to procure goods and commodities for sale, which they know they must sell for money which they esteem bad, or at best doubtful.

The extent and dreadful effects of this are unavoidable and immense. If the industry of the farmer and tradesman is discouraged, and they cease to strive for large crops and fabrics, the consequence must be a universal diminution and scarcity of the produce of the country and of the most important articles of living, as well as commerce. The general industry of the country is of such vast importance—is an object of such magnitude—that to check it is to bring on ruin, poverty, famine, and distress, with idleness, vice, corruption of morals, and every species of evil. As money is the sinews of every business, the introducing of a doubtful medium—and forcing it into currency by penal laws—must weaken and lessen every branch of business in proportion to the diminution of inducement found in the money.

The same thing will render the procurement of supplies for the army difficult, if not utterly impracticable. Most men will hold back their goods from the market rather than sell them for money of a doubtful credit. There will be no possible way of collecting them but to send a superior force into the country and there take them by violence from the owner, which will occasion such an expense as will double the cost of the supplies by the time they get to the army, and be subject to a thousand frauds. This is the most obvious and natural operation of the act if we consider its own nature only, and it is confirmed by such ample experience, recent in the memory of every man, that it can leave no doubt but all this mischief must follow the act from its first operation.

BAD MONEY CORRUPTS MEN

I apprehend the act will, by its natural operation, tend to corrupt the morality of the people, sap the support, if not the very foundation, of our independence, lessen the respect due to our legislature, and destroy that reverence for our laws which is absolutely necessary to their proper operation and the peace and protection of society. Many people will be so terrified with the apprehension of seeing their real substance—the fruit of their labor and anxious attention—converted into a bundle of paper bills of uncertain value, that to avoid this evil they will have strong inducements to rack their invention for all devisable ways and methods of avoiding it. This will give rise to countless frauds, ambiguities, lies, quibbles, and shams. It will introduce the habit and give a kind of facility to the practice of such guile and feats of art as will endanger the uprightness, plain honesty, and noble sincerity which ever mark the character of a happy and virtuous people.

Many, who wish well to our independence and have many necessaries for our army which they would wish to supply, yet will be held back from offering their goods because of the doubtful value of the bills in which those supplies must be paid for. Instances of this sort I conceive will be so numerous as greatly to affect the supplies of our army and, of course, the support of our independence. The injuries and sufferings of people who are compelled to take said bills in satisfaction of contracts for real money will induce them in their rage to use the legislature, who formed the act, with great liberty and, perhaps, gross disrespect. The habit of reproaching the legislature and eluding the injurious act will become general, and pave the way to an habitual and universal abhorrence of our legislature and contempt of our laws, with a kind of facility and artful dexterity in eluding the force of the whole code.

I freely submit it to my readers as to whether these consequences are at all unnatural or ill-drawn, if the surmises are at all groundless, or the painting a whit too strong. No art of government is more necessary than that of keeping up the dignity and respectability of the legislatures and all courts and officers of government, and exciting and preserving in the hearts of the people a high reverence for the laws. And anything which endangers these great supports of the state ought to be avoided as a deadly evil.

BAD MONEY DESTROYS FOREIGN RESPECT

The act, I apprehend, will give a bad appearance to our credit, honor, and respectability in the eyes of our neighbors on this continent, and the nations of Europe, and other more distant parts of the world. For when they learn that our own people must be compelled by the loss of half their estates and imprisonment of their persons to trust the public faith, they will at once conclude there must be some great danger, some shocking mischief dormant there, which the people nearest to and best acquainted with it abhor so much. And of course, as they are out of the reach of our confiscations and imprisonments, they will have little inducement to trust or esteem us.

Finally, the act will give great exultation and encouragement to our enemies, and induce them to prolong the war, and thereby increase the horrid penalty of imprisonment which is to last during the war. When they see that our money has become so detestable that it requires such an act as this to compel our own people to take it, they must at least be convinced that its nature is greatly corrupted and its efficacy and use nearly at an end. When we see the passionate admirers of a great beauty forced by lashes and tortures into her embraces, we at once conclude that she has lost her charms and has become dangerous and loathsome.

It cannot be fairly objected to these strictures that they suppose the bills funded by this act are of less value than hard money. The act itself implies this. The Assembly never thought of wasting time in framing an act to compel people to take English guineas, Portuguese joes, and Spanish dollars under penalty of confiscation and imprisonment.

I dare think that there is not a man to be found, either in the Assembly or out of it, that would esteem himself so rich and safe in the possession of 1000 of these dollars as of 1000 Spanish ones. The most effectual way to impress a sense of the deficiency of the act on the minds of all men, and even discover the idea which the Assembly themselves have of it, is to enforce it by penalties of extreme severity. For if there were no deficiency in the act it could not possibly require such penalties to give it all necessary effect, nor is it likely that the Assembly would add the sanction of horrid penalties to any of their acts unless they thought there was need of them.

The enormity of the penalty deserves remark. The penalty for refusing a dollar of these bills is greater than for stealing ten times the sum.

DESTROYS CONTRACTS AND CREDIT

Further, the act alters, and of course destroys, the nature and value of public and private contracts, and this strikes at the root of all public and private credit. Who can lend money with any security, and of course, who can borrow, let his necessity and distress be ever so great? Who can purchase on credit or make any contract for future payment? Indeed, all confidence of our fellow-citizens in one another is hereby destroyed, as well as all faith of individuals in the public credit.

Upon the whole matter, the bills must rest on the credit of their funds, their quantity, and other circumstances. If these are sufficient to give them a currency at full value, they will pass readily enough without the help of penal laws. If these are not sufficient, they must and will depreciate and thereby destroy the end of their own creation. This will proceed from such strong natural principles, such physical causes, as cannot, in the nature of the thing, be checked or controlled by penal laws or any other application of force.

These strictures are humbly offered to public consideration. The facts alleged are all open to view and well understood. If the remarks and reasonings are just, they will carry conviction; if they are not so, they are liable to anyone's correction.

NOTE FOR THIS CHAPTER

1. On March 18, 1780, the Continental Congress officially had recognized the debauchery of its currency, allowing it to exchange for specie at the rate of 40:1. By the time this piece was written, the unofficial exchange rate had further widened to 100:1. This probably explains Webster's illustration—"two-fifths of the debt."

Fiat Money in France

By Andrew White

In vain did Maury show that, while the first issues of John Law's paper had brought apparent prosperity, those that followed brought certain misery; in vain did he quote from a book published in John Law's time, showing that Law was at first considered a patriot and friend of humanity; in vain did he hold up to the Assembly one of Law's bills, and appeal to their memories of the wretchedness brought on France by them; nothing could resist the eloquence of Mirabeau. Barnave follows; says that "Law's paper was based upon the phantoms of the Mississippi; ours upon the solid basis of ecclesiastical lands," and proves that the assignats can not depreciate further. Prudhomme's newspaper pours contempt over gold as security for the currency, extols real estate as the only true basis, and is fervent in praise of the convertibility and self-adjusting features of the proposed scheme. In spite of all this plausibility and eloquence a large minority stood firm to their earlier principles; but on the 29th of September, by a vote of 508 to 423, the deed was done; a bill was passed authorizing the issue of eight hundred millions of new assignats, but solemnly declaring that in no case should the entire amount put in circulation exceed twelve hundred millions. To make assurance doubly sure, it also provided that, as fast as the assignats were paid into the treasury

for land, they should be burned; and thus a healthful contraction be constantly maintained.

Great were the plaudits of the nation at this relief. Rejoicings were heard on every side. Among the multitudes of pamphlets expressing this joy which have come down to us, the "Friend of the Revolution" is the most interesting. It begins as follows: "Citizens, the deed is done. The assignats are the keystone of the arch. It has just been happily put in position. Now I can announce to you that the Revolution is finished, and there only remain one or two important questions. All the rest is but a matter of detail which can not deprive us any longer of the pleasure of admiring in its entirety this important work. The provinces and the commercial cities which were at first alarmed at the proposal to issue so much paper money, now send expressions of their thanks; specie is coming out to be joined with paper money. Foreigners come to us from all parts of Europe to seek their happiness under laws which they admire; and soon France, enriched by her new property and by the national industry which is preparing for fruitfulness, will demand still another creation of paper money."

To make these prophecies good, every means was taken to keep up the credit of this second issue of assignats. Among the multitudes of pamphlets issued for this purpose was one by Royer; it appeared

September 14, 1790, and was entitled Reflections of a Patriotic Citizen upon the Emission of Assignats. In this Royer gives many excellent reasons why the assignats can not be depressed; and speaks of the argument against them as "vile clamors of people bribed to affect public opinion." He says to the National Assembly, "If it is necessary to create five thousand millions and more of this paper, decree such a creation gladly." He, too, predicts, as Mirabeau and others had done, the time when gold will lose all its value, since all exchanges will be made with this admirably guaranteed paper, and therefore that coin will come out from the places where it is hoarded. He foretells prosperous times to France in case these great issues of paper are continued, and declares this "the only means to insure happiness, glory, and liberty, to the French nation."

France was now fully committed to a policy of inflation; and, if there had been any doubt of this before, it was soon proved by an act of the Government, very plausible, but none the less significant, as showing the exceeding difficulty of stopping a nation once in the full tide of a depreciated currency. The old cry of the "lack of a circulating medium" broke forth again; and especially loud were the clamors for more small bills. This resulted in an evasion of the solemn pledge that the circulation should not go above twelve hundred millions, and that all assignats returned to the treasury for land should immediately be burned. Within a short time there had been received into the treasury for lauds one hundred and sixty million francs in paper. By the terms of the previous acts this amount ought to have been retired. Instead of this, under the plea of necessity, one hundred millions were reissued in the form of small notes.[1]

Yet this was but as a drop of cold water to a parched throat. Although there was already a rise in prices which showed that the amount needed for circulation had been exceeded, the cry for "more circulating medium" was continued. The pressure for new issues became stronger and stronger. The Parisian populace and the Jacobin Club were especially loud in their demands for them; and a few

months later, on June 19, 1791, with few speeches, in a silence very ominous, a new issue was made of six hundred millions more; less than nine months after the former great issue, with its solemn pledges as to keeping down the amount in circulation. With the exception of a few thoughtful men, the whole nation again sang paeans.

In this comparative ease of a new issue is seen the action of a law in finance as certain as the action of a similar law in natural philosophy. If a material body fall from a height, its velocity is accelerated, by a well-known law in physics, in a constantly increasing ratio: so in issues of irredeemable currency, in obedience to the theories of a legislative body, or of the people at large, there is a natural law of rapidly increasing issue and depreciation. The first inflation bill was passed with great difficulty, after a very sturdy resistance, and by a majority of a few score out of nearly a thousand votes; but you observe now that new inflation measures are passed more and more easily, and you will have occasion to see the working of this same law in a more striking degree as this history develops itself.

Nearly all Frenchmen now became desperate optimists, declaring that inflation is prosperity. Throughout France there came temporary good feeling. The nation was becoming fairly inebriated with paper money. The good feeling was that of a drunkard after his draught; and it is to be noted, as a simple historical fact, corresponding to a physiological fact, that, as the draughts of paper money came faster, the periods of succeeding good feeling grew shorter.

Various bad signs had begun to appear. Immediately after this last issue came a depreciation of from eight to ten per cent; but it is very curious to note the general reluctance to assign the right reason. The decline in the purchasing power of paper money was in obedience to one of the simplest laws in social physics; but France had now gone beyond her thoughtful statesmen, and took refuge in unwavering optimism; giving any explanation of the new difficulties rather than the right one. A leading member of the Assembly insisted, in an elaborate speech, that the cause of depreciation was simply want of knowledge and of confidence

---

1 See Von Sybel, History of the Revolution, vol. i, p. 265.

among the rural population, and proposed means of enlightening them. La Rochefoucauld proposed to issue an address to the people, showing the goodness of the currency and the absurdity of preferring coin. The address was unanimously voted. As well might they have attempted to show that, if, from the liquid made up by mixing a quart of wine and two quarts of water, a gill be taken, this gill will possess all the exhilarating value of the original, undiluted beverage.

Attention was next aroused by another menacing fact—specie was fast disappearing. The explanations for this fact also displayed wonderful ingenuity in finding false reasons and evading the true one. A very common explanation may be found in Prud-homme's newspaper, Les Révolutions de Paris, of January 17, 1791, which declared that "coin will keep rising until the people have hung a broker."[2] Another popular theory was that the Bourbon family were in some miraculous way drawing off all solid money to the chief centers of their intrigues in Germany.[3]

Still another favorite idea was that English emissaries were in the midst of the people, instilling notions hostile to paper. Great efforts were made to find these emissaries, and more than one innocent person experienced the popular wrath, under the supposition that he was engaged in raising gold and depressing paper.[4] Even Talleyrand, shrewd as he was, insisted that the cause was simply that the imports were too great and the exports too little.[5] As well might he explain the fact that, when oil is mingled with water, water sinks to the bottom, by saying that it is because the oil rises to the top. This disappearance of specie was the result of a natural law as simple and sure in its action as gravitation: the superior currency had been withdrawn because an inferior could be used.[6] Some efforts were made

to remedy this. In the municipality of Quillebœuf the sum of 817 marks in specie having been found in the possession of a citizen, the money was seized and sent to the Assembly. The good people of that town treated this hoarded gold as the result of some singularly unpatriotic wickedness or madness, instead of seeing that it was but the sure result of a law, working in every land and time, when certain causes are present. Marat followed out this theory by asserting that death was the proper penalty for persons who thus hid their money. In order to supply the specie required a great number of church bells were melted down; but this also proved inadequate.

Still another troublesome fact began now to appear. Though paper money had increased in amount, prosperity had steadily diminished. In spite of all the paper issues business activity grew more and more spasmodic. Enterprise was chilled, and stagnation had set in. Mirabeau, in his speech which decided the second great issue of paper, had insisted that, though bankers might suffer, this issue would be of great service to manufacturers and restore their prosperity. The manufacturers were for a time deluded, but were at last rudely awakened from their delusions. The plenty of currency had at first stimulated production and created a great activity in manufactures, but soon the markets were glutted, and *the demand was vastly diminished. In spite of the wretched financial policy of years gone by, and especially in spite of the Edict of Nantes,* by which religious bigotry had driven out of the kingdom thousands of its most skillful workmen, the manufactures of France had before the Revolution come into full bloom. In the finer woolen and cotton goods, in silk and satin fabrics of all sorts, in choice pottery and porcelain, in manufactures of iron, steel, and copper, they had again taken their old place upon the Continent. All the previous changes had, at the worst, done no more than to inflict a momentary check on this highly developed system of manufactures; but what the bigotry of Louis XIV and the shiftlessness of Louis XV could not do in nearly a century was accomplished by this tampering with the currency in a few months. One manufactory after another stopped. At one town, Lodòve, five thousand workmen were discharged from the cloth

---

2 See also De Goncourt, Société Française, for other explanations.

3 See Les Révolutions de Paris, vol. ii. p 216.

4 See Challamelo. Les Français sons la Révolution; also Senior, On Some Effects of Paper Money, p. 82.

5 See Buchez and Roux, vol. x, p. 216.

6 For an admirable statement and illustration of the general action of this law, see Sumner. History of American Currency, pp. 157, 158; also Jevons, on Money, p. 80.

manufactories. Every cause except the right one was assigned for this. Heavy duties were put upon foreign goods. Everything that tariffs and custom-houses could do was done. Still the great manufactories of Normandy were closed, those of the rest of the kingdom speedily followed, and past numbers of workmen in all parts of the country were thrown out of employment.[7] Nor was this the ease alone in regard to home demand. The foreign demand, which had been at first stimulated, soon fell off. In no way can this be better stated than by one of the most thoughtful historians of modern times: "It is true that at first the assignats gave the same impulse to business in the city as in the country, but the apparent improvement had no firm foundation even in the towns. Whenever a great quantity of paper money is suddenly issued we invariably see a rapid increase of trade. The great quantity of the circulating medium sets in motion all the energies of commerce and manufactures; capital for investment is more easily found than usual, and trade perpetually receives fresh nutriment. If this paper represents real credit, founded upon order and legal security, from which it can derive a firm and lasting value, such a movement may be the starting point of a great and widely extended prosperity, as, for instance, the most splendid improvements in English agriculture were undoubtedly owing to the emancipation of the country bankers. If, on the contrary, the new paper is of precarious value, as was clearly seen to be the case with the French assignats as early as February, 1791, it can have no lasting, beneficial fruits. For the moment, perhaps, business receives an impulse, all the more violent because every one endeavors to invest his doubtful paper in buildings, machines, and goods, which under all circumstances retain some intrinsic value. Such a movement was witnessed in France in 1791, and from every quarter there came satisfactory reports of the activity of manufactures.

"But, for the moment, the French manufacturers derived great advantage from this state of things. As their products could be so cheaply paid for, orders poured in from foreign countries to such a degree that it was often difficult for the manufacturers to satisfy their customers. It is easy to see that prosperity of this kind must very soon find its limit. ... When a further fall in the assignats took place it would necessarily collapse at once, and be succeeded by a crisis all the more destructive the more deeply men had engaged in speculation under the influence of the first favorable prospects."[8]

Thus came a collapse in manufacturing and commerce, just as it had come before in France; just as it came afterward in Austria, Russia, America, and in all other countries where men have tried to build up prosperity on irredeemable paper.[9]

All this breaking down of the manufactures and commerce of the nation made fearful inroads on the greater fortunes; but upon the lesser fortunes, and the little accumulated properties of the masses of the nation who relied upon their labor, it pressed with intense severity.

Still another difficulty appeared. There had come a complete uncertainty as to the future. In the spring of 1791 no one knew whether a piece of paper money representing a hundred francs would, a month later, have a purchasing power of a hundred francs, or ninety francs, or eighty, or sixty. The result was that capitalists feared to embark their means in business. Enterprise received a mortal blow. Demand for labor was still further diminished; and here came an additional cause of misery. By this uncertainty all far-reaching undertakings were killed. The business of France dwindled into a mere living from hand to mouth. This state of things, too, while it bore heavily against the interests of the moneyed classes, was still more ruinous to those in more moderate and, most of all, to those in straitened circumstances. "With the masses of the people, the purchase of every article of supply became a speculation—a speculation in which the professional speculator had an immense

---

7 See De Goncourt, Société Française, p. 214.

8 See Von Sybel, History of the French Revolution, vol. i, pp. 281, 283.

9 For proofs that issues of irredeemable paper at first stimulated manufactures and commerce in Austria, and afterward ruined them, see Storch's Économie Politique, vol iv. p 223, note; and for the same effect produced by the same causes in Russia, see ibid , end of vol. iv. For the same effects in America. see Sumner's History of American Curieney. For general statement of effect of inconvertible issues on foreign exchanges, see MeLeod on Banking, p. 186.

advantage over the ordinary buyer. Says the most brilliant of apologists for French revolutionary statesmanship, "Commerce was dead; betting took its place."[10]

Nor was there any compensating advantage to the mercantile classes. The merchant was forced to add to his ordinary profit a sum sufficient to cover probable or possible fluctuations in value. And while prices of products thus went higher, the wages of labor, owing to the number of workmen who were thrown out of employ, went lower.

But these evils, though very great, were small compared to those far more deep-seated signs of disease which now showed themselves throughout the country. The first of these was the *obliteration of thrift* in the minds of the French people. The French are naturally a thrifty people; but, with such masses of money and with such uncertainty as to its future value, the ordinary motives for saving and care diminished, and a loose luxury spread throughout the country. A still worse outgrowth of this feeling was the increase of speculation and gambling. With the plethora of paper currency in 1791 appeared the first evidences of that cancerous disease which always follows large issues of irredeemable currency—a disease more permanently injurious to a nation than war, pestilence, or famine. At the great metropolitan centers grew a luxurious, speculative, stock-gambling body, which, like a malignant tumor, absorbed into itself the strength of the nation, and sent out its cancerous fibers to the remotest hamlets. At these city centers abundant wealth was piled up. In the country at large there grew dislike of steady labor and contempt for moderate gains and simple living. In a pamphlet published May, 1791, we see how, in regard to this also, public opinion was blinded. The author calls attention to the frightful increase of gambling in values of all sorts in these words: "What shall I say of the stockjobbing, as frightful as it is scandalous, which goes on in Paris under the very eyes of our legislators, a most terrible evil, yet under the present circumstances a necessary evil." The author also speaks of these stock gamblers as using the most insidious means to influence public opinion in favor of their measures; and then proposes, seriously, a change in various matters of detail, thinking that this would prove a sufficient remedy for an evil which had its roots far down in the whole system of irredeemable currency.[11] As well might a physician prescribe a pimple wash for a diseased liver.

Now began to be seen more plainly some of the many ways in which an inflation policy robs the working clashes. As these knots of plotting schemers at the city centers were becoming bloated with sudden wealth, the producing classes of the country, though having in their possession more and more currency, grew lean. In the schemes and speculations put forth by stockjobbers, and stimulated by the printing of more currency, multitudes of small fortunes throughout the country were absorbed, and, while, these many small fortunes were lost, a few swollen fortunes were rapidly aggregated in the city centers. This crippled a large class in the country districts, which had employed a great number of workmen; and created a small class, in the cities, which employed a great number of lackeys.

In the cities now arose a luxury and license which is a greater evil even than the plundering which ministers to it. In the country the gambling spirit spread more and more. Says the same thoughtful historian whom I have already quoted: "What a prospect for a country when its rural population was changed into a great band of gamblers!"[12]

Nor was this reckless and corrupt spirit confined to business men; it began to break out in official circles, and public men who, a few years before, had been pure in motive and above all probability of taint, became luxurious, reckless, cynical, and finally corrupt. Mirabeau himself, who, not many months before, had risked imprisonment and even death to establish constitutional government, was now—at this very time—secretly receiving heavy bribes: when at the downfall of the monarchy, a few years later, the famous iron chest of the Tuileries was opened, there were found evidences that, in this

---

10 See Louis Blanc, Histoire de la Révolution Française, tome xii, p. 113.

11 See Extrait du Registre des Deliberations de la Section de la Bibliothèque, May 3, 1791, pp. 4, 5.

12 Von Sybel, vol, i. p 273

carnival of inflation and corruption, Mirabeau himself had been a regularly paid servant of the court.[13] The artful plundering of the people at large was bad enough, but worse still was this growing corruption in official and legislative circles. Oat of the speculating and gambling of the inflation period grew luxury, and out of this grew corruption. It grew as naturally as a fungus on a muck heap. It was first felt in business operations, but soon began to be seen in the legislative body and in journalism. Mirabeau was by on means the only example. Such members of the legislative body as Jullien, of Toulouse, Delaunay, of Angers, Fabre d'Eglantine, and their disciples, were among the most noxious of those conspiring by legislative action to raise and depress securities for stockjobbing purposes. Bribery of legislators followed as a matter of course. Delaunay, Jullien, and Chabot, accepted a bribe of five hundred thousand francs for aiding legislation calculated to promote the purposes of certain stockjobbers. It is some comfort to know that nearly all concerned lost their heads for it.[14]

It is true that the number of these corrupt legislators was small, far less than alarmists led the nation to suppose, but there were enough to cause widespread distrust, cynicism, and want of faith in any patriotism or any virtue.

Even worse than this was the breaking down of morals in the country at large, resulting from the sudden building up of ostentatious wealth in a few large cities, and the gambling, speculative spirit fostered in the small towns and rural districts.

Yet even a more openly disgraceful result of this paper money was to come, and this was the decay of any true sense of national honor or good faith. The patriotism which the fear of the absolute monarchy, the machinations of a court party, the menaces of the army, and the threats of all monarchical Europe, had been unable to shake, was gradually disintegrated by this same stockjobbing, speculative habit fostered by the new currency. At the outset, in the discussions preliminary to the first issue of paper money, Mirabeau and others who had favored it had insisted that patriotism, as well as an enlightened self-interest, would lead the people to keep up the value of paper money. The very opposite of this was now found to be the case. There now appeared, as another outgrowth of this disease, what has always been seen under similar circumstances. It is a result of previous evils and a cause of future evils. This outgrowth was the creation of a great debtor class in the nation, directly interested in the depreciation of the currency in which their debts were to be paid. The nucleus of this debtor class was formed by those who had purchased the church lands from the Government. Only small payments down had been required, and the remainder was to be paid in small installments spread over much time: an indebtedness had thus been created, by a large number of people, to the amount of hundreds of millions. This large body of debtors, of course, soon saw that their interest was to depreciate the currency in which their debts were to be paid; and soon they were joined by a far more influential class; by that class whose speculative tendencies had been stimulated by the abundance of paper money, and who had gone largely into debt, looking for a rise in nominal values. Soon demagogues of the viler sort in the political clubs began to pander to this debtor class; soon important members of this debtor class were to be found intriguing in the Assembly—often on the seats of the Assembly and in places of public trust. Before long, the debtor class became a powerful body, extending through all ranks of society. From the stock gambler who sat in the Assembly to the small land speculator in the rural districts; from the sleek inventor of *canards* on the Paris Exchange to the lying stockjobber in the market town, all pressed vigorously for new issues of paper; all were able, apparently, to demonstrate to the people that in new issues of paper lay the only chance for national prosperity.

---

13 For general account, see Thiprs's Revolution chapter xiv; also Laeretelle, vol. viii, p. 109: also Memoirs of Mallet Du Pan. For a good account of the intrigues between the court and Mirabeau, and of the prices paid him, see Reeve, Democracy and Monarchy in France, vol. i, pp. 213–220 For a very sinking caricature published after the iron chest in the Tuileries was opened, and the evidence of bribery of Mirabcnu revealed, see Cliallamel, Musée de la Révolution Française, vol. i. p. 341. Minibeau is represented as a skeleton sitting on a pile of letters, holding the French crown in one hand and a purse of gold in the other.

14 Thiers, chapter ix.

This great debtor class, relying on the multitude who could be approached by superficial arguments, soon gained control. Strange as it may seem, to those who have not watched the same causes at work at a previous period in France, and at various periods in other countries, while every issue of paper money really made matters worse, a superstition steadily gained ground among the people at large that, if only *enough* paper money were issued and more cunningly handled, the poor would be made rich. Henceforth all opposition was futile. In December, 1791, a report was made in the Assembly in favor of a fourth great issue of three hundred millions more of paper money. In regard to this report, Chambon says that more money is needed, but asks, "Will you, in a moment when stockjobbing is carried on with such fury, give it new power by adding so much more money to the circulation?" But such high considerations were now little regarded. Dorisy declares that "there is not enough money yet in circulation; that, if there were more, the sales of national lands would be more rapid." And the official report of his speech declares that these words were applauded.

Dorisy declares that the Government lands are worth at least thirty-five hundred million francs, and asks: "Why should members ascend the tribune and disquiet France? Fear nothing; your currency reposes upon a sound mortgage." Then follows a glorification of the patriotism of the French people, which, he asserts, will carry the nation through all its difficulties.

Becquet follows, declaring that the "circulation is becoming more rare every day."

On December 17, 1791, a new issue was ordered of three hundred millions more, making in all twenty-one hundred millions authorized. Coupled with this was the declaration that the total amount of circulation should never reach more than sixteen hundred millions. What such limitations were worth may be judged from the fact that not only had the declaration made hardly a year before, limiting the amount in circulation to twelve hundred millions, been violated, but the declaration, made hardly a *month* before, in which the Assembly had as solemnly limited the amount of circulation to fourteen hundred millions, had also been repudiated. The

evils which we have already seen arising from the earlier issues were now aggravated.

But the most curious thing evolved out of all this chaos was a *new system of political economy*. In the speeches about this time, we begin to find it declared that, after all, a depreciated currency is a blessing; that gold and silver form an unsatisfactory standard for measuring values; that it is a good thing to have a currency that will not go out of the kingdom, and which separates France from other nations; that thus shall manufactures be encouraged; that commerce with other nations is a curse, and every hindrance to it a blessing; that the laws of political economy, however applicable in other times, are not applicable to this particular time, and, however operative in other nations, are not operative in France; that the ordinary rules of political economy are perhaps suited to the minions of despotism, but not to the free and enlightened inhabitants of France at the close of the eighteenth century; that the whole present state of things, so far from being an evil, is a blessing. All these ideas, and others quite as striking, are brought to the surface in the debates on the various new issues.[15]

Within four months comes another report to the Assembly as ingenious as those preceding. It declares: "Your committee are thoroughly persuaded that the amount of circulating medium before the Revolution was greater than that of the assignats to-day; but then the money circulated slowly, and now it passes rapidly, so that one thousand million assignats do the work of two thousand millions of specie." The report foretells further increase in prices, but by some curious jugglery reaches a conclusion favorable to further inflation.

The result was that on April 30, 1792, came the fifth great issue of paper money, amounting to three hundred millions; and at about the same time Cambon sneered ominously at public creditors as "rich people, old financiers, and bankers." Soon payment was suspended on dues to public creditors for all amounts exceeding ten thousand francs.

15 See especially Discours de Fabre d'Eglantme, in Momteur for August 11, 1793; also debate in Moniteur of September 15, 1793; also Prudhomme's Révolutions de Paris.

This was hailed by many as a measure in the interests of the poorer classes of people, but the result was that it injured them most of all. Henceforward, until the end of this history, capital was taken from labor and locked up in all the ways that financial ingenuity could devise. All that saved thousands of laborers in France from starvation was that they were drafted off into the army and sent to be killed on foreign battlefields.

In February, 1792, assignats were over thirty per cent below par.[16]

On the last day of July, 1792, came another brilliant report from Fouquet, showing that the total amount already issued was about twenty-four hundred millions, but claiming that the national lands were worth a little more than this sum. Though it was easy for any shrewd mind to find out the fallacy of this, a decree was passed issuing three hundred millions more. By this the prices of everything were again enhanced save one thing, and that one thing was *labor*. Strange as it may at first appear, while all products had been raised enormously In price by the depreciation of the currency, the stoppage of so many manufactories, and the withdrawal of capital, caused wages in the summer of 1792, after all the inflation, to be as small as they had been four years before—namely, fifteen sous per day.[17] No more striking example can be seen of the truth uttered by Daniel Webster, that "of all the contrivances for cheating the laboring class of mankind, none has been more effectual than that which deludes them with paper money."

Issue after issue followed at intervals of a few months until on December 14, 1792, we have an official statement to the effect that thirty-four hundred millions had been put forth, of which six hundred millions had been burned, leaving in circulation twenty-eight hundred millions. When it is remembered that there was little business to do, and that the purchasing power of the *franc*, when judged by the staple products of the country, was about equal to half the present purchasing power of our own dollar,

it will be seen into what evils France had drifted.[18] As this mania for paper ran its course, even the sous, obtained by melting down the church bells, appear to have been driven out of circulation; parchment money from twenty sous to five was issued, and at last bills of one sou, and even of half a sou, were put in circulation.[19]

But now another source of wealth opens to the nation. There comes a confiscation of the large estates of nobles and landed proprietors who had fled the country. An estimate in 1793 makes the value of these estates three billion francs. As a consequence, the issues of paper money were continued in increased amounts, on the old theory that they were guaranteed by the solemn pledge of these lands belonging to the state. Early in 1793 the consequences of these overissues began to be more painfully evident to the people at large. Articles of common consumption became enormously dear, and the price was constantly rising. Orators in the clubs, local meetings, and elsewhere, endeavored to enlighten people by assigning every reason save the true one. They declaimed against the corruption of the ministry, the want of patriotism among the moderates, the intrigues of the emigrant nobles, the hard-heartedness of the rich, the monopolizing spirit of the merchants, the perversity of the shop keepers, and named these as causes of the difficulty.[20]

The washerwomen of Paris, finding soap so dear that they could scarcely purchase it, insisted that all the merchants who were endeavoring to save something of their little property by refusing to sell their goods for the worthless currency with which France was flooded, should be punished with death; the women of the markets, and the hangerson of the Jacobin Club, called loudly for a law "to equalize the value of paper money and silver coin." It was

---

16   Von Sybel, vol. i, pp. 509, 510.
17   See Von Sybel, vol. i, p. 515; also Villeneuve Bargemont, Histoire de l'Économie Politique, vol. ii, p. 213.

18   As to purchasing power of money at that time, see Arthur Young, Travels in Prance during the Years 1787, 1788, and 1789.
19   For notices of this small currency, with examples of satirical verses written upon it, see Challamel, Les Français sous la Révolution," pp. 307, 308. See also Mercier, Le Nouveau Paris, edition of 1800, chapter cev, entitled Parchemin Monnoie.
20   For Chanmette's brilliant argument to this effect, see Thiers, Shoberl's translation, published by Bentley, vol. in, p. 248.

also demanded that a tax be laid especially on the rich, to the amount of four hundred million francs, to buy bread; and the National Convention, which had now become the legislative body of the French Republic, ordered that such a tax be levied. Marat declared loudly that the people, by hanging a few shopkeepers and plundering their stores, could easily remove the trouble. The result was, that on the 28th of February, 1793, at eight o'clock in the evening, a mob of men and women in disguise began plundering the stores and shops of Paris. At first they demanded only bread; soon they insisted on coffee and rice and sugar; at last they seized everything on which they could lay their hands—cloth, clothing, groceries, and luxuries of every kind. Two hundred shops and stores were plundered. This was endured for six hours, and finally order was restored only by a grant of seven million francs to buy off the mob. The new political economy was beginning to bear its fruits. One of its minor growths appeared at the City Hall of Paris, where, in response to the complaints of the plundered merchants, Roux declared, in the midst of great applause, that "the shopkeepers were only giving back to the people what they had hitherto robbed them of."

This mob was thus bought off, but now came the most monstrous of all financial outgrowths of paper money, and yet it was an outgrowth perfectly logical. *Maximum* laws were passed—laws making the sales of goods compulsory, and fixing their price in paper money. As Von Sybel declares, "it was the most comprehensive attack on the rights of property, as far as our historical knowledge reaches, which was ever made in western Europe—an attack made in the heart of a great and civilized nation, and one which was not confined to the brains of a few idle dreamers, but practically carried out in all its terrible consequences. It was made with fiery fanaticism and unbridled passion, and yet with systematic calculation. Its originators—victorious at home and abroad—were perfectly free in their deliberations, and did not adopt their measures under the pressure of necessity or despair, but from deliberate choice. These are facts of universal significance, on which we ought to fix our attention all the more earnestly, because they have been disregarded,

although they are fraught with the most important consequences."[21]

I have said that these maximum laws were perfectly logical; they were so. Whenever any nation intrusts to its legislators the issue of a currency not based on the idea of redemption in coin, it intrusts to them the power to raise or depress the value of every article in the possession of every citizen. Louis XIV claimed that all property in France was his own, and that what private persons held was as much his as if it were in his coffers.[22] But even this falls short of the reality of the confiscating power exercised in a country where, instead of leaving values to be measured by a standard common to the whole world, they are left to be depressed or raised at the whim, caprice, or interest of a body of legislators,[23] When this power is given, the power of fixing prices is naturally included in it, as the less is included in the greater.

The first result of the *maximum* was that every means was taken to evade the fixed price imposed; the farmers brought in as little produce as they possibly could. This caused scarcity, and the people of the large cities were put on an allowance.

Tickets were issued authorizing the bearer to obtain at the maximum prices a certain amount of bread, or sugar, or soap, or wood, or coal, to cover immediate necessities.[24]

It may be said that these measures were the result of the war then going on. Nothing could be more baseless than such an objection. The war was generally successful. It was pushed mainly upon foreign soil. Numerous contributions were levied upon the

---

21 See Von Sybel, vol. iii, pp. 11, 12. For general statements of theories underlying the *maximum*, see Thiers. For a very interesting picture, by an eyewitness, of the absurdities and miseries it caused, see Mercier, Nouveau Paris, edition of 1800, chapter xhv. For summary of the Report of the Committee, with list of articles embraced under it, and for various interesting details, see Villeneuve Bargemont, Histoire de l'Économie Politique, vol. ii, pp. 213–239. For curious examples of severe penalties for very slight infringements of the law on the subject, see Louis Blanc, Histoire de la Révolution Française, tome x, p. 144.

22 See Memoirs of Louis XIV for the Instruction of the Dauphin.

23 For a simple exposition of the way in which the exercise of this power became simply confiscation of all private property in France, see Mallet Du Pan's Memoirs, London, 1852, vol. ii, p. 14.

24 See specimens of these tickets in A. D. W. Collection.

subjugated countries to support the French armies. The war was one of those of which the loss, falling apparently upon future generations, stimulates, in a sad way, trade and production in the generation in being. The main cause of these evils was the old false system of confiscating the property of an entire nation; keeping all values in fluctuation; discouraging all enterprise; paralyzing all energy; undermining sober habits; obliterating thrift; promoting extravagance and wild riot, by the issue of an irredeemable currency.

Eliminating Runaway Inflation

Lessons from The German Hyperinflation

By Thomas Humphrey

The German hyperinflation of 1923 is a classic example of what can happen when the monetary authorities let themselves be guided by false and misleading theories. In this case the fallacious theories included (1) an external shock or balance of payments theory of inflation and exchange rate depreciation, (2) a reverse causation theory of the link between money and prices, (3) the notion that the real money stock rather than the nominal money stock is the appropriate indicator of monetary ease or tightness, (4) the real bills doctrine according to which the money supply should accommodate itself to the needs of trade, and (5) the idea that the central bank can stabilize nominal market interest rates simply by pegging its discount rate at some arbitrary level.

Misleading Theories The authorities adhered to these theories to. a ludicrous degree. For example, at the height of the inflation when a postage stamp and a newspaper cost 90 billion marks and 200 billion marks respectively, and when the money supply was expanding at a rate of 1300 percent per month and 30 paper mills were working overtime just to keep the Reichsbank supplied with paper for its banknotes, the authorities were actually insisting that money growth had nothing to do with inflation. On the contrary, they blamed inflation on external nonmonetary factors and declared that money growth was the consequence not the cause of inflation. Like modern government officials who attribute our present inflation to the machinations of the OPEC cartel, they located the source of inflation in the postwar punitive actions of the Allies. More specifically, they traced a chain of causation running from reparations burdens to balance of payments deficits to exchange rate depreciation to rising import prices and thence to general price inflation to rising money demand and finally to the money stock itself. That, is, they argued that external shocks operating through the balance of payments caused the inflation, that the resulting rise in prices created a need for more money on the part of business and government to carry on the same level of real transactions, and that it was the duty of the Reichsbank to accommodate this need, a duty which it could accomplish without affecting prices. Far from seeing currency expansion as the source of inflation, they argued that it was the solution to the acute shortage of money caused by skyrocketing prices. In this connection they advanced the peculiar theory that monetary excess could not possibly be the source of German inflation since the real or price-deflated value of the German money stock was smaller than it had been before the inflation started. They failed to realize that excessive nominal money growth itself was responsible for the shrinkage in the real money stock. They did not see that inflationary monetary growth, by generating expectations of future inflation (expectations that constitute the anticipated depreciation cost of holding money) had greatly reduced the demand for money and had stimulated a corresponding rise in velocity. This inflation-induced rise in velocity had caused prices to rise faster than the nominal money stock thus producing the observed shrinkage in the real money stock (see chart on following page). This sequence of events, however, was beyond their comprehension. Hence even though the nominal money stock was several trillion times larger than at the beginning of the inflation, they argued that it was still not large enough because prices had actually risen faster than the money stock. They thought that they could prevent further shrinkage of the real money stock by increasing the nominal money stock. In so doing they succumbed to the fallacy that the policymakers can systematically control real economic variables (e.g., the real money stock) by controlling nominal economic variables (e.g., the nominal money stock).

Real Bills Doctrine   Another fallacious theory to which they adhered was the real bills or needs of trade doctrine, which says that money can never be excessive as long as it is issued against bank loans made to finance real transactions in goods and services. What they overlooked was that the demand for loans also depends on the level of prices at which those real transactions are effected. They forgot that rising prices would require an ever-growing volume of loans just to finance the same level of real transactions. Under the real bills criterion these loans would be granted and the money stock would therefore expand. In this manner price inflation

would generate the very monetary expansion necessary to sustain it and the real bills criterion would not limit the quantity of money in existence. In short, they failed to understand that the real bills criterion cannot distinguish between the price and output components of economic activity and therefore constitutes no bar to the inflationary overissue of money.

Inflationary Discount Rate Policy   They also made the mistake of pegging the discount rate at a level of 90 percent, which they regarded as constituting an appropriate degree of monetary tightness at a time when the market rate of interest on bank loans was more than 7300 percent per year. This huge interest differential of course made it extremely profitable for banks to rediscount bills with the Reichsbank and then to loan out the proceeds, thereby producing additional inflationary expansions of the money supply and further upward pressure on interest rates. If the monetary authorities recognized this, however, they said nothing about it.

Monetary Reform Measures   But I do not intend to dwell on the hyperinflation per se. Rather I wish to discuss the very successful monetary reform that ended it in a prompt and relatively painless manner— an accomplishment that seems beyond our powers today. Regarding the monetary reform the facts are as follows. On November 15, 1923 the government announced that it intended to get inflation under control. Acting quickly, it did four things.

- First, it transferred responsibility for monetary control from the Reichsbank to Dr. Hjalmar H. Schacht, the newly appointed Commissioner for the National Currency.
- Second, it issued a new currency called the Rentenmark to circulate with the old currency. The Rentenmark was declared to be equal in value to one prewar gold mark or one trillion depreciated paper marks.
- Third, it established a fixed upper limit on the amount of Rentenmarks that could be issued. According to Costantino Bresciani-Turroni,

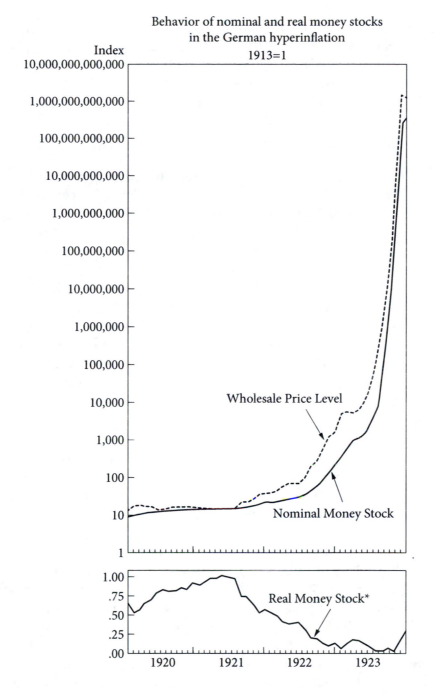

Behavior of nominal and real money stocks
in the German hyperinflation
1913=1

During the German hyperinflation the nominal money stock exploded while the real money stock, reflecting an Inflation-induced flight from cash and a corresponding rise in the circulation velocity of money, declined sharply. The real money stock fell because inflationary nominal monetary growth by generating expectations of future inflation and thereby raising the anticipated depreciation cost of holding money, reduced the demand of real cash balance and stimulated a corresponding rise in velocity. This expectations-induced rise in velocity caused price to rise faster than the nominal money stock thus producing the observed fall in the real or price-deflated money stock. Efforts to arrest this fall via faster nominal money growth only served to prolong it. Not until late 1923 when anti-inflationary monetary reform seemed imminent did the real money stock revive.

*Index of the German Money Stock (1913=1) divided by the Index of Wholesale Prices (1913=1).

Source: Frank D. Graham, **Exchange, Prices and Production in Hyperinflation: Germany, 1920–1923** (Princeton: Princeton University Press, 1930), 105–106.

perhaps the leading authority on the hyperinflation episode, this limitation was crucial to the success of the monetary reform.[1]

- Fourth, it directed the Reichsbank to stop the discounting of Treasury bills, which meant in effect that the Reichsbank would issue no more paper money for the government.

The Miracle of the Rentenmark The reform was an instant success. The new currency was in great demand and circulated at its declared gold value. Within weeks the rate of inflation, which had been raging at an annual rate of 300,000 percent, dropped to virtually zero. And this was accomplished at a cost of only 10 percent lost potential output in 1924 the year following the monetary reform.[2]

To get an idea of the magnitude of this accomplishment were it to be attempted today, we can use the late Arthur Okun's rule of thumb calculation (which he derived from evaluating simulations from six econometric models) that the cost in terms of lost output per each 1 percentage point reduction in the rate of inflation is 10 percent of a year's GNP According to Okun's 10 percent rule, it should have required a 50 percent GNP gap sustained for 600 centuries to eliminate Germany's 300,000 percent inflation rate.[3] In fact, however, the German inflation was virtually eliminated by early 1924 at the cost of only a 10 percent GNP gap.

How did they do it? How did the German authorities manage to eliminate an inflation that was infinitely worse than ours today and yet do it so quickly and painlessly? What recipe for success did they have that our authorities lack today? Most observers correctly note that the key to stopping the inflation was the eradication of inflationary expectations and the restoration of confidence in the German currency. But they offer only the vaguest of explanations as to why that confidence was so easily restored, attributing it either to a yearning of the German national spirit for monetary order and stability or to a naive belief on the part of the public that the new Rentenmark was worth one prewar gold mark simply because it was declared to be worth that much on the face of the note.

The Credibility Hypothesis There is, however, a more plausible explanation that stresses the credibility associated with the government's policy declarations. According to that explanation, when the German officials announced in November 1923 their intention to halt inflation, the public was fully convinced and accordingly swiftly revised downward its expectations of future inflation. People believed the government not only because it had placed the responsibility for stabilization in new hands but also because prior to the monetary reform it had taken decisive steps to reduce the budgetary deficits that were an immediate cause of inflationary money growth.[4] Consisting of drastic cuts in expenditures (particularly welfare relief to striking workers) and the levying of taxes in real (i.e., gold) rather than nominal terms, these measures were widely regarded as an essential prerequisite to monetary stabilization and a clear indication of the government's intention to end inflation. People also believed the government because it had not tried to mislead the public during the preceding hyperinflation. True, the officials had misunderstood the cause of the hyperinflation. But they at least had not lied to the public about the policy rule they were following at the time. On the contrary, throughout the inflationary episode the authorities candidly acknowledged that their main policy objective was to accommodate inflation with sufficient monetary growth to overcome inflation-induced shortages of money and to stabilize the real value of the money stock. In this

---

1   Costantino Bresciani-Turroni, **The Economics of Inflation** (New York: Augustus Kelley, 1968), pp. 347–348, 402.

2   Frank D. Graham, **Exchange, Prices, and Production in Hyperinflation: Germany, 1920–1923** (Princeton: Princeton University Press, 1930), p. 319.

3   The computation is Roy Webb's. See his article, "Depression or Price Controls: A Fictitious Dilemma For Anti-Inflation Policy," Federal Reserve Bank of Richmond, **Economic Review** 66 (May/June 1980), p. 4.

4   On this point see Ragnar Nurkse's comments in **The Course and Control of Inflation** (Geneva: League of Nations, 1946), pp. 22–23, 68–73. Nurkse stresses the contribution made by the fiscal reforms to the success of the stabilization of the mark. In particular, he notes that, since budget deficits were largely financed by inflationary money growth, decisive steps to reduce those deficits and bring the budget under control improved the prospects for monetary stabilization and thereby lowered inflationary expectations.

connection Reichsbank president Rudolf Havenstein even boasted of the installation of new high-speed currency printing presses that would enable money growth to keep up with skyrocketing prices.

Because the authorities had instituted budget reforms compatible with monetary stability and because they had not lied to the public about the policy rule in effect during the preceding hyper-inflation, there was ample reason for the public to believe the authorities' announced intention to change the policy rule and halt inflationary money growth. Consequently, inflationary expectations were swiftly revised to zero when the halt was announced, thereby allowing the speedy removal of inflation without large increases in lost ouput. Evidently, policy credibility was essential to the re-versal of inflationary expectations and the resulting rapid termination of inflation.

Lessons of the Monetary Reform There are at least three lessons to be learned from the monetary reform that ended the German hyperinflation. First, the task of subduing inflation is easier

- if the policymakers have established a record of credibility,
- if they accurately convey their intentions to the public, and
- if they convince the public of their resolve to stop inflation.

Unfortunately, these ingredients have been sadly lacking in many countries in recent years where anti-inflation rhetoric has been accompanied by steady and persistent increases in the basic trend rate of inflation.

Credible Policy Strategies A second lesson to be learned from the German stabilization episode is that a credible anti-inflation policy must focus on a single objective, namely the elimination of infla-tion.[5] A shifting-targets policy that focuses now on inflation, now on unemployment, now on interest rates or the foreign exchange value of the dollar or still some other objective will be largely ineffective in fighting inflation. The public, having observed the past tendency of the authorities to shift from one policy objective to another, will expect monetary restraint to be abandoned upon the first signs of eco-nomic slack as monetary policy shifts from fighting inflation to fighting unemployment. Knowing that monetary restraint will be temporary, wage and price setters will have no incentive to accept lower rates of wage and price increases when such restraint occurs. As a result, the inflation rate will respond but little to the short-lived efforts to reduce it.

The preceding should not be taken to imply that inflation is inherently resistant to all policy strategies. On the contrary, were the government to drop its shifting-targets policy strategy for one devoted solely to eliminating inflation, the inflation rate might subside rapidly once the public was convinced that a true anti-inflation policy was in force. Confronted with a new policy environment, economic agents would have an incentive to alter their wage- and price-setting behavior in a manner consistent with rapid adjustment to lower rates of inflation.

The third lesson is that we should be wary of pessimistic conclusions that inflation can only be removed at the cost of a protracted and painful recession. Those conclusions often are derived from econometric models estimated for the period when the government's shifting-targets policy was in effect. These models usually assume that economic agents will not change their wage-and price-setting strate-gies when the policy environment changes. This assumption is questionable. For as mentioned above, if the focus of monetary policy were to change from a shifting-targets strategy to one of permanently eliminating inflation, the context in which wage and price decisions are made would be drastically altered. Responding to the new policy environment, people would adjust their expectational and price-setting behavior accordingly. Consequently, inflation would be less intractable and costly to subdue than in the past and the inflation rate could be brought down more swiftly and painlessly than indicated by the econometric models. The trick of course would be in convincing the public that the policy environment had indeed changed. But this could be done if the

5 What follows draws heavily from Webb, op. cit., p. 5.

policymakers were to announce anti-inflation targets and then demonstrate that they were meeting those targets. Given a successful track record of meeting stated anti-inflation targets, policy credibility would be restored thus making it easier to get inflation under control.

Conclusion   The preceding has enumerated three lessons taught by the stabilization episode that ended the German hyperinflation. Whether modern policymakers will ever consistently apply these lessons remains to be seen. Certainly the post-World War II policy record in many countries is hardly encouraging on this score, indicating as it does a tendency for the lessons to be more often forgotten than remembered. Over the past year, however, there are signs that the authorities both at home and abroad may have started to apply the lessons and that they may have abandoned their old shifting-targets policy of responding to the most pressing short-run concerns for a new longer run policy of eliminating inflation. The current recession, bringing pressures on the policymakers to shift from fighting inflation to fighting unemployment, should reveal whether this is in fact the case. So should the ensuing recovery when the central bank undoubtedly will be called upon to accelerate money growth to keep interest rates from rising. If the authorities can resist these pressures and stick to their longer term policy of eliminating inflation they will have shown that they have indeed learned the lessons of the German hyperinflation.

REFERENCES

1. Bresciani-Turroni, Costantino. *The Economics of Inflation: A Study of Currency Depreciation in Post-War Germany* (1931). Translated by Millicent E. Sayers. With a Foreward by Lionel Robbins. New York: Augustus Kelley, 1968.

2. Graham, Frank D. *Exchange, Prices, and Production in Hyperinflation: Germany, 1920–1928.* Princeton, Princeton University Press, 1930.

3. League of Nations. *The Course and Control of Inflation: A Review of Monetary Experience in Europe After World War* I. Geneva: League of Nations, 1946.

4. Webb, Roy H. "Depression or Price Controls: A Fictitious Dilemma For Anti-Inflation Policy." *Economic Review*, Federal Reserve Bank of Richmond 66 (May/June 1980), pp. 3–6.

Inflation Data

Review of Hyperinflation

By Thomas Rustici

I n the last few decades of the 20th century, countries all over the world looked to solve their economic problems with inflation. Each of the following painfully learned the lessons of the Quantity Theory: Argentina (May 1989–March 1990); Bolivia (April 1984–September 1985); Brazil (December 1989–March 1990); Nicaragua (April 1987–March 1991); Peru (September 1988–April 1989); Poland (October 1989–January 1990); and Yugoslavia (September 1989–December 1989).[1] And these few are only a small portion of hyper-inflations of the last century! Below is a full list of hyperinflations.

---

1 Sachs, Jeffrey and Felip Larrain. *Macroeconomics in the Global Economy*. Prentice Hall, 1993: 730.

The Monetary Dynamics of Hyperinflation

By Phillip Cagan

Please see next page for table.

Table 1: Monetary Characteristics of Seven Hyperinflations*

			COUNTRY				
	AUSTRIA	GERMANY	GREECE	HUNGARY	HUNGARY	POLAND	RUSSIA
1. Approximate beginning month of hyperinflation.	Oct., 1921	Aug., 1922	Nov., 1943	Aug., 1945	Mar., 1923	Jan., 1923	Dec., 19 21
2. Approximate final month of hyperinflation.	Aug., 1922	Nov., 1923	Nov., 1944	July, 1946	Feb., 1924	Jan., 1924	Jan., 1924
3. Approximate number of months of hyperinflation.	11	16	13	12	10	11	26
4. Ratio of prices at end of final month to prices at first of beginning month.	69.9	1.02×10^{10}	4.70×10^{8}	3.81×10^{27}	44.0	699.0	1.24×10^{5}
5. Ratio of quantity of hand-to-hand currency at end of final month to quantity at first of beginning month.	19.3	7.32×10^{9}*	3.62×10^{6}	1.19×10^{25}†	17.0	395.0	3.38×10^{4}*
6. Ratio of (4) to (5).	3.62	1.40	130.0	320.0	2.59	1.77	3.67
7. Average rate of rise in prices (percentage per month)‡	47.1	322.0	365.0	19,800	46.0	81.4	57.0
8. Average rate of rise in quantity of hand-to-hand currency (percentage per month) §	30.9	314.0	220.0	12,200†	32.7	72.2	49.3
9. Ratio of (7) to (8).	1.52	1.03	1.66	1.62	1.41	1.13	1.16
10. Month of maximum rise in prices.	Aug., 1922	Oct., 1923	Nov., 1944	July, 1946	July, 1923	Oct., 1923	Jan., 1924
11. Maximum monthly rise in prices (percentage per month).	134.0	32.4×10^{3}Π	85.5×10^{5}#	41.9×10^{15}	98.0	275.0	213.0
12. Change in quantity of hand-to-hand currency in month of maximum change in prices (percentage per month).	72.0	1.30×10^{3}**	73.9×10^{3}#	1.03×10^{15}	46.0	106.0	87.0
13. Ratio of (11) to (12).	1.86	24.9	1,160	40.7	2.13	2.59	2.45
14. Month in which real value of hand-to-hand currency was at a minimum.	Aug., 1922	Oct., 1923	Nov., 1944	July, 1946	Feb., 1924	Nov., 1923	Jan., 1924
15. Minimum end-of-month ratio of real value of hand-to-hand currency to value at first of beginning month.	0.35	0.030††	0.0069‡‡	0.0031†	0.39	0.34	0.27

* All rates and ratios have three significant figures except those in row 15, which have two. For sources see Appendix B (pp. 96–117).

† Includes bank deposits.

‡ The value of x that sets $(1 + \dagger x/100\dagger)^t$ equal to the rise in the index of prices (row 4), where t is the number of months of hyperinflation (row 3).

§ The value of x that sets $(1 + \dagger x/100\dagger)^t$ equal to the rise in the quantity of hand-to-hand currency (row 5), where t is the number of months of hyperinflation (row 3).

Π October 2 to October 30, 1923, at a percentage rate per 30 days.

October 31 to November 10, 1944, at n percentage rate per 30 days.

** September 29 to October 31, 1923, at a percentage rate per 30 days.

†† October 23, 1923.

‡‡ November 10, 1944.

World Hyperinflations

By Steve Hanke and Nicholas Krus

Please see next page for tables and data.

Table 1: The Hanke-Krus Hyperinflation Table

LOCATION	START DATE	END DATE	MONTH WITH HIGHEST INFLATION RATE	HIGHEST MONTHLY INFLATION RATE	EQUIVALENT DAILY INFLATION RATE	TIME REQUIRED FOR PRICES TO DOUBLE	CURRENCY	TYPE OF PRICE INDEX
Hungary[1]	Aug. 1945	Jul. 1946	Jul. 1946	4.19×10^{16}%	207%	15.0 hours	Pengő	Consumer
Zimbabwe[2]	Mar. 2007	Mid-Nov. 2008	Mid-Nov. 2008	7.96×10^{10}%	98.0%	24.7 hours	Dollar	Implied Exchange Rate*
Yugoslavia[3]	Apr. 1992	Jan. 1994	Jan. 1994	313,000,000%	64.6%	1.41 days	Dinar	Consumer
Republika Srpska†[4]	Apr. 1992	Jan. 1994	Jan. 1994	297,000,000%	64.3%	1.41 days	Dinar	Consumer
Germany[5]	Aug. 1922	Dec. 1923	Oct. 1923	29,500%	20.9%	3.70 days	Papiermark	Wholesale
Greece[6]	May. 1941	Dec. 1945	Oct. 1944	13,800%	17.9%	4.27 days	Drachma	Exchange Rate‡
China§[7]	Oct. 1947	Mid-May 1949	Apr. 1949	5,070%	14.1%	5.34 days	Yuan	Wholesale for Shanghai
Free City of Danzig[8]	Aug. 1922	Mid-Oct. 1923	Sep. 1923	2,440%	11.4%	6.52 days	German Papiermark	Exchange Rate**
Armenia[9]	Oct. 1993	Dec. 1994	Nov. 1993	438%	5.77%	12.5 days	Dram & Russian Ruble	Consumer
Turkmenistan††[10]	Jan. 1992	Nov. 1993	Nov. 1993	429%	5.71%	12.7 days	Manat	Consumer
Taiwan[11]	Aug. 1945	Sep. 1945	Aug. 1945	399%	5.50%	13.1 days	Yen	Wholesale for Taipei
Peru[12]	Jul. 1990	Aug. 1990	Aug. 1990	397%	5.49%	13.1 days	Inti	Consumer
Bosnia and Herzegovina[13]	Apr. 1992	Jun. 1993	Jun. 1992	322%	4.92%	14.6 days	Dinar	Consumer
France[14]	May 1795	Nov. 1796	Mid-Aug. 1796	304%	4.77%	15.1 days	Mandat	Exchange Rate
China[15]	Jul. 1943	Aug. 1945	Jun. 1945	302%	4.75%	15.2 days	Yuan	Wholesale for Shanghai
Ukraine[16]	Jan. 1992	Nov. 1994	Jan. 1992	285%	4.60%	15.6 days	Russian Ruble	Consumer
Poland[17]	Jan. 1923	Jan. 1924	Oct. 1923	275%	4.50%	16.0 days	Marka	Wholesale
Nicaragua[18]	Jun. 1986	Mar. 1991	Mar. 1991	261%	4.37%	16.4 days	Córdoba	Consumer
Congo (Zaire)[19]	Nov. 1993	Sep. 1994	Nov. 1993	250%	4.26%	16.8 days	Zaïre	Consumer
Russia††[20]	Jan. 1992	Jan. 1992	Jan. 1992	245%	4.22%	17.0 days	Ruble	Consumer
Bulgaria[21]	Feb. 1997	Feb. 1997	Feb. 1997	242%	4.19%	17.1 days	Lev	Consumer
Moldova[22]	Jan. 1992	Dec. 1993	Jan. 1992	240%	4.16%	17.2 days	Russian Ruble	Consumer
Russia/USSR[23]	Jan. 1922	Feb. 1924	Feb. 1924	212%	3.86%	18.5 days	Ruble	Consumer
Georgia[24]	Sep. 1993	Sep. 1994	Sep. 1994	211%	3.86%	18.6 days	Coupon	Consumer
Tajikistan††[25]	Jan. 1992	Oct. 1993	Jan. 1992	201%	3.74%	19.1 days	Russian Ruble	Consumer

Country							
Georgia[26]	Mar. 1992	Apr. 1992	198%	3.70%	19.3 days	Russian Ruble	Consumer
Argentina[27]	May 1989	Mar. 1990	197%	3.69%	19.4 days	Austral	Consumer
Bolivia[28]	Apr. 1984	Sep. 1985	183%	3.53%	20.3 days	Boliviano	Consumer
Belarus††[29]	Jan. 1992	Feb. 1992	159%	3.22%	22.2 days	Russian Ruble	Consumer
Kyrgyzstan††[30]	Jan. 1992	Jan. 1992	157%	3.20%	22.3 days	Russian Ruble	Consumer
Kazakhstan††[31]	Jan. 1992	Jan. 1992	141%	2.97%	24.0 days	Russian Ruble	Consumer
Austria[32]	Oct. 1921	Sep. 1922	129%	2.80%	25.5 days	Crown	Consumer
Bulgaria[33]	Feb. 1991	Mar. 1991	123%	2.71%	26.3 days	Lev	Consumer
Uzbekistan††[34]	Jan. 1992	Feb. 1992	118%	2.64%	27.0 days	Russian Ruble	Consumer
Azerbaijan[35]	Jan. 1992	Dec. 1994	118%	2.63%	27.0 days	Russian Ruble	Consumer
Congo (Zaïre)[36]	Oct. 1991	Nov. 1991	114%	2.57%	27.7 days	Zaïre	Consumer
Peru[37]	Sep. 1988	Sep. 1988	114%	2.57%	27.7 days	Inti	Consumer
Taiwan[38]	Oct. 1948	May 1949	108%	2.46%	28.9 days	Taipi	Wholesale for Taipei
Hungary[39]	Mar. 1923	Jul. 1924	97.9%	2.30%	30.9 days	Crown	Consumer
Chile[40]	Oct. 1973	Oct. 1973	87.6%	2.12%	33.5 days	Escudo	Consumer
Estonia††[41]	Jan. 1992	Feb. 1992	87.2%	2.11%	33.6 days	Russian Ruble	Consumer
Angola[42]	Dec. 1994	May 1996	84.1%	2.06%	34.5 days	Kwanza	Consumer
Brazil[43]	Dec. 1989	Mar. 1990	82.4%	2.02%	35.1 days	Cruzado & Cruzeiro	Consumer
Democratic Republic of Congo[44]	Aug. 1998	Aug. 1998	78.5%	1.95%	36.4 days	Franc	Consumer
Poland[45]	Oct. 1989	Jan. 1990	77.3%	1.93%	36.8 days	Zloty	Consumer
Armenia††[46]	Jan. 1992	Feb. 1992	73.1%	1.85%	38.4 days	Russian Ruble	Wholesale
Tajikistan[47]	Oct. 1995	Nov. 1995	65.2%	1.69%	42.0 days	Tajikistani Ruble	Wholesale
Latvia[48]	Jan. 1992	Jan. 1992	64.4%	1.67%	42.4 days	Russian Ruble	Consumer
Turkmenistan††[49]	Nov. 1995	Jan. 1996	62.5%	1.63%	43.4 days	Manat	Consumer
Philippines[50]	Dec. 1944	Jan. 1944	60.0%	1.58%	44.9 days	Japanese War Notes	Consumer
Yugoslavia[51]	Sep. 1989	Dec. 1989	59.7%	1.57%	45.1 days	Dinar	Consumer
Germany[52]	Jan. 1920	Jan. 1920	56.9%	1.51%	46.8 days	Papiermark	Wholesale

(Continued)

LOCATION	START DATE	END DATE	MONTH WITH HIGHEST INFLATION RATE	HIGHEST MONTHLY INFLATION RATE	EQUIVALENT DAILY INFLATION RATE	TIME REQUIRED FOR PRICES TO DOUBLE	CURRENCY	TYPE OF PRICE INDEX
Kazakhstan[53]	Nov. 1993	Nov. 1993	Nov. 1993	55.5%	1.48%	47.8 days	Tenge & Russian Ruble	Consumer
Lithuania[54]	Jan. 1992	Jan. 1992	Jan. 1992	54.0%	1.45%	48.8 days	Russian Ruble	Consumer
Belarus[55]	Aug. 1994	Aug. 1994	Aug. 1994	53.4%	1.44%	49.3 days	Belarusian Ruble	Consumer
Taiwan[56]	Feb. 1947	Feb. 1947	Feb. 1947	50.8%	1.38%	51.4 days	Taipi	Wholesale for Taipei

Source: Steve H. Hanke and Nicholas Krus (2012) "World Hyperinflations", Cato Working Paper no. 8, August 15. *Forthcoming in*: Randall Parker and Robert Whaples (eds.) (2013) *The Handbook of Major Events in Economic History*, London: Routledge Publishing. (expected publication date: Summer 2013).

Notes:

– When a country experiences periods of hyperinflation that are broken up by 12 or more consecutive months with a monthly inflation rate below 50%, the periods are defined as separate episodes of hyperinflation.

– The currency listed in the chart is the one that, in a particular location, is associated with the highest monthly rate of inflation. The currency may not have been the only one that was in circulation, in that location, during the episode.

– We are aware of one other case of hyperinflation: North Korea. We reached this conclusion after calculating inflation rates using data from the foreign exchange black market, and also by observing changes in the price of rice. Based on our estimates, this episode of hyperinflation most likely occurred from December 2009 to mid-January 2011. Using black-market exchange-rate data, and calculations based on purchasing power parity, we determined that the North Korean hyperinflation peaked in early March 2010, with a monthly rate of 496% (implying a 6.13% daily inflation rate and a price-doubling time of 11.8 days). When we used rice price data, we calculated the peak month to be mid-January 2010, with a monthly rate of 348% (implying a 5.12% daily inflation rate and a price-doubling time of 14.1 days). All of these data were obtained August 13, 2012 from Daily NK, an online newspaper that focuses on issues relating to North Korea (http://www.dailynk.com/english/market.php). We also acknowledge that our investigation was aided by reports from Good Friends USA, a Korean-American advocacy and research organization, as well as from Marcus Noland at the Peterson Institute for International Economics.

(*) The authors calculated Zimbabwe's inflation rate, from August to November 2008, using changes in the price of the stock, Old Mutual, which was traded both on the Harare and London stock exchanges. The stock prices yielded an implied exchange rate for Zimbabwe dollars, under purchasing power parity.

(†) The Republika Srpska is a Serb-majority, semi-autonomous entity within Bosnia and Herzegovina. From 1992 until early 1994, the National Bank of Republika Srpska issued its own unique currency, the Republika Srpska dinar.

(‡) Greece's inflation rate was estimated by calculating the drachma / gold sovereign exchange rate.

(§) The peak monthly inflation rate listed for China in the table differs from that presented in one of the authors' previous pieces on hyperinflation (Hanke and Kwok, 2009). This revision is based on new data from a number of sources, which were recently obtained from the Library of Congress in Washington, D.C.

(**) We calculated the Free City of Danzig's inflation rate using German inflation data. This is case because the last full month in which the German papiermark circulated in the Free City of Danzig was September 1923. Germany continued to circulate the papiermark beyond this point, and subsequently experienced its peak month of hyperinflation (October 1923).

(††) The data for many of the post-Soviet countries were only available in the World Bank's Statistical Handbook: States of the Former USSR. In this publication, the authors stated that the data should be viewed with an extra degree of caution because the statistics were taken from the corresponding official internal government source and not independently reviewed by the World Bank. However, these statistics are official and are the only source of data available for the corresponding time periods for each country.

Cross-Country Data on Inflation and Monetary Growth

By Robert J. Barro

To assess the role of money is a determinant of inflation, let's examine some data. Table 7.1 shows the experiences of 83 countries during the post-World War II period. The table reports the average growth rates of in index of consumer prices and of money, defined as hand-to-hand currency. (The results are similar for the broader monetary aggregate Ml, which includes checkable deposits. However, because of differences in the nature of financial institutions, the meaning of Ml varies more across countries than does that of currency.) The table arranges the countries in descending order with respect to their average rates of inflation. Note the following:

- The average growth rates of prices and money are positive for all countries since World War II.
- The average growth rates are typically high. For example, the median inflation rate for the 83 countries is 7.6% per year, with 23 of them exceeding 10%. For the average growth rate of currency, the median is 11.3% per year, with 57 of the countries above 10%.
- There is a broad cross-sectional range for the average growth rates of prices and money. The average inflation rates vary from "8% for Brazil and 76% for Argentina to 3% for Germany and Switzerland. The rate for the United States is 4.2%. The growth rates of currency have a comparable range, varying from 77% for Brazil and 73% for Argentina to 4% for Belgium. 5% for Switzerland, and 6% for the United States.
- The average growth rate of currency exceeds that of prices in almost all cases. That is, growing real money balances are typical in the post-World War II period. The median growth rate of real currency across the countries is 3.5% per year.
- Most significant, there is a strong positive correlation (0.97) across countries between the average rates of price change and the average rates of monetary growth.

Table 1: Annual Growth Rates of Prices, Money, and Output for 83 Countries in the Post-World War II Period (arranged by decreasing order of the inflation rate)

COUNTRY	ΔP/P	ΔM/M	ΔM/M– ΔP/P	ΔY/Y	TIME SPAN
Brazil	77.8	77.4	–0.4	5.6	1963–90
Argentina	76.0	72.8	–3.2	2.1	1952–90
Bolivia	48.0	49.0	1.0	3.3	1950–89
Peru	47.6	49.7	2.1	3-0	1960–89
Uruguay	43.1	42.4	–0.7	1.5	1960–89
Chile	42.2	47.3	–5.1	3.1	1960–90
Yugoslavia	33.7	38.7	7.0	8.7*	1961–89
Zaire	30.0	29.8	–0.2	2.4	1963–86
Israel	29.4	31.0	1.6	6.7	1950–90
Sierra Leone	21.5	20.7	–0.8	3.1	1963–88
Turkey	20.1	22.9	2.8	5.9*	1915–88
Ghana	19.3	18.6	–0.7	2.5	1950–88
Iceland	18.8	18.4	–0.4	4.3*	1950–90
Mexico	18.7	23.2	4.5	5.4*	1950–89
Somalia	17.2	21.7	4.5	—	1960–88
Colombia	13.9	18.5	4.6	4.7	1950–88
Korea (South)	12.8	22.1	9.3	7.6	1953–90
Paraguay	12.5	16.9	4.4	4.8	1952–88
Sudan	12.0	16.3	4.3	2.3*	1956–86
Costa Rica	11.5	16.5	4.7	4.6	1960–90
Ecuador	11.6	15.7	4.1	4.7	1951–89
Jamaica	11.2	15.6	4.4	1.8	1960–89
Nigeria	10.8	14.2	3.4	4.1	1955–89
Portugal	9.9	11.5	1.6	4.7	1953–86
Iran	9.9	18.5	8.6	4.7*	1959–88
Gambia	9.8	11.5	1.7	3.2*	1904–86
Guyana	9.8	13.8	4.0	–0.4*	1960–88
Greece	9.5	14.9	5.4	4.7	1953–87
Madagascar	9.5	8.8	–0.7	1.5*	1964–86
Spain	9.2	13.1	3.9	4.5	1954–90
Senegal	8.7	12.2	3.5	1.1	1967–86
Mauritius	8.6	12.7	4.1	3.9	1963–90
Dominican Republic	8.6	13.2	4.6	4.7	1950–90
Trinidad and Tobago	8.5	10.5	2.0	1.9	1960–89
Central African Republic	8.3	11.4	3.1	—	1963–89
Egypt	8.0	12.0	4.7	4.1*	1955–89
Nepal	8.0	14.4	6.4	3.1	1964–89
Venezuela	8.0	10.7	2.7	4.4	1950–90
Philippines	7.8	11.3	3.5	4.8*	1950–90
Gabon	7.6	10.0	14	5.3*	1962–87
New Zealand	7.6	6.4	–1.2	2.6	1954–89
El Salvador	7.6	8.1	0.5	3.3	1951–90

South Africa	7.5	10.1	2.6	3.7	1950–90
Cameroon	7.5	10.7	3.2	5.5*	1903–88
Ivory Coast	7.3	12.0	4.7	5.0*	1992–80
Italy	7.3	10.3	3.0	4.6	1950–90
Ireland	7.2	7.9	0.7	3.3	1950–89
India	7.2	10.7	3.5	4.2	1960–89
Pakistan	6.8	10.7	3.9	4.7	1955–80
Syria	6.7	15.0	8.3	5.3	1957–8*
Finland	6.7	8.6	1.9	1.2	1950–90
Togo	6.6	13.8	7.2	4.1*	1963–8*
United Kingdom	6.5	6.4	−0.1	2.4	1951–90
Congo	6.4	9.6	3.2	—	1951–89
Australia	6.4	8.5	2.1	3.9	1990–90
France	6.2	7.0	0.8	4.1	1950–90
Sweden	6.2	7.4	1.2	2.9	1950–90
Denmark	6.1	7.7	1.6	3.0	1950–89
Norway	6.1	6.4	0.3	3.8	1950–90
Burkina Faso	5.9	10.1	4.2	3.6*	1962–85
Sri Lanka	5.9	10.6	4.7	5.8*	1950–90
Chad	5.8	7.2	1.4	—	1960–77
Niger	5.8	9.9	4.1	3.2*	1963–89
Saudi Arabia	5.5	15.0	9.5	6.1	1968–89
Morocco	5.5	11.1	5.6	3.9	1958–80
Tunisia	5.5	11.0	5.5	6.1	1960–90
Libya	5.4	25.0	19.6	5.7*	1964–89
Guatemala	5.4	9.1	3.7	3.9	1950–89
Thailand	4.9	9.4	4.5	6.8	1955–90
Honduras	4.9	9.5	4 6	3.6	1950–90
Haiti	4.8	9.8	5.0	1.8	1953–89
Japan	4.7	11.2	6.5	6.9*	1953–90
Iraq	4.7	14.1	9.4	6.6*	1965–75
Canada	4.6	8.1	3.5	4.2	1950–90
Austria	4.5	7.1	2.6	3.9	1950–90
Cyprus	4.5	10.5	6.0	5.2	1960–90
Netherlands	4.2	6.4	2.2	3.7*	1950–89
United States	4.2	5.7	1.5	3.1*	1950–90

Money Mischief

Episodes in Monetary History

By Milton Friedman

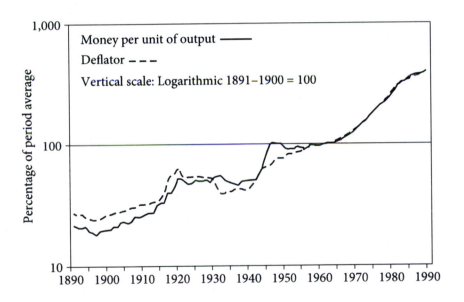

Figure 1: A Century of Money and Prices in the United States, 1891–1990

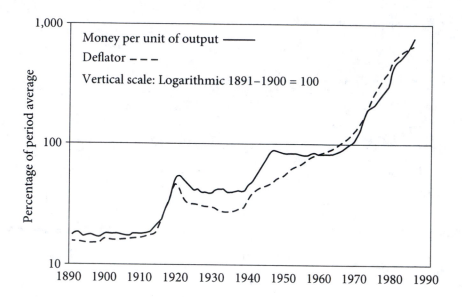

Figure 2: A Century of Money and Prices in the United Kingdom, 1891–1990

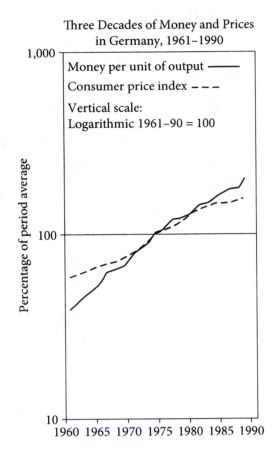

Figure 3: Three Decades of Money and Prices
in Germanny, 1961–1990

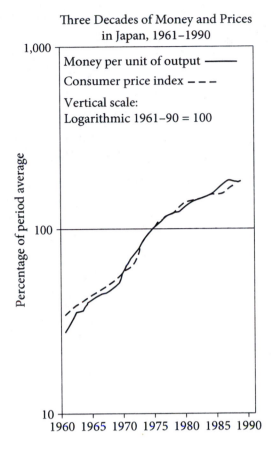

Figure 4: Three Decades of Money and Prices
in Japan, 1961–1990

Source: A Friedman

CHAPTER 6

Classical Macro Model

The Classical Macro Model

By Thomas Rustici

Classical economics had a grand and glorious tradition. The works of Carl Menger, William Stanley Jevons, and Leon Walras in the early 1870s established the principles of micro theory. Values that set prices are subjective in nature, in that they come from the mind of the valuing agent. Moreover, these values have an ordinal rank and therefore the marginal principle holds for the *next unit*. From roughly the 1870s to the early 1930s, most practitioners of the economics profession stood in this neo-classical marginal revolution in micro economics and yet still maintained the traditional classical macro world view. While the Marginal Revolution overturned the Classical Price Theory due to its reliance on the Labor Theory of value, the Classical macro model was fundamentally sound on many points. Exploring this 60 year time frame in the world of ideas will do wonders for our understanding of macro today. While many of the thinkers across this school of thought may disagree on one point or another, there is broad consistency in their acceptance to certain fundamentals. To understand the classical macro model we must get at the five basic propositions.

First and most important idea is the Quantity Theory of money, The idea that the supply of money and its value are inversely related is hugely important. The reason this idea was so critical was because it refuted the fallacies of mercantilist thinkers. Before Adam Smith's *Wealth of Nations*, it was a common mistake to believe that the stock of precious metal or *specie* (often gold and silver) was the determining factor for the nation s standard of living. Mercantilists argued that the countries with more money *per se* were the richer countries. This became an important factor that led governments on voyages of conquest to steal gold and silver from the new world.

THE QUANTITY THEORY

Sophisticated mercantilist writers committed the simple mistake in their thinking that first-year economics students are nowadays not allowed to get away with. That is, the mercantilists confused money with the goods and services being exchanged for money. In short, they were confusing nominal variables with real variables. Understood through the Quantity Theory—or, more generally, the Equation of Exchange—(MV=PQ), the mercantilists believed that the stock of money ("M") was the source of national wealth. However, the increase in quantity of money ("M") *ceteris paribus* yields only a reduction in the value of money because prices ("P") increase. Real goods and services people consume to serve their needs like quantities ("Q") of food, clothing, and shelter, not money, determine the standard of living. In other words, money is not its own purchasing power; it acquires its purchasing power from the real goods and services it can be exchanged for.

Suppose a student visits Zimbabwe today. The African nation recently suffered through a horrendous hyperinflation escalating into the hundreds of billions of percentage points! The people are destitute but have mountains of paper money with numerous zeroes printed on each sheet. How would the economics student advise the people of Zimbabwe on how to improve their life? Would they be told to add *even more* zeroes to their money? Or run the printing presses a little faster? No. These actions are exactly what destroyed the Zimbabwean economy in the first place. Prosperity only originates from production. Money cannot be the wealth of a nation, or scarcity would not exist. Inflationist governments have never printed their way to Nirvana—they simply destroyed their monetary system. Life is never easy, because reality imposes certain economic constraints. The classical thinkers fully understood this point.

THE CLASSICAL DICHOTOMY

Second after the Quantity Theory comes the Classical Dichotomy between nominal and real values, which fundamentally restates or buttresses the long-run implications of the Quantity Theory of money (i.e. that in the long run increasing the money supply changes only nominal prices). The Classical economists since the time of Adam Smith were preoccupied with issues of labor productivity and long run economic growth. It was widely understood by all these pre-Keynesian theorists that, in the short run, money could have transitory affects, often obscuring the underlying real variables; but not in the long run. While new monetary stimulus may affect real output (Q) (and its distribution) in

the short run, eventually monetary expansion shows up in higher nominal prices. The Classical orientation always focused back to the long-run truth that a nation cannot improve its standard of living by the printing press alone.

Thirdly, the **real** or **natural rate of interest** is another important reality check contained in the Classical macro models. The mercantilists not only failed to understand the Quantity Theory or its implications for nominal and real variables, they also demonstrated flawed thinking about the nature of the interest rate. Interest is an extraordinarily important price in every economy. Mercantilists explained positive interest rates of interest as resulting from a shortage or scarcity of money. In other words, interest rates were thought to be a nominal variable, not a real variable. If interest comes from a shortage of money, then it stands to reason that a progressively larger supply of money should, *ceteris paribus*, permanently drive down the interest rate to zero. The classical model openly rejects this mercantilist illusion. Interest is not the price of money; it is the price of time.

Irving Fisher's contribution was to explain how expectations of inflation and deflation factored into the interest rates; it was a tremendous advancement in economic theory. In the short run, money can affect the real interest rate; however, after expectations of money's changing value have formed, the world is back to the Classical Dichotomy. The real or natural rate of interest not only restates the dichotomy between nominal and real magnitudes but also restates the Quantity Theory of money. It is important for students to note that within the Classical tradition there are two schools of thought on exactly what real variable determines interest rates.

CAPITAL AND INTEREST THEORY

The Austrian theory of capital and interest begins with an understanding that *time is a scarce economic good with its own price.* Production occurs through a process using heterogeneous capital goods (factors of production) across time. Carl Menger pointed out in his 1871 *Principles of Economics* that there is a time sequence in the transformation of goods from factors of production to final consumer goods. Factor prices are derived from the demand for final consumer goods that directly serve human needs. Menger points out the production process takes time:

> "However, short the time period lying between the various phases of this process may often appear (and progress in technology and in the means of transport tend to corresponding goods of any lower order by a mere wave of a hand." (Menger 1871)

Production and the corresponding creation of "factor income" occur over time as goods for future sale to consumers are transformed step by step. Consumers must wait for the finalJorder goods to ultimately serve their needs. Look at a simple loaf of bread. A loaf of bread does not magically appear on the grocer s shelf. Before it can be bought as "bread," a long time period of production will have passed. Farmer Jones plants wheat, and he waits 6 months for it to grow. After the harvest, the mill grinds wheat into flour. Eventually, the flour is transported to the bakery and turned into bread. The timeJdistance of intermediate goods away from their ultimate ability to satisfy consumer needs means they are less valuable than consumption goods that are readily available. The rate of interest, therefore, can be explained with the same framework as all other prices. *Interest is a subjective time value.* The interest rate is the marginal value individuals in the aggregate place on time. As Eugen von Bohm Bawerk comments:

> "I think it justifiable to rely on the fact, as a fact, that present goods do have a higher value than identical future goods. The crudest empirical tests of everyday life establish it beyond any question of a doubt. If you ask 1,000 persons to choose between a gift of 1,000 today, and 1,000 50 years from today, all 1,000 of them will prefer to have it today." *History and Critique of Interest Theories* p.265

Human beings always have positive rates of time preference for economic goods. This fact is universally true. The same economic good located through time is not the same good in terms of the satisfaction of our needs. This difference in value between an immediately available economic good and the exact same economic good located through a distance of time is the interest rate. By 1902, Princeton economist Frank Fetter fully articulated a Pure Time Preference Theory of interest (Quarterly Journal of Economics 1902, "*The Roundabout Process of the Interest Theory*").

People trade "time" on the capital market through financial intermediaries called banks. When our own time preferences are lower than the natural rate or real interest rate across the market, we become net lenders. When these time preferences are higher, we become net borrowers.

In 1899, Swedish economist Knut Wicksell made a major contribution to interest theory with his landmark treatise, *Interest and Prices*. Wicksell noticed that the structure of central banks can create a situation where banks often lend more real resources than savers actually deposit. This is called *net credit creation* and it starts what he termed a "cumulative process." New excess reserves lower the market s loan rate of interest. Once the new credit (not based on changes in real time preference values) gets loaned to borrowers, an inflation of nominal prices begins. In the short run, the market's rate of interest deviates from the real underlying natural rate. However, any one-shot injection of new money creation through bank reserves begins an automatic self-reversal process. In the long run, the loan rate gravitates back to the real or natural rate of interest.

A different view of interest rate theory also exists within the classical macro model. In 1899, economist John Bates Clark published a textbook entitled, *The Distribution of Wealth*. Here Professor Clark disputed Bohm Bawerk, Fetter, and Wicksell's claim that interest is the value of time. Many economists have maintained Clark's idea of capital as a homogenous "fund of value." This theory asserts bank deposits represent a pool of capital for future investment. Clark maintains there is *no waiting time* to transform capital goods (factors of production) into consumer goods. He says:

> "I have claimed that no one has to wait for his income through the so-called periods of production, so that in connection with them, this comparison between present and future does not need to be made at all. It is made only in connection with the creation of new capital."

Clark argues that production and consumption are synchronized, because today we work and today we eat (Clark p.308). So what exactly is interest if not a time-value difference? Economists within Clark's tradition, such as Frank Knight, believe capital is a *stock* or fund of value that yields a *flow* of income. The investment of capital increases efficiency and therefore productivity and output. Thus interest is the rate at which the stock of capital organically grows. Since capital (tools, equipment, machines, etc.) makes labor more productive, it will be valued as an input. *Ceteris paribus*, workers that produce more goods per unit of labor input receive more compensation in the form of higher real wages. The same would hold true in the case of capital. Its compensation or return is called interest. If a particular investment yields a rate of return greater than the interest rate, entrepreneurs take out loans to invest and profit on the differences until it is bid away.

The student should note a couple of important principles in this particular strand of Classical thinking. First, time is factored out of capital theory, which then puts the productivity of capital in the center stage of interest theory. Second, the productivity of capital is, like time, a *real* variable. Printing money does not expand the real capital base upon which the economy can grow. In fact, the very attempt to increase capital via rapid inflation leads to the effect that Fisher noted—inflationary expectations impounded into interest rates at best, and destruction of the medium exchange at worst. Thus, we return to the Classical Dichotomy and the Quantity Theory. Even though there are important differences between these contrasting traditions, both end up solidly rejecting mercantilist fallacies about money,

capital, interest rates, and the real foundations for the wealth of nations.

SAY'S LAW OF MARKETS

The fourth Classical macro proposition is Say's Law of Markets. In 1803, French economist J.B. Say refuted another major fallacy in mercantilist doctrine: the *general glut theory of depressions*. In *A Treatise on Political Economy*, Say points out that recessions and cyclical downturns are not caused by a general overproduction of *all* economic goods and services. (This would logically imply that everything is an inferior good with respect to income elasticity of demand.) For this mercantilist idea to be literally true, scarcity would have to cease to exist! Micro theory reminds us that humans do live in a world of scarcity and have an unlimited imagination for an ever-expanding set of needs and desires.

For example, too much salt can be produced (inferior good) relative to not enough oranges and iPods being produced (normal goods). However, it can never be the case that the economy so greatly overproduces all desirable goods such that it causes a recession. The idea that humans can create an economic depression by producing more wealth then they can possibly consume was emphatically rejected by all classical economists, and for good reason. The idea is absurd for this world.

Say demonstrates that production is the limit on our ability to consume things that serve our needs. Scarcity constrains supply. Exchange is also a two-way street. Every exchange is always both an act of both supply and demand. The Classicals understood that a nation's ability to consume (demand) goods was limited only by their ability to create a supply of goods. The printing presses are not a substitute for productivity. Thus, production, and the coordination of that production through the price system, is the central problem of macroeconomics—not consumption, as the mercantilists and later Keynesians will maintain.

Goods and services always ultimately pay for goods and services, *even in a monetary economy*. We are always bartering, however indirectly through money. We trade labor and other real factors of production for money, and then re-trade nominal money amounts for other real consumer goods and services. Apples may pay for oranges directly in a barter economy, and apples still pay for oranges in a monetary economy. The fundamental reality has not changed because of the institution of the medium of exchange. To reiterate: money is not its own purchasing power; rather, it acquires its value from the goods bartered by use of it. Thus, Say's law restates the prior propositions of Classical theory.

PRICE FLEXIBILITY AS A POLICY GOAL

Say's Law of Markets operates through a structure of freely moving relative prices. Given that there can always be disproportionality problems of production the movement of prices to clear markets is critical for macroeconomic coordination. The Classical economists fully understood that a macro economy is made up of micro decisions and conditions. If for any reason one market does not clear because of price frictions, short-sides of the market emerge and dead weight losses result. Some of the gains from trade are never made and some factor income is never earned. For instance, inefficiencies in the corn market (surpluses or shortages) show up negatively in all other markets (tortillas and ethanol). Thus, Say's law connects micro to system wide macro.

For the whole of the Classical tradition, anything that created rigidity of prices, wages, and interest rates was looked upon with great suspicion. Shortages and surpluses cause more potential problems than just for their particular market. The fifth Classical macro proposition was that it was a *policy goal* that prices be fluid or allowed to be flexible. Classical economists often rejected price-fixing schemes by government, monopolies in production, labor union cartels, minimum wage laws, etc. These types of government-induced interventions would make price structures rigid and keep markets from clearing at equilibrium levels. The Classicals *did not assume* that prices wehre always instantly flexible—they argued that it was *desirable* that they be so.

Real and Nominal Prices

The Classical Macro Paradigm

By Thomas Rustici

The works in this chapter apply the fundamentals of Classical macro modeling in economics. There are five basic pieces in the Classical, or pre-Keynesian, school of thought. The essays in these chapters are chosen to highlight these various concepts and how they were integrated into a coherent structure of thought. The general Classical model includes the Quantity Theory of money, the Classical Dichotomy between nominal and real magnitudes, the real or natural rate of interest (as opposed to a monetary theory of interest), Say's Law of Markets, and price flexibility as a *policy goal.*

It is imperative that this section of the book be carefully examined before proceeding into Volume II of this anthology. To understand the Keynesian break from the classical tradition it is critical to actually read the writings of the classical thinkers, rather than passively accepting the routine caricature of their ideas. The editors believe that the Classical macro model exhibits logical consistency, a robust nature, and is much more attuned to the empirical evidence than the modeling and predictions of the Keynesian tradition.

Essay on the Nature of Trade in General

By Richard Cantillon

OF THE INCREASE AND DECREASE IN THE QUANTITY OF HARD MONEY IN A STATE

If Mines of gold or silver be found in a State and considerable quantities of minerals drawn from them, the Proprietors of these Mines, the Undertakers, and all those who work there, will not fail to increase their expenses in proportion to the wealth and profit they make: they will also lend at interest the sums of money which they have over and above what they need to spend.

All this money, whether lent or spent, will enter into circulation and will not fail to raise the price of products and merchandise in all the channels of circulation which it enters. Increased money will bring about increased expenditure and this will cause an increase of Market prices in the highest years of exchange and gradually in the lowest.

Everybody agrees that the abundance of money or its increase in exchange, raises the price of everything. The quantity of money brought from America to Europe for the last two centuries justifies this truth by experience.

M. Locke lays it down as a fundamental maxim that the quantity of produce and merchandise in proportion to the quantity of money serves as the regulator of Market price. I have tried to elucidate his idea in the preceding Chapters: he has clearly seen that the abundance of money makes everything dear, but he has not considered how it does so. The great difficulty of this question consists in knowing in what way and in what proportion the increase of money raises prices.

I have already remarked that an acceleration or greater rapidity in circulation of money in exchange, is equivalent to an increase of actual money up to a point. I have also observed that the increase or decrease of prices in a distant Market, home or Foreign, influences the actual Market prices. On the other hand money flows in detail through so many channels that it seems impossible not to lose sight of it seeing that having been amassed to make large sums it is distributed in little rills of exchange, and then gradually accumulated again to make large payments. For these operations it is constantly necessary to change coins of gold, silver and copper according to the activity of exchange. It is also usually the case that the increase or decrease of actual money in a State is not perceived because it flows abroad, or is brought into the State, by such imperceptible means and proportions that it is impossible to know exactly the quantity which enters or leaves the State.

However all these operations pass under our eyes and everybody takes part in them. I may therefore venture to offer a few observations on the subject, even though I may not be able to give an account which is exact and precise.

I consider in general that an increase of actual money causes in a State a corresponding increase of consumption which gradually brings about increased prices.

If the increase of actual money comes from Mines of gold or silver in the State the Owner of these Mines, the Adventurers, the Smelters, Refiners, and all the other workers will increase their expenses in proportion to their gains. They will consume in their households more Meat, Wine, or Beer than before, will accustom themselves to wear better cloaths, finer linen, to have better furnished Houses and other choicer commodities. They will consequently give employment to several Mechanicks who had not so much to do before and who for the same reason will increase their expenses: all this increase of expense in Meat, Wine, Wool, etc. diminishes of necessity the share of the other inhabitants of the State who do not participate at first in the wealth of the Mines in question. The altercations of the Market, or the demand for Meat, Wine, Wool, etc. being more intense than usual, will not fail to raise their prices. These high prices will determine the Farmers to employ more Land to produce them in another year: these same Farmers will profit by this rise of prices and will increase the expenditure of their Families like the others. Those then who will suffer from this dearness and increased consumption will be first of all the Landowners, during the term of their Leases, then their Domestic Servants and all the Workmen or fixed Wage-earners who support their families on their wages. All these must diminish their expenditure in proportion to the new consumption, which will compel a large number of them to emigrate to seek a living elsewhere. The Landowners will dismiss many of them, and the rest will demand an increase of wages to enable them to live as before. It is thus, approximately, that a considerable increase of Money from the Mines increases consumption, and by diminishing the number of inhabitants entails a greater expense among those who remain.

If more money continues to be drawn from the Mines all prices will owing to this abundance rise to such a point that not only will the Landowners raise their Rents considerably when the leases expire and resume their old style of living, increasing proportionably the wages of their servants, but the Mechanics and Workmen will raise the prices of their articles so high that there will be a considerable profit in buying them from the foreigner who makes them much more cheaply. This will naturally induce several people to import many manufactured articles made in foreign countries, where they will be found very cheap: this will gradually ruin the Mechanics and Manufacturers of the State who will not be able to maintain themselves there by working at such low prices owing to the dearness of living.

When the excessive abundance of money from the Mines has diminished the inhabitants of a State, accustomed those who remain to a too large expenditure, raised the produce of the land and the labour of workmen to excessive prices, ruined the manufactures of the State by the use of foreign productions on the part of Landlords and mine workers, the money produced by the Mines will necessarily go abroad to pay for the imports: this will gradually impoverish the State and render it in some sort dependent on the Foreigner to whom it is obliged to send money every year as it is drawn from the Mines. The great circulation of Money, which was general at the beginning, ceases: poverty and misery follow and the labour of the Mines appears to be only to the advantage of those employed upon them and the Foreigners who profit thereby.

This is approximately what has happened to Spain since the discovery of the Indies. As to the Portuguese, since the discovery of the gold mines of Brazil, they have nearly always made use of foreign articles and manufactures; and it seems that they work at the Mines only for the account and advantage of foreigners. All the gold and silver which these two States extract from the Mines does not supply them in circulation with more precious metal than others. England and France have even more as a rule.

Now if the increase of money in the State proceeds from a balance of foreign trade (i.e. from sending abroad articles and manufactures in greater value and quantity than is imported and consequently receiving the surplus in money) this annual increase of money will enrich a great number of Merchants and Undertakers in the State, and will give employment to numerous Mechanicks and workmen who furnish the commodities sent to the foreigner from whom the money is drawn. This will increase gradually the consumption of these industrial inhabitants and will raise the price of Land and Labour. But the industrious who are eager to acquire property will not at first increase their expense: they will wait till they have accumulated a good sum from which they can draw an assured interest, independently of their trade. When a large number of the inhabitants have acquired considerable fortunes from this money, which enters the State regularly and annually, they will, without fail, increase their consumption and raise the price of everything. Though this dearness involves them in a greater expense than they at first contemplated they will for the most part continue so long as their capital lasts; for nothing is easier or more agreeable than to increase the family expenses, nothing more difficult or disagreeable than to retrench them.

If an annual and continuous balance has brought about in a State a considerable increase of money it will not fail to increase consumption, to raise the price of everything and even to diminish the number of inhabitants unless additional produce is drawn from abroad proportionable to the increased consumption. Moreover it is usual in States which have acquired a considerable abundance of money to draw many things from neighbouring countries where money is rare and consequently everything is cheap: but as money must be sent for this the balance of trade will become smaller. The cheapness of land and labour in the foreign countries where money is rare will naturally cause the erection of Manufactories and works similar to those of the State, but which will not at first be so perfect nor so highly valued.

In this situation the State may subsist in abundance of money, consume all its own produce and also much foreign produce and over and above all this maintain a small balance of trade against the foreigner or at least keep the balance level for many years, that is import in exchange for its work and manufactures as much money from these foreign countries as it has to send them for the commodities or products of the land it takes from them. If the State is a maritime State the facility and cheapness of its shipping for the transport of its work and manufactures into foreign countries may compensate in some sort the high price of labour caused by the too great abundance of money; so that the work and Manufactures of this State, dear though they be, will sell in foreign countries cheaper sometimes than the Manufactures of another State where Labour is less highly paid.

The cost of transport increases a good deal the prices of things sent to distant countries; but these costs are very moderate in maritime States, where there is regular shipping to all foreign ports so that Ships are nearly always found there ready to sail which take on board all cargoes confided to them at a very reasonable freight.

It is not so in States where navigation does not flourish. There it is necessary to build ships expressly for the carrying trade and this sometimes absorbs all the profit; and navigation there is always very expensive, which entirely discourages trade.

England today consumes not only the greatest part of its own small produce but also much foreign produce, such as Silks, Wines, Fruit, Linen in great quantity, etc. while she sends abroad only the produce of her Mines, her work and Manufactures for the most part, and dear though Labour be owing to the abundance of money, she does not fail to sell her articles in distant countries, owing to the advantage of her shipping, at prices as reasonable as in France where these same articles are much cheaper.

The increased quantity of money in circulation in a State may also be caused, without balance of trade, by subsidies paid to this State by foreign powers, by the expenses of several Ambassadors, or of Travellers whom political reasons or curiosity or pleasure may induce to reside there for some time, by the transfer of the property and fortune of some Families who from motives of religious liberty or other causes quit their own country to settle down in this State. In all these cases the sums which come into the State always cause an increased expense and consumption there and consequently raise the prices of all things in the channels of exchange into which money enters.

Suppose a quarter of the inhabitants of the State consume daily Meat, Wine, Beer, etc. and supply themselves frequency with Cloaths, Linen, etc. before the increase in money, but that after the increase a third or half of the inhabitants consume these same things, the prices of them will not fail to rise, and the dearness of Meat will induce several of those who formed a quarter of the State to consume less of it than usual. A Man who eats three pounds of Meat a day will manage with two pounds, but he feels the reduction, while the other half of the inhabitants who ate hardly any meat will not feel the reduction. Bread will in truth go up gradually because of this increased consumption, as I have often suggested, but it will be less dear in proportion than Meat. The increased price of Meat causes diminished consumption on the part of a small section of the People, and so is felt; but the of a small section of the people, and so is felt; but the increased price of bread diminishes the share of all the inhabitants, and so is less felt. If 100,000 extra people come to live in a State of 10 millions of inhabitants, their extra consumption of bread will amount to only 1 pound in 100 which must be subtracted from the old inhabitants; but when a man instead of 100 pounds of bread consumes 99 for his subsistence he hardly feels this reduction.

When the consumption of Meat increases the Farmers add to their pastures to get more Meat, and this diminishes the arable Land and consequently the amount of corn. But what generally causes Meat to become dearer in proportion than Bread is that ordinarily the free import of foreign corn is permitted while the import of Cattle is absolutely forbidden, as in England, or heavy import duties are imposed as in other States. This is the reason why the Rents of meadows and pastures go up in England, in the abundance of money, to three times more than the Rents of arable Land.

There is no doubt that Ambassadors, Travellers, and Families who come to settle in the State, increase consumption there and that prices rise in all the channels of exchange where money is introduced.

As to subsidies which the State has received from foreign powers, either they are hoarded for State necessities or are put into circulation. If we suppose them hoarded they do not concern my argument for I am considering only money in circulation. Hoarded money, plate, Church treasures, etc. are wealth which the State turns to service in extremity, but are of no present utility. If the State puts into circulation the subsidies in question it can only be by spending them and this will very certainly increase consumption and send up all prices. Whoever receives this money will set it in motion in the principal affair of life, which is the food, either of himself or of some other, since to this everything corresponds directly or indirectly.

CONTINUATION OF THE SAME SUBJECT

As Gold, Silver, and Copper have an intrinsic value proportionable to the Land and Labour which enter into their production at the Mines added to the cost of their importation or introduction into States which have no Mines, the quantity of money, as of all other commodities, determines its value in the bargaining of the Market against other things.

If England begins for the first time to make use of Gold, Silver, and Copper in exchanges money will be valued according to the quantity of it in circulation proportionably to its power of exchange against all other merchandise and produce, and their value will be arrived at roughly by the altercations of the Markets. On the footing of this estimation the Landowners and Undertakers will fix the wages of their Domestic Servants and Workmen at so much a day or a year, so that they and their families may be able to live on the wages they receive.

Suppose now that the residence of Ambassadors and foreign travellers in England have introduced as much money into the circulation there as there was before; this money will at first pass into the hands of various Mechanicks, Domestic Servants, Undertakers and others who have had a share in providing the equipages, amusements, etc. of these Foreigners; the Manufacturers, Farmers, and other Undertakers will feel the effect of this increase of money which will habituate a great number of people to a larger expense than before, and this will in consequence send up Market prices. Even the children of these Undertakers and Mechanicks will embark upon new expense: in this abundance of money their Fathers will give them a little money for their petty pleasures, and with this they will buy cakes and patties, and this new quantity of money will spread itself in such a way that many who lived without handling money will now have some. Many purchases which used to be made on credit will now be made for cash, and there will therefore be greater rapidity in the circulation of money in England than there was before.

From all this I conclude that by doubling the quantity of money in a State the prices of products and merchandise are not always doubled. A River which runs and winds about in its bed will not flow with double the speed when the amount of its water is doubled.

The proportion of the dearness which the increased quantity of money brings about in the State will depend on the turn which this money will impart to consumption and circulation. Through whatever hands the money which is introduced may pass it will naturally increase the consumption; but this consumption will be more or less great according to circumstances. It will be directed more or less to certain kinds of products or merchandise according to the idea of those who acquire the money. Market prices will rise more for certain things than for others however abundant the money may be. In England the price of meat might be tripled while the price of corn went up only one fourth.

In England it is always permitted to bring in corn from foreign countries, but not cattle. For this reason however great the increase of hard money may be in England the price of corn can only be raised above the price in other countries where money is scarce by the cost and risks of importing corn from these foreign countries.

It is not the same with the price of Cattle, which will necessarily be proportioned to the quantity of money offered for Meat in proportion to the quantity of Meat and the number of Cattle bred there.

An ox weighing 800 pounds sells in Poland and Hungary for two or three ounces of silver, but commonly sells in the London Market for more than 40. Yet the bushel of flour does not sell in London for double the price in Poland and Hungary.

Increase of money only increases the price of products and merchandise by the difference of the cost of transport, when this transport is allowed. But in many cases the carriage would cost more than the thing is worth, and so timber is useless in many places. This cost of carriage is the reason why Milk, Fresh Butter, Salads, Game, etc. are almost given away in the provinces distant from the Capital.

I conclude that an increase of money circulating in a State always causes there an increase of consumption and a higher standard of expense. But the dearness caused by this money does not affect equally all the kinds of products and merchandise, proportionably to the quantity of money, unless what is added continues in the same circulation as the money before, that is to say unless those who offer in the Market one ounce of silver be the same and only ones who now offer two ounces when the amount of money in circulation is doubled in quantity, and that is hardly ever the case. I conceive that when a large surplus of money is brought into a State the new money gives a new turn to consumption and even a new speed to circulation. But it is not possible to say exactly to what extent.

FURTHER REFLECTION ON THE SAME SUBJECT

We have seen that the quantity of money circulating in a State may be increased by working the Mines which are found in it, by subsidies from foreign powers, by the immigration of Families of foreigners, by the residence of Ambassadors and Travellers, but above all by a regular and annual balance of trade from supplying merchandise to Foreigners and drawing from them at least part of the price in gold and silver. It is by this last means that a State grows most substantially, especially when its trade is accompanied and supported by ample navigation and by a considerable raw produce at home supplying the material necessary for the goods and manufactures sent abroad.

As however the continuation of this Commerce gradually introduces a great abundance of money and little by little increases consumption, and as to meet this much foreign produce must be brought in, part of the annual balance goes out to pay for it. On the other hand the habit of spending increasing the employment of labourers the prices of Manufactured goods always go up. Without fail some foreign countries endeavour to set up for themselves the same kinds of Manufactures, and so cease to buy those of the State in question; and though these new Establishments of crafts and Manufactures be not at first perfect they slacken and even prevent the exportation of those of the neighbouring State into their own country where they can be got cheaper.

Thus it is that the State begins to lose some branches of its profitable Trade: and many of its Workmen and Mechanicks who see labour fallen off leave the State to find more work in the countries with the new Manufacture. In spite of this diminution in the balance of trade the custom of importing various products will continue. The articles and Manufactures of the State having a great reputation, and the facility of navigation affording the means of sending them at little cost into distant countries, the State will for many years keep the upper hand over the new Manufactures of which we have spoken and will still maintain a small Balance of Trade, or at least

will keep it even. If however some other maritime State tries to perfect the same articles and its navigation at the same time it will owing to the cheapness of its manufactures take away several branches of trade from the State in question. In consequence this State will begin to lose its balance of trade and will be forced to send every year a part of its money abroad to pay for its importations.

Moreover, even if the State in question could keep a balance of trade in its greater abundance of money it is reasonable to suppose that this abundance will not arrive without many wealthy individuals springing up who will plunge into luxury. They will buy Pictures and Gems from the Foreigner, will procure their Silks and rare objects, and set such an example of luxury in the State that in spite of the advantage of its ordinary trade its money will flow abroad annually to pay for this luxury. This will gradually impoverish the State and cause it to pass from great power into great weakness.

When a State has arrived at the highest point of wealth (I assume always that the comparative wealth of States consists principally in the respective quantities of money which they possess) it will inevitably fall into poverty by the ordinary course of things. The too great abundance of money, which so long as it lasts forms the power of States, throws them back imperceptibly but naturally into poverty. Thus it would seem that when a State expands by trade and the abundance of money raises the price of Land and Labour, the Prince or the Legislator ought to withdraw money from circulation, keep it for emergencies, and try to retard its circulation by every means except compulsion and bad faith, so as to forestall the too great dearness of its articles and prevent the drawbacks of luxury.

But as it is not easy to discover the time opportune for this, nor to know when money has become more abundant than it ought to be for the good and preservation of the advantages of the State, the Princes and Heads of Republics, who do not concern themselves much with this sort of knowledge, attach themselves only to make use of the facility which they find through the abundance of their State revenues, to extend their power and to insult other countries on the most frivolous pretexts. And all things considered they do not perhaps so badly in working to perpetuate the glory of their reigns and administrations, and to leave monuments of their power and wealth; for since, according to the natural course of humanity, the State must collapse of itself they do but accelerate its fall a little. Nevertheless it seems that they ought to endeavour to make their power last all the time of their own administration.

It does not need a great many years to raise abundance to the highest point in a State, still fewer are needed to bring it to poverty for lack of Commerce and Manufactures. Not to speak of the power and fall of the Republic of Venice, the Hanseatic Towns, Flanders and Brabant, the Dutch Republic, etc. who have succeeded each other in the profitable branches of trade, one may say that the power of France has been on the increase only from 1646 (when Manufactures of Cloths were set up there, which were until then imported) to 1684 when a number of Protestant Undertakers and Artisans were driven out of it, and that Kingdom has done nothing but recede since this last date.

To judge of the abundance and scarcity of money in circulation, I know no better measure than the Leases and Rents of Landowners. When Land is let at high Rents it is a sign that there is plenty of Money in the State; but when Land has to be let much lower it shows, other things being equal, that Money is scarce. I have read in an État de la France that the acre of vineyard which was let in 1660 near Mantes, and therefore not far from the Capital of France, for 200 livres tournois in money of full weight, only let in 1700 for 100 livres tournois in lighter money, though the silver brought from the West Indies in the interval should naturally have sent up the price of Land in Europe.

The author [of the État] attributes this fall in Rent to defective consumption. And it seems that he had in fact observed that the consumption of Wine had diminished. But I think he has mistaken the effect for the cause. The cause was a greater rarity of money in France, and the effect of this was naturally a falling off in consumption. In this Essay I have always suggested, on the contrary, that abundant money naturally increases consumption and contributes above everything to the cultivation of Land. When

abundant money raises produce to respectable prices the inhabitants make haste to work to acquire it; but they are not in the same hurry to acquire produce or merchandise beyond what is needed for their maintenance.

It is clear that every State which has more money in circulation than its neighbours has an advantage over them so long as it maintains this abundance of money.

In the first place in all branches of trade it gives less Land and Labour than it receives: the price of Land and Labour being everywhere reckoned in money is higher in the State where money is most abundant. Thus the State in question receives sometimes the produce of two acres of Land in exchange for that of one acre, and the work of two men for that of only one. It is because of this abundance of money in circulation in London that the work of one English embroiderer costs more than that of 10 Chinese embroiderers, though the Chinese embroider much better and turn out more work in a day. In Europe one is astonished how these Indians can live, working so cheap, and how the admirable stuffs which they send us cost so little.

In the second place, the revenues of the State where money abounds, are raised more easily and in comparatively much larger amount. This gives the State, in case of war or dispute, the means to gain all sorts of advantages over its adversaries with whom money is scarce.

If of two Princes who war upon each other for the Sovereignty or Conquest of a State one have much money and the other little money but many estates which may be worth twice as much as all the money of his enemy, the first will be better able to attach to himself Generals and Officers by gifts of money than the second will be by giving twice the value in lands and estates. Grants of Land are subject to challenge and revocation and cannot be relied upon so well as the money which is received. With money munitions of war and food are bought even from the enemies of the State. Money can be given without witnesses for secret service. Lands, Produce, Merchandise would not serve for these purposes, not even jewels or diamonds, because they are easily recognised. After all it seems to me that the comparative Power and Wealth of States consist, other things being equal, in the greater or less abundance of money circulating in them *hic et nunc*.

It remains to mention two other methods of increasing the amount of money in active circulation in a State. The first is when Undertakers and private individuals borrow money from their foreign correspondents at interest, or individuals abroad send their money into the State to buy shares or Government stocks there. This often amounts to very considerable sums upon which the State must annually pay interest to these foreigners. These methods of increasing the money in the State make it more abundant there and diminish the rate of interest. By means of this money the Undertakers in the State find it possible to borrow more cheaply to set people on work and to establish Manufactories in the hope of profit. The Artisans and all those through whose hands this money passes, consume more than they would have done if they had not been employed by means of this money, which consequently increases prices just as if it belonged to the State, and through the increased consumption or expense thus caused the public revenues derived from taxes on consumption are augmented. Sums lent to the State in this way bring with them many present advantages, but the end of them is always burdensome and harmful. The State must pay the interest to the Foreigners every year, and besides this is at the mercy of the Foreigners who can always put it into difficulty when they take it into their heads to withdraw their capital. It will certainly arrive that they will want to withdraw it at the moment when the State has most need of it, as when preparations for war are in hand and a hitch is feared. The interest paid to the Foreigner is always much more considerable than the increase of public revenue which his money occasions. These loans of money are often seen to pass from one Country to another according to the confidence of investors in the States to which they are sent. But to tell the truth it most commonly happens that States loaded with these loans, who have paid heavy interest on them for many years, fall at length by bankruptcy into inability to pay the Capital. As soon as distrust is awakened the shares or Public stocks fall, the Foreign shareholders do not like to realise them at a loss and prefer to content themselves with the interest,

hoping that confidence will revive. But sometimes it never revives. In States which decline into decay the principal object of Ministers is usually to restore confidence and so attract foreign money by loans of this kind. For unless the Ministry fails to keep faith and to observe its engagements the money of the subjects will circulate without interruption. It is the money of the foreigners which has the power of increasing the circulating currency in the State.

But the resource of these borrowings which gives a present ease comes to a bad end and is a fire of straw. To revive a State it is needful to have a care to bring about the influx of an annual, a constant and a real balance of Trade, to make flourishing by Navigation the articles and manufactures which can always be sent abroad cheaper when the State is in a low condition and has a shortage of money. Merchants are first to begin to make their fortunes, then the lawyers may get part of it, the Prince and the Farmers of the Revenue get a share at the expense of these, and distribute their graces as they please. When money becomes too plentiful in the State, Luxury will instal itself and the State will fall into decay.

Such is approximately the circle which may be run by a considerable State which has both capital and industrious inhabitants. An able Minister is always able to make it recommence this round. Not many years are needed to see it tried and succeed, at least at the beginning which is its most interesting position. The increased quantity of money in circulation will be perceived in several ways which my argument does not allow me to examine now.

As for States which have not much capital and can only increase by accidents and conjuncture it is difficult to find means to make them flourish by trade. No ministers can restore the Republics of Venice and Holland to the brilliant situation from which they have fallen. But as to Italy, Spain, France, and England, however low they may be fallen, they are always capable of being raised by good administration to a high degree of power by trade alone, provided it be undertaken separately, for if all these States were equally well administered they would be great only in proportion to their respective capital and to the greater or less industry of their People.

The last method I can think of to increase the quantity of money actually circulating in a State is by Violence and Arms and this is often blended with the others, since in all Treaties of Peace it is generally provided to retain the trading rights and privileges which it has been possible to derive from them. When a State exacts contributions or makes several other States tributary to it, this is a very sure method of obtaining their money. I will not undertake to examine the methods of putting this device into practice, but will content myself with saying that all the Nations who have flourished in this way have not failed to decline, like States who have flourished through their trade. The ancient Romans were more powerful in this wise than all the other Peoples we know of. Yet these same Romans before losing an inch of the Land of their vast Estates fell into decline by Luxury and brought themselves low by the diminution of the money which had circulated among them, but which Luxury caused to pass from their great Empire into oriental countries.

So long as the luxury of the Romans (which did not begin till after the defeat of Antiochus, King of Asia about A.U.C. 564) was confined to the produce of the Land and Labour of all the vast Estates of their dominion, the circulation of money increased instead of diminishing. The Public was in possession of all the Mines of Gold, Silver, and Copper in the Empire. They had the gold Mines of Asia, Macedonia, Aquilaea and the rich mines both of gold and silver of Spain and other countries. They had several Mints where gold, silver and copper coins were struck. The consumption at Rome of all the articles and merchandise which they drew from their vast Provinces did not diminish the circulation of the currency, any more than Pictures, Statues and Jewels which they drew from them. Though the patricians laid out excessive amounts for their feasts and paid 15,000 ounces of silver for a single fish, all that did not diminish the quantity of money circulating in Rome, seeing that the tribute of the Provinces regularly brought it back, to say nothing of what Praetors and Governors brought thither by their extortions. The amounts annually extracted from the Mines merely increased the circulation at Rome during the whole reign of Augustus. Luxury was however already on a very great scale, and there was much eagerness not only for curiosities produced in the Empire but also for jewels from India, pepper and spices, and all the rarities of Arabia, and the silks which were not made with raw materials of the Empire began to be in demand there. The Money drawn from the Mines still exceeded however the sums sent out of the Empire to buy all these things. Nevertheless under Tiberius a scarcity of money was felt. That Emperor had shut up in his Treasury 2 milliards and 700 millions of sesterces. To restore abundance of circulation he had only to borrow 300 millions on the mortgage of his Estates. Caligula in less than one year spent all this treasure of Tiberius after his death, and it was then that the abundance of money in circulation was at its highest in Rome. The fury of Luxury kept on increasing. In the time of Pliny, the historian, there was exported from the Empire, as he estimated, at least 100 millions of sesterces annually. This was more than was drawn from the Mines. Under Trajan the price of Land had fallen by one-third or more, according to the younger Pliny, and money continued to decrease until the time of the Emperor Septimus Severus. It was then so scarce at Rome that the Emperor made enormous granaries, being unable to collect large treasure for his enterprises. Thus the Roman Empire fell into decline through the loss of its money before losing any of its estates. Behold what Luxury brought about and what it always will bring about in similar circumstances.

OF THE INTEREST OF MONEY AND ITS CAUSES

Just as the Prices of things are fixed in the altercations of the Market by the quantity of things offered for sale in proportion to the quantity of money offered for them, or, what comes to the same thing, by the proportionate number of Sellers and Buyers, so in the same way the Interest of Money in a State is settled by the proportionate number of Lenders and Borrowers.

Though money passes for a pledge in exchange it does not multiply itself or beget an interest in simple circulation. The needs of man seem to have introduced the usage of Interest. A man who lends his money on good security or on mortgage runs at least the risk of the ill will of the Borrower, or of expenses, lawsuits and losses. But when he lends without security he runs the risk of losing everything. For this reason needy men must in the beginning have tempted Lenders by the bait of a profit. And this profit must have been proportionate to the needs of the Borrowers and the fear and avarice of the Lenders. This seems to me the origin of Interest. But its constant usage in States seems based upon the Profits which the Undertakers can make out of it.

The Land naturally produces, aided by human Labour, 4, 10, 20, 50, 100, 150 times the amount of corn sown upon it, according to the fertility of the soil and the industry of the inhabitants. It multiplies Fruits and Cattle. The Farmer who conducts the working of it has generally two thirds of the produce, one third pays his expenses and upkeep, the other remains for the profit of his enterprise.

If the Farmer have enough capital to carry on his enterprise, if he have the needful tools and instruments, horses for ploughing, cattle to make the Land pay, etc. he will take for himself after paying all expense a third of the produce of his Farm. But if a competent Labourer who lives from day to day on his wages and has no capital, can find some one willing to lend him land or money to buy some, he will be able to give the Lender all the third rent, or third part of the produce of a Farm of which he will become the Farmer or Undertaker. However he will think his position improved since he will find his upkeep in the second rent and will become Master instead of Man. If by great oeconomy and pinching himself somewhat of his necessities he can gradually accumulate some little capital, he will have every year less to borrow, and will at last arrive at keeping the whole of his third rent.

If this new Undertaker finds means to buy corn or cattle on credit, to be paid off at a long date when he can make money by the sale of his farm produce, he will gladly pay more than the market price for ready money. The result will be the same as if he borrowed cash to buy corn for ready money, paying as interest the difference between the cash price and the price payable at a future date. But whether he borrow cash or goods there must be enough left to him for upkeep or he will become bankrupt. The risk of this is the reason why he will be required to pay 20 or 30 per cent profit or interest on the amount of money or value of the produce or merchandise lent to him.

Again, a master Hatter who has capital to carry on his manufacture of Hats, either to rent a house, buy beaver, wool, dye, etc. or to pay for the subsistence of his workmen every week, ought not only to find his upkeep in this enterprise, but also a profit like that of the Farmer who has his third part for himself. This upkeep and the profit should come from the sale of the Hats whose price ought to cover not only the materials but also the upkeep of the Hatter and his Workmen and also the profit in question.

Of the Real and Nominal Price of Commodities

or of Their Price in Labour, and Their Price in Money

By Adam Smith

Every man is rich or poor according to the degree in which he can afford to enjoy the necessaries, conveniencies, and amusements of human life.[1] But after the division of labour has once thoroughly taken place, it is but a very small part of these with which a man's own labour can supply him. The far greater part of them he must derive from the labour of other people, and he must be rich or poor according to the quantity of that labour which he can command, or which he can afford to purchase. The value of any commodity, therefore, to the person who possesses it, and who means not to use or consume it himself, but to exchange it for other commodities, is equal to the quantity of labour which it enables him to purchase or command. Labour, therefore, is the real measure of the exchangeable value of all commodities.

The real price of every thing, what every thing really costs to the man who wants to acquire it, is the toil and trouble of acquiring it. What every thing is really worth to the man who has acquired it, and who wants to dispose of it or exchange it for something else, is the toil and trouble which it can save to himself, and which

it can impose upon other people. What is bought with money or with goods is purchased by labour,[2] as much as what we acquire by the toil of our own body. That money or those goods indeed save us this toil. They contain the value of a certain quantity of labour which we exchange for what is supposed at the time to contain the value of an equal quantity. Labour was the first price, the original purchase-money that was paid for all things. It was not by gold or by silver, but by labour, that all the wealth of the world was originally purchased; and its value, to those who possess it, and who want to exchange it for some new productions, is precisely equal to the quantity of labour which it can enable them to purchase or command.

Wealth, as Mr. Hobbes says, is power.[3] But the person who either acquires, or succeeds to a great fortune, does not necessarily acquire or succeed to any political power, either civil or military. His fortune may, perhaps, afford him the means of acquiring both, but the mere possession of that fortune does not necessarily convey to him either. The power which that possession immediately and directly conveys to him, is the power of purchasing; a certain command over all the labour, or over all the produce of labour which is then in the market. His fortune is greater or less, precisely in proportion to the extent of this power; or to the quantity either of other men's labour, or, what is the same thing, of the produce of other men's labour, which it enables him to purchase or command. The exchangeable value of every thing must always be precisely equal to the extent of this power which it conveys to its owner.[4]

But though labour be the real measure of the exchangeable value of all commodities, it is not that by which their value is commonly estimated. It is often difficult to ascertain the proportion between two different quantities of labour. The time spent in two different sorts of work will not always alone determine this proportion. The different degrees of hardship endured, and of ingenuity exercised, must likewise be taken into account. There may be more labour in an hour's hard work than in two hours easy business; or in an hour's application to a trade which it cost ten years labour to learn, than in a month's industry at an ordinary and obvious employment. But it is not easy to find any accurate measure either of hardship or ingenuity. In exchanging indeed the different productions of different sorts of labour for one another, some allowance is commonly made for both. It is adjusted, however, not by any accurate measure, but by the higgling and bargaining of the market, according to that sort of rough equality which, though not exact, is sufficient for carrying on the business of common life.[5]

Every commodity besides, is more frequently exchanged for, and thereby compared with, other commodities than with labour. It is more natural therefore, to estimate its exchangeable value by the quantity of some other commodity than by that of the labour which it can purchase. The greater part of people too understand better what is meant by a quantity of a particular commodity, than by a quantity of labour. The one is a plain palpable object; the other an abstract notion, which, though it can be made sufficiently intelligible, is not altogether so natural and obvious.

But when barter ceases, and money has become the common instrument of commerce, every particular commodity is more frequently exchanged for money than for any other commodity. The butcher seldom carries his beef or his mutton to the baker, or the brewer, in order to exchange them for bread or for beer; but he carries them to the market, where he exchanges them for money, and afterwards exchanges that money for bread and for beer. The quantity of money which he gets for them regulates too the quantity of bread and beer which he can afterwards purchase. It is more natural and obvious to him, therefore, to estimate their value by the quantity of money, the commodity for which he immediately exchanges them, than by that of bread and beer, the commodities for which he can exchange them only by the intervention of another commodity; and rather to say that his butcher's meat is worth threepence or fourpence a pound, than that it is worth three or four pounds of bread, or three or four quarts of small beer. Hence it comes to pass, that the exchangeable value of every commodity is more frequently estimated by the quantity of money, than by the quantity either of labour or of any other commodity which can be had in exchange for it.

Gold and silver, however, like every other commodity, vary in their value, are sometimes cheaper and sometimes dearer, sometimes of easier and sometimes of more difficult purchase. The quantity of labour which any particular quantity of them can purchase or command, or the quantity of other goods which it will exchange for, depends always upon the fertility or barrenness of the mines which happen to be known about the time when such exchanges are made. The discovery of the abundant mines of America reduced, in the sixteenth century, the value of gold and silver in Europe to about a third of what it had been before.[6] As it cost less labour to bring those metals from the mine to the market, so when they were brought thither[7] they could purchase or command less labour; and this revolution in their value, though perhaps the greatest, is by no means the only one of which history gives some account. But as a measure of quantity, such as the natural foot, fathom, or handful, which is continually varying in its own quantity, can never be an accurate measure of the quantity of other things; so a commodity which is itself continually varying in its own value, can never be an accurate measure of the value of other commodities. Equal quantities of labour, at all times and places, may be said to be[8] of equal value to the labourer. In his ordinary state of health, strength and spirits; in the ordinary degree of his skill and dexterity,[9] he must always lay down the same portion of his ease, his liberty, and his happiness. The price which he pays must always be the same, whatever may be the quantity of goods which he receives in return for it. Of these, indeed, it may sometimes purchase a greater and sometimes a smaller quantity; but it is their value which varies, not that of the labour which purchases them. At all times and places that is dear which it is difficult to come at, or which it costs much labour to acquire; and that cheap which is to be had easily, or with very little labour. Labour alone, therefore, never varying in its own value, is alone the ultimate and real standard by which the value of all commodities can at all times and places be estimated and compared. It is their real price; money is their nominal price only.

But though equal quantities of labour are always of equal value to the labourer, yet to the person who employs him they appear sometimes to be of greater and sometimes of smaller value. He purchases them sometimes with a greater and sometimes with a smaller quantity of goods, and to him the price of labour seems to vary like that of all other things. It appears to him dear in the one case, and cheap in the other. In reality, however, it is the goods which are cheap in the one case, and dear in the other.

In this popular sense, therefore, labour, like commodities, may be said to have a real and a nominal price. Its real price may be said to consist in the quantity of the necessaries and conveniencies of life which are given for it; its nominal price, in the quantity of money. The labourer is rich or poor, is well or ill rewarded, in proportion to the real, not to the nominal price of his labour.

The distinction between the real and the nominal price of commodities and labour, is not a matter of mere speculation, but may sometimes be of considerable use in practice. The same real price is always of the same value; but on account of the variations in the value of gold and silver, the same nominal price is sometimes of very different values. When a landed estate, therefore, is sold with a reservation of a perpetual rent, if it is intended that this rent should always be of the same value, it is of importance to the family in whose favour it is reserved, that it should not consist in a particular sum of money.[10] Its value would in this case be liable to variations of two different kinds; first, to those which arise from the different quantities of gold and silver which are contained at different times in coin of the same denomination; and, secondly, to those which arise from the different values of equal quantities of gold and silver at different times.

Princes and sovereign states have frequently fancied that they had a temporary interest to diminish the quantity of pure metal contained in their coins; but they seldom have fancied that they had any to augment it. The quantity of metal contained in the coins, I believe of all nations, has, accordingly, been almost continually diminishing, and hardly ever augmenting.[11] Such variations therefore tend almost always to diminish the value of a money rent.

The discovery of the mines of America diminished the value of gold and silver in Europe. This diminution, it is commonly supposed, though I apprehend without any certain proof, is still going on gradually,[12] and is likely to continue to do so for a long time. Upon this supposition, therefore, such variations are more likely to diminish, than to augment the value of a money rent, even though it should be stipulated to be paid, not in such a quantity of coined money of such a denomination (in so many pounds sterling, for example), but in so many ounces either of pure silver, or of silver of a certain standard.

The rents which have been reserved in corn have preserved their value much better than those which have been reserved in money, even where the denomination of the coin has not been altered. By the 18th of Elizabeth[13] it was enacted, That a third of the rent of all college leases should be reserved in corn, to be paid, either in kind, or according to the current prices at the nearest public market. The money arising from this corn rent, though originally but a third of the whole, is in the present times, according to Doctor Blackstone, commonly near double of what arises from the other two-thirds.[14] The old money rents of colleges must, according to this account, have sunk almost to a fourth part of their ancient value; or are worth little more than a fourth part of the corn which they were formerly worth. But since the reign of Philip and Mary the denomination of the English coin has undergone little or no alteration, and the same number of pounds, shillings and pence have contained very nearly the same quantity of pure silver. This degradation, therefore, in the value of the money rents of colleges, has arisen altogether from the degradation in the value of silver.

When the degradation in the value of silver is combined with the diminution of the quantity of it contained in the coin of the same denomination, the loss is frequently still greater. In Scotland, where the denomination of the coin has undergone much greater alterations than it ever did in England, and in France, where it has undergone still greater than it ever did in Scotland,[15] some antient rents, originally of considerable value, have in this manner been reduced almost to nothing.

Equal quantities of labour will at distant times be purchased more nearly with equal quantities of corn, the subsistence of the labourer, than with equal quantities of gold and silver, or perhaps of any other commodity. Equal quantities of corn, therefore, will, at distant times, be more nearly of the same real value, or enable the possessor to purchase or command more nearly the same quantity of the labour of other people. They will do this, I say, more nearly than equal quantities of almost any other commodity; for even equal quantities of corn will not do it exactly. The subsistence of the labourer, or the real price of labour, as I shall endeavour to show hereafter,[16] is very different upon different occasions; more liberal in a society advancing to opulence, than in one that is standing still; and in one that is standing still, than in one that is going backwards. Every other commodity, however, will at any particular time purchase a greater or smaller quantity of labour in proportion to the quantity of subsistence which it can purchase at that time. A rent therefore reserved in corn is liable only to the variations in the quantity of labour which a certain quantity of corn can purchase. But a rent reserved in any other commodity is liable, not only to the variations in the quantity of labour which any particular quantity of corn can purchase, but to the variations in the quantity of corn which can be purchased by any particular quantity of that commodity.

Though the real value of a corn rent, it is to be observed however, varies much less from century to century than that of a money rent, it varies much more from year to year. The money price of labour, as I shall endeavour to show hereafter,[17] does not fluctuate from year to year with the money price of corn, but seems to be every where accommodated, not to the temporary or occasional, but to the average or ordinary price of that necessary of life. The average or ordinary price of corn again is regulated, as I shall likewise endeavour to show hereafter,[18] by the value of silver, by the richness or barrenness of the mines which supply the market with that metal, or by the quantity of labour which must be employed, and consequently of corn which must be consumed, in order to bring any particular quantity of silver[19] from the mine to the market. But the value of silver, though it sometimes varies greatly from century to century, seldom varies much from year to year, but frequently continues the same, or very nearly the same, for half a century or a century together. The ordinary or average money price of corn, therefore, may, during so long a period, continue the same or very nearly the same too, and along with it the money price of labour, provided, at least, the society continues, in other respects, in the same or nearly in the same condition. In the mean time the temporary and occasional price of corn may frequently be double, one year, of what it had been the year before, or fluctuate, for example, from five and twenty to fifty shillings the quarter.[20] But when corn is at the latter price, not only the nominal, but the real value of a corn rent will be double of what it is when at the former, or will command double the quantity either of labour or of the greater part of other commodities; the money price of labour, and along with it that of most other things, continuing the same during all these fluctuations.

Labour, therefore, it appears evidently, is the only universal, as well as the only accurate measure of value, or the only standard by which we can compare the values of different commodities at all times and at all places. We cannot estimate, it is allowed, the real value of different commodities from century to century by the quantities of silver which were given for them. We cannot estimate it from year to year by the quantities of corn. By the quantities of labour we can, with the greatest accuracy, estimate it both from century to century and from year to year. From century to century, corn is a better measure than silver, because, from century to century, equal quantities of corn will command the same quantity of labour more nearly than equal quantities of silver. From year to year, on the contrary, silver is a better measure than corn, because equal quantities of it will more nearly command the same quantity of labour.[21]

But though in establishing perpetual rents, or even in letting very long leases, it may be of use to distinguish between real and nominal price; it is of none in buying and selling, the more common and ordinary transactions of human life.

At the same time and place the real and the nominal price of all commodities are exactly in proportion to one another. The more or less money you get for any commodity, in the London market, for example, the more or less labour it will at that time and place enable you to purchase or command. At the same time and place, therefore, money is the exact measure of the real exchangeable value of all commodities. It is so, however, at the same time and place only.

Though at distant places, there is no regular proportion between the real and the money price of commodities, yet the merchant who carries goods from the one to the other has nothing to consider but their money price, or the difference between the quantity of silver for which he buys them, and that for which he is likely to sell them. Half an ounce of silver at Canton in China may command a greater quantity both of labour and of the necessaries and conveniencies of life, than an ounce at London. A commodity, therefore, which sells for half an ounce of silver at Canton may there be really dearer, of more real importance to the man who possesses it there, than a commodity which sells for an ounce at London is to[22] the man who possesses it at London. If a London merchant, however, can buy at Canton for half an ounce of silver, a commodity which he can afterwards sell at London for an ounce, he gains a hundred per cent by the bargain, just as much as if

an ounce of silver was at London exactly of the same value as at Canton. It is of no importance to him that half an ounce of silver at Canton would have given him the command of more labour and of a greater quantity of the necessaries and conveniencies of life than an ounce can do at London. An ounce at London will always give him the command of double the quantity of all these, which half an ounce could have done there, and this is precisely what he wants.

As it is the nominal or money price of goods, therefore, which finally determines the prudence or imprudence of all purchases and sales, and thereby regulates almost the whole business of common life in which price is concerned, we cannot wonder that it should have been so much more attended to than the real price.

In such a work as this, however, it may sometimes be of use to compare the different real values of a particular commodity at different times and places, or the different degrees of power over the labour of other people which it may, upon different occasions, have given to those who possessed it. We must in this case compare, not so much the different quantities of silver for which it was commonly sold, as the different quantities of labour which those different quantities of silver could have purchased. But the current prices of labour at distant times and places can scarce ever be known with any degree of exactness. Those of corn, though they have in few places been regularly recorded, are in general better known and have been more frequently taken notice of by historians and other writers. We must generally, therefore, content ourselves with them, not as being always exactly in the same proportion as the current prices of labour, but as being the nearest approximation which can commonly be had to that proportion. I shall hereafter have occasion to make several comparisons of this kind.[23]

In the progress of industry, commercial nations have found it convenient to coin several different metals into money; gold for larger payments, silver for purchases of moderate value, and copper, or some other coarse metal, for those of still smaller consideration. They have always, however, considered one of those metals as more peculiarly the measure of value than any of the other two; and this preference seems generally to have been given to the metal which they happened first to make use of as the instrument of commerce. Having once begun to use it as their standard, which they must have done when they had no other money, they have generally continued to do so even when the necessity was not the same.

The Romans are said to have had nothing but copper money till within five years before the first Punic war,[24] when they first began to coin silver. Copper, therefore, appears to have continued always the measure of value in that republic. At Rome all accounts appear to have been kept, and the value of all estates to have been computed, either in *Asses* or in *Sestertii*. The *As* was always the denomination of a copper coin. The word *Sestertius* signifies two *Asses* and a half. Though the *Sestertius*, therefore, was originally[25] a silver coin, its value was estimated in copper. At Rome, one who owed a great deal of money, was said to have a great deal of other people's copper.[26]

The northern nations who established themselves upon the ruins of the Roman Empire, seem to have had silver money from the first beginning of their settlements, and not to have known either gold or copper coins for several ages thereafter. There were silver coins in England in the time of the Saxons; but there was little gold coined till the time of Edward III. nor any copper till that of James I. of Great Britain. In England, therefore, and for the same reason, I believe, in all other modern nations of Europe, all accounts are kept, and the value of all goods and of all estates is generally computed in silver: and when we mean to express the amount of a person's fortune, we seldom mention the number of guineas, but the number of pounds sterling[27] which we suppose would be given for it.

Originally, in all countries, I believe a legal tender of payment could[28] be made only in the coin of that metal,[29] which was peculiarly considered as the standard or measure of value. In England, gold was not considered as a legal tender for a long time after it was coined into money. The proportion between the values of gold and silver money was not fixed by any public law or proclamation; but was left to be settled by the market. If a debtor offered payment in gold, the creditor might either reject such payment altogether, or accept of it at such a valuation of the gold as he and his debtor could agree upon. Copper is not at present a legal tender, except in the change of the smaller silver coins. In this state of things the distinction between the metal which was the standard, and that which was not the standard, was something more than a nominal distinction.

In process of time, and as people became gradually more familiar with the use of the different metals in coin, and consequently better acquainted with the proportion between their respective values, it has in most countries, I believe, been found convenient to ascertain this proportion, and to declare by a public law[30] that a guinea, for example, of such a weight and fineness, should exchange for one-and-twenty shillings, or be a legal tender for a debt of that amount.[31] In this state of things, and during the continuance of any one regulated proportion of this kind, the distinction between the metal which is the standard, and that which is not the standard, becomes little more than a nominal distinction.[32]

In consequence of any change, however, in this regulated proportion, this distinction becomes, or at least seems to become, something more than nominal again. If the regulated value of a guinea, for example, was either reduced to twenty, or raised to two-and-twenty shillings, all accounts being kept and almost all obligations for debt being expressed in silver money, the greater part of payments could in either case be made with the same quantity of silver money as before; but would require very different quantities of gold money; a greater in the one case, and a smaller in the other. Silver would appear to be more invariable in its value than gold. Silver would appear to measure the value of gold, and gold would not appear to measure the value of silver. The value of gold would seem to depend upon the quantity of silver which it would exchange for; and the value of silver would not seem to depend upon the quantity of gold which it would exchange for. This difference, however, would be altogether owing to the custom of keeping accounts, and of expressing the amount of all great and small sums rather in silver than in gold money. One of Mr. Drummond's notes for five-and-twenty or fifty guineas would, after an alteration of this kind, be still payable with five-and-twenty or fifty guineas in the same manner as before. It would, after such an alteration, be payable with the same quantity of gold as before, but with very different quantities of silver. In the payment of such a note, gold would appear to be more invariable in its value than silver. Gold would appear to measure the value of silver, and silver would not appear to measure the value of gold. If the custom of keeping accounts, and of expressing promissory notes and other obligations for money in this manner, should ever become general, gold, and not silver, would be considered as the metal which was peculiarly the standard or measure of value.

In reality, during the continuance of any one regulated proportion between the respective values of the different metals in coin, the value of the most precious metal regulates the value of the whole coin.[33] Twelve copper pence contain half a pound, avoirdupois, of copper, of not the best quality, which, before it is coined, is seldom worth sevenpence in silver. But as by the regulation twelve such pence are ordered to exchange for a shilling, they are in the market considered as worth a shilling, and a shilling can at any time be had for them. Even before the late reformation of the gold coin of Great Britain,[34] the gold, that part of it at least which circulated in London and its neighbourhood, was in general less degraded below its standard weight than the greater part of the silver. One-and-twenty worn and defaced shillings, however, were considered as equivalent to a guinea, which perhaps, indeed, was worn and defaced too, but seldom so much so. The late regulations[35] have brought the gold coin as near perhaps to its standard weight as it is possible to bring the current coin of any nation; and the order, to receive no gold at the public offices but by weight, is likely to preserve it so, as long as that order is enforced. The silver coin still continues in the same worn and degraded state as before the reformation of the gold coin. In the market, however, one-and-twenty shillings of this degraded silver coin are still considered as worth a guinea of this excellent gold coin.

The reformation of the gold coin has evidently raised the value of the silver coin which can be exchanged for it.

In the English mint a pound weight of gold is coined into forty-four guineas and a half, which, at one-and-twenty shillings the guinea, is equal to forty-six pounds fourteen shillings and six-pence. An ounce of such gold coin, therefore, is worth 3*l*. 17*s*. 10 ½*d*. in silver. In England no duty or seignorage is paid upon the coinage, and he who carries a pound weight or an ounce weight of standard gold bullion to the mint, gets back a pound weight or an ounce weight of gold in coin, without any deduction. Three pounds seventeen shillings and tenpence halfpenny an ounce, therefore, is said to be the mint price of gold in England, or the quantity of gold coin which the mint gives in return for standard gold bullion.

Before the reformation of the gold coin, the price of standard gold bullion in the market had for many years been upwards of 3*l*. 18*s*. sometimes 3*l*. 19*s*. and very frequently 4*l*. an ounce; that sum, it is probable, in the worn and degraded gold coin, seldom containing more than an ounce of standard gold. Since the reformation of the gold coin, the market price of standard gold bullion seldom exceeds 3*l*. 17*s*. 7*d*. an ounce. Before the reformation of the gold coin, the market price was always more or less above the mint price. Since that reformation, the market price has been constantly below the mint price. But that market price is the same whether it is paid in gold or in silver coin. The late reformation of the gold coin, therefore, has raised not only the value of the gold coin, but likewise that of the silver coin in proportion to gold bullion, and probably too in proportion to all other commodities; though the price of the greater part of other commodities being influenced by so many other causes, the rise in the value either of gold or silver coin in proportion to them, may not be so distinct and sensible.

In the English mint a pound weight of standard silver bullion is coined into sixty-two shillings, containing, in the same manner, a pound weight of standard silver. Five shillings and two-pence an ounce, therefore, is said to be the mint price of silver in England, or the quantity of silver coin which the mint gives in return for standard silver bullion. Before the reformation of the gold coin, the market price of standard silver bullion was, upon different occasions, five shillings and four-pence, five shillings and five-pence, five shillings and six-pence, five shillings and seven-pence, and very often five shillings and eight-pence an ounce. Five shillings and seven-pence, however, seems to have been the most common price. Since the reformation of the gold coin, the market price of standard silver bullion has fallen occasionally to five shillings and three-pence, five shillings and four-pence, and five shillings and five-pence an ounce, which last price it has scarce ever exceeded. Though the market price of silver bullion has fallen considerably since the reformation of the gold coin, it has not fallen so low as the mint price.

In the proportion between the different metals in the English coin, as copper is rated very much above its real value, so silver is rated somewhat below it. In the market of Europe, in the French coin and in the Dutch coin, an ounce of fine gold exchanges for about fourteen ounces of fine silver. In the English coin, it exchanges for about fifteen ounces, that is, for more silver than it is worth according to the common estimation of Europe.[36] But as the price of copper in bars is not, even in England, raised by the high price of copper in English coin, so the price of silver in bullion is not sunk by the low rate of silver in English coin. Silver in bullion still preserves its proper proportion to gold; for the same reason that copper in bars preserves its proper proportion to silver.[37]

Upon the reformation of the silver coin in the reign of William III. the price of silver bullion still continued to be somewhat above the mint price. Mr. Locke imputed this high price to the permission of exporting silver bullion, and to the prohibition of exporting silver coin.[38] This permission of exporting, he said, rendered the demand for silver bullion greater than the demand for silver coin. But the number of people who want silver coin for the common uses of buying and selling at home, is surely much greater than that of those who want silver bullion either for the use of exportation or for any other use. There subsists at present a like permission of exporting gold bullion, and a like prohibition of exporting gold coin; and yet the price of gold bullion has fallen below the mint price. But in the English coin silver was then, in the same manner as now, under-rated in proportion to gold; and the gold coin (which at that time too was not supposed to require any reformation) regulated then, as well as now, the real value of the whole coin. As the reformation of the silver coin did not then reduce the price of silver bullion to the mint price, it is not very probable that a like reformation will do so now.

Were the silver coin brought back as near to its standard weight as the gold, a guinea, it is probable, would, according to the present proportion, exchange for more silver in coin than it would purchase in bullion. The silver coin containing its full standard weight, there would in this case be a profit in melting it down, in order, first, to sell the bullion for gold coin, and afterwards to exchange this gold coin for silver coin to be melted down in the same manner. Some alteration in the present proportion seems to be the only method of preventing this inconveniency.

The inconveniency perhaps would be less if silver was rated in the coin as much above its proper proportion to gold as it is at present rated below it; provided it was at the same time enacted that silver should not be a legal tender for more than the change of a guinea; in the same manner as copper is not a legal tender for more than the change of a shilling. No creditor could in this case be cheated in consequence of the high valuation of silver in coin; as no creditor can at present be cheated in consequence of the high valuation of copper. The bankers only would suffer by this regulation. When a run comes upon them they sometimes endeavour to gain time by paying in six-pences, and they would be precluded by this regulation from this discreditable method of evading immediate payment. They would be obliged in consequence to keep at all times in their coffers a greater quantity of cash than at present; and though this might no doubt be a considerable inconveniency to them, it would at the same time be a considerable security to their creditors.[39]

Three pounds seventeen shillings and ten-pence halfpenny (the mint price of gold) certainly does not contain, even in our present excellent gold coin, more than an ounce of standard gold, and it may be thought, therefore, should not purchase more standard bullion. But gold in coin is more convenient than gold in bullion, and though, in England, the coinage is free, yet the gold which is carried in bullion to the mint, can seldom be returned in coin to the owner till after a delay of several weeks. In the present hurry of the mint, it could not be returned till after a delay of several months. This delay is equivalent to a small duty, and renders gold in coin somewhat more valuable than an equal quantity of gold in bullion.[40] If in the English coin silver was rated according to its proper proportion to gold, the price of silver bullion would probably fall below the mint price even without any reformation of the silver coin; the value even of the present worn and defaced silver coin being regulated by the value of the excellent gold coin for which it can be changed.

A small seignorage or duty upon the coinage of both gold and silver would probably increase still more the superiority of those metals in coin above an equal quantity of either of them in bullion. The coinage would in this case increase the value of the metal coined in proportion to the extent of this small duty; for the same reason that the fashion increases the value of plate in proportion to the price of that fashion. The superiority of coin above bullion would prevent the melting down of the coin, and would discourage its exportation. If upon any public exigency it should become necessary to export the coin, the greater part of it would soon return again of its own accord. Abroad it could sell only for its weight in bullion. At home it would buy more than that weight. There would be a profit, therefore, in bringing it home again. In France a seignorage of about eight per cent. is imposed upon the coinage,[41]

and the French coin, when exported, is said to return home again of its own accord.[42]

The occasional fluctuations in the market price of gold and silver bullion arise from the same causes as the like fluctuations in that of all other commodities. The frequent loss of those metals from various accidents by sea and by land, the continual waste of them in gilding and plating, in lace and embroidery, in the wear and tear of coin, and in that of plate;[43] require, in all countries which possess no mines of their own, a continual importation, in order to repair this loss and this waste. The merchant importers, like all other merchants, we may believe, endeavour, as well as they can, to suit their occasional importations to what, they judge, is likely to be the immediate demand. With all their attention, however, they sometimes over-do the business, and sometimes under-do it. When they import more bullion than is wanted, rather than incur the risk and trouble of exporting it again, they are sometimes willing to sell a part of it for something less than the ordinary or average price. When, on the other hand, they import less than is wanted, they get something more than this price. But when, under all those occasional fluctuations, the market price either of gold or silver bullion continues for several years together steadily and constantly, either more or less above, or more or less below the mint price: we may be assured that this steady and constant, either superiority or inferiority of price, is the effect of something in the state of the coin, which, at that time, renders a certain quantity of coin either of more value or of less value than the precise quantity of bullion which it ought to contain. The constancy and steadiness of the effect, supposes a proportionable constancy and steadiness in the cause.

The money of any particular country is, at any particular time and place, more or less an accurate measure of value according as the current coin is more or less exactly agreeable to its standard, or contains more or less exactly the precise quantity of pure gold or pure silver which it ought to contain. If in England, for example, forty-four guineas and a half contained exactly a pound weight of standard gold, or eleven ounces of fine gold and one ounce of alloy, the gold coin of England would be as accurate a measure of the actual value of goods at any particular time and place as the nature of the thing would admit. But if, by rubbing and wearing, forty-four guineas and a half generally contain less than a pound weight of standard gold; the diminution, however, being greater in some pieces than in others; the measure of value comes to be liable to the same sort of uncertainty to which all other weights and measures are commonly exposed. As it rarely happens that these are exactly agreeable to their standard, the merchant adjusts the price of his goods, as well as he can, not to what those weights and measures ought to be, but to what, upon an average, he finds by experience they actually are. In consequence of a like disorder in the coin, the price of goods comes, in the same manner, to be adjusted, not to the quantity of pure gold or silver which the coin ought to contain, but to that which, upon an average, it is found by experience it actually does contain.

By the money-price of goods, it is to be observed, I understand always the quantity of pure gold or silver for which they are sold, without any regard to the denomination of the coin. Six shillings and eight-pence, for example, in the time of Edward I., I consider as the same money-price with a pound sterling in the present times; because it contained, as nearly as we can judge, the same quantity of pure silver.

NOTES FOR THIS CHAPTER

1. ['La richesse en elle-même n'est autre chose que la nourriture, les commodités et les agréments de la vie.'—Cantillon, *Essai*, pp. 1, 2.]

2. ['Everything in the world is purchased by labour.'—Hume, 'Of Commerce,' in *Political Discourses*, 1752, p. 12.]

3. ['Also riches joined with liberality is Power, because it procureth friends and servants: without liberality not so, because in this case they defend not but expose men to envy as a prey.'—*Leviathan*, I., x.]

4. [This paragraph appears first in Additions and Corrections and ed. 3.]

5. [The absence of any reference to the lengthy discussion of this subject in chap. x. is curious.]

6. [Below, I.11.134–138.]

7. [Ed. 1 reads 'there'.]

8. [Ed. 1 reads 'Equal quantities of labour must at all times and places be'.]

9. [The words from 'In his ordinary state of health' to 'dexterity' appear first in ed. 2.]

10. ['Be above all things careful how you make any composition or agreement for any long space of years to receive a certain price of money for the corn that is due to you, although for the present it may seem a tempting bargain.'—Fleetwood, *Chronicon Preciosum*, p. 174.]

11. [Above, I.4.8–10.]

12. [Below, I.11.188–190.]

13. [C. 6, which applies to Oxford, Cambridge, Winchester and Eton, and provides that no college shall make any lease for lives or years of tithes, arable land or pasture without securing that at least one-third of 'tholde' (presumably the whole not the old) rent should be paid in coin. The Act was promoted by Sir Thomas Smith to the astonishment, it is said, of his fellow-members of Parliament, who could not see what difference it would make. 'But the knight took the advantage of the present cheapness; knowing hereafter grain would grow dearer, mankind daily multiplying, and licence being lately given for transportation. So that at this day much emolument redoundeth to the colleges in each university, by the passing of this Act; and though their rents stand still, their revenues do increase.'—Fuller, *Hist. of the University of Cambridge*, 1655, p. 144. quoted in Strype, *Life of the learned Sir Thomas Smith*, 1698, p. 192.]

14. [*Commentaries*, 1765, vol. ii., p. 322.]

15. [Above, I.4.10.]

16. [Below, I.8.16–27.]

17. [Below I.8.27–30,50–56.]

18. [Below, chap. xi., see esp. I.11.134–137.]

19. [Ed. 1 reads 'it.']

20. [Ed. 1 places the 'for example' here.]

21. ['In England and this part of the world, wheat being the constant and most general food, not altering with the fashion, not growing by chance: but as the farmers sow more or less of it, which they endeavour to proportion, as near as can be guessed to the consumption, abstracting the overplus of the precedent year in their provision for the next; and *vice versa*, it must needs fall out that it keeps the nearest proportion to its consumption (which is more studied and designed in this than other commodities) of anything, if you take it for seven or twenty years together: though perhaps the scarcity of one year, caused by the accidents of the season, may very much vary it from the immediately precedent or following. Wheat, therefore, to this part of the world (and that grain which is the constant general food of any other country) is the fittest measure to judge of the altered value of things in any long tract of time: and therefore wheat here, rice in Turkey, etc., is the fittest thing to reserve a rent in, which is designed to be constantly the same for all future ages. But money is the best measure of the altered value of things in a few years: because its vent is the same and its quantity alters slowly. But wheat, or any other grain, cannot serve instead of money: because of its bulkiness and too quick change of its quantity.'—Locke, *Some Considerations of the Consequences of the Lowering of Interest and Raising the Value of Money*, ed. of 1696, pp. 74, 75.]

22. [Ed. 1 reads 'than one which sells for an ounce at London to'.]

23. [Below, chap. xi. *passim.*]

24. Pliny, lib. xxxiii. c. 3. [This note is not in ed. 1.]

25. [Eds. 1 and 2 read 'always'.]

26. [Habere aes alienum.]

27. [Ed. 1 does not contain 'sterling'.]

28. [Ed. 1 places the 'originally' here.]

29. [Ed. 1 places the 'only' here.]

30. [The Act, 19 Hen. VII., c. 5, ordered that certain gold coins should pass for the sums for which they were coined, and 5 and 6 Ed. VI. prescribed penalties for giving or taking more than was warranted by proclamation. The value of the guinea was supposed to be fixed by the proclamation of 1717, for which see *Economic Journal*, March, 1898. Lead tokens were corned by individuals in the reign of Elizabeth. James I. coined copper farthing tokens, but abstained from proclaiming them as money of that value. In 1672 copper halfpennies were issued, and both halfpennies and farthings were ordered to pass as money of those values in all payments under sixpence.—Harris, *Money and Coins*, pt. i., § 39; Liverpool, *Treatise on the Coins of the Realm*, 1805, pp. 130, 131.]

31. [Ed. 1 reads 'sum'.]

32. [*I.e.,* if 21 pounds may be paid with 420 silver shillings or with 20 gold guineas it does not matter whether a 'pound' properly signifies 20 silver shillings or 20/21 of a gold guinea.]

33. [This happens to have been usually, though not always, true, but it is so simply because it has usually happened that the most precious metal in use as money has been made or become the standard. Gold was already the standard in England, though fact was not generally recognised; see Harris, *Money and Coins*, pt. ii., §§ 36, 37, below, vol. ii., IV.6.21–32.]

34. [In 1774.]

35. [These regulations, issued in 1774, provided that guineas should not pass when they had lost a certain portion of their weight, varying with their age.—Liverpool, *Coins Of the Realm*, p. 216, note.]

36. [Magens, *Universal Merchant*, ed. Horsley, 1753, pp. 53–55, gives the proportions thus: French coin, 1 to 14 5803/12279, Dutch, 1 to 14 82550/154425, English, 1 to 15 14295/68200.]

37. [Full weight silver coins would not remain in circulation, as the bullion in them was worth more reckoned in guineas and in the ordinary old and worn silver coins than the nominal amount stamped on them.]

38. [Locke, *Further Considerations Concerning Raising the Value of Money*, 2nd ed., 1695, pp. 58–60. The exportation of foreign coin (misprinted 'kind' in Pickering) or bullion of gold or silver was permitted by 15 Car. II, c. 7, on the ground that it was 'found by experience that' money and bullion were 'carried in greatest abundance (as to a common market) to such places as give free liberty for exporting the same' and in order 'the better to keep in and increase the current coins' of the kingdom.]

39. [Harris, writing nearly twenty years earlier, had said, 'it would be a ridiculous and vain attempt to make a standard integer of gold whose parts should be silver, or to make a motley standard, part gold and part silver.'—*Money and Coins*, pt. i., § 36.]

40. [*I.e.,* an ounce of standard gold would not actually fetch £3 17*s.* 10 1/2*d.* if sold for cash down.]

41. [This erroneous statement is repeated below, p. 501, and also vol. ii., p. 60, where the calculations on which it is based are given. See the note on that passage.]

42. [The question of seignorage is further discussed at some length in the chapter on Commercial Treaties vol. ii., IV.6.15–32,.]

43. [Ed. 1 reads 'in the tear and wear of coin, and in the tear and wear of plate'.]

Of the Rate of Interest

By John Stuart Mill

§ 1. The present seems the most proper place for discussing the circumstances which determine the rate of interest. The interest of loans, being really a question of exchange value, falls naturally into the present division of our subject: and the two topics of Currency and Loans, though in themselves distinct, are so intimately blended in the phenomena of what is called the money market, that it is impossible to understand the one without the other, and in many minds the two subjects are mixed up in the most inextricable confusion.

In the preceding Book[1] we defined the relation in which interest stands to profit. We found that the gross profit of capital might be distinguished into three parts, which are respectively the remuneration for risk, for trouble, and for the capital itself, and may be termed insurance, wages of superintendence, and interest. After making compensation for risk, that is, after covering the average losses to which capital is exposed either by the general circumstances of society or by the hazards of the particular employment, there remains a surplus, which partly goes to repay the owner of the capital for his abstinence, and partly the employer of it for his time and trouble. How much goes to the one and how much to the other, is shown by the amount of the remuneration which, when the two functions are separated, the owner of capital can obtain from the employer for its use. This is evidently a question of demand and supply. Nor have demand and supply any different meaning or effect in this case from what they have in all others. The rate of interest will be such as to equalize the demand for loans with the supply of them. It will be such, that exactly as much as some people are desirous to borrow at that rate, others shall be willing to lend. If there is more offered than demanded, interest will fall; if more is demanded than offered, it will rise; and in both cases, to the point at which the equation of supply and demand is re-established.

Both the demand and supply of loans fluctuate more incessantly than any other demand or supply whatsoever. The fluctuations in other things depend on a limited number of influencing circumstances;

but the desire to borrow, and the willingness to lend, are more or less influenced by every circumstance which affects the state or prospects of industry or commerce, either generally or in any of their branches. The rate of interest, therefore, on good security, which alone we have here to consider (for interest in which considerations of risk bear a part may swell to any amount) is seldom, in the great centres of money transactions, precisely the same for two days together; as is shown by the never-ceasing variations in the quoted prices of the funds and other negotiable securities. Nevertheless, there must be, as in other cases of value, some rate which (in the language of Adam Smith and Ricardo) may be called the natural rate; some rate about which the market rate oscillates, and to which it always tends to return. This rate partly depends on the amount of accumulation going on in the hands of persons who cannot themselves attend to the employment of their savings, and partly on the comparative taste existing in the community for the active pursuits of industry, or for the leisure, ease, and independence of an annuitant.

§2. To exclude casual fluctuations, we will suppose commerce to be in a quiescent condition, no employment being unusually prosperous, and none particularly distressed. In these circumstances, the more thriving producers and traders have their capital fully employed, and many are able to transact business to a considerably greater extent than they have capital for. These are naturally borrowers: and the amount which they desire to borrow, and can obtain credit for, constitutes the demand for loans on account of productive employment. To these must be added the loans required by Government, and by landowners, or other unproductive consumers who have good security to give. This constitutes the mass of loans for which there is an habitual demand.

Now it is conceivable that there might exist, in the hands of persons disinclined or disqualified for engaging personally in business, a mass of capital equal to, and even exceeding, this demand. In that case there would be an habitual excess of competition on the part of lenders, and the rate of interest would bear a low proportion to the rate of profit. Interest would be forced down to the point which would either tempt borrowers to take a greater amount of loans than they had a reasonable expectation of being able to employ in their business, or would so discourage a portion of the lenders, as to make them either forbear to accumulate, or endeavour to increase their income by engaging in business on their own account, and incurring the risks, if not the labours, of industrial employment.

On the other hand, the capital owned by persons who prefer lending it at interest, or whose avocations prevent them from personally superintending its employment, may be short of the habitual demand for loans. It may be in great part absorbed by the investments afforded by the public debt and by mortgages, and the remainder may not be sufficient to supply the wants of commerce. If so, the rate of interest will be raised so high as in some way to re-establish the equilibrium. When there is only a small difference between interest and profit, many borrowers may no longer be willing to increase their responsibilities and involve their credit for so small a remuneration: or some who would otherwise have engaged in business, may prefer leisure, and become lenders instead of borrowers, or others, under the inducement of high interest and easy investment for their capital, may retire from business earlier, and with smaller fortunes, than they otherwise would have done. Or, lastly, there is another process by which, in England and other commercial countries, a large portion of the requisite supply of loans is obtained. Instead of its being afforded by persons not in business, the affording it may itself become a business. A portion of the capital employed in trade may be supplied by a class of professional money lenders. These money lenders, however, must have more than a mere interest; they must have the ordinary rate of profit on their capital, risk and all other circumstances being allowed for. But it can never answer to any one who borrows for the purposes of his business, to pay a full profit for capital from which he will only derive a full profit: and money-lending, as an employment, for the regular supply of trade, cannot, therefore, be carried on except by persons who, in addition to their own capital, can lend their credit, or, in other words, the capital of other people: that is, bankers, and persons (such as bill-brokers) who are virtually bankers, since they receive money in deposit. A bank which lends its notes, lends capital which it borrows from the community, and for which it pays no interest. A bank of deposit lends capital which it collects from the community in small parcels; sometimes without paying any interest, as is the case with the London private bankers; and if, like the Scotch, the joint stock, and most of the country banks, it does pay interest, it still pays much less than it receives; for the depositors, who in any other way could mostly obtain for such small balances no interest worth taking any trouble for, are glad to receive even a little. Having this subsidiary resource, bankers are enabled to obtain, by lending at interest, the ordinary rate of profit on their own capital. In any other manner, money-lending could not be carried on as a regular mode of business, except upon terms on which none would consent to borrow but persons either counting on extraordinary profits, or in urgent need: unproductive consumers who have exceeded their means, or merchants in fear of bankruptcy. The disposable capital deposited in banks; that represented by bank notes; the capital of bankers themselves, and that which their credit, in any way in which they use it, enables them to dispose of; these, together with the funds belonging to those who, either from necessity or preference, live upon the interest of their property, constitute the general loan fund of the country: and the amount of this aggregate fund, when set against the habitual demands of producers and dealers, and those of the Government and of unproductive consumers, determines the permanent or average rate of interest; which must always be such as to adjust these two amounts to one another.[2] But while the whole of this mass of lent capital takes effect upon the *permanent* rate of interest, the *fluctuations* depend almost entirely upon the portion which is in the hands of bankers; for it is that portion almost exclusively which, being lent for short times only, is continually in the market seeking an investment. The capital of those who live on the interest of their own fortunes, has generally sought and found some fixed investment, such as the public funds, mortgages, or the bonds of public companies, which investment, except under peculiar temptations or necessities, is not changed.

§3. Fluctuations in the rate of interest arise from variations either in the demand for loans or in the supply. The supply is liable to variation, though less so than the demand. The willingness to lend is greater than usual at the commencement of a period of speculation, and much less than usual during the revulsion which follows. In speculative times, money-lenders as well as other people are inclined to extend their business by stretching their credit; they lend more than usual (just as other classes of dealers and producers employ more than usual) of capital which does not belong to them. Accordingly, these are the times when the rate of interest is low; though for this too (as we shall hereafter see) there are other causes. During the revulsion, on the contrary, interest always rises inordinately, because, while there is a most pressing need on the part of many persons to borrow, there is a general disinclination to lend. This disinclination, when at its extreme point, is called a panic. It occurs when a succession of unexpected failures has created in the mercantile, and sometimes also in the non-mercantile public, a general distrust in each other's solvency; disposing every one not only to refuse fresh credit, except on very onerous terms, but to call in, if possible, all credit which he has already given. Deposits are withdrawn from banks; notes are returned on the issuers in exchange for specie; bankers raise their rate of discount, and withhold their customary advances; merchants refuse to renew mercantile bills. At such times the most calamitous consequences were formerly experienced from the attempt of the law to prevent more than a certain limited rate of interest from being given or taken. Persons who could not borrow at five per cent, had to pay, not six or seven, but ten or fifteen per cent, to compensate the lender for risking the penalties of the law: or had to sell securities or goods for ready money at a still greater sacrifice.

In the intervals between commercial crises, there is usually a tendency in the rate of interest to a progressive decline, from the gradual process of accumulation: which process, in the great commercial countries, is sufficiently rapid to account for the almost periodical recurrence of these fits of speculation; since, when a few years have elapsed without a crisis, and no new and tempting channel for investment has been opened in the meantime, there is always found to have occurred in those few years so large an increase of capital seeking investment, as to have lowered considerably the rate of interest, whether indicated by the prices of securities or by the rate of discount on bills; and this diminution of interest tempts the possessor to incur hazards in hopes of a more considerable return.

[3]The rate of interest is, at times, affected more or less permanently by circumstances, though not of frequent, yet of occasional occurrence, which tend to alter the proportion between the class of interest-receiving and that of profit-receiving capitalists. Two causes of this description, operating in contrary ways, have manifested themselves of late years, and are now producing considerable effects in England. One is the gold discoveries. The masses of the precious metals which are constantly arriving from the gold countries, are, it may safely be said, wholly added to the funds that supply the loan market. So great an additional capital, not divided between the two classes of capitalists, but aggregated bodily to the capital of the interest-receiving class, disturbs the pre-existing ratio between the two, and tends to depress interest relatively to profit. Another circumstance of still more recent date, but tending to the contrary effect, is the legalization of joint-stock associations with limited liability. The shareholders in these associations, now so rapidly multiplying, are drawn almost exclusively from the lending class; from those who either left their disposable funds in deposit, to be lent out by bankers, or invested them in public or private securities, and received the interest. To the extent of their shares in any of these companies (with the single exception of banking companies) they have become traders on their own capital; they have ceased to be lenders, and have even, in most cases, passed over to the class of borrowers. Their subscriptions have been abstracted from the funds which feed the loan market, and they themselves have become competitors for a share of the remainder of those funds: of all which, the natural effect is a rise of interest. And it would not be surprising if, for a considerable time to come, the ordinary rate of interest in England should bear a higher proportion to the common rate of mercantile profit, than it has borne at any time since the influx of new gold set in.[4]

The demand for loans varies much more largely than the supply, and embraces longer cycles of years in its aberrations. A time of war, for example, is a period of unusual drafts on the loan market. The Government, at such times, generally incurs new loans, and as these usually succeed each other rapidly as long as the war lasts, the general rate of interest is kept higher in war than in peace, without reference to the rate of profit, and productive industry is stinted of its usual supplies. During part of the last war with France, the Government could not borrow under six per cent, and of course all other borrowers had to pay at least as much. Nor does the influence of these loans altogether cease when the Government ceases to contract others; for those already contracted continue to afford an investment for a greatly increased amount of the disposable capital of the country, which if the national debt were paid off, would be added to the mass of capital seeking investment, and (independently of temporary disturbance) could not but, to some extent, permanently lower the rate of interest.

The same effect on interest which is produced by Government loans for war expenditure, is produced by the sudden opening of any new and generally attractive mode of permanent investment. The only instance of the kind in recent history on a scale comparable to that of the war loans, is the absorption of capital in the construction of railways. This capital must have been principally drawn from the deposits in banks, or from savings which would have gone into deposit, and which were destined to be ultimately employed in buying securities from persons who would have employed the purchase money in discounts or other loans at interest: in either case, it was a draft on the general loan fund. It is, in fact, evident, that unless savings were made expressly to be employed in railway adventure, the amount thus employed must have been derived either from the actual capital of persons in business, or from capital which would have been lent to persons in business.

In the first case, the subtraction, by crippling their means, obliges them to be larger borrowers; in the second, it leaves less for them to borrow; in either case it equally tends to raise the rate of interest.

§4.[5] I have, thus far, considered loans, and the rate of interest, as a matter which concerns capital in general, in direct opposition to the popular notion, according to which it only concerns money. In loans, as in all other money transactions, I have regarded the money which passes, only as the medium, and commodities as the thing really transferred—the real subject of the transaction. And this is, in the main, correct: because the purpose for which, in the ordinary course of affairs, money is borrowed, is to acquire a purchasing power over commodities. In an industrious and commercial country, the ulterior intention commonly is, to employ the commodities as capital: but even in the case of loans for unproductive consumption, as those of spendthrifts, or of the Government, the amount borrowed is taken from a previous accumulation, which would otherwise have been lent to carry on productive industry; it is, therefore, so much subtracted from what may correctly be called the amount of loanable capital.

There is, however, a not unfrequent case, in which the purpose of the borrower is different from what I have here supposed. He may borrow money, neither to employ it as capital nor to spend it unproductively, but to pay a previous debt. In this case, what he wants is not purchasing power, but legal tender, or something which a creditor will accept as equivalent to it. His need is specifically for money, not for commodities or capital. It is the demand arising from this cause, which produces almost all the great and sudden variations of the rate of interest. Such a demand forms one of the earliest features of a commercial crisis. At such a period, many persons in business who have contracted engagements, have been prevented by a change of circumstances from obtaining in time the means on which they calculated for fulfilling them. These means they must obtain at any sacrifice, or submit to bankruptcy; and what they must have is money. Other capital, however much of it they may possess, cannot answer the purpose unless money can first be obtained for it; while, on the contrary, without any increase of the capital of the country, a mere increase of circulating instruments of credit (be they of as little worth for any other purpose as the box of one pound notes discovered in the vaults of the Bank of England during the panic of 1825) will effectually serve their turn if only they are allowed to make use of it. An increased issue of notes, in the form of loans, is all that is required to satisfy the demand, and put an end to the accompanying panic. But although, in this case, it is not capital, or purchasing power, that the borrower needs, but money as money, it is not only money that is transferred to him. The money carries its purchasing power with it wherever it goes; and money thrown into the loan market really does, through its purchasing power, turn over an increased portion of the capital of the country into the direction of loans. Though money alone was wanted, capital passes; and it may still be said with truth that it is by an addition to loanable capital that the rise of the rate of interest is met and corrected.

Independently of this, however, there is a real relation, which it is indispensable to recognise, between loans and money. Loanable capital is all of it in the form of money. Capital destined directly for production exists in many forms; but capital destined for lending exists normally in that form alone. Owing to this circumstance, we should naturally expect that among the causes which affect more or less the rate of interest, would be found not only causes which act through capital, but some causes which act, directly at least, only through money.

[6]The rate of interest bears no necessary relation to the quantity or value of the money in circulation. The permanent amount of the circulating medium, whether great or small, affects only prices; not the rate of interest. A depreciation of the currency, when it has become an accomplished fact, affects the rate of interest in no manner whatever. It diminishes indeed the power of money to buy commodities, but not the power of money to buy money. If a hundred pounds will buy a perpetual annuity of four pounds a year, a depreciation which makes the hundred

pounds worth only half as much as before, has precisely the same effect on the four pounds, and cannot therefore alter the relation between the two. The greater or smaller number of counters which must be used to express a given amount of real wealth, makes no difference in the position or interests of lenders or borrowers, and therefore makes no difference in the demand and supply of loans. There is the same amount of real capital lent and borrowed; and if the capital in the hands of lenders is represented by a greater number of pounds sterling, the same greater number of pounds sterling will, in consequence of the rise of prices, be now required for the purposes to which the borrowers intend to apply them.

But though the greater or less quantity of money makes in itself no difference in the rate of interest, a change from a less quantity to a greater, or from a greater to a less, may and does make a difference in it.

Suppose money to be in process of depreciation by means of an inconvertible currency, issued by a government in payment of its expenses. This fact will in no way diminish the demand for real capital on loan; but it will diminish the real capital loanable, because, this existing only in the form of money, the increase of quantity depreciates it. Estimated in capital, the amount offered is less, while the amount required is the same as before. Estimated in currency, the amount offered is only the same as before, while the mount required, owing to the rise of prices, is greater. Either way, the rate of interest must rise. So that in this case increase of currency really affects the rate of interest, but in the contrary way to that which is generally supposed; by raising, not by lowering it.

The reverse will happen as the effect of calling in, or diminishing in quantity, a depreciated currency. The money in the hands of lenders, in common with all other money, will be enhanced in value, that is, there will be a greater amount of real capital seeking borrowers; while the real capital wanted by borrowers will be only the same as before, and the money amount less: the rate of interest, therefore, will tend to fall.

We thus see that depreciation, merely as such, while in process of taking place, tends to raise the rate of interest: and the expectation of further depreciation adds to this effect; because lenders who expect that their interest will be paid and the principal perhaps redeemed, in a less valuable currency than they lent, of course require a rate of interest sufficient to cover this contingent loss.

But this effect is more than counteracted by a contrary one, when the additional money is thrown into circulation not by purchases but by loans. In England, and in most other commercial countries, the paper currency in common use, being a currency provided by bankers, is all issued in the way of loans, except the part employed in the purchase of gold and silver. The same operation, therefore, which adds to the currency also adds to the loans: the whole increase of currency in the first instance swells the loan market. Considered as an addition to loans it tends to lower interest, more than in its character of depreciation it tends to raise it; for the former effect depends on the ratio which the new money bears to the money lent, while the latter depends on its ratio to all the money in circulation. An increase, therefore, of currency issued by banks, tends, while the process continues, to bring down or to keep down the rate of interest. A similar effect is produced by the increase of money arising from the gold discoveries; almost the whole of which, as already noticed, is, when brought to Europe, added to the deposits in banks, and consequently to the amount of loans; and when drawn out and invested in securities, liberates an equivalent amount of other loanable capital. The newly-arrived gold can only get itself invested, in any given state of business, by lowering the rate of interest; and as long as the influx continues, it cannot fail to keep interest lower than, all other circumstances being supposed the same, would otherwise have been the case.

As the introduction of additional gold and silver, which goes into the loan market, tends to keep down the rate of interest, so any considerable abstraction of them from the country invariably raises it; even when occurring in the course of trade, as in paying for the extra importations caused by a bad harvest, or for the high-priced cotton which, under the influence of the American civil war, was imported from so many parts of the world. The money required for these payments is taken in the first instance from the deposits in the hands of bankers, and to that extent starves the fund that supplies the loan market.

The rate of interest, then, depends essentially and permanently on the comparative amount of real capital offered and demanded in the way of loan; but is subject to temporary disturbances of various sorts from increase and diminution of the circulating medium; which derangements are somewhat intricate, and sometimes in direct opposition to first appearances. All these distinctions are veiled over and confounded, by the unfortunate misapplication of language which designates the rate of interest by a phrase ("the value of money") which properly expresses the purchasing power of the circulating medium. The public, even mercantile, habitually fancies that ease in the money market, that is, facility of borrowing at low interest, is proportional to the quantity of money in circulation. Not only, therefore, are bank notes supposed to produce effects as currency, which they only produce as loans, but attention is habitually diverted from effects similar in kind and much greater in degree, when produced by an action on loans which does not happen to be accompanied by any action on the currency.

For example, in considering the effect produced by the proceedings of banks in encouraging the excesses of speculation, an immense effect is usually attributed to their issues of notes, but until of late hardly any attention was paid to the management of their deposits; though nothing is more certain than that their imprudent extensions of credit take place more frequently by means of their deposits than of their issues. "There is no doubt," says Mr. Tooke,[7] "that banks, whether private or joint stock, may, if imprudently conducted, minister to an undue extension of credit for the purpose of speculations, whether in commodities, or in over-trading in exports or imports, or in building or mining operations, and that they have so ministered not unfrequently, and

in some cases to an extent ruinous to themselves, and without ultimate benefit to the parties to whose views their resources were made subservient." But, "supposing all the deposits received by a banker to be in coin, is he not, just as much as the issuing banker, exposed to the importunity of customers, whom it may be impolitic to refuse, for loans or discounts, or to be tempted by a high interest? and may he not be induced to encroach so much upon his deposits as to leave him, under not improbable circumstances, unable to meet the demands of his depositors? In what respect, indeed, would the case of a banker in a perfectly metallic circulation differ from that of a London banker at the present day? He is not a creator of money, he cannot avail himself of his privilege as an issuer in aid of his other business, and yet there have been lamentable instances of London bankers issuing money in excess."

In the discussions, too, which have been for so many years carried on respecting the operations of the Bank of England, and the effects produced by those operations on the state of credit, though for nearly half a century there never has been a commercial crisis which the Bank has not been strenuously accused either of producing or of aggravating, it has been almost universally assumed that the influence of its acts was felt only through the amount of its notes in circulation, and that if it could be prevented from exercising any discretion as to that one feature in its position, it would no longer have any power liable to abuse. This at least is an error which, after the experience of the year 1847, we may hope has been committed for the last time. During that year the hands of the bank were absolutely tied, in its character of a bank of issue; but through its operations as a bank of deposit it exercised as great an influence, or apparent influence, on the rate of interest and the state of credit, as at any former period; it was exposed to as vehement accusations of abusing that influence; and a crisis occurred, such as few that preceded it had equalled, and none perhaps surpassed, in intensity.

§5. Before quitting the general subject of this chapter, I will make the obvious remark, that the rate of interest determines the value and price of all those saleable articles which are desired and bought, not for themselves, but for the income which they are capable of yielding. The public funds, shares in joint-stock companies, and all descriptions of securities, are at a high price in proportion as the rate of interest is low. They are sold at the price which will give the market rate of interest on the purchase money, with allowance for all differences in the risk incurred, or in any circumstance of convenience. Exchequer bills, for example, usually sell at a higher price than consols, proportionally to the interest which they yield; because, though the security is the same, yet the former being annually paid off at par unless renewed by the holder, the purchaser (unless obliged to sell in a moment of general emergency), is in no danger of losing anything by the resale, except the premium he may have paid.

The price of land, mines, and all other fixed sources of income, depends in like manner on the rate of interest. Land usually sells at a higher price, in proportion to the income afforded by it, than the public funds, not only because it is thought, even in this country, to be somewhat more secure, but because ideas of power and dignity are associated with its possession. But these differences are constant, or nearly so; and in the variations of price, land follows, *cæteris paribus,* the permanent (though of course not the daily) variations of the rate of interest. When interest is low, land will naturally be dear; when interest is high, land will be cheap. The last long war presented a striking exception to this rule, since the price of land as well as the rate of interest was then remarkably high. For this, however, there was a special cause. The continuance of a very high average price of corn for many years had raised the rent of land even more than in proportion to the rise of interest and fall of the selling price of fixed incomes. Had it not been for this accident, chiefly dependent on the seasons, land must have sustained as great a depreciation in value as the public funds: which it probably would do, were a similar war to break out hereafter; to the signal disappointment of those landlords and farmers who, generalizing from the casual circumstances of a remarkable period, so

long persuaded themselves that a state of war was peculiarly advantageous, and a state of peace disadvantageous, to what they chose to call the interests of agriculture.

NOTES FOR THIS CHAPTER

1. Supra, book ii. ch. xv. § 1.
2. I do not include in the general loan fund of the country the capitals, large as they sometimes are, which are habitually employed in speculatively buying and selling the public funds and other securities. It is true that all who buy securities add, for the time, to the general amount of money on loan, and lower *pro tanto* the rate of interest. But as the persons I speak of buy only to sell again at a higher price, they are alternately in the position of lenders and of borrowers: their operations raise the rate of interest at one time, exactly as much as they lower it at another. Like all persons who buy and sell on speculation, their function is to equalize, not to raise or lower, the value of the commodity. When they speculate prudently, they temper the fluctuations of price; when imprudently, they often aggravate them.
3. [This paragraph and the accompanying note were added in the 6th ed. (1865).]
4. [1865] To the cause of augmentation in the rate of interest, mentioned in the text, must be added another, forcibly insisted on by the author of an able article in the *Edinburgh Review* for January, 1865; the increased and increasing willingness to send capital abroad for investment. Owing to the vastly augmented facilities of access to foreign countries, and the abundant information incessantly received from them, foreign investments have ceased to inspire the terror that belongs to the unknown; capital flows, without misgiving, to any place which affords an expectation of high profit; and the loan market of the whole commercial world is rapidly becoming one. The rate of interest, therefore, in the part of the world out of which capital most freely flows,

cannot any longer remain so much inferior to the rate elsewhere, as it has hitherto been.

5. [The first three paragraphs of this section were added in the 6th ed. (1865).]

6. [The text of this and the next seven paragraphs is an expansion in the 6th ed. (1865) of two paragraphs of the earlier editions.]

7. *Inquiry into the Currency Principle*, ch. xiv.

A Glance at the Money Illusion

By Irving Fisher

INTRODUCTION

As I write, your dollar is worth about 70 cents. This means 70 cents of pre-war buying power. In other words 70 cents would buy as much of all commodities in 1913 as 100 cents will buy at present. Your dollar now is not the dollar you knew before the War. The dollar seems always to be the same but it is always changing. It is unstable. So are the British pound, the French franc, the Italian lira, the German mark, and every other unit of money. Important problems grow out of this great fact—that units of money are not stable in buying power.

A new interest in these problems has been aroused by the recent upheavals in prices caused by the World War. This interest, nevertheless, is still confined largely to a few special students of economic conditions, while the general public scarcely yet know that such questions exist.

Why this oversight? Why is it that we have been so slow to take up these fundamental problems which are of vital concern to all people? It is because of the "Money Illusion"; that is, the failure to perceive that the dollar, or any other unit of money, expands or shrinks in value. We simply take it for granted that "a dollar is a dollar"—that "a franc is a franc," that all money is

stable, just as centuries ago, before Copernicus, people took it for granted that this earth was stationary, that there was really such a fact as a sunrise or a sunset We know now that sunrise and sunset are illusions produced by the rotation of the earth around its axis, and yet we still speak of, and even think of, the sun as rising and setting!

We need a somewhat similar change of ideas in thinking about money. Instead of thinking of a "high cost of living" as a rise in price of many separate commodities which simply happen, by coincidence, to rise at the same time, we shall find instead that it is really the dollar, or other money unit, which varies.

THE MONEY ILLUSION WITHIN YOUR COUNTRY

Almost every one is subject to the "Money Illusion" in respect to his own country's currency. This seems to him to be stationary while the money of other countries seems to change. It may seem strange but it is true that we see the rise or fall of foreign money better than we see that of our own.

For instance, after the War, we in America knew that the German mark had fallen, but very few Germans knew it. This was certainly true up to 1922 when with another economist (Professor Frederick W. Roman) I studied price changes in Europe. On my way to Germany I stopped in London and consulted with Lord D'Abernon, then British Ambassador to Germany. He said: "Professor Fisher, you will find that very few Germans think of the mark as having fallen." I said: "That seems incredible. Every schoolboy in the United States knows it." But I found he was right. The Germans thought of commodities as rising and thought of the American gold dollar as rising. They thought we had somehow cornered the gold of the world and were charging an outrageous price for it. But to them the mark was all the time the same mark. They lived and breathed and had their being in an atmosphere of marks, just as we in America live and breathe and have our being in an atmosphere of dollars. Professor Roman and I talked at length with twenty-four men and women whom we met by chance in our travels in Germany. Among these only one had any idea that the mark had changed.

Of course, all the others knew that prices had risen, but it never occurred to them that this rise had anything to do with the mark. They tried to explain it by the "supply and demand" of other goods; by the blockade; by the destruction wrought by the War; by the American hoard of gold; by all manner of other things,— exactly as in America when, a few years ago, we ourselves talked about the "high cost of living," we seldom heard anybody say that a change in the dollar had anything to do with it.

I remember particularly a long talk with one very intelligent German woman who kept a shop in the outskirts of Berlin. She gave all kinds of trivial reasons for the high prices. There was a grain of truth in some of them, just as there is a grain of truth in the idea that a small part of the seeming motion of the stars is real. But the main fact of the tremendous increase in the volume of "marks" and of the action of this paper money inflation on prices was not even glimpsed by the German shop woman. For eight years she had been victimized by the changing mark but had never once suspected the true cause—inflation. When I talked with her the inflation had gone on until the mark had depreciated by more than ninety-eight per cent, so that it was only a fiftieth of its original value (that is, the price level had risen about fifty fold), and yet she had not been aware of what had really happened. Fearing to be thought a profiteer, she said: "That shirt I sold you will cost me just as much to replace as I am charging you." Before I could ask her why, then, she sold it at so low a price, she continued: "But I have made a profit on that shirt because I bought it for less."

She had made no profit; she had made a loss. She *thought* she had made a profit only because she was deceived by the "Money Illusion." She had assumed that the marks she had paid for the shirt a year ago were the same sort of marks as the marks I was paying her, just as, in America, we assume that the dollar is the same at one time as another. She had kept her accounts in what was in reality a fluctuating unit, the mark. In terms of this changing unit her accounts did indeed show a profit; but if she had translated her accounts into dollars, they would have shown a large loss, and if she had translated them into units of commodities in general she would have shown a still larger loss—because the dollar, too, had fallen.

Chart I shows her apparent gain and actual loss.

We found the same complacent assumption of stability in other countries. Austrians, Italians, French, English,—all peoples assumed that their own respective moneys had not fallen in value, but that goods had risen.

WHEN TWO COUNTRIES COMPARE NOTES

It follows, of course, that when people from different countries with different moneys compare notes they find that their ideas are in conflict. This is well illustrated by the case of an American woman who owed money on a mortgage in Germany. The World War came and she had no communication with Germany for two years. After the War she visited Germany, intending to pay the mortgage. She had always thought of it as a debt of $7,000. It was legally a debt of 28,000 marks, in terms of German money. She went to the banker who had the matter in charge and said: "I want to pay that mortgage of $7,000." He replied: "The amount isn't $7,000; it is 28,000 marks; that sum today is about $250." She said: "Oh! I am not going to take advantage of the fall of the mark. I insist upon paying the $7,000." The banker could not see the point; he showed that legally this was not necessary and he could not understand her scruples. As a matter of fact, however, she herself failed to take account of a corresponding, though lesser, change in the dollar. She was thinking in terms of American dollars, just as the banker was thinking in terms of German marks. She insisted on paying $7,000 instead of paying $250, but she would have rebelled if she had been told that the dollar also had fallen, that the equivalent in buying power of the original debt was not $7,000, but $12,000, and that she ought, therefore, to pay $12,000! Then she would not have seen the point!

THE MONEY ILLUSION IN AMERICA

Thus, we Americans are no exception in regard to the "Money Illusion." An American is quite lost if he tries to think of the dollar as varying. He cannot easily think of anything by which to measure it. Even

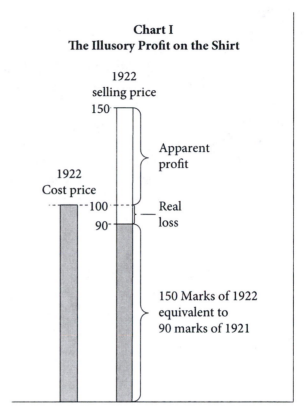

Chart I
The Illusory Profit on the Shirt

1922
selling price
150

Apparent
profit

1922
Cost price
100

Real
loss

90

150 Marks of 1922
equivalent to
90 marks of 1921

with our gold standard we have a dollar fluctuating in buying power. Yet we think of the dollar as fixed. It is fixed only in the sense that it is redeemable in a fixed number of grains of gold. It is not fixed in the amount of goods and benefits it can command.

A very able American business man said to me some years ago: "I have made a great deal of money and I have been on the boards of directors of a great many concerns. I haven't before heard anyone talk about an unstable dollar as having anything to do with hard times; I take no stock in any such idea."

It is refreshing to note, however, that many far-sighted business men are now aware of the changeableness of the dollar. In 1925, at a time when people were marvelling at how high the stock market seemed, Secretary Mellon pointed out that, if we took account of the depreciated dollar, prices on the stock market really were not so high as they had been before the War. He was right; for a depreciated dollar tends to raise prices of commodities and property in general, including stocks representing shares in property.

Earlier in the same year, Mr. James H. Rand, Jr., now President of Remington Rand Inc., had pointed put in some detail the same fact.

Having been interested for a long time in this subject of the fluctuating dollar, he had, from time to time, kept two accounts, one in actual prices, the other translated into such prices as would have prevailed if the dollar had remained stable in buying power. This he did to make sure that he was not being victimized, like the shop woman in Berlin, by unstable money. Without such a translation into actual buying power, we are all likely to deceive ourselves.

In 1919, which was in a period of inflation, a leading banker learned, for the first time, of translating accounts into stable dollar values. When he saw the point, he took a pad out of his pocket and made some calculations. Then he exclaimed: "I have been boasting about how my bank has expanded its deposits and loans. But now I see, when I take into account the depreciated dollar, that I am only doing about the same business as before the War at twice the old level of prices. The expansion of which I have been boasting has been an illusion."

The United States Steel Corporation has the reputation of having grown rapidly—and it has grown very rapidly; but its growth seems to be more than it is because in comparing the company's present and past records the depreciation of the dollar is overlooked. This comparison of real with seeming growth has been made in detail by Mr. Ernest F. DuBrul in a pamphlet mentioned in the Supplement

APPLICATION TO INVESTORS

Apply the idea of the unstable dollar to your own case. Suppose that you received before the War a dividend of four dollars per share, and that now you are receiving five dollars per share. Perhaps you cherish the idea that your dividend is now twenty-five per cent more than it used to be. But when you consider what your dividend dollar will buy, you will find that the real return to you is actually 12½ per cent less!

Work it out and see. The dollar of today, as compared with the dollar of 1913, is worth about 70 pre-war cents, as already mentioned; that is, it will buy about seventy per cent as much goods, on the average, as the dollar of 1913 bought Using this figure, suppose you translate your five dollar dividend of today back into the old 1913 dollars. Since each of these five present-day dollars is really only 70 cents, of pre-war standard, you will find that you actually have only five times 70 cents, or three dollars and a half, of pre-war standard. You used to get four dollars in your dividend and now you are getting only three dollars and a half of the same standard of buying power.

Two investigators in the banking and brokerage business have recently shown what this means to the American investor, and have published their findings in two excellent books: Edgar Lawrence Smith's "Common Stocks as Long Term Investments" and Kenneth Van Strum's "Investing in Purchasing Power." Both of these men, working by independent methods, have startled many conservative investors by showing that the bondholder does not necessarily have a safe investment, as measured in buying power, even in this country. The reason is simple. As long as a dollar is not safe, any agreement to pay a dollar is not safe. However certain it may be that you are going to get the promised dollar, it is not at all sure what the dollar is going to be worth when you get it. These investigators have found that, on some occasions, the bondholder, instead of getting interest, was really taking a loss in terms of real buying power. He was actually losing part of his principal; but, like the German shopkeeper, he did not know it

IS GOLD STABLE?

The Money Illusion is strong even in countries which have lost the gold standard and are on a paper money basis, despite two reminders which business men have before their eyes. These are the ever-changing quotations of their former gold money—mark, franc, crown or whatever—and the ever-changing quotations of foreign moneys. But stronger yet is the Money Illusion in gold standard countries, where these two reminders are absent. In fact their absence is often pointed to, with pride, as proof that the money is sound and stable.

One form of such "proof" of this stability is that the "price of gold" never varies in a gold standard country. In the United States pure gold sells at about twenty dollars an ounce (exactly $20.67) and has remained at that fixed price ever since 1837 when the pure gold content of the dollar was fixed at about one-twentieth of an ounce (exactly 23.22 grains) of pure gold. Of course the two figures mutually imply each other and afford absolutely no evidence that gold is constant in its buying power over other commodities. They merely mean that gold is constant in terms of gold.

I once jokingly asked my dentist—at a time when people were complaining about "the high cost of living"—whether the cost of gold for dentistry had risen. To my surprise he took me seriously and sent his clerk to look up the figures. She returned and said: "Doctor, you are paying the same price for your gold that you always have."

Turning to me the dentist said: "Isn't that surprising? Gold must be a very steady commodity."

"It's exactly as surprising," I said, "as that a quart of milk is always worth two pints of milk."

"I don't understand," he said.

"Well, what is a dollar?" I asked.

"I don't know," he replied.

"That's the trouble," I said. "The dollar is approximately one-twentieth of an ounce; there are, therefore, twenty dollars in an ounce of gold, and naturally an ounce of gold must be worth $20. The dollar is a unit of weight, just as truly as the ounce. It is a unit of weight masquerading as a stable unit of value, or buying power."

CONCLUSION

Our fixed-weight dollar is as poor a substitute for a really stable dollar as would be a fixed weight of copper, a fixed yardage of carpet, or a fixed number of eggs. If we were to define a dollar as a dozen eggs, thenceforth the price of eggs would necessarily and always be a dollar a dozen. Nevertheless, the supply and demand of eggs would keep on working. For instance, if the hens failed to lay, the price of eggs would not rise but the price of almost everything else would fall. One egg would buy more than before. Yet, because of the Money Illusion, we would not even suspect the hens of causing low prices and hard times.

In what sense, then, should a dollar be fixed, if not in weight? Evidently, in buying power. We use a dollar as a unit of value, or buying power, not as a unit of weight. We have other units of weight, the pound, ounce, grain, gram. We use these units of weights for weighing. But the dollar is a unit of weight never used for weighing. 23.22 grains of silver or copper is not a dollar. Only 23.22 grains of gold is a dollar and even then, while the grain means to us weight, the dollar does not. We never think of it in any such way. We think of it as a unit of value. No one cares, or should care, what a dollar weighs. What it buys is the vital question. As an economist, General F. A. Walker, said, "money is as money does" or "the dollar is what the dollar buys." To confuse the fixed weight of the dollar with a fixed value is like confusing a fixed weight of a yardstick with a fixed length. If the Bureau of Standards should put out yardsticks always weighing the same, that would not insure their having the same length. They could be used accurately for weighing sugar but not, with any great accuracy, for measuring cloth.

It follows that our dollar could be used accurately for weighing sugar, but it cannot at present be used, with accuracy, for measuring value. This fact nevertheless is hidden from us by the Money Illusion.

In which they were traded in, and such that the whole assortment could be bought in 1913 for one dollar.

Then let us suppose that, while the 1913 dollar would buy that market basketful, the dollar of 1919 would buy only half of it. That is, the price of that basket in 1919 was two dollars instead of one dollar; the goods in the basket, taken all together, had doubled in price. It follows, according to these figures, that the 1919 index number of commodity prices is twice the 1913 level; that is, it is 200, if we take 100 as the price level of 1913.

This statement does not, of course, mean that every one of the goods had doubled in price. Some kinds of goods had more than doubled in price and some had less than doubled; a few even had fallen.

Such a doubling of prices, on the average, did actually occur between 1913 and 1919. We can express it in either of two ways. We may say that the price index, or price of the assortment of goods in the imaginary basket, was doubled, or we may say that the dollar was worth half as much.

Today the value of the dollar is higher than in 1919; it will buy more than two-thirds of the market basket which cost a dollar in 1913. That is, as before stated, today's dollar is worth about 70 pre-war cents.

As already said, the market basket is supposed to contain the various commodities in their right proportions. But, in actual practice, it usually makes very little difference whether the proportions are carefully chosen or not. This is partly because most of the commodities usually go up and down in sympathy and partly for other reasons. But of the fact there is no question, surprising as it may seem to those not familiar with index numbers. Chart II constructed from the figures published in Bulletin 181 of the United States Bureau of Labor Statistics illustrates two curves, one curve "weighted," according to the amounts bought and sold, the other "unweighted," giving equal weight to each and every commodity.

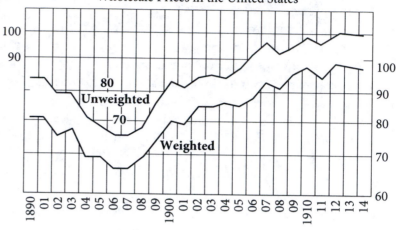

Chart II
Weighted and Unweighted Indes Numbers
Wholesale Prices in the United States

The reader can see for himself that usually the two curves move up and down together.

The United States Bureau of Labor Statistics publishes monthly an index based on the wholesale prices of 550 commodities. I publish one weekly based on 120 commodities. Carl Snyder, economist of the Federal Reserve Bank of New York, has constructed a general index, compiled from the prices of goods, property and services of all descriptions, not only commodities, wholesale and retail, but stocks, bonds, real estate, wages, rents, and freights.

Indexes are increasingly used by statisticians, by the statistical departments of banks, by business men, and, in recent years, even by the general public. A number of commercial houses and some official agencies have adjusted wages by an index of the cost of living. The Dawes Plan for Germany's reparation payments makes some use of index numbers. The World Economic Conference at Geneva, in 1927, recommended that various kinds of indexes be constructed for world-wide use.

As already implied, if we, so to speak, turn an index of prices upside down, we get an index of the buying power of the dollar. The two indexes play seesaw with each other, one going up or down as the other goes down or up. So there are always these two indexes, one of prices and the other of the buying power of the dollar. Both tell us the same story but in opposite ways.

FLUCTUATIONS IN EUROPE

When we apply this instrument, the index, to the facts of history, what do we find has happened to price levels and money? Indexes show that the German commodity price level rose during, and following, the World War more than a trillion fold as compared with the level of the year 1913, or, to reverse the index, that the buying power of the German mark was reduced to less than one-trillionth part of what it was in 1913. In Russia the rise of prices was far less, yet it was over a billion fold. In Poland the rise was again, far less; yet it was over a million fold. In Austria the rise was still less; yet it was twenty thousand fold. In Italy and France and several other countries it was still less; yet it was five to ten fold. In England, Canada, and in the United States it was still less; yet it was two to three fold; that is, the dollar and the pound fell to a half or a third of their pre-war buying powers.

FLUCTUATIONS IN AMERICA

During the Civil War the dollar fell rapidly, so that in 1865 its buying power was only two-fifths of that of 1860. Next, the dollar's buying power rose again until it was multiplied four fold in the 31 years between 1865 and 1896. Once more the tide turned and the dollar fell until its buying power in 1920 was only one-fourth what it had been in 1896. Finally, from May 1920 to June 1921 the dollar again rose rapidly in buying power, from 40 to 70 pre-war cents. All these figures are based on wholesale prices. If other sorts of prices are included the extreme fluctuations are reduced. Since 1921 the dollar has remained fairly stable, with comparatively minor changes, up to the present time.

Chart III shows what the dollar was worth in various years, five years apart, beginning with 1850. All figures are in terms of "pre-war cents," that is, 1913 cents.

These facts show that, while the changes in our dollar are small compared with the extreme changes in the German mark or in the Russian ruble, they have nevertheless been very great. An expansion in the dollar's worth of nearly four fold within a generation, an equal shrinkage within a still shorter time, followed by another great expansion in a little more than a year, show that our dollar has been far from stable. That is to say, even in the United States, a gold standard country, money changed in buying power just as truly, even if not as much, as it did in the paper standard countries.

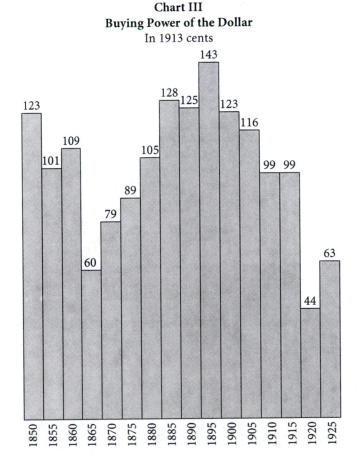

Chart III
Buying Power of the Dollar
In 1913 cents

DIFFERENT INDEXES AGREE

The indexes used in Chart III are made from wholesale prices but the results will not be far different if we use an index made from retail prices, or even one from "general" prices—of goods and services of all descriptions. Discrepancies between the wholesale index and the general index are shown in the accompanying table. It is interesting to see how closely these different indexes agree. The wholesale figures are repeated from Chart III. The general index, given in the last column, is that calculated by Carl Snyder.

The differences are, successively: 1, 3, 6, 3, 2, 1, 0, 5, 2, 8, 4 cents. The greatest difference is 8 cents (52-44 for 1920) the average difference is 3.2 cents and there are only two cases out of the eleven over 5 cents.

While it is a highly technical question what is the very best index or indexes to be used to guide stabilization the facts prove that even at the worst, as shown in this table, the various available indexes agree with each other fairly well. Each one shows an extremely variable dollar.

Buying Power of the Dollar in 1913 cents

	WHOLESALE	GENERAL
1875	89	88
1880	105	102
1885	128	122
1890	125	122
1895	143	145
1900	123	122
1905	116	116
1910	99	104
1915	99	97
1920	44	52
1925	63	59

COMMENTS

What would we say if our yardstick, pound avoirdupois, bushel basket, gallon, or kilowatt were to shrink and swell—nearly four fold:—back and forth? Suppose that a railway company were to order railway ties six feet long and that the foot rule were to quadruple in length before the time they were delivered! Or suppose that a grain elevator were to buy 1000 bushels of wheat, but the bushel basket meanwhile were to shrink to one-fourth its original size! Our dollar, the measure of value, nevertheless changes as the yardstick might if it were a rubber band, or as the pound might if the standard pound weight were made of something that takes up moisture from the air and afterward dries out again.

The reason the World War aroused us a little to the importance of this subject of unstable money was that it made almost all moneys in the world far more unstable than they had ever been before. Yet it required, in Germany for instance, a change of over a hundred fold occurring within the period of a few years to make any large number of people realize that there had been any change at all, so difficult is it to rid ourselves of the Money Illusion.

Even under such extreme conditions, the Money Illusion did not end. The idea of the stability of money was merely transferred by the Germans from their money to ours. Like a passenger who discovers, to his surprise, that his train is moving and not the one on the next track, the ordinary German, after the German price level had risen some hundreds of times, suddenly realized that the mark was falling and immediately assumed that the Swiss franc, or the American dollar, was stationary. It was then that the general public began, for the first time, to watch daily the foreign exchanges and promptly to adjust their own prices accordingly. They envied the foreigner for having what they now falsely assumed was a stable money. One result was a desire to "get back" to such a gold standard themselves; that any standard still better might be obtained was an idea never thought of. Thus the very instability of the paper mark, as soon as discovered, blinded them to the instability of the gold standard. The fact that gold was so very much more stable than unregulated paper money caused it to be idealized. But it is not, and never has been, ideal—far from it,—as the indexes just quoted clearly show.

Real Interest Rate

Interest

Human Action: A Treatise on Economics

By Ludwig Von Mises

1. THE PHENOMENON OF INTEREST

It has been shown that time preference is a category inherent in every human action. Time preference manifests itself in the phenomenon of originary interest, i.e., the discount of future goods as against present goods.

Interest is not merely interest on capital. Interest is not the specific income derived from the utilization of capital goods. The correspondence between three factors of production—labor, capital, and land—and three classes of income—wages, profit, and rent—as taught by the classical economists is untenable. Rent is not the specific revenue from land. Rent is a general catallactic phenomenon; it plays in the yield of labor and capital goods the same role it plays in the yield of land. Furthermore there is no homogeneous source of income that could be called profit in the sense in which the classical economists applied this term. Profit (in the sense of entrepreneurial profit) and interest are no more characteristic of capital than they are of land.

The prices of consumers' goods are by the interplay of the forces operating on the market apportioned to the various complementary factors cooperating in their production. As the consumers'

goods are present goods, while the factors of production are means for the production of future goods, and as present goods are valued higher than future goods of the same kind and quantity, the sum thus apportioned, even in the imaginary construction of the evenly rotating economy, falls behind the present price of the consumers' goods concerned. This difference is the originary interest. It is not specifically connected with any of the three classes of factors of production which the classical economists distinguished. Entrepreneurial profit and loss are produced by changes in the data and the resulting price changes which occur in the passing of the period of production.

Naïve reasoning does not see any problem in the current revenue derived from hunting, fishing, cattle breeding, forestry, and agriculture. Nature generates deer, fish, and cattle and makes them grow, causes the cows to give milk and the chickens to lay eggs, the trees to put on wood and to bear fruit, and the seeds to shoot into ears. He who has a title to appropriate for himself this recurring wealth enjoys a steady income. Like a stream which continually carries new water, the "stream of income" flows continually and conveys again and again new wealth. The whole process appears as a natural phenomenon. But for the economist a problem is presented in the determination of prices for land, cattle, and all the rest. If future goods were not bought and sold at a discount as against present goods, the buyer of land would have to pay a price which equals the sum of all future net revenues and which would leave nothing for a current reiterated income.

The yearly recurring proceeds of the owners of land and cattle are not marked by any characteristic which would catallactically distinguish them from the proceeds stemming from produced factors of production which are used up sooner or later in the processes of production. The power of disposal over a piece of land is the control of this field's cooperation in the production of all the fruit which can ever be grown on it, and the power of disposal over a mine is the control of its cooperation in the extraction of all the minerals which can ever be brought to the surface from it. In the same way the ownership of a machine or a bale of cotton is the control of its cooperation in the manufacture of all goods which are produced with its cooperation. The fundamental fallacy implied in all the productivity and use approaches to the problem of interest was that they traced back the phenomenon of interest to these productive services rendered by the factors of production. However, the serviceableness of the factors of production determines the prices paid for them, not interest. These prices exhaust the whole difference between the productivity of a process aided by a definite factor's cooperation and that of a process lacking this cooperation. The difference between the sum of the prices of the complementary factors of production and the products which emerges even in the absence of changes in the market data concerned, is an outcome of the higher valuation of present goods as compared with future goods. As production goes on, the factors of production are transformed or ripen into present goods of a higher value. This increment is the source of specific proceeds flowing into the hands of the owners of the factors of production, of originary interest.

The owners of the material factors of production—as distinct from the pure entrepreneurs of the imaginary construction of an integration of catallactic functions—harvest two catallactically different items: the prices paid for the productive cooperation of the factors they control on the one hand and interest on

the other hand. These two things must not be confused. It is not permissible to refer, in the explanation of interest, to the services rendered by the factors of production in the turning out of products.

Interest is a homogeneous phenomenon. There are no different sources of interest. Interest on durable goods and interest on consumption-credit are like other kinds of interest an outgrowth of the higher valuation of present goods as against future goods.

2. ORIGINARY INTEREST

Originary interest is the ratio of the value assigned to want-satisfaction in the immediate future and the value assigned to want-satisfaction in remote periods of the future. It manifests itself in the market economy in the discount of future goods as against present goods. It is a ratio of commodity prices, not a price in itself. There prevails a tendency toward the equalization of this ratio for all commodities. In the imaginary construction of the evenly rotating economy the rate of originary interest is the same for all commodities.

Originary interest is not "the price paid for the services of capital."[1] The higher productivity of more time-consuming roundabout methods of production which is referred to by Böhm-Bawerk and by some later economists in the explanation of interest, does not explain the phenomenon. It is, on the contrary, the phenomenon of originary interest that explains why less time-consuming methods of production are resorted to in spite of the fact that more time-consuming methods would render a higher output per unit of input. Moreover, the phenomenon of originary interest explains why pieces of usable land can be sold and bought at finite prices. If the future services which a piece of land can render were to be valued in the same way in which its present services are valued, no finite price would be high enough to impel its owner to sell it. Land could neither be bought nor sold against definite amounts of money, nor bartered against goods which can render only a finite number of services. Pieces of land would be bartered only against other pieces of land. A super-structure that can yield during a period of ten years an annual revenue of one hundred dollars would be priced (apart from the soil on which it is built) at the beginning of this period at one thousand dollars, at the beginning of the second year at nine hundred dollars, and so on.

Originary interest is not a price determined on the market by the interplay of the demand for and the supply of capital or capital goods. Its height does not depend on the extent of this demand and supply. It is rather the rate of originary interest that determines both the demand for and the supply of capital and capital goods. It determines how much of the available supply of goods is to be devoted to consumption in the immediate future and how much to provision for remoter periods of the future.

People do not save and accumulate capital because there is interest. Interest is neither the impetus to saving nor the reward or the compensation granted for abstaining from immediate consumption. It is the ratio in the mutual valuation of present goods as against future goods.

The loan market does not determine the rate of interest. It adjusts the rate of interest on loans to the rate of originary interest as manifested in the discount of future goods.

Originary interest is a category of human action. It is operative in any valuation of external things and can never disappear. If one day the state of affairs were to return which was actual at the close of the first millennium of the Christian era when some people believed that the ultimate end of all earthly things was impending, men would stop providing for future secular wants. The factors of production would in their eyes become useless and worthless. The discount of future goods as against present goods would not vanish. It would, on the contrary, increase beyond all measure. On the other hand, the fading away of originary interest would mean that people do not care at all for want-satisfaction in nearer periods of the future. It would mean that they prefer to an apple available today, tomorrow, in one year or in ten years, two apples available in a thousand or ten thousand years.

We cannot even think of a world in which originary interest would not exist as an inexorable element in every kind of action. Whether there is or is not division of labor and social cooperation and whether society is organized on the basis of private or of public control of the means of production, originary interest is always present. In a socialist commonwealth its role would not differ from that in the market economy.

Böhm-Bawerk has once for all unmasked the fallacies of the naïve productivity explanations of interest, i.e., of the idea that interest is the expression of the physical productivity of factors of production. However, Böhm-Bawerk has himself based his own theory to some extent on the productivity approach. In referring in his explanation to the technological superiority of more time-consuming, roundabout processes of production, he avoids the crudity of the naïve productivity fallacies. But in fact he returns, although in a subtler form, to the productivity approach. Those later economists who, neglecting the time-preference idea, have stressed exclusively the productivity idea contained in Böhm-Bawerk's theory cannot help concluding that originary interest must disappear if men were one day to reach a state of affairs in which no further lengthening of the period of production could bring about a further increase in productivity.[2] This is, however, utterly wrong. Originary interest cannot disappear as long as there is scarcity and therefore action.

As long as the world is not transformed into a land of Cockaigne, men are faced with scarcity and must act and economize; they are forced to choose between satisfaction in nearer and in remoter periods of the future because neither for the former nor for the latter can full contentment be attained. Then a change in the employment of factors of production which withdraws such factors from their employment for want-satisfaction in the nearer future and devotes them to want-satisfaction in the remoter future must necessarily impair the state of satisfaction in the nearer future and improve it in the remoter future. If we were to assume that this is not the case, we should become embroiled in insoluble contradictions. We may at best think of a state of affairs in which technological knowledge and skill have reached a point beyond which no further progress is possible for mortal men. No new processes increasing the output per unit of input can henceforth be invented. But if we suppose that some factors of production are scarce, we must not assume that all processes which—apart from the time they absorb—are the most productive ones are fully utilized, and that no process rendering a smaller output per unit of input is resorted to merely because of the fact that it produces its final result sooner than other, physically more productive processes. Scarcity of factors of production means that we are in a position to draft plans for the improvement of our well-being the realization of which is unfeasible because of the insufficient quantity of the means available. It is precisely the unfeasibility of such desirable improvements that constitutes the element of scarcity. The reasoning of the modern supporters of the productivity approach is misled by the connotations of Böhm-Bawerk's term *roundabout methods of production* and the idea of technological improvement which it suggests. However, if there is scarcity, there must always be an unused technological opportunity to improve the state of well-being by a lengthening of the period of production in some branches of industry, regardless of whether or not the state of technological knowledge has changed. If the means are scarce, if the praxeological correlation of ends and means still exists, there are by logical necessity unsatisfied wants with regard both to nearer and to remoter periods of the future. There are always goods the procurement of which we must forego because the way that leads to their production is too long and would prevent us from satisfying more urgent needs. The fact that we do not provide more amply for the future is the outcome of a weighing of satisfaction in nearer periods of the future against satisfaction in remoter periods of the future. The ratio which is the outcome of this valuation is originary interest.

In such a world of perfect technological knowledge a promoter drafts a plan *A* according to which a hotel in picturesque, but not easily accessible, mountain districts and the roads leading to it should be built. In examining the practicability of this plan he discovers that the means available are not sufficient for its execution. Calculating the prospects of the profitability of the investment, he comes to the conclusion that the expected proceeds are not great enough to cover the costs of material and labor to be expended and interest on the capital to be invested. He renounces the execution of project *A* and embarks instead upon the realization of another plan, *B*. According to plan *B* the hotel is to be erected in a more easily accessible location which does not offer all the advantages of the picturesque landscape which plan *A* had selected, but in which it can be built either with lower costs of construction or finished in a shorter time. If no interest on the capital invested were to enter into the calculation, the illusion could arise that the state of the market data—supply of capital goods and the valuations of the public—allows for the execution of plan *A*. However, the realization of plan *A* would withdraw scarce factors of production from employments in which they could satisfy wants considered more urgent by the consumers. It would mean a manifest malinvestment, a squandering of the means available.

A lengthening of the period of production can increase the quantity of output per unit of input or produce goods which cannot be produced at all within a shorter period of production. But it is not true that the imputation of the value of this additional wealth to the capital goods required for the lengthening of the period of production generates interest. If one were to assume this, one would relapse into the crassest errors of the productivity approach, irrefutably exploded by Böhm-Bawerk. The contribution of the complementary factors of production to the result of the process is the reason for their being considered as valuable; it explains the prices paid for them and is fully taken into account in the determination of these prices. No residuum is left that is not accounted for and could explain interest.

It has been asserted that in the imaginary construction of the evenly rotating economy no interest would appear.[3] However, it can be shown that this assertion is incompatible with the assumptions on which the construction of the evenly rotating economy is based.

We begin with the distinction between two classes of saving: plain saving and capitalist saving. Plain saving is merely the piling up of consumers' goods for later consumption. Capitalist saving is the accumulation of goods which are designed for an improvement of production processes. The aim of plain saving is later consumption; it is merely postponement of consumption. Sooner or later the goods accumulated will be consumed and nothing will be left. The aim of capitalist saving is first an improvement in the productivity of effort. It accumulates capital goods which are employed for further production and are not merely reserves for later consumption. The boon derived from plain saving is later consumption of the stock not instantly consumed but accumulated for later use. The boon derived from capitalist saving is the increase of the quantity of goods produced or the production of goods which could not be produced at all without its aid. In constructing the image of an evenly rotating (static) economy, economists disregard the process of capital accumulation; the capital goods are given and remain, as, according to the underlying assumptions, no changes occur in the data. There is neither accumulation of new capital through saving, nor consumption of capital available through a surplus of consumption over income, i.e., current production minus the funds required for the maintenance of capital. It is now our task to demonstrate that these assumptions are incompatible with the idea that there is no interest.

There is no need to dwell, in this reasoning, upon plain saving. The objective of plain saving is to provide for a future in which the saver could possibly be less amply supplied than in the present. Yet, one of the fundamental assumptions characterizing the imaginary construction of the evenly rotating economy is that the future does not differ at all from the present, that the actors are fully aware of this fact and act accordingly. Hence, in the frame of this construction, no room is left for the phenomenon of plain saving.

It is different with the fruit of capitalist saving, the accumulated stock of capital goods. There is in the evenly rotating economy neither saving and accumulation of additional capital goods nor eating up

of already existing capital goods. Both phenomena would amount to a change in the data and would thus disturb the even rotation of such an imaginary system. Now, the magnitude of saving and capital accumulation in the past—i.e., in the period preceding the establishment of the evenly rotating economy—was adjusted to the height of the rate of interest. If—with the establishment of the conditions of the evenly rotating economy—the owners of the capital goods were no longer to receive any interest, the conditions which were operative in the allocation of the available stocks of goods to the satisfaction of wants in the various periods of the future would be upset. The altered state of affairs requires a new allocation. Also in the evenly rotating economy the difference in the valuation of want-satisfaction in various periods of the future cannot disappear. Also in the frame of this imaginary construction, people will assign a higher value to an apple available today as against an apple available in ten or a hundred years. If the capitalist no longer receives interest, the balance between satisfaction in nearer and remoter periods of the future is disarranged. The fact that a capitalist has maintained his capital at just 100,000 dollars was conditioned by the fact that 100,000 present dollars were equal to 105,000 dollars available twelve months later. These 5,000 dollars were in his eyes sufficient to outweigh the advantages to be expected from an instantaneous consumption of a part of this sum. If interest payments are eliminated, capital consumption ensues.

This is the essential deficiency of the static system as Schumpeter depicts it. It is not sufficient to assume that the capital equipment of such a system has been accumulated in the past, that it is now available to the extent of this previous accumulation and is henceforth unalterably maintained at this level. We must also assign in the frame of this imaginary system a role to the operation of forces which bring about such a maintenance. If one eliminates the capitalist's role as receiver of interest, one replaces it by the capitalist's role as consumer of capital. There is no longer any reason why the owner of capital goods should abstain from employing them for consumption. Under the assumptions implied in the imaginary construction of static conditions (the evenly rotating economy) there is no need to keep them in reserve for rainy days. But even if, inconsistently enough, we were to assume that a part of them is devoted to this purpose and therefore withheld from current consumption, at least that part of capital will be consumed which corresponds to the amount that capitalist saving exceeds plain saving.[4]

If there were no originary interest, capital goods would not be devoted to immediate consumption and capital would not be consumed. On the contrary, under such an unthinkable and unimaginable state of affairs there would be no consumption at all, but only saving, accumulation of capital, and investment. Not the impossible disappearance of originary interest, but the abolition of payment of interest to the owners of capital, would result in capital consumption. The capitalists would consume their capital goods and their capital precisely because there is originary interest and present want-satisfaction is preferred to later satisfaction.

Therefore there cannot be any question of abolishing interest by any institutions, laws, or devices of bank manipulation. He who wants to "abolish" interest will have to induce people to value an apple available in a hundred years no less than a present apple. What can be abolished by laws and decrees is merely the right of the capitalists to receive interest. But such decrees would bring about capital consumption and would very soon throw mankind back into the original state of natural poverty.

3. THE HEIGHT OF INTEREST RATES

In plain saving and in the capitalist saving of isolated economic actors the difference in the valuation of want-satisfaction in various periods of the future manifests itself in the extent to which people provide in a more ample way for nearer than for remoter periods of the future. Under the conditions of a market economy the rate of originary interest is, provided the assumptions involved in the imaginary construction of the evenly rotating economy are present, equal to the ratio of a definite amount of money available today and the amount available at a later date which is considered as its equivalent.

The rate of originary interest directs the investment activities of the entrepreneurs. It determines the length of waiting time and of the period of production in every branch of industry.

People often raise the question of which rate of interest, a "high" or a "low," stimulates saving and capital accumulation more and which less. The question makes no sense. The lower the discount attached to future goods is, the lower is the rate of originary interest. People do not save more because the rate of originary interest rises, and the rate of originary interest does not drop on account of an increase in the amount of saving. Changes in the originary rates of interest and in the amount of saving are—other things, especially the institutional conditions, being equal—two aspects of the same phenomenon. The disappearance of originary interest would be tantamount to the disappearance of consumption. The increase of originary interest beyond all measure would be tantamount to the disappearance of saving and any provision for the future.

The quantity of the available supply of capital goods influences neither the rate of originary interest nor the amount of further saving. Even the most plentiful supply of capital need not necessarily bring about either a lowering of the rate of originary interest or a drop in the propensity to save. The increase in capital accumulation and the per capita quota of capital invested which is a characteristic mark of economically advanced nations does not necessarily either lower the rate of originary interest or weaken the propensity of individuals to make additional savings. People are, in dealing with these problems, for the most part misled by comparing merely the market rates of interest as they are determined on the loan market. However, these gross rates are not merely expressive of the height of originary interest. They contain, as will be shown later, other elements besides, the effect of which accounts for the fact that the gross rates are as a rule higher in poorer countries than in richer ones.

It is generally asserted that, other things being equal, the better individuals are supplied for the immediate future, the better they provide for wants for the remoter future. Consequently, it is said, the amount of total saving and capital accumulation within an economic system depends on the arrangement of the population into groups of different income levels. In a society with approximate income equality there is, it is said, less saving than in a society in which there is more inequality. There is a grain of truth in such observations. However, they are statements about psychological facts and as such lack the universal validity and necessity inherent in praxeological statements. Moreover, the other things the equality of which they presuppose comprehend the various individuals' valuations, their subjective value judgment in weighing the pros and cons of immediate consumption and of postponement of consumption. There are certainly many individuals whose behavior they describe correctly, but there also are other individuals who act in a different way. The French peasants, although for the most part people of moderate wealth and income, were in the nineteenth century widely known for their parsimonious habits, while wealthy members of the aristocracy and heirs of huge fortunes amassed in commerce and industry were no less renowned for their profligacy.

It is therefore impossible to formulate any praxeological theorem concerning the relation of the amount of capital available in the whole nation or to individual people on the one hand and the amount of saving or capital consumption and the height of the originary rate of interest on the other hand. The allocation of scarce resources to want-satisfaction in various periods of the future is determined by value judgments and indirectly by all those factors which constitute the individuality of the acting man.

4. ORIGINARY INTEREST IN THE CHANGING ECONOMY

So far we have dealt with the problem of originary interest under certain assumptions: that the turnover of goods is effected by the employment of neutral money; that saving, capital accumulation, and the determination of interest rates are not hampered by institutional obstacles; and that the whole economic process goes on in the frame of an evenly rotating economy. We shall drop the first two of these assumptions in the following chapter. Now we want to deal with originary interest in a changing economy.

He who wants to provide for the satisfaction of future needs must correctly anticipate these needs. If he fails in this understanding of the future, his provision will prove less satisfactory or totally futile. There is no such thing as an abstract saving that could provide for all classes of want-satisfaction and would be neutral with regard to changes occurring in conditions and valuations. Originary interest can therefore in the changing economy never appear in a pure unalloyed form. It is only in the imaginary construction of the evenly rotating economy that the mere passing of time matures originary interest; in the passage of time and with the progress of the process of production more and more value accrues, as it were, to the complementary factors of production; with the termination of the process of production the lapse of time has generated in the price of the product the full quota of originary interest. In the changing economy during the period of production there also arise synchronously other changes in valuations. Some goods are valued higher than previously, some lower. These alterations are the source from which entrepreneurial profits and losses stem. Only those entrepreneurs who in their planning have correctly anticipated the future state of the market are in a position to reap, in selling the products, an excess over the costs of production (inclusive of net originary interest) expended. An entrepreneur who has failed in his speculative understanding of the future can sell his products, if at all, only at prices which do not cover completely his expenditures plus originary interest on the capital invested.

Like entrepreneurial profit and loss, interest is not a price, but a magnitude which is to be disengaged by a particular mode of computation from the price of the products of successful business operations. The gross difference between the price at which a commodity is sold and the costs expended in its production (exclusive of interest on the capital invested) was called profit in the terminology of British classical economics.[5] Modern economics conceives this magnitude as a complex of catallactically disparate items. The excess of gross receipts over expenditures which the classical economists called profit includes the price for the entrepreneur's own labor employed in the process of production, interest on the capital invested, and finally entrepreneurial profit proper. If such an excess has not been reaped at all in the sale of the products, the entrepreneur not only fails to get profit proper, he receives neither an equivalent for the market value of the labor he has contributed nor interest on the capital invested.

The breaking down of gross profit (in the classical sense of the term) into managerial wages, interest, and entrepreneurial profit is not merely a device of economic theory. It developed, with progressing perfection in business practices of accountancy and calculation, in the field of commercial routine independently of the reasoning of the economists. The judicious and sensible businessman does not attach practical significance to the confused and garbled concept of profit as employed by the classical economists. His notion of costs of production includes the potential market price of his own services contributed, the interest paid on capital borrowed, and the potential interest he could earn, according to the conditions of the market, on his own capital invested in the enterprise by lending it to other people. Only the excess of proceeds over the costs so calculated is in his eyes entrepreneurial profit.[6]

The precipitation of entrepreneurial wages from the complex of all the other items included in the profit concept of classical economics presents no particular problem. It is more difficult to sunder entrepreneurial profit from originary interest. In the changing economy interest stipulated in loan contracts is always a gross magnitude out of which the pure rate of originary interest must be computed by a particular process of computation and analytical repartition. It has been shown already that in every act of lending, even apart from the problem of changes in the monetary unit's purchasing power, there is an element of entrepreneurial venture. The granting of credit is necessarily always an entrepreneurial speculation which can possibly result in failure and the loss of a part or of the total amount lent. Every interest stipulated and paid in loans includes not only originary interest but also entrepreneurial profit.

This fact for a long time misled the attempts to construct a satisfactory theory of interest. It was only the elaboration of the imaginary construction of the evenly rotating economy that made it possible to distinguish precisely between originary interest and entrepreneurial profit and loss.

5. THE COMPUTATION OF INTEREST

Originary interest is the outgrowth of valuations unceasingly fluctuating and changing. It fluctuates and changes with them. The custom of computing interest pro anno is merely commercial usage and a convenient rule of reckoning. It does not affect the height of the interest rates as determined by the market.

The activities of the entrepreneurs tend toward the establishment of a uniform rate of originary interest in the whole market economy. If there turns up in one sector of the market a margin between the prices of present goods and those of future goods which deviates from the margin prevailing in other sectors, a trend toward equalization is brought about by the striving of businessmen to enter those sectors in which this margin is higher and to avoid those in which it is lower. The final rate of originary interest is the same in all parts of the market of the evenly rotating economy.

The valuations resulting in the emergence of originary interest prefer satisfaction in a nearer period of the future to satisfaction of the same kind and extent in a remoter period of the future. Nothing would justify the assumption that this discounting of satisfaction in remoter periods progresses continuously and evenly. If we were to assume this, we would imply that the period of provision is infinite. However, the mere fact that individuals differ in their provision for future needs and that even to the most provident actor provision beyond a definite period appears supererogatory, forbids us to think of the period of provision as infinite.

The usages of the loan market must not mislead us. It is customary to stipulate a uniform rate of interest for the whole duration of a loan contract[7] and to apply a uniform rate in computing compound interest. The real determination of interest rates is independent of these and other arithmetical devices of interest computation. If the rate of interest is unalterably fixed by contract for a period of time, intervening changes in the market rate of interest are reflected in corresponding changes in the prices paid for the principal, due allowance being made for the fact that the amount of principal to be paid back at the maturity of the loan is unalterably stipulated. It does not affect the result whether one calculates with an unchanging rate of interest and changing prices of the principal or with changing interest rates and an unchanging amount of the principal, or with changes in both magnitudes.

The terms of a loan contract are not independent of the stipulated duration of the loan. Not only because those components of the gross rate of market interest which made it deviate from the rate of originary interest are affected by differences in the duration of the loan, but also on account of factors which bring about changes in the rate of originary interest, loan contracts are valued and appraised differently according to the duration of the loan stipulated.

NOTES FOR THIS CHAPTER

1. This is the popular definition of interest as, for instance, given by Ely, Adams, Lorenz, and Young, *Outlines of Economics* (3d ed. New York, 1920), p. 493.

2. Cf. Hayek, "The Mythology of Capital," *The Quarterly Journal of Economics*, L (1936), 223 ff. However Professor Hayek has since partly changed his point of view. (Cf. his article "Time-Preference and Productivity, a Reconsideration," *Economica*, XII [1945], 22–25.) But the idea criticized in the text is still widely held by economists.

3. Cf. J. Schumpeter, *The Theory of Economic Development*, trans. by R. Opie (Cambridge, 1934), pp. 34-46, 54.

4. Cf. Robbins, "On a Certain Ambiguity in the Conception of Stationary Equilibrium," *The Economic Journal*, XL (1930), 211 ff.

5. Cf. R. Whately, *Elements of Logic* (9th ed. London, 1848), pp. 354 ff.; E. Cannan, *A History of the Theories of Production and Distribution in English Political Economy from 1776 to 1848* (3d ed. London, 1924), pp. 189 ff. But, of course, the present-day intentional confusion of all economic concepts is conducive to obscuring this distinction. Thus, in the United States, in dealing with the dividends paid by corporations people speak of "profits." There are, of course, also deviations from this usage.

Expected Inflation and Interest Rates

By J. H. McCulloch

GIBSON'S PARADOX

Around the turn of the century, an English statistician named Gibson observed the following paradox: As the banks increase the money supply, one would think that they would drive prices up because of the Quantity Theory. At the same time, one would think that their loan expansion would drive interest rates down. Gibson therefore expected to see the highest price levels coinciding with the lowest interest rates and the lowest price levels coinciding with the highest interest rates. Yet when he looked at actual price and interest rate data for the 19th century, he observed just the opposite: The highest values of the price level coincided with the highest values of interest rates, and vice versa.

Graphically, what Gibson expected to see was something like the graphs of *P* and *i* in Figure 1. What he actually saw looked more like Figure 2. In fact, Gibson was looking at data for only the 19th century. Figure 4-2 covers almost a quarter of a millennium and shows that the same tendency prevailed during the 18th and 20th centuries.

Gibson's paradox was later solved by the famous American economist, Irving Fisher. Fisher pointed out that what Gibson was observing was the nominal interest rate, rather than the real interest rate. After a long period of inflationary monetary expansion, when prices are at their highest levels, people will have come to expect further inflation. This means that the nominal interest rate will exceed the real interest rate. Although the bank expansion may have the effect of lowering the real interest rate somewhat, the increase in inflationary expectations is liable to completely offset this effect, so that nominal interest rates will actually be at their highest. This means that a peak in the price level should actually correspond to a peak in the nominal interest rate.

Similarly, a prolonged period of deflationary monetary contraction (or a deflationary constant money supply during a period of real growth)

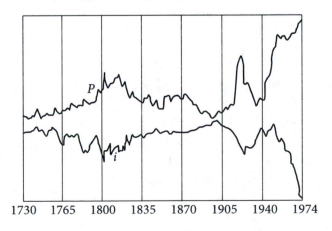

| 1730 | 1765 | 1800 | 1835 | 1870 | 1905 | 1940 | 1974 |

Figure 1: What Gibson expected to see.

413

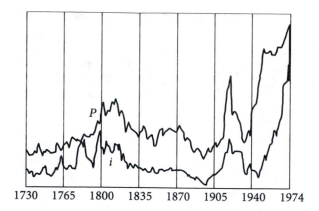

1730 1765 1800 1835 1870 1905 1940 1974

Figure 2: What Gibson actually saw.

The lo of the British price index (P) and the long-term interest rate (i). Figure 4-1 is copied from this one, but with the i-series turned upside down.

will result in *deflationary* expectations when the price level is at its minimum. This implies that the troughs in the price level will coincide with the troughs in nominal interest rates.

The phenomenon that Gibson observed, given Fisher's explanation, has an important implication for the formation of the expected inflation rate. It indicates that to a large degree expected inflation is based on the experience of inflation over the preceding several years.

Another implication has to do with the effect of monetary expansion on interest rates. In the short run, a higher rate of monetary expansion will probably reduce the interest rate, whether through the direct effect of bank expansion on the loan market, or through the "liquidity" effect of the temporary excess supply of money (see Chapter 2, pp. 23–24); however, the monetary expansion will increase the inflation rate. In the long run, inflationary expectations will catch up with actual inflation, and the nominal interest rate (which is the one that is observed) will end up higher than it started. A recent statistical study found that a sustained increase in the rate of monetary growth makes interest rates lower and lower, but only for about 6 to 8 months. Then they

start to come back up again. After 12 to 18 months, they pass their original level, and continue to climb.[1]

THE REAL CASH BALANCES MIRAGE

An interesting argument tends to crop up during inflationary times. Its advocates observe that as inflation rises, real cash balances often fall. They therefore argue that the monetary authorities, far from creating too much money, have actually created too *little* money. They go on to argue that the monetary authorities should get busy making the nominal money supply catch up with nominal income, so that real cash balances are restored to their original' level, relative to real income.

The fallacy in this argument lies in its failure to recognize that in an inflation caused by excessive monetary expansion, we would expect desired real cash balances to fall as inflationary expectations and nominal interest rates rise. Once an inflation is under way with excessive monetary expansion, real cash balances will be reduced to a lower level as prices are driven up by the increased supply of nominal cash balances and even further by the decreased demand for real balances. Measured real cash balances can *temporarily* be restored to their earlier level by even greater expansion of the nominal money supply, because monetary expansion causes prices to rise only with a lag in time. But eventually this greater expansion rate will cause prices to rise even faster, further lowering the equilibrium demand for real cash balances. To restore *m* to its original level now requires greater monetary expansion than ever. As the inflation rate rises higher and higher, the gap between real cash balances supplied and the equilibrium

1   Phillip Cagan and Arthur Gandolfi, "The Lag in Monetary Policy as Implied by the Time Pattern of Monetary Effects on Interest Rates," *American Economic Review* (May, 1969), pp. 277–284.

demand for real cash balances becomes larger and larger, so there will be no end to the growth of the monetary expansion and inflation rates. As with the passive accommodation doctrine, there will be a runaway money supply and a runaway inflation.

It is true that one of the real costs of inflation is that it forces individuals and firms to operate with smaller real cash balances than they would choose to employ without inflation. But the monetary authorities cannot permanently restore real cash balances through additional monetary expansion. With every step they take in that direction, their goal will recede like a mirage in the desert. It is actually worse than a mirage. A mirage moves one step away from you with every step you take toward it. But the goal of restoring real cash balances to their preinflationary level recedes two steps with every step of monetary expansion. The only way to increase real cash balances permanently without runaway inflation is by *slowing* the rate of monetary expansion long enough for inflationary expectations to fall.

A policy of printing money to keep up with inflation would in itself be sufficient to destabilize the price level.

Say's Law

Of the Demand or Market for Products

A Treatise on Political Economy

By Jean-Baptiste Say

It is common to hear adventurers in the different channels of industry assert, that their difficulty lies not in the production, but in the disposal of commodities; that products would always be abundant, if there were but a ready demand, or market for them. When the demand for their commodities is slow, difficult, and productive of little advantage, they pronounce money to be scarce; the grand object of their desire is, a consumption brisk enough to quicken sales and keep up prices. But ask them what peculiar causes and circumstances facilitate the demand for their products, and you will soon perceive that most of them have extremely vague notions of these matters; that their observation of facts is imperfect, and their explanation still more so; that they treat doubtful points as matter of certainty, often pray for what is directly opposite to their interests, and importunately solicit from authority a protection of the most mischievous tendency.

To enable us to form clear and correct practical notions in regard to markets for the products of industry, we must carefully analyse the best established and most certain facts, and apply to them the inferences we have already deduced from a similar way of proceeding; and thus perhaps we may arrive at new and important truths, that may serve to enlighten the views of the agents of industry, and to give confidence to the measures of governments anxious to afford them encouragement.

A man who applies his labour to the investing of objects with value by the creation of utility of some sort, can not expect such a value to be appreciated and paid for, unless where other men have the means of purchasing it. Now, of what do these means consist? Of other values of other products, likewise the fruits of industry, capital, and land. Which leads us to a conclusion that may at first sight appear paradoxical, namely, that it is production which opens a demand for products.

Should a tradesman say, "I do not want other products for my woollens, I want money," there could be little difficulty in convincing him that his customers could not pay him in money, without having first procured it by the sale of some other commodities of their own. "Yonder farmer," he may be told, "will buy your woollens, if his crops be good, and will buy more or less according to their abundance or scantiness; he can buy none at all, if his crops fail altogether. Neither can you buy his wool nor his corn yourself, unless you contrive to get woollens or some other article to buy withal. You say, you only want money; I say, you want other commodities, and not money. For what, in point of fact, do you want the money? Is it not for the purchase of raw materials or stock for your trade, or victuals for your support?[1] Wherefore, it is products that you want, and not money. The silver coin you will have received on the sale of your own products, and given in the purchase of those of other people, will the next moment execute the same office between other contracting parties, and so from one to another to infinity; just as a public vehicle successively transports objects one after another. If you can not find a ready sale for your commodity, will you say, it is merely for want of a vehicle to transport it? For, after all, money is but the agent of the transfer of values. Its whole utility has consisted in conveying to your hands the value of the commodities, which your customer has sold, for the purpose of buying again from you; and the very next purchase you make, it will again convey to a third person the value of the products you may have sold to others. So that you will have bought, and every body must buy, the objects of want or desire, each with the value of his respective products transformed into money for the moment only. Otherwise, how could it be possible that there should now be bought and sold in France five or six times as many commodities, as in the miserable reign of Charles VI.? Is it not obvious, that five or six times as many commodities must have been produced, and that they must have served to purchase one or the other?"

Thus, to say that sales are dull, owing to the scarcity of money, is to mistake the means for the cause; an error that proceeds from the circumstance, that almost all produce is in the first instance exchanged for money, before it is ultimately converted into other produce: and the commodity, which recurs so repeatedly in use, appears to vulgar apprehensions the most important of commodities, and the end and object of all transactions, whereas it is only the medium. Sales cannot be said to be dull because money is scarce, but because other products are so. There is always money enough to conduct the circulation and mutual interchange of other values, when those values really exist. Should the increase of traffic require more money to facilitate it, the want is easily supplied, and is a strong indication of prosperity—a proof that a great abundance of values has been created, which it is wished to exchange for other values. In such cases,

merchants know well enough how to find substitutes for the product serving as the medium of exchange or money:[2] and money itself soon pours in, for this reason, that all produce naturally gravitates to that place where it is most in demand. It is a good sign when the business is too great for the money; just in the same way as it is a good sign when the goods are too plentiful for the warehouses.

When a superabundant article can find no vent, the scarcity of money has so little to do with the obstruction of its sale, that the sellers would gladly receive its value in goods for their own consumption at the current price of the day: they would not ask for money, or have any occasion for that product, since the only use they could make of it would be to convert it forthwith into articles of their own consumption.[3]

This observation is applicable to all cases, where there is a supply of commodities or of services in the market. They will universally find the most extensive demand in those places, where the most of values are produced; because in no other places are the sole means of purchase created, that is, values. Money performs but a momentary function in this double exchange; and when the transaction is finally closed, it will always be found, that one kind of commodity has been exchanged for another.

It is worth while to remark, that a product is no sooner created, than it, from that instant, affords a market for other products to the full extent of its own value. When the producer has put the finishing hand to his product, he is most anxious to sell it immediately, lest its value should diminish in his hands. Nor is he less anxious to dispose of the money he may get for it; for the value of money is also perishable. But the only way of getting rid of money is in the purchase of some product or other. Thus, the mere circumstance of the creation of one product immediately opens a vent for other products.

For this reason, a good harvest is favourable, not only to the agriculturist, but likewise to the dealers in all commodities generally. The greater the crop, the larger are the purchases of the growers. A bad harvest, on the contrary, hurts the sale of commodities at large. And so it is also with the products of manufacture and commerce. The success of one branch of commerce supplies more ample means of purchase, and consequently opens a market for the products of all the other branches; on the other hand, the stagnation of one channel of manufacture, or of commerce, is felt in all the rest.

But it may be asked, if this be so, how does it happen, that there is at times so great a glut of commodities in the market, and so much difficulty in finding a vent for them? Why cannot one of these superabundant commodities be exchanged for another? I answer that the glut of a particular commodity arises from its having outrun the total demand for it in one or two ways; either because it has been produced in excessive abundance, or because the production of other commodities has fallen short.

It is because the production of some commodities has declined, that other commodities are superabundant. To use a more hackneyed phrase, people have bought less, because they have made less profit;[4] and they have made less profit for one or two causes; either they have found difficulties in the employment of their productive means, or these means have themselves been deficient.

It is observable, moreover, that precisely at the same time that one commodity makes a loss, another commodity is making excessive profit.[5] And, since such profits must operate as a powerful stimulus to the cultivation of that particular kind of products, there must needs be some violent means, or some extraordinary cause, a political or natural convulsion, or the avarice or ignorance of authority, to perpetuate this scarcity on the one hand, and consequent glut on the other. No sooner is the cause of this political disease removed, than the means of production feel a natural impulse towards the vacant channels, the replenishment of which restores activity to all the others. One kind of production would seldom outstrip every other, and its products be disproportionately cheapened, were production left entirely free.[6]

Should a producer imagine, that many other classes, yielding no material products, are his customers and consumers equally with the classes that raise themselves a product of their own; as, for example, public functionaries, physicians, lawyers, churchmen, &c., and thence infer, that there is a class of demand other than that of the actual producers, he would but expose the shallowness and superficiality of his ideas. A priest goes to a shop to buy a gown or a surplice; he takes the value, that is to make the purchase, in the form of money. Whence had he that money? From some tax-gatherer who has taken it from a tax-payer. But whence did this latter derive it? From the value he has himself produced. This value, first produced by the tax-payer, and afterwards turned into money, and given to the priest for his salary, has enabled him to make the purchase. The priest stands in the place of the producer, who might himself have laid the value of his product on his own account, in the purchase, perhaps, not of a gown or surplice, but of some other more serviceable product. The consumption of the particular product, the gown or surplice, has but supplanted that of some other product. It is quite impossible that the purchase of one product can be affected, otherwise than by the value of another.[7]

From this important truth may be deduced the following important conclusions:—

1. That, in every community the more numerous are the producers, and the more various their productions, the more prompt, numerous, and extensive are the markets for those productions; and, by a natural consequence, the more profitable are they to the producers; for price rises with the demand. But this advantage is to be derived from real production alone, and not from a forced circulation of products; for a value once created is not augmented in its passage from one hand to another, nor by being seized and expended by the government, instead of by an individual. The man, that lives upon the productions of other people, originates no demand for those productions; he merely puts himself in the place of the producer, to the great injury of production, as we shall presently see.

2. That each individual is interested in the general prosperity of all, and that the success of one branch of industry promotes that of all the others. In fact, whatever profession or line of business a man may devote himself to, he is the better paid and the more readily finds employment, in proportion as he sees others thriving equally around him. A man of talent, that scarcely vegetates in a retrograde state of society,

would find a thousand ways of turning his faculties to account in a thriving community that could afford to employ and reward his ability. A merchant established in a rich and populous town, sells to a much larger amount than one who sets up in a poor district, with a population sunk in indolence and apathy. What could an active manufacturer, or an intelligent merchant, do in a small deserted and semi-barbarous town in a remote corner of Poland or Westphalia? Though in no fear of a competitor, he could sell but little, because little was produced; whilst at Paris, Amsterdam, or London, in spite of the competition of a hundred dealers in his own line, he might do business on the largest scale. The reason is obvious: he is surrounded with people who produce largely in an infinity of ways, and who make purchases, each with his respective products, that is to say, with the money arising from the sale of what he may have produced.

This is the true source of the gains made by the towns' people out of the country people, and again by the latter out of the former; both of them have wherewith to buy more largely, the more amply they themselves produce. A city, standing in the centre of a rich surrounding country, feels no want of rich and numerous customers; and, on the other hand, the vicinity of an opulent city gives additional value to the produce of the country. The division of nations into agricultural, manufacturing, and commercial, is idle enough. For the success of a people in agriculture is a stimulus to its manufacturing and commercial prosperity; and the flourishing condition of its manufacture and commerce reflects a benefit upon its agriculture also.[8]

The position of a nation, in respect of its neighbours, is analogous to the relation of one of its provinces to the others, or of the country to the town; it has an interest in their prosperity, being sure to profit by their opulence. The government of the United States, therefore, acted most wisely, in their attempt, about the year 1802, to civilize their savage neighbours, the Creek Indians. The design was to introduce habits of industry amongst them, and make them producers capable of carrying on a barter trade with the States of the Union; for there is nothing to be got by dealing with a people that have nothing

to pay. It is useful and honourable to mankind, that one nation among so many should conduct itself uniformly upon liberal principles. The brilliant results of this enlightened policy will demonstrate, that the systems and theories really destructive and fallacious, are the exclusive and jealous maxims acted upon by the old European governments, and by them most impudently styled *practical truths,* for no other reason, as it would seem, than because they have the misfortune to put them in practice. The United States will have the honour of proving experimentally, that true policy goes hand-in-hand with moderation and humanity.[9]

3. From this fruitful principle, we may draw this further conclusion, that it is no injury to the internal or national industry and production to buy and import commodities from abroad; for nothing can be bought from strangers, except with native products, which find a vent in this external traffic. Should it be objected; that this foreign produce may have been bought with specie, I answer, specie is not always a native product, but must have been bought itself with the products of native industry; so that, whether the foreign articles be paid for in specie or in home products, the vent for national industry is the same in both cases.[10]

4. The same principle leads to the conclusion, that the encouragement of mere consumption is no benefit to commerce; for the difficulty lies in supplying the means, not in stimulating the desire of consumption; and we have seen that production alone, furnishes those means. Thus, it is the aim of good government to stimulate production, of bad government to encourage consumption.

For the same reason that the creation of a new product is the opening of a new market for other products, the consumption or destruction of a product is the stoppage of a vent for them. This is no evil where the end of the product has been answered by its destruction, which end is the satisfying of some human want, or the creation of some new product designed for such a satisfaction. Indeed, if the nation be in a thriving condition, the gross national re-production exceeds the gross consumption. The consumed products have fulfilled their office, as it is natural and fitting they should; the consumption, however, has opened no new market, but just the reverse.[11]

Having once arrived at the clear conviction, that the general demand for products is brisk in proportion to the activity of production, we need not trouble ourselves much to inquire towards what channel of industry production may be most advantageously directed. The products created give rise to various degrees of demand, according to the wants, the manners, the comparative capital, industry, and natural resources of each country; the article most in request, owing to the competition of buyers, yields the best interest of money to the capitalist, the largest profits to the adventurer, and the best wages to the labourer; and the agency of their respective services is naturally attracted by these advantages towards those particular channels.

In a community, city, province, or nation, that produces abundantly, and adds every moment to the sum of its products, almost all the branches of commerce, manufacture, and generally of industry, yield handsome profits, because the demand is great, and because there is always a large quantity of products in the market, ready to bid for new productive services. And, *vice versâ*, wherever, by reason of the blunders of the nation or its government, production is stationary, or does not keep pace with consumption, the demand gradually declines, the value of the product is less than the charges of its production; no productive exertion is properly rewarded; profits and wages decrease; the employment of capital becomes less advantageous and more hazardous; it is consumed piecemeal, not through extravagance, but through necessity, and because the sources of profit are dried up.[12] The labouring classes experience a want of work; families before in tolerable circumstances, are more cramped and confined; and those before in difficulties are left altogether destitute. Depopulation, misery, and returning barbarism, occupy the place of abundance and happiness.

Such are the concomitants of declining production, which are only to be remedied by frugality, intelligence, activity, and freedom.

NOTES FOR THIS CHAPTER

1. Even when money is obtained with a view to hoard or bury it, the ultimate object is always to employ it in a purchase of some kind. The heir of the lucky finder uses it in that way, if the miser do not; for money, as money, has no other use than to buy with.

2. By bills at sight, or after date, bank-notes, running-credits, write-offs, &c. as at London and Amsterdam.

3. I speak here of their aggregate consumption, whether unproductive and designed to satisfy the personal wants of themselves and their families, or expended in the sustenance of reproductive industry. The woollen or cotton manufacturer operates a two-fold consumption of wool and cotton: 1. For his personal wear. 2. For the supply of his manufacture; but, be the purpose of his consumption what it may, whether personal gratification or reproduction, he must needs buy what he consumes with what he produces.

4. Individual profits must, in every description of production, from the general merchant to the common artisan, be derived from the participation in the values produced. The ratio of that participation will form the subject of Book II., *infrà*.

5. The reader may easily apply these maxims to any time or country he is acquainted with. We have had a striking instance in France during the years 1811, 1812, and 1813; when the high prices of colonial produce of wheat, and other articles, went hand-in-hand with the low price of many others that could find no advantageous market.

6. These considerations have hitherto been almost wholly overlooked, though forming the basis of correct conclusions in matters of commerce, and of its regulation by the national authority. The right course where it has, by good luck been pursued, appears to have been selected by accident, or, at most, by a confused idea of its propriety, without either self-conviction, or the ability to convince other people.

7. *Sismondi*, who seems not to have very well understood the principles laid down in this and the three first chapters of Book II. of this work, instances the immense quantity of manufactured products with which England has of late inundated the markets of other nations, as a proof, that it is impossible for industry to be too

productive. (*Nouv. Prin.* liv. iv. c. 4.) But the glut thus occasioned proves nothing more than the feebleness of production in those countries that have been thus glutted with English manufactures. Did Brazil produce wherewithal to purchase the English goods exported thither, those goods would not glut her market. Were England to admit the import of the products of the United States, she would find a better market for her own in those States. The English government, by the exorbitance of its taxation upon import and consumption, virtually interdicts to its subjects many kinds of importation, thus obliging the merchant to offer to foreign countries a higher price for those articles, whose import is practicable, as sugar, coffee, gold, silver, &c. for the price of the precious metals to them is enhanced by the low price of their commodities, which accounts for the ruinous returns of their commerce.

8. I would not be understood to maintain in this chapter, that one product can not be raised in too great abundance, in relation to all others; but merely that nothing is more favourable to the demand of one product, than the supply of another; that the import of English manufactures into Brazil would cease to be excessive and be rapidly absorbed, did Brazil produce on her side returns sufficiently ample; to which end it would be necessary that the legislative bodies of either country should consent, the one to free production, the other to free importation. In Brazil every thing is grasped by monopoly, and property is not exempt from the invasion of the government. In England, the heavy duties are a serious obstruction to the foreign commerce of the nation, inasmuch as they circumscribe the choice of returns. I happen myself to know of a most valuable and scientific collection of natural history, which could not be imported from Brazil into England by reason of the exorbitant duties.

9. The views of *Sismondi*, in this particular, have been since adopted by our own Malthus, and those of our author by Ricardo. This difference of opinion has given rise to an interesting discussion between our author and Malthus, to whom he has recently addressed a correspondence on this and other parts of the science. Were any thing wanting to confirm the arguments of

this chapter, it would be supplied by a reference to his *Lettre* 1, à M. Malthus. Sismondi has vainly attempted to answer Ricardo, but has made no mention of his original antagonist. *Vide Annales de Legislation*, No. 1. art. 3. Geneve, 1820. Translator.

10. The capitalist, in spending the interest of his capital, spends his portion of the products raised by the employment of that capital. The general rules that regulate the ratio he receives will be investigated in Book II., *infrà*. Should he ever spend the principal, still he consumes products only; for capital consists of products, devoted indeed to reproductive, but susceptible of unproductive consumption; to which it is in fact consigned whenever it is wasted or dilapidated.

11. A productive establishment on a large scale is sure to animate the industry of the whole neighbourhood. "In Mexico," says Humboldt, "the best cultivated tract, and that which brings to the recollection of the traveller the most beautiful part of French scenery, is the level country extending from Salamanca as far as Silao, Guanaxuato, and Villa de Leon, and encircling the richest mines of the known world. Wherever the veins of precious metal have been discovered and worked, even in the most desert part of the Cordilleras, and in the most barren and insulated spots, the working of the mines, instead of interrupting the business of superficial cultivation, has given it more than usual activity. The opening of a considerable vein is sure to be followed by the immediate erection of a town; farming concerns are established in the vicinity; and the spot so lately insulated in the midst of wild and desert mountains, is soon brought into contact with the tracts before in tillage." *Essai pol. sur. la Nouv. Espagne.*

12. It is only by the recent advances of political economy, that these most important truths have been made manifest, not to vulgar apprehension alone, but even to the most distinguished and enlightened observers. We read in Voltaire that "such is the lot of humanity, that the patriotic desire for one's country's grandeur, is but a wish for the humiliation of one's neighbours;—that it is clearly impossible for one country to gain, except by the loss of another." (*Dist. Phil. Art. Patrie.*) By a continuation of the same false reasoning, he goes on to

declare, that a thorough citizen of the world cannot wish his country to be greater or less, richer or poorer. It is true, that he would not desire her to extend the limits of her dominion, because, in so doing, she might endanger her own well-being; but he will desire her to progress in wealth, for her progressive prosperity promotes that of all other nations.

Effects of Accumulation and Profit of Interest

Principles of Political Economy and Taxation

By David Ricardo

From the account which has been given of the profits of stock, it will appear, that no accumulation of capital will permanently lower profits, unless there be some permanent cause for the rise of wages. If the funds for the maintenance of labour were doubled, trebled, or quadrupled, there would not long be any difficulty in procuring the requisite number of hands, to be employed by those funds; but owing to the increasing difficulty of making constant additions to the food of the country, funds of the same value would probably not maintain the same quantity of labour, If the necessaries of the workman could be constantly increased with the same facility, there could be no permanent alteration in the rate of profits or wages, to whatever amount capital might be accumulated. Adam Smith, however, uniformly ascribes the fall of profits to accumulation of capital, and to the competition which will result from It, without ever adverting to the increasing difficulty of providing food for the additional number of labourers which the additional capital will employ. "The increase of stock," he says, "which raises wages, tends to lower profit. When the stocks of many rich merchants are turned into the same trade, their mutual competition naturally tends to lower its profit; and when there is a like increase of stock in all the different trades carried on in the same society, the same competition must produce the same effect in ail." Adam Smith speaks here of a rise of wages, but it is of a temporary rise, proceeding from increased funds before the population is increased; and he does not appear to see, that at the same time that capital is increased, the work to be effected by capital, is increased in the same proportion. M. Say has, however, most satisfactorily shewn, that there is no amount of capital which may not be employed in a country, because demand is only limited by production. No man produces, but with a view to consume or sell, and he never sells, but with an intention to purchase some other commodity, which may be immediately useful to him, or which may contribute to future production. By producing, then, he necessarily becomes either the consumer of his own goods, or the purchaser and consumer of the goods of some other person. It is not to be supposed that he should, for any length of time, be ill-informed of the commodities which he can most advantageously produce, to attain the object which he has in view, namely, the possession of other goods; and, therefore, it is not probable that he will continually produce a commodity for which there is no demand.[1]

There cannot, then, be accumulated in a country any amount of capital which cannot be employed productively, until wages rise so high in consequence of the rise of necessaries, and so little consequently remains for the profits of stock, that the motive for accumulation ceases.[2] While the profits of stock are high, men will have a motive to accumulate. Whilst a man has any wished-for gratification unsupplied, he will have a demand for more commodities; and it will be an effectual demand while he has any new value to offer in exchange for them. If ten thousand pounds were given to a man having £100,000 per annum, he would not lock it up in a chest, but would either increase his expenses by £10,000; employ it himself productively, or lend it to some other person for that purpose; in either case, demand would be increased, although it would be for different objects. If he increased his expenses, his effectual demand might probably be for buildings, furniture, or some such enjoyment. If he employed his £10,000 productively, his effectual demand would be for food, clothing, and raw material, which might set new labourers to work; but still it would be demand.[3]

Productions are always bought by productions, or by services; money is only the medium by which the exchange is effected. Too much of a particular commodity may be produced, of which there may be such a glut in the market, as not to repay the capital expended on it; but this cannot be the case with respect to all commodities; the demand for corn is limited by the mouths which are to eat it, for shoes and coats by the persons who are to wear them; but though a community, or a part of a community, may have as much corn, and as many hats and shoes, as it is able or may wish to consume, the same cannot be said of every commodity produced by nature or by art. Some would consume more wine, if they had the ability to procure it. Others having enough of wine, would wish to increase the quantity or improve the quality of their furniture. Others might wish to ornament their grounds, or to enlarge their houses. The wish to do ail or some of these is implanted in every man's breast; nothing is required but the means, and nothing can afford the means, but an increase of production. If I had food and necessaries at my disposal, I should not be long in want of workmen who would put me in possession of some of the objects most useful or most desirable to me.

Whether these increased productions, and the consequent demand which they occasion, shall or shall not lower profits, depends solely on the rise of wages; and the rise of wages, excepting for a limited period, on the facility of producing the food and necessaries of the labourer. I say excepting for a limited period, because no point is better established, than that the supply of labourers will always ultimately be in proportion to the means of supporting them.

There is only one case, and that will be temporary, in which the accumulation of capital with a low price of food may be attended with a fall of profits; and that is, when the funds for the maintenance of labour increase much more rapidly than population;—wages will then be high, and profits low. If every man were to forego the use of luxuries, and be intent only on accumulation, a quantity of necessaries might be produced, for which there could not be any immediate consumption. Of commodities so limited in number, there might undoubtedly be an universal glut, and consequently there might neither be demand for an additional quantity of such commodities, nor profits on the employment of more capital. If men ceased to consume, they would cease to produce. This admission does not impugn the general principle. In such a country as England, for example, it is difficult to suppose that there can be any disposition to devote the whole capital and labour of the country to the production of necessaries only.

When merchants engage their capitals in foreign trade, or in the carrying trade, it is always from choice, and never from necessity: it is because in that trade their profits will be somewhat greater than in the home trade.

Adam Smith has justly observed "that the desire of food is limited in every man by the narrow capacity of the human stomach, but the desire of the conveniences and ornaments of building, dress, equipage, and household furniture, seems to have no limit or certain boundary." Nature then has necessarily limited the amount of capital which can at any one time be profitably engaged in agriculture, but she has placed no limits to the amount of capital that may be employed in procuring "the conveniences and ornaments" of life. To procure these gratifications in the greatest abundance is the object in view, and it is only because foreign trade, or the carrying trade, will accomplish it better, that men engage in them in preference to manufacturing the commodities required, or a substitute for them, at home. If, however, from peculiar circumstances, we were precluded from engaging capital in foreign trade, or in the carrying trade, we should, though with less advantage, employ it at home; and while there is no limit to the desire of "conveniences, ornaments of building, dress, equipage, and household furniture," there can be no limit to the capital that may be employed in procuring them, except that which bounds our power to maintain the workmen who are to produce them.

Adam Smith, however, speaks of the carrying trade as one, not of choice, but of necessity; as if the capital engaged in it would be inert if not so employed, as if the capital in the home trade could overflow, if not confined to a limited amount. He says, "when the capital stock of any country is increased to such a degree, *that it cannot be all employed in supplying the consumption, and supporting the productive labour of that particular country,* the surplus part of it naturally disgorges itself into the carrying trade, and is employed in performing the same offices to other countries."

"About ninety-six thousand hogsheads of tobacco are annually purchased with a part of the surplus produce of British industry. But the demand of Great Britain does not require, perhaps, more than fourteen thousand. If the remaining eighty two thousand, therefore, could not be sent abroad *and exchanged for something more in demand at home,* the importation of them would cease immediately, *and with it the productive labour of all the inhabitants of Great Britain, who are at present employed in preparing the goods with which these eighty-two thousand hogsheads are annually purchased.*" But could not this portion of the productive labour of Great Britain be employed in preparing some other sort of goods, with which something more in demand at home might be purchased? And if it could not, might we not employ this productive labour, though with less advantage, in making those

goods in demand at home, or at least some substitute for them? If we wanted velvets, might we not attempt to make velvets; and if we could not succeed, might we not make more cloth, or some other object desirable to us?

We manufacture commodities, and with them buy goods abroad, because we can obtain a greater quantity than we could make at home. Deprive us of this trade, and we immediately manufacture again for ourselves. But this opinion of Adam Smith is at variance with ail his general doctrines on this subject. "If a foreign country can supply us with a commodity cheaper than we ourselves can make it, better buy it of them with some part of the produce of our own industry, employed in a way in which we have some advantage. *The general industry of the country being always in proportion to the capital which employs it,* will not thereby be diminished, but only left to find out the way in which it can be employed with the greatest advantage."

Again, "Those, therefore, who have the command of more food than they themselves can consume, are always willing to exchange the surplus, or, what is the same thing, the price of it, for gratifications of another kind. What is over and above satisfying the limited desire, is given for the amusement of those desires which cannot be satisfied, but seem to be altogether endless, The poor, in order to obtain food, exert themselves to gratifying those fancies of the rich; and to obtain it more certainly, they vie with one another in the cheapness and perfection of their work. The number of workmen increases with the increasing quantity of food, or with the growing improvement and cultivation of the lands; and as the nature of their business admits of the utmost subdivisions of labours, the quantity of materials which they can work up increases in a much greater proportion than their numbers. Hence arises a demand for every sort of material which human invention can employ, either usefully or ornamentally, in building, dress, equipage, or household furniture; for the fossils and minerals contained in the bowels of the earth, the precious metals, and the precious stones."

It follows then from these admissions that there is no limit to demand—no limit to the employment of capital while it yields any profit, and that however abundant capital may become, there is no other adequate reason for a fall of profit but a rise of wages, and further it may be added, that the only adequate and permanent cause for the rise of wages Is the increasing difficulty of providing food and necessaries for the increasing number of workmen.

Adam Smith has justly observed, that it is extremely difficult to determine the rate of the profits of stock. "Profit is so fluctuating, that even in a particular trade, and much more in trades in general, it would be difficult to state the average rate of it, To judge of what it may have been formerly, or in remote periods of time, with any degree of precision must be altogether impossible." Yet since it is evident that much will be given for the use of money, when much can be made by it, he suggests that "the market rate of interest will lead us to form some notion of the rate of profits, and the history of the progress of interest afford us that of the progress of profits." Undoubtedly if the market rate of interest could be accurately known for any considerable period, we should have a tolerably correct criterion, by which to estimate the progress of profits.

But in all countries, from mistaken notions of policy, the State has interfered to prevent a fair and free market rate of interest, by imposing heavy and ruinous penalties on all those who shall take more than the rate fixed by law. In ail countries probably these laws are evaded, but records give us little information on this head, and point out rather the legal and fixed rate, than the market rate of interest. During the present war, Exchequer and Navy Bills have been frequently at so high a discount, as to afford the purchasers of them 7, 8 per cent, or a greater rate of interest for their money. Loans have been raised by Government at an interest exceeding 6 per cent and individuals have been frequently obliged, by indirect means, to pay more than 10 per cent for the interest of money; yet during this same period the legal rate of interest has been uniformly at 5 per cent. Little dependence for information then can be placed on that which is the fixed and legal rate of interest, when we find it may differ so considerably from the market rate. Adam Smith informs us, that from the 37th of Henry VIII. to 21st of James I. 10 per cent continued to be the legal rate of interest. Soon after

the Restoration it was reduced to 6 per cent, and by the 12th of Anne, to 5 per cent. He thinks the legal rate followed, and did not precede the market rate of interest. Before the American war, Government borrowed at 3 per cent, and the people of credit in the capital, and in many other parts of the kingdom at 3½, 4, and 4½ per cent.

The rate of interest, though ultimately and permanently governed by the rate of profit, is however subject to temporary variations from other causes. With every fluctuation in the quantity and value of money, the prices of commodities naturally vary. They vary also, as we have already shewn, from the alteration in the proportion of supply to demand, although there should not be either greater facility or difficulty of production. When the market prices of goods fall from an abundant supply, from a diminished demand, or from a rise in the value of money, a manufacturer naturally accumulates an unusual quantity of finished goods, being unwilling to sell them at very depressed prices. To meet his ordinary payments, for which he used to depend on the sale of his goods, he now endeavours to borrow on credit, and is often obliged to give an increased rate of interest. This, however, is but of temporary duration; for either the manufacturer's expectations were well grounded, and the market price of his commodities rises, or he discovers that there is a permanently diminished demand, and he no longer resists the course of affairs: prices fall, and money and interest regain their real value. If by the discovery of a new mine, by the abuses of banking, or by any other cause, the quantity of money be greatly increased, its ultimate effect is to raise the prices of commodities in proportion to the increased quantity of money; but there is probably always an interval, during which some effect is produced on the rate of interest.

The price of funded property is not a steady criterion by which to judge of the rate of interest. In time of war, the stock market is so loaded by the continual loans of Government, that the price of stock has not time to settle at its fair level, before a new operation of funding takes place, or it is affected by anticipation of political events. In time of peace, on the contrary, the operations of the sinking fund, the unwillingness, which a particular class of persons feel to divert their funds to any other employment than that to which they have been accustomed, which they think secure, and in which their dividends are paid with the utmost regularity, elevates the price of stock, and consequently depresses the rate of interest on these securities below the general market rate. It is observable too, that for different securities, Government pays very different rates of interest. Whilst £100 capital in 5 per cent stock is selling for £95, an exchequer bill of £100, will be sometimes selling for £100 5s., for which exchequer bill, no more interest will be annually paid than £4 11s, 3d.: one of these securities pays to a purchaser at the above prices, an interest of more than 5¼ per cent, the other but little more than 4¼; a certain quantity of these exchequer bills is required as a safe and marketable investment for bankers; if they were increased much beyond this demand, they would probably be as much depreciated as the 5 per cent stock. A stock paying 3 per cent per annum will always sell at a proportionally greater price than stock paying 5 per cent, for the capital debt of neither can be discharged but at par, or £100 money for £100 stock. The market rate of interest may fall to 4 per cent, and Government would then pay the holder of 5 per cent stock at par, unless he consented to take 4 per cent or some diminished rate of interest under 5 per cent: they would have no advantage from so paying the holder of 3 per cent stock, till the market rate of interest had fallen below 3 per cent per annum. To pay the interest on the national debt, large sums of money are withdrawn from circulation four times in the year for a few days. These demands for money being only temporary, seldom affect prices; they are generally surmounted by the payment of a large rate of interest.[4]

NOTES FOR THIS CHAPTER

1. Adam Smith speaks of Holland, as affording an instance of the fall of profits from the accumulation of capital, and from every employment being consequently overcharged, "The Government there borrow at 2 per cent, and private people of good credit, at 3 per cent." But it should be remembered, that Holland was obliged to import almost all the corn which she consumed, and by imposing heavy taxes on the necessaries of the labourer, she further raised the wages of labour. These facts will sufficiently account for the low rate of profits and interest in Holland.

2. Is the following quite consistent with M. Say's principle? "The more disposable capitals are abundant in proportion to the extent of employment for them, the more will the rate of interest on loans of capital fall."—Vol. ii. p. 108, If capital to any extent can be employed by a country, how can it be said to be abundant, compared with the extent of employment for it?

3. Adam Smith says, that "When the produce of any particular branch of industry exceeds what the demand of the country requires, the surplus must be sent abroad, and exchanged for something for which there is a demand at home. *Without such exportation, a part of the productive labour of the country must cease, and the value of its annual produce diminish.* The land and labour of Great Britain produce generally more corn, woollens, and hardware, than the demand of the home market requires. The surplus part of them, therefore, must be sent abroad, and exchanged for something for which there is a demand at home. It is only by means of such exportation, that this surplus can acquire a value sufficient to compensate the labour and expense of producing it." One would be led to think by the above passage, that Adam Smith concluded we were under some necessity of producing a surplus of corn, woollen goods, and hardware, and that the capital which produced them could not be otherwise employed. It is, however, always a matter of choice in what way a capital shall be employed, and therefore there can never, for any length of time be a surplus of any commodity; for if there were, it would fall below its natural price, and capital would be removed to

some more profitable employment. No writer has more satisfactorily and ably shewn than Dr. Smith, the tendency of capital to move from employments in which the goods produced do not repay by their price the whole expenses, including the ordinary profits, of producing and bringing them to market.*

4. "All kinds of public loans", observes M. Say, "are attended with the inconvenience of withdrawing capital, or portions of capital, from productive employments, to devote them to consumption; and when they take place in a country, *the Government of which does not inspire much confidence,* they have the further inconvenience of raising the interest of capital. Who would lend at 5 per cent per annum to agriculture, to manufacturers and to commerce, when a borrower may be found ready to pay an interest of 7 or 8 per cent? That sort of income, which is called profit of stock, would rise then at the expense of the consumer. Consumption would be reduced, by the rise in the price of produce; and the other productive services would be less in demand, less well paid, The whole nation, capitalists excepted, would be the sufferers from such a state of things." To the question: "who would lend money to farmers, manufacturers, and merchants, at 5 per cent per annum, when another borrower, having little credit, would give 7 or 8?" I reply, that every prudent and reasonable man would. Because the rate of interest is 7 or 8 per cent there, where the Sender runs extraordinary risk, is this any reason that it should be equally high in those places where they are secured from such risks? M. Say allows, that the rate of interest depends on the rate of profits; but it does not therefore follow, that the rate of profits depends on the rate of interest. One is the cause, the other the effect, and it is impossible for any circumstances to make them change places.

---

* See Chap. X. Book I.

Say's Principle, What it Means and Doesn't Mean

By Axel Leijonhufvud and Robert Clower

The doctrine in question only appears a paradox, because it has usually been so expressed as apparently to contradict ... well-known facts; which, however, were equally well known to the authors of the doctrine, who, therefore, can only have adopted from inadvertence any form of expression which could to a candid person appear inconsistent with it.

J. S. Mill, *Some Unsettled Questions of Political Economy* (1844)

Students with some exposure to macroeconomics will recall that the standard verbal statement of "Say's Law" (SL) is "Supply creates its own demand." Students will also recall—at least if they have had the usual indoctrination in these matters—that the rejection of SL was associated with the development of Keynesian macroeconomics. Classical (pre-Keynesian) economists, so it is said, could not explain prolonged unemployment because they believed in SL, but Keynes denied the validity of SL and so was able to lay the foundations for a modern and reasonably adequate theory of income and employment ... etc.[1]

Like most fairytales, this one contains an element of truth. Anyone who bothers to delve into the matter[2] will discover that textbook discussions of SL are seldom fair to pre-Keynesian writers; this is not surprising. Doubts about the meaning and significance of SL have been perplexing economists more or less continuously for nearly two centuries. The extensive literature since Keynes has done little to resolve these doubts, largely because it has failed to address squarely the main issues in dispute and so has got bogged down in a mire of conceptual and semantic confusions.

To avoid the same mistake, we shall ignore the previous literature for the time being and start by explaining and analyzing a simple but fundamental proposition that we shall call "Say's Principle" (SP). This principle, though elementary and outwardly trivial, is crucial for clear understanding of macrotheory. Indeed, there is hardly a single problem in macrotheory (or, for that matter, micro-theory) that can be consistently analyzed without it. The same principle permits us to resolve all issues of substance associated with earlier discussions of SL. It is essential, therefore, that students acquire a clear understanding not only of what SP means and does not mean, but also of what it implies and does not imply.

I. FUNDAMENTALS

In the following paper the term "commodity" will refer to any exchangeable object. Thus the usual macro-model, involving labor services, goods, bonds and money, has four commodities. Similarly, we shall use the term "transactor" (or individual) to refer to any economic agent or decision-making unit.[3] For reasons that will become clear later, we shall deal directly with just one type of economic activity, namely exchange. Occasional references to consumption, production and other non-trade activities are introduced only by way of illustration.

To lend direction to the argument, we begin by associating SP with a brief verbal statement that is easy to remember—not, however, with the phrase "Supply creates its own demand." A mnemonic much to be preferred is: *the net value of an individual's planned trades is identically zero.* (Notice, for reasons to be made clear later, we do not say net market value.) This is a restriction that we impose on the commodity trades that transactors are permitted to contemplate within the conceptual framework of economic theory, trades that we shall later refer to as theoretically admissible. It is not an assertion about the income and expenditure plans of flesh-and-blood humans (the world is full of thieves and philanthropists as well as people who can't calculate the cost of their weekly groceries). Neither is it an assertion that applies to all commodity transfers that occur in the real world (the acquisition of cash by a pickpocket is a case in point). What the restriction does and does not entail, however, is better indicated by argument than example.

Starting from familiar ground, consider one of the first exercises encountered in microeconomics, namely, the household decision problem of determining how a given amount of money, $s_{m,o}$, will be allocated to purchase quantities d_x and d_y of two commodities that are available at given money prices p_x and p_y. In this problem, the set of all possible budgets may be associated with the set of all points $d^* = (d_x, d_y)$ in the nonnegative (northeast) quadrant of the diagram shown in Figure 1. However, if the head of the household is presumed to be honest—or merely risk-averse—the set of all theoretically admissible trades of money for commodities will consist of points that lie on a single budget line (shown as L in Figure 1). This line is defined by the equation:

$$p_x d^*_x + p_y d^*_y - s_{m,0} = O, \qquad (1)$$

where (by hypothesis) p_x, p_y and $s_{m,0}$ are given decision parameters (i.e., constants, from the point of view of the individual). Points to the northeast of L represent budgets that have a value greater than $s_{m,0}$ dollars, while points to the southwest represent budgets that have a value less than $s_{m,0}$ dollars. Only those points that lie on the budget line represent budgets that have a value of precisely $s_{m,0}$ dollars. Let us denote budgets that satisfy equation (1) by $d = (d_x, d_y)$. The set of budgets d is, of course, a subset of the set of all possible budgets d^*. By definition it is literally true that

$$p_x d_x + p_y d_y - s_{m,0} \equiv O; \qquad (2)$$

that is to say, all theoretically admissible budgets d identically satisfy equation (1).[4] This zero-net-value

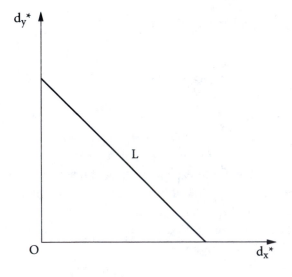

Figure 1:

identity, i.e., identity (2), is an exact rendition of SP as it appears in the context of the present discussion.

At first sight, the preceding argument might seem to suggest that SP is implied by the assumption that household purchases are constrained by the budget equation (1). On closer inspection, however, it will be seen that the true relation between SP and the budget equation is precisely the reverse of this, for the validity of SP is tacitly presupposed in our initial definition of the budget equation. Thus SP appears in this instance as an independent assumption rather than a derived conclusion. In fact, this instance illustrates the general rule rather than the exceptional case; i.e., the restriction on individual trading behavior that we call SP is a fundamental postulate of economic theory that holds quite independently of other behavior assumptions.

The full significance of the last observation will become clear later. Meanwhile, the following comments may be helpful:

> The budget equation (and so the budget line) is a special case of a class of behavioral restrictions that occur over and over again in economic analysis, restrictions that follow from a completely general proposition that we shall call *Say's Principle*. This proposition asserts, broadly speaking, that trade is a two-way street; i.e., individuals can expect to acquire commodities from other individuals only by giving commodities (or money) of equal market value in exchange. Say's Principle might seem almost too obvious to be worth stating, but it is as well to take nothing for granted at this point. It should be remarked, for example, that Say's Principle (and the budget equation) refers not to quantities actually purchased or to prices actually paid, but rather to expected purchase prices and planned quantities purchased. It is evident that if one pays, say, $10 for all groceries that he *actually* acquires in a supermarket, the total value of the separate items purchased must add up to $10—or else the supermarket checkout clerk has made a mistake. But it is neither obvious nor always true that a shopper who *plans* to spend $10 on groceries in a supermarket also plans to walk out of the store with a collection of goods that is valued at just $10; the shopper may be a shoplifter as well as a customer! In effect, Say's Principle constitutes an implicit definition of the concept of a transactor as distinguished from the concept of a thief or a philanthropist. Thus it restricts our vision as economists to just one aspect of individual behavior, for it excludes (by assumption) facets of behavior which, although they involve the acquisition and disposal of commodities—and so are of economic interest in some sense—fall outside the purview of formal economic analysis.[5]

II. EXTENSIONS

In keeping with the logical primacy of SP, let us now reverse direction and consider the consequences of applying SP to situations that are more general (and less obviously contrived) than the problem of household choice outlined in the previous section. Let us start by considering a simple generalization of the household choice model in which we permit some of the money available for expenditure to be retained by the household for future disposal. Applying SP to this case, we may suppose that the set of theoretically admissible budgets, $d = (d_x, d_y, d_m)$, is defined by the zero-net-value identity:

$$p_x d_x + p_y d_y + (dm - s_{m,0}) \equiv O, \qquad (3)$$

where d_m denotes the quantity of money that the household plans to hold for future disposal (other variables are defined just as before).

Another easy extension of our model is accomplished by admitting the possibility that the household may be a supplier of non-money commodities as well as a supplier of money. In this case, application of SP yields the zero-net-value identity:

$$p_x(d_x - s_{x,0}) + p_y(d_y - S_{y,0}) + (d_m - S_{m,0}) \equiv O,[6] \quad (4)$$

where the symbols $s_{x,0}$ and $s_{y,0}$, like the symbol $s_{m,0}$, represent decision parameters and denote (non-negative) stocks of nonmoney commodities currently available for possible sale (the values of $s_{x,0}$ and $s_{y,0}$ may be zero, of course, for one or both commodities).

Yet another extension of our model is obtained by supposing that the individual is a potential trader of a large but finite number of commodities. Using numerical subscripts, 1, 2, ... , m to distinguish different commodities, and treating the m-th commodity as money, we obtain:

$$p_1(d_1 - s_{1,0}) + p_2(d_2 - s_{2,0}) + \dots$$
$$p_{m-1}(d_{m-1} s_{m-1,0}) + (d_m - s_{m,0}) \equiv O, \quad (5)$$

as the zero-net-value identity implied by SP. Notice that this condition—like analogous relations set out earlier—holds for all values of the price variables, p_i; and not just for one or a few specially chosen price lists. Further notice that the validity of identity (5) does not depend in any way on the assumption that the symbols $s_{i,0}$ represent (given) decision parameters rather than (unknown) decision variables whose values have to be determined by the individual decision maker. This being so, it is superfluous to work with gross demands and gross supplies when we are considering transactors as commodity traders, for only net demands and net supplies are relevant in this case. Accordingly, to simplify notation let us define the individual's excess demand (ED) for the i-th commodity by the relation:

$$x_i = d_i - s_i \ (i = 1, \dots ,m). \quad (6)$$

In general, x_i may be positive, zero or negative. In the last case, the individual would appear as a potential seller rather than buyer (or non-trader) of the i-th

commodity, in which event we might call x_i the individual's excess supply (ES) of the i-th commodity. Using the notation of equation (6), identity (5) now takes the simpler but logically equivalent form:

$$p_1x_1 + p_2x_2 \dots + p_{m-1}x_{m-1} + x_m = O.[7] \quad (7)$$

As a final generalization consider a large (but finite) collection of transactors; we distinguish among quantities associated with different transactors by adding a second numerical subscript, 1, 2, ... , k to relevant variables (e.g., the variable x_{ij} denotes the j-th transactor's ED for the i-th commodity). For simplicity, suppose that all transactors face the same money prices; this uniform price assumption is so conventional in general equilibrium theory that its presence is sometimes not even recognized.[8] We also assume (as usual) that the trading behavior of each and every transactor is constrained in accordance with SP. On these assumptions, we obtain not one, but rather a set of K zero-net-value identities to characterize the set of admissible net trades that transactors as a group are permitted to contemplate. These relations are displayed in matrix form in Table 1.

Each row in Table 1 show the money value of the corresponding transactor's EDs—valued at some arbitrary set of money prices (the same set for all transactors). In accordance with SP, the sum of these money values is identically zero (right-hand column). Of course, some of the individual terms in each sum may also be zero, indicating that the transactor in question neither plans to buy nor sell units of those commodities. In particular, if the i-th commodity is assumed to be an imaginary object, or a commodity that has no concrete counterpart (e.g., the English monetary unit called the "Guinea"), then $x_{ij} \equiv O$ for all transactors since, by its very definition, such a commodity cannot seriously be contemplated as an object of trade by any transactor.[9]

The first K terms in each of the first M columns of Table 1 indicate which transactors are net suppliers and which are net demanders of the corresponding commodity. We shall refer to the sum of the individual EDs in each column as the aggregate ED for the corresponding commodity. In symbols:

Table 1: Matrix of Admissible Trades

Transactors			COMMODITIES (C_i)					(Money)		Net Value
(I_j)	C_1		C_2			C_{m-1}		C_m		
I_1	$p_1 x_{1,1}$	$+$	$p_2 x_{2,1}$	$+ \cdots \cdots$	$+$	$p_{m-1} x_{m-1,1}$	$+$	$x_{m,1}$	$\equiv$	0
I_2	$p_1 x_{1,2}$	$+$	$p_2 x_{2,2}$	$+ \cdots \cdots$	$+$	$p_{m-1} x_{m-1,2}$	$+$	$x_{m,2}$	$\equiv$	0
.										
.										
.										
I_k	$p_1 x_{1,k}$	$+$	$p_2 x_{2,k}$	$+ \cdots \cdots$	$+$	$p_{m-1} x_{m-1,k}$	$+$	$x_{m,k}$	$\equiv$	0
Aggregate excess demands	$p_1 X_2$		$p_2 X_2$	$+ \cdots \cdots$	$+$	$p_{m-1} X_{m-1}$		$X_{m,}$	$\equiv$	0

$$\sum_{j=1}^{j=k} x_{ij} \equiv X_i, (i = 1, \dots, m) \quad (8)$$

On the assumption that a common price is relevant for valuing all individuals EDs, we may then write the money value of aggregate ED for the *i*-th commodity as:

$$\sum_{j=1}^{j=k} p_i x_{ij} \equiv p_i \sum_{j=1}^{j=k} x_{ij} \equiv p_i X_i, (i = 1, \dots, m) \quad (9)$$

Because the money value of individual EDs may be negative as well as positive or zero, the magnitude and sign of $p_i X_i$ may be positive, negative or zero. However, since the (row) sum of the money values of any single transactor's EDs is identically zero, and since the sum of K zeroes is zero, it follows that the money value of all individual EDs summed over all transactors and all commodities, is identically zero.[10] Even though we can place no restrictions on the size or sign of any of the first M terms in the bottom row of Table 1 we may assert unequivocally that the last term is zero; i.e., the money value of the sum of all aggregate EDs is identically equal to zero.[11] In symbols,

$$\sum_{i=1}^{i=m} p_i X_i \equiv 0, (i = 1, \dots, m) \quad (10)$$

This proposition effectively summarizes the whole of the preceding argument. In the final analysis it asserts much the same concept as the simple individual version of SP defined earlier; however, it applies to a group of transactors rather than a single individual. Where we specially wish to emphasize that we are referring to the group identity (10), we shall identify it henceforth as the aggregative version of SP (where the sense of our argument is not in doubt, however, we shall omit qualifying phrases and speak simply of SP).

Three features of the aggregative version of SP merit special emphasis before we proceed:

1. *The proposition is valid for any (uniform) set of prices and for every theoretically admissible set of aggregate EDs;*

2. *No general statement can be made about the sum of the money values of any proper subset of the aggregate EDs; i.e., if one or more of the terms $p_i X_i$ is excluded from the summation in identity (10), we can place no restrictions whatever on the sign or magnitude of the sum of the remaining terms;*

3. The aggregate ED for each commodity in identity (10) is defined by identity (8) as the sum over all transactors of planned (notional, intended, desired) purchases or sales of the same commodity. *If aggregate EDs were defined in*

terms of anything other than planned quantities, we should have no assurance that the aggregative version of SP would still hold.

III. STANDARD THEMES AND DOCTRINES

We are now in a position to discuss certain interpretations of SP that appear frequently in the economic literature.

A. Old Familiar Phrases

1. "A general glut of commodities is impossible." This sounds archaic ... which is natural, since it is a version of SP that was much in vogue among early nineteenth century economists. Glut means ES (negative ED). If general glut is interpreted to mean notional ES prevailing for all commodities simultaneously, then such a situation is flatly inconsistent with SP in any of its variants and, in that sense, the statement is true.

2. "Supply creates its own demand." This is perhaps the most ambiguous statement that students of economics are ever asked to ponder. Consider, for example, the following alternatives:

    i. "Supply of a commodity at some price gives rise to an equal demand for the same commodity at that price." This version is, of course, false. But it illustrates one possible interpretation of a special case of the version of SL that the Classical economists are often accused of believing (see Section C, below).

    ii. "No one plans to supply anything of value without also planning some use for the proceeds from the sale, which may include simply planning to hold money until a later

decision is made to purchase other commodities." This statement is correct and sensible.

    iii. "Confronted with given prices, each transactor must plan to supply commodities of sufficient value to finance all his planned net demands." This statement is also correct.

    iv. "If prices are given, each transactor's planned sales will create the means to finance his planned purchase." This statement resembles (ii) but it is quite different—false rather than true. Suppose that aggregate ES exists for all commodities that the transactor plans to sell; it is then likely that actual sales will be less than planned (perhaps nil). Hence, planned receipts will not serve to finance planned purchases. SP refers only to purchase and sale intentions; it asserts absolutely nothing about the possibility of their realization.

B. General Equilibrium

An economic system may be said to be in equilibrium when the values of all variables that are considered relevant for describing its observable behavior are equal over time to the values of a corresponding set of theoretical variables that define the virtual (notional) behavior of the system along a postulated equilibrium path. This very general concept is consistent with the existence of non-stationary equilibrium paths. In elementary accounts of general equilibrium theory, however, equilibrium paths are typically defined in terms of constancy over time in the values of a set of relative prices, $\bar{P} = (p_1, p_2, \ldots, pm)$ where one commodity, say the m-th, serves as a unit of account or *numeraire* so that $\bar{p}_m = 1$. This simple definition of economic equilibrium is arrived at by conceptualizing the economic system as a collection of named, but otherwise nondescript, transactors whose trading activities are centrally coordinated by some kind of "trading authority" that acts as a bargaining agent and commodity distribution center for all transactors. At the beginning of any given bargaining period (implicitly defined as a time interval of sufficient length for everything we wish to talk about to occur), each transactor formulates a definite trading plan on the basis of a set of provisional prices, P_0, which are announced by the trading authority. These plans are communicated to the trading authority who first checks each plan to see that it satisfies SP (individual version), and then sums all plans to arrive at a set of provisional aggregate EDs, $X_0 = (X_{1,0}, X_{2,0}, ..., X_{m,0})$. If X_0 includes some elements that are non-zero (by SP—the aggregate version—at least *two* elements must be non-zero in this case), the trading authority knows that individual plans are not mutually consistent at the price vector P_0 (i.e., not all planned net trades can be executed as scheduled). It then selects and announces a new set of provisional prices, P_1, and requests the assembled mob of transactors to formulate new plans. This process continues until at some stage, say the i-th when the trading authority manages to announce a price vector P_t at which each and every aggregate ED is exactly equal to zero: i.e., $X_{i,t} = O$ ($i = 1, ..., m$). In this case, all individual trades can be executed as planned (through the collection and distribution facilities conveniently—and costlessly—provided by the authority), and the prices, P_t, are called equilibrium prices for the current trading period. In the absence of changes in technology, preferences, or other data that might influence individual trading plans, the same prices should yield equilibrium in all subsequent periods.

Such, in brief, is the story that underlies the condition $P = \bar{P} = $ constant, as a comprehensive criterion for equilibrium in elementary general equilibrium theory. According to this story, constancy of prices over time implies corresponding constancy of trading plans. But neither of these conditions can prevail unless, in every period, $X_i = O$ for all commodities. Hence the condition $P = \bar{P} = $ constant, is logically equivalent to the economically more informative requirement:

$$X_i = O \quad (i = 1, ..., m). \tag{11}$$

We emphasize that this simple requirement is in no sense sufficient. to characterize general equilibrium except in very simple models; however, it is usually (but not always) a necessary condition and, for the purposes of the present argument, it may be regarded as both necessary and sufficient. In what follows, therefore, we shall refer to equation (11) as the general equilibrium condition.

Whether or not we wish to regard equation (11) as the only condition for general equilibrium (as in fact we do here), we might treat it as a universally valid, necessary condition for what might be called full coordination of economic activities, that is, situations in which, for each and every commodity, purchase and sale intentions are consistent in the aggregate. In a world without a central trading authority, knowing that equation (11) is fulfilled does not assure us that all trading plans can in fact be executed. It is conceivable (just barely) that each and every transactor could actually carry out each of his intended purchases and sales and not end up in a situation where all the sellers known to him are out of stock and all the buyers he contacts are unwilling to buy. As a practical matter, however, even this weak requirement that all aggregate EDs be zero is unlikely ever to be realized in any real-world situation; hence, the probability that all transactors should ever simultaneously achieve full execution of their individual trading plans may be set at zero.

Having run through essential preliminaries, we turn now to the relation between SP and the concept of general equilibrium. Without being too formal let us suppose that we have to deal with an economy in which there exists one and only one price vector, $\bar{P}$, for which the general-equilibrium condition equation (11) is satisfied.[12] We know that SP is satisfied in the present model for *all* price vectors P; the rules imposed by the trading authority positively guarantee this. But not all price vectors are consistent with general equilibrium; indeed, under our present assumptions only one such vector exists. Hence we conclude: the satisfaction of SP implies nothing whatever about the satisfaction of the general equilibrium condition; neither has general equilibrium any bearing on SP. If the general equilibrium condition is satisfied, it is obvious that:

$$\sum_{i=1}^{i=m} x_i \equiv 0,$$

but this fatuous proposition should never be confused with Say's Principle.[13]

Suppose that the general equilibrium condition is not satisfied, so that aggregate ED for at least two commodities is nonzero. In this case, the economy may be said to be in a state of disequilibrium. It is impossible for all trades to be executed as planned, so prices and trading plans must be revised. Some of the commodities in aggregate ES may be labor services. It follows that SP is entirely consistent with the existence of large- scale unemployment.

SP is also consistent with indefinite persistence of unemployment on a large scale, for it involves no assumptions and yields no implications about the dynamic adjustment behavior of the economic system. Imagine observing the system in a state of serious disequilibrium. Knowing that SP holds true for the system will *not* permit us to predict whether or not this disequilibrium will tend automatically to disappear with the passage of time. (Hence, SP is totally irrelevant to any ideological discussion and in particular to discussion of the pros and cons of so- called *laissez-faire).* For example, SP would still hold in a system where *every* commodity was subject to effectively enforced price-control. (Shortages and surpluses would be felt everywhere, but aggregate EDs would still have a total zero money value.)

That a general glut is impossible is not an empty statement. SP refutes, for example, the recurrent, fearful popular notion that productivity increasing innovations (automation, nuclear power, or whatever) will create or increase aggregate ESs for some commodities without affecting the aggregate EDs for the others. But the reassurance that this knowledge entails is very limited. It is utter nonsense, for example, to maintain (as some students, unfortunately, have a tendency to do) that, although the Principle is consistent with each and every aggregate ED being non-zero and large, it still asserts that the economy will be in overall equilibrium in that total demand and total supply are equal in money value. It is nonsense, because the statement completely empties the term equilibrium of all meaning. This particular piece of nonsense is not always so easy to spot. Quite a few otherwise reputable economists have put in print the proposition that Classical economists were unable to provide a meaningful and useful theory of large-scale unemployment because they believed in SL. This is simply inane: SP, by itself, could not possibly pose a mental block to the development of unemployment theory. On the contrary, correct and systematic application of it is necessary for the construction of a consistent theory of any disequilibrium (or equilibrium) phenomenon.

Needless to say, it does not follow that all, or even most, Classical economists fully understood what the Principle means and does not mean. A doctrinal investigation might well show, for example, that some notable writers muddled the conceptual distinctions between SP and propositions relating to the existence and stability of general equilibrium. We do not lack, after all, latter-day examples of the confounding of these separate issues.[14] The existence problem concerns the question whether a price vector exists such that, if it were to be obtained, aggregate ED for each commodity would be zero. SP alone will not allow one to deduce an answer one way or another to this question. The stability problem concerns the question whether it can be deduced that prices will adjust so as to reduce the absolute magnitude of aggregate EDs until, eventually, all aggregate EDs are zero (presuming such an equilibrium solution exists). SP contains no laws of motion of prices, nor is it even helpful in deducing what these laws might be. A fairly large set of assumptions completely independent of the Principle, must be made in order to obtain answers to stability questions.

Many pre-Keynesian writers, who simply believed in the existence of general equilibrium, assumed "flexible prices"; they also assumed or argued that flexible prices would tend to move in such a manner as to reduce aggregate EDs to zero. Some of them may have been unable to conceive of persistent mass unemployment as a realistic possibility; however, it was clearly these sundry beliefs and assumptions— *not* SP—that constituted mental blocks for them.

C. National Income Analysis

In macroeconomics texts, SP (aggregative version) is sometimes said to imply that aggregate demand always equals aggregate supply. If one's definitions of aggregate demand and aggregate supply are, respectively, the summed money value of all commodities in aggregate ED and the summed money value of all commodities in aggregate ES, then, naturally, this is what SP means. (It is not an implication of the Principle, but simply a restatement.) However, the accepted, conventional definitions of aggregate demand and aggregate supply are quite different. The coinage of both terms is associated with the development of Keynesian macroeconomics, and it is the usage within that body of doctrine that must be decisive. In macroeconomics, aggregate demand is defined as the summed value of the demands for all final goods and services; similarly, aggregate supply is defined as the summed value of supplies of all final goods and services.

Final goods and services are a subset of all currently-produced commodities. (Current production of intermediate goods and services is excluded.) Current output is, in turn, a subset of all commodities in the system that excludes not just money but also all existing assets and many inputs as well. Suppose, then, that of the commodities in Table 1, those indexed 4 through 17 are designated as final goods and services. It is immediately apparent that the sum of the values of the demands for these goods (aggregate demand) cannot be asserted to equal the sum of the values of the supplies of the same goods. To assert this we should have to know—in addition to SP—that the sum of the values of the EDs for goods 1 through 3, and 18 through m were zero, and the latter condition, of course, will not in general be fulfilled. This example suffices to disprove the general validity of the proposition that SP implies equality between aggregate demand and aggregate supply.

There is another point to be made in this connection. In national income analysis, the term aggregate demand has come to mean the total value of actual spending—not *planned spending*—on final goods and services. If actual prices differ from equilibrium prices, actual spending will almost certainly differ

from planned purchases (since not all plans can be carried out). SP, to repeat, is a proposition about trading *plans* and carries with it no direct implications about the realization of plans. On this account, therefore, the assertion that SP implies equality between aggregate demand and supply is seen to be the product of muddled thinking.[15]

D. General Deflation

Of all the innumerable disequilibria that are consistent with SP, one subset is particularly worth singling out because of the potential practical seriousness of the conditions defining it; namely, disequilibria in which the sum of the values of EDs for all currently produced commodities is negative and equal in value to the positive ED for money. This means, on balance, that the entire business sector is under general deflationary pressure.[16] The typical industry will be laying off workers. If there are some industries hiring, they won't hire enough; unemployment will be widespread.

If the real money supply (i.e., the stock of money in relation to the general price level) could be increased in this situation, prevailing deflationary pressures could be relieved—though that alone would not necessarily permit the economy to snap into general equilibrium. The supply of money in real terms might be increased in two ways: 1) by letting excess supplies drive prices down so that the general price level is reduced in relation to an unchanged stock of nominal money balances; 2) by increasing the nominal money stock at prevailing prices. Alternative 1 is the automatic solution; but if prices and wages are rigid downward, this way out is simply not open to us. Even if prices and wages are not rigid, the process envisaged in this solution may be a long-drawn-out affair that entails heavy costs in terms of resource unemployment and human misery and which, therefore, might well be regarded as unacceptable. Alternative 2, the interventionist solution, might seem more promising than 1 as a procedure for accomplishing the same results more quickly and at less social cost. But its use raises other issues. To whom is "the engine of inflation" to be entrusted? What limits to that party's discretionary use of the throttle would it be advisable to impose?

The Classical economists were not unaware of this class of disequilibria or of their seriousness. John Stuart Mill, for example, diagnosed general depressions of trade in precisely these terms. It is also true, however, that many British Classical economists tended to discuss the problem as if the automatic alternative 1 offered the only way out. Some of them did not regard the nominal money supply as a policy instrument that the Bank of England of the time could control. Others were of the view that the central bank had or could be endowed with the powers to control the money stock, but believed very strongly that the central bank on the whole ought to let balance-of-payments deficits and surpluses determine variations over time in the monetary base and, hence, in the money stock.[17]

Reliance on the automatic solution, in this view, is argued to be the lesser of two evils. Naive *laissez-faire* notions do not figure at all in the theory of economic policy of the British Classical school. Nor was Classical thinking on this subject in any way inhibited by prevailing views about "Say's Law of Markets." SP is entirely consistent with confirmed disbelief in the possibility of general gluts and, simultaneously, with clear recognition of the actuality of frequent and prolonged bouts of general deflation. John Stuart Mill's *Principles,* the "Bible of Economics" during the later Classical period, is the perfect illustration.

E. Lange's Laws: A Restatement and Criticism

The aggregative version of SP as we have defined it earlier, is formally equivalent to a proposition that is known more familiarly in the literature as Walras' Law, a label that was first attached to it by Oscar Lange (Lange [1942]). Two names for the same concept is, in general, a luxury that economics can well do without. But we have good reasons for making an exception in the present case. The central portions

of Lange's argument are concerned with conceptual experiments that involve just two models, namely:

i. A model of a barter economy with $m-1$ commodities, all of which are either currently produced final goods and services or currently supplied factor services. Commodities not classified in this manner cannot be traded at all. In particular, nothing called money is included in the set of tradable commodities, which means that the system is "equivalent to a barter economy."[18]

ii. A model of a money economy that is identical with the first in all respects except that an m-th commodity called money is added to the set of tradable commodities—functioning as "medium of exchange as well as numeraire ..."

Since money does not exist in the first economy, it cannot be traded. However, it still can be regarded by us as a unit of account (*numeraire*) for expressing prices, so we may continue to speak of the money value of aggregate EDs even when referring to the barter system.[19]

The proposition that the sum of the money values of all EDs in system i is identically zero is called Say's Law by Lange.[20] The proposition that the sum of the money values of all EDs in system ii is identically zero Lange then called Walras' Law. Since the two propositions are identical, the reader may well wonder why Lange assigns them different names. The answer to this apparent mystery is that Lange, unlike us, starts by considering only a so-called "money economy" (system ii). He defines Walras' Law in relation to this kind of system, and then asks, in effect: In what circumstances will the total money value of ED for all commodities exclusive of money be zero? Not very surprisingly, he discovers that his condition will be satisfied if and only if the ED for money is zero, a state of affairs that he calls "monetary equilibrium." He then defines SL *not* as a proposition that holds only for situations of monetary equilibrium, but rather as a proposition that together with Walras' Law, holds identically for all possible states of system *ii.* These two stipulations effectively make system *ii* indistinguishable from system *i.*

From this point onward, Lange's argument is all downhill. In order to elaborate the implications of what he calls "Say's Law," he first asks: What conclusions follow if we suppose that aggregate EDs in a money economy such as *ii* simultaneously satisfy *both* Walras' Law and SL? The words in which the ensuing discussion are couched strongly suggest that the simultaneous assumption of Walras' Law and SL leads one to economically nonsensical results. Thus, he argues that money prices are indeterminate (obviously, since only ratios of money prices are relevant in system *i*). Lange argues further that people will never desire to change their money balances (obviously, since money in system *i* is like romantic love—you take what you can get, but it's not for sale!). He goes on to observe that money in such a system is merely a worthless medium of exchange and standard of value. (Here the nonsense is Lange's, for whatever else money may be in system *i*, it can't be a medium of exchange, worthless or otherwise). Clearly, if one focuses attention not on the words Lange uses but rather on the properties of the system he is talking about (namely, system *i* rather than system *ii*) all of his results appear to be either entirely sensible or to involve confusion or errors of logic on his part. An example of the latter is his assertion that, "... under Say's Law an excess supply of primary factors and direct services *always* implies an excess demand of equal amount for products, and vice versa. This tends directly to restore equilibrium." As we have emphasized in earlier remarks, SP has no bearing whatever on the dynamic adjustment properties of any economic system.

Using the terms as he defines them, Lange concludes that Walras' Law is true in general and that SL is true for barter but not for money economies. Since Lange's distinction between the two types of economies is purely verbal, not analytical, this conclusion is fatuous. In Lange's article (and in the present paper) the word "money" serves only to name one commodity, specifically, that commodity (it might be any of them) that serves as a unit of account for expressing prices. At no stage in Lange's formal analysis is money endowed with any other special properties as compared with other commodities.[21]

Attributing a belief in SL (in his sense) to Classical economists, Lange also argues that pre-Keynesian theories of employment, interest and money are (a) logically false, and (b) economically nonsensical because they rest on the assumption that SL is valid for a monetary economy. In this part of his argument, Lange is guilty not only of repeated sins of verbal sophistry but also of gross historical inaccuracy. As argued earlier the statement that the summed values of aggregate EDs over a subset of tradable commodities is identically zero involves a most elementary error.[22]

So what remains of Lange's analysis when all is said and done? Our answer is, quite bluntly: nothing of value. Nonetheless, Lange's terminological innovations—including, in particular, the entirely superfluous term Walras' Law—somehow have taken root in macroeconomics; and his associated criticisms of Classical economics are now part of the mythology of the subject.

F. Say's Principle and Walras' Law

As we remarked at the outset of the preceding section, what we have called the aggregative version of SP is formally equivalent to what Lange called Walras' Law. Formally equivalent, they certainly are, but economically equivalent they sometimes are not. Two observations will suffice to make clear the sense and validity of this distinction.

1. Walras' Law is sometimes described as asserting that, if prices are such that all markets for non-money commodities satisfy the general-equilibrium condition (i.e., if $X_i = O$ for i = 1,2, ... , m-1), then the money market must also be in equilibrium (i.e., $X_m = O$ also);[23] or, more shortly, that if supply equals demand on M-l markets then the same equality must also hold on the m-th.[24]

Now, our definition of SP (aggregative version) involves the concept of aggregate demand in an essential way, but it does not in any way depend upon or refer to the concept of a market. Our avoidance of any reference to the word market was quite deliberate. The term market, as used in ordinary discourse, carries with it a host of intuitive associations that have no counterpart in standard accounts of individual decision-making behavior. In common parlance, a market is (among other things) a place where one pays (receives) money to (from) another person in exchange for some other commodity at some date in time. To establish a theoretical analog to this conception, we should have to specify the logistics of commodity trade in fine detail—fine enough detail, indeed, to permit us to assert within the framework of formal theory precisely when and where each transactor trades what commodities with whom and in exchange for which other commodities. No such specification is even attempted in existing accounts of macro- or micro-economic theory.[25] Thus, to speak of markets for labor services, goods, bonds, money, etc. in connection with conventional theoretical models is, strictly speaking, meaningless. It is entirely sensible to speak of aggregate ED for these commodities but to link aggregate EDs with markets is to invite needless confusion and misunderstanding.[26]

To insist on this terminological distinction between aggregate ED for a commodity and market ED (for the same commodity) may seem overly fastidious. And it is, in fact, not necessary in a discussion that does not go beyond SP. In more general contexts, however, the distinction is far from pointless. When one moves on to the task of constructing a theory that describes how the economic system adjusts when in disequilibrium, it is traditional to use the term "market excess demand" to denote the relevant forces governing price adjustment. It is a distinct and potentially dangerous jump in logic, however, to take it for granted that these forces are always measured by aggregate EDs (which is the custom in the existing literature). For example, in models where market ED cannot be obtained by aggregating over individual planned net demands and supplies, we have no assurance whatsoever that the sum of measured market EDs, valued at the prevailing market prices, is equal to zero or any other number (though SP, in the

generalized form given by equation (9), above, holds as usual for the aggregate of individual planned EDs).

2. Most statements of Walras' Law in the existing literature, unlike our statement of SP, tacitly presuppose that the trading plans of individual transactors satisfy one or another of the optimality conditions (i.e., maximize some criterion function) in addition to relevant behavior constraints. This is certainly true for the statements of Lange, Patinkin, Debreu and Arrow and Hahn, all of whom assume that individual ED functions (or correspondences) are defined independently of Walras' Law. This corresponds to the point of view adopted in the first section of this paper, where we first illustrated the nature of SP. It differs sharply, however, from the view adopted later. While we have no logical objection to the approach of other writers, we should remark that such a procedure makes SP appear much more limited in application than it actually is. SP is also significantly diminished as a theoretical proposition by suggesting incorrectly that it is valid only if all individuals in the economic system are behaving optimally.

NOTES FOR THIS CHAPTER

1. For example, McConnell (1972), pp. 203–7.

2. A good book to start with is Sowell (1972).

3. We will not bother to distinguish among households, business firms, financial intermediaries, government agencies, and so on.

4. It may help clarify the distinction between d and d*, and the related distinction between the conditional equation (1) and the identical equation. (2), if we consider a simple analog. Suppose that an algebraist is assigned the problem of choosing one value of the variable x^* that satisfies the equation $x^{*2} = 9$. Clearly, most values of x^* that might be considered won't do. However, two values of x^*, namely, $x^* = 3$ and $x^* = -3$, do satisfy the equation. The set of theoretically admissible solutions to the original problem thus consists of two numbers. The original problem, which involves choosing some element x^* of the set of all real numbers is thus transformed into the

more restricted problem of choosing some element x of the set of just two real numbers, [3,-3], Since the latter set is defined in such a way that all of its elements satisfy the conditional equation $x^{*2} = 9$, it follows trivially that any element x of the set {3,-3} satisfies the same equation *identically*, i.e., $x^2 = 9$. The algebraist, like the household, still has a choice to make, but the choice is narrowed down considerably by the requirement that $x^2 = 9$ as compared with the weaker requirement that $x^{*a} = 9$.

5. Quoted from Clower and Due (1972), pp. 64–65.

6. More accurately, SP yields the set of budgets defined by identity (4) if, as is conventional, we assume that each of the non-money commodities (x) and (y) can be traded directly for each other as well as for money. We shall not elaborate on this theme here; for additional details see Clower (1967) and Veendorp (1970). However, in general, a single constraint such as identity (4) can be used to define the set of admissible budgets only in a world where individuals consider themselves able to trade any given collection of commodities directly for any other collection in a *single* exchange transaction.

7. The money price of a unit of money is necessarily unity, $p_m = 1$; so identity (7) is equivalent to the more symmetrical identity:

$$P_1 x_1 + P_2 x_2 + \cdots + P_{m-1}, x_{m-1} + P_m x_m \equiv 0 \qquad (7')$$

8. For future reference, we observe here that the assumption involves a drastic over-simplification; it means we ignore differences in price for the same good between different localities, bid-ask spreads for the same good in the same locality, discrepancies in prices charged for different sellers, etc. These omissions represent serious abstractions from reality. However, they do not affect the logic of our argument (which would merely become more complicated if the assumption of uniform prices were relaxed).

9. The relevance of this outwardly trivial observation will become clear below.

10. Notice that this proposition is valid even if the prices used to value individual EDs are not the same for different transactors:

$$\sum_{j=1}^{j=k} \sum_{j=1}^{i=m} P_{ij} X_{ij} \equiv 0, (i = 1, \ldots, m) \text{ and } (j = 1, \ldots, k) \qquad (9)$$

where p is represents the money price of the *jth* commodity as seen by the *jth* transactor. Hence, the proposition holds even more strongly if prices are uniform over all transactors (i.e., if $Pij = P_i$ for all values of j).

11. For the record we can find no hints of any such aggregative proposition in J. B. Say's economic writings. In our view, however, it would be historically accurate to credit J. B. Say with the weaker (but still fairly powerful) proposition (9') where the sum of all individual notional EDs, valued at money prices as seen by individual transactors is identically zero. This, or some similar disaggregative version of SP is, we believe, what most pre-Keynesian writers had in mind when referring to "Say's Law of Markets."

12. For any specified state of resource endowments, production technology, property and contract laws, and consumer tastes, there exists a unique price vector P⁻ for which $X_1 = 0$ for all commodities.

13. Even great economists sometimes nod: "… Say's Law is valid only in a state of perfect equilibrium …" Schumpeter (1954), p. 619.

14. "However, the satisfaction of *all* the stability conditions … is not implied in Say's Law. Say's Law implies only that enough of the stability conditions of the system hold, to assure the existence of a stable equilibrium for two broad classes of commodities, namely, the class of products and the class of factors and direct services." Cf. O. Lange (1942), p. 59. A proposition that states that the money values of some or all aggregate EDs sum to a certain number implies nothing about the fulfillment of any stability condition. Moreover, the notion of equilibrium for broad classes of commodities is just as empty and misleading as that of overall equilibrium which we have just criticized.

15. Another version of the same muddle consists of the assertion that SP implies coincidence at every point between the aggregate demand function and the 45° line in standard "Keynesian Cross" diagrams.

16. General deflationary pressure means here a situation in which ESs cannot be eliminated by merely changing relative prices.

17. From the standpoint of domestic stabilization policy, this is a self-denying ordinance—the monetary authorities cannot at one and the same time be bound by such a rule and retain discretion to intervene in domestic economic affairs whenever they deem it advisable.

18. Lange (1942), p. 64.

19. Individuals in system i would be concerned, of course, only with *ratios* of such money prices, i.e., with rates of exchange between pairs of tradable commodities.

20. Lange simply assumes that the proposition is true for the system described, but the proposition could be shown to hold as a consequence of standard assumptions underlying the definition of the demand and supply functions that Lange introduced at the outset of his analysis.

21. This may be seen most easily by noticing that if what Lange calls money were a liquid asset that came in bottles marked "100 proof Scotch Whisky" rather than pieces of paper labelled "In God We Trust," no one would notice it.

22. As far as we know, no major Classical economist has ever been shown to commit this error outright; but even if such a sinner could be found by hunting around among lesser figures, we (the authors) should follow Mill's gracious example and attribute the blunder to inadvertence.

23. Patinkin (1965), p. 25.

24. Arrow and Hahn (1971), p. 4.

25. An instructive example of just such a careful specification is provided by Ostroy (1973).

26. A common example of such confusion arises in macroeconomic theory in the mere listing of four markets, one for each distinct commodity. Since exchange necessarily involves at least two commodities, the very phrase "market for commodity Z" presupposes that we know what commodity or commodities Z is traded for or else it must he regarded as a contradiction in terms.

Price Flexibility

The Significance of Price Flexibility

The Critics of Keynesian Economics

By W. H. Hutt

The period 1932–1953 has witnessed a revolution and counterrevolution in thought on the function and consequences of price flexibility.

In considering this remarkable phase in the history of theory, it is useful to begin by referring to a related field of hardly disturbed agreement. There has been no controversy during the period of our survey among serious economists about the desirability of a system which tends to ensure that different kinds of prices shall stand in a certain optimum relation to one another, or about the desirability, in a changing world, of continuous *relative* price adjustment in order to bring about some conformance to the ideal relation. From the so-called "socialist economists" of the Lange-Lemer type to the so-called "individualist economists" of the Mises-Röpke type, there has been agreement that the price system has important equilibrating and co-ordinative functions. Moreover, until the appearance of Keynes's *General Theory,* in 1936, the measure of agreement about the *aims* of institutional reform for the better working of the price system seemed to be slowly but definitely growing.

There was not the same marked tendency towards agreement about *methods*. Some thought that improved pricing could be achieved through a greater centralisation or sectionalisation of economic power, with the final voice to decide both preferences (choice of ends) and productive policy (choice of means) entrusted to elected representatives or syndicates. Others thought that the required reforms involved exactly the reverse—the breaking up and diffusion of economic authority so that the final voice about ends rested with the people as consumers, whilst the final voice about the choice of means rested with those who stood to gain or lose according to the success with which they allocated scarce resources in accordance with consumer-determined ends. But in spite of this apparently basic clash, as soon as explicit plans for the devising of a workable economic system were attempted, even the divergence of opinion about methods appeared to be narrowing. The so-called "socialist economists" were clearly attempting to restore *the market* and the *power of substitution.* So much was this so, that I believed the result of their labours would ultimately be the re-building of *laissez-faire* institutions, in elaborate disguises of name are superficial form, the result being regarded as the perfect pricing system.[1]

This interesting trend towards unanimity of opinion in several fields was overlapped by and rudely disturbed by Keynes's *General Theory.* Since 1936, the economists have become sharply divided about the nature of the price changes which ought, in the interests of "full employment," to take place in any given situation.[2] Consider trade union or State enforced wage-rates. At one extreme, we have the Keynesians who argue that, in maintaining wage-rates, we are maintaining consumer demand, creating a justification for new investment, and so preventing the emergence of depression. At the other extreme, we have those who argue that each successive increase of wage-rates so brought about renders essential a further element of inflation in order to maintain "full employment"—a development which tends permanently to dilute the money unit.

The Keynesian theory on this point proved enormously attractive. The idea as such was not novel; but before *The General Theory* it had enjoyed a negligible following in respectable economic circles. After 1936, it gave many economists what they seemed to have been waiting for, a non-casuistic argument for the tolerance of the collective enforcement or State fixation of minimum wage-rates.

Curiously enough, Keynes's challenge was based on a sort of admission of the evils of current collective bargaining and a further admission (by no means explicit, but an inevitable inference[3]), that labour in general was unable to benefit in real terms at the expense of other parties to production, by forcing a rise in the price of labour. Gains achieved by individual groups of organised workers were paid out of the pockets of other workers. At the same time, Keynes's new teachings seemed to support strongly those who cried, "Hands off the unions!" Although his thesis was accompanied by the charge—not wholly without foundation—that orthodox economists had closed their eyes to the consequences of the wage rigidity caused by trade union action, he always seemed to range himself on the side of the unions in their resistance to wage-rate adjustments. The reasons for his views on this question were two-fold.

Firstly, he argued that the price of labour had to be regarded as *inevitably* rigid. This empirical judgment about economic reality is, of course, not confined to the Keynesians. Where Keynes was original was in the subsidiary and supporting assumption that what other economists have called "the money illusion" was a basic cause of the rigidity.

Secondly, he argued that, in any case, wage-rate flexibility downwards, even if other prices were flexible, would aggravate and not alleviate depression. For even under perfect wage-rate flexibility and perfect flexibility generally, an equilibrium with unemployment could exist.[4] As I have previously argued,[5] Keynes would have preferred to rely wholly upon the second argument. But he kept the first, as Schumpeter has put it, "on reserve." In this survey I shall be dealing only with this second argument.

The contention is that wage-rate cuts must in any case be ineffective, as a means of restoring employment in labour, because it is possible to cut money rates only and not real wage-rates. Reduced money rates, Keynes explained, would mean reduced wages in the aggregate and lead to reduced demand. Hence the wage-rate rigidity, which former economists had been inclined to criticise ought, in his opinion, to be regarded as a virtue in times of depression.

At two points; Keynes appeared to have some misgivings about this thesis. He admitted firstly that if the price of labour *could* be flexible, things would be different, i.e., "if it were always open to labour to reduce its real wage by accepting a reduction in its money wage. ... " This condition assumed, he said, ". ... free competition among employers and no restrictive combinations among workers."[6] And he explicitly admitted later that, if there were competition between unemployed workers, "there might be no position of stable equilibrium except in conditions consistent with full employment.[7] But he did not attempt to reconcile these passages with apparently contradictory passages.

We are left, then, with the principal contention, namely, that changes in wage-rates are "double-edged," affecting both individual outputs and general demand. As this infectious doctrine has been developed by Keynes's disciples, costs as a whole are no longer regarded as merely *limiting* output, but as *calling forth* output through demand.

The objection to regarding costs as a source of demand can be simply stated. The only cost adjustments which defenders of price flexibility advocate are those which must always increase real income, and hence always increase money income under any system in which the value of the money unit remains constant. If we concentrate attention upon wages, it can be said that, on the reasonable assumption that the growth of real income will not mean a re-distribution against the *absolute* advantage of the wage-earners, the effect of the wage-rate reductions which are advocated must always mean an increase and not a decrease in aggregate wages received, and hence an increased demand for wage-goods. (The possibility of hoarding being induced is discussed later.)

In part, the Keynesian attempt to handle the problem in terms of the crude concept of "the price of labour" has confused the issue. We are concerned with the prices of different kinds of labour, whilst the index number concept of "the wage level" screens off from scrutiny all the issues which seem to me to be important.[8] Throughout Chapter 19 of *The General Theory* Keynes talked simply of "reduction of money wages." And he discussed the orthodox view of the desirability of price adjustments as though it was based on a "demand schedule for labour in industry as a whole relating the quantity of employment to different levels of wages."[9]

Through thus thinking rather uncritically about aggregates, the Keynesians appear to have *assumed* that wage-rate reductions imply reduction of aggregate earnings,[10] irrespective of whether the labour price which is cut is that of workers in an exclusive, well-paid trade, or that of workers doing poorly paid work because they are excluded from well-paid opportunities. When the Keynesians do think of adjustments in individual wage-rates, they think of blanket changes. At one point Keynes objected to price flexibility as a remedy for idleness in labour on the grounds that "there is, as a rule, no means of securing a simultaneous and equal reduction of money-wages in all industries."[11] But it is not *uniform* reductions which are wanted, it is selective reductions, the appropriate selection of which can be entrusted to markets when non-market *minima* have been adjusted.[12]

But even if equi-proportional wage-cuts were enacted, in a régime in which there was much unemployment, aggregate and average earnings might still tend to increase,[13] owing to the redistribution of workers over the different wage-rate groups. It would become profitable to employ more in the higher-paid types of work, whilst in the lower-paid

types there would have to be rationing.[14] Keynes's static, short-term methods exclude consideration of these reactions.[15] Clarity will not be gained whilst we try to think in terms of "wage levels." We have to think in terms of changing frequency distributions. This is important enough for the consideration of employment in individual industries, but still more important in relation to employment as a whole.

The Keynesian argument is that it is no use cutting the wage-rates of say, carpenters, if there is unemployment among them because, even if *their* employment fully recovers, their incomes and expenditure will fall and so cause the demand for the labour of other workers to fall.[16] But the case for price flexibility by no means assumes that a moderate fall in carpenters' wage-rates, together with a corresponding fall in the price of the product will, in itself, greatly increase the employment of *carpenters*. Such a reaction, although *possible*, is most unlikely.[17]

The correct proposition can be put this way. *Increased employment among carpenters can be most easily induced as the result of wage-rate and price reductions on the part of those persons who ultimately buy the carpenters' services.* The assumption is that the reductions result in the release of withheld capacity in the industries which do not compete with carpenters, whilst the increasing flow of products becomes demand through being priced to permit its full sale. This is the argument which the Keynesians should answer.

In his *Prosperity and Depression*, Haberler expressed doubts about this type of argument. He stated the case for it briefly, in a footnote,[18] but added that it assumed MV to be constant. I shall try to show that whatever MV may be, the value adjustments needed to secure the consumption or use of all goods and services may still be brought about. Haberler argues also that we cannot infer the truth of the proposition from facts which appear to support it. During the depression, outputs and employment were maintained in the agricultural field, in which the fall of prices *could not be* effectively resisted, but shrank in industry, in which prices *could be* effectively maintained. It would seem, then, that full employment and outputs could have been maintained. It would seem, then, that full employment and outputs could have been maintained in industry also, had price competition been effective. That, says Haberler, "has not yet been rigorously proven."[19] But is it not self-evident that, given any monetary policy, *selective* reduction of the prices of industrial goods would, in general, have made smaller reductions of agricultural prices necessary (in order to secure full employment in that field), whilst the maintenance of outputs as a whole would have eased the task of financing full production without diluting the money unit?[20] And is it not equally obvious that, had the price of agricultural products been maintained, so that these products absorbed a greater proportion of the total power to purchase, industrial unemployment would have been still more serious?

The relation between wage-rates and the aggregate pay-roll cannot, I suggest, be effectively considered, except in relation to the price system as a whole. But the Keynesians appear to take the co-ordinative effects of the value mechanism for granted and concentrate upon what they regard as the motive power behind it, namely, money income. They do not continuously envisage and consider the *synchronising function*, of prices, the fact that the prices attaching to individual commodities or services determine the *rate of flow* at which these commodities or services move into consumption or into the next stage of production. The co-ordination of the rates of flow of materials, services, etc., is brought about through the raising or lowering of prices. *Ceteris paribus*, a rise in price causes a falling off in the rate of flow, and a fall in price causes a rise in the rate of flow of anything through the stage of production at which it is priced. If certain prices cannot change, other prices (i.e., other rates of flow) must adjust themselves accordingly if the economy is to be synchronised in any sense.[21]

"Full employment" is secured when all services and products are so priced that they are (i) brought within the reach of people's pockets (i.e., so that they are purchasable' by existing money incomes) or (ii) brought into such a relation to predicted prices, that no postponement of expenditure on them is induced. For instance, the products and services used in the manufacture of investment goods, must be so priced that anticipated future money incomes will be able to buy the services and depreciation of new equipment or replacements.

Admittedly, the view that co-ordinative reductions or increases of wage-rates must always tend to increase real income (and probably real wages in the aggregate also) does not imply that money income (and money wages) will *also* increase, except on certain assumptions about the nature of the monetary system which exists. Perhaps the pre-Keynesian economists could be criticised for having made tacit instead of explicit assumptions on this point. But orthodox economics (as I understand it) did not overlook what is now called "the income effect." The tacit assumption[22] was that the monetary system was of such a nature that the increased real income due to the release of productive power in individual trades (through the acceptance of lower wage rates) would not result in a reduction of money income. No-one suggested that the monetary system *had* necessarily to be like that; but from the actual working of the credit system, it seemed to be unnecessary to consider the case in which an expansion of production would not be accompanied by an increase in money income induced by this expansion. The assumption on which Keynes built, namely, that the number of money units is fixed, would have seemed absurd to most pre-Keynesian economists, unless they were considering the economics of a community so primitive that a fixed number of tokens (shells, for instance) served as the sole medium of exchange, whilst no lending or credit of any kind existed.

In a credit economy, there could never be any difficulty, due to the mere fact that outputs had increased, about purchasing the full flow of production at ruling prices. That is, expanding real income could not have, in itself, any price depressing tendencies. Only monetary policy was believed to be able to explain that. But given any monetary policy, they believed that unemployment of any type of labour was due to wage-rates being wrongly related to the "amount of money" existing at any time.[23] It followed that downward adjustments of minimum wage-rates and prices could never *aggravate*—on the contrary would always *mitigate*—the consequences of any deflationary tendency caused by monetary policy.

Ought we not now to recognise that it is unnecessary to modify this pre-Keynesian view? Under *any* monetary system, the price situation which permits ideal co-ordination, in the sense which I have explained, must maximise the source of real demand-real income. Whilst this may be clear enough in the case in which monetary policy precipitates *primary* deflation, it may be less obvious when *secondary* deflation is induced. But postponements of demand, with their self-perpetuating consequences, arise when current costs or prices are higher than anticipated costs or prices.[24]

In more general terms, expected changes in costs or prices, unaccompanied by immediate cost and price co-ordination to meet expectations, lead to "secondary" reactions. A *cut in costs* does not induce demand postponement; nor, indeed, do *falling costs* have this effect. Postponements arise because it is judged that a cut in costs (or other prices) is less than will eventually have to take place, or because the rate of fall of costs (or other prices) is insufficiently rapid. It follows that "secondary" deflations are attributable to the unstable rigidities which prevent continuous co-ordination of prices. Confusion arises because secondary deflation can be brought to an end, not by true coordination, but at the expense of a prospective permanent sacrifice of real income, i.e., through the imposition of cost and price rigidities (in the form of minima) which are expected to continue indefinitely.[25]

Now if, for any reason, a change in the value of the money unit becomes the declared object of policy, or the expected consequence of policy, *the whole price system is immediately thrown out of co-ordination.* Thus, if the value of the money unit is expected to rise, then until the necessary adjustments have all taken place, "willingness to buy" must necessarily fall off—most seriously where values of services and materials in the investment goods industries do not at once respond.[26]

We turn finally to explicit criticisms of the reasoning on which Keynes based his suggestion of unemployment equilibrium under wage-rate flexibility or, as his disciples were later forced to argue, under price flexibility.

Through the attempts of disciples[27] like Lange, Smithies, Tobin, Samuelson, Modigliani and Patinkin to defend or strengthen the new creed, successive refinements have gradually paved the way for the ultimate abandonment, by would-be Keynesians, of the view that wage-rate and price adjustments are powerless to secure full employment. The contributions of these very friendly critics, said Schumpeter, "might have been turned into very serious criticisms" if they had been "less in sympathy with the spirit of Keynesian economics."[28] He added that this is particularly true of Modigliani's contribution. He could have made the same remark about that of Patinkin, which appeared two years later. But the criticisms of these writers *were* very serious in any case. Their apparent reluctance to abandon standpoints which their own logic was urging them to reject, clouded their exposition; but it did not weaken the implications of their reasoning.

Modigliani (whose 1944 article[29] quietly caused more harm to the Keynesian thesis than any other single contribution) seems, almost unintentionally, to reduce to the absurd the notion of the co-existence of idle resources and price flexibility. He does this by showing that its validity is limited to the position which exists when there is an *infinitely elastic* demand for money units ("the Keynesian case"). Modigliani does not regard this extreme case as absurd and, indeed, declares that interest in such a possibility is "not purely theoretical." [30] Yet Keynes himself, in dealing explicitly with this case, described it as a "possibility" of which he knew of no example, but which "might become practically important in future,"[31] although there are many passages in *The General Theory* which (as Haberler has pointed out[32]) rely upon the assumption of an infinitely elastic demand. "The New Keynesians" appear to be trying to substitute this, "special theory" (Hicks's description) for the "general theory" which they admit must be abandoned.

It is my present view that any attempt to envisage the "special theory" operating in the concrete realities of the world we know—even under depression conditions—must bring out its inherent absurdity.[33]

But let us keep the discussion to the theoretical plane. If one can seriously imagine a situation in which heavy net saving persists in spite of its being judged unprofitable to acquire non-money assets, with the aggregate real value of money assets being inflated, and prices being driven down catastrophically, then one may equally legitimately (and equally extravagantly) imagine continuous price co-ordination accompanying the emergence of such a position. We Can conceive, that is, of prices falling rapidly, keeping pace with expectations of price changes, but never reaching zero, with full utilisation of resources persisting all the way.[34] We do not really need the answer which first Haberler, and then Pigou, gave on this point, namely, that the increase in the real value of cash balances is inversely related to the extent to which the individual (or for that matter the business firm) prefers to save, whilst the rate of saving is a diminishing function of the accumulation of assets which the individual holds.[35]

I have argued above that the weakness of Keynes's case rests on his static assumptions; and that once we bring dynamic repercussions into the reckoning (*via* the co-ordination or disco-ordination of the economic system) his arguments for unemployment equilibrium under price flexibility fall away. Strangely enough the new Keynesians have themselves transferred the fight to the dynamic field. The position they now seem to assume is that, whilst Keynes's own analysis (essentially static) cannot be defended, his propositions survive if they are explained through dynamic analysis. But in their attempt to retain Keynes's conclusions, they have abandoned the very roots of his own reasoning.

Thus, Patinkin[36] is equally specific in rejecting the original Keynesian arguments concerning unemployment equilibrium. He says, "it should now be definitely recognised that this is an indefensible position."[37] Even so, Keynes's errors on this point, and the similar errors of his manifold enthusiastic supporters over the period 1936–1946, are represented by Patinkin as quite unimportant. The truth which the early critics of *The General Theory* fought so hard to establish (against stubborn opposition at almost every point[38]), namely, that price flexibility is inconsistent with unemployment, he describes

as "uninteresting, unimportant and uninformative about the real problems of economic policy."[39] In spite of the mistakes which led Keynes to his conclusions, he did stumble upon the truth.

Let us consider, then, the conclusions concerning price flexibility of what Patinkin continues to describe as "Keynesian economics" (meaning by that an economics which rejects the logic but retains the conclusions of *The General Theory*). This version of "the New Keynesianism" contends—again in Patinkin's words—"that the economic system may be in a position of under-employment *disequilibrium* (in the sense that wages, prices, and the amount of unemployment are continuously changing over time) for long or even indefinite, periods of time"[40] (Patinkin's italics). "In a dynamic world of uncertainty and adverse anticipations; even if we were to allow an infinite adjustment period, there is no certainty that full employment will be generated. I.e., we may remain indefinitely in a position of under-employment dis-equilibrium."[41]

This sounds like pure orthodoxy. Indeed, the use of the word "*disequilibrium*" implies that some Keynesians have now completely retreated. And the reference to "uncertainty and adverse anticipations" seems to refer to hypothetical situations which, using my own terminology, can be described as follows:

> Given price rigidities regarded as unstable, deflation will cause the emergence of withheld capacity. Three cases arise: (a) general expectations (i.e., typical or average expectations) envisage a fall of prices towards a definite ultimate scale which is regarded as most probable; or (b) general expectations are constantly changing so that the generally expected ultimate scale of prices becomes continuously lower; or (c) general expectations envisage a certain rate of decline of the scale of prices in perpetuity.

> In case (a), the withholding of capacity will last over a period which will be longer the more slowly the predicted price

adjustments come about. In cases (b) and (c), the withholding of capacity will last over an indefinite period, *unless downward price adjustments take place as rapidly as or more rapidly than (i) the changes in expectations, or (ii) the generally expected rate of decline,* in which case full employment will persist throughout. In short, when the scale of prices is moving or is expected to move in any direction, the notion of perfect price flexibility must envisage current prices being adjusted sufficiently rapidly in the same direction, if the full utilisation of all productive capacity is sought.

In admitting that Keynes cannot be said "to have demonstrated the co-existence of unemployment equilibrium and flexible prices," Patinkin explains that this is because "flexibility means that the money wage falls with excess supply, and rises with excess demand; and equilibrium means that the system can continue through time without change. Hence, *by definition,* a system with price flexibility cannot be in equilibrium if there is unemployment." [42] Now if by "excess supply" is meant more than can be sold at current prices, and by "excess demand" more than can be bought at current prices, *it remains true, equally "by definition," that price flexibility so conceived is inconsistent with wasteful idleness, even when we take into account the full dynamic reactions which are theoretically conceivable under a condition of falling or rising prices.* For price flexibility then requires that all prices shall be continuously adjusted so as to bring the spot and future values of the money unit into consistency; in other words, to establish harmony between current and expected prices. Under such adjustments, even unemployment *disequilibrium* is ruled out.

Do not the words "adjustment period" in the passage quoted above show that Patinkin, in using the term "*disequilibrium,*" is in fact still envisaging some price rigidity? What other adjustments, apart from changes in prices and effective exchange values can he be envisaging? How else can the terms "uncertainty" and "adverse expectations" be explained, unless in relation to unstable price rigidities? And

the same tacit assumption of rigidity is present in his statement of what he terms, "the Keynesian position, closest to the 'classics.' " In this position, he says, although price flexibility would eventually "generate" full employment, "the length of time that might be necessary for the adjustment makes the policy impractical."[43] He tells us that this statement (like that in the previous quotation) is *not* "dependent upon the assumption of wage rigidities."[44] But what "adjustments" other than tardy cuts in rigid wage-rates has he in mind? He must be thinking of unstable price rigidities *somewhere* in the system.

A critic writes that this argument seems to overlook *inevitable* rigidities. In practice, contracts cannot be varied constantly, so that costs tend to follow prices with some interval. Thus, copper miners' wages can hardly change every time the price of copper changes. But for Patinkin's argument to hold, it would be essential for the wage-rates of the miners to be maintained when actual or expected copper prices had fallen to such an extent that formerly marginal seams became unworkable at current costs. The most complete measure of price flexibility practically attainable involves discontinuities at both the cost—and the final product ends.[45] But periodic adjustments through recontract (as idleness threatens) can meet that situation.[46]

In short, the kind of price flexibility for which we can reasonably hope is one in which the price inconsistencies which must exist at any point of time *are never in process of material or cumulative worsening.* That need not mean unemployment. Contract covers the short run. And inconsistencies need not accumulate: they can be in process of rectification at about the same rate as that at which they arise.

Hence, "the dynamic approach" does not, as Patinkin maintains, obviate the necessity for the assumption of rigidities and revalidate the Keynesian fallacies. On the contrary, it was largely Keynes's neglect of the dynamic co-ordinative consequences of price adjustment which led him into the error that wage-rate and price adjustments are no remedy for unemployment.[47]

What are the implications? In my judgment, the abandonment of the theory of unemployment equilibrium under price flexibility means that the

Say Law stands once again inviolate as the basic economic reality in the light of which all economic thinking is illuminated. But I do not think that all the critics of Keynes on the point at issue will immediately accept this inference. Indeed, Haberler adheres to a rejection of the Law at the very stage at which his own reasoning seems to be prompting him to recognise it.[48]

Yet even so extreme a Keynesian as Sweezy has been rash enough (and right enough) to admit, in his obituary article on Keynes, that the arguments of *The General Theory* "all fall to the ground if the validity of the Say Law is assumed."[49] If my own view is right, then the apparent revolution wrought by Keynes after 1936 has been reversed by a bloodless counterrevolution conducted unwittingly by higher critics who tried, very hard to be faithful. Whether some permanent benefit to our science will have made up for the destruction which the revolution left in its train, is a question which economic historians of the future will have to answer.

We are now forced back to the stark truth that the elimination of wasteful idleness in productive capacity is attainable only through the continuous adjustment of prices or the continuous dilution of the money unit. But the latter is a tragically evil method of attempting to rectify disco-ordination due to inertias or sectionalism. For the harmful repercussions of inflation become the more serious (and force an accelerated inflation) the more successfully entrepreneurs and consumers, in the free sectors of the economy, correctly forecast monetary policy. But the new Keynesians, like the old, appear to believe that monetary or fiscal policy, through the control of spending, can act as a universal solvent of all price disharmonies and, like an invisible hand, make unnecessary, or less necessary, the difficult task of overhauling the institutions which make up the price system.

We must remember that the attack on wage-rate adjustment as a policy of securing full employment in labour is an attack on a policy which has never been experimentally tested. For whilst there is a great deal of evidence of wage-rate adjustments forced by depression being followed by recovery, no deliberate attempt to increase income (including the flow of wages) by reducing all prices which appear to be above the natural scarcity level (including wage-rates) so that all prices and wage-rates below the natural scarcity level may rise, has ever been purposely pursued. Actual policies have, for decades, been based precisely upon the politically attractive rule, justified by Keynesian teaching, that disharmony in the wage-rate structure must not be tackled but offset; whilst the current tendency is to assume dogmatically with no examination of the institutional and sociological factors involved, that to advocate wage and price adjustments is to recommend the conquest of the moon.

NOTES FOR THIS CHAPTER

1. In a discussion with A. P. Lemer about 1933, I pointed out to him that, however opposed our approaches might seem superficially to be, the Institutions which we were seeking would in the end, turn out to be exactly the same things. He refers to this conversation in the Preface to his *Economic of control*.

2. J. Viner, *The Role of Costs in a System of Economic Liberalism in Wage Determination and the Economics of Liberalism* (Chamb. of Com. of U.S.), p. 31; To-day, different groups of economists "give diametrically opposite advice as to policy when unemployment prevails or is anticipated."

3. Compare A. Smithies's statement of the implications of *The General Theory*,—in his article, "Effective Demand and Employment," in Harris, *The New Economics*, page 561—" … concerted action by the whole labour movement to increase money wages will leave real wages unchanged. Real wage gains by a single union are won at the expense of real wages elsewhere."

4. These two propositions were very much confused in Keynes's exposition and it is usually difficult to know, at any point, on which proposition he was relying. The exceptions are in passages which are rather puzzling, when related to the rest of his argument, as on pages 191 and 267 of *The General Theory*.

5. In this *Journal*, March, 1952, p. 53.

6. *General Theory,* page 11.

7. *I bid.,* p. 253.

8. Compare criticisms of "the wage level" concept by R. A. Gordon (A.E.R. Proceedings, May, 1948, page 354) who refers to "… the concentration of attention upon aggregates and upon distressingly broad and vaguely defined index number concepts—with insufficient attention being paid to those inter-relationships among components which may throw light upon the behaviour of those aggregates … "

9. *The General Theory,* p. 259.

10. It is an interesting commentary on the uncritical nature of current assumptions that Professor Viner has felt it necessary to remind economists that it does not necessarily follow, "and I think that many economists have taken that step without further argument," that an increase of wage-rates at a time of unemployment will increase the pay-off. "An increase of wage-rates may quite conceivably reduce the pay-roll." (Viner, *op. cit.,* page 32).

11. *The General Theory,* page 264. It was partly this which led him to argue that wage-rate adjustment would be possible only in a Communist or Fascist State. (*Ibid.,* page 269).

12. Actually, Professor Pigou has shown that equi-proportional wage-cuts, even under Keynes's other assumptions, must mean increased employment of labour if the reaction is a reduction of the rate of interest. Professor Pigou suggests that this reaction is "fairly likely." "Money Wages and Unemployment," *Economic Journal,* March, 1938, p. 137.

13. As measured by money units of unchanging value.

14. For simplicity, I am assuming that *maxima* are enacted.

15. The possibilities of transfers of workers from low-paid to high-paid work are magnified in the long run, because it will be possible to train for the well-paid employment opportunities which are brought within reach of income.

16. Professor K. Boulding has used this actual example and argument in his *Economics of Peace,* pp. 141–2.

17. Moreover, whilst wage-rate and price adjustments are required to dissolve withheld capacity among carpenters, to adopt that remedy *in individual trades* and on a small scale would bring severe distributive injustices in its train. Indeed, the aggregate wage receipts of the larger number employed in any trade might be smaller than before the increased employment.

18. Haberler, *Prosperity and Depression,* p. 493.

19. *Ibid.,* p. 243.

20. I feel that Haberler would now admit this argument, in view of his unequivocal rejection, in 1951, of Keynesian teaching about unemployment equilibrium under price flexibility. "Welfare and Freer Trade," *Economic Journal,* Dec., 1951, pp. 779–80. See also his article in *The New Economics,* pp. 166 *et seq.*

21. What is commonly expressed as changes in cost-price ratios, i.e., in the price of output in relation to the price of labour, I think of in terms of divergencies from, or conformance with, synchronizing prices at various stages of production. (The last stage is, of course, sale for consumption.)

22. Some economists in the pre-Keynesian era, in attempting to deal with the relations of employment and wage-rates, made *explicit*, highly simplified assumptions consistent with the assumption as I have worded it, for purposes of abstract analysis. But I do not know of any economist who has stated the fundamental assumption as I have done. Quite possibly the point was made.

23. Compare F. Modigliani, "Liquidity Preference and the Theory of Interest and Money," *Econometrica,* January, 1944, and this symposium, pp. 132–184.

24. My article in the issue of this *Journal* for December, 1953, is an attempt to deal rigorously with this situation.

25. Imposed cost and price rigidities in the form *of maxima* (i.e., ceilings) may similarly prevent secondary inflation, but in this case, *the effect is the opposite.* In so far as the maxima force down monopoly prices nearer to marginal cost, there is a mitigating co-ordinative and deflationary action which creates an incentive to increased outputs (i.e., increased real income).

26. It should be stressed, however, that this is no conclusive argument against policies seeking to increase the value of the money unit, as tardy rectifications of the distributive injustices of inflations. Nor is it a good argument against rectifying price disharmonies which have been allowed to develop and strain the ability to honour a convertibility obligation.

27. I do not include Haberler, whose criticisms have been damaging, as a Keynesian. It is difficult to pick out the other non-Keynesian economists who have been most

influential on the point at issue; but Marget, Knight, Viner and Simons must take much of the credit.

28. Schumpeter, in *The New Economics*, p. 92.

29. "Liquidity Preference and the Theory of Interest and Money," *Econometrica*, January, 1944. Reprinted in this symposium, pp. 132–184.

30. Pigou regards the contemplation of this possibility as "an academic exercise." He describes the situation envisaged (although he is not criticising Modigliani) as extremely improbable, and he adds, "Thus the puzzles we have been considering ... are academic exercises, of some slight use perhaps for clarifying thought, but with very little change of ever being posed on the cheque board of actual life." "Economic Progress in a Stable Environment," *Economica*, 1947, pp. 187–8.

31. *General Theory*, p. 207.

32. *Op. cit.*, p. 221.

33. No condition which even distantly resembles infinite elasticity of demand for money assets has even been recognized, I believe, because general expectations have always envisaged either (a) the attainment in the not too distant future of some definite scale of prices, or (b) so gradual a decline of prices that no cumulative postponement of expenditure has seemed profitable. General expectations appear to have rejected the possibility of a scale of prices which sags without limit, because of such things as convertibility obligations, or the necessity to maintain exchanges, or the political inexpediency of permitting prices to continue to all.

34. See below, and compare Pigou, op. cit., pp. 183–184; Haberler, Prosperity and Depression, pp. 499–500.

35. In any case, this argument is no answer to the case in which the nature of saving is speculative hoarding. For this reason Haberler claims only that there is "a strong probability" and no "absolute certainty" of there being a lower limit to MV so caused. (*Op. cit.*, p. 390.)

36. Patinkin, "Price Flexibility, and Full Employment" (*A.E.R.*, 1948). Quotations are from the revised version in the A.E.A. *Readings in Monetary Theory*.

37. *Ibid.*, p. 279.

38. For an example of the stubbornness, see Keynes's reply to criticisms in his "Relative Movements of Real Wages and Output" *Economic Journal*, March, 1939.

39. Patinkin, *op. cit.*, p. 279.

40. *Ibid.*, p. 280.

41. *Ibid.*, p. 281.

42. *Ibid.*, p. 279.

43. *Op. cit.*, p. 282.

44. *Op. cit.*, p. 282.

45. That is not, *in itself*, likely to mean discontinuity in movements of the scale of prices (i.e., in a price index).

46. Sliding scales can render the need for recontract less frequent.

47. The confusion in this field ultimately stems, I feel, from a failure to achieve conceptual clarity, and particularly owing to the absence of a sufficiently rigorous definition of price flexibility.

48. Haberler, in Harris, *op. cit.*, pp. 173–176. The acceptance of the Say Law does not imply, as Haberler suggests, the absurd assumption that the phenomena of hoarding or dishoarding cannot exist. It merely accords to money assets and the services which they provide the same economic status and significance as all other assets and the services which they provide. Nor does the existence of depression or idle resources (under unstable price rigidity) prove that this law does not hold, any more than balloons and aeroplanes invalidate the law of gravity.

49. In *Science and Society*, 1946, p. 400.

CHAPTER 7

Conclusion

The Pretence of Knowledge

By F. A. Hayek

The particular occasion of this lecture, combined with the chief practical problem which economists have to face today, have made the choice of its topic almost inevitable. On the one hand the still recent establishment of the Nobel Memorial Prize in Economic Science marks a significant step in the process by which, in the opinion of the general public, economics has been conceded some of the dignity and prestige of the physical sciences. On the other hand, the economists are at this moment called upon to say how to extricate the free world from the serious threat of accelerating inflation which, it must be admitted, has been brought about by policies which the majority of economists recommended and even urged governments to pursue. We have indeed at the moment little cause for pride: as a profession we have made a mess of things.

It seems to me that this failure of the economists to guide policy more successfully is closely connected with their propensity to imitate as closely as possible the procedures of the brilliantly successful physical sciences—an attempt which in our field may lead to outright error. It is an approach which has come to be described as the "scientistic" attitude—an attitude which, as I defined it some thirty years ago, "is decidedly unscientific in the true sense of the word, since it involves a mechanical and uncritical application of habits of thought to fields different from those in which they have been formed."[1] I want today to begin by explaining how some of the gravest errors of recent economic policy are a direct consequence of this scientistic error.

The theory which has been guiding monetary and financial policy during the last thirty years, and which I contend is largely the product of such a mistaken conception of the proper scientific procedure, consists in the assertion that there exists a simple positive correlation between total employment and the size of the aggregate demand for goods and services; it leads to the belief that we can permanently assure full employment by maintaining total money expenditure at an appropriate level. Among the various theories advanced to account for extensive unemployment, this is probably the only one in support of which strong quantitative evidence can be adduced. I nevertheless regard it as fundamentally false, and to act upon it, as we now experience, as very harmful.

This brings me to the crucial issue. Unlike the position that exists in the physical sciences, in economics and other disciplines that deal with essentially complex phenomena, the aspects of the events to be accounted for about which we can get quantitative data are necessarily limited and may not include the important ones. While in the physical sciences it is generally assumed, probably with good reason, that any important factor which determines the observed events will itself be directly observable and measurable, in the study of such complex phenomena as the market, which depend on the actions of many individuals, all the circumstances which will determine the outcome of a process, for reasons which I shall explain later, will hardly ever be fully known or measurable. And while in the physical sciences the investigator will be able to measure what, on the basis of a *prima facie* theory, he thinks important, in the social sciences often that is treated as important which happens to be accessible to measurement. This is sometimes carried to the point where it is demanded that our theories must be formulated in such terms that they refer only to measurable magnitudes.

It can hardly be denied that such a demand quite arbitrarily limits the facts which are to be admitted as possible causes of the events which occur in the real world. This view, which is often quite naively accepted as required by scientific procedure, has some rather paradoxical consequences. We know: of course, with regard to the market and similar social structures, a great many facts which we cannot measure and on which indeed we have only some very imprecise and general information. And because the effects of these facts in any particular instance cannot be confirmed by quantitative evidence, they are simply disregarded by those sworn to admit only what they regard as scientific evidence: they thereupon happily proceed on the fiction that the factors which they can measure are the only ones that are relevant.

The correlation between aggregate demand and total employment, for instance, may only be approximate, but as it is the *only* one on which we have quantitative data, it is accepted as the only causal connection that counts. On this standard there may thus well exist better "scientific" evidence for a false theory, which will be accepted because it is more "scientific", than for a valid explanation, which is rejected because there is no sufficient quantitative evidence for it.

Let me illustrate this by a brief sketch of what I regard as the chief actual cause of extensive unemployment—an account which will also explain why such unemployment cannot be lastingly cured by the inflationary policies recommended by the now fashionable theory. This correct explanation appears to me to be the existence of discrepancies between the distribution of demand among the different goods and services and the allocation of labour and other resources among the production of those outputs. We possess a fairly good "qualitative" knowledge of the forces by which a correspondence between demand and supply in the different sectors of the economic system is brought about, of the conditions under which it will be achieved, and of the factors likely to prevent such an adjustment. The separate steps in the account of this process rely on facts of everyday experience, and few who take the trouble to follow the argument will question the validity of the factual assumptions, or the logical correctness of the conclusions drawn from them. We have indeed good reason to believe that unemployment indicates that the structure of relative prices and wages has been distorted (usually by monopolistic or governmental price fixing), and that to restore equality between the demand and the supply of labour in all sectors changes of relative prices and some transfers of labour will be necessary.

But when we are asked for quantitative evidence for the particular structure of prices and wages that would be required in order to assure a smooth continuous sale of the products and services offered, we must admit that we have no such information. We know, in other words, the general conditions in which what we call, somewhat misleadingly, an equilibrium will establish itself: but we never know what the particular prices or wages are which would exist if the market were to bring about such an equilibrium. We can merely say what the conditions are in which we can expect the market to establish prices and wages at which demand will equal supply. But we can never produce statistical information which would show how much the prevailing prices and wages *deviate* from those which would secure a continuous sale of the current supply of labour. Though this account of the causes of unemployment is an empirical theory, in the sense that it might be proved false, e.g. if, with a constant money supply, a general increase of wages did not lead to unemployment, it is certainly not the kind of theory which we could use to obtain specific numerical predictions concerning the rates of wages, or the distribution of labour, to be expected.

Why should we, however, in economics, have to plead ignorance of the sort of facts on which, in the case of a physical theory, a scientist would certainly be expected to give precise information? It is probably not surprising that those impressed by the example of the physical sciences should find this position very unsatisfactory and should insist on the standards of proof which they find there. The reason for this state of affairs is the fact, to which I have already briefly referred, that the social sciences, like much of biology but unlike most fields of the physical sciences, have to deal with structures of *essential* complexity, i.e. with structures whose characteristic properties can be exhibited only by models made up of relatively large numbers of variables. Competition, for instance, is a process which will produce certain results only if it proceeds among a fairly large number of acting persons.

In some fields, particularly where problems of a similar kind arise in the physical sciences, the difficulties can be overcome by using, instead of specific information about the individual elements, data about the relative frequency, or the probability, of the occurrence of the various distinctive properties of the elements. But this is true only where we have to deal with what has been called by Dr. Warren Weaver (formerly of the Rockefeller Foundation), with a distinction which ought to be much more widely understood, "phenomena of unorganized complexity," in contrast to those "phenomena of organized complexity" with which we have to deal in the social sciences.[2] Organized complexity here means that the character of the structures showing it depends not only on the properties of the individual elements of which they are composed, and the relative frequency with which they occur, but also on the manner in which the individual elements are connected with each other. In the explanation of the working of such structures we can for this reason not replace the information about the individual elements by statistical information, but require full

information about each element if from our theory we are to derive specific predictions about individual events. Without such specific information about the individual elements we shall be confined to what on another occasion I have called mere pattern predictions—predictions of some of the general attributes of the structures that will form themselves, but not containing specific statements about the individual elements of which the structures will be made up.[3]

This is particularly true of our theories accounting for the determination of the systems of relative prices and wages that will form themselves on a wellfunctioning market. Into the determination of these prices and wages there will enter the effects of particular information possessed by every one of the participants in the market process—a sum of facts which in their totality cannot be known to the scientific observer, or to any other single brain. It is indeed the source of the superiority of the market order, and the reason why, when it is not suppressed by the powers of government, it regularly displaces other types of order, that in the resulting allocation of resources more of the knowledge of particular facts will be utilized which exists only dispersed among uncounted persons, than any one person can possess. But because we, the observing scientists, can thus never know all the determinants of such an order, and in consequence also cannot know at which particular structure of prices and wages demand would everywhere equal supply, we also cannot measure the deviations from that order; nor can we statistically test our theory that it is the deviations from that "equilibrium" system of prices and wages which make it impossible to sell some of the products and services at the prices at which they are offered.

Before I continue with my immediate concern, the effects of all this on the employment policies currently pursued, allow me to define more specifically the inherent limitations of our numerical knowledge which are so often overlooked. I want to do this to avoid giving the impression that I generally reject the mathematical method in economics. I regard it in fact as the great advantage of the mathematical technique that it allows us to describe, by means of algebraic equations, the general character of a pattern even where we are ignorant of the numerical values which will determine its particular manifestation. We could scarcely have achieved that comprehensive picture of the mutual interdependencies of the different events in a market without this algebraic technique. It has led to the illusion, however, that we can use this technique for the determination and prediction of the numerical values of those magnitudes; and this has led to a vain search for quantitative or numerical constants. This happened in spite of the fact that the modern founders of mathematical economics had no such illusions. It is true that their systems of equations describing the pattern of a market equilibrium are so framed that if we were able to fill in all the blanks of the abstract formulae, i.e. if we knew all the parameters of these equations, we could calculate the prices and quantities of all commodities and services sold. But, as Vilfredo Pareto, one of the founders of this theory, clearly stated, its purpose cannot be "to arrive at a numerical calculation of prices", because, as he said, it would be "absurd" to assume that we could ascertain all the data.[4] Indeed, the chief point was already seen by those remarkable anticipators of modem economics, the Spanish schoolmen of the sixteenth century, who emphasized that what they called *pretium mathematician,* the mathematical price, depended on so many particular circumstances that it could never be known to man but was known only to God.[5] I sometimes wish that our mathematical economists would take this to heart, I must confess that I still doubt whether their search for measurable magnitudes has made significant contributions to our *theoretical* understanding of economic phenomena—as distinct from their value as a description of particular situations. Nor am I prepared to accept the excuse that this branch of research is still very young: Sir William Petty, the founder of econometrics, was after all a somewhat senior colleague of Sir Isaac Newton in the Royal Society!

There may be few instances in which the superstition that only measurable magnitudes can be important has done positive harm in the economic field: but the present inflation and employment problems are a very serious one. Its effect has been that what is probably the true cause of extensive unemployment has been disregarded by the scientistically minded majority of economists, because its operation could not be confirmed by directly observable relations between measurable magnitudes, and that an almost exclusive concentration on quantitatively measurable surface phenomena has produced a policy which has made matters worse.

It has, of course, to be readily admitted that the kind of theory which I regard as the true explanation of unemployment is a theory of somewhat limited content because it allows us to make only very general predictions of the *kind* of events which we must expect in a given situation. But the effects on policy of the more ambitious constructions have not been very fortunate and I confess that I prefer true but imperfect knowledge, even if it leaves much indetermined and unpredictable, to a pretence of exact knowledge that is likely to be false. The credit which the apparent conformity with recognized scientific standards can gain for seemingly simple but false theories may, as the present instance shows, have grave consequences.

In fact, in the case discussed, the very measures which the dominant "macro-economic" theory has recommended as a remedy for unemployment, namely the increase of aggregate demand, have become a cause of a very extensive misallocation of resources which is likely to make later large-scale unemployment inevitable. The continuous injection of additional amounts of money at points of the economic system where it creates a temporary demand which must cease when the increase of the quantity of money stops or slows down, together with the expectation of a continuing rise of prices, draws labour and other resources into employments which can last only so long as the increase of the quantity of money continues at the same rate—or perhaps even only so long as it continues to accelerate at a given rate. What this policy has produced is not so much a level of employment that could not have been brought about in other ways, as a distribution of employment which cannot be indefinitely maintained and which after some time can be maintained only by a rate of inflation which would rapidly lead to a disorganisation of all economic activity. The fact is that by a mistaken theoretical view we have been led into a precarious position in which we cannot prevent substantial unemployment from re-appearing; not because, as this view is sometimes misrepresented, this unemployment is deliberately brought about as a means to combat inflation, but because it is now bound to occur as a deeply regrettable but inescapable consequence of the mistaken policies of the past as soon as inflation ceases to accelerate.

I must, however, now leave these problems of immediate practical importance which I have introduced chiefly as an illustration of the momentous consequences that may follow from errors concerning abstract problems of the philosophy of science. There is as much reason to be apprehensive about the long run dangers created in a much wider field by the uncritical acceptance of assertions which have the *appearance* of being scientific as there is with regard to the problems I have just discussed. What I mainly wanted to bring out by the topical illustration is that certainly in my field, but I believe also generally in the sciences of man, what looks superficially like the most scientific procedure is often the most unscientific, and, beyond this, that in these fields there are definite limits to what we can expect science to achieve. This means that to entrust to science—or to deliberate control according to scientific principles—more than scientific method can achieve may have deplorable effects. The progress of the natural sciences in modern times has of course so much exceeded all expectations that any suggestion that there may be some limits to it is bound to arouse suspicion. Especially all those will resist such an insight who have hoped that our increasing power of prediction and control, generally regarded as the characteristic result of scientific advance, applied to the processes of society, would soon enable us to mould society entirely to our liking. It is indeed true that, in contrast to the exhilaration which the discoveries of the physical sciences tend to produce, the insights which we gain from the study of society more often have a dampening effect on our aspirations; and it is perhaps not surprising that the more impetuous younger members of our profession are not always prepared to accept this. Yet the confidence in the unlimited power of science is only too often based on a false belief that the scientific method consists in the application of a ready-made technique, or in imitating the form rather than the substance of scientific procedure, as if one needed only to follow some cooking recipes to solve all social problems. It sometimes almost seems as if the techniques of science were more easily learnt than the thinking that shows us what the problems are and how to approach them.

The conflict between what in its present mood the public expects science to achieve in satisfaction of popular hopes and what is really in its power is a serious matter because, even if the true scientists should all recognize the limitations of what they can do in the field of human affairs, so long as the public expects more there will always be some who will pretend, and perhaps honestly believe, that they can do more to meet popular demands than is really in their power. It is often difficult enough for the expert, and certainly in many instances impossible for the layman, to distinguish between legitimate and illegitimate claims advanced in the name of science. The enormous publicity recently given by the media to a report pronouncing in the name of science on *The Limits to Growth*, and the silence of the same media about the devastating criticism this report has received from the competent experts[6], must make one feel somewhat apprehensive about the use to which the prestige of science can be put. But it is by no means only in the field of economics that far-reaching claims are made on behalf of a more scientific direction of all human activities and the desirability of replacing spontaneous processes by "conscious human control". If I am not mistaken, psychology, psychiatry and some branches of sociology, not to speak about the so-called philosophy of history, are even more affected by what I have called the scientistic prejudice, and by specious claims of what science can achieve.[7]

If we are to safeguard the reputation of science, and to prevent the arrogation of knowledge based on a superficial similarity of procedure with that of the physical sciences, much effort will have to be directed toward debunking such arrogations, some of which have by now become the vested interests of established university departments. We cannot be grateful enough to such modern philosophers of science as Sir Karl Popper for giving us a test by which we can distinguish between what we may accept as scientific and what not—a test which I am sure some doctrines now widely accepted as scientific would not pass. There are some special problems, however, in connection with those essentially complex phenomena of which social structures are so important an instance, which make me wish to restate in conclusion in more general terms the reasons why in these fields not only are there only absolute obstacles to the prediction of specific events, but why to act as if we possessed scientific knowledge enabling us to transcend them may itself become a serious obstacle to the advance of the human intellect.

The chief point we must remember is that the great and rapid advance of the physical sciences took place in fields where it proved that explanation and prediction could be based on laws which accounted for the observed phenomena as functions of comparatively few variables–either particular facts or relative frequencies of events. This may even be the ultimate reason why we single out these realms as "physical" in contrast to those more highly organized structures which I have here called essentially complex phenomena. There is no reason why the position must be the same in the latter as in the former fields. The difficulties which we encounter in the latter are not, as one might at first suspect, difficulties about formulating theories for the explanation of the observed events—although they cause also special difficulties about testing proposed explanations and therefore about eliminating bad theories. They are due to the chief problem which arises when we apply our theories to any particular situation in the real world. A theory of essentially complex phenomena must refer to a large number of particular facts; and to derive a prediction from it, or to test it, we have to ascertain all these particular facts. Once we succeeded in this there should be no particular difficulty about deriving testable predictions—with the help of modern computers it should be easy enough to insert these data into the appropriate blanks of the theoretical formulae and to derive a prediction. The real difficulty, to the solution of which science has little to contribute, and which is sometimes indeed insoluble, consists in the ascertainment of the particular facts.

A simple example will show the nature of this difficulty. Consider some ball game played by a few people of approximately equal skill. If we knew a few particular facts in addition to our general knowledge of the ability of the individual players, such as their state of attention, their perceptions and the state of their hearts, lungs, muscles etc. at each moment of the game, we could probably predict the outcome. Indeed, if we were familiar both with the game and the teams we should probably have a fairly shrewd idea on what the outcome will depend. But we shall of course not be able to ascertain those facts and in consequence the result of the game will be outside the range of the scientifically predictable, however well we may know what effects particular events would have on the result of the game. This does not mean that we can make no predictions at all about the course of such a game. If we know the rules of the different games we shall, in watching one, very soon know which game is being played and what kinds of actions we can expect and what kind not. But our capacity to predict will be confined to such general characteristics of the events to be expected and not include the capacity of predicting particular individual events.

This corresponds to what I have called earlier the mere pattern predictions to which we are increasingly confined as we penetrate from the realm in which relatively simple laws prevail into the range of phenomena where organized complexity rules. As we advance we find more and more frequently that we can in fact ascertain only some but not all the particular circumstances which determine the outcome of a given process; and in consequence we are able to predict only some but not all the properties of the result we have to expect. Often all that we shall be able to predict will be some abstract characteristic of the pattern that will appear—relations between kinds of elements about which individually we know very little. Yet, as I am anxious to repeat, we will still achieve predictions which can be falsified and which therefore are of empirical significance.

Of course, compared with the precise predictions we have learnt to expect in the physical sciences, this sort of mere pattern predictions is a second best with which one does not like to have to be content. Yet the danger of which I want to warn is precisely the belief that in order to have a claim to be accepted as scientific it is necessary to achieve more. This way lies charlatanism and worse. To act on the belief that we possess the knowledge and the power which enable us to shape the processes of society entirely to our liking, knowledge which in fact we do *not* possess, is likely to make us do much harm. In the physical sciences there may be little objection to trying to do the impossible; one might even feel that one ought not to discourage the over-confident because their experiments may after all produce some new insights. But in the social field the erroneous belief that the exercise of some power would have beneficial consequences is likely to lead to a new power to coerce other men being conferred on some authority. Even if such power is not in itself bad, its exercise is likely to impede the functioning of those spontaneous ordering forces by which, without understanding them, man is in fact so largely assisted in the pursuit of his aims. We are only beginning to understand on how subtle a communication system the functioning of an advanced industrial society is based—a communications system which we call the market and which turns out to be a more efficient mechanism for digesting dispersed information than any that man has deliberately designed.

If man is not to do more harm than good in his efforts to improve the social order, he will have to learn that in this, as in all other fields where essential complexity of an organized kind prevails, he cannot acquire the full knowledge which would make mastery of the events possible. He will therefore have to use what knowledge he can achieve, not to shape the results as the craftsman shapes his handiwork, but rather to cultivate a growth by providing the appropriate environment, in the manner in which the gardener does this for his plants. There is danger in the exuberant feeling of ever growing power which the advance of the physical sciences has engendered and which tempts man to try, "dizzy with success", to use a characteristic phrase of early communism,

to subject not only our natural but also our human environment to the control of a human will. The recognition of the insuperable limits to his knowledge ought indeed to teach the student of society a lesson of humility which should guard him against becoming an accomplice in men's fatal striving to control society—a striving which makes him not only a tyrant over his fellows, but which may well make him the destroyer of a civilization which no brain has designed but which has grown from the free efforts of millions of individuals.

NOTES FOR THIS CHAPTER

1. "Scientism and the Study of Society", *Economica*, vol. IX, no. 35, August 1942, reprinted in *The Counter-Revolution of Science*, Glencoe, Ill., 1952, p. 15 of this reprint.

2. Warren Weaver, "A Quarter Century in the Natural Sciences", *The Rockefeller Foundation Annual Report 1958*, chapter I, "Science and Complexity".

3. See my essay "The Theory of Complex Phenomena" in *The Critical Approach to Science and Philosophy. Essays in Honor of K. R. Popper*, ed. M. Bunge, New York 1964, and reprinted (with additions) in my *Studies in Philosophy, Politics and Economics*, London and Chicago 1967.

4. V. Pareto, *Manuel d'économie politique*, 2nd. ed., Paris 1927, pp. 223–4.

5. See, e.g., Luis Molina, *De iustitia et iure*, Cologne 1596–1600, tom. II, disp. 347, no. 3, and particularly Johannes de Lugo, *Disputationum de iustitia et iure tomus secundus*, Lyon 1642, disp. 26, sect. 4, no. 40.

6. See *The Limits to Growth: A Report of the Club of Rome's Project on the Predicament of Mankind*, New York 1972; for a systematic examination of this by a competent economist cf. Wilfred Beckerman, *In Defence of Economic Growth*, London 1974, and, for a list of earlier criticisms by experts, Gottfried Haberler, *Economic Growth and Stability*, Los Angeles 1974, who rightly calls their effect "devastating".

7. I have given some illustrations of these tendencies in other fields in my inaugural lecture as Visiting Professor at the University of Salzburg, *Die Irrtümer des Konstruktivismus und die Grundlagen legitimer Kritik gesellschaftlicher Gebilde*, Munich 1970, now reissued for the Walter Eucken Institute, at Freiburg i.Brg. by J. C. B. Mohr, Tübingen 1975.

APPENDICES

Appendix 1

Trade Accounting, Exchange Rates, and Purchasing Power and Real Interest Parities

There is no such thing as a "trade deficit." By the very logic of double--entry book-keeping, trade always balances.

CURRENT MERCHANDISE ACCOUNT +
CAPITAL ACCOUNT = 0
(Value of goods counted through customs) (Net Foreign Investment)

All funds used to purchase imports come back, either as exports moving through customs, or by entering into the capital account as foreign investment into the United States. This statistic is reported once a month on the news, yet it is an entirely meaningless statistic!

5 MAJOR PROBLEMS IN THE CURRENT ACCOUNT

1. Doesn't count foreign investment (capital account).
2 Doesn't properly count services or tourism (70% + of economy).
3. Doesn't account for value of title transfers.
4. Doesn't count underground economy.
5. Counts goods from point of shipment (What about IBM Japan shipping goods to America? Counted as imports!)

Suppose the government allows Americans to export to other nations, but shuts off all imports of goods and capital. This is a clear--cut case of foreign aid to other nations! If the government subsidizes our exports to other countries, again we (taxpayers) are giving away gifts. In the limit of price subsidy, we reach a "zero--price" and are just giving gifts in kind. When other nations subsidize their exports to the United States, we are receiving foreign aid from their taxpayers.

Usually a congressman or a senator picks up the capital account in an indirect manner. Since U.S. dollars are not generally spent in local Japanese shops (the dollars must be converted to Yen first), and the dollars are recycled through the international banks back to the U.S. as foreign investment. It is at this stage that the politicians see "foreigners" buying up the United States and decry the haunting specter of "foreign ownership." This fear is very silly indeed! Foreigners have given us "real" economic goods (automobiles, DVDs, TVs, etc.), and they hold mere "claims" to our wealth. They are simply completing the cycle of trade through money by executing the final transaction. Ultimately, we are just trading goods and services for other goods and services through the intermediation of money.

Suppose we import goods from country (Z) and send them "dollars" in exchange. What would occur if we strictly prohibited country (Z) from investing in the United States (assuming a two country model)? We would be in effect stealing from country (Z), since they shipped us real wealth for cheap little green pictures of George Washington. This analysis is not weakened by the fact of a multi--nation world. Country (Z) might send those dollars to country (M) to send through to the U.S. However, if the United States can prevent those dollars from returning from country (M), then country (M) is the nation being plundered not (Z).

THERE IS NO PROBLEM WITH FOREIGN OWNERSHIP

What exactly is a foreign company? In the global marketplace, strategic alliances make the corporate nationality idea really trivial. For example, major U.S. corporations have large equity positions in Japanese firms.

Who is made more vulnerable by foreign investment, the investor or the recipient? It is always the investor that takes all the risks. Suppose hostilities arise between the United States and Japan, and Japan owns all of our farmland. The U.S. could simply nationalize the land and back it up with the Army. When Iranian terrorists took hostages in the U.S. Embassy in Tehran, President Carter responded by freezing Iranian assets worth billions of dollars in this country, After Batiste fell to the Cuban communists, U.S. investors saw all their capital expropriated by Castro and his military. The same was true for all foreign investment into Russia after Lenin took

power. Nationalization occurred in similar fashion all over the continent of Africa after decolonization.

Why do industrial countries tend to invest little capital in many parts of Africa, South America, or Asia? Because investors fear the very high risks associated with foreign nationalization. This is a sad fact of international life. When a poor country cancels its foreign debt or seizes foreign-owned property, how do the investors repossess roads, bridges, hydroelectric dams, or factories?

Would foreign investment assist poor countries in their economic development? Yes it would, but often the risks associated with expropriation are prohibitive. This is why most foreign investment occurs within the industrial world, not between the developed and underdeveloped nations. This is also why countries with high levels of mutual foreign investment do not have tendencies to go to war. Canada, United States, United Kingdom, France, Japan, and Germany have too much vulnerable property that could be at risk they in the event of a military conflict. We are interconnected by mutual comparative advantages in production, and cross--national ownership binds our mutual fate together.

THE ECONOMIC THEORY OF EXCHANGE RATES

International trade occurs through the institution of money. However, in the international arena, there are hundreds of different mediums of exchange. To buy goods or assets in a foreign country, you generally need to access the domestic currency. This process of converting one currency into another, therefore, leads to a price emerging from exchange: the exchange rate. There are two alternative, although not incompatible, views of exchange rates between currencies.

PURCHASING POWER PARITY (PPP)

The purchasing power parity theory is the relative-inflation-rate theory of exchange rates. Relative inflation rates between currencies govern changes in the exchange rate. This theory in essence says: "like goods should cost the same in different countries." For example, suppose we have two currencies, dollars and yen, and one good: apples. Let's say apples cost one dollar in DC and one yen in Tokyo. Also, suppose the exchange rate is one dollar to one yen.

Now suppose the U.S. government doubles the money supply. What happens to the price of apples in terms of dollars? The nominal price doubles to $2 per apple. Japan has no inflation and therefore apples still cost only one yen. At the old exchange rate, apples in Japan are a bargain for Americans. Dollars will migrate to Japan since apples now only cost 50 cents! The "relative price" of apples has fallen in Japan because of the U.S. inflation. In order to actually buy those apples in Tokyo, however, one needs to get access to the yen which can be bought at a Foreign Exchange Bank with dollars. The supply of dollars in Japanese banks expands and the exchange rate for the dollar will fall. At the old exchange rate, there is a "surplus" of dollars, and their "price" falls to 2 to 1.

This process of dollars going to Japan stops when apples cost the same again in both markets. The dollar devalues against the yen to account for the U.S. inflation. If the exchange rate did not adjust, we could simply steal from foreigners by printing money. Remember, money is simply an intermediary in the exchange process. Money is a claim against existing stocks of wealth. If we give the Japanese one dollar for one yen and get their apple, we have the "real wealth" of one extra apple. They hold a "claim" to one apple from America. However, when they come back to get an apple's equivalent in value, they will find they can only get 1/2 apple with that dollar at the old exchange rate. We in effect have stolen 1/2 apple from them and they are not oblivious to this fact which makes expropriation through inflation in the long run a very difficult task.

WEIMAR GERMANY

In 1919, the exchange rate stood at eight marks to one dollar. When the hyperinflation ended, the "official" exchange rate stood at 4.2 trillion marks to the dollar, while it stood at 11.2 trillion to one dollar on the black market!

BRAZIL 1985

In 1985, the Brazilian currency was the cruzeiro, and it was being inflated at the rate of about 300- to 400-percent per year. The government therefore fixed exchange rate of 6400 cruzeiros to the dollar (the bank would take dollars for cruzeiros but not the reverse!). In Rio Di Janeiro, some jewelry stores, next door to the foreign exchange banks, engaged in black market currency transactions and they were dealing 9000 cruzeiros to one dollar. At the end of three weeks the "official" exchange rate stood at 7200 to the dollar, while the black market rate was 13,500 to the dollar. The largest Rio daily newspaper published both official and black market exchange rates!

INTEREST PARITY, OR ASSET PARITY

Interest parity, or asset parity, is the second explanation for changes in the exchange rate. This theory states that the exchange rate is governed by the relative differentials in the real interest rate between countries. Suppose the "real interest rate," the nominal rate minus expected inflation rate, in the U.S. is 10% and is 15% in Japan. What will happen to the old exchange rate at one dollar to one yen? It will fall as dollars move to Japan to capture this extra 5% profit differential. Again, there will be excess supply of dollars in Japan, or excess demand of yen relative to dollars. The yen rises and the dollar falls in value. This fall of the dollar will continue until the rates of return are equalized in both countries.

IMPORTANT NOTE

Both of these explanations are mutually compatible. Both have a vast array of supporting evidence backing up the theory. Interest parity is the short-run explanation for exchange rate changes because capital moves around the world in minutes to capture interest differentials between the forward exchange rate and the spot exchange rate. In the long run, the relative inflation rates (purchasing power parity) set the exchange rate. It all depends on the time horizon for the analysis.

Appendix 2

Central Banking and Money Creation

KEYNESIAN THEORY

According to Keynesian theory, the free market is inherently unstable because the economy is chronically deficient in aggregate demand. Money demand is volatile because consumers and bond traders periodically hoard cash. Therefore, the government must offset the "excessive" money demand with the requisite expansionary fiscal and monetary policy. Thus, Keynesians believe active government policy can "fine tune" or stabilize the macro economy.

It is important to understand that the Keynesian theory of government-spending, "stimulus," to offset contractionary effects of excessive monetary hoarding occurs only if it impacts real factors. This can only happen under the constellation of four conditions: (1) the spending arises from a budget deficit, (2) the deficit is monetized by printing money or credit creation, (3) the inflation is unanticipated, and (4) the workers having their real wage reduced to the full-employment equilibrium are unemployed workers in group 3 of the monetary flow.

The Keynesian theory of discretionary policy rests on three assumptions: (1) government has "superior" knowledge (quantitative and qualitative) about the macro economy as compared to the private sector,

(2) it can act in time on that knowledge with the right monetary and fiscal instruments, and (3) it does not face any public choice problems of incentives.

The idea that government has "superior knowledge" over the private sector is wrong. If government actually possesses accurate and superior knowledge, it can offset the business cycle by selling that information to the vested parties that can profit with that information (speculators on options markets). In fact, the Great Depression vividly illustrated that Federal Reserve governors thought the money supply was expanding for 3 years, while it was dramatically collapsing! Conversely, when America was a couple steps away from a hyperinflation disaster in the late 1970s, G. William Miller believed real interest rates were too high when they were negative!

Keynesians assume the relevant data can be in government hand in time to effectively implement a proper counter-cyclical response. This is not plausible. Tax and expenditure appropriations are made with glacial speed. The federal budgetary process takes nearly the entire year to get a budget approved. This is far too late as a response. Can the Federal Reserve act quickly? Not really. The data on monetary aggregates, employment, real output, etc. often take months to collect and synthesize. What is done are provisional "estimates" (guessing) with seasonal adjustments (corrections) in later quarters! The data the government has at its disposal is no better than "speculative data" (what the private sector already has). GDP statistics for any given quarter are "fully adjusted" three months after the end of the quarter (and readjusted again, one and two years later). This is far too late to be used, let alone for national policy. While the monetary authorities can act quickly, they are acting on data not relevant to the current economic situation.

There is also the time problem of "implementation lag" effect. Suppose government has relevant information and tries to counter an economic downturn. How does the government know the policy has had its desired effect? Changes in behavior arising from tax and spending policy often take years to detect. This also is far too late. On the monetary side, there is a period of anywhere between 6 to 18 month before changes in the monetary aggregates begin showing up in the relevant indexes, such as unemployment, CPI, etc. Again, this is far too late. Therefore, government policy can aggravate the business cycle instead of fine tune it!

Finally, there is the issue of public choice. The Keynesian benevolent view of government is questionable. Do the agents of various state bureaus really care about the overall macro economy, or only about their particular piece of it? No member of Congress has ever been elected on the prosperity found in other voting districts; rather, pork barrel transfer to their own district takes priority. Likewise, would the Federal Reserve-member banks care more about their own members' portfolios or the overall economy? In fact, Robert Tollison had demonstrated that during the Great Depression the vast majority of banks allowed to collapse were non-Federal Reserve member banks!

MONETARISM: THE MONETARY GROWTH RULE

Monetarists take a very different view of counter-cyclical "rules versus discretion". Friedman argues the free market is inherently stable and government is a destabilizing influence. If we examine the historical record (especially the Great Depression), it is very obvious Friedman's point is true. All too often government uses the wrong instruments, at the wrong time, and in the wrong proportions.

Since there are political market incentive problems, information-data collection problems, implementation lags, and policy effectiveness lags, Friedman argues the government should be restrained from as much discretion as absolutely possible. The constraints: rigidly fixed fiscal and monetary rules.

With respect to fiscal policy, Friedman has advocated constitutional limitations on taxation and spending. Given the tax and reckless spending absurdity occurring during the Great Depression and from the Great Society to the present, anything that takes arbitrary discretion away politicians and bureaucrats (flat tax, national sales tax, balanced budget amendment) is generally an improvement on the status quo. Government discretion leads to disaster.

On the monetary side, Friedman did at some point advocate a monetary growth rule. Since the Federal Reserve cannot know how much money to put into the system at any point in time, the best we can do is fix rigid limits and boundaries over its discretion.

The Monetarists advocate a growth rule that would track the long-term growth in the real output of the economy. If we look at the "Q" in the quantity equation over long periods of time, e.g., the last 100 years, the trend rate in economic growth is about 3% per annum.

Friedman argues the Federal Reserve can stabilize the price level and the purchasing power of the monetary unit by predictably expanding the money supply by the same amount (e.g., 2-4% range). In doing so, the business cycle can also be dampened, because there would be fewer errors of expectation. There would be no monetary contractions such as the Great Depression, or any inflations which are a one way path to hyperinflation.

Friedman's proposal was challenged by the Keynesians. How does the Federal Reserve know which monetary aggregate to track by a growth rule? Friedman responded that it does not matter, just so long as it is consistently tracked. For instance, if the Federal Reserve picks M2 and keeps it growing at 3% year in and year out, all of the other M's will eventually begin to move in correspondence with M2.

Monetarists want to maintain the existing fiscal and monetary institutions but take away discretion used by decision makers in those institutions. They believe the free market is inherently stable. Therefore the proper course of action is the implementation of rigidly pre- fixed rules constraining the choices of fiscal and monetary planners. Since no one really knows what to do and when to do it, monetarists advocate amendments to the

Constitution to balance the budget, limit taxation, limit spending, and fixing limits on the growth rate of the money supply. If M is growing at roughly the long-term growth rate of Q, the price level, expectations about it, employment, and the business cycle are stabilized.

THE AUSTRIAN POSITION: COMMODITY STANDARDS (GOLD) AND FREE BANKING

Economists from the Austrian School of Economics, like Mises, Rothbard, and Hayek, take a very different approach to monetary policy and banking institutions. There are no public goods problem with respect to the origin of money or its evolution from livestock to metals, from irregular weight metals to

standardized coins, from coins to paper money. This is radically different from the Walrasian treatment of money as only the "nth" good in the system of excess demand equations, or the "state theory of money," which maintained that the government invented money. Money is not just another economic good, it is the most important economic good in the economy. If we erase "paper clips" or papayas from economic life we have easy substitutes. In a highly specialized division of labor economy of today, the destruction of money via hyperinflation is detrimental. How does New York City feed itself without a medium of exchange?

Like the monetarists, Austrians believe the unhampered free market is also macroeconomically stable, and that depressions and inflations are caused by government policy. However, while a monetarist wants to bind the Federal Reserve under rules, the Austrians emphatically want to entirely separate government from money and banking.

Governments can never be trusted with such an important institution given Caesar's greed. The current banking system is a cartelized (monopolized) central banking structure based on a fractional reserve. This is highly unstable, either causing runaway inflation or severe contractions. Austrians universally want to abolish the Federal Reserve.

THE GOLD STANDARD AND 100% RESERVE REQUIREMENTS

The Austrian economists desiring a return to the gold standard include George Reisman, Joseph Salerno, and Mark Skousen. What they advocate is not some government-manipulated gold standard with a Federal Reserve system and government mint, but a genuine 100% pure gold coin standard. Government would have no role in setting or maintaining a legal price of gold. Rather, gold's price would be determined on the free market without any influence at all.

The classical gold standard had a relatively obvious advantages and disadvantages. First, Mother Nature hides the world's gold stock in mines and shafts; therefore, governments cannot manipulate its actual quantity. However, there is a real problem when there have been sudden gold discoveries (California and Alaska Gold Rushes), which in the past caused short-term inflation especially in the immediate mining regions. Also, mining technology can improve causing a rapid expansion on the gold stock. But, there is a shut-off mechanism: as the value of gold falls because of increased quantity, and its cost of production (due to bidding for inputs) rises, the profitability of gold mining is diminished. The lower price of gold also encourages its use in jewelry and industry, further reducing the supply and stabilizing the price.

Second, if the money supply is gold coins and bullion, it can never collapse or be destroyed. Only if a ship full of gold sinks in the ocean would the stock of money decline. Even under the government-manipulated gold standard of America's past, the price level, although experiencing short-run fluctuations was stable over the long run. In fact, the purchasing power of the dollar was the same in 1930 as it was in 1830!

Murray Rothbard from the Austrian school of economics advocated a 100% reserve requirement for all bank demand deposits. Under this requirement, all the money you deposit in your checking account which is redeemable on demand would always be in the vault of the bank when it is legally demanded. Naturally, time deposits would not have this requirement and they would make up the body of loanable funds. This would prevent multiple credit creation or credit destruction. All loans would be time deposits as demand deposits, i.e., checking accounts, are not loans. During the time specified on the deposit (e.g., a 6-month CD) the bank could loan all the money out as credit (real savings loaned to borrowers). No loans could be made on demand deposits. What this leaves us with is real savings and investment made on real time preferences, therefore, there is no possibility of (1) a Wicksellian divergence in interest rates (cumulative process), (2) mal-invested capital and depressions, (3) bank runs

instigated because only a fraction of deposits are in the vault, and (4) inflation.

There is one issue that some take with Rothbard's proposal. That is, they believe that zero price checking accounts would be effectively eliminated. Given the enormous efficiency and convenience associated with checking accounts, most economists have thus rejected Rothbard's original proposal. However, this is quite a misrepresentation of the situation. Most "free" checking accounts today require a minimum balance; this is just one way of paying for the account. It is not the free account represented in the argument for fractional reserve banking. And Rothbard would argue that it is costly to society as well, as the fragility of the fractional reserve system, combined with its inflationary tendencies, can cause harm to the entire economy. In fact free checking accounts are already becoming a casualty of the system they help support, as government regulations in the wake of the bank bailouts are driving them to extinction. It appears that the fundamental contradictions of the fractional reserve system may leave us with the worst of both worlds: an expensive and fragile banking industry.

MONETARY DYNAMICS

Mises's Micro Cash-Balance Approach

Ludwig von Mises has made four major contributions to monetary theory. First, Mises links monetary theory with marginal utility theory. Second, he demonstrates the monetary dynamics of new money on individual cash holdings. Third, he answers what was once called the circularity problem involved with the value of money. Finally, Mises links monetary theory to the capital structure to formulate a theory of the trade cycle.

Monetary theorists before Mises believed that the principle of subjective diminishing marginal utility applicable to economic goods was impossible in the case of money. For any particular economic good, there is some satiation point in which diminishing marginal utility reaches zero or even becomes a negative, i.e., a "bad." This is never the case of money. These economists argued that micro-economic value theory was not a proper framework for understanding the value of money. Mises disagreed. People hold Cash balances and every individual has an unlimited demand for wealth in general (cash balances + goods). They do not have an unlimited demand to hold all their wealth in the form of cash balances, however. The demand for money is a demand for a certain portion of wealth in liquid form.

When the marginal utility of the next dollar is less than some other economic good, that person spends that new lower-valued dollar for another economic good. If the marginal utility of the new dollar exceeds the marginal utility of other economic goods, the person saves that new dollar in their cash balances. The maintenance of desired cash balances is a continual wealth-portfolio decision for the individual. We accumulate and spend down our cash balances based on our marginal utility attached to money and all other economic goods.

Mises uses the micro-economic cash balance approach to explain the dynamics of a monetary injection. While the older (aggregative) quantity theorists, like Irving Fisher, see the effect of inflation as primarily a long-run increase in average nominal prices, Mises reveals that a real redistribution of wealth occurs as well. In other words, nominals can affect reals according to the following mechanism.

There are two sources of government revenue:

1. Taxes which can be direct (income tax, sales tax, etc.) or indirect (through inflation).
2. Borrowing which changes the interest rate (not assuming Ricardian Equivalence)

Government wants to build a road costing one billion dollars. If it raises taxes by one billion, this is non-inflationary. The government has more cash or purchasing power to bid up the prices of road-related commodities (land, cement, earth moving equipment, etc.), but taxpayers have exactly that much less to spend on goods they desire, causing those prices to fall (clothes, food, etc.). This is a pure diversion of wealth from the private sector to the government sector. The price changes cancel each other out with no net effect on average.

Suppose the government builds the road but does not tax the people. It now runs a one billion dollar deficit. Government borrows cash from the capital market to finance the deficit. As an extra borrower on the loan market, the government outbids marginal borrowers to divert loans from the private sector to itself to build the road. The government's new borrowing changes the interest rate. However, this is also non-inflationary. Government has one billion more cash balances to bid up road-related prices. Private investors and consumers have exactly one billion less to borrow from the loan market and non-road-related prices fall exactly as before. On net these price changes cancel each other out on average, no inflation.

However, if the government runs a deficit, builds the road, and borrows the money from the Federal Reserve System, new money and credit is created out of thin air. This is pure inflation. The prices of road related goods rise as before because government has greater cash balances; but there are no fewer cash balances in taxpayer hands or private borrowers to offset the price increases. Remember: the money supply is the sum total of all cash balances across the economy (there is no un-owned money), therefore, there is a net addition to the stock of aggregate cash balances. The fact is that the road did not materialize itself out of thin air. Real resource must have been diverted from the private sector to the government.

One cannot "print" a real asset like a road. Mises pierces this illusion in his explanation of monetary dynamics. New money or credit enters into the system at specific points, falling into certain people's cash balances before it spreads to others. The Fed's creation of money increases the government's cash balances first. As it spends those new cash balances on road related goods and services, the cash balances get dispersed into an ever-expanding array of cash balances (the road worker spends his higher wage on TV sets and so on).

Some prices are bid up before other prices, depending on the direction of where the new cash balances are spent. Eventually, the original billion dollars is spread across most cash balances across the economy.

Those groups that received higher rates of cash balances before prices have risen are wealthier by one billion in the aggregate. Others receive this money only after a time delay as money circulates. Some sets of people receive higher cash balances at about the same rate as increased prices; they tread inflationary water. However, there is a final group that receives new cash balances only after prices have risen (people on the periphery). They cannot keep up with inflation and lose real purchasing power. Thus:

Group 1: wins from new inflation

Group 2: breaks even

Group 3: pays for the real wealth transferred to Group 1

Group 3 ultimately pays for the road. Inflation is a tax on cash balances of people in Group 3. Therefore, money and credit creation not only increases nominal prices (*ceteris paribus*), but it also redistributes wealth depending on who gets the new money first, second, and last. This micro-economic dynamic is last if we only look at the aggregative quantity theory MV=PQ. All prices do not move up or down at the same rate. Money does not enter evenly from a money helicopter. Anyone to receive any new money or credit first in any way gets positioned to be in Group 1. This is true even under a commodity standard such as the gold standard during a "gold rush."

Finally, Mises points out that individuals hold cash balances (money demand), which also helps determine money's value, or purchasing power. Our expectations of the value of money play a large role in determining its actual exchange value. Our expectations today are based on the value of money determined yesterday, plus any new changes in expectations. However, what set the expectations of yesterday? Mises argued that those expectations were set based on those held the day before and so on. This is called the Misesian regression theorem. Economist Benjamin Anderson claimed Misesian monetary theory of exchange value was based on an infinite regress. Mises' answer to Anderson points back to Merger's evolution of money. All monetary regimes start out in a barter context where the good ultimately emerging to be money originally has use-value. People originally valued the monetary commodity for its consumption utility. Only later does the most marketable good acquire exchange-value in its evolution into a medium of exchange.

CONCLUSION

Ludwig von Mises's contribution to the quantity theory is substantial. He takes the quantity-theory construct and its insight about the money supply and inflation, and breaks it down to the microeconomic level of individually held cash balances. In doing so, he relinks subjective marginal utility analysis with money. We can also understand the real wealth redistribution involved with an inflationary "injection" of new money or credit.

Finally, Mises's theory of expectations and the exchange value of money circumvented infinite regress problems by connecting the current monetary regime to the Mengerian evolution of money.

Deposit and Money Multiplier

The Narrowest Measure: M1

M1=Currency in circulation + traveler's checks + demand deposits (checking accounts) + other checkable deposits

The Broader Measure: M2

M2=M1 + small denomination time deposits (CDs) + savings deposits + non-institutional money market fund shares + overnight repurchase agreements + overnight Eurodollars

The Broadest Measure: M3

M3=M2 + large-denomination time deposits + institutional money market fund balances + term repurchase agreements + term Eurodollars

Important Relations

Monetary base = currency in circulation + bank reserves

Currency in circulation = total currency outstanding - vault cash

Bank reserves = deposits with Fed + vault cash

Reserves = Required reserves (part-vault, part-Fed) + excess reserves

The Deposit Multiplier D

$$D = CR * 1 / RR$$

where:

D = change in total deposits

CR = Change in reserves (initial injection of new money)

RR = Legal Reserve Requirement Ratio

The Money Multiplier MM

$$MM = \frac{1 + (D/C)}{(D/C) + (RR)}$$

where: D/C = deposit to currency ratio

To calculate the overall money supply we use the following formula:

monetary base x money multiplier = money supply

The Fed and the Monetary Base: T-accounts

The monetary base of money supply is all currency and coin in circulation plus all reserves held by the banking system. This reiterates our earlier point that the "money supply" is nothing more than the cash balances held throughout the entire economy. From the monetary base, banks create credit, which is part of the overall money supply as well. But, exactly how does the banking system create new money or credit? It does this through the fractional reserve deposit system.

Balance Sheet of Federal Reserve System

It is important to note that the bank deposits at the Federal Reserve pay no interest to the member bank. The foregone interest operates like a franchise tax on those cash balances.

Suppose the Fed decides to buy securities on the capital markets. The Fed gets this new money to purchase the financial asset by printing it. Suppose the Fed buys $1 billion in new securities. Also, suppose the fractional reserve requirement is 10%. How much is the total money supply increased? By $10 billion. Bank 1 receives that billion first and it will

Assets	Liabilities
U.S. Government Securities (T-Bills)	Currency in circulation (Federal Reserve Notes)
Discount Loans to Banks	Reserves (deposits at Fed by banks)

loan out 90% of that billion and hold 10% for required reserves. The borrowers of that $900 million in loans eventually deposit those checks in Bank 2. Bank 2 takes $90 million out as required reserves and loans out $810 million, which is in turn deposited into Bank 3, and so on. Once the entire original $1 billion is turned into required reserves, the process of loan creation stops. When this multiple expansion of loans and deposits ends, the banking system as a whole has increased total deposits by $10 billion (1 billion + 900 million +

810 million +. .). The total increase in bank loans or credit is $9 billion (900 million + 810 million +...). The total increase in required reserves increase by $1 billion (100 million + 90 million +...).

It is very important to remember that individual banks are not multiplying the quantity of loans and deposits, rather, the system as a whole is. Each individual bank loans out its excess reserves, and those loans become another bank's excess reserves minus the required fraction of reserves until all excess reserves are a part of required reserves. The summation of those deposits and loans add up to the multiple expansion or contraction of the money supply. The deposit multiplier operates in exact reverse for multiple contractions. If the Fed sells securities to the banking system, it takes bank reserves out of the loan market. Thus, a multiple contraction of money and credit.

Appendix 3

Price Level, National Income Accounting, Aggregate Demand and Supply, and Unemployment

GDP

National income accounting is a methodology first developed by Simon Kuznets to measure how much total value is produced in a country in a unit of time (e.g., a year, a quarter). The particular measure was named Gross Domestic Product (GDP) (Gwartney 2014).

The first natural question that arises is how can one measure the total value added from the production of goods and services without double counting? Take for example, a car. Do we count the price that the car manufacturer paid to the steel and glass manufacturers as well as the price paid by the consumer for the car? The answer is no. GDP should measure the *flow* of value added to each stage of a production. In other words, the value added by the car manufacturer in making the car in its final form above the value added by the steel and glass manufacturers. As long as the manufacturer of each stage of production is able to sell his product to someone in the economy profitability, then each stage adds a layer of positive value. The sum of layers (all denominated in dollars) is what should be counted in GDP, or, alternatively, only the final consumer expenditure (price in dollars paid for final product), as the two must be equal to each other (Gwartney 2014).

PRICE LEVEL

What do economists mean when they speak of a rising price level or a falling price level? Are they talking about the price of meat? But why would that matter to a vegetarian? Is it the price of fruits, vegetables, or dairy? Generally, when economists refer to a price level, they are referring to a measure called the Consumer Price Index (CPI). The CPI tracks the prices of *a basket of goods and services*, i.e., a bundle of consumer products the average American family is expected to consume. The CPI is then used to track change in prices over time; a rising CPI is translated into a rising price level, or inflation, where a falling CPI is translated into a falling price level, or deflation (Gwartney 2014). Of course, in order for the CPI to be an adequate measure of changes in the price level, the goods and services that form the basket of goods used to compute the CPI must remain constant over time.

PROBLEMS WITH THE CPI

One major problem with calculating an accurate price index is called the **weights problem**. Very few individuals will buy items in the exact proportions set up by the consumer price index. For example, suppose the price of meat represents 10% of the overall index. Suppose the price of meat doubles. If you are a large meat eater, that price change effects you more than it would a vegetarian. So price changes compromising a large percentage of the index create disproportionate changes in the measured inflation rate. It is always important to remember, the bundle is an assumed representative consumer bundle.

A second major problem is called the **composition problem**. This involves what goes in the index bundle. For example, in the CPI base of 1979, personal computers were not in the index. So updating the index requires adding new goods and services that are a part of a typical consumer's expenditures. Every year thousands of products leave the marketplace and thousands of entirely new products and services enter the market. This can cause problems of what should be counted at any point of time.

A third problem is called the **quality problem**. How about quality? Automobile prices are included in the index, but if new cars are better than older made cars, because quality improves, then their real price has gone down! It is a very important assumption that the average quality of index goods remain unchanged. If newer cars have air conditioning, stereo systems, anti-lock brakes, air bags etc. these cars include a different bundle of goods in the price of the car. Thus, quality improvements via technology tend to overstate the measured inflation rate. The recent Boskin Commission (led by Stanford economist Michael Boskin) concluded that the CPI is over-stated by about 1% per year.

What GDP Does Not Count

There are a few caveats you need to keep in mind with respect to GDP statistics as measures of human well-being. First, the GDP does not include **leisure** as an economic good. We can always increase real GDP fast by forcing people to work 20 hours a day, 7 days a week (Stalin did this). But, leisure is of value and is not included in the statistic. An assumption is made that workers supply their labor voluntarily by choice to earn income by trading off leisure time. If workers are coerced into laboring by government, how is it possible to infer anything about their well-being?

Second, GDP does not count **environmental quality**. Again, it's easy to boost GDP by polluting the air and water with dangerous toxins, since the loss of the quality loss in value are often not registered on formal markets and traded through money (Stalin did this too). If production is increased at the expense of environmental amenities and consumers' value the previous qualities of environmental goods forgone, then how can anything be inferred about the consumer's welfare?

Third, GDP does not count the value of **non-market production** such as the family output of consumer goods and services. If your mom cooks a meal worth $150 at dinner time, while spending only $50 on ingredients for the meal ($100 of her productive efforts); then only her $50 purchase at the grocery store shows up in official statistics. If the family goes out to eat in a restaurant the exact same meal and the bill comes to $150 this is all counted in GDP. Thus, non-market, non-cash intermediated transactions such as direct bartering is uncounted.

Finally, all **underground** economic activity is excluded from GDP statistics. It is impossible to directly count what is being hidden from those that count the statistics. This can be a huge factor since there are always two economies: official and underground. This underground sector is of two components: legal and illegal. Legal underground actions occur from hidden actions because of tax and regulatory compliance purposes i.e. working off the books to escape tax burdens. Illegal underground is the contraband sector: the activity itself has been criminalized such as narcotics, prostitution etc. Whatever the case, both are activities not counted in GDP statistics.

AGGREGATE DEMAND FOR GOODS AND SERVICES

The micro view of demand describes the relationship between the price of a good or service and the quantity demanded at each price. The macro view of demand, called the Aggregate Demand, describes a relationship between the price level and *real GDP*. Real GDP is GDP adjusted for inflation. In other words, it computes how much today's GDP can buy of yesterday's goods.

Like the demand curve in any market, the aggregate demand also slopes downward, and there are three reasons for the negative slope (Gwartney 2014). First, *purchasing power of money*: when the price level falls, then the income that you earn can buy you more goods and services, which translates into an increase in GDP. Second, the *interest rate effect*: when the price level falls, less money from earned income needs to be spent to cover expenditures, and thus households and businesses alike have an incentive to shift some of their income to interest-earning assets such as bonds. The increased amount of funds puts a downward pressure on the interest rate which, in turn, makes borrowing cheaper, i.e., buying goods and services on credit. Therefore, the amount of goods and services increases. Third, the *price of domestic goods and services*: a lower price level makes domestic goods and services cheaper on the world market and so more Americans switch to buying more domestic relative to foreign goods and services. Also, domestic goods are cheaper to foreign consumers, who have an incentive to switch to buying more American goods.

AGGREGATE SUPPLY OF GOODS AND SERVICES

The aggregate supply of goods and services is also a relationship between the price level and GDP. For the aggregate supply, however, a distinction is made between the short-run and the long-run. The short-run supply curve describes how much of particular goods and services firms are willing to supply as the demand for goods and services fluctuates inducing changes in the price level. As with the supply curve in any market, the short-run supply curve slopes upward as producers increase their output in response to an increase in the price level. Since costs for producers in the short-run are determined by long-term contracts, input prices for producers lag behind the prevailing price increase (Gwartney 2014). Therefore, producers foresee a profit opportunity in increasing their quantity supplied of goods and services in the short-run. The dynamic changes slightly in the long-run. In the long-run, input producers have had time to change the terms of contracts to reflect the new higher prices, diminishing the profit opportunity that existed in the short-run. Therefore, the long-run aggregate supply curve is vertical, implying that the quantity supplied in the long-run is unaffected by changes in the price level (Gwartney 2014).

EQUILIBRIUM IN THE LONG-RUN VS. EQUILIBRIUM IN THE SHORT-RUN

Figures 1 and 2 contrast equilibrium in the short-run and equilibrium in the long-run. As Figure 1 demonstrates, output in the short-run is determined by the intersection between the aggregate demand (AD) and short-run aggregate supply curve (SRAS). The equilibrium output also occurs at the equilibrium price level. Prices above the equilibrium price reduce the quantity demanded of goods and services relative to that supplied, pushing the price level down to the equilibrium price; alternatively, prices below the equilibrium price increase the quantity demanded of goods and services relative to that supplied, putting

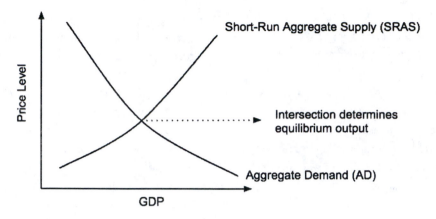

Figure 1: Equilibrium in the Short-Run

an upward pressure on the price level to the equilibrium price.

Figure 2, on the other hand, demonstrates equilibrium in the long-run with a vertical supply curve at the full rate of employment output. Two conditions prevail in such scenario (Gwartney 2014). First, the quantity demanded and supplied must be equal at the prevailing price. Second, all the parties to the market have the same expected price level, which is the prevailing equilibrium price level.

UNEMPLOYMENT

The supply of labor is intimately tied to the aggregate supply curve. Just as an increase in the price level, ceteris paribus, incentivizes owners of resources to employ those resources for production, an increase in wages incentivizes workers to contribute their labor toward production. However, not all workers who are willing to work always find gainful employment. Those who desire to work, but cannot work are considered unemployed. The unemployment rate reflects the number of workers who are unemployed as a portion of the labor force:

$$\text{Unemployment Rate} = \frac{(\text{Unemployed Workers})}{(\text{Unemployed Workers} + \text{Employed Workers})}$$

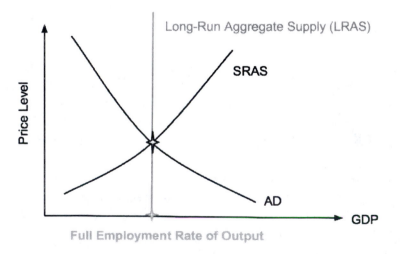

Figure 2: Equilibrium in the Long-Run

Only those who are either employed or looking for work are included in this statistic. Those individuals who were unemployed but have stopped looking for a job are not considered. Unemployment can be divided into three categories: frictional, structural, and cyclical. **Frictional unemployment** includes those workers who are unemployed because they are currently searching for work. These individuals have the skills required to gain employment, but must spend time looking for a job that suits those skills. **Structural unemployment** includes those who are not employed because their current skillset is obsolete. For example, a horse carriage driver who became unemployed consumers substituted away from horse carriages and toward Henry Ford's Model-T fit into this category. These drivers needed to learn to operate an automobile if they wanted to continue to earn a living by transporting passengers. The first two categories comprise the natural rate of unemployment. Unemployment is not always at the natural rate. During the economic expansions and contractions, the unemployment rate oscillates above and below the natural rate of unemployment. This fluctuation is due to **cyclical unemployment**. Cyclical unemployment occurs due to changes in demand for labor. When the economy expands, demand for labor increases. Producers employ more workers as they expand output and the unemployment rate falls. Likewise, demand for labor falls when the economy is in a period of contraction. The temporary fall in production reduces demand for workers, and thus the unemployment rate increases.

Credits

Paul Heyne, "Do Trade Deficits Matter?" Cato Journal, vol. 3, no. 3 , pp. 705-716. Copyright © 1983 by Cato Institute. Reprinted with permission.

Henry Hazlitt, "Who's "Protected" by Tariffs?" Economics in One Lesson, pp. 74-83. Copyright © 1946 by Random House LLC. Reprinted with permission.

Theodore Shamoun, Thomas Rustici and Dina Yazji Shamoun, "The Smoot-Hawley Tariff and the Great Depression," The Freeman. Copyright © 2012 by Foundation for Economic Education.

Rondo Cameron, "World's First Coins," A Concise Economic History of the World From Paleolithic Times to the Present, pp. 35-37, 65-68. Copyright © 2002 by Oxford University Press. Reprinted with permission.

Adam Smith, An Inquiry into the Nature and Causes of the Wealth of Nations, pp. 37-46. Methuen Publishing Ltd., 1904. Copyright in the Public Domain.

Murray Rothbard, What Has Government Done to Our Money?, pp. 23-30. Copyright © 2005 by Ludwig von Mises Institute. Reprinted with permission.

Carl Menger, "The Theory of Money," Principles of Economics, pp. 257-271. Copyright © 2013 by Cengage Learning, Inc. Reprinted with permission.

Armen Alchain, "Why Money?" Journal of Money, Credit and Banking, vol. 9, pp. 133-140. Copyright © 1977 by Ohio State University Press. Reprinted with permission.

David Glasner, "An Evolutionary Theory of the State Monopoly over Money," Money and the Nation State: The Financial Revolution, Government, and the World Monetary System, ed. Kevin Dowd and Richard H. Timberlake, pp. 22-28, 40. Copyright © 1998 by Transaction Publishers. Reprinted with permission.

Milton Friedman, "The Island of Stone Money," Monetary Mischief, pp. 3-7. Copyright © 1994 by Houghton Mifflin Harcourt. Reprinted with permission.

Edwin Vieira, "What is a Dollar?" The Freeman. Copyright © 1994 by Foundation for Economic Education.

Nicolas Copernicus, Essay on Money, ed. Ralph Benko and Charles Kadlec, trans. Gerald Malsbary. Copyright © by Ralph Benko. Reprinted with permission.

Marjorie Grice-Hutchinson, The School of Salamanca, pp. 89-96, 99-103. Copyright © 1952 by Interpares. Reprinted with permission.

Ashley Montagu, "Vignette: Importing Inflation: Conquistadores and the Quantity Theory of Money," The Last Two Million Years, pp. 202-203, 234. Reader's Digest Association, 1973.

David Hume, "Of Money," Essays, Moral, Political, and Literary. Copyright in the Public Domain.

John S. Mill, "Of the Value of Money, as dependent on Demand and Supply," Principles of Political Economy with some of their Applications to Social Philosophy, ed. William J. Ashley. Copyright in the Public Domain.

Ludwig von Mises, The Theory of Money and Credit, trans. H. E. Batson. Copyright in the Public Domain.

Ralph Hawtrey, Currency and Credit, pp. 33-40. Copyright in the Public Domain.

Armen Alchian, "Problems of Rising Prices," Governmental Controls and the Free Market: The U.S. Economy in the 1970's, ed. Svetozar Pejovich, pp. 19-40. Copyright © 1976 by Texas A&M University Press. Reprinted with permission.

Jerome Smith, Swiss Economic Viewpoint. Foreign Commerce Bank, 1976.

"Not Worth a Continental: Editor's Note," Free Market Economics: A Basic Reader, ed. Bettina Bien Greaves, pp. 127. Copyright © 1982 by Foundation for Economic Education.

Pelatiah Webster, "Structures on Tender Acts," 1780. Copyright in the Public Domain.

Andrew Dickson White, Fiat Money in France. D. Appleton & Company, 1896. Copyright in the Public Domain.

Thomas Humphrey, "Eliminating Runaway Inflation: Lessons from German Hyperinflation," Essays on Inflation, pp. 150-154. Copyright © 1980 by Federal Reserve Bank of Richmond. Reprinted with permission. Views expressed in this article are those of the author and not necessarily those of the Federal Reserve Bank of Richmond or the Federal Reserve System.

Philip Cagan, "Table 1: Monetary Characteristics of Seven Hyperinflations," Studies in the Quantity Theory of Money, pp. 26. Copyright © 1956 by University of Chicago Press.

Steve H. Hanke and Nicholas Krus, "The Hanke-Krus Hyperinflation Table," Cato Working Paper, no. 8. Copyright © by Cato Institute.

Robert J. Barro, "Cross-Country Data on Inflation and Monetary Growth," Macroeconomics, pp. 166. Copyright © 1993 by John Wiley & Sons, Inc. Reprinted with permission.

Robert J. Barro, "Table 7.1," Macroeconomics, pp. 167-168. Copyright © 1993 by John Wiley & Sons, Inc.

Milton Friedman, Figures 1-5, Money Mischief: Episodes in Monetary History, pp. 197-201. Copyright © 1994 by Houghton Mifflin Harcourt.

Richard Cantillon, "Of the Increase and Decrease in the Quantity of Hard Money in a State," Essay on the Nature of Trade in General, ed. and trans. Henry Higgs. Copyright © 1931 by Royal Economic Society. Reprinted with permission.

Adam Smith, "Of the Real and Nominal Price of Commodities, or of Their Price in Labor and Their Price in Money," An Inquiry into the Nature and Causes of the Wealth of Nations, ed. Edwin Cannan. Methuen Publishing Ltd., 1904. Copyright in the Public Domain.

John Stuart Mill, "Of the Rate of Interest," Principles of Political Economy with Some of their Applications to Social Philosophy, ed. William J. Ashley. Longmans, Green and Co., 1909. Copyright in the Public Domain.

Irving Fisher, "A Glance at the Money Illusion," The Money Illusion, pp. 3-30. Adelphi Company, 1928. Copyright in the Public Domain.

Ludwig von Mises, "Interest," Human Action: A Treatise on Economics, pp. 524-537. Copyright © 1996 by Foundation for Economic Education.

J. Huston McCulloch, "Chapter 4: Expected Inflation and Interest Rates," Money and Inflation: A Monetarist Approach, pp. 47-49, 60-61. Copyright © 1982 by Elsevier Science and Technology. Reprinted with permission.

Jean-Baptiste Say, "Of the Demand or Market for Products," A Treatise on Political Economy, ed. Clement C. Biddle, trans. C. R. Prinsep. Copyright in the Public Domain.

David Ricardo, "The Effects of Accumulation and Profit on Interest," On the Principles of Political Economy and Taxation. John Murray Publishers Limited, 1817. Copyright in the Public Domain.

Axel Leijionhufvud and Robert Clower, "Say's Principle, What It Means and Doesn't Mean," Intermountain Economic Review, pp. 79-102. Oxford University Press, 1981.

W. H. Hutt, "The Significance of Price Flexibility," The South African Journal of Economics, vol. 22, issue 1, pp. 40-51. Copyright © 1954 by John Wiley & Sons, Inc. Reprinted with permission.

F. A. Hayek, "The Pretence of Knowledge," http://www.nobelprize.org/nobel_prizes/economic-sciences/laureates/1974/hayek-lecture.html. Copyright © 1992 by Nobel Foundation. Reprinted with permission.